Lecture Notes in Computer Scie

Commenced Publication in 1973
Founding and Former Series Editors:
Gerhard Goos, Juris Hartmanis, and Jan van Leeuwen

Frank Ortmeier   Peter Daniel (Eds.)

Computer Safety, Reliability, and Security

SAFECOMP 2012 Workshops: Sassur, ASCoMS,
DESEC4LCCI, ERCIM/EWICS, IWDE
Magdeburg, Germany, September 25-28, 2012
Proceedings

 Springer

Volume Editors

Frank Ortmeier
Otto-von-Guericke-Universität, Fakultät für Informatik
Institut für Technische und Betriebliche Informationssysteme (ITI)
Universitätsplatz 2, 39106 Magdeburg, Germany
E-mail: frank.ortmeier@ovgu.de

Peter Daniel
SELEX ELSAG, Liverpool Innovation Park
Edge Lane, Fairfield, Liverpool, L7 9NJ, UK
E-mail: ewicstc7@prdaniel.co.uk

ISSN 0302-9743   e-ISSN 1611-3349
ISBN 978-3-642-33674-4   e-ISBN 978-3-642-33675-1
DOI 10.1007/978-3-642-33675-1
Springer Heidelberg Dordrecht London New York

Library of Congress Control Number: 2012947423

CR Subject Classification (1998): K.6.5, D.2, C.2, F.3, H.4, D.3, I.2

LNCS Sublibrary: SL 2 – Programming and Software Engineering

Typesetting: Camera-ready by author, data conversion by Scientific Publishing Services, Chennai, India

Printed on acid-free paper

Springer is part of Springer Science+Business Media (www.springer.com)

Preface

Safety, reliability, and security are becoming vital in almost all technical domains. The reason is that computer pervasion is steadily increasing and more and more systems are becoming networked. This often leads to the term of cyber-physical systems, i.e., systems influencing our environment that are connected by modern computer networks. Examples are smart traffic guidance, intelligent power lines, or autonomous vehicles. Despite the commonality in safety challenges, each domain has very specific stakeholders, requirements, standards, etc.

To account for this, we decided to give various domain experts a common meeting place in the form of domain-specific workshops at SAFECOMP. The common theme is safety and security. Bringing these experts together at one place and collecting their articles in one volume fosters collaboration and the exchange of ideas.

For SAFECOMP 2012, we accepted five domain-specific, high-quality workshops. Each workshop had well-known chairs and an international program committee. Altogether 69 researchers from 15 countries reviewed the following 44 articles.

Architecting safe collaborative mobile systems was the aim of the ASCoMS workshop (chairs: António Casimiro and Jörg Kaiser). Building autonomous mobile systems is already challenging. However, for transition from academia to real-world scenarios, safety guarantees are mandatory and a prerequisite for acceptance.

Our daily life heavily depends upon the correct functioning of many complex large-scale infrastructures such as communication, power, or water supply. The DESEC4LCCI workshop (chairs: Christian Esposito, Marco Platania, and Francesco Brancati) focused on dependable and secure computing for such systems. Until recently, security for such systems could be reduced to physical security (i.e., protecting the infrastructure by security personal). As systems become widely connected, this is no longer sufficient and new approaches must be developed.

The emergence of cyber-physical systems is speeding up exponentially. The ERCIM/EWICS/DECOS workshop (chairs: Erwin Schoitsch and Amund Skavhaug) brought together stakeholders from many major European research projects and programs to exchange ideas on making such systems safer and more reliable.

Design and operation of most technical systems is no longer only an engineering challenge. It requires the interaction of mechanical, electrical, and software engineers for digitally engineering such a system. The 3rd International Workshop on Digital Engineering – IWDE (chairs: Gunter Saake and Veit Köppen) brought together researchers from these domains, which share the common vision of jointly digitally engineering safe and secure systems.

Safety assurance and certification are amongst the most expensive and time-consuming tasks in the development of safety-critical systems. The SASSUR workshop (chairs: Alejandra Ruiz, Tim Kelly, Mehrdad Sabetzadeh, and Didier Van den Abeele) focused exactly on bridging this gap. It covered new methods, approaches, and tools on tackling this problem.

Summarizing, I have to say that correspondence and organization of these five workshops for SAFECOMP took a lot of my time. But when looking at the program now, I would like to express my deepest thanks to all workshop chairs. You did a fantastic job. The program was very tempting and a great extension to SAFECOMP 2012. I would also like to thank in particular Michael Lipaczewski, who did a great job in organizing this volume and collecting all the articles, introductions, copyright forms, etc.

I hope you are all enjoying this volume and are maybe even benefitting from some new ideas and achievements presented here.

August 2012   Frank Ortmeier

Organization

Next Generation of System Assurance Approaches for Safety-Critical Systems Workshop (Sassur 2012)

Chairs

Didier Van Den Abeele	Alstom Transport, France
Tim Kelly	University of York, UK
Alejandra Ruiz	Tecnalia, Spain
Mehrdad Sabetzadeh	Simula Research Laboratory, Norway

Steering Committee

Annie Combelles	Inspearit, France
Javier Díaz	University of Granada, Spain
Huascar Espinoza	TECNALIA, Spain
John Favaro	Intecs, Italy
Paolo Panaroni	Intecs, Italy
Fulvio Tagliabò	Centro Ricerche FIAT, Italy

Program Committee

Katrina Attwood	University of York, UK
Fabien Belmonte	Alstom, France
Ronald Blanrue	EADS/Eurocopter, France
Marc Born	ikv++ technologies ag, Germany
Sergio Campos	Tecnalia Research & Innovation, Spain
Daniela Cancilla	Atego, France
Cedric Chevrel	Thales Avionics, France
C. Michael Holloway	NASA Langley Research Center, USA
Olaf Kath	ikv++ technologies ag, Germany
Andreas Keis	EADS/Innovation Works, UK
Uwe Kremer	TÜV SÜD, Germany
Xabier Larrucea	TECNALIA, Spain
Mark Nicholson	University of York, UK
Jürgen Niehaus	Safetrans, Germany
Kenji Taguchi	AIST, Japan
Jose Luis De La Vara	Simula Research Laboratory, Norway
Harold Weffers	Eindhoven University of Technology, The Netherlands

Workshop on Architecting Safety in Collaborative Mobile Systems (ASCoMS 2012)

Chairs

António Casimiro   University of Lisbon, Portugal
Jörg Kaiser   Otto-von-Guericke-University of Magdeburg,
                            Germany

Program Committee

Luis Almeida   FEUP, Portugal
Leandro Becker   UFSC, Brazil
Andrea Bondavalli   University of Florence, Italy
Thomas Fuhrman   GM, USA
Karl Goeschka   Vienna University of Technology, Austria
Rolf Johansson   SP, Sweden
Marcelo Lemes   EMBRAER, Brazil
Priya Narasimhan   Carnegie Mellon University, USA
Edgar Nett   Otto-von-Guericke-University of Magdeburg,
                            Germany
Stefan Schemmer   RT Solutions, Germany
Elad Michael Schiller   Chalmers University of Technology, Sweden
Paulo Verissimo   University of Lisbon, Portugal

Workshop on Dependable and Secure Computing for Large-scale Complex Critical Infrastructures (DESEC4LCCI 2012)

Chairs

Francesco Brancati   Resiltech, Italy
Christian Esposito   Institute of High Performance Computing
                            and Networking (ICAR), Italy
Marco Platania   Sapienza University of Rome, Italy

Program Committee

Angelo Corsaro   PrismTech, UK
Michele Colajanni   University of Modena, Italy
Bojan Cukic   West Virginia University, USA
Francesco Flammini   University "Federico II" of Naples, Italy
Felicita Di Giandomenico ISTI-CNR, Italy

Abdelmajid Khelil   TU Darmstadt, Germany
Catello Di Martino   University of Illinois at Urbana-Champaign, USA
Edgar Nett   Otto-von-Guericke-University of Magdeburg,
                             Germany
Ricardo Jimenez Peris   Universidad Politecnica de Madrid, Spain
Sara Tucci Piergiovanni   CEA LIST, Italy
Luigi Romano   Parthenope University of Naples, Italy
Nuno Silva   Critical Software SA, Portugal
Paulo Verissimo   University of Lisbon, Portugal
Marco Vieira   University of Coimbra, Portugal

ERCIM/EWICS/Cyberphysical Systems Workshop

Chairs

Erwin Schoitsch   Austrian Institute of Technology, Austria
Amund Skavhaug   NTNU, Trondheim, Norway

Program Committee

Friedemann Bitsch   Germany
Sandro Bologna   Italy
Wolfgang Ehrenberger   Germany
Francesco Flammini   Italy
Robert Genser   Austria
Janusz Gorski   Poland
Maritta Heisel   Germany
Floor Koornneef   The Netherlands
Peter Ladkin   Germany
Meine van der Meulen   Norway
Odd Nordland   Norway
Frank Ortmeier   Germany
Thomas Pfeiffenberger   Austria
Francesca Saglietti   Germany
Christoph Schmitz   Switzerland
Erwin Schoitsch   Austria
Rolf Schumacher   Germany
Amund Skavhaug   Norway

International Workshop on Digital Engineering (IWDE 2012)

Chairs

Veit Köppen   Otto-von-Guericke-University Magdeburg,
                            Germany
Gunter Saake   Otto-von-Guericke-University Magdeburg,
                            Germany

Program Committee

Abdel-Badeeh M. Salem   Ain Shams University, Egypt
Andreas Brenke   HS Niederrhein, Germany
Raimund Dachselt   TU Dresden, Germany
Matthias Güdemann   Inria, Grenoble, France
Frank Ortmeier   Otto-von-Guericke University Magdeburg,
                            Germany
Dirk Reiners   University of Louisiana at Lafayette, USA
Hermann Rohling   TU Hamburg, Germany
Michael Schenk   FhG IFF Magdeburg, Germany
Gunter Saake   Otto-von-Guericke University Magdeburg,
                            Germany

Table of Contents

Workshop on Architecting Safety in Collaborative Mobile Systems (ASCoMS 2012)

Workshop on Dependable and Secure Computing for Large-Scale Complex Critical Infrastructures (DESEC4LCCI 2012)

ERCIM/EWICS/Cyberphysical Systems Workshop

International Workshop on Digital Engineering (IWDE 2012)

Next Generation of System Assurance Approaches for Safety-Critical Systems Workshop (Sassur 2012)

Introduction to Sassur 2012

Alejandra Ruiz[1], Tim P. Kelly[2], Mehrdad Sabetzadeh[3], and Didier Van Den Abeele[4]

[1] ICT-European Software Institute, TECNALIA, Parque Tecnológico Ed. 202, Zamudio, Spain
[2] Department of Computer Science, University of York, York, United Kingdom
[3] Simula Research Laboratory, Norway
[4] Alstom Transport, France
alejandra.ruiz@tecnalia.com, tim.kelly@york.ac.uk,
mehrdad@simula.no, didier.van-den-abeele@transport.alstom.com

Abstract. Safety assurance and certification are amongst the most expensive and time-consuming tasks in the development of safety-critical systems. The increasing complexity and size of these systems combined with their growing market demand requires the industry to implement a coherent reuse strategy. A key difficulty appears when trying to reuse products from one application domain in another, because different domains are subject to different safety regulations. Subsequently, for a reused product, the full safety assurance and certification process has to be applied, just as for a new product. This reduces the return on investment of such reuse. Further, market trends strongly suggest that many future safety-critical systems will be comprised of heterogeneous, dynamic coalitions of systems of systems. For this type of systems, it is crucial to develop sound strategies that would allow safety assurance and certification to be done compositionally.

1 Overview

The innovation and productivity in the market of safety-critical embedded systems is curtailed by the lack of affordable safety assurance and (re)certification approaches. Major problems arise when evolutions to a system entail reconstruction of the entire body of certification arguments and evidence.

Modern engineering and business practices use massive subcontracting and Commercial Off The Shelf (COTS) component-based development that provide little visibility into subsystem designs. In the aerospace domain, experience shows that despite the difficulties and costs incurred over the certification of COTS components, these components pose relatively few problems, and in most cases, with only minor negative impact. This observation suggests that the required levels of safety can be met by adopting broadly-used COTS products, thus laying the groundwork for a reuse strategy in aerospace system design. In the automotive domain, ISO 26262 has introduced the concept of SEooC (Safety Element out of Context) where a component is evaluated against "presumed" operational context conditions. Once the component becomes part of a specific system in an actual operational context, the evaluation is

F. Ortmeier and P. Daniel (Eds.): SAFECOMP 2012 Workshops, LNCS 7613, pp. 3–7, 2012.
© Springer-Verlag Berlin Heidelberg 2012

optimised by comparing assumed context conditions against actual context conditions. This is in the right direction though it deserves to be investigated further.

Incremental and modular certification is a hot topic on the different European R&D agendas. For instance, the ARTEMIS platform of embedded systems has included this topic as one of the most challenging and influential for the next generation of systems and systems of systems (Annual Programme 2012 and Strategic Research Agenda). The EU FP7 program has recently launched several projects on safety certification as result of its Call 7 for embedded systems.

2   Objectives

SASSUR aims at bringing together experts, researchers, and practitioners, from diverse communities, such as safety and security engineering, certification processes, model-based technologies, software and hardware design, safety-critical systems and applications communities (railway, aerospace, automotive, health, industrial manufacturing).

The topics of the proposed workshop are extremely important from an economical and social view and yet some of them still constitute emerging research areas, possibly without well-established or recognized results and require integration of knowledge and cross fertilization from different domains. SAFECOMP is an excellent opportunity to bring together people from diverse critical systems communities, such as automotive, avionics, railway... Jointly, these communities can help create a critical mass of research, development and innovation in safety critical areas. An open exchange of ideas and experiences will benefit the global community, leading to new insights and stimulating further development.

The SASSUR workshop is intended to explore new ideas on compositional and evolutionary safety assurance and certification. In particular, SASSUR will provide a platform for thematic presentations and in-depth discussions about reuse and composition of safety arguments, safety evidence, and contextual information about system components, in a way that makes assurance and certification more cost-effective, precise, and scalable.

3   Topics

Contributions were sought in (but are not limited to) the following topics:

- Industrial challenges for cost-effective safety assurance and certification
- Cross-domain product certification
- Integration of process-centric and product-centric assurance
- Compliance management of standards and regulations
- Evidence traceability
- Transparency of the safety assurance and certification processes: metrics and business cases
- Evolutionary approaches for safety and security assurance and certification

- Case-based assurance approaches
- Open-source tools for supporting of safety assurance
- Mixed-criticality systems and multi-core platforms
- Model-based methods and tools for safety assurance and certification support .

4   Workshop Contributions

Safety assurance and safety certification processes are some of the main concerns on the industry. On one hand industry needs to be competitive so new technologies are being included on the developments. The Integrated Modular Avionics (IMA) architecture on the avionics domain is becoming popular but still innovative and brings questions for the reuse of the certification artefacts. Also multi-core technologies are an important issue while dealing with certification and continue being an area for research. Also on the certification topic evidence evolution is an open issue.

Model based developments are emerging on critical systems, and new frameworks and methods need to be discussed to help decrease the entrance barrier on the industry.

For safety assurance, the use of safety cases is very popular however this area is willing to improve on confidence and some support on automation.

The papers presented on SASSUR deal with the topics mentioned before and create topics for discussion and address new areas for research. Overall 6 long presentations and 4 short presentations have been accepted for the workshop. A synopsis of each presentation is given below.

AdvoCATE: An Assurance Case Automation Toolset : It introduces a tool suite for construction of safety cases and further provides a number of quantitative metrics to analyze the progress of safety case construction. An architectural view of the tool suite is provided and explained, along with illustrations and interoperability features. While the paper is focused primarily on tooling aspects, it manages to provide a concise outline of some of the authors' earlier work on automated generation of safety cases from proofs, and how that work blends into the tool suite. Behind the description of the tool capabilities, authors introduce a number of principles supporting the toolset. Among them, interoperability of the specification is a topic carefully considered in AdvoCATE, both with similar tools (e.g. for safety case specification) and with complementary tools (e.g. formal verification tools). Finally, authors present the measurement capabilities built on metrics derivation

Modelling for Safety in a Synthesis-Centric Systems Engineering Framework: This paper presents a framework for model-based systems engineering relying on formal methods to automatically synthesize control designs. It gives an overview about the principles of Supervisory Control Synthesis, describes the systems engineering framework and a case study involving control of theme park vehicles (3 other case studies are briefly mentioned, too).

Towards a Case-Based Reasoning Approach for Safety Assurance Reuse: The authors address certification issues for Modular Avionics (IMA) platform and presents an approach using case-based reasoning (CBR) to facilitate the production of safety cases. In order to take into account new challenges, which are related to the use of multi-core and mixed-criticality technologies, the authors discuss the importance of techniques based on modular argumentation.

A model based approach for safety analysis: This paper describes a model-based safety analysis approach applied to the railway domain. It covers Preliminary Hazard Analysis (PHA) and Failure Mode and Effect Analysis (FMEA) as two safety engineering activities running in paralell with development activities. The approach is based on SysML and some extensions incrementally done in the IMOFIS and VERDE projects. The paper presents the on-going work to define the modeling bridges between the proposed graphical modeling language (SysML-based) and the Altarica language. The focus of the paper is the adds to support FMEA in the SysML-based language extensions and the formalization of the model transformation.

A Preliminary Fault Injection Framework for Evaluating Multicore Systems: The paper describes an experimental fault injection mechanism and framework for evaluating multicore systems. The general background of multicore architecture issues compared to single core architectures is being introduced, followed by an intro to the framework itself and its application in two scenarios with Linux as application. A preliminary case study using the Machine Check Architecture of the Intel Core i7 to analyse error handling in the Linux Operating System is provided.

Meeting Real-Time Requirements with Multi-Core Processors: The paper concerns WCET analysis for multi-core systems, an open industrial challenge and obstacle to the adoption of multicore architectures for safety-critical embedded systems. The papers reviews timing anomalies due to concurrent access to shared resources and high-performance architectural features and techniques, provides experimental results and summarize some important recommendations for obtaining predictable multi-core architectures for hard real-time systems.

A New Approach to Assessment of Confidence in Assurance Cases: This paper presents an approach to assessing the confidence in safety arguments through converting ARM-based representations into Toulmin form and then using Hitchcock's reasoning assessment criteria as the basis of a of Bayesian Belief Networks model of confidence.

An Unified Meta-Model for Trustworthy Systems Engineering: The paper aims to provide the theoretical principles and associated meta-model of systems engineering. It presents and explains a meta (meta) model for Systems Engineering of potentially safety-critical systems. It talks around a number of concepts including requirements vs. specifications, product vs. process views.

Assessing Software Interference Management When Modifying Safety-Related Software: This paper is about an important issue in safety-related software development, unintended interference, and its associated assessment. It introduces and refines a workflow to identify interference and how to manage it systematically.

Towards a Model-Based Evolutionary Chain of Evidence for Compliance with Safety Standards: The development and evolution of chains of evidence underlying a compliance / safety case are clearly of high relevance to industry. Making the way that elements are addressed to be as standardised as possible across multiple regulators in a domain is laudable and challenging. This paper gives a clear overview of the current state of a number of issues that need to be addressed with respect to evidence chains. It is not so detailed on solutions and validations of these solutions.

We hope that you enjoy SASSUR 2012.

General Chairs:
Mehrdad Sabetzadeh - Simula Research Laboratory, Norway
Tim Kelly - University of York, UK
Didier Van Den Abeele - Alstom Transport, France
Alejandra Ruiz - TECNALIA, Spain

Steering Commitee
Annie Combelles - Inspearit, France
John Favaro & Paolo Panaroni - Intecs, Italy
Huascar Espinoza - TECNALIA, Spain
Fulvio Tagliabò - Centro Ricerche FIAT, Italy
Javier Díaz - University of Granada, Spain

Program Committee:
Fabien Belmonte - Alstom Transport Information Solution, France
Jose Luis De La Vara - Simula Research Laboratory, Norway
Kenji Taguchi - AIST, Japan
Daniela Cancilla – Atego, France
Olaf Kath - ikv++ technologies ag, Germany
Harold Weffers - Eindhoven University of Technology, Holland
Sergio Campos – TECNALIA, Spain
Marc Born - ikv++ technologies ag, Germany
C. Michael Holloway - NASA Langley Research Center, USA
Ronald Blanrue - EUROCOPTER
Uwe Kremer – TUEV, Germany
Jürgen Niehaus- Safetrans, Germany
Xabier Larrucea – TECNALIA, Spain
Andreas Keis – EADS, Germany
Mark Nicholson - University of York, UK

Acknowledgment. We would like to give special thanks to OPENCOS Project (FP7 programme) and to RECOMP Project (ARTEMIS programme) that have kindle sponsor this workshop.

AdvoCATE: An Assurance Case Automation Toolset

Ewen Denney, Ganesh Pai, and Josef Pohl

SGT / NASA Ames Research Center
Moffett Field, CA 94035, USA
{ewen.denney,ganesh.pai,josef.pohl}@nasa.gov

Abstract. We present AdvoCATE, an Assurance Case Automation ToolsEt, to support the automated construction and assessment of safety cases. In addition to manual creation and editing, it has a growing suite of automated features. In this paper, we highlight its capabilities for (i) inclusion of specific metadata, (ii) translation to and from various formats, including those of other widely used safety case tools, (iii) composition, with auto-generated safety case fragments, and (iv) computation of safety case metrics which, we believe, will provide a transparent, quantitative basis for assessment of the state of a safety case as it evolves. The tool primarily supports the Goal Structuring Notation (GSN), is compliant with the GSN Community Standard Version 1, and the Object Modeling Group Argumentation Metamodel (OMG ARM).

Keywords: Assurance cases, Safety cases, Metrics, Safety management, Safety process, Safety toolset, Formal methods.

1 Introduction

Structured, evidence-based arguments are increasingly being adopted as a means for assurance, e.g., as dependability or assurance cases [15], and more popularly as *safety cases* [18], for safety assurance in several domains including automotive, medical devices, and aviation. Safety cases have already been in use for some time in the defense, rail, and oil & gas sectors. The practitioner has a broad choice of tools, e.g., [1, 13, 14, 17], to use in creating structured safety assurance arguments (manually) in a variety of notations such as the Goal Structuring Notation (GSN) [10], and the Claims Argument Evidence (CAE) notation. This is, by no means, a comprehensive list of available safety case construction tools, each of which have different foci, e.g., linking to type theory, use of different notations for graphical representation of safety cases, etc. However, common to all the tools is manual safety case creation with limited support for auto-generation or automatic assembly. Creating safety cases manually can be time consuming and costly.

Our goal is to develop a framework for the automated creation and assembly of assurance cases, using model-based transformation. In particular, we want to (i) leverage our earlier work on using the output of formal methods to create auto-generated safety case fragments [3], and additionally (ii) automatically combine them with the results of traditional safety analyses, also transforming these into safety case fragments [8]. The latter is aimed at supporting lightweight, automatic assembly and integration of safety

F. Ortmeier and P. Daniel (Eds.): SAFECOMP 2012 Workshops, LNCS 7613, pp. 8–21, 2012.

cases into traditional safety, and development processes [6]. We aim to support the more general notion of assurance cases, although in this paper we focus on safety cases.

We present AdvoCATE, the Assurance Case Automation ToolsEt, a suite of tools and applications based on the Eclipse platform[1], to build and transform safety cases. The core of the system is a graphical safety case editor, integrated with a set of model-based transformations that provide functionality for translating and merging pre-existing safety cases from other formats, and for incorporating automatically generated content from external formal verification tools. The tool metamodel (Section 2.1) extends the GSN, e.g., through the inclusion of metadata (Section 2.2). The tool (Section 3) supports basic manual creation and editing (Section 4.1), and interoperability with other safety case tool formats (Section 4.2). The metadata supports automation in safety case creation, for assembly of safety case fragments that have themselves been auto-generated using formal methods (Section 5), generation of safety case metrics (Section 6), and transformations to generate "to-do" lists, textual narratives, and tabular representations (Section 7).

We are using AdvoCATE in the ongoing construction of a safety case for the Swift Unmanned Aircraft System (UAS), under development at NASA Ames.

2   Extended Goal Structuring Notation

2.1   Metamodel

In AdvoCATE, we have defined and implemented an Extended Goal Structuring Notation (EGSN) metamodel, to extend "traditional" GSN with additional information, e.g., node metadata, to be used to define more features and operations. The EGSN metamodel has been developed as a combination of several different safety and assurance case models; it is compatible both with the GSN standard [10], and the Argumentation Metamodel (ARM)[2], from the Object Management Group. There is a mapping from any EGSN-based model to ARM, and vice versa; the major difference is that EGSN explicitly contains all of the standard constructs, and only the two relationships as defined in the GSN. This is, of course, extensible and extra relationships and/or reasoning elements (in ARM terminology), can be added as needed.

The top level of any safety case model based on the EGSN metamodel (Fig. 1) is a *SafetyCase* element. Essentially, this is the container that holds all elements of the safety case; it has no attributes, and children of *SafetyCase* can be concrete instances of either of the the abstract elements *Node* or *Link*. A *Node* generalizes the different types of GSN elements, i.e., *Goal, Strategy, Assumption, Justification, Context*, and *Evidence*[3]. The attributes of a *Node* are:

– *identifier*, which holds a unique name for a given node.
– *description*, which is user-supplied content describing/defining the node.

---

[1] http://www.eclipse.org
[2] GSN is itself in compliance with ARM, which is available at:
    http://www.omg.org/spec/ARM/
[3] Strictly speaking, the GSN uses the term *Solution*. We use the term *Evidence* interchangeably with *Solution*.

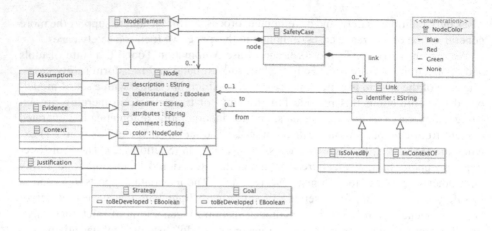

Fig. 1. EGSN metamodel in UML, representing model elements, attributes and relationships

- *color*, an attribute which is meant to indicate the color used for display; informally, we use it to convey the relative importance, source, or node state.
- *comment*, which we use to give informal information about a node.
- *toBeInstantiated*, which we use to denote abstract GSN elements that require further instantiation of specific content within the *description*, and
- *attributes*, which are used to hold extra metadata about the node, e.g., classification of the node as a high- or low-level requirement, and merging points with auto-generated content.

We can modify the attributes (above) as required and they are inherited by each node specialization. The *Goal* and *Strategy* elements also contain an additional attribute, *toBeDeveloped*, which denotes that the elements are yet to be developed, e.g., by using strategies to connect them to sub-goals/solutions. The GSN standard limits applying the *toBeDeveloped* annotation to only *Goal* and *Strategy* elements, whereas the attribute *toBeInstantiated* applies to any node.

A *Link* is also an abstract entity and contains the attribute *identifier*. Links have containment relationships, which relate the *Node*, *from* which the link comes, and *to* which it goes. These relationships refer to the abstract entity *Node* and not directly to the derived entities. The *InContextOf* link, represents a one-way association between the *Goal* (*Strategy*) element, and the *Context*, *Assumption* or *Justification* elements respectively; the *IsSolvedBy* link, denotes a one-way association between *Goal*, *Strategy*, and *Evidence* elements.

2.2   Node Metadata

We tag nodes with metadata to convey meaning about the significance or provenance of particular nodes in a safety case, such as whether they relate to the mitigation of a specific hazard, or whether they represent requirements that can be formally verified using external tools.

Node metadata is expressed as a set of attributes associated with each node. We use metadata to define transformations on the safety case and during metrics computation. At present, we have a pre-defined list of attributes that may be used. Eventually, this will be replaced with a user-definable dictionary of attributes based on an ontology. There is a strict syntax for defining attributes, as below, and multiple attributes are comma-separated.

1. High-level and Low-level requirements
   – High-Level Requirement
   – Low-Level Requirement
2. Risks
   – Risk[Likelihood,Severity]
   where
   – Likelihood ::= Extremely Improbable | Extremely Remote | Remote | Probable
   – Severity ::= Catastrophic | Hazardous | Major | Minor | No Safety Effect
3. Hazards
   – Hazard[Identifier]
   where identifier is a string giving a reference identifier in a hazard table.
4. Provenance
   – autocert:n
   where n is a number giving an AUTOCERT [9] requirement. The auto-generated fragment produced by verifying the formal requirement number n, will be merged into the safety case at this node (described in more detail in Section 5).

The tool has been designed so that different attributes affect the display (color) of the nodes, e.g., the attributes *Risk*, *Hazard*, and *Requirement* affect node color. The idea is to provide a visual indicator to the user to convey specific semantics.

For instance, for requirement attributes, *High-Level Requirement* will assign a red node color, whereas *Low-Level Requirement* will assign a green color. The *Hazard* attribute will turn a node red as well. For the *Risk* attribute, the color scheme is dependent on the combination of *Severity* and *Likelihood*, and is based on a risk categorization matrix, e.g., such as the one defined in [19]. Node color will turn red, green, or remain blue depending on whether the risk region in the risk categorization matrix is *high*, *medium*, or *low*. Once a color has been set by an attribute, it cannot be manually changed. In the case of multiple attributes, the color set by the first attribute takes precedence. The rules used to determine node colors are currently hard-coded, but we plan to make it user-definable in future.

3   Tool Chain Architecture and Implementation

In this section, we briefly describe the different frameworks and components that comprise the AdvoCATE tool chain (Fig. 2), and their integration.

Eclipse. AdvoCATE is distributed as a set of plug-ins to the Eclipse platform. Eclipse uses a number of utilities of the underlying frameworks, namely the Eclipse Modeling Framework (EMF) and the Graphical Editing Framework (GEF). AdvoCATE

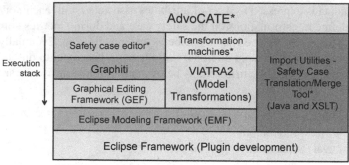

Fig. 2. Frameworks in the AdvoCATE tool chain architecture

uses the generated EMF editing tools. In principle, we could provide *extension points*[4] to extend AdvoCATE as well.

Graphical Editing. The graphical component, at the core of the safety case editor, permits the addition and manipulation of elements of a safety case. It also provides a visual representation of the relationships between the safety case model elements. The safety case model created is maintained as a separate resource from its visual representation, and the diagram. In this way, the model can be used and manipulated separately without affecting the graphical representation. Similarly, none of the information of the graphical representation affects the model except when explicitly specified, e.g., *color* can be stored as part of the properties. The two files are combined to create the diagram that is rendered on the screen and is editable by the user. Both representations are contained inside an Eclipse project. The model data file is connected to the Ecore metamodel, i.e., it must be a well-formed representation of that metamodel.

Graphiti. We built the graphical component in the Graphiti framework, an application interface (API) built upon the GEF. As shown in Fig. 2, the GEF is itself built on top of EMF. Graphiti simplifies the development of graphical tools for editing and displaying models, by automating much of the low-level implementation used to manipulate graphical objects such as rendering, moving, selecting, etc.

Translation. The tool uses XSLT to convert external data into the appropriate XML format (such as the AUTOCERT-generated XML, Section 5), which can be merged with a pre-existing assurance case. The file formats for assurance cases developed in other tools, such as ASCE, are parsed using Java DOM XML libraries.

VIATRA2. *VIATRA*2 (*VI*sual *A*utomated model *TRA*nsformations) [20], a project developed within the Generative Modeling Technology (GMT) framework, is a toolset designed for engineering life-cycle support from specification to maintenance. In the scope of AdvoCATE, it is used to hold intermediate model representations (such

---

[4] Plug-ins typically will provide extension points, by connecting to any of which we gain access to their functionality, e.g., the context menus and diagram creation utilities are extended from the core Eclipse user interface.

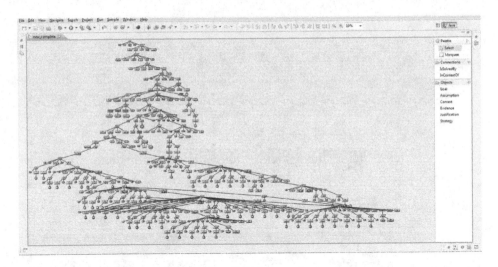

Fig. 3. AdvoCATE screenshot displaying auto-layout on the auto-assembled Swift UAS safety case fragment, which contains both manually created and auto-generated fragments

as the EGSN Ecore representation) and enact transformations on those models. Through the transformation system, we can manipulate and transform safety case models into other models (such as text, a CSV table, or a modified safety case).

4   Basic Functionality and Interoperability

Although the primary goal of AdvoCATE is to support automation, it also contains the basic manual functionality that one would expect from a safety case tool, i.e., creating and editing. In this section, we describe this manual functionality, giving an overview of some basic use-cases for the tool: to create a new safety case diagram/model, and to open a pre-existing model (as a diagram) for further editing or manipulation. Additional basic functionality includes saving, printing, translating from/to other formats, and merging external data.

4.1   Creating and Editing Safety Cases

Fig. 3 shows a bird's eye view of the structure of an end-to-end safety case fragment for the Swift UAS. It has been automatically assembled/composed from a manually created fragment and an auto-generated fragment, after which it underwent auto-layout.

Editing a diagram typically takes place within a more detailed view (Fig. 4) that shows more node information, as well as the editing features. We can select, move and resize nodes as required; node descriptions are editable either directly on the canvas, or in the properties panel, whereas attributes are edited only via the latter. Edits are reflected in the diagram in real-time, through automatic refresh. In Fig. 4, the canvas shows that the goal with identifier N48087573 (at the top right of the canvas) is selected and being edited. The properties panel beneath the canvas shows the corresponding

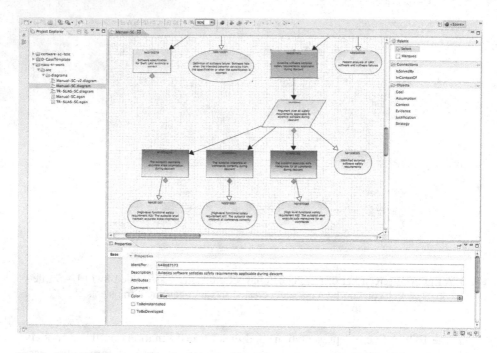

Fig. 4. AdvoCATE screenshot showing a zoomed-in view for editing, with a *Properties* panel underneath the canvas, the *Project explorer* as the left panel, and the *Palette* containing EGSN constructs in the right panel

attributes that can be edited, and we can add new values directly, as required. Attribute editing uses specialized syntax (Section 2.2) to include pre-defined node metadata.

Safety cases can be split up into separate interconnected diagrams using the *Goal Developed Elsewhere* symbol ([16], p. 66). Note that this does not provide true modularity in the sense of the modular GSN notation [10], which we do not yet support, but it does make large safety cases more manageable.

We can link to other documents such as webpages, spreadsheets, or text documents. These documents can either be local to the system or remotely stored, e.g., on a web server. We provide a specific syntax to make references to external documentation: in the *description* attribute for a node, the reference to the external document is specified as a fully qualified URL in the properties panel. The resource will be displayed in a web browser or the user will be prompted to open/save the resource.

Diagrams can be exported as an image in scalable vector graphics (SVG) format, and subsequently converted[5] to portable document format (PDF).

4.2   Interoperability

AdvoCATE supports the import/export of a variety of safety case formats—currently those produced from the ASCE [1], CertWare [13], and D-Case [14] tools. A translation

---
[5] Using the Batik toolkit: http://xmlgraphics.apache.org/batik/

engine acts as an import/export utility translating file formats from these tools into EGSN, and vice versa. If an EGSN file already exists it can be imported directly.

The translation works by using ARM as the interoperability metamodel, i.e., there are bidirectional translations between ARM and the different safety case formats. Consequently we only need to define a translation from each format to/from ARM rather than defining point-to-point connections between each tool. The ARM is also convenient for merging external information.

One of the challenges in model transformation, as between EGSN and other safety case formats, is that each metamodel has different attributes, and sometimes differing model elements. To preserve information between translations, we annotate the information as comments in the EGSN metamodel. The annotations indicate the source metamodel and what the information actually represents. For instance, in EGSN, we label nodes with a user-modifiable identifier. In ASCE, there is both a unique "reference" and a user specified identifier. If, in ASCE, the user specified identifier is not provided, the unique reference is used instead. This information is preserved by storing it in the EGSN metamodel, tagging it as being from ASCE and by labeling it as the "user-id". This way, if translating back to ASCE, the information is preserved and the ASCE model can be regenerated without information loss. There are a number of such cases which we handle in a similar way.

The one exception to this is layout data; in most cases, the model is stored separately from the layout. As a design decision, we decided not to preserve layout information.

5   Automated Assembly

AdvoCATE can automatically assemble safety cases by combining manually created fragments with content produced by external tools. Currently, this is limited to the formal verification tool AUTOCERT [9], though we plan further tool integrations in future.

Rather than perform formal verification itself, AdvoCATE integrates results from formal verification or formal methods with safety case construction. In general, there are two ways to achieve this: (i) the output of a tool can produce evidence or, depending on the level of detail it provides, be transformed into an actual argument fragment of a safety case [8], and (ii) safety case fragments can be transformed into formal specifications that are then input to a tool.

An AUTOCERT specification formalizes software requirements that we derive from system safety requirements, during safety analysis. Formal verification takes place in the context of a logical domain theory, i.e., a set of axioms and function specifications. To verify the software, we use formal verification of the implementation against a mathematical specification and test low-level library functions against their specifications.

5.1   From Formal Proofs to Safety Cases

AUTOCERT generates a document (in XML) with information describing the formal verification of requirements. The core of this is the chain of information relating requirements back to assumptions.

Each step is described by (i) an annotation schema for the definition of a program variable [4], (ii) the associated verification conditions (VCs) that must be shown for the correctness of that definition, and (iii) the variables on which that variable, in turn, depends. We derive the goals (and subgoals) of the safety case from the annotation schema. The subgoals are the dependent variables from those annotation schema. We represent each VC related to a goal as a subgoal. An argument for a VC is a proof, generated using a subset of the axioms. This proof forms the evidence connected to the VC goal, and includes the prover used as a context. Function specifications from external libraries used in the software and its verification also appear as goals. Arguments for these goals can be made with evidence such as testing or inspection. Each subgoal derived from an annotation schema is a step in the verification process.

During the process of merging the manually created and the auto-generated safety cases, we replace specific nodes of the manually created safety case with the tree fragments generated from AUTOCERT; specifically, the top-level goals of the latter are grafted onto the appropriate lowest-level nodes of the former. These nodes are denoted with unique attributes, autocert:n, relating the node to a tree in the automatically created file, meaning that the goal with tag n is to be solved with AUTOCERT. Additionally, these nodes are formal equivalents of informally stated goals, developed through an explicit strategy of formalization, though the formalization at this stage is both performed and checked manually.

5.2   From Safety Cases to Formal Specifications

Often, a safety case fragment may be created before the software verification is completed. In this case, we can use the autocert:n annotations on the nodes to generate a formal specification. Based on the type of node in which the identifier occurs, the tool infers whether the labeled node is a requirement or an assumption. Thereafter, we can transform and graft back onto the safety case the proofs that result after running AUTOCERT on the generated specification.

6   Generation of Safety Case Metrics

6.1   Metrics Derivation

There has been some criticism of safety cases as lacking a measurement basis and, therefore, impeding systematic, repeatable evaluation [21]. We attempt to address this weakness of safety cases, using AdvoCATE, by defining and implementing a (preliminary) set of safety case metrics. Our goal is to create a transparent, quantitative foundation for assessment/review. It is worth noting that metrics alone (including those given here) do not necessarily constitute an assessment; rather, together with a model for interpretation, they can provide a convenient mechanism for decision-making by summarizing the state and key properties of a safety case during its evolution.

We distinguish between (i) *base* metrics, which express a direct measurement of, or value assignment to, a safety case property, e.g., the number of claims in a safety argument, and (ii) *derived* metrics, which are an analytical combination of base metrics, expressing a measure of, or a value assignment to, a safety case property that is not directly measurable, e.g., coverage.

Table 1. (Excerpt) GQM based derivation of safety case metrics and their specification

Goal G1. Coverage of Claims: *Analyze* the argument structure *for the purpose of* establishing the extent of coverage *with respect to* the claims made and the evidence presented *from the viewpoint of* the assessment team *in the context of* the safety case of the Swift UAS.	
Questions	**Metrics**
Q1.1. What is the total number of claims made?	BM1.1. Total #(Claims)
Q1.2. What is the total number of claims that end in evidence, i.e., developed claims?	DM1.2. Total #(Developed claims)
Q1.3. What fraction of the total number of claims are developed claims?	DM1.3. Coverage (Claims)
Specification: – BM1.1. Total #(Claims) = C, $C \geq 1$. – DM1.2. Total #(Developed claims) = C_D, $C_D \geq 0$. – DM1.3. Coverage (Claims) = Fraction of developed claims = $COV_C = \frac{C_D}{C}$.	

We consider an underlying process for safety case assessment, e.g., based on inspections [11], or reviews [12] to get insights into where metrics can be useful for decision making during assessment, and the interpretation models required. Thereafter, we use the Goal-Question-Metric (GQM) method [2] to define appropriate measurement goals, identify questions that characterize the goal, and specify the relevant metrics.

For instance, in a staged argument review [12], quantitative measures applied at the step of checking well-formedness can summarize the relevant properties, e.g., the number of goals with missing evidence/strategies. This can be useful when assessing large argument structures, where manual review of the entire structure, for well-formedness, can be time consuming. Similarly, during the argument criticism and defeat step, coverage of the top-level claim by evidence is a property for which metrics can be defined.

Table 1 gives an example of how GQM has been used to define metrics that, we believe, meet the goal of analyzing claims coverage. We state the measurement goal by instantiating the GQM template (the *italicized* text in Table 1), identify questions that characterize the goal, and define the metrics that answer the questions quantitatively. In Table 1, the base and derived metrics are distinguished by the prefixes BM and DM respectively. In this way, by defining additional measurement goals, we have specified[6] a preliminary set of safety case metrics (Table 2). For this paper, we have mainly focused on metrics that address the structural and syntactical properties of argument structures described using the GSN.

Note that although tool support can also be used to highlight violations, e.g., of well-formedness properties, this is mainly useful during argument development, where the intent would be to "find and fix". From the perspective of an assessor, however, the broad intent is to evaluate the argument for essential qualities [11]. When properly defined and interpreted, we hypothesize that metrics can be indicators of these qualities.

6.2 Metrics Implementation

The generation of the safety case metrics, as given in Table 2, is an automated operation, which uses some of the node metadata (Section 2.2) to count the nodes in the

---

[6] The full GQM-based derivation of the metrics, and their formal specifications, are out of the scope of this paper.

Table 2. Safety case metrics, with their valid values

Metric	Symbol	Type	Valid Values
Measures of Size			
Total #(Hazards considered in the safety case)	H	Base	≥ 0
Total #(Hazards identified in hazard analysis)	HI	Base	≥ 0
#(High-level safety requirements per hazard H_i)	$r(H_i)$	Base	≥ 0
Total #(High-level safety requirements)	R_{HL}	Base	≥ 0
Total #(Low-level safety requirements)	R_{LL}	Base	≥ 0
#(Developed claims per hazard H_i)	$c_D(H_i)$	Base	≥ 0
#(Claims per high-level safety requirement HLR$_i$)	$C(\text{HLR}_i)$	Base	≥ 0
#(Claims per low-level safety requirement LLR$_i$)	$C(\text{LLR}_i)$	Base	≥ 0
Total #(Claims)	C	Base	≥ 1
Total #(Developed claims)	C_D	Derived	≥ 0
Total #(Undeveloped claims)	C_{UD}	Derived	≥ 0
Total #(Uninstantiated claims)	C_{UI}	Derived	≥ 0
Total #(Strategies)	S	Base	≥ 0
Total #(Undeveloped strategies)	S_{UD}	Derived	≥ 0
Total #(Uninstantiated strategies)	S_{UI}	Derived	≥ 0
Total #(Contexts)	K	Base	≥ 0
Total #(Assumptions)	A	Base	≥ 0
Total #(Justifications)	J	Base	≥ 0
Total #(Evidence)	E	Base	≥ 0
Measures of Coverage			
Coverage (Claims)	COV_C	Derived	$[0,1]$
Coverage (High-level safety requirements)	$COV_{R_{HL}}$	Derived	$[0,1]$
Coverage (Low-level safety requirements)	$COV_{R_{LL}}$	Derived	$[0,1]$
Coverage (Hazards considered)	COV_{CH}	Derived	$[0,1]$
Coverage (Hazards Identified)	COV_{HI}	Derived	$[0,1]$

EGSN-based safety case model, e.g., counting the nodes containing "high-level require-ment" as an attribute gives the value assignment for the metric R_{HL}. Presently, only certain node types can be distinguished based on node attributes and metadata. Conse-quently, only a subset of the metrics identified in Table 2 have been implemented.

Fig. 5 shows the implemented metrics and the computed values when applied to the Swift UAS safety case fragment [8] (also shown as a bird's eye view in Fig. 3). As we define more expressive/detailed node metadata, we can implement the remainder of the metrics from Table 2, as well as additional metrics such as "confidence in a claim" [7].

7   Transformation Operations

We describe three automated operations defined in AdvoCATE, for generating artifacts that support safety case development and assessment:

To-do Lists. One simple form of assessment is determining those parts of the safety case that need further development. AdvoCATE uses a *Model2Text* transformation to create a simple to-do list, listing the undeveloped and uninstantiated nodes. Fig. 6 shows an excerpt of such a to-do list, for the Swift UAS safety case fragment.

```
---SIZE METRICS---
Goals: 220
        Developed: 157
        Undeveloped: 63
        Uninstantiated: 6
Strategies: 107
        Undeveloped: 13
        Uninstantiated: 0
Contexts: 133
Assumptions: 5
Justifications: 3
Evidence: 65
TOTAL NODES: 533


R_HL : Number of High-Level Requirements = 3
R_LL : Number of Low-Level Requirements = 2
R1_HL : Number of claims (High-Level Requirement 1) = 182
R2_HL : Number of claims (High-Level Requirement 2) = 1
R3_HL : Number of claims (High-Level Requirement 3) = 1
R1_LL : Number of claims (Low-Level Requirement 1) = 32
R2_LL : Number of claims (Low-Level Requirement 2) = 122


--- COVERAGE METRICS ---
COV_C : Developed claims to total claims = 0.71
COV_R_HL : Coverage of High-Level Requirements = 0.8
COV_R_LL : Coverage of Low-Level Requirements = 0.88
```

Fig. 5. AdvoCATE calculation of metrics for the Swift UAS safety case fragment

```
Undeveloped Goals To Do:
      ID:N43752193 :: Failure hazards during Cruise phase are mitigated
      ID:AC486 :: srcWpPos is a position in the NE frame (i.e. has_unit(srcWpPos, pos(ne)) holds.)
      ID:N63112384 :: Modem interface is correct ID:N11943209 :: FMS design is correct
      ...
Uninstantiated Goals To Do:
      ID:N87102962 :: Autopilot module satisfies {Higher-level Requirement X}
      Derived from parent ID: N92654598 :: Argument that Autopilot module satisfies higher level
                                        requirements
      ID:N59408212 :: {Subsystem X} failure hazard during descent is mitigated
      Derived from parent ID: N3143972 :: Argument over all Swift UAV subsystems (identified
                                        failure hazards)
```

Fig. 6. (Excerpt) To-do list generated by AdvoCATE, for the Swift UAS safety case fragment

Narrative Form. The generation of a safety case narrative form, i.e., a structured document providing the content of the safety case in a readable form, uses an intermediate tree model. The safety case can then be flattened into a sequence that is a pre-order traversal of the tree, giving a description of the content of the safety case without the diagrammatic form.

Tabular Form. We generate a comma separated value (CSV) format of the document (Fig. 7) using an intermediate model for the transformation. The CSV template relates a goal with an arbitrary number of contexts and strategies. The strategies are further related to any number of assumptions, contexts, justifications, and subgoals. For each goal the operation generates these relationships. The operation then repeats the process for each sub-goal related to each strategy. The rationale for a specific CSV format of a safety case, and the resulting tabular form, is based on the experiences gained [5] from the ongoing creation of the Swift UAS safety case.

PARENT GOAL	CONTEXT	STRATEGY				SUBGOAL/SOLUTION
		Strategy Type	Context	Assumptions	Justifications	
N27216417: SWIFT UAS is safe	N80058283: Range (Location and Site) of operation	N18584532: Argument of safety over all UAS subsystems and interactions between subsystems	N91753638: SWIFT UAS Design Management Plan and Design Documentation			N2946770: SWIFT UAS Communication Infrastructure is safe
	N24389172: Specified configuration					N20743322: Airborne system (SWIFT UAV) is safe
	N44679952: Weather conditions					N83345544: SWIFT UAS subsystem interactions are safe
	N86072314: Specified Mission					N67094880: SWIFT Ground stations are safe
N2946770: SWIFT UAS Communication Infrastructure is safe						
N20743322: Airborne system (SWIFT UAV) is safe		N70618522: Argument of hazard mitigation over all identified SWIFT UAV hazards	N49558532: Definition of acceptable risk and risk categories			N44519454: Interaction hazards
			N2965510: Identified hazards and hazard categories during Swift UAV Hazard analysis			N69623828: SWIFT UAV failure hazards are mitigated
			N84863913: Definition of hazard from MIL-STD-882D			N40609843: Hazards arising from the operating environment of SWIFT UAV are mitigated

Fig. 7. (Excerpt) CSV format of the Swift UAS safety case generated using AdvoCATE, subsequently imported into a spreadsheet, resulting in a tabular view

8 Conclusion

In this paper, we have described AdvoCATE, an Eclipse-based toolset that uses model-based transformation and extended GSN to support the automated construction and assessment of safety cases.

We have just begun to develop the wealth of functionality for automated construction that can be implemented using transformations, e.g., a simple extension will be the generation of traceability matrices linking requirements, hazards and evidence. A more involved transformation will be argument refactoring. Our next step will be to include modular extensions to GSN, patterns, and to provide automated features for their use. To support safety case assessment, we have defined and implemented a preliminary set of metrics based on the syntactic/structural properties of argument structures documented using GSN. As future work, we intend to define integrated measures that combine the metrics based on both syntactic and semantic properties, building on our previous work on confidence quantification [7]. We will also define interpretation models based upon which metrics can be used, during assessment, for decision making.

For tool validation, we continue regression testing of the interface and transformations, and we also plan to verify the algorithms that AdvoCATE implements. We believe that the capabilities of AdvoCATE, highlighted in this paper, are promising steps towards cost-effective safety assurance, and transparency during assessment and certification. Eventually, our goal is to support "round-trip engineering" of safety cases, linking safety-relevant, operational, and development artifacts.

Acknowledgements. This work was funded by the VVFCS element under the SSAT project in the Aviation Safety Program of the NASA Aeronautics Mission Directorate. We also thank Ábel Hegedüs and Michael Wenz for their help with VIATRA2 and Graphiti, respectively, and Corey Ippolito for access to the Swift UAS data.

References

[1] Adelard LLP: Assurance and safety case environment (ASCE), http://www.adelard.com/asce/ (last accessed May 2011)

[2] Basili, V., Caldiera, G., Rombach, D.: Goal question metric approach. In: Encyclopedia of Software Engineering, pp. 528–532. John Wiley (1994)

[3] Basir, N., Denney, E., Fischer, B.: Deriving Safety Cases for Hierarchical Structure in Model-Based Development. In: Schoitsch, E. (ed.) SAFECOMP 2010. LNCS, vol. 6351, pp. 68–81. Springer, Heidelberg (2010)

[4] Denney, E., Fischer, B.: Generating customized verifiers for automatically generated code. In: Proc. Conf. Generative Programming and Component Eng., pp. 77–87 (October 2008)

[5] Denney, E., Habli, I., Pai, G.: Perspectives on software safety case development for unmanned aircraft. In: Proc. 42nd Intl. Conf. Dependable Systems and Networks (June 2012)

[6] Denney, E., Pai, G.: A Lightweight Methodology for Safety Case Assembly. In: Ortmeier, F., Daniel, P. (eds.) SAFECOMP 2012. LNCS, vol. 7612, pp. 1–12. Springer, Heidelberg (2012)

[7] Denney, E., Pai, G., Habli, I.: Towards measurement of confidence in safety cases. In: Proc. 5th Intl. Symp. Empirical Soft. Eng. and Measurement, pp. 380–383 (September 2011)

[8] Denney, E., Pai, G., Pohl, J.: Heterogeneous aviation safety cases: integrating the formal and the non-formal. In: 17th IEEE Intl. Conf. Engineering of Complex Computer Systems (July 2012)

[9] Denney, E., Trac, S.: A software safety certification tool for automatically generated guidance, navigation and control code. In: IEEE Aerospace Conf. Electronic Proc. (2008)

[10] Goal Structuring Notation Working Group: GSN Community Standard Version 1 (November 2011), http://www.goalstructuringnotation.info/

[11] Graydon, P., Knight, J., Green, M.: Certification and safety cases. In: Proc. 28th Intl. System Safety Conf. (September 2010)

[12] Kelly, T.P.: Reviewing Assurance Arguments - A Step-by-Step Approach. In: Proc. Workshop on Assurance Cases for Security - The Metrics Challenge, Dependable Systems and Networks (July 2007)

[13] Kestrel Technology LLP and NASA Langley Research Center: CertWare tool, http://nasa.github.com/CertWare/ (last accessed May 2011)

[14] Matsuno, Y., Takamura, H., Ishikawa, Y.: Dependability case editor with pattern library. In: Proc. 12th IEEE Intl. Symp. High-Assurance Systems Eng., pp. 170–171 (2010)

[15] National Research Council Committee on Certifiably Dependable Software Systems: Software for Dependable Systems: Sufficient Evidence? National Academies Press (2007)

[16] Spriggs, J.: GSN - The Goal Structuring Notation. Springer (2012)

[17] Steele, P., Collins, K., Knight, J.: ACCESS: A toolset for safety case creation and management. In: Proc. 29th Intl. Systems Safety Conf. (August 2011)

[18] UK Ministry of Defence (MoD): Safety Management Requirements for Defence Systems. Defence Standard 00-56, Issue 4 (2007)

[19] U.S. Department of Transportation, Federal Aviation Administration: System Safety Handbook. FAA (December 2000)

[20] Varró, D., Balogh, A.: The model transformation language of the VIATRA2 framework. Science of Computer Programming 68(3), 214–234 (2007)

[21] Wassyng, A., Maibaum, T., Lawford, M., Bherer, H.: Software Certification: Is There a Case against Safety Cases? In: Calinescu, R., Jackson, E. (eds.) Monterey Workshop 2010. LNCS, vol. 6662, pp. 206–227. Springer, Heidelberg (2011)

Towards a Case-Based Reasoning Approach
for Safety Assurance Reuse

Alejandra Ruiz[1], Ibrahim Habli[2], and Huáscar Espinoza[1]

[1] ICT-European Software Institute, TECNALIA, Parque Tecnológico Ed. 202, Zamudio, Spain
[2] Department of Computer Science, University of York, York, United Kingdom
{alejandra.ruiz,huascar.espinoza}@tecnalia.com,
ibrahim.habli@york.ac.uk

Abstract. The increasing complexity and size of electronic systems in the aerospace industry, combined with the growing market demand, requires the industry to implement an efficient safety assurance strategy. Reuse of safety argumentation and evidence for certification is one of the potential means for achieving such a strategy. Typically, major problems arise when the evolution of complex avionics entails the reconstruction of the entire body of safety justification, often resulting in expensive and time-consuming assurance and certification processes. This paper investigates the use of Case-Based Reasoning (CBR) as a strategy for representing, retrieving and reusing previously assured safety cases. This is supported by the existence of patterns of safety cases, which determine a unified knowledge representation scheme for retrieving further safety cases. We illustrate the approach with the development of modular argumentation for an Integrated Modular Avionics (IMA) platform.

Keywords: cased-based reasoning, safety assurance, avionics, certification.

1   Introduction

In the aerospace industry, safety-critical systems are increasingly more reliant on software, with millions of lines of software code running onboard advanced aircraft. The higher complexity and size of software combined with the growing market demand requires the industry to implement a coherent and an efficient safety assurance strategy. Driven by these considerations, the avionics domain in particular is transitioning from federated architectures to Integrated Modular Avionics (IMA) architectures. IMA defines a logically centralized and shared computing platform, which is physically distributed on the aircraft to meet redundancy requirements [10]. IMA promotes flexibility and enforces temporal and physical segregation of application components that are integrated in a single system. More precisely, IMA aims at reducing space, weight and power requirements. Further, it aims at reducing maintenance and certification costs by allowing incremental certification of avionics building blocks.

As described in [23], one of the most important issues in the reuse of an IMA platform in a given project is to reuse as much certification credit as possible from

F. Ortmeier and P. Daniel (Eds.): SAFECOMP 2012 Workshops, LNCS 7613, pp. 22–35, 2012.

previous projects. DO-297/ED-124 is the current guidance document for IMA, but it still lacks sufficient support for dealing with changes made in existing IMA systems or when reusing design elements of an IMA. The number of acceptance criteria (e.g., safety requirements and characteristics such as fault/error handling and failure modes) and the combination of safety arguments and evidence that need to be considered in a new integration project, strongly suggest that the pre-qualification documents of an IMA platform are not reusable without a appropriate *justification*.

The concept of reuse is not limited to the reuse of software and hardware components. It is also applicable to the reuse of safety assurance artefacts, including safety argumentation used for certification. Over recent years, there has been an increasing interest in the use of safety cases for providing justification for system safety. A safety case provides a means to *"communicate a clear, comprehensive and defensible argument that a system is acceptably safe to operate in a particular context"* [4]. The development of a safety case has been a common practice for the assurance of safety-critical systems, particularly in the UK [19]. Recently, the requirement for a safety case has been included in emerging standards, e.g. the new automotive functional safety standard ISO 26262 [20], the US Food and Drug Administration's guidance on the production of infusion pump systems [21] and the aerospace guidelines for the development of civil aircraft and system ARP 4754A [22].

One of the goals of the underlying work, which is still in its early stages, is to define a framework to manage the reuse of safety assurance artefacts –evidence, argumentation and contextual information – from system components across IMA-based systems. The intention is to reuse the safety arguments across different IMA configurations. There are a number of barriers affecting reuse of safety assurance in this context. For instance, if the knowledge of the rationale behind safety-case construction is not explicit and is owned by only a few experts, the reuse opportunity is quite low. *Safety case patterns* [5] are considered to be one of the main approaches for managing reuse of safety assurance. A safety case pattern provides a means of explicitly and clearly documenting common elements found in safety cases, and it also promotes the reuse of best practices for safety assurance.

This paper presents our preliminary research on the use of safety case patterns in combination with Case-Based Reasoning (CBR) as a reuse strategy that could be used to represent and retrieve previously examined safety cases. CBR is a knowledge-based technique for solving new problems by referring to similar previously experienced concrete problems and solutions, captured as cases [25]. This is supported by the existence of repeatable patterns of safety cases, which emerge through common approaches to arguing safety. These patterns determine a unified knowledge representation scheme which will be used to retrieve further safety cases. We illustrate the approach with the development of modular argumentation for an IMA platform.

This paper is organised as follows. Section 2 describes the domain background and related work. Section 3 provides details on the proposed approach as well as the challenges of using CBR for safety assurance. Finally, Section 4 presents our preliminary conclusions.

2   Background and Related Work

2.1   Regulatory Scenario in the Avionics Domain

The avionics domain is highly regulated where multiple standards apply in the process of safety certification. Fig. 1. shows some of these standards (more precisely guidelines and guidance documents).

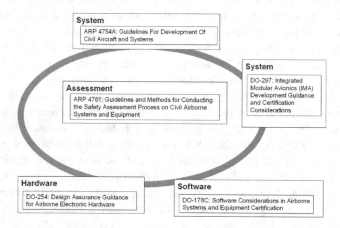

Fig. 1. Standards in the avionics domain

ARP 4754A [11] and ARP 4761 [12] provide guidelines for the development and safety assessment of aircraft and aircraft systems, targeting reduction of the number and severity of failure conditions in aircraft/system designs. These processes iterate down through systems and subsystems but at some point they establish requirements for hardware and software items. DO-254/ED-80 [9] and DO-178 [8] are quite similar in concepts and application but one is related to the production of hardware and the other to software. Both standards are objective-based and process-centred. They define objectives that should be satisfied by the chosen development, verification and support processes.

One important concept from these standards is the risk criteria. A Functional Hazard Assessment (FHA) should be conducted at the beginning of the aircraft/system development lifecycle. The result of the failure conditions addressed in the FHA will determine the assurance levels. The Development Assurance Level (DAL) *"is the measure of rigor applied to the development process to limit, to a level acceptable for safety, the likelihood of errors occurring during the development process of aircraft/system..."* [12]. The DAL, ranging from Level A (the highest) down through Levels B, C, D to E, is assigned in correspondence with the severity classification of failure conditions. These levels will affect to the number of objectives to comply with. For instance, DO-178B describes 66 objectives and requires that all of them must be applied to Level A, 65 to Level B, 57 to Level C, and 28 to Level D.

DO-297 [10] applies where IMA architecture is deployed. IMA is the term used for a distributed computing network aboard aircraft, which supports avionics applications of many different assurance levels, and is designed for flexibility in configurations and modularity. It supports assurance evidence reuse to reduce effort required when reusing components in different systems.

IMA technology has introduced the possibility to fragment the certification process into several tasks: (a) module and/or platform acceptance, (b) application acceptance (software and hardware), (c) IMA system acceptance (integration of multiple applications), (d) aircraft integration (e) change of modules or applications and (f) reuse of modules or applications.

2.2   The Multi-Core and Mixed-Criticality Technology Case

A challenging issue in the aerospace industry is that in some cases, new technologies emerge before certification processes can be adapted. This is the situation of multi-core technologies. In the avionics domain, functions are allocated to systems and subsequently to items. Some critical functions are supposed to work independently on a single core with their dedicated resources. When this is not the case, partitioning is used for which an argument is needed in order to justify that spatial and temporal independence exist between each partition.

With the introduction of multi-core computers into IMA architectures, multiple partitions may run concurrently on a single computing card all accessing memory or I/O interfaces at the same time. As a consequence, such deployments may exhibit mutual influences at the IMA execution platform, which has to be addressed by system and application designers.

The use of multi-core technologies is particularly a challenge in mixed-criticality IMA configurations. Mixed criticality is the concept of allowing applications at different levels of criticality to co-exist on the same computational platform. In a mixed-criticality system, low-critical and high-critical applications coexist and must therefore share processing time in a 'safe' way. Unfortunately, certification of such systems is more difficult, because it requires that even the components of less criticality be certified at the highest criticality level. An alternative is to present sufficient evidence so as to show that lower-critical applications do not interfere with the high-critical applications. This is one of the objectives of the underlying work.

2.3   Argumentation and Modular Safety Cases

The idea behind a safety case [4] is that the application of an argumentation approach to the concept of target compatibility would require definitions, assumptions, and limitations to be made visible. This allows a much clearer evaluation for the contribution and limit to the overall correctness of the software and therefore its contribution to safety of the system. The underlying work subscribes to the view of using such kind of argumentation in the avionics domain as a basic pre-condition to improve safety assurance reuse.

As systems are becoming more and more complex, so does the safety assurance process. One of the solutions in the context of safety argumentation is the concept of modular safety cases. In [16], Kelly proposes a contract-based approach for assuring safety across the argument modules within the safety cases. Modular safety cases can increase its reuse level by means of patterns. Kelly in [4] proposes the use of safety case patterns as a way for reusing successful safety strategies. Several patterns have been published [5]. In [6] a different approach to safety case patterns is presented, where patterns are related to certification objectives and how they help introducing conformance items for the IEC 61508 [7] standard on safety cases and improving transparency in certification processes.

2.4   The Case-Based Reasoning Approach

Case-based reasoning is an analysis technique for solving new problems by referring to similar previously experienced concrete problems and solutions, captured as cases. This is based on the hypothesis that similar problems are likely to have similar solutions [24]. Case-based reasoning is an effective analysis technique when it is infeasible to rely solely on general domain knowledge or generic associations between problem attributes and conclusions. Research has shown that experts in technical fields such as medicine, engineering, planning and finance rely on past cases to generate hypotheses about new situations.

There are a number of reasons for choosing CBR as a safety assurance reuse strategy. The main requirement for our problem context (certification in avionics and IMA) is that the solution should be able to support a significant variability from one project to another in terms of justification diversity (See Section 2.3). Additionally the reuse solution is intended to deal with a fairly wide range of kinds of arguments and certification data. Traditional rule-based knowledge approaches are not suitable for this requirement, as they require strong domain knowledge and representation. In CBR, as opposed to rule-based approaches, knowledge about the domain is acquired and maintained through unrelated but similar cases and does not need a domain expert or knowledge about the problem domain. The generic concept of our approach hence moves away from a rule-based implementation, as for each type of IMA platform and company context, specific rule-sets would need to be encoded.

CBR applied to safety assurance is new and few published work exists in this area. However some examples on how these techniques have been applied to safety related topics have been reviewed. A web-based system is presented in [1] for managing the Hazard and Operability (HAZOP) analysis based on a case based reasoning support The system shows the end user previous result from HAZOP analysis on similar environments so it can be adapted for the new case. Instead of doing the analysis from the scratch, the system tries to reuse the best practices from previous situations.

PHASUITE [2] is another CBR system for HAZOP analysis in a systematic way. PHASUITE framework consists of four main parts: information sharing, representation, knowledge base and reasoning engine. CBR techniques are used for the management of models which capture the knowledge concerning the system.

The work in [3] explains a framework that shows the first results for an industrial application where their conceptual semantic case-based framework for safety analysis is tested. Their framework facilitates the reuse of previous HAZOP and FMEA experiences in order to reduce the time and effort associated with these analyses.

A prototype is described in [17] for a semantic-case framework used in the aerospace domain, using a specific ontology. The prototype is able to guide the user for the definition of well-structured requirements.

3   Outlining a CBR Approach for Safety Assurance Reuse

3.1   Problem Description

We were particularly interested in evaluating a CBR approach for a case study on certification activities related to *IMA platform integration*, including computing and networking. The input of this certification activity is the qualification data of hardware and software components (e.g. computing unit or operating system) of IMA platforms. The outcomes of this incremental activity in certification will be used to build the certified IMA system's certification data (this includes the IMA platform plus applications on top of it).

In this context, the IMA platform architect role establishes a certification baseline about sizing hypothesis (memory, processor throughput), certification standards applicable (DO254, DO178), and functionality expected (e.g. API A653). The IMA platform architect also fixes the execution platform perimeter for the module supplier, including hardware (e.g., processing unit, IO units, and memory units) and software (OS, drivers, platform system functions, etc.). The module supplier provides what DO-297 calls the *usage domain* (characteristics and usage constraints). The module supplier also provides qualification material for certification demonstrations. Finally, the IMA platform architect validates the module supplier's data and provides formal acceptation. Acceptance of a module can only be performed in the context of the aircraft or engine certification program or modification project [10].

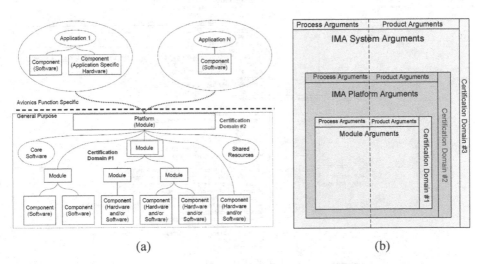

(a)   (b)

Fig. 2. Relationship of IMA elements and the incremental certification concept

Fig. 2.a describes the incremental aspects that are related to the IMA concept. The IMA platform (certification domain #2) that is built from modules (certification domain #1) and associated configuration tools are in correlation with the IMA platform Usage Domain. The *usage domain* defines the set of rules and constraints that allow the customization of the IMA platform for a specific use while keeping the certification credits obtained for the platform.

In this case study, we focus on the development of safety argumentation and patterns to demonstrate compliance with avionics standards, as part of the justifications needed to integrate the module into the IMA platform. The strategy is to define a set of claims related to IMA platform level hazards. The claims are decomposed using sub-claims, evidence, and other argumentation elements that are represented using the Goal Structuring Notation (GSN) [13].

As the argumentation in GSN models must reflect a modular approach of the reference IMA architecture, it is necessary to identify possible architectural elements that could be used to construct a specific IMA assurance argumentation. Fig. 2.b shows the hierarchy of argumentation and its link to the IMA architecture. We have also added two kinds of arguments: process arguments and product arguments [25]. Process arguments are related to the assurance processes that should be used, the intermediate artefacts to be produced (requirements, specifications, test plans etc.), the kinds of reviews, tests, and analyses that should be performed, and the documentation required to tie all these together. The product arguments consider the potentially hazardous behaviours exhibited by the system and how they are mitigated.

Table 1. DO-297 objectives and hazards regarding partitioning associated

Objective	Life Cycle Data Description	LEVEL	Product	Elements asociated with hazards

Partitioning ensures that the behavior of any hosted application is prevented from adversely affecting the behavior of any other application or function.	Partitioning Analysis Data	Module	Product	* Interrupts and interrupt inhibits (software and hardware)
				 * Real time correspondence:
				   + frame overrun,
				   + interference with real time clock,
				   + counter/timer corruption,
				   + pipeline and caching)
				 * Memory, I/O contention
				 * Data flags
				 * Recursion termination
				 * Control Flow defects :
				   + incorrect branching into a partition or protected area (timing and space aspects)
				 * External device interaction (e.g. displays):
				   + loss of data (e.g. overwritten)
				   + delayed data
				   + incorrect data (unlikely across systems)
				   + protocol haits (e.g. ack nacks)

	V&V Data	Module	Product	* Software traps:
				   + divide by zero,
				   + un-implemented instruction,
				   + specific software interrupt instructions,
				   + unrecognized instruction)
				 * Program overlays
				 * Buffer sequence (double jeopordy)
				 * Indirect non terminating call loops
				 * Holdup commands (performance hedges)
				 * Loops (e.g. infinite loops)

	Failure Analyses and Safety Analyses	Module	Product	* Control Flow defects (timing and space aspects):
				   + incorrect branching into a partition or protected area,
				   + corruption of a jump table (double duty?)
				   + corruption of the processor sequence control
				   + corruption of return addresses
				   + unrecoverable hardware state corruption (e.g., mask and halt))
				 * Loss of input or output data
				 * Corruption of input or output data
				 * Corruption of internal data:
				   + direct or indirect memory writes
				   + table overrun
				   + incorrect linking
				   + calculations involving time
				 * Delayed data

For example, when building the safety argument for IMA platform/modules, we take advantage of a Certification Authorities Software Team (CAST) document [18] that gives some guidelines for assuring partitioning. Given these guidelines, we can align our argumentation to the assessment required by the standards. The decisions made on the architecture implementation have effects on the structure of the fault tree so they will be part of the features analysed in the case representation. One of the most dependable decisions made on architecture is how partitioning and sharing resources are implemented. In order to work in a methodical way, we propose that architecture services can be mapped with an IMA module and so they should follow the DO-297 requirements for certification.

Table 1 shows the objective of the DO-297 standard regarding partitioning and the lifecycle data required for the certification of IMA platform modules. Associated with the hazards there are the items that can be considered as the causes of hazards. These items need to be taken into account for satisfying that specific objective. In order to deal with these elements, we should offer evidence that the resources are accessible in time and space. How each resource is accessible depends on the architecture design and implementations decisions.

While the previous table describes a generic set of hazards extracted from standards and guidelines, the project-specific hazards define technology-specific arguments identified from preliminary hazard analyses. In Fig. 3, we show an excerpt of safety argumentation used for safe access to shared resources.

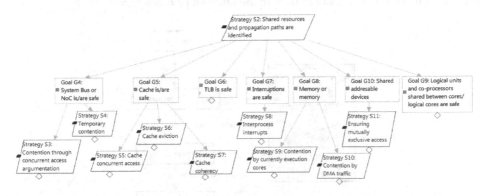

Fig. 3. Excerpt of safety argumentation used for safe access to shared resources

One of the ideas that were implemented in this approach is the use of safety case patterns. This is the key to reuse the good practices accepted by experts in the sector. Patterns are widely used in engineering, and in relation to safety, some catalogues have been designed [5] [6]. The same methodology is applied while representing the knowledge for the domain. The cases are represented by the procedure follow in order to fulfil the standard's objectives and the product, that is, safety requirements that the platform implementation must fulfilled.

For the next step, we propose to define a common pattern regarding sharing resources so all instantiations of the pattern will have a similar structure that will help the system on a future step to compare decisions from past cases and how the decisions have affected the arguments. On Fig 4 a preliminary pattern used an example of the proposal.

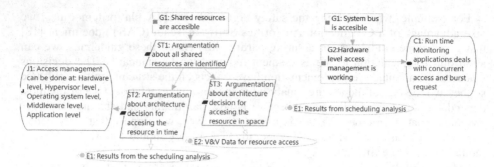

Fig. 4. Preliminary pattern and its use on an example for shared resources

For the case characterization in a CBR approach, we will use the elements described before (safety case patterns and hazards) as case and knowledge bases.

3.2   Case Characterization

The phases for CBR are shown in Fig. 5. The process starts when a new case arrives and needs to be processed and finalized when the case is solved and the information learned from the process is stored back in the knowledge repository.

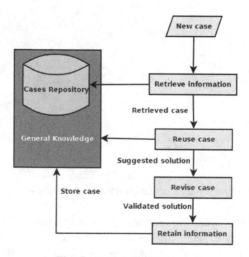

Fig. 5. CBR general flow

One of the main tasks that should be done and is not described in the figure is case characterization and how the knowledge for the cases is represented in the repository. The cases should represent information balancing complexity and richness with efficiency. Case descriptions are not just a feature vector with some values, but a representation of an argumentation (goals, claims and evidence). This is one of the challenges that must be achieved in order to apply these techniques to safety assurance reuse.

Before defining the case characterisation, we identify all the "resources" to build the CBR approach. These should be at least three:

1. **New project data (new case).** The set of data used to certify an IMA Platform by integrating: (i) pre-qualification data of an IMA Platform (e.g., owned by the Platform Integrator), and (ii) Module data (certification data for module acceptance)
2. **Safety case patterns (general knowledge).** The set of "experience" information to be used as initial case base in the form of modular arguments organized in safety case patterns.
3. **Previous projects' safety cases (case repository).** The set of "experience" information to be used in future projects as case base in the form of safety cases. They must also contain "context" information.

Additionally, we identify the inputs and outputs in a specific CBR reuse project:

1. **Inputs (new case):** The set of data related to the module pre-qualification, which must be adapted in the form of an "IMA module safety case". The adapted inputs (target) must be structured: safety cases plus additional structure (argument variables, arguments ontology).
4. **Outputs (validated solution):** The set of candidate safety cases related to the IMA platform with a trust measure for each, which will be the "IMA platform safety cases". These may be incomplete safety cases that will provide a basis to humans for completing the final safety case. This means that CBR does not need provide conclusive solutions but at least advice to humans in decision making and reusing as much previous experience as possible. The outputs must be also structured: safety cases plus additional structure (argument variables, arguments ontology)

As a starting point to characterize cases, we take typical safety cases as they may be presented for argumentation of product assurance or compliance with standards. Typical safety cases will have the following concept types:

1. **Types of goals** as organized by the type of argumentation modules: conformance arguments, risk reduction arguments, etc.
5. **Types of claims** as described in the current version of the paper (arguments to demonstrate IMA segregation, partition, distribution, integration, etc.)
6. **Types of evidences** that may be based on an ontology/taxonomy and their characteristics.

Within each of these three elements, we may find additional aspects, including:

— **A lexical structure given by the textual information.** This may lead to a structured textual language. This also raises the question of converting the textual information (inputs) in the structured format required for a kind of propositional language.
— **Variables.** Some of the elements of a safety case would need to be variables taking values from a value space (variable types) which will include dependencies between variables. E.g., the "evidence" (option branch in a use case) to be provided depends on the "DAL" identified for the function.

— **Values for variables**. These could be extracted from safety cases for previous projects or a library of possible values specific to a given company. For instance: concrete means of compliance used by a company, technical information on IMA platform (size, time constraints, computing capacity, etc)
— **Relations between the aspects above**. The main challenge is to find a way to keep consistency between the three aspects above when authoring a safety case. The decisions on how to build a safety case in a specific project may depend on the intricate relation between all these aspects.

3.3   Case Retrieving and Reuse

The system should learn how the similarity among cases is defined and assessed in order to retrieve the cases whenever a new situation arises. Commonalities should be studied in each of the attributes that conforms and identifies the cases. At the same time it should analyse the weight that each attribute should have when calculating the general similarity.

The first step is to identify what will be the elements that will help index cases: basically they will be the types of goals, claims and evidences. Then we need to establish a voting approach to select the best similar cases.

Once the cases are retrieved, general knowledge also plays its part, as among the retrieved cases, the system should be able to suggest a possible solution for the new situation. When a past case matches exactly with the new situation, there is no need for the retrieved solution to be adapted. However as it has been mentioned, this is not a frequent situation. The information on how cases are reused is directly related to the information on how the matching between cases is done.

The suggested solution is presented but must be validated with information. As the domain where the system is intended to apply is avionics, information on how the authorities understand the assessment. In this domain it is difficult to validate a solution in an automatic way, safety argumentations and evidence depth could vary from one project to another and from one assessor to another.

The information on why a solution is valid or not will help to improve the matching process and the task to adapt retrieving cases to a new situation in order to make a plausible solution.

3.4   Discussion

One of the reasons that validate the CBR approach is that while dealing with certification, standards can be vague and need interpretation. The quantity of evidence and/or the depth needed could vary from one project to another. The use of past experiences is informally applied in industry and argumentation about past experiences is accepted by some authorities. A CBR system could help certification related teams to store and share the knowledge gathered on previous projects to future situations even when the team change.

The approach presented here is intended to decrease the efforts needed while designing safety cases. According to [15], it is the argument that, product testing has some limitations and so many regulatory authorities have recommended the use of process-based techniques. However the process-oriented approach do not guarantee the elimination of all potential risk. We plan to balance both approaches, use a process oriented approach to fulfil the objectives of the standards and product-oriented while testing the safety of a specific platform implementation.

The IMA architecture will be referenced for all cases on the example developed to validate the case based reasoning approach. Although the same architecture is maintained, the implementation from one to another could differ and even different hardware implementation will be under study for this example. Habli in [18] indicates that architecture design and its variations are key to discover the elements that could contribute to system failure conditions.

The methods and techniques used for gathering evidence have been selected for the safety method database that is mentioned in [14]. The database relates to the different methods not only with the domain but also with the different stages if the safety assessment when they are used.

New cases are defined by the safety goal that should be in the argument, and the design decisions taken for the implementation of the specific safety requirement. The case based reasoning approach should provide the safety argumentation related to those decisions that have been used on previous cases that have certain level of similarity. It is also considered the different types of evidence which can support the argumentation planned; it is in this aspect where the safety database could play an important role.

For the retrieval activity, we propose a list of ranked similar cases, those will be the cases to base the reuse of argumentation. The only case where the reuse will be direct will be those cases where the similarity is total and all features have equal values. On the cases where this similarity is not complete, we should study the sum of similarities among all from the features that identify the case and weigh those similarities in correspondence with the importance of each feature.

The revision in the proposed example is always done manually where the suggested solution is shown to the user who should be an expert on safety assessment and certification. The solution shows a safety case which integrates the safety argumentation about the platform implementation, the certification objectives that should be fulfilled and the possible evidences that support those arguments. The end user should validate the solution or modify it to adjust it to the requirements. This validated solution will be stored on the cases repository to serve for future enquires.

This approach only serves when the patterns are used and integrated in the way it is explained. When we have a safety case that does not follow that structure this approach cannot be followed.

If a new hazard is identified then the architecture pattern should be updated and consequently all the cases that use it.

4   Conclusions

CBR techniques provide a promising approach for assisting engineers in their assurance task while creating safety argumentations in relation with a specific architecture for a specific standard. A CBR system could help in creating a methodology for safety assessment and in this way decrease the time needed for assessing certain products, particularly those developed in a modular way. This approach could help engineers to maintain the best practice updated and at the same time helps engineers to focus on the safety implications that one design could have compared to other.

Future work, beyond solution implementation, is to define a propositional language based on a domain-specific language. The expected CBR user interface to collect inputs and show safety case as outputs would be as a graphical interface for safety cases but with support of this propositional language (auto-completion assistant, type checking, semantic checking).

Acknowledgment. The research leading to these results has received funding from the FP7 programme under grant agreement n° 289011 (OPENCOSS) and from the ARTEMIS programme under the project RECOMP. We would also like to thank Integrasys, 7 solutions and University of Granada that are part of the project and have conceived the ACP platform that was key for the pattern example described here.

References

1. Sahar, B., Ardi, S., Kazuhiko, S., Yoshiomi, M., Hirotsugu, M.: HAZOP Management System with Dynamic Visual Model Aid. American Journal of Applied Sciences 7(7), 943–948 (2010)
2. Zhao, C., Bhushan, M., Venkatasubramanian, V.: PHASUITE: An automated HAZOP analysis tool for chemical processes Part I: Knowledge Engineering Framework. Process Safety and Environmental Protection 83(B6), 509–532 (2005)
3. Daramola, O., Stalhane, T., Moser, T., Biffl, S.: A conceptual framework for semantic case-based safety analysis. In: 2011 IEEE 16th Conference on Emerging Technologies & Factory Automation (ETFA), pp. 1–8 (2011)
4. Kelly, T.: Arguing Safety - A Systematic Approach to Managing Safety Cases. PhD thesis, Department of Computer Science, The University of York (1998)
5. Hawkins, R., Kelly, T.: A software Safety Argument Pattern Catalogue, Department of Computer Science, The University of York (2008)
6. Stensrud, E., Skramstad, T., Li, J., Xie, J.: Towards Goal-based Software Safety Certification Based on Prescriptive Standards. In: International Workshop on Software Certification, WoSoCER (2011)
7. IEC61508, 61508 - Functional Safety of Electrical/Electronic/Programmable Electronic Safety-Related Systems. International Electrotechnical Commission (2011)
8. RTCA DO-178/EUROCAE ED-12, Software Considerations in Airborne System and Equipment Certification
9. RTCA DO-254/EUROCAE ED-80 Design Assurance Guidance for Airborne Electronic Hardware
10. RTCA DO-297/EUROCAE ED-124 Integrated Modular Avionics (IMA) Development Guidance and Certification Considerations
11. SAE ARP4754/EUROCAE ED-79, Certification Considerations for Highly Integrated or Complex Aircraft Systems
12. SAE ARP4761, Guidelines and Methods for Conducting The Safety Assessment Process on Civil Airborne Systems and Equipment
13. Origin Consulting GSN Community Standard Version 1 (2011)
14. Everdij, M.H.C., Blom, H.A.P., Kirwan, B.: Development of a structured database of safety methods. In: 8th International Conference on Probabilistic Safety Assessment and Management, PSAM8 (2006)

15. Johnson, C.W., Robins, D.A.: Mith and barriers to the Introduction of Safety Cases in Space-Based Systems

16. Kelly, T.: Using Software Architecture Techniques to Support the Modular Certification of Safety-Critical Systems. In: Cant, T. (ed.) Proceedings of Eleventh Australian Workshop on Safety-Related Programmable Systems, Melbourne, Australia. CRPIT. ACS (August 2005)

17. Hayhurst, K.J., Maddalon, J.M., Miner, P.S., Szatkowski, G.N., Ulrey, M.L., DeWalt, M.P., Spitzer, C.R.: Preliminary Considerations for Classifying Hazards of Unmanned Aircraft Systems. NASA (2007)

18. Certification Authorities Software Team (CAST): Guidelines for Assessing Software Partitioning/Protection Schemes. FAA (2001)

19. Bloomfield, R., Bishop, P.: Safety and Assurance Cases: Past, Present and Possible Future – an Adelard Perspective. In: 18th Safety-Critical Systems Symposium (SSS 2010), Bristol, UK (2010)

20. International Organization for Standardization (ISO), ISO26262 Road vehicles – Functional safety, ISO (November 2011)

21. U.S. Food and Drug Administration, Guidance for Industry and FDA Staff - Total Product Life Cycle: Infusion Pump – Premarket Notification, Draft Guidance (April 2010)

22. Aerospace guidelines for the development of civil aircraft and system ARP 4754A

23. Eveleens: Integrated Modular Avionics Development Guidance and Certification Considerations (2006)

24. Aamodt, A., Plaza, E.: Case-Based Reasoning: Foundational Issues, Methodological Variations, and System Approaches. Artificial Intelligence Communications 7(1), 39–52 (1994)

25. Habli, I., Kelly, T.: Process and Product Certification Arguments – Getting the Balance Right. Workshop on Innovative Techniques for Certification of Embedded Systems, the Proceedings of 12th IEEE Real-Time and Embedded Technology and Applications Symposium, San Jose, California, USA (April 2006)

Modeling for Safety in a Synthesis-Centric Systems Engineering Framework

Jasen Markovski* and J.M. van de Mortel-Fronczak

Eindhoven University of Technology,
P.B. 513, 5600MB, Eindhoven, The Netherlands
{j.markovski,j.m.v.d.mortel}@tue.nl

Abstract. The ever-increasing complexity of safety-critical systems puts high demands on safety assurance and certification. We focus on the development of control software, where safety) requirements engineering plays a crucial and delicate role. Nowadays, most of the safety features are ensured by the (embedded) control software and, consequently, a great deal of the operational failures primarily originate from requirement errors. We apply formal methods to systematically specify, model, and validate safety (control) requirements, which we then employ to automatically synthesize a control design based on a formal model of the system at hand. The synthesized designs are correct by definition, provided that the models capture all safety aspects of the system. We structure the process in a synthesis-centric model-based systems engineering framework that we apply in an industrial case study involving safe coordination of movement of theme park vehicles. The framework provides rigorous means for modeling of safety requirements, and it supports evolvable product design, requirement reuse, and early integration with hardware prototypes for validation and testing.

1 Introduction

The constant increase in complexity of safety-critical systems combined with the growing market demand for products with improved quality promotes safety assurance and certification amongst the most costly undertakings in product development. To cope with complex systems and reduce development costs, most of the global safety requirements are ensured by coordinating (off-the-shelf) system components, which themselves ensure local safe behavior by embedded control software. This puts pressure on requirements engineering, which plays a crucial role in determination of the quality of the end product. According to the overview of [1], nearly three quarters of failures found in operational software originate from errors or oversights in (safety) requirements. Cases in point are many, cf. [33], some with catastrophical consequences, furthermore fortifying the need for high-quality requirements specifications and rigorous analysis.

---

* Supported by Dutch NWO project ProThOS, no. 600.065.120.11N124.

F. Ortmeier and P. Daniel (Eds.): SAFECOMP 2012 Workshops, LNCS 7613, pp. 36–49, 2012.
© Springer-Verlag Berlin Heidelberg 2012

Formal Methods for Safety-Critical Systems. On the one hand, formal methods are advocated by [16,29] as cost- and time-effective alternative for formal and rigorous specification, modeling, verification, validation, and testing of safety requirements. Moreover, they are already encouraged as appropriate, even mandatory, methodologies in the development of safety-critical software by several standards, like [32,38]. However as noted in [17], relatively little emphasis is placed on how formal methods integrate into the safety-critical system development process, despite their successful application in multiple industrial cases studies for the purpose of verification and validation like [20,9,21]. On the other hand, it has been recognized in [23] that traditional approaches to software development employing (re)coding-(validation-)testing loops have proven not entirely adequate to handle the challenge, as safety (control) requirements frequently change during the design process inducing a large number of time-consuming design iterations. Thus, simply employing formal methods for certain product design and development phases alongside or supporting the main design process might not suffice, calling in [4] for a shift from process-based towards model-based development from early stage to certification, deployment, evaluation, evolution, and decommission of the system.

Supervisory Control. Our proposal for a synthesis-centric model-based systems engineering framework partly addresses some of these issues in the development of supervisory controllers for high-tech complex machines. Supervisory controllers observe and coordinate high-level discrete(-event) system behavior. They observe the discrete-event behavior of the uncontrolled system, make a decision on which activities the system can safely perform, and send back control signals that actuate the system. We note that the layer of supervisory control is on a high level of abstraction, residing between the user and the resource control of the machine [8]. The automated synthesis of control designs is supported by supervisory control theory of [31,8], which investigates synthesis of models of supervisory controllers based on the models of the uncontrolled system and the *safety or control requirements*. Thereafter, the synthesized models can be employed to generate the control software or, alternatively, they can be directly coupled with the prototype hardware using appropriate interfaces.

The models of supervisory controllers are referred to as *supervisors*, whereas the model of the uncontrolled hardware is referred to as *plant*. Typically, it is assumed that the supervisory controller can react sufficiently fast on system sensory input, which enables modeling of the supervised system as a synchronization between the plant and the supervisor, known as *supervised plant*. Plants are usually represented by sets of sequences of events, or discrete-event automata that generate formal languages, which model and correspond to sequences of observed activities of the uncontrolled system. In the following, we simplify the role of events for the sake of a more gentle introduction to the topic. The events are split to *uncontrollable events*, which model activities like observations of sensors, and *controllable events*, which model actions like interaction with actuators of the plant. Consequently, supervisors cannot disable uncontrollable events, as controllers cannot change sensor signals and need the feedback they carry.

On the other hand, they can disable controllable events in order to actuate the machine in a safe manner, i.e., to prevent potentially unsafe state of the system or dangerous situations. The safe behavior of the system is prescribed by a model of the safety or control requirements.

Consequently, the supervisory controller synthesis problem is to synthesize models of software controllers that observe discrete(-event) system behavior and ensure their safe execution by disallowing activities of the system that might lead to dangerous or otherwise undesired situations. The advantage is that the synthesized controllers are correct by definition, i.e., the supervised system adheres to all prescribed safety rules, provided that the plant and the control requirements were correctly modeled. Therefore, validation of the synthesized control software is always required, but the focus of the designers is no longer on interpreting informal requirement specifications, coding, and testing, but on analyzing requirements, their correct modeling, and validating system behavior.

Motivation and Contributions. Supervisory control has already been successfully applied in a broad range of industrial cases: in [37] to ensure safety of patients in a patient support system of Philips MRI scanners, in [19] to prevent deadlock behavior of parallel programs, in [10] to enable safe and secure access of web services, or in [27] to guarantee proper maintenance of high-tech Océ printers. We noted that the control designs, which implement the modeled safety requirements, describe unambiguously the safety aspects of the control system. Therefore, they can serve as means of communication between the industrial producer of the equipment and the client that makes the order.

Here, we focus on the formal modeling of safety requirements and the validation of the control design. We illustrate the application of our framework, directly applied in an industrial case study involving safe movement coordination of theme park vehicles. We developed control design that successfully coordinated the movement of the vehicles. The flexibility and advantage of supervisory controller synthesis was highlighted by a last minute addition of a new sensory component. It took us only four hours to model the new component, add it to the existing models, adjust the control requirements, synthesize a supervisor, and validate it by directly interfacing it with the vehicle prototype.

The remainder of this paper is organized as follows. We present and discuss the proposed systems engineering framework in the following section. Then, we present the industrial case study and summarize the whole process from specification to validation of control designs with early integration of prototype hardware. We finish with a discussion involving challenges in supervisory control and its integration with system safety engineering.

2   Synthesis-Centric Model-Based Systems Engineering

To structure the process of supervisory control synthesis we employ the framework of [34,26,5] depicted in Fig. 1. The modeling process begins with an informal specification of the desired system, written by domain engineers. A design of the

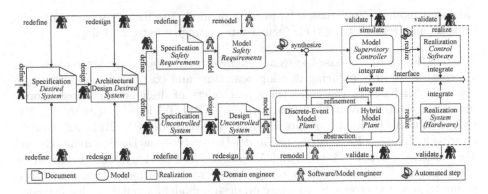

Fig. 1. Model-based engineering framework for supervisory controller synthesis

architecture of the system follows, contrived by domain and software engineers together. The design most importantly defines the modeling level of abstraction and the control architecture. Subsequently, it is used to separate the plant and the control or safety requirements, a joint task of domain and software engineers. Here, a decision is made to which extent the control is managed by the software, and which part is implemented in hardware. The resulting informal documents specify the plant and control requirements, respectively. In the following, we omit the roles of the engineers as they are clear from the context.

Most plants typically exhibit hybrid (discrete-event and continuous) behavior, whereas supervisor synthesis requires a discrete-event abstraction. The hybrid model is suitable for simulation purposes, and it can be abstracted to a discrete-event model for synthesis purposes, required by [31,8]. This abstraction only eliminates timing behavior, while preserving the sequencing of the events and their consequence on the control design. In the design of the plant, decisions are made on the level of abstraction that is used, and what is significant discrete-event and hybrid behavior. Moreover, in many cases, the hardware prototype of the system is already in place, and it only needs to be modeled for synthesis purposes, or it has already been modeled for simulation and validation of its components, resulting in a hybrid model that needs to be abstracted. In parallel, a model of the control requirements is made following the specification documents, referring to the plant. The discrete-event version of the plant together with the model of the control requirements are input to the synthesis tool, which automatically generates a supervisor.

Software-in-the-loop simulation can be used to validate the supervisor coupled with the hybrid plant, and hardware-in-the-loop simulation can be used to validate the supervisor against a hardware prototype. The latter offers an early integration alternative before the actual control software is built as in [7]. If the validation is not satisfactory, the control requirements and/or the plant model need to be remodeled or redefined. In certain cases, a complete revision proves to be necessary, which might even require redefining the specification of the whole system. Finally, the control software is generated automatically, based on the validated models. Note that software engineers in the framework act more as 'model' engineers, shifting their focus from writing code to modeling.

Related Work. Model-based systems engineering methods are state-of-the-art approaches towards reducing development time and cost, while retaining high level of confidence in the correctness and safety of designs. The most prominent commercially available frameworks are IBM Telelogic Harmony-SE, IN-COSE Object-Oriented Systems Engineering Method, IBM Rational Unified Process for Systems Engineering for Model-Driven Systems Development, Esterel Technologies SCADE System, and Vitech Model-Based Systems Engineering Methodology. They achieve a paradigm shift from traditional document-based to model-based approach by focusing on design model formulation, as discussed in [12]. These frameworks do provide methodologies and tools that support the process of (manual) development of system models, but they do not support automated model derivation as enabled by supervisory control synthesis. Our academic framework is still under development and the way of specifying safety requirements comes closest to the approach of Event-B, described in [2]. To specify models in Event-B, safety invariants need to be defined similar to the ones that we employ in our framework. In Event-B, it is a task of the modeler to prove these invariants correct with the available tools, whereas in our approach correct models are synthesized automatically, satisfying specified safety requirements.

Framework Implementation. The proposed framework can be coupled to several specification, synthesis, and verification state-of-the-art tools, depending on the control architecture, the form of the safety requirements, and the additional progress or liveness and performance requirements. For the traditional approach to supervisory control, we employ discrete-event models in the form of automata. The safety requirements are also given in the form of automata, which generate the allowed sequences of events. To this end, we employ tools like TCT [13] and Supremica [3] for monolithic synthesis, or the techniques introduced in [36] for synthesis of distributed supervisors. We noticed in [26,27], however, that specifying safety requirements in terms directly in terms of states provides high-quality transparent safety formal specifications, supported by the tools NBC [24] and the extended finite automata with data of Supremica [30].

As the supervision caters only for safe system behavior, and it does not guarantee liveness properties of the supervised system, so several extensions of the theory were proposed to extend modeling convenience and to increase the expressiveness of the control requirements. To this end, standard safety control requirements are reinforced with liveness requirements, which specify intended activities the supervised system should be capable of performing. The work of [39] extends the NuSMV model checker for synthesis employing the branching temporal logic CTL*. Similarly, control requirements in CTL* are proposed and analyzed in [18]. In [35] a proposal to translate temporal logic to standard event-based control requirements is presented, subsequently enabling the usage of standard synthesis tools. However, all of these approaches suffer from (doubly-)exponential complexity due to enforcing of liveness requirements during the synthesis procedure. Consequently, the proposed frameworks can handle only systems with $10^4 - 10^5$ states reported in [39,18,35,11].

Industrial Applications. Thus, for industrial application we remain in the domain of event-based [8,3] or state-based properties [24], decoupling supervisor synthesis and liveness verification, and employing the most efficient specialized tools. To this end, we developed several transformation tools that align the synthesis tool Supremica [3] with the model checkers UPPAAL [22] and mCRL2 [15], which can be employed for the purpose of verification of progress properties of the supervised plant. The supervised plant is transformed to an input model for the corresponding tool, preserving both state- and event-based information in the format required by the temporal logic supported by the tool. For UPPAAL the same data-structures can be employed, whereas for mCRL2, we have to encode the state-based information into events. In any case, the post-synthesis verification is a valuable tool that provides relatively early feedback to the modeler, bringing higher confidence in the control design. The synthesis-based systems engineering framework has been applied to several industrial case studies like [37,27,14]. The synthesized supervisors have been successfully tested using hardware-in-the-loop integration, where the hardware is directly supervised by the model of the supervisory controller. Control software has also been generated and integrated within the software architecture of the machines, but this step is not yet fully automated and it requires a manual intervention.

The goal of the case study reported in [37] is safe positioning of patients inside a Philips MRI scanner. To this end, models of the patient support system and the user interface of the machine have been made, comprising $6.3 \cdot 10^9$ states of the uncontrolled system. The control requirements that ensure patient safety among else define the conditions for manual and automatic movements of the tabletop on which the patient lies, prevent collisions of the tabletop with the magnet, and enable the operator to safely control the system by means of the user interface. The case study of [27] deals with coordination of maintenance procedures of the printing process of a high-tech Océ printer. The printing process applies a toner image onto a paper sheet. To maintain high printing quality, several maintenance operations have to be carried out after a certain number of prints. However, if possible, the execution of the maintenance operations should not interrupt an ongoing printing procedure. Still, print quality must not be compromised and, if necessary, a print job can be interrupted. The plant model consist of the printing process comprised 25 automata with 2 to 24 states. For this case, we employed parameterized state-based control requirements, which translated to 500 state-based expressions as required for input to the synthesis tool NBC [24]. In addition, several re-iterations of this case study has led us to a framework based on the tool Supremica [3], which provides an extension with performance evaluation in [25,28], bringing additional confidence to the design.

3 Industrial Case Study: Theme Park Vehicle

The case study elaborated in [14] illustrates industrial application of supervisory control theory, in which safety plays a prominent rôle. Using this case study, we explain how safety requirements can be modeled and coped with in the synthesis-centric systems engineering framework described in Section 2.

The multimover, a theme park vehicle shown in Fig. 2, is a relatively new concept in the amusement park business. It is an Automated Guided Vehicle that drives around following an invisible track: an electrical wire integrated in the floor. It offers the possibility for new rides with crossings, switches, junctions and driving into and out of dead-end tracks, as opposed to the conventional roller coaster or ferris wheel. It acts and drives according to a scene program that is specified by the theme park. The track wire produces a magnetic field that can be measured by sensors. Next to the track wire, floor codes are positioned that can be read by means of a metal detector. These floor codes give additional information about the track, e.g. the start of a certain scene program, a switch, junction or a dead-end. The scene program, which is read by the scene program handler, defines at what speed the vehicle should ride at a certain position, when it should follow other vehicles, stop, rotate or play music, and in which direction the vehicle should move at a junction. An operator is responsible for powering up and deploying vehicles into the ride manually. He also controls the dispatching of the vehicles in the passenger boarding and outboarding area. Ride Control coordinates all vehicles and sends start/stop commands. The messages are sent as wireless signals or by means of the track wire. Multimovers can interact with each other so that passengers have influence on the ride experience, for example with target shooting systems and similar competitive features. By gaining a certain score, new scenes can be unlocked. This interactivity and the fact that the passengers cannot see the actual track makes the ride more exciting because of the unexpectedness of the vehicle's actions. This concept makes the multimover a very flexible vehicle that can be used in theme parks, museums and in other recreational activities.

Safety is the most important aspect of this vehicle. Therefore, several sensors are integrated in it to avoid collisions. Proximity sensors are used to avoid physical contact with other objects. We can distinguish two types of proximity sensors. A *long* proximity sensor that detects obstacles in the vicinity of six meter and a *short* proximity sensor that detects obstacles in the vicinity of one meter. The vehicle should ride slower when an object is only detected by a long proximity sensor and stop when an object is detected by the short proximity sensor. This stop is not an emergency stop. When the short proximity sensor does not detect an object any more, the vehicle should start riding automatically. Additionally, a bumper switch is mounted on the vehicle that can detect physical contact with other objects. The vehicle should respond to such a situation with an emergency stop. After the emergency stop, the operator has to deploy the vehicle back into the ride. Finally, an emergency stop has to executed when the battery power is too low or when a system failure occurs. The vehicle should not become active when the bumper switch is still active or the battery power is still too low.

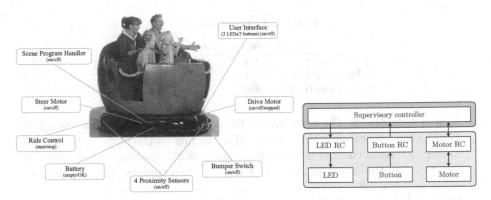

Fig. 2. Multimover and its components   **Fig. 3.** Control architecture

Safety Requirements. The functionality described above refers to the closed-loop system, that is, the hardware and the controller. To facilitate further discussion on safety requirements, we give an overview of the control architecture in Fig. 3.

At the lowest level, the components (transducers) of the multimover are depicted: a LED, a button and a motor. The next level is the level of resource control. This resource control contains feedback control of these individual components, e.g. a PID-controller for a motor. The upper level, supervisory control, coordinates the discrete behavior of all components so that safety requirements are satisfied. Specifically, two aspects are taken into account:

- **Proximity handling.** The supervisory controller has to assure that the multimover does not collide with other vehicles or obstacles. To this end, proximity sensors are integrated at the front and back which can detect an obstacle if it is within a certain range of the multimover. To avoid collisions, the multimover should drive with a safe speed and stop if the obstacle is too close to it.
- **Emergency and error handling.** The system should stop immediately and should be powered off to prevent any further wrong behavior when a collision or a system failure occurs (e.g. a malfunction of a motor). To detect collisions, a bumper switch is mounted on the multimover. The same applies when the battery level is too low. The LED interface should give a signal when an emergency stop has been performed. The multimover should be deployed back into the ride by an operator manually.

To structure the control problem and enable distributed synthesis techniques, we divide the control problem of the multimover into following five subproblems:

- **LED actuation.** The operator must be able to check in which state the multimover is by looking at the Interface LEDs. This means that the states of the LEDs represent the current state of the multimover. It is a task of the supervisor to actuate the LEDs according to the state of the multimover, as defined in Table 1.

Table 1. LED actuation

	Emergency	Reset	Active
ResetLED	On	Off	Off
ForwardLED	Off	On	Off
BackwardLED	Off	On	Off

- **Motor actuation.** The drive motor, the steer motor and the scene program handler have to be switched on and off according to the state of the multi-mover. If the multimover is in the state **Active**, the motors can be switched on. If the multimover is in the state **Reset** or **Emergency**, the motors have to be switched off.
- **Button handling.** The user interface of the multimover contains three buttons. First, the reset button is used to reset the vehicle if the multimover is active and deployed into the ride or is in the state **Emergency**. Subsequently, the forward button and the backward button is used to deploy the vehicle into a certain direction. A control task of the supervisor is to enter the corresponding state when a button is pushed.
- **Proximity and Ride Control handling.** On each side of the multimover, two proximity sensors are mounted: one long proximity sensor and one short proximity sensor. If the long proximity sensor detects an object in the traveling direction, the multimover should slow down to a safe driving speed. If an obstacle is detected by the short proximity sensor, the multimover should stop to prevent a collision.

  Ride Control can send a 'general start/stop' command to all multimovers in order to stop and start the complete ride. Since a 'general stop' command of Ride Control can be considered as a short proximity stop, this control task is similar to proximity handling. If Ride Control is sending a 'general start' command again, the multimover should start riding automatically (depending of the state of the proximity sensors in the current driving direction).

  The control task of the supervisor is to slow down or stop the multimover if a proximity sensor is activated in the travelling direction of the multimover or if Ride Control is sending a 'general stop' command.
- **Emergency handling.** To guarantee passenger safety, the multimover should be deactivated immediately when an emergency situation occurs. We can distinguish the following emergency situations: battery power too low, bumper switch collision detection, drive motor driver failures (including not connected or defect motor), wire signal lost, steering motor driver failures (including not connected or defect motor).

  It should not be possible to reset the multimover if the bumper switch is still activated or the battery power is still too low. A control task of the supervisor is to enter the **Emergency** state of the multimover when an emergency situation occurs.

Models of Safety Requirements. To guarantee that the closed-loop system satisfies safety requirements, the supervisor can be synthesized based on the models

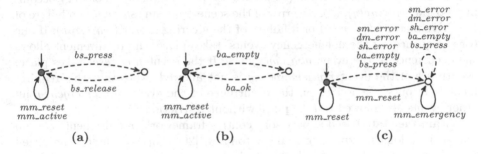

Fig. 4. Requirement models of the emergency handling module

of components and requirements mentioned previously. The component models represent the actual behavior of the transducers and their resource (low-level) control. For supervisory control synthesis, component models are defined by automata. Each transducer including its resource control is modeled by one automaton. Automata consist of states and transitions labeled by controllable and uncontrollable events. States of the component models represent all relevant states of each resource (e.g. on, off, empty, active). Controllable events represent relevant discrete commands/tasks (function calls) to the resource control (e.g. *enable*, *disable*). These actions are controlled by the supervisor. Uncontrollable events represent messages that are sent from the resource control layer to the supervisory controller (e.g. a failure notification, a sensor event). These events are not controlled by the supervisor. The component models are made with the assumption that the resource control of the multimover is working correctly. This means that if a command is given, the command is carried out correctly. For example, if a command is sent to enable the drive motor, we assume that in response the drive motor is switched on by its resource controller. Furthermore, we assume that the communication between the resource layer and the supervisor is fast enough so that if an event occurs, e.g a button is pressed, the supervisor timely receives the information about this occurrence. This also means that events cannot overtake each other and cannot get lost.

As already mentioned, requirements have to be modeled by automata in the event-based approach. The state-based approach allows the user to define requirements also by logical specifications. As an example, we discuss the automata modeling the requirements of the emergency handling module depicted in Fig. 4. The first requirement, Fig. 4a, specifies that the events *mm_active* (representing the transition from the **Reset** state to the **Active** state of the multimover) and *mm_reset* (representing the transitions from the **Active** and **Emergency** states to the **Reset** state of the multimover) are only allowed to take place if the bumper switch is not activated. The second requirement, Fig. 4b, specifies that the events *mm_active* and *mm_reset* are only allowed to take place if the power level of the battery is sufficient. The last requirement, Fig. 4c, specifies that the event *mm_emergency* (representing the transitions from the **Reset** and **Active** states to the **Emergency** state of the multimover) is only allowed to occur after activation of the bumper switch (*bs_press*), the power level of the battery becoming too low (*ba_empty*), a parse error of the scene program (*sh_error*), a failure of the drive motor (*dm_error*) or a failure of the steering motor (*sm_error*). If one (or a sequence) of these 'emergency events' takes place, the requirement allows the occurrence of the event *mm_emergency*. If the event *mm_reset* takes place, occurrence of the event *mm_emergency* is not allowed. Note that this requirement only puts restrictions on the occurrence of the event *mm_emergency*, all other events are allowed to take place without restrictions.

Within the state-based supervisory control framework, requirements can be modeled by logical expressions and automata. [26] proposes three generalized state-based expressions, described as logical expressions based on propositional logic. In the emergency handling module, we are only using one type of generalized state-based expression, namely a generalized transition-state formula:

$$\rightarrow \{ \; mm\_reset, \; mm\_active \; \} \Rightarrow \textbf{BS\_Released} \downarrow \wedge \textbf{BA\_OK} \downarrow$$

This generalized transition-state formula specifies that the multimover may only switch to active or reset (*mm_active* or *mm_reset*) if the battery level is ok (**BA_OK**) and the bumper switch is released (**BS_Released**).

Supervisor Synthesis, Implementation, Validation, and Testing. Based on the component and requirement models, an optimal supervisor is synthesized, validated and implemented. Both a centralized (monolithic) supervisor and a distributed supervisor are synthesized for the supervisory control problem of the multimover. A centralized supervisor has been synthesized with the state-based framework based on state tree structures of [24]. Furthermore, a distributed supervisor has been synthesized with an aggregated approach of [36]. Both supervisors guarantee that the supervised system fulfills the requirements specified.

We validated the control design in several phases as outlined in [26]. First, the control requirements where checked for conflicts. Then, the synthesized supervisors were evaluated to check whether the models of the controlled system are consistent with the intended behavior. For this purpose, discrete-event simulation was used persistently. Specifically, the state-space stepper was used to check whether the supervisor disables the right transitions in the right states when evaluating the closed-loop system behavior. The toolset described in [6] was used for discrete-event simulation. Moreover, validation of the models was performed by interfacing the supervisor with a hardware prototype. Finally, a prototype of a supervisory controller with the synthesized supervisors is implemented in the existing control software of the multimover. This implementation is first tested by means of simulation, and thereafter, on the existing implementation platform where the developed control software is tested.

The synthesis-centric framework was employed in parallel with the traditional approach in the development of the movement controller for the theme park vehicle. The flexibility of the approach and the advantage of the automated synthesis and early integration capabilities was highlighted when the number of proximity sensors was to be extended. The engineering process used presently requires approximately two days for making necessary changes to the control system and software testing. The synthesis-based engineering process described in this paper requires approximately four hours to cope with the same change and deliver a validated control design.

4 Concluding Remarks

We gave a compact overview of a model-based engineering framework relying on supervisory controller synthesis, as we find it employed in systems engineering. We find that the use of formal models is a key element for successful application of a synthesis-based systems engineering process. Model-based specifications are consistent and less ambiguous than informal specification documents, forcing the engineers to clarify all aspects of the system early in the design process. The proposed framework most importantly affects the control design development process, switching the focus from interpreting requirements, coding, and testing to analyzing requirements, modeling, and validating the behavior of the system. It is typically remarked that introducing formal models early in the development process prolongs the production time of initial control design, but it greatly improves the validation phase, reducing the number of reiterations needed for correct control design and mitigating testing costs. Moreover, the framework provides for automated synthesis of supervisory controllers, which implement the safety requirements by definition, so one can directly proceed with model validation and test the control design by integration with the prototype of the hardware early in the design process. Finally, the proposed framework is flexible, as it gives early feedback to the modeler regarding conflicting requirements and wrongful assumptions, and it can easily withstand changes in the control design or validation and testing errors.

The promise of automatic control software generation captured the interest of the industry, with supervisory control becoming even more captivating as engineers nowadays are familiar with building models for simulation and validation purposes. Moreover, this technique enables rapid prototyping, i.e., the obtained models can be coupled with (prototype) hardware components to evaluate the control requirements before building and testing expensive control software. However, we foresee the need for deeper integration with the design process, as we believe that the developed models provide a sound basis for ensuring safety and quality of the developed products. Since we are developing our systems engineering framework for application in an industrial environment, we are working towards supporting the process of safety certification as well, based on the developed models of the system and the safety requirements.

References

1. A systematic literature review to identify and classify software requirement errors. Information and Software Technology 51(7), 1087–1109 (2009)
2. Abrial, J.R.: Modeling in Event-B: System and Software Engineering. Cambridge University Press (2010)

3. Akesson, K., Fabian, M., Flordal, H., Malik, R.: Supremica - an integrated environment for verification, synthesis and simulation of discrete event systems. In: Proceedings of WODES 2006, pp. 384–385. IEEE (2006)
4. Anderson, S., Felici, M.: Safety, reliability and security of industrial computer systems. Reliability Engineering & System Safety 81(3), 235–238 (2003)
5. Baeten, J.C.M., van de Mortel-Fronczak, J.M., Rooda, J.E.: Integration of Supervisory Control Synthesis in Model-Based Systems Engineering. In: Proceedings of ETAI/COSY 2011, pp. 167–178. IEEE (2011)
6. Baeten, J., van Beek, D., Cuijpers, P., Reniers, M., Rooda, J., Schiffelers, R., Theunissen, R.: Model-based engineering of embedded systems using the hybrid process algebra Chi. ENTCS 209, 21–53 (2008)
7. Braspenning, N., van de Mortel-Fronczak, J., Rooda, J.: A model-based integration and testing method to reduce system development effort. ENTCS 164(4), 13–28 (2006)
8. Cassandras, C., Lafortune, S.: Introduction to discrete event systems. Kluwer Academic Publishers (2004)
9. Cha, S., Son, H., Yoo, J., Jee, E., Seong, P.H.: Systematic evaluation of fault trees using real-time model checker UPPAAL. Reliability Engineering & System Safety 82(1), 11–20 (2003)
10. Darondeau, P., Dubreil, J., Marchand, H.: Supervisory control for modal specifications of services. In: Proceedings of WODES 2010, pp. 428–435. IFAC (2010)
11. D'Ippolito, N.R., Braberman, V., Piterman, N., Uchitel, S.: Synthesis of live behaviour models. In: Proceedings of SIGSOFT 2010, pp. 77–86. ACM (2010)
12. Estefan, J.: Survey of Model-Based Systems Engineering (MBSE) methodologies. Tech. rep., INCOSE (2008), http://www.incose.org
13. Feng, L., Wonham, W.M.: TCT: A computation tool for supervisory control synthesis. In: Proceedings of WODES 2006, pp. 388–389. IEEE (2006)
14. Forschelen, S.T.J., Mortel-Fronczak, J.M., Su, R., Rooda, J.E.: Application of supervisory control theory to theme park vehicles. Discrete Event Dynamic Systems, 1–30 (to appear, 2012)
15. Groote, J.F., Mathijssen, A.H.J., Reniers, M.A., Usenko, Y.S., van Weerdenburg, M.J.: Analysis of distributed systems with mCRL2. In: Process Algebra for Parallel and Distributed Processing, pp. 99–128. Chapman & Hall (2009)
16. Hinchey, M., Bowen, J.: Applications of Formal Methods. International Series in Computer Science. Prentice Hall (1995)
17. Iwu, F., Galloway, A., McDermid, J., Toyn, I.: Integrating safety and formal analyses using UML and PFS. Reliability Engineering & System Safety 92(2), 156–170 (2007)
18. Jiang, S., Kumar, R.: Supervisory control of discrete event systems with CTL* temporal logic specifications. SIAM Journal on Control and Optimization 44(6), 2079–2103 (2006)
19. Kelly, T., Wang, Y., Lafortune, S., Mahlke, S.: Eliminating concurrency bugs with control engineering. Computer 42(12), 52–60 (2009)
20. Kim, T., Stringer-Calvert, D., Cha, S.: Formal verification of functional properties of a SCR-style software requirements specification using PVS. Reliability Engineering & System Safety 87(3), 351–363 (2005)
21. Lahtinen, J., Valkonen, J., Bjorkman, K., Frits, J., Niemela, I., Heljanko, K.: Model checking of safety-critical software in the nuclear engineering domain. Reliability Engineering & System Safety (to appear, 2012)
22. Larsen, K.G., Pettersson, P., Yi, W.: UPPAAL in a Nutshell. International Journal on Software Tools for Technology Transfer 1(1-2), 134–152 (1997)

23. Leveson, N.: The challenge of building process-control software. IEEE Software 7(6), 55–62 (1990)
24. Ma, C., Wonham, W.M.: Nonblocking Supervisory Control of State Tree Structures. LNCIS, vol. 317. Springer (2005)
25. Markovski, J.: Towards supervisory control of Interactive Markov chains: Controllability. In: Proceedings of ACSD 2011, pp. 108–117. IEEE (2011)
26. Markovski, J., van Beek, D.A., Theunissen, R.J.M., Jacobs, K.G.M., Rooda, J.E.: A state-based framework for supervisory control synthesis and verification. In: Proceedings of CDC 2010, pp. 3481–3486. IEEE (2010)
27. Markovski, J., Jacobs, K.G.M., van Beek, D.A., Somers, L.J.A.M., Rooda, J.E.: Coordination of resources using generalized state-based requirements. In: Proceedings of WODES 2010, pp. 300–305. IFAC (2010)
28. Markovski, J., Reniers, M.A.: Verifying performance of supervised plants. In: Proceedings of ACSD 2012. IEEE (to appear, 2012)
29. Mertke, T., Menzel, T.: Methods and tools to the verification of safety-related control software. In: Proceedings of SMC 2000, vol. 4, pp. 2455–2457 (2000)
30. Miremadi, S., Akesson, K., Lennartson, B.: Extraction and representation of a supervisor using guards in extended finite automata. In: Proceedings of WODES 2008, pp. 193–199. IEEE (2008)
31. Ramadge, P.J., Wonham, W.M.: Supervisory control of a class of discrete-event processes. SIAM Journal on Control and Optimization 25(1), 206–230 (1987)
32. RTCA Inc. and EUROCAE: DO-178B: Software considerations in airborne systems and equipments certification (1992)
33. Schauf, A.: Safety implications of software in safety-critical devices. Journal of System Safety 47(6), 1–5 (2011)
34. Schiffelers, R.R.H., Theunissen, R.J.M., van Beek, D.A., Rooda, J.E.: Model-based engineering of supervisory controllers using CIF. Electronic Communications of the EASST 21, 1–10 (2009)
35. Seow, K.T.: Integrating temporal logic as a state-based specification language for discrete-event control design in finite automata. IEEE Transactions on Automation Science and Engineering 4(3), 451–464 (2007)
36. Su, R., van Schuppen, J.H., Rooda, J.: Aggregative synthesis of distributed supervisors based on automaton abstraction. IEEE Transactions on Automatic Control 55(7), 1627–1640 (2010)
37. Theunissen, R.J.M., Schiffelers, R.R.H., van Beek, D.A., Rooda, J.R.: Supervisory control synthesis for a patient support system. In: Proceedings of ECC 2009, pp. 1–6. EUCA (2009)
38. UK Ministry of Defence: Defence standard 00-55 – The procurement of safety critical software in defence equipment (1997)
39. Ziller, R., Schneider, K.: Combining supervisor synthesis and model checking. ACM Transactions on Embedded Computing Systems 4(2), 331–362 (2005)

A Model Based Approach for Safety Analysis

Fabien Belmonte and Elie Soubiran

Alstom Transport, 48 rue Albert Dhalenne
93484 Saint-Ouen cedex, France
{fabien.belmonte,elie.soubiran-ext}@transport.alstom.com

Abstract. This paper deals with model based safety engineering in Railway signaling systems development. Recently, model based system engineering (MBSE) has brought new specification means for large industrial system. Alstom Transport develops its own MBSE methodology supported by the SysML notation. In this context, a domain specific modeling language (DSML) has been developed for the safety studies enabling tight coupling with the MBSE environment. The paper describes a model to model translation. The translation developed takes the functional part of the system model and the dysfunctional viewpoint modeled within the safety DSML to generate an Altarica model of the system. The generated Altarica model is formal and allows, one from another, the dysfunctional simulation of the system and the generation of sequences of events leading to accidents.

1 Introduction

In Railways domain, signaling systems are highly safety critical. Those systems are intended to prevent the trains from colliding and from derailing. The development life-cycle of signaling systems is regulated by process-and-performance oriented norms defined (for Europe but widely used around the world) in CENELEC standards (EN 50126 [2], EN 50128 [3], EN 50129 [4]). Concretely, the development life-cycle is twofold, on one hand the designers develop a safe system by observing a safety methodology, on the other hand the safety engineers identify the accidental scenarios and insure that the system hazards leading to these scenarios are mitigated within the design of the system.

Up to now, system design is generally described with textual requirements in large documentation and the safety analyses are also performed within textual documentation. But the documentation reveals only the result of system design activity and the rationale of the retained solution is not recorded. Furthermore, the results included in documentation are difficult to trace and to reuse because of the manual operations required by the safety engineers. Recently, Alstom Transport introduced a MBSE methodology, supported by the SysML notation [8] to tackle the limitations of the textual approach. Given the fact that the SysML notation does not fit the specific dysfunctional[1] semantic required to perform safety

---

[1] A dysfunctional viewpoint highlights the way a system or function does not work properly.

F. Ortmeier and P. Daniel (Eds.): SAFECOMP 2012 Workshops, LNCS 7613, pp. 50–63, 2012.

analysis, a Domain Specific Modeling Language (DSML) has been developed for the safety activities [5]. It enables the traceability between each safety model element with its corresponding object element in the model of the system. This DSML has been developed during the French IMOFIS R&D research program and further extended during the ITEA2 R&D research program VERDE. In particular, the work presented here extends the IMOFIS safety DSML to apply formal analysis and enables early validation. The remainder of this paper is the following: the first part gives an overview of the safety process, the second part describes our MBSE approach, finally the last part proposes a formal model to model transformation that targets the Altarica language.

2   Overview of the Safety Analysis

The safety process stems from the system development process. More precisely, each safety step depends on a corresponding system development step (cf. Figure 1). The aim of the overall safety analysis is to preserve traceability within a deep causal analysis (from elementary faults to system accidents) and to allow analysts to provide explanation of causation link from cause to effect at every levels of the V descendant phase. Firstly, a Preliminary Hazard Analysis (PHA) is performed to identify the accidental scenarios, secondly an iterative System Hazard Analysis is conducted at each level of description of the system. These are twofold, a causal and a consequence analysis insures an exhaustive analysis of the events leading to the accidents.

In the PHA, accidents are identified by the hazardous situation and by the operational concept in which they occur; this is the consequence analysis. Then a causal analysis is performed in order to identify the barriers that prevent hazards to be developed into accident. Accident is the result of the conjunction of the hazard occurrence event and the barrier failure event both conditioned by a specific operational context.

At the end of the PHA, the system designers start the definition of the functional breakdown structure (FBS). The Figure 2 presents a typical hierarchy of activities and operations that represent the FBS of a system. The tree structure of the FBS ranges from high-level abstract functions allocated to (sub)systems

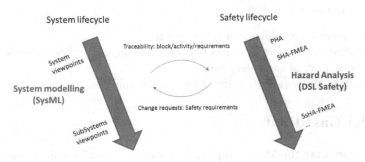

Fig. 1. Parallel and collaborative V process for system and safety

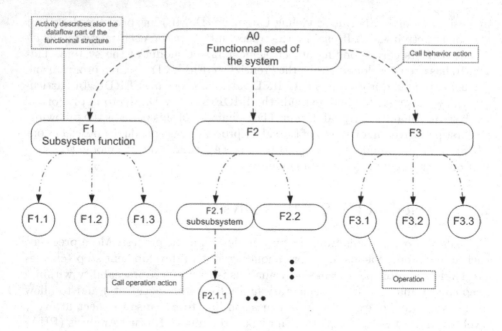

Fig. 2. FBS

to concrete functions allocated to software or hardware components. Then, a detailed failure mode analysis is applied systematically to every single function of the FBS. This is the role of the Failure Mode and Effect Analysis (FMEA) technique [1]. Each system's function shall be analyzed in order to discover its failure modes. A failure mode of a function is the manner by which a failure is observed; it generally describes the way the failure occurs. Then for each failure mode of a function their causes and their consequences are identified. This analysis uses inductive reasoning: from particular established fact (the failure mode occurs) the analyst entails a more general fact (what could be deduce on a larger set, in our case the system). Up to now this safety process was performed within documentation. The traceability between system specification artifacts and safety artifacts was established manually. Since the system specification uses semi-formal modeling language (SysML), the use of a safety DSML offers the following opportunities:

- To share a single repository of requirements;
- To formalize the traceability links between system and safety model artifacts;
- To generate part of the safety model;
- To automate the top-down part of the safety analysis.

3   Model Based Safety

This section presents the MBSE approach of this work and is split in four parts. The first part concerns the system modeling approach, the second part presents the contributed safety DSL, the third part proposes Altarica as the formal target of safety modeling and the last part describes the proposed process.

3.1 SysML and MARTE

SysML is now widely accepted as the general-purpose modeling language for system engineering. In contrast to UML, it provides a requirement-driven approach and proposes modeling elements, like blocks and constraint blocks, that mitigates the software-centered vision of UML. However, it stays interoperable with other modeling languages since it is based on the XMI interchange format [7]. Hence, SysML can be used with specific modeling languages or profiles like our DSML or MARTE [6].

In order to tackle the complexity of system modeling, Alstom decomposes system models into several viewpoints. Each one has a clearly defined purpose and the whole allows to present all facets of the system. We find, beyond others, an operational view, a functional view, and a constructional view. For safety analysis purpose, we are mainly interested by the operational and functional views. Indeed, the operational view identifies for each subsystem the external entities, the contexts, and the operational missions. On its side, the functional view describes services and functions the system and subsystems must realize, and results in the FBS presented above. Concretely, we get from these views a structured description of the system environment and a data/control flow oriented description of the functions. Finally, the MARTE profile allows us to add to the system model real-time artifacts that can be exploited for safety analysis. For instance, the loose semantic of SysML can be greatly enriched by adding VSL based constraints on activities and sequences that will be furthermore traced in the safety model for dysfunctional analysis purpose. A typical example consists in a constraint that expresses the validity time of a message. These real-time specification artifacts together with the requirements management of SysML are mandatory to conduct a precise safety analysis.

3.2 The Safety DSML

The risk assessment starts with the identification of accidental scenarios. This analysis is called Preliminary Hazard Analysis (PHA). Based on the definition of accidental scenarios, fault trees are built to identify the causes of the accidents, this is the deductive phase of the risk assessment called System Hazard Analysis - Fault Tree (SHA-FT). Then, the safety analysts take into account the elementary failures of the system one by one and identify their effects on the system. This is the inductive process named SHA-FMEA. The PHA is modeled with event tree formalism, the SHA-FT with fault-trees and SHA-FMEA with transition systems. PHA needs to be linked with structural and operational model elements of the system design model, and SHA are linked to structural and functional model elements of the system design model. A DSL supported by semi-formal modeling tool for risk assessment has been developed. It is able to communicate with any system engineering modeling language as long as the model follows the Eclipse Modeling Framework format. The main features are:

- Graphical representation of PHA and SHA;
- One model serialized, many views are available;
- Serialization of the global risk analysis into one fault tree;
- Requests on system design model and references of model element into risk assessment;
- Customization of requests based on system engineering method used in system design (e.g. which model element represents function?);
- Automatic layout of graphical representation (very useful for large model);
- Requirements repository and traceability purpose.

Structure of the PHA. The PHA aims at identifying the accidental scenarios of the system. A scenario is defined by a hazard event that may develop into accident. The consequence of this accident is identified. The principle of the PHA is then to identify the barrier that prevents the hazard to be developed into accident and the barrier that reduces the severity of the consequence of the accident. The PHA (all the scenarios) are encoded in the model with a fault tree formalism. One scenario is shown to the user within an event tree formalism (The reader interested [5]).

Structure of the SHA-FMEA. The Safety meta-model (MM) has been extended during the Verde project to enhance its expressiveness relatively to FMEA modeling. The basic idea is to bring an adequate semantic, closely related to the Altarica's one, for FMEA constructions. The SHA-FMEA is built as a hierarchy of FMEAs, where each FMEA is associated to an activity or an operation of the system model (cf. Figure 3). The relations sub/super FMEA, depicted as dashed arrows, follow the relation induced by the use of callBehaviorAction and callOperationAction objects in the FBS. In other words, the overview diagram gives the hierarchical presentation of the system from a safety point of view. The top level node is the previously presented PHA, at depth 1 we have the system FMEA, at depth 2 the subsystems FMEAs and so on until software FMEAs. Furthermore, the causes of a failure at depth i are explained by failures at depth $i + 1$. These cross-level references gives the ability to the safety analyst to navigate quickly between related FMEAs. Finally, it allows us to have, in our safety models, both a vertical traceability (system/subsystem/...) of failure modes and a horizontal traceability (subsystem$_1$/subsystem$_2$...) that is mainly supported by the dataflow part of the system model. The overview diagram also allows one to edit the dysfunctional characterization of the data, by default we propose a three valued characterization: correct, erroneous, and void, it then can be extended with custom values (TooHigh, TooLate...).

As shown in Figure 4, a FMEA object is roughly a transition system. For a given system object, the states of the associated FMEA are the nominal state and the failure states, transitions from nominal to failure states are guarded by

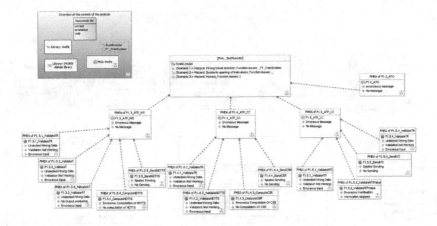

Fig. 3. The overview diagram

constraints and/or events, they represent the causes of a failure. More precisely, a failure mode is characterized by a system effect and a local effect. Beside natural language descriptions, the system effect references a failure mode of the super level[2], on its side the local effect characterizes outputs of the considered system component from a dysfunctional point of view. A failure cause may reference one or part of the following objects:

- Atomic events, for instance "bug", "shutdown"...
- Input events, they associate to parameters or ports of the system model a dysfunctional value. The event is raised if the value is observed on the port.
- System model constraints expressed in VSL or OCL. The guard is true if the constraint evaluates to false.
- Failure states of lower levels for hierarchical propagation and traceability of failures.
- An operational context that narrows the scope of a failure

From this short presentation, one may notice the high density of traceability links within and between models (system and safety). The systematic use of cross-reference allows us to gain in productivity since information is always one-click distant, but also in completeness and coherence since it becomes quite easy to write a set of OCL rules to perform ad hoc checking on models.

Finally, we propose for models that are conforms to our Safety MM a translation based semantic that targets Altarica's guarded transition system. The main benefit in fixing a precise semantic is that it allows us to automatize a part of the safety analysis.

---

[2] For the system FMEA, the system effects reference either hazards or barrier failures that are used in accident cases of the PHA.

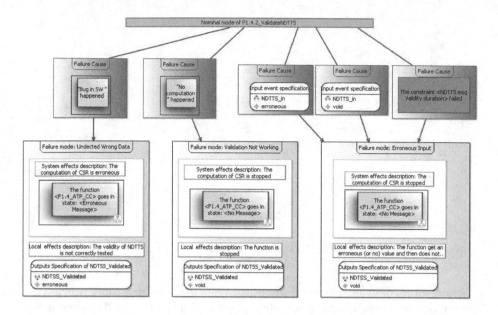

Fig. 4. FMEA diagram for an operation

3.3   The Need of Formal Language: Altarica

The DSML presented above allows one to describe the dysfunctional viewpoint
of the system, but does not provide a formal semantic that enables automated
computational analysis. The scientific dependability community developed in
the 90's a formal language, called Altarica, to perform such analysis [9]. Altarica
language provides a way to describe constrained automata. Furthermore, these
automata can be interfaced together through a concept of flow and hierarchically
organized by instantiating sub-automata. Hence this language is able to answer
the challenge of modeling together the functional behavior of the system, the
triggering of failures, and their propagation. An Altarica model consists in a set
of interrelated nodes. A node is composed of sub-nodes, flow and state variables,
events, transitions, and assertions. The meaning given, in this work, for each
item is the following:

- Sub-nodes provide a mean to describe the functional hierarchy (FBS).
- Flows encode the functional interfaces, but are typed with dysfunctional
  values.
- States correspond to the failure modes described in FMEAs.
- Events are the failure occurrences.
- Transitions encode the condition to trigger a failure occurrence and the re-
  sulting failure mode of the function.
- Assertions allow to specify the values of the outputs of the node considering
  the values of the input and the failure modes.

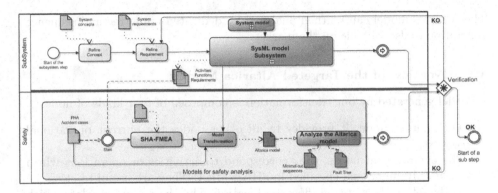

Fig. 5. The process

Traditional safety formalism, such as Fault Trees, Event trees, Petri Nets, *etc.* can be extracted from the Altarica model of the system. Furthermore, the executable semantic of Altarica allows to compute directly the traditional safety analysis result sets (*e.g.* minimal cut-sets and accident sequences). Today, FMEAs are performed manually. Since it is an exhaustive and inductive technique, hand-made production are highly cost-consuming. By designing a safety DSML and a system model transformation to Altarica, a productivity and quality gain is expected. The following sections describes the methodology to achieve this goal.

3.4   The Proposed Process

In order to generate the Altarica model, the following process is proposed. The figure shows a sub-system development phase. It is assumed that the above system model is available. The first task of the sub-system designer is to refine the requirements of the system level specification. Then the modeling phase aims at specifying within three viewpoints (operational, functional and constructional) the system to be developed. The parallel safety life-cycle depends on the SysML model of the sub-system. Then, the SHA-FMEA is performed by the safety engineer with the safety DSML workbench. Finally, the model transformation developed in this work takes the functional specification of the model of the sub-system and the FMEA of each function and generates the Altarica model. A dedicated tool is used to perform the analyses of the Altarica model. As a result, the set of accident sequences and the fault-tree of the sub-system is generated. With this result-set the safety engineers validates the safety criteria. The case should arises that some criteria are not fulfilled, the safety engineer requests changes in the design of the system.

4   Model Transformation

In this section we present the model transformation developed during the Verde project. It aims at providing an automatic and transparent translation tool which is able to extract an Altarica model from both safety and system models.

The Altarica model can be then analyzed by dedicated fault tree and sequence generation tools available on the market.

4.1 Overview of the Targeted Altarica Models

A model generated by our transformation is composed of four kinds of nodes:

1. The context node, it provides to all other nodes the current operational context.
2. The environment nodes, they correspond to activities or operations which are not dysfunctional specified in SHA-FMEA. They are useful to close the model relatively to its dataflow specification. They basically send data which can be corrupted to the rest of the model.
3. The FMEA nodes, they are the core of the Altarica model. They encode the dysfunctional specification given in the safety model and the dataflow specification given by the system model.
4. The PHA node, it is the top level node of the model. It acts as an observer that checks if the state of the whole system triggers an accident.

The model transformation takes into account both system and safety viewpoint. This allows us to extract the dataflow part from activities and the control part from FMEAs. More precisely, pins and parameters are mapped to flow variables, object flow to assertion on flow variables, while FMEAs provide guards, events, and states to specify transitions.

4.2 Formalization of the Model Transformation

In this section, we assume that an Altarica model is a set of nodes and that a node can be expressed as an octuple $(l, SI, F, S, E, I, T, A)$ where:

- l is an identifier, it represents the name of the node
- SI is a set of subnode instances. A subnode instance is represented as a pair of identifiers, the first projection is the name of the instance, and the second projection is the name of the node.
- F is a set of flow definitions. A flow is defined by an identifier and a type[3].
- S is a set of state variable definitions. Like flows, state variables are defined by an identifier and a type.
- E is a set of identifier and represents the set of events.
- I is an initial state, it associates to each state variable an expression.
- T is a set of guarded transitions. A guarded transition is made of a boolean expression acting as the guard, a triggering event, and a valuation of state variables.
- A is a set of boolean assertions, linking flow values to states of the node.

---

[3] Models generated by the proposed translation only use enumerated type.

Notation:

i. $||\cdot||$ (resp. $||\cdot||_{foo}$) denotes the translation function (resp. the foo subfunction)

ii. The rule $||X|| \rightarrow Y$ expresses "the translation applied to X evaluates into Y"

iii. We denote by M the system model, m ranges over elements of M and $A_0 \in M$ is the top level activity

iv. We denote by S the safety model, P is the PHA, F is the SHA-FMEA and L the library

v. We say that $m \in M$ and $f \in F$ are in relation if and only if the FMEA f describes the dysfunctionnal behavior of m, and we write $m \sim f$

vi. $X.a$ denotes the attribute a of the element X. In the following, we have tried to give self-explanatory names for attributes.

Translation Rules:
In the following, we use two type abbreviations:

$$Ctxt := ||L.ownedCtx||_{ident}$$

$$Ddys := ||L.dataDys||_{ident}$$

$Ctxt$ is the datatype which represents the operationnal context of the system. $Ddys$ is datatype that abstracts system data to dysfunctionnal data (correct, erroneous, too high...). The translation subfunction $ident$ is given at the end of rules description.

• The **main** rule:

$$||(M,S)|| \rightarrow ||L||_{ctxt} \cup ||(A_0, F)||_{env} \cup ||(M, F)||_{fmea} \cup ||(A_0, P)||_{pha}$$

The main translation rule is applied to a pair composed of a system model and a safety model. It evaluates to a set of Altarica nodes computed by four subfunctions. The first one computes the context node and is applied to the library of the safety model. The second one computes the environment and takes as arguments both top level activity and SHA-FMEA. The third one computes the set of nodes that encodes the dysfunctionnal behavior of the system. The last one translates the PHA.

• The **ctxt** rule produces the singleton node $CtxtProvider$:

$$||L||_{ctxt} \rightarrow (CtxtProvider, \emptyset, F_l, S_l, E_l, I_l, T_l, A_l)^4$$

The state variables, flow variables and events range over the operationnal contexts of the model:

$$F_l := (C_{flow}, Ctxt)$$

$$S_l := (C_{state}, Ctxt)$$

$$E_l := ||L.ownedCtx||_{event}$$

---

[4] We intentionally omit braces for singleton sets.

$$I_l := (C_{state}, c_1)_{c_1 \in Ctxt}$$

The transitions define a complete transition system over operationnal contexts:

$$T_l := \{\ldots, (\top, ||c_i||_{event}, (C_{state}, ||c_i||_{ident})), \ldots\}_{\forall c_i \in L.ownedCtx}$$

Finally, the assertion links the state of the node to its output flow:

$$A_l := (C_{state} = C_{flow})$$

• The **env** rule gathers operations and behaviors that are called in A_0 but are not dysfunctionally specified in the safety model. It then generates a set of nodes that closes the Altarica model relatively to its dataflow part.

$$||(A_0, F)||_{env} \rightarrow \bigcup_{st\ \forall f \in S,\, !m \sim f}^{\forall m \in A_0} ||(m, f)||_{env}$$

$$||(m, f)||_{env} \rightarrow (m.name, \emptyset, F_e, S_e, E_e, I_e, T_e, A_e)$$

The flow and state variables correspond to the output parameters of system component m and are typed by the dysfunctionnal datatype. Assertions enforce the equality between state, initialized with the *correct* dysfunctionnal value, and flow variables

$$F_e := \{\ldots, (||p_i||_{flow}, Ddys), \ldots\}_{\forall p_i \in m.parameter\ st\ isout(p_i)}$$

$$S_e := \{\ldots, (||p_i||_{ident}, Ddys), \ldots\}_{\forall p_i \in m.parameter\ st\ isout(p_i)}$$

$$A_e := \{\ldots (||p_i||_{flow} = ||p_i||_{ident}) \ldots\}_{\forall p_i \in m.parameter\ st\ isout(p_i)}$$

$$I_e := \{\ldots, (||p_i||_{ident}, d_1), \ldots)\}_{d_1 \in Ddys}$$

We define events as the cartesian product of the set of output parameters and the set of dysfunctionnal values, and we map it to a set of labels. Guarded transistions map each event to the corresponding valuation of the state variable:

$$E_e := \{\ldots, (||p_i||_{ident} + d_j), \ldots)\}_{\forall (p_i, d_j) \in m.parameter \times Ddys}{}^5$$

$$T_e := \{\ldots, (\top, ||p_i||_{ident} + d_j, (||p_i||_{ident}, d_j)), \ldots\}_{\forall (p_i, d_j) \in m.parameter \times Ddys}$$

• The **fmea** rule produces the set of node which elements correspond to the pairs (system component, safety component) of the input models:

$$||(M, F)||_{fmea} \rightarrow \bigcup_{st\ \exists f \in S,\, m \sim f}^{\forall m \in M} ||(m, f)||_{fmea}$$

$$||(m, f)||_{fmea} \rightarrow (m.name, SI_f, F_f, S_f, E_f, I_f, T_f, A_f)$$

---

[5] The + operator denotes identifier concatenation.

The subnode instances are given by the subFMEA of f in the safety model:

$$SI_f := \{\ldots, (||m_i||_{inst}, ||m_i||_{ident}), \ldots\}_{\forall f_i \in f.SubFmea \; st \; m_i \sim f_i}$$

The flow variables correspond to the parameters of the system component, the state variable of the node ranges over failure and nominal modes specified in the FMEA:

$$F_f := \{(C_{flow}, Ctxt)\ldots, (||p_i||_{ident}, Ddys), \ldots\}_{\forall p_i \in m.parameter}$$

$$S_f := (F_{state}, ||f.failMod||_{ident} \cup ||f.nominalMode||_{ident})$$

$$I_f := \{(F_{State}, ||f.nominalMode||)\}$$

The events are the atomic events and constraint failures defined in the failure causes:

$$E_f := ||f.failureCause.AtomicEvent||_{ident}$$

$$\cup ||f.failureCause.Constraintfailure||_{ident}$$

The guarded transitions of the node correspond to failure causes of the FMEA. Input events, operationnal context restrictions, subsystem failures are translated as guards while atomic event and constraint failure are trigering events.

$$T_f := \{\ldots (g_i, e_i, (F_{State}, ||fc_i.dest||_{ident}))\ldots\}_{\forall fc_i \in f.failureCause}$$

$$g_i := (C_{flow} = ||fc_i.opCtx||_{ident} \wedge ||fc_i.inEv||_{input}$$

$$\wedge ||fc_i.SubFail.owner||_{ident}.F_{state}^{sub} = ||fc_i.SubFail||_{ident})$$

$$e_i := (||fc_i.AtomEvent||_{ident})_{fc_i.AtomEvent \neq Null}$$

$$e_i := (||fc_i.CstrFail||_{ident})_{fc_i.CstrFail \neq Null}$$

For assertions, we need to consider two cases, either the system component m is an activity either it is an operation. If it is an activity then the assertions will encode the object flows of the activity:

$$A_f := \{\ldots (||o.target||_{ident} = ||o.source||_{ident})\ldots\}_{\forall o \in m.edge}{}^6$$

$$\cup \{\ldots (||m_i||_{ident}.C_{flow} = C_{flow})\ldots\}_{\forall f_i \in f.SubFmea \; st \; m_i \sim f_i}$$

If it is an operation then the local effect description of the failures modes gives the specification of outgoing flows.

$$A_f := \{\ldots (||p_i||_{ident} = ||(p_i, f.failMod)||_{case})\ldots\}_{\forall p_i \in m.parameter \; st \; isout(p_i)}$$

The case rule produces conditionnal branching represented here as a set of pair condition value. In the current context, the conditionnal branching expresses that

---

[6] The long names that are mandatory to access subnode flows are not specified here but can be easily extracted from $o.target.owner.behavior$ or $o.target.owner.operation$

if the node is in a given failure mode the flow variable takes the value specified in this failure mode. The default branch always returns the *correct* value.

$$||p, FM||_{case} \rightarrow \{\ldots (F_{state} = ||fm_i||_{ident}, ||fm_i.ouput(p)||_{ident}) \ldots \}_{\forall fm_i \in FM}$$

- The **PHA** rule produces the node *PHA*, it is the main node of the model:

$$||(A_0, P)||_p \rightarrow (PHA, SI_p, \emptyset, S_p, \emptyset, I_p, T_p, A_p)$$

The set of instances of subnode in PHA is composed of a context provider, the nodes forming the environment, and the FMEA nodes associated to (sub)sytem.

$$SI_p := (ctxtInst, CtxtProvider)$$
$$\cup \{(||m||_{inst}, ||m||)\}_{\forall f \in P.SubFmea, m \sim f}$$
$$\cup \{(||m||_{env}, ||m||)\}_{\forall m \in A_0 \text{ st } \forall f, !m \sim f}$$

The state variable of PHA node is typed by the set of accident bounded in the accident cases of the PHA, and the initial state is the "no accident" state $\bar{a}$.

$$S_p := (Ac_{State}, \bar{a} \cup ||P.AccidentCase||_{ident})$$
$$I_p := (Ac_{State}, \bar{a})$$

In the PHA context, guarded transitions encode the accident scenarios. A guard is then the conjunction of a hazard, a functionnal issue and an operationnal context. Both hazard and issue result from failures at subsystem level.
$$T_p :=$$

$$\bigcup_{\substack{\forall (h,i,c,a) \\ \in P.AccidentCase}} (C_{flow} = ||c||_{ident} \wedge ||h||_{cause} \wedge ||i||_{cause}, \epsilon, (Ac_{State}, ||a||_{ident}))$$

Where the **cause** rule builds the disjunction of possible causes for a given hazard or issue:

$$||x||_{cause} \rightarrow \bigvee_{\substack{\forall fm \in P.subfmea.failMod \\ \text{st } fm.syseffect=x}} ||fm.owner||_{ident}.F_{state}^{sub} = ||fm||_{ident}$$

Finally, the assertion translation scheme is roughly the same as in **fmea**:

$$A_p := \{\ldots (||o.target||_{ident} = ||o.source||_{ident}) \ldots \}_{\forall o \in A_0.edge}$$

$$\cup \{\ldots (||m_i||_{ident}.C_{flow} = CtxtProvider.C_{flow}) \ldots \}_{\forall f \in P.SubFmea, m_i \sim f_i}$$

- The **ident** rule extracts identifiers from named elements of the model:

$$||N||_{ident} \rightarrow \bigcup_{\forall n_i \in N} ||n_i||_{ident}$$

$$||n_i||_{ident} \rightarrow n_i.name$$

The **event** (resp. **inst, flow**) rule is a variant of the **ident** rule and appends "ev" (resp. "inst", "flow") to the generated identifier.

- The **input** rule translates input events to a boolean expression. It is used by the **fmea** rule

$$||InEv||_{input} \rightarrow \bigwedge_{\forall (p_i, d_i) \in InEv} ||p_i||_{ident} = ||d_i||_{ident}$$

5 Conclusion

This work is an on-going research activity related to the overall MBSE methodology within Alstom Transport and will pursue in the Artemis MBAT project. This work follows the development of a specific modeling environment for safety activities. Based on the existing DSML for safety, the system hazard analysis viewpoint has been improved in order to enable translation of the safety model conjointly with the functional specification of the system to a dysfunctional model of the system. This later, modeled with the Altarica language, allows the computation of the fault-tree analysis, the accident sequences and allows the simulation of dysfunctional events. For the safety engineers, it improves both its productivity and the accuracy of its study. Indeed, the MBSE approach, by enabling tight coupling of the engineering environment, facilitates the information traceability application and maintenance. Document based FMEA describes only one level of consequence of failure occurrences, the formalization of all these one-shot causal events with Altarica allows the analyze of the propagation of the failure in the system. Additionaly, the results of Altarica analyses provide feedbacks to the safety engineer on the criticity of the functions at each description levels of the system. Hence, justifications of the Safety Integrity Level of the barrier functions are provided to the safety case. The next step of this work will be the validation of the overall transformation chain from specifications to minimal cut-sets and accecibility sequences generation. The functional validation will stem from the formal transformation presented in this paper.

References

1. Villemeur, A.: Reliability, availability, maintainability, and safety assessment. Wiley J. (1992)
2. CENELEC, Railway applications. The specification and demonstration of reliability, availability, maintainability and safety (RAMS), EN50126
3. CENELEC, Railway applications. Communications, signalling and processing systems. Software for railway control and protection systems, EN50128
4. CENELEC, Railway applications. Communication, signalling and processing systems. Safety related electronic systems for signalling, EN50129
5. Belmonte, F., Blas, A., Mejia, L.-F., Thomas, F.: Risk Evaluation in Railway Systems Supported By Modeling Languages and Tools. Lambda-Mu, 17ème Congrès de Maîtrise des Risques et de Sûreté de Fonctionnement. IMDR, La Rochelle (2010)
6. OMG. UML Profile for MARTE: Modeling and Analysis of Real-time Embedded Systems, v1.1 (June 2011), http://www.omg.org/spec/MARTE
7. OMG. MOF 2 XMI Mapping, v2.4.1 (August 2011), http://www.omg.org/spec/XMI/
8. OMG. OMG Systems Modeling Language (OMG SysML), v1.2, http://www.omg.org/spec/SysML
9. Point, G.: AltaRica: Contribution à l'unification des méthodes formelles et de la sûreté de fonctionnement. LaBRI, Université Bordeaux I (January 2000)

Towards a Model-Based Evolutionary Chain of Evidence for Compliance with Safety Standards

Jose Luis de la Vara[1], Sunil Nair[1], Eric Verhulst[2], Janusz Studzizba[3],
Piotr Pepek[3], Jerome Lambourg[4], and Mehrdad Sabetzadeh[1]

[1] Simula Research Laboratory,
P.O. Box 134, 1325 Lysaker, Norway
{jdelavara,sunil,mehrdad}@simula.no
[2] Altreonic
Gemeentest. 61A, B3210 Linden, Belgium
eric.verhulst@altreonic.com
[3] Parasoft S.A.
Kielkowskiego 9, Krakow, 30-704, Poland
{januszst,piotr}@parasoft.com
[4] AdaCore
46 rue d'Amsterdam, 75009 Paris, France
lambourg@adacore.com

Abstract. Compliance with safety standards can greatly increase the development cost and time of critical systems. Major problems arise when evolutions to a system entail reconstruction of the body of safety evidence. When changes occur in the development or certification processes, identification of the new evidence to provide, the evidence that is no longer adequate, or the evidence that can be reused poses some challenges. Therefore, practitioners need support to identify how a chain of evidence evolves as a result of the changes. Otherwise, execution of the above activities can be very costly, and it can even result in abandonment of certification efforts. This paper outlines a solution to deal with these challenges. The solution is based on the use of model-driven engineering technology, which has already been applied for safety certification but not from an evolutionary chain of evidence-based perspective. The paper also sets the background for developing the solution, describes real situations in which the solution can help industry, and discusses possible challenges for developing it. The solution will be developed as part of OPENCOSS, a research project on cross-domain evolutionary certification.

Keywords: safety, safety certification, evidence, chain of evidence, evidence evolution, model-driven engineering, impact analysis, OPENCOSS.

1 Introduction

Most critical systems in domains such as avionics, railways, and automotive are subject to some form of safety assessment as a way to ensure that the systems do not pose undue risks to people, property, or the environment. The most common type of

F. Ortmeier and P. Daniel (Eds.): SAFECOMP 2012 Workshops, LNCS 7613, pp. 64–78, 2012.

assessment is safety certification [18], whose goal is to provide a formal assurance that a system is deemed safe by a licensing or regulatory body. Certification is typically performed based on one or more standards that apply in a given domain. Examples of standards include IEC61508, DO-178C for avionics, the CENELEC standards for railways, and ISO26262 for the automotive sector [7, 13].

Demonstrating compliance with a safety standard involves the provision of evidence to show that the relevant criteria in the standard are met. This imposes unavoidable, high costs on companies [15]. Furthermore, system evolution often becomes costly because it entails regenerating the entire body of evidence. The evidence should be re-examined whenever the system is modified and, if the evidence is no longer adequate, new evidence should be generated. This is closely related to (change) impact analysis [4], which aims at identifying the potential consequences of a change, or at estimating what needs to be modified to accomplish it.

As a result, when a system is certified, subsequent modifications are usually avoided. This can also hinder innovation, as use of new technologies would require re-certification. Consequently, new approaches centred on evidence evolution, including chains of evidence (Section 2.1), are necessary.

This paper presents a solution sketch for managing evolutionary chains of evidence and thus how to deal with the above challenges for safety certification. The solution will be developed as part of the work in OPENCOSS [26], a large-scale European research project whose goal is to devise a common certification framework for the railway, avionics and automotive domains, addressing evidence evolution.

The solution is based on the use of model-driven engineering (MDE) [37], thus it supports a model-based evolutionary chain of evidence. As we discuss below, MDE is an enabler for performing several tasks related to evidence and chains of evidence management. For example, MDE can facilitate standard interpretation, electronic evidence management, and identification of chains of evidence.

In addition, the paper (1) sets the background on which the solution is based and that makes us believe that it is necessary and feasible, (2) describes realistic situations in which evidence and thus chains of evidence evolve, and (3) outlines the challenges that we might face. The set of challenges are related to both technology issues and business issues (e.g., industrial acceptance).

The rest of the paper is organized as follows. Section 2 presents background work. Section 3 describes situations in which evidence evolves. Section 4 outlines the envisioned solution, whereas Section 5 discusses the challenges that we foresee. Finally, Section 6 summarises our conclusions and future work.

2   Background

This section introduces: (a) safety certification; (b) OPENCOSS; (c) two surveys on certification and evidence management; (d) past work on evidence management and on model-based safety certification, and; (e) some related projects and initiatives. Overall, past work has not focused enough on evolution of chains of evidence.

2.1   Safety Certification

Safety-critical systems are typically subject to a rigorous safety certification process. The purpose of certification is to provide assurance that the system is safe to use in a specific environment under specific conditions [7].

Satisfaction of safety objectives according to a specific standard involves gathering convincing evidence during the lifecycle of the system. In general, evidence can be defined as "the available body of facts or information indicating whether a belief or proposition is true or valid" [28]. However, one can seldom argue that evidence for safety certification serves as a definitive proof of the truth or validity of safety claims, but only whether the evidence is sufficient for building (adequate) confidence in the claims. Hence, we define evidence for safety certification as "information or artefacts that contribute to developing confidence in the safe operation of a system". Such information or artefacts must also be linked to the requirements/objectives of the safety standard(s) that need to be met.

A chain of evidence is a set of pieces of evidence that are related (e.g., the agent that has created a requirements specification, the test cases derived from the requirements, etc.). Therefore, traceability between these pieces of evidence exists. By evolutionary, we mean that a chain of evidence can suffer changes (e.g., a requirement is modified), and thus it can evolve. As a result, the chain of evidence might not be adequate anymore (e.g., the related test cases might have to be updated).

Safety evidence can be supported by argumentation. Safety arguments are a set of inferences between claims and evidence that leads from the evidence forming the basis of the argument to a top-level safety claim. This claim is typically that the system is safe to operate in its intended environment [7].

2.2   OPENCOSS

OPENCOSS [26] is a FP7 European project that aims (1) to devise a common certification framework that spans different vertical markets for railway, avionics and automotive industries, and (2) to establish an open-source safety certification infrastructure. The ultimate goal of the project is to bring about substantial reductions in recurring safety certification costs, and at the same time increase product safety through the introduction of more systematic certification practices. Both are expected to boost innovation and system upgrades considerably. The project consortium consists of 17 partners from 9 different countries.

The problems that OPENCOSS addresses are: (1) lack of precision and large variety of certification requirements; (2) lack of composable/system view for certification; (3) high and non-measured costs for (re)certification, and; (4) lack of openness to innovation and new approaches. The project will deal with: (1) creation of a common certification language (metamodel); (2) compositional certification; (3) evolutionary chains of evidence (whose envisioned solution is outlined in this paper); (4) transparent certification process, and; (5) compliance-aware development process.

2.3   Earlier Surveys on Certification Issues and Evidence Management

This section summarises part of the results of two surveys that have been conducted at the beginning of OPENCOSS in order to gain an overall understanding of practices related to the project.

In the first survey [1], a total of 85 valid responses were obtained on certification issues. The main conclusions related to this paper are:

- Certification was considered as important for 68% of the respondents.
- The demotivating factors for certification are:
  - o Effort, cost, complexity, inconsistency, bureaucratic (paperwork) (60.7%)
  - o Change management (evolving standards, evolving products), differences national/ international (21.4%)
  - o Rigidity, lagging market and technology (17.9%)

In the second survey [25], a total of 15 responses were obtained from OPENCOSS partners. It aimed to set a baseline concerning the state of the practice on safety certification within the consortium. The main conclusions related to this paper are:

- Traceability between evidence was acknowledged as a major concern for safety certification by most of the partners.
- 11 partners selected MDE as a suitable way to manage traceability, and only matrices were selected more times.
- Most of the partners recommended using models to structure certification documentation.
- 27 types of traceability between types of evidence were identified.

The results of the surveys suggest (1) the need of mitigating the demotivating factors for certification, (2) the importance of chains of evidence (traceability), and (3) the suitability of using MDE technology for evidence management.

2.4   Safety Evidence Management and Evolution

This section reviews some existing research and tools that have dealt with safety evidence, its management, and its evolution.

Some works on the nature of safety evidence (e.g., [17]) have discussed process-based evidence (i.e., about the process followed) and product-based evidence (i.e., about system characteristics), and what type of evidence can be regarded as better suited for demonstrating safety. In general, the conclusion is that both types of evidence are necessary and are related.

Other works have defined evidence items for IEC61508 [35] and for the nuclear domain [16], have provided classifications of artefacts that can be used as evidence (e.g., [12]), or have proposed ways to structure evidence in certification documentation (e.g., [39]). Within OMG, there are two initiatives aimed at standardizing the notion of and the concepts related to assurance evidence [22] and arguments [24]. In relation to this paper, the main weakness of these works is that they have not dealt with chains of evidence. Other works have modelled standards such as IEC61508 [29] and DO-178B [42], identifying their main concepts and relations. However, they have not dealt with evolutionary chains of evidence.

Research-based prototypes have been developed for (1) specification of certificates associated to source code [34], V&V activities [38], and the activities of the development process [41], and (2) expert judgement-based quantification of confidence on evidence [35]. MDE-based prototypes for evidence management are presented in the following subsection.

Some existing commercial tools that directly or indirectly deal with evidence management are:

- Atego Workbench [3], which supports traceability, impact analysis, and versioning of software development work products.
- GoedelWorks [2], which supports IEC61508, IEC62061, ISO26262, ISO13849, ISO-DIS25119 and ISO15998, supports the specification of dependencies between (evidence) entities, and provides an entity lifecycle (Defined, InWork, FrozenForApproval, and Approved).
- Medini Analyze [19], which supports ISO 26262 and allows specification of traceability to express dependencies between (evidence) elements.
- Parasoft Concerto [33], which supports management (i.e., lifecycles) of requirements, test and defects, as well as traceability between them and impact analysis.

In summary, we consider that new research efforts that address and study in detail chains of evidence (of more types) and their evolution are necessary.

2.5   Model-Driven Compliance with Safety Standards

MDE can be a suitable and very useful technology for safety evidence management [32]. It is based on the use of models as main artefacts for concept representation and for communication, and of supporting tools for model verification and transformation.

MDE supports: (1) creation of interpretations of standards; (2) specialization of standards to industrial contexts (Fig. 1); (3) alignment of standards to organizational practices; (5) planning for certification; (6) electronic evidence management, and; (7) evidence reuse. Future, open issues to be addressed are: (1) facilitation of analysis and determination of the correspondence between different standards; (2) link of MDE-based safety certification with MDE-based development; (3) link of MDE-based evidence with argumentation, and; (4) use of MDE for management of evolutionary chains of evidence. The latter point would be the main contribution of the envisioned solution presented in this paper.

MDE has been used as basis for the development of prototypes aimed at: (1) facilitating the agreement upon the evidence to provide [9]; determining traceability between requirements and design [21]; (3) creating evidence repositories [30], and; (4) tailoring standards to specific companies, systems, and projects [31].

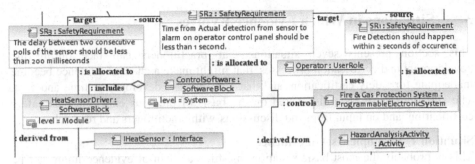

Fig. 1. Example of IEC61508-baed evidence information [29]

Model-based impact analysis is also related to MDE-based evolutionary chains of evidence. Various techniques exist for this purpose, with often differing requirements about the traceability links that need to be defined and also the semantics of the links. For example, a traceability information model and an algorithm based on this model for automatically analysing the impacts of change in UML models have been proposed in [5]. While useful, the conceptualization of the traceability links in most of the existing work is at a coarse level of abstraction, hindering their application for safety certification. A reference, better-suited approach can be found in [21], which addressed impact analysis regarding requirements and design.

2.6   Related Projects and Initiatives

When reviewing existing work on evidence management as a part of the work in OPENCOSS, and in addition to some works mentioned above, we have found several projects and initiatives that addressed or are addressing this issue:

- DECOS [6], which dealt with reuse of pre-validated hardware and software components and of functional blocks for design and certification purposes.
- EVOLVE [8], which aimed to create of a methodological framework for early V&V of evolutionary products.
- FormalSafe [11], which provided a framework to reuse development artefacts targeted at providing evidence for safety certification.
- ModelME! [20], which studied the use of MDE technologies for supporting safety certification.
- Open-DO [27], which aims to build a community around certification-oriented free software tools and libraries, addressing continuous certification.
- SafeCer [36], which aims to increase system development efficiency and reduce time-to-market by facilitating compositional certification.

More details about these and other projects can be found in [25]. Although they have addressed evidence evolution and/or management, application of MDE for evolutionary chains of evidence has seldom been explored.

3   Situations in Which Evidence Evolves

This section presents seven situations that practitioners can face during the development and certification processes, that might make a chain of evidence become inadequate for safety certification, and that can increase development time and cost. The situations have been discovered on the basis of previous experience on safety certification, and on input from and discussions with practitioners and researchers.

Situation 1) Incomplete set of evidence
This is probably the most basic situation in which a chain of evidence might not be adequate. It corresponds to the development scenario in which evidence is gathered and structured for a non-certified system. Therefore, evidence is collected, or at least structured, progressively. Until all the pieces of evidence that are part of a chain of evidence have not been gathered and structured, such a chain is inadequate.

This situation is related to other scenarios reported in research such as incremental certification and compositional/modular certification [10]. Nonetheless, the envisioned solution presented in this paper does not address adequate composition of evidence, beyond having all the necessary pieces of evidence of a chain. That is, the envisioned solution will not deal with composition adequacy assessment in a semantic way, but simply in a syntactic way (i.e., a chain of evidence must be complete). Such a semantic analysis will also be addressed in OPENCOSS, but not mainly by the authors of this paper.

Situation 2) System modification and recertification
This situation corresponds to a development scenario in which an already-certified system is modified and thus a new certification (i.e., recertification) is required. For example, a new system can be developed on the basis of an existing one (system modification). Such a new system can include, for instance, some new component.

In relation to tools for development of critical system, the safety assessment of the tools is not referred to as certification, but as qualification [18]. A tool is not certified "as safe", but qualified in the sense that its results (e.g., source code) can be used as evidence for safety certification without needing, for instance, to review them.

For these tools, the situation outlined would be referred to as requalification. For example, a tool aimed at verifying coding standards can require requalification as new versions are released, or clients request configurations of the tool that have not been qualified before. Qualification documentation consists of a tool qualification plan, the tool operation requirements and test cases, and the test results. Requalification would require identification of the necessary changes in these documents, based on new evidence to provide.

Situation 3) Modifications during the development process of a system
While a critical system is developed, and even though a waterfall process is followed, changes in a system and its associated documentation (which can be used as evidence) can occur at any moment. For example, (a) a new hazard might be identified as a result of an accident in another system. Such a hazard should be analysed, and would impact other artefacts (safety requirements, design, test cases, etc.). Another scenario

is, for instance, (b) a necessary change in the architecture of system. This might impact other artefacts such as design specifications, test cases, or even source code, which might become inadequate.

In this situation, a chain of evidence might become inadequate because of (a) missing pieces of evidence or (b) the impact of the change of other piece of evidence.

Situation 4) Change in the confidence on evidence

Another situation in which evidence can evolve and thus a chain of evidence can become inadequate is the result of the change of the confidence on a piece of evidence. Confidence refers to how adequate the piece is on the basis of some criterion. For example, an expert can judge evidence adequacy, or evidence linked to an argument can be regarded as stronger (i.e., more adequate). A piece of evidence can be considered better or worse than another based on adequacy assessment.

The simplest way of adequacy assessment is probably to determine if a set of evidence is complete (i.e., it allows justification of the fulfilment of all the criteria of a safety standard). Such a type of approach can be found, for instance, in [31]. Nonetheless, there are cases in which adequacy assessment can be more complex, based on specific pieces of evidence that are qualitative or quantitative assessed (e.g., [35]). In these cases, a change in the adequacy of a piece of evidence can affect the adequacy of the rest of pieces of a chain of evidence. For example, a change during the development of a system (e.g., related to requirements specification) that is made by an agent whose competence is not "high" (no "top confidence" on the agent) can negatively affect the confidence of the related pieces of evidence (e.g., a test case).

Situation 5) New context for a system

When an already certified system is to be used in a context other than what the system was certified for, then some pieces of evidence might become inadequate or new evidence might have to be provided. For example, a system for a type of train and a specific line (e.g., from Brussels to Paris) that is to be reused for the same type of train but in another line (e.g., from Rome to Milan) would not be certified per se, but new evidence (or arguments) would have to be provided. In the railway domain, this situation also matches the use of generic, certified applications in a specific train or line, in which impact analysis is necessary in order to determine what chains of evidence are not adequate and thus what new evidence must be generated.

Another situation related to context change is certification against another safety standard. That is, adequate evidence and chains of evidence for a standard might not be so for another (second standard). The second standard could correspond to a new standard, a new version of a standard, or a different interpretation of a standard (e.g., by a different certification authority). For example, new evidence might have to be provided for a system certified against DO-178B because of the release of DO-178C.

Situation 6) Agreement with a certification authority

This situation corresponds to scenarios in which new or different evidence is requested by a certification authority. For example, an authority might request new evidence for some safety criteria at some moment, after having agreed previously upon how to show compliance with such criteria, in order to gain more confidence on the global safety of a system. As a result, a chain of evidence might be inadequate, for instance, in relation to Situation 1 (incomplete evidence).

Situation 7) Component reuse
The last situation presented and in which evidence for safety certification can evolve is related to component reuse in a system. Although closely related to Situation 1, they are not exactly the same. As a result of component reuse, new evidence might have to be provided in order to have an adequate set of chains of evidence. For example, reuse of an event recorder system for different trains might require provision of different evidence, or new evidence about the system might have to be provided.

As mentioned in Situation 1, semantic analysis (of a component-based chain of evidence) is out of the scope of the envisioned solution presented in this paper.

4   Envisioned Solution

This section outlines the envisioned solution for model-based evolutionary chains of evidence. More concretely, a (research) process for realising the solution is presented. In addition, MDE technologies such as those described in [30, 31] will be used as a reference for the development of the tool support resulting from the solution. These technologies might be also combined with non-MDE ones (e.g., with [41]).

The process consists of six activities: (1) specification of the lifecycle of a chain of evidence; (2) identification of chains of evidence in safety standards; (3) impact analysis of the change of a piece of evidence on the rest of pieces of a chain; (4) validation of the chains identified; (5) analysis of the chains of evidence in actual projects, and; (6) determination of how the chains can be mapped into the common certification language specified in OPENCOSS. An activity that is not described is the evaluation of the (improvement) effect of the solution on practice.

Although the process is presented sequentially, backward steps might be necessary as the solution is developed. For example, "validation of the chains identified" might result in the discovery of some new piece of evidence of a chain. Some activities might also be performed in parallel. For example, "determination of how the chains can be mapped into the common certification language" can be executed at any moment of the process, which will be performed in parallel to the OPENCOSS tasks aimed at specifying the language.

The activities of the process are described as follows.

1) Specification of the lifecycle of a chain of evidence
The first activity will be to define and model a lifecycle for chains of evidence. Although no proposal for such a lifecycle exists yet, we plan to base it on existing proposal for evidence lifecycle. We will focus on the lifecycle proposed in the safety assurance evidence metamodel by OMG [24] because of being a standard. Nonetheless, we will also analyse other alternatives in order to try to specify the most suitable lifecycle for chains of evidence. We will study current practice (i.e., other lifecycles for evidence or chains of evidence used in industry, such as the one proposed by GoedelWorks [2]) and the notion of (software) certificate [34, 38].

The main issue for this activity will be to determine how evidence lifecycle relates to the lifecycle of a chain of evidence, having to address the possible needs found. In addition, since automation of management of chains of evidence is planned, we will have to analyse which transitions between states might be fully automatic. Others might require validation by users. In this sense, we think that fully automation will depend on the chains of evidence (i.e., the evidence types of its pieces). For example, a change in a requirement can automatically make its associated test case inadequate. Indeed, tools such as Parasoft Concerto [33] provide this functionality. However, human intervention might necessary, for instance, in scenarios related to the change of the confidence on a piece of evidence.

2) Identification of chains of evidence in safety standards
The second activity will aim to discover chains of evidence. For this purpose, (1) existing metamodels of safety standards (e.g., [29, 42]) will be used, and/or (2) metamodels for relevant standards will be created (e.g., for CENELEC standards of the railway domain), and subsequently used.

For each relation between two entities of the metamodel, it will have to be determined if the change of one of the entities can affect the other. For example, and using Fig. 2 as a reference, if (an instance of) "Source Code" changes, then its associated "Software Module Testing" will not be adequate. In addition, a finer analysis might be necessary. Once the chains of evidence have been identified, we will have to analyse what characteristics of the evidence types (i.e., attributes of the entities) can make a chain inadequate as a results of a change. That is, a change in some attributes might not have any impact on the adequacy of a chain of evidence.

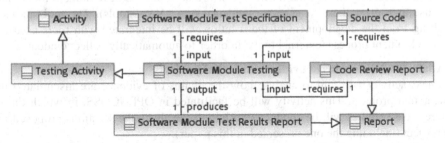

Fig. 2. Fragment of an IEC61508-based metamodel regarding software module testing [29]

3) Impact analysis of the change of a piece of evidence on the rest of pieces of a chain of evidence
After identification of the chains of evidence, mechanisms for model-based impact analysis must be determined in order to assess the effect that the change of a piece of evidence of a chain will have on the rest of pieces of the chain.

The most basic mechanism will be the specification of constraints (probably in the form of OCL [23]) aimed at enforcing the syntactic correctness of a chain of evidence. Evaluation of such constraints can automatically detect if some piece of evidence of a chain is missing.

Impact analysis related to, for instance, the change of the confidence on a piece of evidence will require further study. Using existing works as a reference (e.g., [5, 21]), we will have to decide on the most suitable and precise way to assess change impact. Probabilistic-based approaches such as the one proposed in [35] seem to be a promising possibility. However, it is based on quantitative assessment, which might pose challenges related to elicitation of expert knowledge. An alternative is qualitative assessment (e.g., [24]). Even a combination of both types of approaches might be the most suitable solution.

For deciding on the final alternative to adopt, we think that we will need input from practitioners in relation to (1) how they assess evidence adequacy, and (2) how they would like to do it, if they consider that improvements are necessary. At the end, the goal is to develop a solution that fits practice and meets industry needs and wishes.

4) Validation of the chains of evidence identified
Another activity that will follow the identification of chains of evidence is their validation. Even though we find (potentially) relevant chains, they might not be so in practice. At the same time, we might miss some chain when analysing the metamodels of the standards.

Two tasks are planned for validation of the chains of evidence. First, we will aim to obtain feedback from practitioners (both suppliers and certifiers). They will indicate if the chains identified are so in practice, as well as how they deal with their evolution. Second, we will aim to analyse data from real projects in order to determine if the chains can be found in documentation of past projects, and how traceability was kept (e.g., by means of hyperlinks in electronic documentation).

When interacting with practitioners, we will also study the development tools that they use and allow them to generate evidence (e.g., V&V tools). The tool support resulting from the development of the solution will be integrated with tools used in the development process (external tools) in order to automatically collect evidence.

5) Analysis of the chains of evidence in actual projects
The next activity will aim to analyse how the chains of evidence are instantiated in new, actual projects. This activity will be facilitated in OPENCOSS, in which three different case studies will be conducted to initially evaluate the solutions proposed in the project (including the one presented in this paper).

In addition, we will try to reach other companies that might be interested in the solution developed. For this purpose, we will make use of our industry network, for instance, in the maritime and energy domain.

We expect that it will be necessary to tailor (the metamodels of) the safety standards to the specific projects used in this activity. That is, specific interpretations and instantiations of the standards will be necessary.

6) Determination of how the chains of evidence can be mapped into the common certification language
The last activity will correspond to the mapping of the chains of evidence identified in specific standards to the common certification language defined in OPENCOSS. Otherwise, a cross-domain solution would not be provided.

The chains of evidence must be reflected and supported, in an abstract way, by the common certification language. In addition, the solution must be flexible and customizable, allowing adaptation of the chains of evidence to the specific characteristics of a development/certification project (e.g., requirements imposed by a certification authority).

A goal of the common certification language is to facilitate cross-domain (or cross-standard) certification. The language must help practitioners to determine, on the basis of a set of evidence compliant with a given standard, the degree of compliance with another standard. As a result, the need of providing new evidence could be indicated. In relation to chains of evidence, the common certification language must make their cross-domain correspondence possible. Therefore, (1) the language must support (cross-domain) chains of evidence (i.e., the relations between evidence types of a chain must be reflected in the language), and (2) it must be possible to determine, for a given standard, how its chains of evidence correspond to the ones of the common certification language.

5   Challenges

The previous section has outlined our envisioned solution for model-based evolutionary chains of evidence. However, a realisation of the solution might be curtailed because of the existence of challenges (and open issues) related to execution of the process described and to the adoption of the solution.

We have identified the following eight main challenges.

1) Involvement of practitioners. Practitioners (both system suppliers and certifiers) will have to participate in the project for (1) validation of the interpretations of the standards, (2) validation of the chains of evidence identified, and (3) provision of input about current industry practices and needs. Otherwise, the solution might not fit practice and thus might not be accepted in industry.

2) Development of a common, cross-standard, and cross-domain solution. OPENCOSS aims to provide common solutions for the railway, avionics and automotive domain. Therefore, this aspect must be taken into account in the solution, which must be suitable for the three domains. Each domain has its own standards, with a different approach and terminology. There is certainly an overlap, but they are different from a certification point of view.

3) Need of agreement with certification authorities. Also in relation to their involvement, it is essential that certifiers agree upon the solution. For example, they should agree upon and accept the results of impact analysis provided by the solution.

4) Intellectual property issues. This challenge is related to the need of (1) using data from actual projects, and (2) being provided with suppliers and certifiers' know-how. In both cases, sensitive information must be properly handled.

5) Immature MDE technology. Based on past experience, we think that some problems might arise as a result of the use of some MDE technologies. For example, we might face problems regarding model scalability, transformation and management.

6) Evidence collection from external tools. Although this challenge has been and is being addressed in other projects (e.g., [14]), the need of collecting evidence from external tools can pose interoperability problems in the tool support for the solution.

7) Impact of changes in a chain of evidence on arguments, and vice versa. An aspect that will require further study is the possible relationships between chains of evidence and arguments, and how their changes can affect each other. This might also affect safety case development and maintenance.

8) Determination of the best-suited perspective for impact analysis. So far, we have focused on information-based impact analysis (i.e., based on the information provided as evidence). However, it must be determined if an activity-based perspective would be more suitable for industry. That is, practitioners might prefer to explicitly know what activities they have to (re)execute for having adequate evidence.

Finally, Table 1 shows a summary of the impact of the challenges on the solution. Such an impact indicates if the corresponding challenge can hinder development, validation, or acceptance by industry of the solution.

Table 1. Summary of the impact of the challenges

Aspect affected	Challenge							
	1	2	3	4	5	6	7	8
Development		X	X	X	X	X	X	X
Validation	X		X	X				
Industry Acceptance	X	X	X		X	X		X

6   Conclusions and Future Work

Safety assurance and certification can become very costly as a result of changes in the development and certification processes of a system, or in the system itself. Industry thus needs effective and efficient means that support identification of the evidence that becomes inadequate after such changes, and of the new evidence to provide.

This paper has presented a possible solution to deal with evidence and chain of evidence evolution. The solution will be developed as part of the OPENCOSS project, and is mainly based on the use of model-driven technology. The suitability of this technology can be argued on the basis of current practice and past research.

For realising the solution, we plan to (1) define the lifecycle of a chain of evidence (2) identify chains of evidence in safety standards, (3) analyse the impact of the changes of a piece of evidence on the rest of pieces of a chain, (4) validate the chains, (5) analyse the chains in actual projects, and (6) determine how the chains of evidence can be translated in an abstract, common certification language. We have also identified eight challenges that could hinder development, validation, and acceptance by industry of the solution.

As future work, we plan to continue working on the development of the envisioned solution presented in this paper. Therefore, modifications might be made based on, for instance, the challenges faced. Once the solution has been implemented, it will be validated in case studies as part of the work in OPENCOSS. Validation will allow us to assess the actual, potential improvements that the solution can provide to industry.

Acknowledgments. The research leading to these results has received funding from the FP7 programme under grant agreement n° 289011 (OPENCOSS) and from the Research Council of Norway under the project Certus SFI. The authors would also like to thank the OPENCOSS partners who have provided information and feedback about evidence evolution, chains of evidence, and possible solutions to manage them, and Leon Moonen for his suggestions regarding impact analysis literature.

References

1. Altreonic: Survey on Certification Issues, http://www.altreonic.com/content/survey-certification-issues (accessed May 15, 2012)
2. Altreonic: Trustworthy Systems Engineering with GoedelWorks, http://www.altreonic.com/category/products/goedelworks (accessed May 15, 2012)
3. Atego Workbench, http://www.atego.com/products/atego-workbench/ (accessed May 15, 2012)
4. Bohner, S.A., Arnold, R.S.: Software Change Impact Analysis. IEEE Press (1996)
5. Briand, L., Labiche, Y., Yue, T.: Automated traceability analysis for UML model refinements. Information & Software Technology 51(2), 512–527 (2009)
6. DECOS project, http://www.decos.at (accessed May 15, 2012)
7. Ericson, C.A.: Concise Encyclopedia of System Safety. Wiley (2011)
8. EVOLVE project, http://www.evolve-itea.org (accessed May 15, 2012)
9. Falessi, D., et al.: Planning for Safety Evidence Collection. IEEE Software 29(3), 64–70 (2012)
10. Fenn, J., et al.: The Who, Where, How, Why and When of Modular and Incremental Certification. In: 2nd IET International Conference on System Safety (2007)
11. FormalSafe project, http://www.dfki.de/web/research/projects/base_view?pid=456 (accessed May 15, 2012)
12. Habli, I.M.: Model-based assurance of safety-critical product lines. PhD thesis, University of York (2009)
13. Herrmann, D.S.: Software Safety and Reliability. IEEE Press (1999)
14. iFEST project, http://www.artemis-ifest.eu (accessed May 15, 2012)
15. Jackson, D., Thomas, M., Millet, L.I.: Software for Dependable Systems. NAP (2007)
16. Johansson, M., Nevalainen, R.: Additional requirements for process assessment in safety–critical software and systems domain. J. Softw. Maint. Evol. (2010), doi: 10.1002/smr.499
17. Kelly, T.P.: Can Process-Based and Product-Based Approaches to Software Safety Certification be Reconciled? In: Improvements in Systems Safety. Springer (2008)
18. Kornecki, A., Zalewski, J.: Certification of software for real-time safety-critical systems: state of the art. Innovations in Systems and Software Engineering 5(2), 149–161 (2009)
19. Medini Analyze, http://www.ikv.de/index.php/en/products/functional-safety (accessed May 15, 2012)

20. ModelME! project, http://modelme.simula.no/ (accessed May 15, 2012)
21. Nejati, S., et al.: A SysML-Based Approach to Traceability Management and Design Slicing of Safety Certification. Info. & Software Technology (accepted paper, 2012)
22. OMG: Argumentation Metamodel (ARM) 1.0 – Beta 1 (2010), http://www.omg.org/spec/ARM/ (accessed May 15, 2012)
23. OMG: Object Constraint Language (OCL) Version 2.3.1 (2006), http://www.omg.org/spec/OCL/2.3.1/ (accessed May 15, 2012)
24. OMG: Software Assurance Evidence Metamodel (SAEM) 1.0 – Beta 1 (2010), http://www.omg.org/spec/SAEM/ (accessed May 15, 2012)
25. OPENCOSS: Deliverable D6.1 - Baseline for the evidence management needs of the OPENCOSS platform (2012)
26. OPENCOSS, http://www.opencoss-project.eu/ (accessed May 15, 2012)
27. Open-DO initiative, http://www.open-do.org/ (accessed May 15, 2012)
28. Oxford Dictionaries: evidence, http://oxforddictionaries.com/definition/evidence?q=evidence (accessed May 15, 2012)
29. Panesar-Walawege, R.K., et al.: Characterizing the Chain of Evidence for Software Safety Cases: A Conceptual Model Based on the IEC 61508 Standard. In: ICST 2010 (2010)
30. Panesar-Walawege, R.K., Skyberg Knutsen, T., Sabetzadeh, M., Briand, L.: CRESCO: Construction of Evidence Repositories for Managing Standards Compliance. In: De Troyer, O., Bauzer Medeiros, C., Billen, R., Hallot, P., Simitsis, A., Van Mingroot, H. (eds.) ER Workshops 2011. LNCS, vol. 6999, pp. 338–342. Springer, Heidelberg (2011)
31. Panesar-Walawege, R.K., Sabetzadeh, M., Briand, L.: Using UML Profiles for Sector-Specific Tailoring of Safety Evidence Information. In: Jeusfeld, M., Delcambre, L., Ling, T.-W. (eds.) ER 2011. LNCS, vol. 6998, pp. 362–378. Springer, Heidelberg (2011)
32. Panesar-Walawege, R.K., Sabetzadeh, M., Briand, L.: Using Model-Driven Engineering for Managing Safety Evidence: Challenges, Vision and Experience. In: WoSoCER 2011 (2011)
33. Parasoft Concerto, http://www.parasoft.com/jsp/products/concerto/home.jsp (accessed May 15, 2012)
34. Programatica project, http://programatica.cs.pdx.edu/index.html (accessed May 15, 2012)
35. Sabetzadeh, M., et al.: MODUS: A goal-based approach for quantitative assessment of systems, http://modelme.simula.no/assets/modus.pdf (accessed May 15, 2012)
36. SafeCer project, http://www.safecer.eu/ (accessed May 15, 2012)
37. Schmidt, D.C.: Model-Driven Engineering. IEEE Computer 39(2), 25–31 (2006)
38. Sherriff, M., Williams, L.: DevCOP. In: ISSRE 2006 (2006)
39. Sommerville, I.: Software Engineering, 7th edn. Pearson (2004)
40. Squair, M.J.: Issues in the Application of Software Safety Standards. In: SCS 2005 (2005)
41. The Qualifying Machine: In: [27]
42. Zoughbi, G., Briand, L., Labiche, Y.: Modeling safety and airworthiness (RTCA DO-178B) information: conceptual model and UML profile. SoSyM 10(3), 337–367 (2011)

A New Approach
to Assessment of Confidence in Assurance Cases

Xingyu Zhao, Dajian Zhang, Minyan Lu, and Fuping Zeng

School of Reliability and System Engineering, Beihang University, Beijing, P.R. China
{zhaoxingyu,djz}@dse.buaa.edu.cn, {lmy,zfp}@buaa.edu.cn

Abstract. An assurance case is a body of evidence organized into an argument demonstrating that some claims about a system hold. It is generally developed to support claims in areas such as safety, reliability, maintainability, human factors, security etc. Practically, both argument and evidence are imperfect, resulting in that we can hardly say the claim is one hundred percent true. So when we do decision-making against assurance cases, we need to know how much confidence we hold in the claims. And the quantitative confidence would provide benefits over the qualitative one. In this paper, an approach is proposed to assess the confidence in assurance cases (mainly arguments) quantitatively. First we convert Argument Metamodel based (ARM-based) cases into a set of Toulmin model instances; then we use Hitchcock's evaluative criteria for solo-verb-reasoning to analyze and quantify the Toulmin model instances into Bayesian Belief Network (BBN); running the Bayesian Belief Network, we get quantified confidence from each claim of the assurance case. Finally, we illustrate our approach by using a simplified fragment from safety cases and discuss several future work.

Keywords: Assurance case, quantified confidence, informal logic, Toulmin model, Bayesian Belief Network.

1   Introduction

The increasing complexity of software-intensive systems raises a new question that how manufacturers and regulators could gain confidence in the dependable operation of such software-intensive systems. Instead of assessing manufacturer compliance with process-based regulations and standards, recently the industry areas have paid much attention to the assurance cases which focused on demonstrating the dependability of product-specific system. An assurance case is a body of evidence organized into an argument demonstrating that some claims about a system hold [1]. As arguments and evidences are practically imperfect, we are difficult to determine that the claim is true with 100 percent. So when we do decision-making against assurance cases, we may ask questions like: How confident are we that the claim is true? How do we express confidence quantitatively [9]?

Argument is the most commonly used concept in the area of both assurance cases development and informal logic [2]. Borrowing ideas from the informal logic area to

F. Ortmeier and P. Daniel (Eds.): SAFECOMP 2012 Workshops, LNCS 7613, pp. 79–91, 2012.

assess and review cases qualitatively or quantitatively is not innovation. In [2], Yuan argued that the informal logic argument schemes have important roles to play in safety arguments construction and review process. In [3], Goodenough et al. outlined an approach for determining the confidence based on the notion of defeasible reasoning which is a concept from informal logic. We propose an approach based on Hitchcock's Toulmin model [5] arguments assessment criteria to quantitatively assess the confidence of assurance cases.

In the next section of this paper, some related work and backing theories are briefly introduced. After that, a detailed description of our approach to assess the confidence in assurance cases is presented. First we convert the ARM-based [4] cases into the Toulmin model instances. Then we use Hitchcock's arguments assessment criteria to analyze the Toulmin models and construct the basic structure of BBN. Furthermore, we quantify the BBN and calculate the confidence of each claim in the assurance cases. Finally, in section 4, a case study on a simple fragment of safety case is discussed. The conclusion and future work to improve this approach are presented in Section 5.

2   Related Work

2.1   Assurance Case and Its Confidence

Assurance cases are generally developed to support claims in areas such as safety, reliability, maintainability, human factors, operability, and security, although these assurance cases are often called by some more specific names, e.g. safety case or reliability and maintainability (R&M) case. The assurance case has one or more top-level claims in which confidence is needed and has supporting arguments connecting the top-level claims with multiple levels of sub-claims. The sub-claims are in turn supported by evidences and, where appropriate, assumptions. An assurance case is a means to provide the grounds for confidence and to assist decision making [7]. One typical application is the decision-making processes of safety certification in medical device industry [1].

As both arguments and evidences are practically imperfect, we could never say the claims in our assurance case are 100 percent true. So we consider the confidence of each claim in the case should be provided as other elements (e.g. assumptions, context) to facilitate the decision making. In addition, we need confidence due to we need to work on 'stopping rules' of the case, i.e. when to stop expanding claims. This is related to the degree of confidence that the claim is correct without the need for any further supporting evidence, as stated by Bloomfield [8].

Currently the confidence in a safety case is often assessed by appealing to qualitative reasoning. However, as indicated in [8], expressed in simplistic terms (e.g. using traffic lights) is not clear how a lack of confidence will propagate through to higher level claims. In addition, without quantitative confidence, we could not provide guidance about how much benefit will ensue, or how confident one would be in a claim after taking steps to enhance an assurance argument e.g., by adding additional argument legs to support a claim [9]. So it is more than nature that we want a claim with a quantified confidence rather than a qualified one. Once a proper method which could quantify the confidence of claims is accepted, the quantified claims could be merged into a wider assessment of system quantitative risk analysis and play an important role in decision making under uncertainty. Especially, it will be the basis to support the As Confident As Reasonably Practicable (ACARP) principle [9], which will in turn affect the software certification and engineering process.

Littlewood, Bloomfield, Bishop and Wright have done a series of work related to a formal quantitative treatment of confidence since 2003 [10] [11] [12]. After their work, Denney et al. proposed an approach for measuring the confidence by integrating probabilistic reasoning with Bayesian Networks for uncertainty modeling and assessment [13]. Goodenough et al. outlined an approach for determining the confidence based on the notion of eliminative induction and the defeasible reasoning. In other words, they use Baconian probability to provide a measure of confidence based on how many defeaters have been eliminated [3]. In this paper, we use the Hitchcock's evaluative criteria for solo-verb-reasoning as guidance to construct BBN more systematically and then quantify the confidence with traditional Pascalian probability instead of Baconian probability.

2.2   Good Reasoning on Toulmin Model

Toulmin model addresses all types of reasoning such as scientific, legal, aesthetic, colloquial and management. Its general shape is shown in Figure 1. The claim is a conclusion which is to be demonstrated. The data is the facts that we appeal to as a foundation for the claim. The warrant links data and other grounds to the claim. The qualifier represents the degree of confidence that can be placed on the claim. The rebuttal represents counter arguments that can be used. Toulmin introduces the notion of backing to support the warrant.

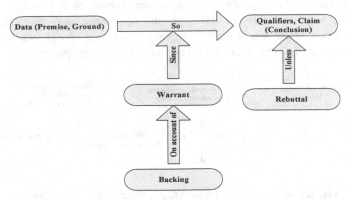

Fig. 1. Toulmin's Argument Model

Case method has a close relationship with Toulmin's model which is the basis of the Adelard goal-based justification approach ASCAD [14]. Also following Toulmin, Kelly proposed a graphical argumentation notation - Goal Structuring Notation [15] and Gorski proposed an argument model for trust cases which had been implemented in Trust-IT framework [16].

As stated by Hitchcock [6], Toulmin's model applies not only to argumentations (authors address verbalized reasoning to someone else) but also to solo verbal reasonings in which reasoners draw conclusions for themselves from information at their disposal. Hitchcock proposed an evaluative criterion for solo verbal reasoning [6], which we choose as the guidance in our approach. Such reasoning is good if and only if its grounds are justified and adequate, its warrant is justified, and the reasoner is justified in assuming that no defeaters apply. These four conditions are individually necessary and jointly sufficient for good solo reasoning aimed at working out a correct answer to a question. Further explanation of these four conditions could be found later in this paper. Why Hitchcock's solo verbal reasoning criteria instead of argumentation assessment criteria? First, the basis is the common view that case should be developed by all stakeholders (such as designers, operators, maintainers, managers, the public, government etc.) [20] rather than only system manufacturers. So the concept of solo verbal reasoning is in line with the reality of how we should develop and use the assurance cases, i.e. aiding decision-making for all stakeholders instead of merely convincing other stakeholders for system manufacturers. Second, we believe, when assessing assurance cases, one should pay more attention to the logic and pragmatic aspects than rhetoric and dialectics aspects. As all stakeholders are case developers, the different viewpoints of stakeholders and argumentation among stakeholders could be treated as self-argumentation which could be reflected in Hitchcock's solo verbal reasoning criteria.

3   Proposed Approach

Following [17], where a safety case comprises two complementary arguments: safety argument and qualitative confidence argument, we propose an approach to construct the confidence argument through BBN. In our confidence argument, Hitchcock's reasoning assessment criteria is the decomposition strategy. As shown in Figure 2, more detailed steps of our approach could be found later in this paper.

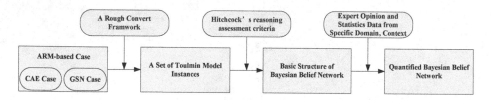

Fig. 2. Overview Steps to Assess Confidence in Assurance Cases

3.1   Convert ARM-Based Case to Toulmin Model Instance

In [4], Object Management Group (OMG) defined a meta-model, i.e. ARM, for representing structured arguments, as illustrated in Figure 3. The scope of ARM is to allow the interchange of structured arguments between diverse tools by different vendors. So both CAE style cases and GSN style cases can be treated as ARM-based cases instances. To generalize the application scope of our method, we propose a rough convert framework from ARM-based Case into a set of Toulmin model Instances, as illustrated in Figure 4.

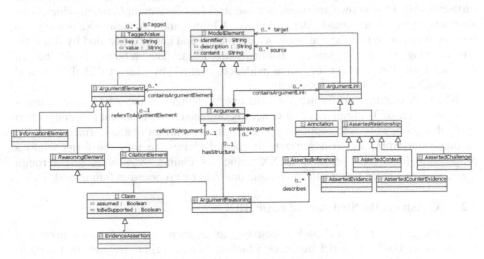

Fig. 3. Overview of Argument Metamodel

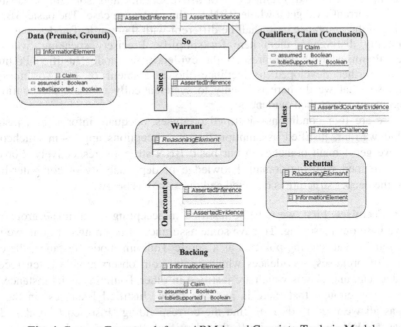

Fig. 4. Convert Framework from ARM-based Case into Toulmin Models

Rectangles in the framework are the classes of ARM. The Data (Premise, Ground) could be directly observed evidence or claims which are justified in related lower level Toulmin model instance, respectively linked by the AssertedEvidence class and AssertedInference class to the Claim of this Toulmin model instance. As there are two kinds of warrants, namely the warrant can be self-evident and the warrant can be further justified by its own argument, we use the class ReasoningElement which is an abstract class that could derive class Claim and ArgumentReasoning to present Warrant. When the warrant is a claim itself and need be justified by Backing, the Backing is in the same situation with Data. The rebuttal could be an exception of the warrant or count-evidence, linked by AssertedChallenge and AssertedCounterEvidence respectively.

When this framework is iterated until every element in the ARM-based case is analyzed, a set of Toulmin model instances is obtained. One practical difficulty when apply this framework is to explicitly present a proper warrant in a uniformed form. To facilitate our work, we treat warrants as special claims, so they are formed into a proposition form 'XX property is XX value' as claims. Now it is just a rough framework and more systematic, automatic one will be proposed in future work

3.2   Construct the Structure of Basic BBN

Under the guidance of Hitchcock's reasoning assessment criteria, for each argument in the set of Toulmin model instances which obtained earlier, we construct a basic structure of BBN, as shown in Figure 5. Then all basic BBNs are connected through interface nodes 'Justified Premises', 'Justified Claim' and sometimes 'Justified Applicable Warrant', we get a whole BBN for the assurance case. The basic BBN for leaf nodes in the assurance case shall be different with the non-leaf nodes, but we do not explicitly distinguish them here for simplify. Precisely speaking, when the 'Justified Premises' directly represents the evidence, the node 'Justified Premises' should be further developed to facilitate the assessment of trustworthiness of evidence, so what we do here is mainly to systematically measure the confidence from arguments rather than evidences.

As there are four conditions—justified premises, adequate information, justified applicable warrant, justified assumption that no exceptions apply—in Hitchcock's criteria, we get 4 main branches in our basic BBN structure respectively. For each branch, combined with the domain knowledge of dependability of computer-based systems, the deeper structure is depicted and discussed as below.

Justified Premises. First, we must be justified in accepting the ultimate grounds on which we base our reasoning. To have some assurance of reaching our goal, we need justification for our starting-points. For a single Toulmin model instance, there are two types of premises – evidences which come from observation, written records, history data etc. and claims which are justified in other Toulmin model instance. For the latter, it is enough that there is just one node 'Justified Premises' in the first branch, as all we need to do is to find the corresponding 'Justified Claim' node in other basic BBN and replace it. If the 'Justified Premises' node represents an evidence (i.e. a leaf node in the case), we directly quantify it with expert opinion at the present stage.

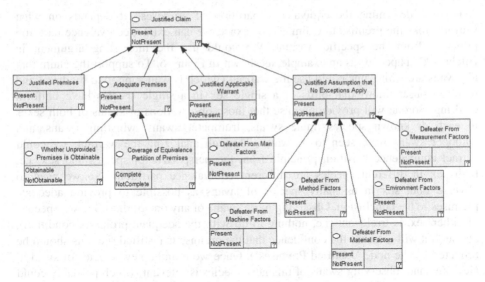

Fig. 5. Basic BBN Structure for Each Toulmin Model Instance

Adequate Premises. If one tries to answer a question correctly on the basis of obtainable information, one needs to take into account all the good relevant information that is practically obtainable. So we develop two sub-nodes of 'Adequate Premises', namely the node 'Whether Unprovided Premise is Obtainable' and the node 'Coverage of Equivalence Partition of Premises'.

The node 'Whether Unprovided Premise is Obtainable' is easily to be understood that we could not provide all the relevant premises due to the time and cost in practical engineering project. So if we provide all obtainable premises we could to some extent say the adequate premises condition is justified.

Second, the premises must be relevant, in the sense that it could make a difference to the answer one reaches. That is, considering all the new and old information, to answer the question that could be different than the one justified by the information already obtained. We grasp it with an example in software testing activity. Assume that we have tested the target software with 5000 test cases without any failure, so the tester may have a 'confirmation bias' that the software is good enough. But are these 5000 test cases adequate? The answer depends on the coverage of equivalence partitions of test cases. If the 5000 test cases come from all different equivalence partitions, we have high confidence to say the software is good enough. In contrary, if the 5000 test cases represent only one equivalence partition, we are hardly to say the software is good and we need generate more test cases. We need relevant test cases, namely from different equivalence partitions which could make the test result fail, instead of irrelevant test cases from the same equivalence partition which we know will pass the test. So we add a node 'Coverage of Equivalence Partition of Premises' which will affect the adequate premises condition. We believe this idea is a possible way to solve the 'confirmation bias' problem [18] of case method.

How to determine the equivalence partition of premises? It depends on what warrant links the premise to claim. To be exact, we can extract equivalence partition principle from the specific warrant. We could use the interesting argument in Hitchcock's paper [6] as an example, as shown in Figure 6. To support the claim that all swans are white, one could use the warrant (which is well supported by direct and reported observation) that birds of a single sex in a single species have uniform coloring. So one will provide premise that those observations of swans of both sexes in each of known species: mute swans, trumpeter swans, whistling swans, and whooper swans were seen to be white. Through analyzing the warrant, we could extract equivalence partition principle from the perspective of species and sex, i.e. both sex in different species are different equivalence partitions. So we need to obverse both sex in as many species of swans as possible to provide adequate premises to the conclusion. Observing more swans of any one of those known species, of either sex, is irrelevant (i.e. nothing to do with the adequate promises condition), although it will increase the confidence that the premise is justified (i.e. this should be reflected by the node 'Justified Premises'). Once we found a new species of swan in New Zealand, observing swans of this new species is relevant, which probably could turn over the conclusion. So as the equivalence partition principle indicates, we should observe swans of both sexes, of as many species as possible to provide the adequate premises.

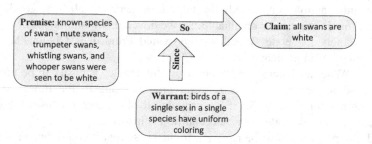

Fig. 6. Toulmin Model Instance

Justified Applicable Warrant. Conclusion must follow from one's premises in accordance with a justified general warrant. Hitchcock first emphasized that the phase 'in accordance with' means that the warrant actually applies to the inference. In other words, the warrant is semantically equivalent to some generalization of the reasoning's associated conditional 'if p_1 and ... and p_n, then c', where p_1 ..., p_n stand for the premises and c for the conclusion. We do not present this idea in our basic BBN structure, as we believe this work should be correctly done in the framework which converts the ARM into Toulmin model, to be specific, when refining the ReasoningElement class of ARM into a warrant. As aforementioned, there are two kinds of warrants, namely warrant can be self-evident and warrant can be further justified by its own argument. For the former, like the situation that premises represent evidence in the assurance case, we directly quantify it. For the latter, we just treat it as a claim which could be found justified in another Toulmin model instance, so in this situation the node 'Justified Applicable Warrant' becomes an interface when connecting the whole BBN.

Justified Assumption That No Exceptions Apply. As stated in [6], a well-known feature of Toulmin's model is that many warrants come with rebuttals, or exceptional conditions under which the conclusion is incorrect. If the warrant which justifies one's inference is not universal, it must be justified by assuming that no exceptional condition exists. Such exceptional conditions include not only the circumstances that show the conclusion is incorrect but also the circumstances that show the warrant is inapplicable to a particular system.

In order to aid quantify this last condition of Hitchcock's criteria in BBN, we have to ask ourselves, how to systematically find the exceptional circumstances? Or in other words, what are the factors that could make these exceptional circumstances different from the ideal circumstances? When consider this question in the field of quality of computer-based systems, the question may be transformed into what factors could make the product (in case) different from the ideal product where the general warrant will be smoothly applied? Borrowing ideas from the product quality control and management, 5M1E analysis method is the answer we proposed, namely machine, man, material, method, measurement and environment factors. For instance, one general warrant may be 'a component with correct input and correct computation process could provide correct output'. This self-evidence warrant is justified applicable on most programmable electronic component. But when the operation environment is full of electromagnetic interference, the warrant is no longer applicable in this exceptional circumstance. In other words, there is exception from the perspective of environment factors. Following this idea, the last branch of basic BBN structure is constructed.

3.3   Quantify BBN and Measure Confidence

To quantify the BBN and measure confidence for each claim in the assurance case, we need assign a conditional probability table (CPT) to each non-leaf node of BBN, and assign the prior probabilities or set observed evidence probabilities for the leaf nodes and then connect the basic BBN into a whole BBN.

As Toulmin stated, criteria for evaluating arguments has strong field and context dependency, which we believe becomes unquestionably true when there is an attempt to quantitatively assess the argument. All the parameters used to quantify the BBN should be obtained from the field-related statistical data, and inevitably domain expert judgments, in the context of the target system. Here, combined with our structure of basic BBN, we only propose brief, general guidelines on how to quantify the basic BBN.

- **Guideline 1:** For the CPT of node 'Justified Claim', we could use the Noisy-And [19] function to quantify it. So the parameters, 4 link probabilities and the leakage k, should be discussed by stakeholders and settled down. The same for the CPT of the node 'Justified Assumption that No Exceptions Apply' with Noisy-Or function.

- **Guideline 2:** For the CPT of node 'Adequate Premises', we only concern how to give P(Adequate Premises| Obtainable= obtainable, Coverage =not complete), as the other 3 conditional probabilities we could simply set 100% present.
- **Guideline 3:** For the nodes 'Justified Premises' and 'Justified Applicable Warrant', how to quantify them depends on whether they present the leaf nodes in the assurance case, i.e. whether they are the claims which need further argument or they are self-evidence. For the former, we quantify the node with parameters read from the corresponding node in other basic BBN. For the latter, it is to some extent equal to give the trustworthiness of evidence, so we directly quantify them with domain expert judgments at the present stage. Intuitively, we should go deeper into the taxonomy of evidence and self-evidence warrants. For example, if a warrant is mathematic theorem or settled law items, we could treat it as 100 percent justified. If a warrant is a common sense concluded from history data, then we should use the statistical probability to quantify it.
- **Guideline 4:** For the serials of nodes which find exceptions from perspective of 5M1E, we should quantify them with the likelihood probability that the exceptions happen in this case. Still, the likelihood probability comes from domain experts or statistical data, which should be discussed and accepted by all stakeholders.

4   Simplified Case Study

In this section, a simplified case study on a fragment of safety case is discussed. The scalability of this proposed approach will be tested upon a big example in the future work.

Figure 7 is a typical argument in safety cases. It is not hard to convert this case into Toulmin model instance where the premise is 'hazard A and B of system S are both eliminated', the warrant is 'systems without any hazards are safe' and the conclusion is 'system S is safe'. Given an argument shown in figure 7, how confident should we believe that the system is actually safe and what is the basis for this confidence? To answer this question, we adopt the approached depicted above. And the corresponding basic BBN for this typical safety argument is shown in Figure 8.

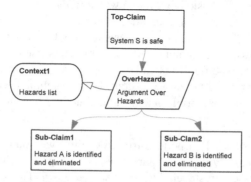

Fig. 7. Simplified Typical Safety Argument

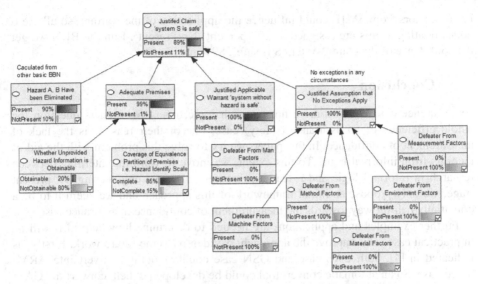

Fig. 8. Corresponding Basic BBN for the Typical Safety Argument

In this case, for simplify, the CPT of the node 'system S is safe' is quantified by the traditional logical AND operator, i.e. only when all the 4 main branches - justified premises, adequate information, justified applicable warrant, justified assumption that no exceptions apply -are presented, the claim is 100 percent justified, and in any other conditions the claim is 100 percent not justified. Similarly, when quantify the CPT of the node 'Justified Assumption that No Exceptions Apply', only in the condition that all the 5M1E factors are not presented, we 100 percent no exceptions presented, and in any other conditions the node is quantified 100 percent 'NotPresent'. The CPT for node 'Adequate Premises' is shown in Figure 9. It is very arbitrary here and in practice it should be discussed by experts and stakeholders.

Coverage of Equivalence Partition of Premises i.e. Hazard Identify Scale	Complete		NotComplete	
Whether Unprovided Hazard Information is Obtainable	Obtainable	NotObtainable	Obtainable	NotObtainable
Present	1	1	0.8	1
NotPresent	0	0	0.2	0

Fig. 9. CPT for Node 'Adequate Premises'

Now we assign prior probabilities to leaf nodes. For the node 'Hazard A, B Have Been Eliminated' we just get the numbers from two low level basic BBN which support claims like 'Hazard A has been eliminated' (0.94 justified) and 'Hazard B has been eliminated' (0.96 justified), and then multiply them and quantify the node (0.94*0.96=0.9024 justified). In this case, the prior probabilities for 'Coverage of Equivalence Partition of Premises i.e. Hazard Identify Scale' and 'Whether Unprovided Hazard Information is Obtainable' directly comes from hazard analysis expert. In practice they also could come from statistic data against some forecast algorithm, like based on the lines of codes to predict the defects in software. As the warrant 'system without any hazards is safe' has no exceptions in any circumstances i.e. no factors from 5M1E could influence the application of the warrant, so all the 6 nodes relating to this are assigned as 100 percent 'NotPresent'. Run the BBN we get the confidence of the claim 'system S is safe', 89% justified.

5   Conclusion

As assurance case has become a hot research topic, many researchers question the whole efficiency of an assurance (safety) case, one of their reasons is the lack of measurement of confidence. In this paper, we try to solve this problem with the aid of theories from informal logic. To this extent, we move forward the interplay between research in informal logic and research in computer system engineering. At present stage, we only propose an initial framework of this approach and we deem it to be a potentially helpful way towards the measurement of confidence in assurance cases.

Further examples and applications are needed to determine how helpful it will be in practical cases. To improve the approach, we identify some future work. Firstly, as indicated in [4], both CAE case and GSN case could smoothly convert into ARM-based case. So an automatic convert tool could be developed to help convert the CAE, GSN, ARM-based cases and Toulmin model instance. Secondly, combining with domain knowledge (e.g. safety, security), the basic BBN structure should be further developed and refined. Thirdly we should closely integrate domain knowledge with the guideline of how to quantify the BBN. Domain statistics data and expert will definitely play an important role here, and only go deeper into different fields we get better efficiency. Finally and more significantly, once we got an acceptable confidence, how should we use it to facilitate our decision-making e.g. perfect the ACARP principle. Existing certification process might be modified accordingly.

References

1. Weinstock, C.B., Goodenough, J.B.: Towards an Assurance Case Practice for Medical Devices. CMU/SEI-2009-TN-018 (2009)
2. Yuan, T., Kelly, T.: Argument Schemes in Computer System Safety Engineering. Informal Logic 31(2), 89–109 (2011)
3. Goodenough, J.B., Weinstock, C.B., Klein, A.Z.: Assessing Confidence in an Assurance Case. CMU/SEI-2011-TR-Draft (2011)
4. Argumentation Metamodel (ARM). OMG Document Number: ptc/2010-08-36. Standard document (2010), http://www.omg.org/spec/ARM
5. Toulmin, S.: The Uses of Argument. Cambridge University Press (1958)
6. Hitchcock, D.: Good Reasoning on the Toulmin Model. Argumentation 19(3), 373–391 (2005)
7. ISO/IEC TR 15026-1:2010, Systems and Software Engineering - Systems and Software Assurance – Part 1: Concepts and Vocabulary (2010)
8. Bloomfield, R., Bishop, P.: Safety and Assurance Cases: Past, Present and Possible Future - an Adelard Perspective. In: Making Systems Safer, pp. 51–67 (2010)
9. Bloomfield, R., Littlewood, B., Wright, D.: Confidence: Its Role in Dependability Cases for Risk Assessment. In: International Conference on Dependable Systems and Networks, Edinburgh, pp. 338–346 (2007)

10. Bloomfield, R., Littlewood, B.: Multi-legged Arguments: the Impact of Diversity Upon Confidence in Dependability Arguments. In: International Conference on Dependable Systems and Networks (DSN 2003), pp. 25–34 (2003)
11. Littlewood, B., Wright, D.: The Use of Multilegged Arguments to Increase Confidence in Safety Claims for Software-based Systems: A Study Based on a BBN Analysis of an Idealized Example. IEEE Trans. Soft. Eng. 33(5), 347–365 (2007)
12. Bishop, P., Bloomfield, R., Littlewood, B., Povyakalo, A., Wright, D.: Towards a Formalism for Conservative Claims about the Dependability of Software-based Systems. IEEE Trans. Soft. Eng. 37(5), 708–717 (2011)
13. Denney, E., Pai, G., Habli, I.: Towards Measurement of Confidence in Safety Cases. In: 2011 International Symposium on Empirical Software Engineering and Measurement, pp. 380–383 (2011)
14. Bloomfield, R., Bishop, P., Jones, C., Froome, P.: ASCAD-Adelard Safety Case Development Manual. Adelard (1998) ISBN 0953377105
15. Kelly, T.: Arguing safety-a systematic approach to managing safety cases. York, University of York. PhD thesis (1998)
16. Górski, J.: Trust-IT - a Framework for Trust Cases. In: Workshop on Assurance Cases for Security - The Metrics Challenge, DSN 2007, Edinburgh, UK (2007)
17. Hawkins, R., Kelly, T., Knight, J., Graydon, P.: A New Approach to Creating Clear Safety Arguments. In: Safety Critical Systems Symp. (2011)
18. Leveson, N.: The Use of Safety Cases in Certification and Regulation. Journal of System Safety 47(6) (2011)
19. Hobbs, C., Lloyd, M.: The Application of Bayesian Belief Networks to Assurance Case Preparation. In: Achieving Systems Safety, pp. 159–176 (2012)
20. Sun, L., Zhang, W., Kelly, T.: Do Safety Cases Have a Role in Aerospace Certification? In: 2nd International Symposium on Aircraft Airworthiness, Beijing, China (2011)

An Unified Meta-model
for Trustworthy Systems Engineering

Eric Verhulst and Bernhard H.C. Sputh

Altreonic NV, Gemeentestraat 61A Bus 1, B3210 Linden, Belgium
{eric.verhulst,bernhard.sputh}@altreonic.com
http://www.altreonic.com

Abstract. This paper describes the theoretical principles and associated meta-model of a unified trustworthy systems engineering approach. Guiding principles are "unified semantics" and "interacting entities". Proof of concept projects have shown that the approach is valid for any type of process, also non technical engineering ones. The meta-model was used as a guideline to develop the GoedelWorks internet based platform supporting the process view (focused on requirements engineering), the modelling process view as well as the workplan development view. Of particular interest is the integration of the ASIL process, an automotive safety engineering process that was developed to cover multiple safety standards.

Keywords: unified semantics, interacting entities, systems engineering, safety engineering, systems grammar.

1   Introduction

Systems Engineering (SE) is considered to be the process that transforms a need into a working system. Discovering what the real need is, is often already a challenge as it is the result of the interaction of many stakeholders, each of them expressing their "requirements" in the language specific to their domain of expertise. The problem is partly due to the fact that we use natural language and that our domain of expertise is always limited. In order to overcome these obstacles, formalization is required. The meta-model we developed is an attempt to achieve this in the domain of SE. In terms of the guiding principles, unified semantics comes down to defining univocal and orthogonal concepts. The interacting entities paradigm defines how these concepts are linked. The result is called a "systems grammar" in analogy with the rules of language that allow us to construct meaningful sentences (an entity), a chapter (a system) or a book (a system of systems). It defines the SE terms (standing for conceptual entities) and the rules on how to combine the conceptual entities in the right way to obtain a (trustworthy) system. What complicates the matter is that a system in the end is defined not only by its final purpose but also by its history (e.g. precursors), by the process that was followed to develop it and by the way its

F. Ortmeier and P. Daniel (Eds.): SAFECOMP 2012 Workshops, LNCS 7613, pp. 92–105, 2012.

composing entities were selected and put together. Each corresponds to a different view and it is the combination of these views that result in a unique system. Note, that a process can also be considered as a system. The main difference with a system that is being developed is that the composing entities and they way they interact are different. For example humans will communicate and execute a process that delivers one or more results. The system being developed will be composed of several sub-systems that in combination execute a desired function, often transforming inputs into outputs. A process can therefore be seen as a meta-level system model for a concrete project.

An important aid in the formalisation of SE is abstraction, an activity whereby lower level concepts are grouped in separate, preferably orthogonal meta-level entities and whereby the specific differences are abstracted away. One could call this categorisation, but this ignores that the meta-level entities still have meta-level links (or interactions). This process can be repeated to define a next higher level, the meta-meta-level, until only one very generic concept is left. The exercise is complete if the reverse operation allows to derive the concrete system by using refinement. One could say that this is not different from what modelling defines. There is certainly an overlap, but what makes the approach different is that our approach does not just try to describe what exists, but tries to find the minimum set of conceptual entities and interactions that are sufficient to be used as meta-models across different domains. This is often counter intuitive because it doesn't align with our use of natural language. The latter is often very flexible, but therefore also very imprecise. Natural language is also associative whereby human communication is full of unspoken context information. Engineers have here a source of a fundamental conflict. To prove the "correctness" of a system, it must be described in unambiguous terms. At the same time even when using formal techniques, the use of natural language is unavoidable to discuss about the formal properties and architecture of the system. Precise mathematical expressions are by convention bounded with imprecise natural language concepts. In this paper we present a middle ground. As a full mathematical approach is not yet within reach of the scale of systems engineering in general, we defined a meta-model that formalises the SE domain in a generic way. Only 17 orthogonal concepts were needed to define most SE domains. The resulting framework was proven to be capable importing a specific safety engineering process. Also many explicit guidelines or requirements of traditional safety engineering standards are found back.

1.1   Related Work

The work presented in this paper is closely related with work going on in other domains, such as architectural modelling. This has resulted in a number of graphical development tools and modelling languages such as UML [1] and SysML [2]. Without examining them in detail, these approaches suffer from a number of shortcomings:

- Often architectural models are developed bottom-up, e.g. as a means of representing graphically what was first defined in a textual format. Hence, such approaches are driven by the architecture of the system and its implementation. As we witnessed often, even when formal methods are used, such an approach biases the stakeholders to think in terms of known design patterns and results in less optimal system solutions [3].

- Many modelling approaches focus only on a specific domain, requiring other tools to support the other SE subdomains. This poses the problem of keeping semantic consistency and hence introduces errors.
- Most of the tools have no formal basis and hence have too many terms and concepts that semantically overlap. In other words, orthogonality and separation of concerns is lacking.

Despite these short comings, when properly used, architectural modelling contribute to a better development process. The approach we propose and implemented in GoedelWorks [4,5] emphasizes the cognitive aspect of the SE process whereby the different activities are actually just different "views" on the system under development.

Note that the issues GoedelWorks aims to address are more and more being recognised as revelant. Safety is an increasingly necessary property of systems, but at the same time certification costs are escalating. A project that in particular looks at reducing certification costs by taken a cross-domain approach is OPENCOSS [6].

The remainder of the paper is organized as follows. The motivation behind the formalization of concepts and their relations are described in the next section, which also presents the link between the abstract, domain independent meta-ontological level, and the domain specific ontological level. The concepts and the unified systems grammar itself are further described in section 3. This formalization can also guide the definition and implementation of a concrete instantiation of a SE process. We conclude by a short description of the import of a large automotive focused safety engineering process flow, called ASIL [7]. Other pilot projects were executed as well, but not included by lack of space.

2   A Generic Framework for Systems Engineering

Here we give an introduction to our view on Systems Engineering, which provides the framework of understanding the 17 concepts of System Engineering detailed in section 3.

2.1   Intentional Approach to Systems Engineering

Systems Engineering is the process that transforms a "need" into a working system. Initially we describe the system from the "intentional" perspective. Example: "We want to put a human on the moon". From this perspective we can derive what the system is supposed to be (or to do). Another perspective is the architectural one. This perspective shows us how the system can be implemented. Part of the systems engineering work is to make the right trade-off decisions.

The "mission" is the top level requirement that the system must meet. In order to achieve the mission, a system will be composed of sub-elements (often called components, modules or subsystems). We call these elements "entities" and the way they relate to each other are called "interactions". The term system is used when multiple combined interacting entities fulfil a functionality, that they individually do not fulfil.

Note, that any system component has often been developed in a prior project, hence the notion of "System of Systems" emerges naturally. Similarly an embedded system is often assembled from standardised hardware and software components, but it's only when put together and an application specific layer is added that the embedded system can provides us with the required functionality.

As entities and interactions form a system architecture, all requirements achieve the mission of a system as an aggregate. Unfortunately, requirement statements are often vague or imprecise, because they assume an unspoken context. To be usable in the engineering domain we need to refine them into quantifiable statements. We say that we derive specifications. In doing so, we restrict the SE state space guided by the constraints that we must be able to meet by selecting from all the possible implementations the ones that meet all our requirements. In the SE domain we link specifications with test cases allowing us to confirm that a given implementation meets the derived specifications in a quantifiable way. An example requirement statement could be "a fast car". The derived specification could be "Topspeed 240 km/hr, 0 to 100 km/hr in 6 seconds". We can then define a test that will measure a given implementation. The specification also defines boundary conditions (e.g. cost, size) for the implementation choices and the context in which the system will meet the requirements. Hence, the input for the architectural design is taken from the specifications and not directly from the requirements.

In practice the use of the terms requirements and specifications is not always consistent and the terms are often confused. Even the term "requirement specifications", a rather ambiguous one, is often used. Hence, we consistently use the term "Requirement" when the required systems properties are not linked with a measurable test case. Once this is done, we can speak of a "Specification".

From the structural or architectural perspective a system is defined by entities and interactions between entities. An entity is defined by its attributes and functional properties. Attributes reflect intrinsic qualitative and quantitative properties of an entity (e.g. colour, speed, etc.) and have their own names, types and values. A function defines the intended behaviour of an entity. An entity can have more than one function. We use the term function in two ways:

1. The traditional "use case" of entities (corresponding with the intentional view above);
2. The entities' internal behaviour.

Functions define the internal behaviour as opposed to external interactions. In a first approach, interactions are defined using a partial order, i.e. implemented as a sequence of messages. Interactions are caused by events and are implemented by messages. An interaction structure corresponds to a protocol and can be defined with inputs and outputs in form of a functional flow diagram. State diagrams can be used to show event-function pairs on the transition lines between states.

An event is any transition that can take place in a system. An event can be the result of an entity attribute change (i.e. of changing the entity's state). A message can cause and can be caused by an event whereby the interaction between entities results in changes to their attributes and their state.

Interfaces belong to the structural part of an entity. An interface is the boundary domain of interaction between an entity and another entity. Interfaces can have input or output types, which define data, energy or information directions at interaction areas between the entities.

Interfaces and interactions are related by the fact that an interface transforms an entity internal event into an external message. A second entity will receive such a message through its interface, transforming the external message into an internal form. An interface can also filter received messages and invoke the appropriate entity internal functions. It should be noted that while an interaction happens between two entities, the medium, that enables the interaction, can be a system in its own right. We also need to take into account that its properties may affect the system behaviour. One should also note that the use of the terms "events", "messages" and "protocol" is more appropriate for embedded systems, but an interaction can also be an energy or force transfer between mechanical components. Or even two people discussing a topic.

Another important view in systems engineering is the project development view, which is derived from the architectural decomposition of the system. In this view, once all entities have been identified, they are grouped into work packages for project planning. Each work package is divided into tasks with attributes, such as: duration, resources, milestones, deadlines, responsible person, etc. Defining the timeline of the workplan and the workplan tasks are important system development stages. Selecting such metrics and attaching them to work packages leads to the workplan specification.

2.2 Intentional Requirements, Concrete Specifications

As mentioned previously, a system is described at the highest level by its requirements. Requirements are captured at the initial point of the system definition process and must be transformed into measurable specifications. These specifications are to be fulfilled by structured architectural elements (i.e. entities-interactions, attributes-values, event-function pairs).

This means that at the cognitive level the qualitative requirements produce entities, interactions (i.e. architectural descriptions) and specifications (i.e. normal cases, test cases, failure cases), work plans, and also issues, to be resolved. The order of this sequence is essential and constitutes a process of refinement whereby we go from the more abstract to the more concrete. Fig. 1 illustrates this dependency using an extract of a 'Shift by Wire' project, done as part of the ASIL project [7].

Using a coherent and unified systems grammar provides us with the basis for building cognitive models from initially disjoint user requests. Requirements and

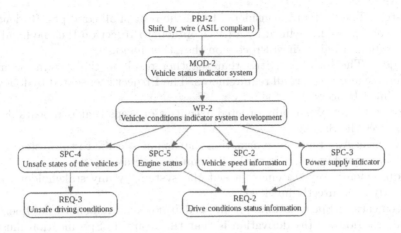

Fig. 1. Graphical Representation of Dependency Links in a GoedelWorks Project

specifications are not just a collection of statements, but represent a cognitive model of the system with a structure corresponding to the system grammar's relations.

Capturing requirements and specifications is a process of system description. Specifications are derived from the more general requirements. This is necessary in order to make requirements verifiable by measurements.

Specifications are often formulated with the (hidden) assumption that the system operates without observable or latent problems. We call these the "normal cases". However, this is not enough. Specifications are met when they pass "test cases", which often describe the specific tests that must be executed to verify the specifications. In correspondence to test cases we define "failure cases", i.e. a sequence of events that can result in a system fault and for which the system design should cater. Note that security properties are considered as a sub-type of safety cases.

3   The Notion of a Systems Grammar as a Meta-model

In this section we outline the meta-model and its 17 concepts. We first list and define these concepts. To differentiate from the natural language terms, we use upper case for the first letter. Next we discuss the relationships between the concepts, the different views in SE and how this results in a process flow.

3.1   Overview of the Meta-model

When we use the term System we assume it is being developed in the context of a Project. During the Project a defined Process is followed. The Meta-Model consists of the following 17 concepts:

1. System: The System is considered to be the root of all concepts. It identifies a System as being defined by a (development) Project on the one hand and a (Systems Engineering) Process on the other hand.
2. Project: The set of activities that together result in the system becoming available and meeting all requirements. The Project is executed by following a defined Process.
3. Process: A set of partially ordered activities or steps that is repeatable and produces the System.
4. Reference: Any relevant information that is not specific to the system under development but relevant to the domain in general.
5. Requirement: Any statement about the system by any stakeholder who is directly or indirectly involved.
6. Specification: Specifications are derived from Requirements by refinement. The criterion for the derivation is that the resulting Specification must be testable.
7. Work Product: The result of a Work Package.
8. Model: A model is a specific system-level implementation of a partial or full set of specifications. A model is composed of Entities and is a Project related Work Product.
9. Entity: An Entity is a composing subset of a model. The interactions create the emerging system properties.
10. Work Package: A set of Tasks that, using Resources, produce a Work Product which meets its Requirements and Specifications. A Work Package shall at least have a Development-, a Verification-, a Test- and a Validation-Task.
11. Development-Task: A Task that takes as input the specifications and develops the Work Products.
12. Verification-Task: A task that verifies that the work done in the Development-Task meets the Process related Requirements and Specifications.
13. Test-Task: A Task that verifies that the result of a verified Work Product meets the System related Specifications.
14. Validation-Task: A Task that verifies that the tested Work Product meets the System related Requirements after integration with all Work Products constituting the System.
15. Resource: A Resource is anything that is needed for a Work Package to be executed.
16. Issue: An issue is anything that comes up during development that requires further investigation, mainly to determine if the issue is a real concern.
17. Change Request: A Change Request is an explicit request to modify an already approved Project Entity.

We make abstraction here from often domain specific sub-typing (often introduced by qualifying attributes). One must be careful to keep the subtypes to a minimal and orthogonal set. Otherwise, the terminology confusion creeps in again.

The attentive reader will notice that the definitions above might not fully agree with his own notions and still leave some room for interpretation.

This is largely due to the ambiguities of natural language and established but not necessarily coherent practices in how people use the natural language terms. While we cannot really change language we stick to the terms as they are but clarify the definitions and why they were chosen. In addition, in the GoedelWorks environment the structure helps to enforce a specific meaning.

3.2   Requirements vs. Specifications

It might come as a surprise, but many but bot all safety standards don't even use the term "specification". Most standards use the term "requirement" often with a qualifying prefix. An example are the High Level Requirements (HLR) and Low Level Requirements (LLR) in DO-178C.[8] In ISO-26262 [9] a specification is defined as a set of requirements which, when taken together, constitute the definition of the functions and attributes of item or element.

To eliminate the ambiguity we clearly distinguish between Requirements and Specifications. A Requirement only becomes a Specification when it is sufficiently precise and constrained that we can define a way to test it. We can say that a Specification is a quantified Requirements statement. It comes into being by a refinement process that often will include trade-off decisions driven by the Project constraints. The point is that development engineering activities can really only start when the Specification stage has been reached, else we have too many degrees of freedom. The latter does not exclude early proof-of-concept prototypes.

3.3   Development, Verification, Testing and Validation

Another distinction is in the terms used to differentiate the Work Package Tasks. Verification is here linked with Process Specifications whereas Development and Testing are linked with System or Project Specifications. In the case of Development, Specification statements are necessary input to guide the Development. Although, we say that Testing verifies that the system Specifications were met, we reserve the term Verification for verifying the way the Development was done. The logic behind this is that testing should not be used to find the errors and deviations of the development activities but to find the deviations from the System's specified properties. Similarly, Validation comes after Testing and is meant to verify that the System as a whole (which implies that it includes Integration) meets the original Requirements statements. Note, that Validation will include Testing activities, typically by operating the System in its intended environment.

3.4   The Main Complementary Views in SE

The meta-model we introduced covers three main views that together define the system being developed. Before we elaborate on these, we should clarify what we mean with the term "System". In the SE context, the System is what is being developed in a SE Process. However, a System is never alone, it is an Entity that always interacts with two other Systems. The first one is the environment in which it will be used. This can literally be the rest of the real-world or a higher level system. The second one is the (human) operator actively interacting with the System. When developing a System, one must always take these two other Systems into account. Their interactions influence the System under development (typically by changing the System's state, either by changing its energy level, either by changing the operating mode). The reader will notice that both Systems are characterised by the presence of elements that one never has fully under control. A human operator can be assumed to always give correct commands, but this cannot be guaranteed. The same for the environment. It can be anticipated, but not predicted, how these two systems will behave. This is the essence of safety engineering.

In the end SE can be seen as the converge of three views. The first one is the well known requirements view. It is concerned with the properties that Systems should and must have and relates to the well known question of "What is the right System?". The second is the Work Plan view. It consists of the activities that centered around the development that produces the system. It is related to the "what system?" question. The third one is the Process view. It answers the question: "How is the System to be developed?". It defines on the one hand a partial order for the different Work Packages of the Work Plan, but it also defines the evidence that needs to be present at the end of a SE Project. What is less understood is that the deliverables of a SE engineering project are on the one hand the System itself (a collection of Entities that create the System after integration) and on the other hand the Process Work Products. In a systematic, controlled SE Project all these Work Products together define the System. The Work Products document it and together with the dependency chain provide the evidence that it meets the Specifications and Requirements. The Process Work Products are sometimes called the artefacts as if they were by-products, which underestimates their value. They make the difference between development as an engineering activity and development as a crafting activity.

3.5 Morphing Work Products as Templates, Resources and Deliverables

Another important aspect to see is that a Process is also something that has to be developed like any other System. Developing a Process also requires a Work Plan and a set of Process Requirements resulting in Process Specifications. The deliverables of such a Process developing Project are on the one hand the Process itself (i.e. defined activities) and on the other hand the Specifications for the Work Products to be developed in a concrete Project. In essence, a Process will define Templates that need to be filled in during a concrete Project. Hence, the Template becomes a Resource in a concrete Project whereby the Deliverable is again a Work Product. A simple example is a test plan. A Process will define what we can expect from a test plan in generic terms (e.g. completeness, confidence, etc.). It acts as a Reference for further instantiation. Therefore, an organisation will have to derive an organisation, often domain specific test plan, but still a template enhanced with organisation specific procedures and guidelines. In a concrete Project this enhanced template is a Resource. After the Work Package developing an Entity has been approved it becomes part of the evidence that the Entity meets the Requirements and Specifications.

This "morphing" of entities is another reason why terminology can be confusing. It is related to implicit or explicit reuse of previously developed "Entities" and actually this is what engineering does all the time. All new developments somehow always include prior knowledge or reuse previously developed Entities that become components or Resources for new Projects. On the other hand it simplifies the understanding of SE by being aware that the finality of a SE Project is always a (coherent) set of Work Products. The Project and the Process are never the finality but the main means to reach the approved state of the Work Products.

3.6   Links and Entity Dependencies

In a real Project, the number of Entities grows quickly. This induces the need to group and structure them. Therefore, we define "structural" links, i.e. an Entity can be composed of sub-Entities. This is not an operation of refinement but one of decomposition.

If we now make these Requirements concrete, we obtain Specifications that are derived from them by refinement. For example, we can first build a physical simulation Model that given parameters allow us to determine the Entity Specifications. The exercise of linking Specifications with Model Entities is one of mapping.

The different Process steps actually create dependency relationships. The Specifications depend on the Requirements. The Work Package related to developing will also depend on Resources. The composing Tasks also define dependency relationships. The Validation will depend on the Testing with the Testing depending on the Verification and the Verification depending on the Development.

These dependency relationships give us also the traceability requirements, allowing to trace back e.g. from the source code back to the original Requirements. If the dependency chain is broken, we know that something was overlooked or not fully analysed. This property is further discussed in the next section.

Using a car as example, we illustrate another aspect that is tightly related with Requirements management. Assume that we have Requirements saying "The car shall drive like a sports car", "Fuel consumption shall be the lowest on the market" and "The car must be bullet proof". These Requirements are likely in conflict. While the examples are straightforward, in practice this conclusion is less trivial. This is why different Models are needed. Simulation modelling or virtual prototyping allows us to verify the consistency of the Requirements in view of the available technology (found back as parameters of the model). For example, the designer will have to make trade-offs between either a fuel-efficient and light car, either a powerful and light car but with a higher fuel consumption or a very safe but heavy and fuel-inefficient car. Similarly, when using formal models we use them to verify critical properties. Often there is a relationship between being able to prove such properties and the complexity, read: architecture, of the System. For example if safety properties can't be proven, often the System will need to be restructured and simplified.

3.7 State Transitions and Process Flow

The dependency chains identified earlier seem to indicate that a Project always proceeds top-down, from Requirements till implementation. When taken literally (like in the waterfall process model), this cannot work because as we have seen that Requirement statements do not necessarily form a coherent set and at least some modelling will be needed to weed out overlapping or to make the trade-off decisions. In practice, some Entities will already exist or have been selected (e.g. when using COTS) and the dependency link is created later on. The way to introduce iterative processes is by assigning a "state" to the Project entities and combining them with the dependency relationships. Typically a Project entity will be created and becomes "Defined". At some point in time it will become "In Work" and when it has been properly worked on, it can become "Frozen for Approval". Following a subsequent review, it can then become "Approved". More subtler states can be defined but we illustrate the principle using the main ones.

The state "Approved" can only be reached if we follow the dependency chain in the reverse order. An entity can only be approved if the preceding entities in the chain have been approved. If any of them is not, or loses that status, e.g. because of an approved Issue or Change Request, all depending entities loose that status as well. The result is that we have for each Work Product (that includes Models) a separate iterative flow, even if the overall Process flow is following a V-model, illustrated in Fig. 2. The order doesn't come from having predefined a temporal partial order between the Work Packages but from the precedence-dependency chains. Nothing prevents us from starting to work on all entities concurrently. The only order that is imposed is the order in which entities can be approved.

4   Unified SE vs. Domain Specific Engineering

Another aspect that is worth highlighting is that the unified Process flow and meta-model we described is not specific to a particular domain. The reasoning applies to business processes, which can be classified as social engineering processes, as well as to technical engineering processes. In all cases, once we have agreed on what we need, we can define what will meet the needs and how we will reach that goal.

In the industry, much attention goes to supporting the development of safety critical systems and as such safety standards often define for each domain which process to follow. Each of them also has it own terminology. By introducing the generic meta-model (actually a meta-meta-model) we can cater for the different domains by defining subtypes. We illustrate this by analysing Requirements.

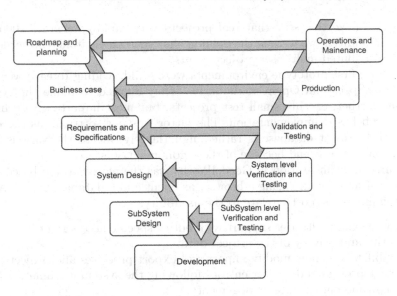

Fig. 2. The overall V-Model Process Flow of GoedelWorks

Requirements are often obtained by defining "use cases", often descriptions of scenarios that highlight some operational aspect of the system. We subtype a Requirement into three classes, i.e. the "normal case", the "test case" and the "fault case", as refinements of the generic "use case". These are defined as follows:

- Normal case: This related to a Requirement that covers the normally expected behaviour or properties.
- Test case: This relates to a Requirement that covers a mode in which the system is "tested". Test cases do not modify the "normal case" Requirements but have an impact on the architectural design.
- Fault case: This relates to a Requirement whereby faults in the system are considered. Faults are defined as occurrences whereby some components no longer meet their "normal case" Specifications (derived from "normal case" Requirements). Safety engineering then prescribes what we expect of the System when these occur. Hence we can consider a "safety case" as a subtype of a "fault case".

The approach whereby we start from a higher level more abstract meta-model allows us also to e.g. consider security aspects as a fault case. We can say that e.g. a security case is a fault case whereby the fault is maliciously injected versus a safety case whereby the fault is often physical in origin. This allows us to reuse a safety engineering approach (for which documented standards exist) to a security engineering approach (for which documented standards are often lacking).

4.1   GoedelWorks as a Supporting Environment

While the unifoied SE approach this paper presents, provides us with a coherent framework, it's applicability can only be validated by applying it to a real project whereby we have the issue that real projects very rapidly generate 1000's of entities. In addition we were of the opinion that such an environment needed to support distributed multi-user project teams.

Therefore, first prototype environments were build, leading to early versions called OpenSpecs and OpenCookBook [5]. They allowed to refine the system grammar further, execute small test projects, but most importantly to find a suitable web based implementation. The latter was not so trivial as the complexity of a project database is rather high (largely due to the various links between the entities) and because of the ergonomic needs.

The final implementation in GoedelWorks was therefore entirely based on a client-server architecture using a browser as client and a database server. Additional requirements mostly relate to the useability:

- International multi-user support with entity specific access rights;
- Security and privacy of the project data;
- Capability to define, modify import and export processes and projects;
- Manage process and project entities following the system grammar;
- Change and entity state management;
- Queries and dependency analysis;
- Creating "snapshot" documents (in HTML or PDF format);
- Resource and Task planning.

Without going into detail, such an environment acts as a unique and central repository for Processes and Projects, facilitating concurrent team work and communication from early Requirements capturing till implementation.

4.2   Importing the ASIL Automotive Centered Safety Integrity Level Process Flow

While in principle GoedelWorks can support any type of Project and Process, its meta-model was tuned for Systems engineering Projects with a particular emphasis on safety critical Processes and certification, hence the importance of traceability links. Organizations can add and develop their own Processes as well.

To validate the approach an existing safety engineering process was imported, called ASIL. It is a Process based on several safety engineering standards, but with a focus on the automotive and machinery domain. It was developed by a consortium of Flanders Drive [7] members and combines elements from IEC 61508, IEC 62061, ISO DIS 26262, ISO 13849, ISO DIS 25119, ISO 15998, CMMI and Automotive Spice. These were obtained by dissecting the standards in semi-atomic Requirement statements and combining them in a iterative V-Model Process. It was enhanced with templates for the Work Products and domain specific guidelines.

In total the ASIL Process identified about 3800 semi-atomic Requirement statements and about 100 Process Work Products. Also 3 Process domains were identified (Organizational Processes. Safety engineering and development Processes, Supportive Processes. More details can be found in [4].

The imported ASIL still needs to be completed to create an organization or Project specific Process. It is also likely that organization specific Processes will need to be added. As each Entity in GoedelWorks can be edited, this is directly possible on a GoedelWorks portal. Without going into details, the import of ASIL proved that the meta-model approach works and is consistent. For the interested reader, we refer to a generic description of the ASIL process flow in the reference document [4].

5 Conclusions

This paper presented a unified meta-model to develop and execute System Engineering Processes and Projects. SE was formalized through the use of a unifying paradigm based on the observation that systems, including a process, can be described at an abstract level as a set of interactions and entities. A second observation is that a key problem in SE is the divergence in terminology, hence the use of unified semantics by defining a univoque and orthogonal set of concepts. GoedelWorks as a practical implementation of a supporting environment was developed. It was validated by importing a generic automotive focused process flow.

References

1. Object Management Group: UML, http://www.uml.org/
2. OMG Systems Modeling Language, http://www.omgsysml.org/
3. Verhulst, E., Boute, R.T., Faria, J.M.S., Sputh, B.H.C., Mezhuyev, V.: Formal Development of a Network-Centric RTOS. Software Engineering for Reliable Embedded Systems. Springer, Amsterdam (2011)
4. Trustworthy Systems Engineering with GoedelWorks. Booklet published by Altreonic NV (January 2012),
   http://www.altreonic.com/sites/default/files/Systems
   %20Engineering%20with%20GoedelWorks.pdf
5. Mezhuyev, V., Sputh, B., Verhulst, E.: Interacting entities modelling methodology for robust systems design. In: 2010 Second International Conference on Advances in System Testing and Validation Lifecycle (VALID), pp. 75–80 (August 2010)
6. Espinoza, H., Ruiz, A., Sabetzadeh, M., Panaroni, P.: Challenges for an open and evolutionary approach to safety assurance and certification of safety-critical systems. In: 2011 First International Workshop on Software Certification (WoSoCER), November 29-December 2, pp. 1–6 (2011)
7. Automotive Safety Integrity Level Public Results (2011),
   http://www.flandersdrive.be/_js/plugin/ckfinder/userfiles/files/
   ASIL%20public%20presentation.pdf
8. Software Considerations in Airborne Systems and Equipment Certification (2012),
   http://en.wikipedia.org/wiki/DO-178C
9. Automotive functional safety (2012), http://en.wikipedia.org/wiki/ISO_26262

A Preliminary Fault Injection Framework for Evaluating Multicore Systems

Anna Lanzaro[1], Antonio Pecchia[1], Marcello Cinque[1], Domenico Cotroneo[1],
Ricardo Barbosa[2], and Nuno Silva[2]

[1] Dipartimento di Informatica e Sistemistica
Universitá degli Studi di Napoli Federico II
Via Claudio 21, 80125, Naples, Italy
[2] ASD-T Aeronautics, Space, Defense and Transportation
Critical Software SA
Parque Industrial de Taveiro, Lt 48, Coimbra, Portugal
{anna.lanzaro,antonio.pecchia,macinque,cotroneo}@unina.it,
{rbarbosa,nsilva}@criticalsoftware.com

Abstract. Multicore processors are becoming more and more attractive in embedded and safety-critical domains because they allow increasing the performance by ensuring reduced power consumption. However, moving to multicore systems raises novel dependability challenges: the number of cores, concurrency issues, shared resources and interconnections among cores make it hard to develop and validate software deployed on the top of multicore processors.

This paper discusses a preliminary fault injection framework, which aims to investigate dependability properties of multicore-based systems. The proposed framework leverages the error reporting architecture provided by modern processors and has been instantiated in the context of the Intel Core i7 processor. Fault injection campaigns have been conducted under the Linux OS to show the benefits of the framework.

Keywords: Dependability, Multicore, Fault Injection, Machine Check Error, Intel Core i7.

1 Introduction

High performance, reduced size and weight, and power efficiency are key features that make **multicore processors** desirable for several industrial domains. Recent market trends indicate that safety-critical and embedded system domains, such as *avionic* [4], [3], *automotive* [1], [2] and *medical* [5], are moving towards multicore-based solutions. Even of more relevance, the adoption of multicore can support achieving safety requirements imposed by standards (e.g., ISO-26262, IEC-61508, and DO-178B) because it makes it possible running independent tasks on each core so to ensure properties such as, space and temporal isolation. Furthermore, the inherent presence of replicated cores allows implementing fault-tolerant solutions by means of virtualization [8]. Overall these features

F. Ortmeier and P. Daniel (Eds.): SAFECOMP 2012 Workshops, LNCS 7613, pp. 106–116, 2012.

exacerbate the need for strategies to evaluate dependability characteristics of multicore systems.

Modern processors, e.g., Intel, AMD, ARM, IBM, Freescale, incorporate hardware-implemented detection and fine-grained **error-reporting architecture** to notify problems affecting processor units, such as memory and caches hierarchy, TLB, bus. These mechanisms produce precise notifications and context information about the errors reported by the hardware, which are valuable to the software components running on the top of the processor. Among them, software addressing *recovery* and *isolation* capability plays a key role in the development of multicore systems due to the complexity introduced by the number of cores, concurrency issues, shared resources and interconnections among cores. Evaluating the overall system behavior under errors is crucial and requires specific methodologies in the context of multicore systems.

This paper proposes a preliminary fault injection framework to support dependability evaluation of multicore systems. The key idea underlying the framework is emulating **machine check errors**, i.e., errors occurring when the processor detects problems affecting hardware components. Emulation is accomplished by writing into the registers of the error reporting architecture of the processor rather than physically interfering with the actual hardware units. In this way, the approach allows performing low-cost and controllable fault injection campaigns. The proposed framework has been instantiated in the context of the Intel Core i7 processor. Explorative fault injection campaigns have been conducted under the Linux OS to validate and to show the benefits of the framework.

The rest of the paper is organized as follows. Section 2 introduces related work in the area of fault injection. Section 3 discusses the framework and design challenges concerning its functional components. Section 4 introduces the reference processor adopted in the study. Section 5 describes a preliminary implementation of the fault injection framework and results obtained in the context of the Linux OS. Section 6 concludes the work and indicates future research directions.

2 Related Work

Fault injection is a well-established technique for dependability evaluation of systems in both industry and academia. It allows introducing faults into a given system with the aim of observing its dependability behavior and assessing fault tolerant mechanisms. More important, fault injection is currently recommended, if not mandatory, and regulated by many **international standards**, to support the system validation and certification process and to develop robust software. For example, fault injection is an important constituent of the ISO 26262 [10] standard to supplement software unit and integration testing.

Several fault injection techniques were proposed in order to inject **hardware faults**. Hardware-based fault injection techniques insert into the system real hardware errors by means of special-purpose and architecture-dependent equipment or by interfering with the physical unit (e.g., by lowering the device voltage, increasing the temperature, radiations introducing electromagnetic interferences) [9], [11]. This approach has the advantage of reproducing real hardware faults, but it is costly and risky to implement. Moreover, it makes it hard the observation of the effect of the faults in the processor because of the interferences caused by the injectors. For these reasons, **software-implemented** fault injection (SWIFI) techniques, which are closer to our work, have gained popularity. SWIFI consists of reproducing via software the effects of hardware errors. The injection can be performed at compile time inserting the effects of hardware errors in the target code or at run time using time-out, exceptions or code insertion to trigger the fault injection. Tools implementing SWIFI technique are [12] [13], [14], [15].

The use of fault injection techniques for the assessment of **multicore systems** is still recent. Appropriate fault models encompassing faults that were not a concern in single-core architectures (e.g., adopting SWIFI technique, the execution of additional software for the injection could affect the scheduling of the system tasks impacting real-time requirements) are required to guarantee effective and low cost fault injection campaigns. Challenges in tolerating faults in parallel execution on multicore systems are discussed in [6]. In [16], mSWAT is presented. It is a detection and diagnosis technique for permanent and transient hardware faults in multicore architectures running multithreaded software. The authors adopt fault injection by simulation in order to validate the detection mechanisms. However, assuming that at most one core is faulty, the fault model encompasses only in-core faults and not faults that can occur in I/O controller, memory sub-system, etc. In both [18] and [7] a simulation-based fault injection analysis for multicore is presented. In [17] the use of NFTAPE tool for the evaluation of operating system behavior running on multicore processor is proposed. In [20], the authors describe a method for predicting failures based on the monitoring of the execution units in a Quad-core Intel processor.

3   Proposed Framework

Machine check errors (MCE) indicate the occurrence of problems affecting hardware units of the processor. Modern processors usually notify MCEs by means of an error-reporting architecture (exemplified in Fig. 1) composed by a set of *global* and *per-core* registers. The idea underlying our proposal is emulating the occurrence of MCEs by **writing into the registers** of the error-reporting architecture rather interfering with the device, such as in the mentioned hardware fault injection approaches. The knowledge about MCEs and error codes reported by the processor during the execution is inferred from the documentation provided by the manufacturer of the processor [19]. Modifying the registers of the error-reporting architecture allows implementing a low-cost and controllable fault injection framework.

Fig. 1 shows the functional components of the framework implementing the injection approach. The system under test is composed by the multicore processor and a **target workload**. The latter could be an operating system, software for embedded systems, or a virtualization-based solution, and represents the software whose robustness is assessed under the occurrence of MCEs. The role of

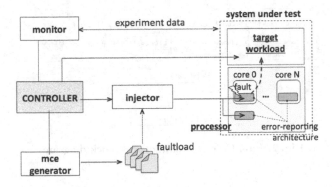

Fig. 1. Proposed fault injection framework

the remaining components depicted in Fig. 1 is described in the following along with relevant design challenges:

- **MCE generator** is the entity that automates the generation of the *faultload*, i.e., the set of MCEs that will be injected in the target system during the campaign. It should be noted that the number of combinations representing all the possible error codes reported by the processor is extremely large. The faultload generation should be optimized with criteria aiming to narrow down the number of experiments. For examples, experiments might focus on a given hardware unit or specific border values assigned to the error-reporting registers of the processor.

- **Injector** is the component responsible for injecting MCEs into the error-reporting architecture of the target processor, as shown in Fig. 1. The injector should not distort the actual behavior of the system under test. For this reason, if injection is accomplished via a software module, isolation between the injector and the injection target can be achieved by running them on different cores. A better solution is represented by the use of specialized hardware supports, such as a debugger; however, this might not always be available to analysts and requires additional costs. Even of more relevance, injector must address spatial and timing features of the experiment.

- **Monitor** is responsible for collecting data concerning the fault-injection outcomes. Data might include notifications reported in the system log, output produced by the target workload, or state variables. Monitor should cope with data loss caused by experiments leading to critical system failures, such as reboot or panic. Again, monitoring and data collection features should not impact the behavior of the target system.

- **Controller** is the entity responsible for iterating fault injection experiments and coordinating the described components. For each experiment it activates/deactivates the injector module, and stores monitoring data. Moreover, controller should ensure that the workload is actually running at the time injection is performed. To this objective, controller might leverage

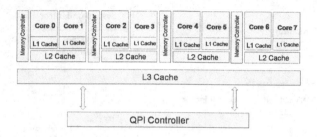

Fig. 2. Intel Core i7 architectural block diagram

operating system support (e.g., Linux OS get/set CPU affinity mask) to cope with processes scheduling issues.

4 Case Study

The multicore processor targeted by the study is the **Intel Core i7** 2670QM [21]. Fig. 2 shows a simplified block diagram of the architecture. It is a distributed shared memory system consisting of 4 physical cores integrated on the same chip. Cores are connected by a point-to-point and high-speed communication link (Quick Path Interconnect). Each core appears to software as two logical cores by means of the Hyper Threading Technology (e.g. Intel's implementation of Simultaneous Multi-Threading). Moreover, the processor introduces several new features (e.g., integrated memory controller for each core, a memory hierarchy with 3 caches levels) that assure high performance and power efficiency.

The processor provides a sophisticated error-reporting architecture called **Machine Check Architecture** (MCA). The MCA is composed by a set of registers (Machine Specific Register - MSR) for reporting errors detected by hardware components, such as memory, caches, and buses. As shown in the Fig. 3, the MCA consists of 9 banks of registers replicated for **each core** and associated to specific hardware units. Each bank is composed by 5 registers for reporting hardware errors: two *control* registers (MCi_CTL and MCi_CTL2), a *status* register (MCi_STATUS), an *address* register (MCi_ADDR), and a *miscellaneous* error information register (MCi_MISC). By means of the bank of registers, the MCA notifies different category of errors:

- **uncorrected errors** (UC): errors not corrected by the processor;
- **uncorrected recoverable errors** (UCR): errors not corrected by the processor and for which system software can attempt recovery actions. In particular, the recovery actions can be *required* (SRAR), *optional* (SRAO) or *not required* (UCNA).
- **corrected errors** (CE): errors corrected by the processor without impacting running processes.

Additional information about the type of errors affecting hardware units of the processor is available in the first 16 bits of the status register (again, MCi_STATUS).

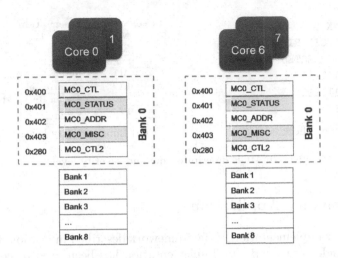

Fig. 3. Machine Check Architecture

Details about the error codes adopted in the study are reported in the Table 1, which has been taken from the processor documentation. This information supported the definition of realistic fault model for the target processor. Moreover, 3 **global registers** are provided by the processor: MCG_CAP, MCG_STATUS and MCG_CTL registers. In the context of our work, we considered the MCG_CAP register, which gives information about the capabilities of the MCA available in the processor (e.g., bit SER_P of such register indicates if the processor supports recovery actions) and MCG_STATUS register, which reports the status of the processor at the time a MCE occurs.

Table 1. Status Register [15:0]

Type	Format*
Generic Cache hierarchy	0001 0000 0000 11LL
TLB	0001 0000 0001 TTLL
Memory controller	0001 1MMM 11LL CCCC
Cache hierarchy	0001 0001 RRRR TTLL
Bus and interconnections	0001 1PPT RRRR IILL

*TT - Type of transaction
LL - Level in the memory hierarchy
RRRR - Type of action associated with the error
MMM and CCCC - Memory transaction type and Channel
PP and T - Partecipation and Timeout
II - Memory or I/O

CPU 2   BANK 8
MCGSTATUS MCIP RIPV EIPV
STATUS UNCORRECTED 0x0186
ADDR 0x11111111
MISC 0x11111111
NOBROADCAST

Level	Severity	Description
0	NO	No Action
1	KEEP	No panic
2	SOME	No panic
3	AO	Action Optional
4	UC	Uncorrectable
5	AR	Action Required
6	PANIC	Panic

(a) Machine check error   (b) Linux severity levels

Fig. 4. MCE description file and severity levels

5   Preliminary Application

A preliminary implementation of the framework described in Section 3 has been developed under the Linux OS. Implementation has been used to conduct explorative fault-injection campaigns to validate the proposed approach in a real testbed adopting the Intel i7 processor.

In the proposed implementation the **injector** consists of mce-inject [22], which is a well-known tool in Intel/Linux community. Each MCE is represented by a textual description providing information about the location (i.e., cpu and bank number) where the MCE will be injected and values assigned to MCG_STATUS, MCi_STATUS, MCi_ADDR, and MCi_MISC registers of the MCA architecture. Fig. 4a provides an example of MCE to be injected in the *bank 8* of the *cpu 2*. It emulates an *uncorrected error* affecting data of L2 cache during the snoop protocol by means of the error code *0x0186* that will be written in the status register. A bash script has been implemented to automatically generate the *faultload*, i.e., the set of MCEs that are injected during a campaign. Given the textual description, *mce-inject* sets the values of the registers of the MCA by means of a specific kernel module of the Linux OS.

The **workload** is represented by the Linux OS (kernel version 3.1.10) running on the top of the Intel i7 processor. Preliminary experiments aim to explore the Linux error-handling capabilities initiated by the do_machine_check procedure. This is the OS exception handler that is actually triggered when a real machine check occurs (interrupt 18 in the case of Intel processors). For each MCE-injection experiment, the **monitor** component collects the error *severity* determined by the kernel as a result of the injected MCE and the *recovery action* triggered by the kernel based on the severity level. Values assumed by the severity parameter under the Linux OS are reported in Fig. 4b.

5.1   Campaign #1

The faultload of the first campaign consists of 4,096 MCEs. It emulates cache, memory controller, and TLB errors by changing the bits of the status registers according to the codes reported in Table 1. The set of emulated errors contains uncorrected recoverable errors (UCR), uncorrected recoverable errors with action

(a) Severity   (b) Recovery actions

Fig. 5. SER_P=0: recovery actions not supported by the processor

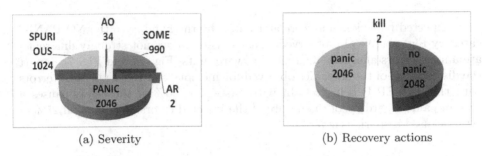

(a) Severity   (b) Recovery actions

Fig. 6. SER_P=1: recovery actions supported by the processor

required (SRAR), optional (SRAO) or not required (UCNA). Moreover, the same faultload has been injected into two different scenarios, i.e., (i) with the processor not supporting recovery actions (i.e., the bit SER_P is clean); (ii) with processor supporting recovery by software (i.e., the bit SER_P is set).

Fig.5a and Fig.5b show the MCEs severities and related recovery actions provided by the Linux OS, when the **bit SER_P is clean**. All the errors have classified as uncorrectable; however, this set of experiments did not cause the triggering of any specific a recovery action.

The same set of 4,096 errors has been emulated with the **bit SER_P set**. Experiments made it possible to highlight a rather different behavior of the error handling mechanism indicated by Fig. 6a and Fig. 6b, respectively. Fig. 6a shows the severity levels. The 50% of the injected MCEs is classified as PANIC: as a result, the injection of this subset of errors actually caused the panic of the machine, such as reported in Fig. 6b. Errors causing SOME and AO severities represent total 24% and the 0.8%, respectively. These errors did not trigger any specific action of the handler. Only 2 error codes affecting the cache unit, i.e., 0x0134 - *data load error* and 0x0150 - *instruction fetch error* were actually recognized by the handler, i.e., AR severity, and caused the 2 process kills shown in Fig. 6b.

More important, experiments revealed a possible bug in the code that determines the error severity (Fig.6a). Around 25% of experiments caused a **spurious** severity value, i.e., a numeric value that is not a severity level according to Fig. 4b. Spurious values prevent to correctly determine the severity of errors leading

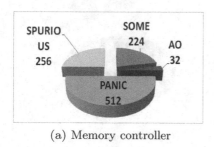

(a) Memory controller

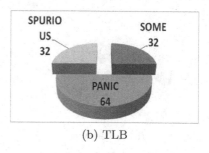

(b) TLB

Fig. 7. Severity and recovery actions grouped by error categories

to unexpected behaviors and were attributed by the handler to the NO PANIC category Fig. 6b. We also observed that the kernel does not strongly differentiate among errors affecting different hardware units. Fig. 7a and Fig. 7b report the distribution of the severities observed for memory controller and TLB errors with the bit SER_P being set. In both cases, the 50% of the errors causes a system panic regardless of the nature of the injected errors. Again, total 25% of errors caused a spurious severity.

5.2   Campaign #2

Because of the inability of the handler to differentiate among error codes, a further campaign has been performed to explore its recovery behavior. In this campaign, rather than exhaustively trying different error codes, we used different combinations of the diagnostic information provided by the MCA along with the error notification (such as, the error is recoverable or not, an action is required to recover from the error, the error corrupted or not the processor state, etc).

The campaign encompassed 192 MCEs injected when the bit SER_P is set, i.e., recovery actions are supported. Results reported in Fig. 8a and 8b confirm that the target handler mainly provides coarse-grained recovery actions, i.e., system panic (82%) and process kill (3%). Again, the handler was not able to correctly manage around 11% of the errors due to the presence of spurious severity values, possibly causing an improper recovery action.

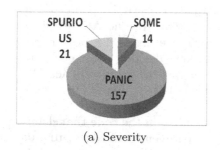

(a) Severity

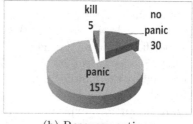

(b) Recovery actions

Fig. 8. Severity and recovery action for Campaign #2

6   Conclusion

This paper proposed a fault injection framework developed for supporting dependability analysis of multicore systems. The approach leverages the notion of machine check error and the error-report mechanism implemented by modern processors. So far, fault injection campaigns have been conducted to test the functionalities of the framework under the Linux OS running on the top of the Intel i7 processor.

In the future, we will improve the framework by addressing the emulation of simultaneous errors affecting different cores, burst of errors, errors propagation among cores. The framework will be used to validate error handling of different operating systems, to analyze fault-tolerant mechanisms implemented across cores, to assess the resiliency of a given system under errors, and to benchmark the dependability behavior of different solutions adopting multicore.

Acknowledgment. This work has been supported by the European project CRITICAL Software Technology for an Evolutionary Partnership (CRITICAL STEP, http://www.critical-step.eu), Marie Curie Industry-Academia Partnerships and Pathways (IAPP) number 230672, in the context of the EU Seventh Framework Programme (FP7).

References

1. Aussaguès, C., Chabrol, D., David, V.: PharOS, a multicore OS ready for safety-related automotive systems: results and future prospects. In: Software and Systems, pp. 1–10 (2010)
2. Navet, N., Monot, A., Bavoux, B.: Multi-source and multicore automotive ECUs-OS protection mechanisms and scheduling, vol. 2010 (2010)
3. Agrou, H., Sainrat, P., Gatti, M.: A design approach for predictable and efficient multi-core processor for avionics. Digital Avionics (2011)
4. Kinnan, L.: Use of multicore processors in avionics systems and its potential impact on implementation and certification. In: Avionics Systems Conference, DASC 2009 (2009)
5. Zhu, Y.: Medical Image Viewing on Multicore Platforms Using Parallel Computing Patterns. IT Professional 12(2), 33–41 (2010)
6. Mushtaq, H., Al-Ars, Z., Bertels, K.: Survey of fault tolerance techniques for shared memory multicore/multiprocessor systems. In: 2011 IEEE 6th International Design and Test Workshop (IDT), pp. 12–17 (December 2011)
7. Lee, D., Na, J.: A Novel Simulation Fault Injection Method for Dependability Analysis. IEEE Design & Test of Computers 26(6), 50–61 (2009)
8. Leveraging virtualization in Aerospace and Defense applications, Radisys white paper (November 2011)
9. Madeira, H., Rela, M., Moreira, F., Silva, J.G.: RIFLE: A General Purpose Pin-Level Fault Injector. In: Echtle, K., Powell, D.R., Hammer, D. (eds.) EDCC 1994. LNCS, vol. 852, pp. 199–216. Springer, Heidelberg (1994)
10. International Organization for Standardization. Product Development: Software Level. ISO/DIS 26262-6 (2009)

11. Gunneflo, U., Karlsson, J., Torin, J.: Evaluation of Error Detection Schemes Using Fault Injection by Heavy Radiation. In: Proceedings of the Fault Tolerant Computing Symposium - FTCS-19, pp. 340–347 (1989)
12. Segall, Z., Vrsalovic, D., Siewiorek, D., Kownacki, J., Barton, J., Dancey, R., Robinson, A., Lin, T.: FIAT - Fault Injection Based Automated Testing Environment. In: Proceedings of the 18th IEEE International Symposium on Fault Tolerant Computing - FTCS 1988, pp. 102–107 (1988)
13. Kanawati, G.A., Kanawati, N.A., Abraham, J.A.: FERRARI: A Tool for the Validation of System Dependability Properties. In: Proceedings of the 22nd IEEE International Fault Tolerant Computing Symposium, FTCS-22, pp. 336–344 (1992)
14. Kao, W.-L., Iyer, R.K., Tang, D.: FINE: A Fault Injection and Monitoring Environment for Tracing the UNIX System Behavior under Faults. IEEE Transactions on Software Engineering 19, 1105–1118 (1993)
15. Carreira, J., Madeira, H., Silva, J.G.: Xception: Software Fault Injection and Monitorintg in Processor Functional Units. IEEE Transactions on Software Engineering 24 (1998)
16. Hari, S.K.S., Li, M.-L., Ramachandran, P., Choi, B., Adve, S.V.: mSWAT: Low-Cost Hardware Fault Detection and Diagnosis for Multicore Systems. In: MICRO 2009, New York (December 2009)
17. Jacques-Silva, G., Kalbarczyk, Z., Iyer, R.K.: Dependability Assessment of Operating Systems in Multi-core Architectures. In: Fast Abstract in the 38th Int. Symp. on Dependable Systems and Networks, Anchorage, Alaska (June 2008)
18. Faraji, I., Didehban, M., Zarandi, H.R.: Analysis of Transient Faults on a MIPS-Based Dual-Core Processor. In: Int. Conf. on Availability, Reliability, and Security - ARES 2010, Krakow, Poland (2010)
19. Lanzaro, A., Cotroneo, D., Duraes, J., Silva, N., Barbosa, R.: Multicore Systems: Challenges for creating a representative fault model for fault injection. In: DASIA Int'l Space System Engineering Conference, Dubrovnik, Croatia (May 2012)
20. Salfner, F., Troger, P., Tschirpke, S.: Cross-Core Event Monitoring for Processor Failure Prediction. In: Int. Conf. on High Performance Computing & Simulation, HPCS 2009, Leipzig, Germany (2009)
21. Intel 64 and IA-32 Architectures Software Developer's Manual vol. 3: System Programming Guide, http://www.intel.com/
22. Kleen, A.: Machine check handling on Linux. SUSE Labs (August 2004)

Meeting Real-Time Requirements
with Multi-core Processors

Daniel Kästner, Marc Schlickling, Markus Pister, Christoph Cullmann,
Gernot Gebhard, Reinhold Heckmann, and Christian Ferdinand

AbsInt GmbH, Science Park 1, D-66123 Saarbrücken, Germany

Abstract. Many multi-core processors exhibit characteristics that make
it difficult or even impossible to use them in safety-critical real-time systems. To prevent sporadic failures and late-stage integration problems,
the hardware properties of the processor and its peripherals have to be
checked for their real-time capability at an early project stage. Selecting
a configuration which enables predictable performance is an important
requirement to achieve compliance with current safety standards, e.g.,
ISO-26262, IEC-61508, EN-50128, or DO-178B.

For timing-predictable hardware configurations safe worst-case execution time bounds can be computed by static analysis tools. Combined
with scheduling analysis at the system level the correct end-to-end timing
can be guaranteed. This article gives an overview of hardware features
leading to predictability problems, shows examples of predictability-
oriented multi-core configurations, and describes a tool-based methodology to ensure the correct timing behavior.

1   Introduction

In recent years multi-core processing has evolved to be the predominant hardware
paradigm for desktop computers. Performing parallel computations by several
cores per chip makes it possible to significantly accelerate systems consisting of
multiple independent threads. Moreover compared to single-core processors the
lower clock rates contribute to a better energy efficiency of multi-core processors.
Also in embedded systems multi-core processors are increasingly used – a trend
facilitated by availability considerations and a significant price drop.

Whereas for desktop applications the predominant goal is to achieve a high average performance, safety-critical embedded systems impose other requirements.
A real-time system not only has to be logically correct, it must also exhibit the
correct timing behavior. A real-time task missing its deadline can cause severe
damage. In order to show that a task always terminates before its deadline its
worst-case execution time (WCET) has to be known. In multi-tasking systems
tasks can be preempted or blocked. This is considered in the worst-case response time of the task (WCRT) which is computed from the WCET and the
time penalties due to preemptions or task blocking.

F. Ortmeier and P. Daniel (Eds.): SAFECOMP 2012 Workshops, LNCS 7613, pp. 117–131, 2012.

With direct timing measurements by using logic analyzers, debuggers, or hardware simulators timing information is only determined for one concrete input. However, usually no full test coverage can be achieved and there is no safe test end criterion. With modern processors the timing behavior of an instruction depends on the instructions previously executed, e.g., due to cache or pipeline effects. In consequence even MC/DC coverage is not enough to determine WCET information since different execution paths cannot be distinguished and there is no control which paths have been covered. Techniques based on code instrumentation modify the code which can significantly change the cache behavior. The times measured for the instrumented software do not necessarily correspond to the timing behavior of the original software at all.

A safe method for timing analysis is static analysis by Abstract Interpretation which provides guaranteed upper bounds for the WCET of tasks [19]. Static analysis based on Abstract Interpretation is recommended by many safety standards and can be considered as the state-of-the-art for verifying non-functional program properties. Combined with a system-level scheduling analysis guaranteed upper bounds for the WCRT can be derived. Static analysis tools for computing WCET and WCRT are in industrial use, like AbsInt's aiT WCET Analyzer [17] and Symtavision's scheduling analyzer SymTA/S [8]. Dedicated tool couplings enable a seamless timing analysis from code to system level [11].

Static WCET analyzers are available for complex processors and yield precise results. However, a basic requirement is that the timing behavior of the processor is *predictable*: it must be possible to determine an upper bound of the maximal execution time which is guaranteed to hold. Additionally the behavioral variance, i.e., the influence of processor state or execution history on the execution time should be as low as possible.

In general, the main obstacle to predictable performance is *resource sharing*. Even in single-core processors accesses to shared resources by concurrent tasks can cause interferences since the ordering of accesses can vary significantly. With speculative hardware mechanisms like caches, out-of-order pipelining, or branch prediction predictability degrades.

On multi-core processors not only the interferences within each core have to be considered. Now there may be additional interferences due to concurrent accesses to shared resources by different applications executed on different cores. Existing multi-cores typically have not been developed with the goal of achieving predictable performance unless configured for lockstep execution. Interferences may be caused by accesses to common caches, common memory banks, or common flash memory prefetch buffers. Since different applications usually are only combined in the integration phase there is the risk of severe timing problems detected very late in the development process.

For a given multi-core architecture interferences have to be carefully examined. Then a configuration can be determined which enables or facilitates predictable performance. Developing multi-core processors with predictable timing is an active area of research (cf. the research projects PREDATOR, MERASA, CERTAINTY, or T-CREST).

This article gives an overview of predictability challenges when using multi-core architectures for applications with real-time constraints. Whereas [4] focuses on the consequences of hardware features for static timing analysis this article discusses the requirements of current safety standards and provides guidelines for predictable hardware designs and configurations. Experiments are reported which demonstrate the timing variance on multi-core architectures induced by interferences between different cores.

2 Requirements of Safety Standards

All current safety standards, including DO-178B [14], DO-178C, IEC-61508 [9], ISO-26262 [10], or EN-50128 [2], require the WCET and the WCRT of real-time tasks to be known. Task interferences both in the spatial and temporal domain have to be addressed. In mixed-criticality applications the entire software is subject to the highest criticality level used unless spatial and temporal independence of all safety functions can be demonstrated. This has significant consequences for hardware selection and system configuration: it has to be ensured that there are no unpredictable timing-related interferences that might affect real-time safety functions. Cache-related preemption costs, pipeline effects, and timing anomalies have to be taken into account. For multi-core processors it has to be shown that there are *no inherent timing interferences between the cores*. The latter aspect is especially important for standardized development frameworks focusing on integrating components from different suppliers on Electronic Control Units (ECUs). Examples are IMA in the avionics and AUTOSAR in the automotive domain.

From a methodological perspective, all safety standards discuss the limitations of dynamic tests and measurements methods. According to the DO-178B for verification testing alone is not enough since testing cannot show the absence of errors. The ISO-26262 points out typical limitations of dynamic testing: it has to be shown that sufficient coverage has been achieved and it has to be argued that code modification and instrumentation does not affect the test results. IEC-61508 and EN-50128 take similar positions. In general, the standards recommend to use static techniques to determine safe upper bounds on the WCET.

3 Static Timing Analysis

Static program analyzers compute information about the software under analysis without actually executing it. Semantics-based static analyzers use an explicit (or implicit) program semantics that is a formal (or informal) model of the program executions in all possible or a set of possible execution environments. In general, the state space of input data and initial states is too large to exhaustively explore all possible executions for determining the exact worst-case execution times. The theory of abstract interpretation [3] offers a semantics-based methodology for static program analyses where the concrete semantics is mapped to a simpler abstract model, the so-called abstract semantics. The static analysis is computed with respect to that abstract semantics. Compared to an analysis of the concrete semantics, the analysis result may be less precise, i.e., overestimate the exact WCET, but the computation may be significantly faster. This means that upper bounds for the execution times of basic blocks are determined, from which upper bounds for the whole system's execution time are derived. The most important characteristics of static analyzers is whether they are *sound* or *unsound*. A static analyzer is called *sound* if the computed results hold for any possible program execution. The WCET bounds computed by a sound WCET analyzer will never be exceeded by any possible program execution.

In addition to soundness, further essential requirements for static WCET analyzers are *efficiency* and *precision*. The analysis time has to be acceptable for industrial practice, and the overestimation must be small enough to be able to prove the timing requirements to be met.

Over the last few years, a more or less standard architecture for timing analysis tools has emerged [5, 6] which is composed of three major building blocks:

− control-flow reconstruction and static analyses for control and data flow,
− micro-architectural analysis, computing upper bounds on execution times of basic blocks,
− path analysis, computing the longest execution paths through the whole program.

The data flow analysis of the first block also detects infeasible paths, i.e., program points that cannot occur in any real execution. This reduces the complexity of the following micro-architectural analysis. There, basic block timings are determined using an abstract processor model (*timing model*) to analyze how instructions pass through the pipeline taking cache-hit or cache-miss information into account. This model defines a cycle-level abstract semantics for each instruction's execution yielding in a certain set of final system states. After the analysis of one instruction has been finished, these states are used as start states in the analysis of the successor instruction(s). Here, the timing model introduces non-determinism that leads to multiple possible execution paths in the analyzed program. The pipeline analysis has to examine all of these paths.

The commercially available tool aiT by AbsInt GmbH implements this architecture. The tool is successfully employed in the avionics [7, 6, 17] and automotive [13] industries to determine precise bounds on execution times of safety-critical software (visit http://www.absint.com/ait for more information).

4   Predictability Challenges

The notion of *timing predictability* encompasses two important aspects:

− It must be possible to determine an upper bound of the maximal execution time which is guaranteed to hold. This guarantee has to be statically determined which means that the hardware architecture has to be amenable to static analysis techniques.

– The behavioral variance, i.e., the different states the hardware can accept, e.g., due to different cache fillings, or internal pipeline states, should be as low as possible. This is important for timing measurements: the larger the behavioral variance is

- the more the execution time depends on the execution history,
- the less meaningful is a measurement in a given execution context, and
- the larger can be the gap between the largest measured execution time and the true worst-case execution time.

In fact, both aspects are related: the higher the behavioral variance of an architecture is the more complex will be the internal state of a static WCET analyzer. In the following we will give an overview of hardware features affecting timing predictability, first focusing on single-core architectures, then on multi-cores.

Modern embedded processors try to maximize the instruction-level parallelism by the implementation of specific and *sophisticated performance enhancing features*. For non-pipelined architectures one can simply add up the execution times of individual instructions to obtain a bound on the execution time of a basic block. Pipelines increase performance by overlapping the executions of consecutive instructions. Hence, a timing analysis cannot consider individual instructions in isolation. Instead, they have to be analyzed collectively – together with their mutual interactions – to obtain tight timing bounds.

In general, the challenges for a timing analysis of single-core architectures originate from the complexity of the particular execution pipeline and the connected hardware devices. Commonly used performance-enhancing features are caches, static/dynamic branch prediction, speculative execution, out-of-order execution, branch history tables, or branch target instruction caches. Many of these hardware features can cause *timing anomalies* [16] which render WCET analysis more difficult. Intuitively, a timing anomaly is a situation where the local worst-case does not contribute to the global worst-case. For instance, a cache miss – the local worst-case – may result in a globally shorter execution time than a cache hit because of hardware scheduling effects. In consequence, it is not safe to assume that the memory access causes a cache miss; instead both states have to be taken into account. An especially difficult class of timing anomalies are domino effects [12]: A system exhibits a *domino effect* if there are two hardware states a, b s.t. the difference in execution time (of the same program starting in a, b respectively) may be arbitrarily high. E.g., given a program loop, the executions never converge to the same hardware state and the difference in execution time increases in each iteration. In consequence, loops have to be analyzed very precisely and the number of machine states to track can grow high.

As the runtime of embedded control software often is dominated by load/store operations, memory subsystems nowadays introduce queues before the caches to buffer them and overcome stall conditions like cache misses. Often this is complemented by fast data forwarding for consecutive accesses into cache lines that have already been requested by previous pending instructions, where the requested data might already be present in the core. This reduces the number of transactions over the system bus. In the abstract model of the timing analysis, the representation of these features has to be close to the concrete hardware to achieve satisfactory analysis precision. Due to their size especially the dynamic branch prediction and the branch history tables consume a mentionable number of bits in the abstract state representation which increases the memory consumption of the analysis. Unknown or not precisely known effective addresses of memory requests further increase the timing analysis search space due to the number of possible scenarios (cache hit/miss, fast data forward or not, ...).

Concerning processor caches, both precision and efficiency depend on the predictability of the employed *replacement policy* [15, 4]. The Least-Recently-Used (LRU) replacement policy has the best predictability properties. Employing other policies, like Pseudo-LRU (PLRU), or First-In-First-Out (FIFO), or Random, yield less precise WCET bounds because fewer memory accesses can be precisely classified. Furthermore, the efficiency degrades because the analysis has to explore more possibilities. Another deciding factor is the write policy. Typically there are two main options: *write-through* where a store is directly written to the next level in the memory hierarchy, and *write-back* where the data is written into the next hierarchy level if the concrete memory cell is evicted from the cache. Here, the write-back policy is difficult to analyze because due to uncertainties in the cache analysis, the precise occurrence of such a write-back operation is not known, increasing the search space. This complexity multiplies in the presence of multiple cache levels.

Another timing analysis challenge is to model processor external devices which are typically connected with the caches over the system bus. Such devices are memory controllers for static (SRAM, Flash) or dynamic memory (SDRAM, DDR) or controllers for communication (CAN, FlexRay, AFDX). The corresponding bus protocol and memory chip timing have to be modeled precisely.

Individually, each of the above features can be modeled without complexity problems. Only their combination actually could result in a huge number of possible system states during the abstract simulation of a basic block. However, a smart configuration can decrease analysis complexity (cf. Sections 4.2 and 4.3). Then, timing analysis is feasible even for modern and complex processors like the Freescale MPC7448. Other space-reducing approaches like local worst-case considerations cannot be used in general due to the presence of timing anomalies.

Some events in modern architectures are either asynchronous to program execution (e.g., interrupts, DMA) or not predictable in the model (e.g., ECC errors in RAM, hardware exceptions). Their effect on the execution time has to be incorporated externally, i.e., by adding penalties based on the computed WCET and the worst-case occurrence of the events or by statistical means.

4.1   Multi-core Processors

Whereas timing analysis of single-core architectures already is quite challenging, multi-core architectures are even more complex to predict. A multi-core processor is a single computing component with two or more independent cores; it is called *homogeneous* if it includes only identical cores, otherwise it is called *heterogeneous*. Thus, all characteristic challenges from single-cores are still present in the multi-core design, but the multiple cores can run multiple instructions at the same time. Some multi-core processors can be run in *lockstep* mode where all cores execute the same instruction stream in parallel. This typically eliminates interferences between the cores, so from a timing perspective the processor behaves like a single-core.

When the processor is not run in lockstep mode, the inter-core parallelism becomes relevant. To interconnect the several cores, buses, meshes, crossbars, and also dynamically routed communication structures are used. Most multi-core architectures offer a sophisticated memory hierarchy including private L1 caches, but also some shared caches. Access to the interconnect usually requires an arbitration of accesses from the different cores. The shared physical address space requires additional effort in order to guarantee a *coherent* system state: Data resident in the private cache of one core may be invalid since modified data may already exist in the private cache of another core, or data might have already been changed in the main memory. Thus, additional communication between different cores is required. In general, access to a shared resource might cause the following traffic to appear on the processor's interconnect:

A cacheable read access issued by one core

- may cause no communication in case of a cache hit,
- may initiate a read request in case of a cache miss, and
- may initiate a write access first to evict modified data from the cache.

A write access to a cacheable memory area issued by one core

- may cause no traffic in case of a cache hit,
- may cause coherency traffic in case of a cache hit to update directories of other cores,
- may initiate a read access in case of a cache miss, and
- may initiate a write access first to evict modified data from the cache.

Hence, interconnect traffic initiated by one core in order to process an instruction is composed of *data traffic*, *eviction traffic*, and *coherency traffic*.

To summarize, depending on the system configuration a single-core timing analysis is feasible even for modern and complex systems. In general, the complexity arising from the cross-product between processor pipelining features and synchronization overhead between the different cores multiplies the search space of the single-core case and may degrade the observable average case performance (cf. Section 5). When all available performance-enhancing hardware features are freely used the resulting timing bounds would prohibitively overestimate the concrete WCET. This overestimation originates in the combination of execution paths with events that cannot happen in the real execution, but, due to core synchronization uncertainties, cannot be statically excluded from the analysis. However, such systems would also exhibit a significant observable timing variance which makes them unsuitable for hard real-time systems.

The next two sections now give examples for smart system configurations that increase the predictability of WCET bounds on multi-core systems.

4.2 Configuring the MPC5668G

The Freescale MPC5668G is a dual-core processor designed for automotive applications that integrates several automotive features on a single chip, e.g., CAN and FlexRay support. It comprises an e200z6 core and an e200z0 core, which is a stripped-down version of the e200z6. The e200z6 core utilizes a seven-stage pipeline for single-issue in-order execution and retirement of instructions. The z6 core uses an eight entry branch target buffer (BTB) for branch prediction. The BTB entries are updated using the FIFO replacement algorithm. The cache is unified, 32KB large, and 4-way (or 8-way) set-associative.

The MPC5668G offers significant leeway for configuration. To improve predictability we recommend the following:

No unified cache. The cache can be configured as a unified cache, used for storing instructions and data, or as a disjoint cache where instructions and data are separated. Unified caches are more challenging to analyze: If there is a memory access whose address cannot be statically determined the analyzer has to assume that both instruction and data cache are affected, causing a further loss of precision. Hence the cache should be configured s.t. disjoint ways are available for code fetches and data accesses (disjoint cache).

Cache locking. The cache uses a pseudo round-robin replacement algorithm to determine which cache line to evict upon a miss. There is a single replacement counter for all cache sets. This design is prone to high performance variations and can have domino effects [1]. To avoid this, we recommend to lock the cache down to one way for code and one way for data. The locked ways should be filled with frequently accessed data or code. This improves the analysis results.

Disable Branch Target Buffer. The e200z6 core uses a branch target buffer (BTB) for dynamic branch prediction, which is updated using the FIFO replacement policy. As FIFO has domino effects, the BTB should be entirely disabled to make the core more predictable.

No shared SRAM. In general the whole memory is shared among the two cores. However, the hardware allows for some partitioning s.t. conflicts on the internal SRAM memory modules can be avoided. The MPC5668G features two disjoint SRAM memory modules: an 80KB module, and a 512KB module. To avoid any interferences on the internal SRAM, the application software could be designed s.t. one SRAM module only is used by the z0 core, whereas the z6 core solely uses the other SRAM module.

Handle flash prefetch buffers. To reduce access delays on the internal Flash memory, the MPC5668G core implements four prefetch buffers that allow for zero-cycle access delays in case a buffer already contains the requested data. The prefetch buffers are shared between the two processors, and are used for both instruction and data accesses. For predictability reasons, the prefetch buffers should only be enabled for one of the cores, to avoid any interferences. Furthermore, the prefetch buffers should be split up s.t. disjoint buffers are used to satisfy instruction fetches and data accesses. This configuration does not redeem the Flash module of all interferences. An access of any of the cores might still be delayed by an access of the other one (address pipelining).

To get rid of those inferences as well, the code executed by one core should be put into the privately used SRAM module – where applicable.

The above configuration allows for an efficient static WCET analysis that yields results that are quite precise.

4.3   Configuring the MPC8641D

The MPC8641D is a dual-core derivate of the MPC7448, which is a complex single-core architecture employed in the avionics industry. The MPC7448 consists of an e600 core with a complex, eight-level pipeline that allows out-of-order and speculative execution and features first- and second-level caches with PLRU and random replacement. Already as a single-core, this architecture is non-compositional, exhibiting both domino-effects in the pipeline and the caches. The MPC8641D tightly couples two such cores with a single shared bus. Each access, either for the instruction fetches or any data access must pass this one shared resource. Given the non-compositionality of the two cores, any clash on the shared bus during execution could trigger a timing anomaly or even a domino effect. This makes the timing behavior of the entire system very unpredictable, unless interference on the shared bus can be avoided.

The individual cores can be made more predictable by configuration:

L1 Caches. Locking down the first level caches to have a LRU replacement policy and using the write-through policy.

L2 Cache. Completely locking the random replacement second level cache for use as scratchpad memory.

Performance Features. Deactivate non-predictable features like the dynamic branch prediction.

Still the domino-effects which are possible in the complex e600 pipelines are not avoidable. Therefore, to get a predictable multi-core system, clashes on the shared bus need to be avoided. Two features of the *IMA architecture* and the employed cores are very helpful for this goal:

Long Time Slices. The *IMA architecture* features time slices for the individual tasks in the ten milliseconds range. Inside each time slice, the input/output activities, which only make up a fraction of the slice, can be moved to the beginning and the end of the individual time slice to create local copies of the working set. Then the largest remaining fraction of the time slice can be used for lengthy computations on the local copies of the data. This is beneficial compared to the one millisecond time slices typically seen in the automotive domain.

Private L2 Caches. The two cores are supported by private 1MB second level caches. One of the cores can use its cache as local private memory for instructions and data by locking it. This avoids bus accesses by this core during the long computation phases of its tasks. During this time, the other core has interference-free bus access.

Given the above design of the system, in which one core works on its private memory most of the time and only short time slices are needed for bus accesses, a clever scheduling can completely avoid clashes of accesses. Therefore, the normal static timing analysis, which assumes continuous execution without interferences, can be used to deal with each of the cores separately.

4.4 Other Multi-core Architectures

Whereas the processors described above require quite extensive modifications in the hardware configuration there exist multi-core architectures whose off-the-shelf hardware configuration is better suited for static timing analysis. An example of such an embedded architecture is the Freescale MPC5643L, which is designed for applications that require a high level of safety and provides lock-step execution. This processor comprises two e200z4 cores that, contrary to the e200z6, feature a less versatile, dual-issue five-stage in-order execution pipeline. Both cores feature private L1 instruction caches, which use the pseudo-round robin cache replacement policy similar to the unified cache of the MPC5668G.

To enable a static analysis with high precision it is advisable to use the same cache locking approach as described above (see 4.2). The user may also choose to disable the lockstep computation mode and allow the two cores to operate in decoupled parallel mode so that they execute independently from each other. However from the timing predictability point of view the decoupled parallel mode is not advisable, because all internal memories and I/O channels are shared between both cores.

5   Experimental Observations

This section describes an experiment using the MPC8641D processor (cf. Section 4.3) conducted at THALES Research and Technology within the CER-TAINTY research project. It clearly demonstrates the execution time variance of tasks executed on one core induced by parallel activities on the second core.

The experiment is composed of two parts. First, the second core of the processor is disabled by setting the DEVDISR[e600_1] bit to 1. By doing so, the core enters its stop state, in which it does not respond to interrupts. Also instruction

Table 1. Runtime increase of parallel running tasks compared to the isolated runtime.

	bezier	bsort	canny	fdct	mult	ndes	qsort	vecadd	vecsum
bezier	38.8%	-	-	-	-	-	-	-	-
bsort	30.8%	38.1%	-	-	-	-	-	-	-
canny	20.6%	21.2%	21.8%	-	-	-	-	-	-
fdct	39.9%	32.1%	24.8%	55.9%	-	-	-	-	-
mult	30.8%	30.1%	21.9%	28.4%	31.6%	-	-	-	-
ndes	34.6%	30.4%	21.5%	47.8%	27.4%	43.4%	-	-	-
qsort	28.7%	30.0%	20.2%	31.6%	32.8%	30.3%	33.0%	-	-
vecadd	29.7%	33.4%	22.1%	30.7%	32.1%	28.6%	30.4%	33.3%	-
vecsum	28.3%	29.8%	19.5%	26.8%	27.0%	25.6%	28.2%	31.1%	26.7%

fetching is stopped, snooping is disabled, and clocks are shut down to all functional units of the core. Thus, it is guaranteed that the core does not have any influence on shared resources of the processor.

The remaining core is now utilized to execute several benchmark programs (e.g., bezier, ndes, etc.) in isolation and their runtimes are recorded. To guarantee reliability of the measured runtimes, the core is brought to a deterministic starting state before executing a task T_i, and runtime measurement is repeated several times leading to an average isolated runtime for the executed task rt_i.

Afterwards, the second core is re-enabled, and the benchmark programs are duplicated forming benchmark groups B_I and B_{II}. Each task from B_{II} is adjusted to guarantee full spatial isolation from all tasks B_I, i.e., by providing disjoint data and address spaces. The experiment described above is now repeated with the tasks of B_I running on the first core and the tasks of B_{II} running on the second core. Tasks running on both cores are started synchronously. Again, the runtime of the tasks in B_I running on core 1 – where each task is exactly the same as in the first experiment – is measured and the experiment is repeated several times. Then the resulting average runtime rt_{ij} for the task $T_i \in B_I$ when executed in parallel with task $T_j \in B_{II}$ is computed.

Using the runtime rt_i from above, i.e., the runtime of task T_i running in isolation on core 1, and the runtime rt_{ij} of task $T_i \in B_I$ when executed in parallel with task $T_j \in B_{II}$, the percentage of deviation is formed by

$$\Delta_{ij} = \left(\frac{rt_{ij}}{rt_i} - 1 \right) * 100.$$

The results are given in Table 1. Tasks from the first benchmark group B_I are listed in rows, tasks from the second group B_{II} are given in columns. Compared to the isolated runtime of the tasks, an average runtime increase of 30% is observed. The largest increase of 56% was observed when running one instance of task fdct on each core.

Even though an increase in execution time was to be expected, an increase by 56% is surprisingly high. Note that there was full spatial isolation between all tasks executed in parallel. Each task was started with a deterministic hardware state. The MPC8641D has two DDR controllers, and L1/L2 caches are fully private to each core. Data and address space of the concurrently executed tasks are separated. Hence, the observed increase in runtime was mostly caused by bus conflicts on the MPX bus and can be considered an ideal-case scenario.

Furthermore, note that the experiment considers the average task execution times, not the WCETs. Obviously the gap between the isolated WCET bound $wcet_i$ and the concurrent WCET bound $wcet_{ij}$ will be greater or equal to the gap Δ_{ij} described above.

If additional conflicts could occur, e.g., due to accesses to shared caches or DDR controllers, by variations of the hardware start state, or by asynchronous execution, not only the penalty Δ_{ij} would be much higher. Also the overestimation of the WCET analysis induced by uncertainties will be higher.

The experimental observation clearly shows that both minimizing accesses to shared resources and using deterministic arbitration mechanisms are essential for guaranteeing safe and precise bounds on the execution time of tasks within multi-core environments.

The results are not specific for the MPC8641D processor, but illustrate the potential performance impact of interferences due to shared resources. In [18] similar results have been reported for the Intel SCC and the Texas Instruments TMS320-C6678 processors.

6   Design for Predictability

Whereas the preceding sections mostly dealt with existing multi-core architectures, here we will summarize how to assess predictability and list criteria for predictable multi-core designs.

Most of the challenges of static timing analysis for multi-core architectures are caused by the *interference on shared resources*. Resources are shared for cost, energy, and communication reasons. Even if the sharing of a resource only slightly increases the concrete execution times of a task, it might be difficult for a static analysis to prove this: If a resource is shared among several (resource-)users, their accesses to this resource may be interleaved in a huge amount of ways, in particular if the users are not tightly synchronized. Different access sequences may result in different states of the shared resource. In addition to the different interleaved access sequences that may already exhibit different execution times, the resulting resource states may cause even more differences in the future timing behavior. This behavior is not a technical limitation of the static analysis approach. Also dynamic measurement-based approaches would be difficult to apply because of the high observable variance in execution time.

It is an open problem how to limit the information loss about concurrently running tasks by suitable abstractions. Hence, limiting interferences must be a high-priority design goal. If there can be no interferences *at all* in the concrete system, it is easy for an analysis to exclude interferences even when abstracting completely from other tasks. One obvious solution for multi-core processors is to run them in *lockstep* mode – however, this means that the potential parallelism of the processor is not exploited. To avoid this, it is essential to strive for a good compromise between cost, performance, and predictability, *concerning the sharing or duplication of resources.*

6.1   Design Principles

The PROMPT (PRedictability Of Multi-Processor Timing) design principles [4] aim at embedded hard real-time systems in the avionics and automotive industry requiring *efficiently predictable good worst-case performance.*

Often, the inherent amount of sharing within the set of applications is very small. This makes it possible to design a target architecture with little interference on shared resources and thus little variance of execution times and high predictability. According to the PROMPT principles the architecture is designed in a multi-phase process. It starts with the design or the selection of the cores that exhibit good predictability. Then the set of applications is considered:

- *Hierarchical privatization* decomposes the set of applications according to their sharing characteristics on the shared global state. The resulting partitioning of the set of applications can be used to define an isomorphically structured target architecture with no more shared resources than required by the set of applications.
- *Sharing of lonely resources* introduces sharing of costly and infrequently accessed resources. Input/output devices will most likely have to be shared, for cost and space reasons.
- *Controlled socialization* tries to satisfy cost constraints with an acceptable loss of predictability by the introduction of sharing.

We conjecture that without this or a similar design discipline the required modular development process will not be realizable without an unacceptable loss of guaranteed performance. The improved precision of the execution-time bounds will increase the chance to show the satisfaction of timing requirements, and thereby avoid the need of over-commissioning and save resources.

6.2   Design Guidelines

In the following we will summarize some important recommendations for obtaining predictable multi-core architectures for hard real-time systems. The first three guidelines aim at the predictability of a single core, whereas the remaining guidelines discuss the predictability of the overall system.

1. *A fully timing compositional architecture*: Since an exhaustive enumeration of architectural states is practically infeasible an abstract hardware model of the analyzed architecture has to be used in static timing analysis. Timing anomalies in combination with interferences on shared resources introduce a high computational complexity and lead to imprecise WCET bounds. Ideally an architecture without any timing anomalies – a so-called fully timing-compositional architecture – is used.
2. *Disjoint instruction and data caches*: When unified instruction and data caches are used, in case of uncertainty about the address of a memory access or about the order between a data and an instruction cache access the interferences between data and instruction accesses impairs the precision and additionally leads to an inefficient analysis. Therefore, if possible, the hardware should be configured for disjoint instruction and data caches.
3. *Caches with LRU replacement policy*: Employing replacement strategies like FIFO or PLRU yields less precise WCET bounds and less efficient timing analysis than when using LRU. Employing such strategies even introduces domino effects. The recommended cache replacement strategy is LRU.
4. *A shared bus protocol with bounded access delay*: An unbounded access delay leads to a potentially unbounded execution time of tasks that access the shared resource. Guaranteeing the timing constraints is only possible for bounded access delays.
5. *Private caches*: The uncertainty about cache contents of shared caches impairs the precision and leads to a complexity explosion of the analysis. Each core should have separate, private caches.

6. *Private memories*, or, *only share lonely resources*: The delay to access a shared resource depends on the utilization of the resource. Too much sharing may lead to a system that is not schedulable. Ideally each core should have a private memory.

7 Conclusion

Ensuring the correct timing behavior of real-time systems is an essential part of overall system correctness. Static analyzers based on Abstract Interpretation provide safe upper bounds for the WCET of tasks. From these bounds response time guarantees can be computed by schedulability analysis at the system level. Abstract Interpretation based static analyzers can be considered as the state of the art for WCET analysis and are recommended by all current safety standards. Especially on multi-core architectures for safety-critical real-time systems the hardware has to be carefully examined with respect to predictable performance and has to be appropriately configured to avoid timing and stability problems. The most important aspect is to eliminate interferences induced by shared resources. In this paper we have given an overview of WCET analysis by Abstract Interpretation and discussed the perspective of the current safety standards. We have analyzed the relevant features of contemporary single-core and multi-core processors with respect to predictability and examined the timing variance of a typical multi-core processor. Configuration and design recommendations are presented to enable predictable performance.

Acknowledgements. The work presented in this paper has been supported by the European FP7 projects PREDATOR and CERTAINTY, and by the ARTEMIS-JU project MBAT. The authors would like to thank THALES Research and Technology for permitting use of the benchmark results within CERTAINTY.

References

[1] Berg, C.: PLRU Cache Domino Effects. In: Proceedings of the International Workshop on Worst-Case Execution Time Analysis, WCET (2006)

[2] CENELEC DRAFT prEN 50128. Railway applications – Communication, signalling and processing systems – Software for railway control and protection systems (2009)

[3] Cousot, P., Cousot, R.: Abstract Interpretation: A Unified Lattice Model for Static Analysis of Programs by Construction or Approximation of Fixpoints. In: Proceedings of the 4th ACM Symposium on Principles of Programming Languages, pp. 238–252 (1977)

[4] Cullmann, C., Ferdinand, C., Gebhard, G., Grund, D., Maiza, C., Reineke, J., Triquet, B., Wilhelm, R.: Predictability Considerations in the Design of Multi-Core Embedded Systems. In: Proceedings of Embedded Real Time Software and Systems, pp. 36–42 (May 2010)

[5] Ermedahl, A.: A Modular Tool Architecture for Worst-Case Execution Time Analysis. PhD thesis, Uppsala University (2003)

[6] Ferdinand, C., Heckmann, R., Langenbach, M., Martin, F., Schmidt, M., Theiling, H., Thesing, S., Wilhelm, R.: Reliable and Precise WCET Determination for a Real-Life Processor. In: Henzinger, T.A., Kirsch, C.M. (eds.) EMSOFT 2001. LNCS, vol. 2211, pp. 469–485. Springer, Heidelberg (2001)

[7] Ferdinand, C., Wilhelm, R.: Fast and Efficient Cache Behavior Prediction for Real-Time Systems. Real-Time Systems 17(2-3), 131–181 (1999)

[8] Henia, R., Hamann, A., Jersak, M., Racu, R., Richter, K., Ernst, R.: System Level Performance Analysis – the SymTA/S Approach. IEEE Proceedings on Computers and Digital Techniques 152(2) (March 2005)

[9] IEC 61508. Functional safety of electrical/electronic/programmable electronic safety-related systems (2010)

[10] ISO/FDIS 26262. Road vehicles – Functional safety (2011)

[11] Kästner, D., Ferdinand, C., Heckmann, R., Jersak, M., Gliwa, P.: An Integrated Timing Analysis Methodology for Real-Time Systems. In: Embedded World Congress (2011)

[12] Lundqvist, T., Stenström, P.: Timing Anomalies in Dynamically Scheduled Microprocessors. In: Real-Time Systems Symposium, RTSS (December 1999)

[13] NASA Engineering and Safety Center. Technical Support to the National Highway Traffic Safety Administration (NHTSA) on the Reported Toyota Motor Corporation (TMC) Unintended Acceleration (UA) Investigation (2011)

[14] Radio Technical Commission for Aeronautics. RTCA DO-178B. Software Considerations in Airborne Systems and Equipment Certification

[15] Reineke, J., Grund, D., Berg, C., Wilhelm, R.: Timing Predictability of Cache Replacement Policies. Real-Time Systems 37(2), 99–122 (2007)

[16] Reineke, J., Wachter, B., Thesing, S., Wilhelm, R., Polian, I., Eisinger, J., Becker, B.: A Definition and Classification of Timing Anomalies. In: Proceedings of the International Workshop on Worst-Case Execution Time Analysis (2006)

[17] Souyris, J., Le Pavec, E., Himbert, G., Jégu, V., Borios, G., Heckmann, R.: Computing the Worst Case Execution Time of an Avionics Program by Abstract Interpretation. In: Proceedings of the 5th Intl Workshop on Worst-Case Execution Time (WCET) Analysis, pp. 21–24 (2005)

[18] Verhulst, E., Sputh, B.: Hard Real-Time on Multicores: Shared Resources are the Challenge. White paper, Altreonic (2012)

[19] Wilhelm, R., Engblom, J., Ermedahl, A., Holsti, N., Thesing, S., Whalley, D., Bernat, G., Ferdinand, C., Heckmann, R., Mitra, T., Mueller, F., Puaut, I., Puschner, P., Staschulat, J., Stenström, P.: The Worst-Case Execution-Time Problem – Overview of Methods and Survey of Tools. ACM Transactions on Embedded Computing Systems 7(3), 1–53 (2008)

Assessing Software Interference Management When Modifying Safety-Related Software

Patrick J. Graydon and Tim P. Kelly

University of York, York, YO10 5GH, UK
{patrick.graydon,tim.kelly}@cs.york.ac.uk

Abstract. Many systems deliberately manage interference between software components, e.g. through partitioning. When engineers modifying such software determine which items of verification evidence have been invalidated by changes, they consider interference management measures. A complete understanding of interference and its management is crucial when engineers re-use evidence. In prior work, we suggested: (a) a guided process for identifying interference and means of managing it; and (b) a strategy for arguing about interference management. In this paper, we present the results of a case study meant to answer two questions raised by this prior work: (i) which views of the system engineers should consider when identifying interference and its management; and (ii) whether our argument pattern captures a practical way to argue about interference management.

Keywords: software partitioning, interference, software change management, safety argument.

1 Introduction

Many software systems deliberately manage *interference* between software components. For example, many operating systems provide spatial partitioning based on hardware memory management. When modifying software, engineers assess change impact and decide what evidence to regenerate. *Complete* understanding of interference and how well it is managed is essential for making these choices.

Interference is typically assessed using ad hoc means. In some cases, engineers use standardised partitioning schemes or refer to lists of considerations derived from experience. A systematic method of assessing interference and its management would both provide more rigour than ad hoc means and be better suited to systems built on novel architectures. In prior work, we suggested such a method and proposed patterns for arguing about interference management [8]. In this paper, we present the results of a case study intended to drive further refinement of the approach with a view toward eventual evaluation of its efficacy relative to existing approaches.

In prior work, we suggested that analysts assessing interference systematically consider the system from multiple views [8]. For completeness, we proposed using each of the four views in a standard architectural model: (1) a *conceptual*

F. Ortmeier and P. Daniel (Eds.): SAFECOMP 2012 Workshops, LNCS 7613, pp. 132–145, 2012.
© Springer-Verlag Berlin Heidelberg 2012

view describing software in terms of domain elements; (2) a *module view* that describes the decomposition of the software; (3) an *execution view* that maps modules to physical resources; and a (4) *code view* that maps modules, interfaces, and run-time images to source and executable files [10,11]. That work raised questions of whether each of the four views is necessary, whether use of all four is sufficient, and whether other standard views would be more useful. In this work, we conducted a case study application of our method to a hypothesised embedded control system to answer the first two of these questions.

In prior work, we proposed a pattern for arguing about how well a system manages interference [8]. In that pattern, analysts decompose the goal of adequate management over *forms* of interference. They then decompose goals of adequately managing each form of interference over *circumstances* in which the system manages interference differently. In this work, we investigated whether applying this pattern to our specimen system would result in a combinatorial explosion that would make the argument impractical.

In section 2, we discuss guidance and practice for software modification and interference management assessment. In section 3, we present a model of interference and its management. In section 4, we relate our method for identifying interference and interference management. In section 5, we present our pattern for arguing about how well systems manage interference. In section 6, we report the results of our case study assessment. Finally, we conclude in section 7.

2   Current Guidance and Practice

Modifications to existing software are frequently limited to a few modules. It is expensive to repeat testing, review, and analyses for portions of the system not impacted by the changes. Consequently, typical software safety standards do not require this [12,14,19]. Instead, engineers must analyse the impact of the proposed changes and plan verification and validation activities accordingly.

The effects of change can spread beyond the modified modules. For example, modifying one component could affect the data that it passes to an unmodified component, changing that component's behaviour. Some standards explicitly recognise this. For example, RTCA DO-178B advises engineers analysing the impact of change to consider "coupling between several software components that may result in reverification effort involving more than the modified area" [19].

Typical software safety standards do not define how change impact analysis should consider interference management. However, the planned changes might affect the interference that software generates, its reaction to received interference, or both. Clearly, engineers performing change impact assessment must understand how a system manages interference and how well it does so.

2.1   Current Approaches to Assessing Interference Management

Current guidance for assessing interference and its management is limited. Some standards list considerations [12,14,19]. For example [19]:

These aspects of the system should be considered when designing partitioning protection to determine their potential for violating that protection:

(1) Hardware resources: processors, memory devices, I/O devices, interrupts, and timers.
(2) Control coupling: vulnerability to external access.
(3) Data coupling: shared or overlaying data, including stacks and processor registers.
(4) Failure modes of hardware devices associated with the protection mechanisms.

However, RTCA DO-178B offers no guidance on how to carry out a conforming assessment [6,19]. It requires review and/or analysis of the software architecture to "ensure that partitioning breaches are prevented" and testing that could reveal "violations of software partitioning" [19]. However, the standard offers no guidance on how to perform these activities well enough to justify reverification decisions. Other standards offer similarly little guidance [12,14].

Recognising this lack, the Certification Authorities Software Team (CAST) has developed guidelines for assessing software partitioning schemes [6]. The CAST guidance, drawing from Rushby's work [20], advises developers to "first categorize the type of protection being claimed" and then demonstrate that it has been provided. Its guidance on how to accomplish this is limited to a list of considerations that it cautions "is not intended to be all inclusive".

Existing guidance is undoubtedly helpful. However, it is not a complete, general-purpose approach to assessing what interference a system might be subject to and how well it manages this. Lists of considerations capture insight gained through experience. However, experience alone is not an adequate basis for evaluating novel systems. For example, some modern multicore microprocessors can scale clock rates in response to changing temperatures. This mechanism gives rise to a form of interference wherein the workload of one core affects the clock rate of adjacent core(s) and thus the runtime of the software they execute [7]. The CAST guidance, predating this feature, cannot counsel consideration of it. A general method is needed.

2.2 Standards for Partitioning

There are standards describing partitioning schemes. For example, ARINC 653 defines a partitioning scheme for integrated avionics applications [3]. In it, a single processor or processor core may host multiple partitions, each isolated from the others in both time and space. That is, partitions cannot overwrite each other's memory and are guaranteed a portion of execution time. Each partition can, if needed, run a guest operating system to sequence multiple tasks.

ARINC 653 partitioning is robust but coarse-grained. Whilst it is desirable to isolate applications sharing a processor from each other, it is also desirable to protect smaller pieces of each application from other small pieces. Thus, the existence of ARINC 653 and compatible operating systems does not obviate the need for a general-purpose method for assessing interference management.

3   A Model of Interference and Its Management

In this work, we model software as a set of *elements* and consider how these might interfere with each other. An element might be a procedure, a module, a task, a process, a complete binary, or all of the software running on one processor core. When analysing interference, analysts should define elements that identify the parts of the software to be reasoned about. We adopt the definition of interference proposed by the UK Civil Aviation Authority and used in prior work [5,8]:

> **Interference** — Unintended (and thus undesigned) interaction between elements of a software system.

Interference might be either *spatial* or *temporal*. Spatial interference occurs when an element writes to storage it should not write to. For example, if an uninitialised pointer points to another element's private memory, writing to it results in spatial interference. For completeness, 'storage' includes microprocessor registers, peripheral registers, flash devices, hard disk drives, and any other components that store state. Temporal interference occurs when one element's activities have an unintended impact on the timing of another's. For example, elements running on different cores of the same processor might create temporal interference through contention for shared memory devices.

Potential interference might be managed in three ways:

1. **Prevention.** Prevention precludes interference from arising during operation or shows that it does not. For example, static analysis can show that procedures written in SPARK use no access types (i.e., pointers) and assign values only to shared variables named in the procedure specification [1].
2. **Blocking.** Blocking prevents one element's interference from reaching another. For example, hardware memory management can prevent an element's stray write operations from affecting the private memory of other elements.
3. **Tolerance.** Tolerance allows elements to function acceptably despite interference. For example, elements can use checksums or canary values to detect interference and trigger remedial action.

Most means of interference management are imperfect. Consequently, it is useful to combine forms of management so that each compensates for the others' weaknesses. For example, consider the two processes communicating using shared memory depicted in Figure 1. Static analysis might verify that element 5 cannot interfere with elements 1–4, but cannot show that element 2 is similarly well-behaved. Hardware memory management might block interference between elements 1 and 4. However, memory management at the process level cannot block interference between elements 4 and 5 (or elements 5 and 3). Interference between elements 2 and 3 (in the form of writes to Value i or Value ii) cannot be blocked. Testing of element 2 might justify a claim of prevention, but only if it is

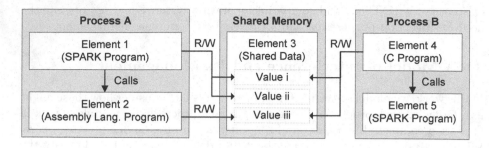

Fig. 1. Example elements

adequately rigorous and conducted in a way that would detect spurious writes. Moreover, a single event upset might still result in a write that is not predicted by testing. Accordingly, it is useful to tolerate interference to element 3.

When modifying software, engineers must reason about how well a combination of mechanisms manages interference. Simply reasoning about partitioning at one (coarse) level is not sufficient. Existing guidance typically comprises reminders to consider aspects of interference management that have proved important in the past. It is advisable to learn from the past. However, it is also important to have a general method for assessing interference management in any system, no matter how novel.

4   A Method for Identifying Interference and How a System Manages It

In this section, we present a refined version of the method introduced in prior work [8]. Our method is based on the guided enumeration techniques used in software and system safety analyses, e.g. Hazard and Operability Studies (HAZOP) [13,21], Software Hazard Analysis and Resolution in Design (SHARD) [18], and Low-level Interaction Safety Analysis (LISA) [16,18]. Figure 2 depicts the method, which comprises the ten steps detailed below.

Identify Views. The analysts select views from which to analyse the system. It is necessary to consider multiple views because interference visible in one view may not be obscured in others. Engineering documents describe systems from diverse viewpoints using different notations. For example, some developers produce Unified Modelling Language (UML) diagrams [17]. Others use the Modular Approach to Software Construction Operation and Test (MASCOT) [15]. In yet other projects, architects describe the system using the Architecture Analysis and Design Language (AADL) [2]. In prior work, we proposed considering four standard architectural views: conceptual, modular, execution, and code [10,11].

Select Team. The analysis team must include experienced people who understand the system from each identified viewpoint. Their knowledge of the system

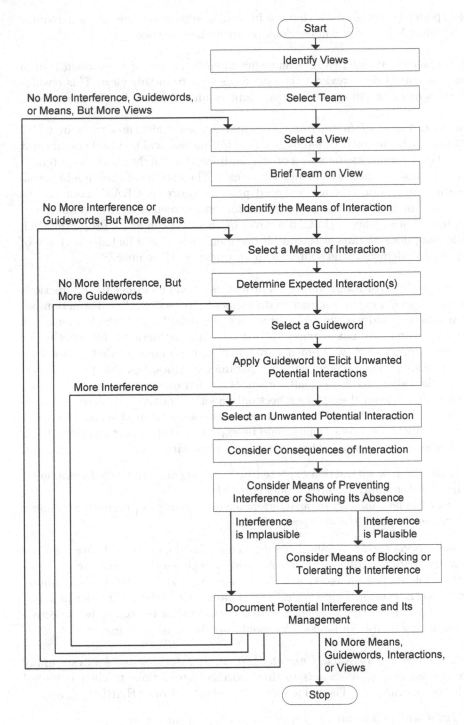

Fig. 2. Method for identifying potential interference and means of managing it

and experience assessing interference in similar systems is crucial, as it reduces the likelihood that they will overlook potential interference.

Brief Team on View. Before attempting identify means of interaction from a view, the team briefly reviews the system as seen from this view. This ensures that each member can draw upon as complete an understanding as practicable.

Identify a Means of Interaction. The analysis team identifies ways in which elements might interact. Different means of interaction will be visible in different views. For example, examination of the modular view might show the potential for interaction by messages or procedure call. The execution view might reveal potential interaction through a shared processor core or DRAM module. The code view might illustrate the potential for one element's source to affect the compilation of another's. (In C, directives in .h file(s) can affect properties such as the compiler's alignment setting. If one element's source includes a .h file of another, the elements might interact in an unexpected manner [8].)

Determine Expected Interaction(s). The analysis team identifies the interactions that are expected over each identified means of interaction. The distinction between expected and unexpected interactions is crucial because the former is not interference and need not be pursued. However, the distinction is also subtle. For example, suppose that two elements are meant to communicate via function call, that there are no documented limits on parameter values, and that previous versions of the caller exercise a small portion of the parameter value space. Testing, analysis, and historical evidence reflect only a subset of these element's possible function call interactions. When interference assessment is used in change impact analysis, only those interactions should be expected. If the caller is modified and might pass unprecedented values, developers must either:

- *Make* the new interaction expected by verifying that the called component handles the unprecedented inputs correctly
- Treat the new interaction as interference and manage it, perhaps by using a wrapper to block the unexpected inputs

Interactions via caches are another subtle case. Developers of real-time software are aware that executing one element could change another's runtime by altering the contents of a shared cache. However, typical approaches to determining Worst-Case Execution Time (WCET) treat each task as though it will run in isolation. Thus, interaction through a shared cache cannot be said to be expected. If there is any doubt, an interaction should not be considered expected.

Apply Guidewords to Elicit Unwanted Potential Interactions. Analysts apply each of a set of five *guidewords* to the identified interactions to elicit potential unwanted interactions. The guidewords, are adapted from SHARD [18], are:

1. **Omission** — The interaction does not occur as intended
2. **Commission** — The interaction occurs when it is not intended

3. **Early** — The interaction occurs before it is intended to
4. **Late** — The interaction occurs after it is intended to
5. **Value** — The content of the interaction is not what was intended

The concrete meaning of each guideword will depend upon the type of interaction that it is applied to. For example, when applied to a function call, *value* refers to the parameter values. In contrast, when applied to interaction through a shared cache, *value* refers to the data blocks that are loaded or evicted. Some guidewords might be inapplicable to some types of interaction.

Consider the Consequences of Interference. If an interaction might occur but is not expected, that interaction is potential interference. The risks that interference might give rise to define the importance of managing that interference.

There are several approaches to risk assessment. If a project must conform to a standard that defines an approach, the analyst should use that approach. If not, analysts can perform a basic risk assessment by estimating the probability and severity of risks arising from interference and characterising each form of interference according to the highest risk that *might* result if the interference arises. For example, consider the case of element *A* unexpectedly writing to element *B*'s private memory. Suppose that *B* could give rise to a system hazard by failing to operate as intended. Depending upon events beyond the system's control, it is judged `probable` that this would lead to a `catastrophic` loss. System safety concerns dictate that *B*'s functionality must be assured to a degree of confidence appropriate for this risk. Because this form of interference brings this hazard as a consequence, managing it is of proportionately high importance.

Consider Means of Preventing Interference or Showing Its Absence. For each form of potential interference, analysts consider both means of preventing interference and means of showing its absence. For example, consider interference in the form of writes to private memory. Some efforts might preclude this form of interference by selecting a programming language subset that does not include pointers. Alternatively or in combination, testing (in an appropriate manner) might yield confidence that the tested code does not perform such writes.

Consider Means of Blocking or Tolerating the Interference. Where interference has not been prevented or cannot be shown to be absent, analysts consider means of blocking or tolerating that interference. For example, flushing shared caches during a task switch can block temporal interference arising from cache contention in uniprocessors. Interference might be detected by computing and checking an error-correcting code, prompting the system to take remedial action.

Document Potential Interference and Its Management. Finally, the analysts document each form of potential interference and how the system manages it. At a minimum, they record:

- A description of the form of interference
- The consequences of the interference
- How the interference is prevented, shown to be absent, blocked, or tolerated

Using Experience and Standard Lists. Our method does not replace either experience with similar systems or the use of standard lists of considerations. Where possible, analysts should consider these sources of insight.

5 Reasoning about Interference Management

In prior work, we proposed a pattern for reasoning about how well a system manages interference [8]. Figure 3 presents an elaboration of this pattern depicted in Goal Structuring Notation (GSN) [4]. Goal G1 depicts the main claim that the system adequately manages interference. The argument decomposes this claim over forms of interference (strategy ST1 and context C2), yielding several sub-claims of the form of goal G2. The argument further decomposes those sub-claims over means of management (strategy ST3). This further decomposition yields one to four sub-claims of the form(s) of goals G4, G5, G6, and/or G7. Evidence of prevention, absence, blocking, or toleration supports each sub-claim.

In some cases, means of managing interference apply only in different but overlapping circumstances. Returning to the example developed in section 3, writes to undefined addresses might be prevented in a subset of the code, blocked between elements in different processes, or tolerated when they impact a shared memory block. In such cases, the argument must decompose claims over the circumstances in which each combination of means applies (strategy ST2). This form of argument makes clear to readers those circumstances that are covered by multiple means of management and those that aren't.

6 A Case Study to Answer Questions from Prior Work

This work does not assess the value of our as-yet incomplete method. Because there is no baseline data on how completely existing ad hoc methods enumerate interference, comparing our method to these would require a head-to-head experiment. A control group would use their existing methods whilst a treatment group would use ours, and the experimenters would assess the completeness of the results. Since experience might affect the outcome, the participants would have to be seasoned professional developers. Application and architecture novelty might also affect the outcome, so the experiment would have to be replicated.

Our case study aims instead to answer three questions raised by the prior work in which we proposed the method and argument pattern [8]:

1. Does consideration of each of the four of the views discussed in section 4 produce insight that consideration of the others does not?
2. Are there insights not produced by consideration of the four views?
3. Is it practical to divide interference and its management into "forms" and "circumstances", or are there too many permutations for this to be feasible?

We expect that the answers to these questions will drive further development of the method. Once complete, the method can be subject to a rigorous evaluation of its efficacy and value.

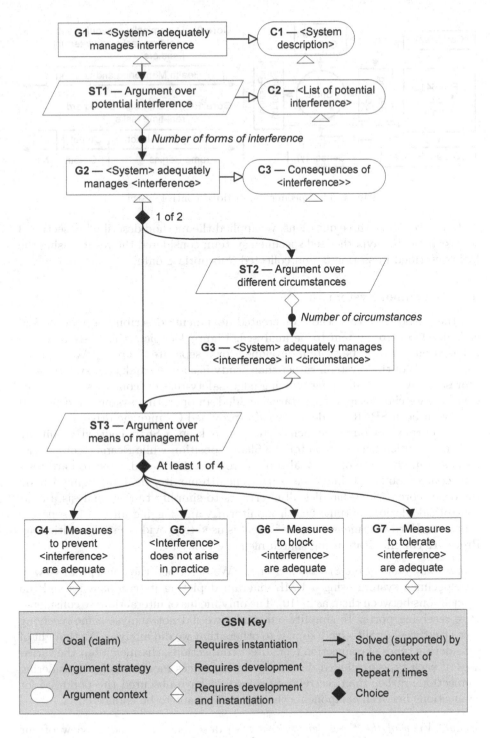

Fig. 3. Top-level non-interference argument pattern

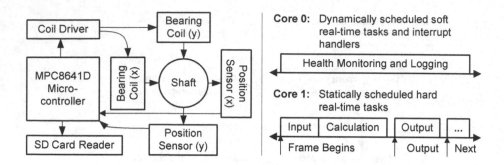

Fig. 4. The specimen embedded control system

To answer these three questions, we applied the method described in section 4 to a realistic but hypothesised specimen system, considered the results using the logic described in section 5, and collected appropriate data.

6.1   Specimen System

For the purposes of this study, we created documents describing a hypothetical embedded control system to be analysed. Figure 4 depicts this system, which is based on a prototype system developed for a separate study [9]. We changed some details of that system, rather than study it as-is, to make the system more representative of challenging, cutting-edge safety-related control systems. For example, we chose a multi-core target, added an operating system, and posited the use of both SPARK code and vendor-provided C language drivers.

The purpose of our specimen system is to keep a Shaft centred within its housing. Position Sensors monitor the Shaft's position while Bearing Coils adjust its position. One core of the dual-core microcontroller is dedicated to hard real-time control. Soft real-time tasks, such as health monitoring and logging, run on the other core. Core 0 handles all interrupts to simplify timing analysis. Input, control calculation, output, health monitoring, and logging all run in separate processes. Hardware memory management is used to provide spatial partitioning. Processes communicate using shared memory blocks.

Conceptual View of the Specimen System. We described the conceptual view of our specimen system using a UML diagram depicting its components and the connections between them as in [10]. The only means of interaction we considered were receiving ports. To simplify our study, we did not analyse some receiving ports that were qualitatively similar to others that we did analyse. We thought of considering types of connection (e.g. direct connections, channels), but the varied uses of each type precluded discussing consequences meaningfully. Considering connections rather than receiving ports would have obscured the potential for connections between components that are not meant to be connected.

Module View of the Specimen System. We described the module view of our specimen system using: (1) a UML package diagram showing the mapping from modules to packages; (2) a UML class diagram showing the mapping from implementation classes to modules; and (3) a UML class diagram showing the static relationship between implementation classes. We analysed only one module, a sensor input module comprising vendor-sourced C-language code and application-specific SPARK code. The means of interaction that we considered were: (a) modification of class attributes; and (b) method invocations.

Execution View of the Specimen System. We described the execution view of our specimen system using a UML class diagram to map modules to processes and a timing diagram. The means of interaction that we considered were: (a) accesses to a process's private memory; (b) accesses to a shared memory area; (c) system calls; and (d) competition for CPU time. We omitted consideration of access to some processes' private memory and some shared memory areas because these were similar to others that we did analyse.

Code View of the Specimen System. We described the code view of our specimen system using tables to map classes to source files and document source file dependencies. The means of interaction that we considered were: (a) source inclusion (e.g. #include in C); and (b) build procedure steps.

6.2   Study Results

Applying the method described in section 4 to the specimen system described in subsection 6.1, we identified 71 unwanted potential interactions. Organising these into forms of interaction in order to apply the pattern shown in Figure 3 yielded 19 distinct forms of interference. Identifying circumstances in which each form is managed differently yielded 39 distinct permutations of form and circumstance.

Question 1 (necessity of each view). Of the four architectural views that we used in analysis, only the conceptual view failed to illuminate interference in this system. While the view informed our understanding of the system, examining interactions revealed by the view did not help us to find interference that we could not have found using other views. Moreover, the other views better illuminated circumstances and means of management. For example, it was more obvious from the module viewpoint than from the conceptual viewpoint that some components comprise classes implemented in multiple languages, each of which was associated with different interference prevention measures.

The SHARD technique uses a view similar to our conceptual view [18]. SHARD has been useful as a means of gaining understanding of software hazards early in the development lifecycle so that they can be addressed by design [18]. However, in software modification scenarios, a detailed design already exists; there is no need to trade detail for early feedback. Consequently, effort might be better spent analysing more detailed views.

Question 2 (sufficiency of views). In prior work, we considered a different hypothesised system from a perspective that included low-level hardware details such as general purpose registers, special-purpose registers, buses, caches, and memory modules [8]. That perspective was identical to the perspective used in LISA [16,18]. Using that low-level hardware view, we identified forms of interference that we did not identify in this effort, such as competition for shared memory units [8]. Unfortunately, an execution view of a software architecture might not contain the necessary low-level detail. We conclude that a low-level hardware view, such as that used in LISA, should be used when assessing interference and its management in software modification scenarios.

Question 3 (practicality of argument pattern). We did not create multiple forms of non-interference argument for our specimen system. Thus, we cannot comment on whether such an argument would be more compact if organised as shown in Figure 3 than if organised in some alternative way. However, we can report that no form of interference that we identified was managed differently in more than 11 different circumstances. Interference in the form of unintended writes to shared memory areas was managed by 11 combinations of memory management, dataflow analysis, use of redundant sensors, or re-use of the last frame's control outputs. The remaining 18 of 19 forms were managed differently in 3 or fewer different circumstances. The size of this argument is not unreasonable.

7   Conclusion

In prior work, we proposed both a method for identifying interference and how systems manage it and a pattern for arguing about that interference [8]. That work raised questions about which architectural views analysts should consider and the practicability of the proposed argument pattern. In this work, we conducted a case study to address these questions. Our findings suggest that analysis of software using a conceptual view, while useful during initial system design, might be less useful when analysing interference in software change scenarios. We also find that analysis from the conceptual, module, execution, and code architectural views might be insufficient: detailed analysis from a view including low-level hardware details is needed. Finally, we find no evidence that a combinatorial explosion in interference circumstances would make it impractical to argue about our specimen system using the pattern shown in Figure 3.

This work does not present a complete method for assessing and reasoning about interference in software modification scenarios. Instead, it describes a work in progress. The study results, gained from analysis of a single hypothesised system, cannot show that our method and pattern are valuable or even feasible for all systems. Instead, they are a contribution toward refining our method and constructing a complete and compelling approach to assuring modified software systems. Further work will be needed to assess a complete method and approach.

Acknowledgement. We thank the CAA for collaboration that produced the ideas refined in this paper.

References

1. AdaCore: Spark pro > language & toolsuite. Web page (October 2011),
   http://www.adacore.com/home/products/sparkpro/language_toolsuite/
2. AADL | getting started. Web page (2011),
   http://www.aadl.info/aadl/currentsite/start/index.html
3. ARINC 653P1-3: Avionics application software standard interface, Part 1, Required services. Specification, ARINC (November 2010)
4. Attwood, K., et al.: GSN Community Standard v. 1. Origin Consulting (2011),
   http://www.goalstructuringnotation.info/documents/GSN_Standard.pdf
5. CAP 670: Air Traffic Services Safety Requirements. Civil Aviation Authority, West Sussex, United Kingdom (October 2010), http://www.caa.co.uk
6. Certification Authorities Software Team (CAST): Guidelines for assessing software partitioning/protection schemes. Position Paper CAST-2 (February 2001)
7. Charles, J., Jassi, P., Ananth, N.S., Sadat, A., Fedorova, A.: Evaluation of the Intel® Core™ i7 Turbo Boost feature. In: Proceedings of the International Symposium on Workload Characterization (IISWC), pp. 188–197 (October 2009)
8. Graydon, P.: Classifying, analysing, and arguing about barriers in modified software systems. Technical Report SSEI-TR-000107, Software Systems Engineering Initiative (May 2011)
9. Graydon, P.J., Knight, J.C., Yin, X.: Practical Limits on Software Dependability: A Case Study. In: Real, J., Vardanega, T. (eds.) Ada-Europe 2010. LNCS, vol. 6106, pp. 83–96. Springer, Heidelberg (2010)
10. Hofmeister, C., Nord, R.L., Soni, D.: Describing software architecture with UML. In: Proceedings of the 1st Working IFIP Conference on Software Architecture (1999)
11. Hofmeister, C., Nord, R., Soni, D.: Applied Software Architecture. Addison-Wesley, Reading (1999)
12. IEC 61508-3: Functional safety of electrical/electronic/programmable electronic safety-related systems — Part 3: Software requirements. International Electrotechnical Commission, 2nd edn. (April 2010)
13. IEC 61882: Hazard and operability studies (HAZOP studies) — Application guide. International Electrotechnical Commission, 1st edn. (May 2001)
14. ISO 26262-6:2011: Road vehicles — Functional safety — Part 6: Product development at the software level. International Organization for Standardization (2011)
15. Joint IECCA and MUF Committee on Mascot (JIMCOM): The Official Handbook of Mascot, Version 3.1, Issue 1. Royal Signals and Radar Establishment, UK (1987)
16. McDermid, J.A., Pumfrey, D.J.: Safety analysis of hardware/software interactions in complex systems. In: Proceedings of the 16th International System Safety Conference, Seattle, WA, pp. 231–241 (1998)
17. OMG: OMG Unified Modeling Language™ (OMG UML): Infrastructure, Version 2.3. Object Management Group (May 2010)
18. Pumfrey, D.J.: The Principled Design of Computer System Safety Analyses. DPhil thesis, University of York, York, UK (September 1999)
19. RTCA DO-178B: Software Considerations in Airborne Systems and Equipment Certification. RTCA, Inc., Washington, DC, USA (December 1992)
20. Rushby, J.: Partitioning in avionics architectures: Requirements, mechanisms, and assurance. Technical report NASA/CR-1999/209347, National Aeronautics and Space Administration, Hampton, VA, USA (March 2000),
   http://www.tc.faa.gov/its/worldpac/techrpt/ar99-58.pdf
21. The Chemical Industry Safety and Health Council: A Guide to Hazard and Operability Studies. Chemical Industries Association (1977)

Workshop on Architecting Safety in Collaborative Mobile Systems (ASCoMS 2012)

Introduction to ASCoMS 2012

António Casimiro and Jörg Kaiser

The continuous emergence and improvement of sensor and communication technologies creates new opportunities for designing embedded and mobile systems that are able to interact with their environment, and exhibit "smart" and autonomous behaviour. Furthermore, collaboration between mobile entities can also be envisaged for improving their functionality. However, a fundamental challenge is to ensure that safety requirements are satisfied despite the increased system complexity and the uncertainties introduced by the operation in open and not well defined environments. In particular, it is necessary to deal with temporal uncertainties that may affect the environment perception as well as the coordination of mobile entities. In general, the problem might be equated in terms of achieving functional safety. Then, the challenge is to adapt the system to different performance levels as needed to ensure safety according to the existing operational conditions (e.g. system and environment state). In any case, some minimal level of performance is always needed to ensure that safety can be achieved, which should be reflected on the architectural design.

This workshop on Architecting Safety in Collaborative Mobile Systems is intended to address the multiple facets of this problem, with a special focus on applications in the automotive and avionics domains. In fact, there are many reasons today for the use of autonomous mobile systems, like unmanned aerial vehicles (UAVs) or smart cars. For instance, UAVs can be used for environmental surveillance and control, and smart vehicles coordinating their behaviours can be used to increase traffic throughput and improve mobility without the need of using more space for the respective traffic infrastructures. However, so far the existing solutions to ensure the needed safety despite the uncertainties affecting their operation are still insufficient or inadequate. Therefore, these systems are not allowed to operate in the public air space or on public roads because the risk of causing severe damage or even threaten human lives cannot be excluded with sufficient certainty. This justifies the importance of research in this area, namely on topics such as:

- Architectural design for safety-critical systems
- Aspects of functional safety
- Reliable perception of the environment
- Coordination and adaptation strategies for safety-critical systems
- System safety guidelines and standards

The workshop includes an invited talk and two sessions addressing safety issues in automotive applications and dependability of sensor based systems. The invited talk intends to bring an industrial perspective on the main problems lying ahead, and on expectations on how research can contribute to address these problems. The session on safety issues in automotive applications includes three presentations, focusing on modelling of safety related timing constraints, on challenges for the software

F. Ortmeier and P. Daniel (Eds.): SAFECOMP 2012 Workshops, LNCS 7613, pp. 149–150, 2012.
© Springer-Verlag Berlin Heidelberg 2012

engineering of safer cars and on the use of quality metrics for functional safety. Finally, the session on dependability of sensor based systems provides two contributions, on dependable and stable perception despite timing and value faults and on supporting fault-propagation analysis.

Towards Dependable and Stable Perception in Smart Environments with Timing and Value Faults*

Luís Marques and António Casimiro

FC/UL
lmarques@lasige.di.fc.ul.pt, casim@di.fc.ul.pt

Abstract. Future physical environments are expected to be pervasively enriched with sensors, which mobile embedded applications can use to safely interact in and with that environment. Unfortunately, due to the open and uncertain nature of the environment and the wireless communication, it is not possible to provide strict a priori guarantees with regard to the quality and timeliness with which such environments can be perceived.

In this paper we take a look at the threats to a reliable perception of the environment, considering both timing and value faults. We discuss how such threats can be mitigated and we explore possible paths towards an integrated architecture to efficiently achieve a dependable and stable perception of smart environments in the presence of timing and value faults.

Keywords: smart environments, dependability, adaptation, stability, real-time, fault-tolerance.

1 Introduction

For more than a decade now, there has been a significant interest in the area of distributed sensors which communicate through wireless networking. This is reflected in such concepts as "Cyber-physical Systems", "Internet of Things", "Wireless Sensor Networks" (WSNs) and "Smart Environments". What is common to all of these concepts is the vision of highly pervasive sensors which allow the environment to be monitored at large scales, through the cooperation of many individual systems.

This mesh of highly ubiquitous sensors can support a wide range of different applications, some of which have already received significant attention, such as habitat monitoring [1][2], object tracking [3], target tracking [4], detection of pollutants [5], climate monitoring [6], energy consumption awareness [7], early disaster warning systems [8], and smart vehicles [9].

---

* This work was partially supported by the EU through the KARYON project (FP7-288195) and the FCT through the Multiannual Funding Program.

F. Ortmeier and P. Daniel (Eds.): SAFECOMP 2012 Workshops, LNCS 7613, pp. 151–161, 2012.

Different applications have different requirements with regard to the accuracy and timeliness with which the physical environment must be perceived. For instance, a pollutant monitoring application may only require that gas concentrations be measured every few minutes or hours, and it may be that this data does not need to be collected in real-time. Furthermore, the data may be able to be collected and processed in a centralized fashion, allowing for sensor readings to be compared and correlated in a batch and non-real-time manner, such as to remove outlier values due to faulty sensors.

On the other hand, other applications can have strict accuracy and timeliness requirements. For instance, target tracking and smart vehicles operating as part of vehicular networks are examples of applications which require both a highly accurate and a timely perception of the environment, to assure operational safety. In general, mobile and cooperative systems, that cooperate in and with the physical environment, will require stricter guarantees than more "passive" systems, such as habitat monitoring.

Yet, the problem arises that in open and uncertain environments it is not possible to provide a priori guarantees regarding the accuracy and timeliness with which the information from the surrounding environment and other cooperative systems can be obtained. Without such guarantees it becomes harder for mobile systems, such as vehicles, to safely cooperate and interact.

Part of the problem stems from the way in which embedded systems have, traditionally, been designed, which is not compatible with such open environments. Traditionally, embedded systems — particularly safety-critical systems — have been engineered in a systematic way which allows providing the required properties in terms of timeliness, accuracy and validity of the sensed environment.

To provide timeliness guarantees, all scenarios are previously studied, all operations are given deadlines, critical communication is performed using real-time networks, and every task is scheduled using carefully crafted algorithms, which execute code paths with worst case execution times designed to respect such deadlines. To provide the necessary accuracy, the type and amount of sensors used is carefully planned at system design time. The necessary redundancy is built-in, to provide protection against both timing and value faults.

Since traditional systems are engineered in such a way that all requirements are assured by design, their architectures have generally not focused on being aware, at runtime, of how well system assumptions are being covered, nor do they generally exhibit a large degree of runtime adaptability.

We argue that in open environments, in which the environment state information is obtained with uncertain timeliness and accuracy, such systems must be engineered to be adaptable and aware of their operational environment. We must transition from hard limits to adaptable bounds, from no awareness of the operating environment conditions to an awareness of runtime timing and accuracy bounds, and from uncertainty to dependable perception and operation.

We previously proposed a generic technique to be aware of, and to dependably adapt to, the varying communication timings of WSNs [10]. Such technique, based on a stochastic analysis of the runtime latencies of the wireless network, allows one to overcome the communication uncertainties of these open environments. In fact, we evaluated the proposed technique and confirmed its dependability in 802.15.4-based WSNs [11].

In this paper we discuss how similar techniques can incorporate the presence of sensors with varying margins of error, sensor heterogeneity and value faults, and how to achieve adaptation stability. We look at the various threats to a reliable perception of the environment, discuss how they can be mitigated and how to incorporate such strategies in an efficient architecture to achieve a stable and dependable perception of the environments, even in the presence of timing and value faults.

In the following section we start by exploring the desired properties of smart environments and various threats to a reliable perception.

2   Threats to Reliable Perception

We can identify several properties of smart environments upon which a dependable perception of the environment relies. With regard to the values which represent the current state of the perceived physical environment, or the production thereof, the following are four important properties.

- **Accuracy** — reflects the expected or computed margin of error of the considered value;
- **Validity** — indicates if the value may be outside of the expected or computed margin of error, due to a value fault;
- **Timeliness** — the ability to produce and deliver the desired value within a given deadline;
- **Efficiency** — the relation between the amount of resources expended and the accuracy, validity and timeliness of the obtained value.

These properties are not completely orthogonal but, as defined here, are useful constructs to allow reasoning about the threats to a reliable perception of the environment.

The properties of accuracy, validity and timeliness will determine the perception reliability and, therefore, the **application performance**. The relationship between these properties of the smart environment and the obtained performance is necessarily application-specific. In open environments these properties will also vary throughout time and space. As such, the reliability of the environment perception, and consequent application performance, will depend on: (1) the performance with which the applications or the smart environment itself adapt to varying conditions; (2) the stability of the three properties; (3) the relationship between (1) and (2).

Therefore, we must not only be aware of current environment conditions, but also of how such conditions can vary throughout time and space. Only that way can the application or the smart environment avoid adapting to new conditions more frequently (or faster) than would be optimal for a given application.

Based on this understanding of the requirements to a reliable perception of the environment, we can identify several threats and challenges to this reliability.

- **The amount of information** — with the amount of sensors spread out throughout the environment expected to grow exponentially, there will be added pressure on scarce resources like bandwidth (which will likely grow slower than the amount of information) and computational power (which is probably even more crucial in small and limited sensors);
- **Sensor heterogeneity** — the availability of sensors which provide the same state information with different accuracies, or which provide complementary state information, is an opportunity for optimization, but can also impair perception quality if the best information sources are not chosen;
- **The variability of information** — for mobile systems, the geographical variability of sensor information can have an impact on performance, by jeopardizing adaptation stability;
- **CPU hardware / software faults** — computational faults in the systems comprising either the smart environment itself or the cooperative systems can compromise safety, by corrupting sensor information or coordination information;
- **Sensor transducer faults** — in a world with a very large number of sensors, possibly from many different manufacturers, it can be expected that faulty sensor readings are a common occurrence, in absolute terms. The faults can derive from transducer miscalibrations, transducer aging, environmental effects, electromagnetic interferences, and various other sources;
- **Communication interferences** — both intra-network interferences (network nodes competing for the transmission medium) and external interferences (e.g. background noise) can threaten reliable environment perception, essentially by means of timing failures. Value faults can also occur, through packet corruption, but those faults can be transformed into omissions;
- **Network inaccessibility** — communication interferences may also lead the network to temporarily refrain from providing service, even if it is not considered to have failed. Network inaccessibility can be characterized by the specification of limits for inaccessibility duration and rate, where the violation of those limits implies a permanent failure of the network.
- **Clock desynchronization** — clock drift and other sources of desynchronization can impact distributed sensors, when relying on a notion of global time;

3   Accurate and Timely Perception

The reliability of the environment perception and consequent application performance will depend not only on the accuracy and timeliness of the sensed information, but also on the stability of these metrics. In this section we discuss existing work to achieve value accuracy, fault tolerance and timeliness, and to what extent these techniques can provide the required properties in a stable way, or be augmented to do so.

3.1   Timeliness

In the work described in [10], we previously proposed a technique to achieve probabilistic timely behavior in WSNs. A central assumption of that work was that although the timing variables had unknown bounds, which in addition could change at any time due to the open nature of the environment, such bounds were not completely arbitrary and unpredictable but that, instead, they were probabilistic. Furthermore, we considered that these probabilistic bounds changed slowly enough compared with the capacity of the application or the WSN itself to recognize and adapt to new bounds.

In [11] we indirectly evaluated these assumptions in 802.15.4-based WSNs, by measuring the adaptation effectiveness with regard to the end-to-end latencies, under a variety of scenarios. We concluded that, even with the adaptation occurring only at the application level (and not at the level of the WSN itself), we could meet deadlines with the desired probability, plus or minus a small margin of error (generally 1 or 2%, with some scenarios having a maximum margin of slightly over 5%).

There are three important issues to adaptation stability which this work did not cover. One is that these deadline fulfillment metrics are long-term averages; the work in [11] did not focus on the short-term variability. A second is that it was assumed that an application could adapt instantly after the new network behavior was recognized. Yet a third is that we had devised this technique mostly with stationary WSNs in mind.

Regarding this last point, notwithstanding our initial assumptions, in our evaluation we verified that the proposed technique was effective not only in stationary networks but also when sensor mobility was introduced. Despite the significant additional dynamics, we observed only a small increase in the margin of error of the probability of deadlines being fulfilled. In networks with more spatial heterogeneity and/or faster node movement it might be necessary to take proactive measures to assure that adaptation stability remains.

Regarding the short-term stability of the deadline fulfillment probability, although this was not specifically tested we informally observed that there were no significant variations from period to period. If stronger guarantees are needed, one option that is likely viable is to dynamically change the WSN behavior to adjust at runtime the amount of resources expended, to decrease variability. The challenge is how to do this in a decentralized and efficient way.

Likewise, while applications may not be able to adapt instantly, especially if they are far away from the source of network disruption, having the adaptation occur at the level of the WSN will likely be an effective strategy to assure temporal stability of timing bounds.

In fact, one of our conclusions from our evaluation in [11] supports the effectiveness of this strategy. We observed that in more complex networks, with more sources of uncertainty, we achieved (seemingly paradoxically) *better* adaptation effectiveness than in simpler networks. The reason for this is that all of these sources of uncertainty can average out. Hence, in future smart environments, with large amounts of sensors and network nodes, we can expect that decentralized network-level adaptations will be highly effective in smoothing out short term timing variabilities.

3.2   Accuracy and Value Faults

In traditional embedded systems, the type and number of sensors are predetermined according to the application requirements, and therefore fault masking can be planned in a straightforward manner using the sensors' manufacturer specification sheet. In smart environments the amount and type of available sensors is unknown at design time and can vary unpredictably. Therefore, the accuracy and fault behavior cannot be assumed in such a black box style, but must instead be checked and enforced at runtime.

An architecture for a dependable distributed sensor system is described in [12], which allows for an efficient detection and masking of common types of sensor faults. This architecture integrates a set of ideas that were previously developed in isolation into a coherent and unifying concept. We here review some of the underlying concepts and its suitability to be extended into an architecture for accurate, timely and stable environment perception.

One strategy to implement fault detection is through the classical paradigm of hardware replication. The work presented in [13] had previously identified the necessary number of sensors to tolerate different types of transducer faults; a different method was described in [14], based on maximizing the consistency of sensor fusion results.

Another strategy is to detect anomalous values from a single sensor, by comparing the sensor output to a model of the system and noticing discrepancies, or through a signal analysis of the sensor output; different approaches to implement this are detailed in [15], [16] and [17].

The distributed sensor architecture proposed in [12] combines ideas from these different approaches, by performing each kind of fault checking as close as possible to the source of error, for efficiency. This architecture follows the model of distributed fusion architecture, which had already been developed but which generally do not consider fault tolerance [18], extending previous work on fault-tolerant sensors [19].

This architecture performs a series of tests and, in the end, outputs sensor values together with a measure of their validity, which is a computed probability of the respective value being faulty. This final validity is a combination of the computed probabilities for each of the possible fault types.

One important aspect of this architecture is that it seems to be compatible with the technique proposed in [10] to achieve probabilistic real-time guarantees. For instance, regarding the distributed sensor fusion, the architecture does not specify any particular protocol for the dissemination and aggregation of sensor values, and therefore does not introduce incompatibilities with real-time network protocols. Also, no specific algorithms are mandated for the local transducer fault checks, so the algorithms can be chosen considering on their impact on timeliness, for example based on their worst-case execution times.

The architecture considers that the accuracy and fault model of the sensors is discoverable but does not contribute mechanisms to assure the provision of specific accuracy or fault probabilities. There are two considerations here for adaptation stability. One is that, even in stationary networks, the identified fault probability can (and will likely) vary throughout time. This can happen either because of changes in the sensor themselves or because of variations in the amount and type of aggregated sensor information. The other is that, in scenarios of mobility, such as vehicular scenarios, the quality of sensor information will likely vary spatially.

3.3   Adaptation Stability and Application Performance

We consider that an adaptation is stable for a given application if another adaptation will *not* be required, with a given probability p, in the immediate interval δ after it becomes effective. The values of p and δ will vary with the considered application and desired application performance.

In this subsection we clarify the impact of the adaptation stability in the application performance through a hypothetical scenario.

Figure 1 illustrates a scenario with moving vehicles and heterogenous perception quality regions. Vehicle A is shown in its current position (black) and a past position (grey).

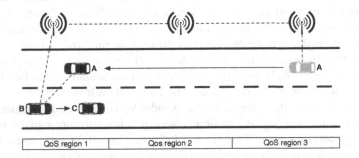

Fig. 1. Timing Variables (Example)

The operational performance of vehicle B, for instance with regard to the distance that must be kept to vehicle C, will be depend on the perception quality and stability that is achievable in QoS region 1. Since vehicles cannot instantaneously change their speed, and since frequent speed changes have a cost in terms of fuel consumption and passenger comfort, the optimal distance will depend on the expected probability of receiving within a given period sensory updates that are accurate and valid. If such information is not received then the operational performance will have to be degraded, if necessary to the point of switching to a fail-safe mode (e.g. vehicle immobilization).

Due to the spatial QoS heterogeneity, as vehicles move they will have to adapt to maintain operational safety and performance. If a more global awareness of perception quality is available then this adaptation can be optimized to maximize application performance. For instance, if QoS region 3 has a lower quality and that information is available in QoS region 1 then the vehicles can preemptively and gradually transition to the new optimal state, as they approach the region with lower quality. In particular, an adaptation can be made at QoS region 1 or 2 which is stable enough that, with high probability, no further adaptation is required when the vehicle reaches QoS region 3.

A possible way to achieve such awareness is for the smart environment participants to disseminate their local awareness of perception quality and temporal stability thereof. With regard to the timeliness, the historical latencies that are collected already contain information about the temporal variability of network latencies. In terms of sensor accuracy and validity, the distributed sensor fusion architecture should be extended to collect historical information and to compute the probability of valid updates being received within a period.

There are several challenges to an effective and efficient dissemination of the achievable perception quality information. For instance, in Figure 1 we can observe that the perception quality achievable in region 3 can be disseminated to other vehicles either directly by vehicle A or indirectly, by using the road-side infrastructure. Which is the best choice can depend on a wide variety of factors. If bandwidth is particularly scarce, then it might be more efficient for vehicle A to directly communicate with vehicle B. If vehicle A is moving slowly, then it might be preferable for the information to be disseminated through the road-side infrastructure, so that it is available in a timely manner, before vehicle B is too close to region 3. If multiple applications can benefit from that information, then it might be preferable to use the road-side infrastructure as a central hub of dissemination. Also, we can expect vehicles to host and support specific applications, while a smart environment sensor infrastructure can be expected to be more general purpose. Therefore, while vehicles might be preprogrammed to disseminate the quality of certain specific environment attributes, the generic environment sensors will have to learn what information is most beneficial to surrounding applications.

A more specific consideration is how to predict future sensor validities based on the disseminated past sensor information and/or validities. The non-parametric approach, based on order statistics, used in [10] may not be (fully) applicable to this task. It will be necessary to evaluate what model best approximates the variations over time of such validities. This model will have to integrate an awareness of both (1) how likely a fault is to occur in a specific sensor value, given past faults, and (2) how likely a valid value is to be available until a given deadline, given what fusible sensor values are expected to arrive.

4   Towards an Architecture for Dependable and Stable Environment Perception

Although no specific architecture is proposed in this paper, from the issues previously examined we can start enumerating components, services, design aspects and guiding principles that should comprise an architecture for dependable and stable environment perception.

In general, we suggest an architecture which uses fault-tolerant distributed sensor fusion to handle sensor accuracy and faults, that has an awareness of network latencies, and where the communication deadlines can be probabilistically assured by dynamically varying the amount of resources expended by the networked sensors of the smart environment, to counteract network and application dynamics.

The CPU hardware and/or software faults which change sensor values can be dealt with by enforcing fail-silent behavior. Other techniques can be compared for efficiency and performance in different scenarios, such as value voting and the elimination of outliers.

The threat introduced by network inaccessibility can be dealt with using specialized techniques, as has already been done for other kinds of networks [20][21]. These techniques can be compared for efficiency and performance with using redundant networks paths, which are unlikely to suffer of inaccessibility at the exact same times.

Clock synchronization is assumed in both the probabilistic timeliness solution and in the fault-tolerant distributed sensor fusion architecture. Such clock synchronization can be achieved by using algorithms specially optimized for smart environments. There already exist algorithms optimized for WSNs [22][23]. These can be improved upon to take into consideration factors that would be specific to an architecture for smart environments. For instance, synchronization accuracy may not need to be homogenous; it may be more efficient for the accuracy to be relatively better between nodes which are more relevant for sensor fusion, which may rely on the transformation of sensed values according to the elapsed time, as considered in [12]. Also, an awareness of network latencies may be exploited for a more efficient synchronization algorithm, at no additional cost if this information is already collected to assure timeliness.

There are many ways to mitigate network interferences [24]. To the extent that such interferences are not unpredictable they will not have an impact on timeliness, when using the considered probabilistic approach, but instead will only affect the efficiency of the environment perception. Strategies for improving that efficiency must not jeopardize timing properties. With regard to fault tolerance, the architecture can integrate the provision of timeliness properties with sensor fusion, so that guarantees of accuracy and validity will not be threatened by the necessary sensor information not being available in a timely manner.

A central aspect of this architecture is the components, protocols and/or services for the discovery of sensor information, which should work in such a way that the most beneficial combinations of fusible sensor state are made available. Another fundamental aspect, as identified in section 3.3, is how to provide stable perception quality properties to applications, throughout not only time but also space.

We propose exploring architectural mechanisms that can efficiently satisfy both of these aspects. In particular, we propose researching a mechanism for the decentralized dissemination of both the available sensors and their fault models, as well as what validity can be achieved in a given spatial region, according to the combination of perceived network latency conditions, available sensors and historical sensor validities.

5   Conclusion

The trend is clear that an ever increasing amount of sensors will be part of the physical environment, eventually culminating in smart environments where sensors are pervasive. While this presents an opportunity for increased autonomy and performance of mobile applications, the lack of guarantees offered by these environments creates a very hard challenge for application dependability and, in particular, their operational safety.

We identified the main threats to dependability and presented various possibilities of how both accuracy and timeliness might be achievable in an architecture for a dependable and stable environment perception. We built upon previous work, and explored how to combine and extend one solution devised to provide probabilistic timeline guarantees and an architecture for fault-tolerant distributed sensor fusion.

We identified the limitations of these previous efforts in terms of perception/performance stability, and we suggested various research venues of how such stability might be supplemented.

References

1. Tolle, G., Polastre, J., Szewczyk, R., Culler, D., Turner, N., Tu, K., Burgess, S., Dawson, T., Buonadonna, P., Gay, D., Hong, W.: A macroscope in the redwoods. In: SenSys 2005: Proceedings of the 3rd International Conference on Embedded Networked Sensor Systems, pp. 51–63. ACM Press (2005)
2. Szewczyk, R., Osterweil, E., Polastre, J., Hamilton, M., Mainwaring, A., Estrin, D.: Habitat monitoring with sensor networks. Communications of the ACM 47, 34–40 (2004)
3. Priyantha, N.B., Chakraborty, A., Balakrishnan, H.: The Cricket Location-Support System. In: 6th ACM MOBICOM, Boston, MA (August 2000)
4. Simon, G., Maróti, M., Lédeczi, A., Balogh, G., Kusy, B., Nádas, A., Pap, G., Sallai, J., Frampton, K.: Sensor network-based countersniper system, pp. 1–12. ACM Press (2004)
5. Tsujita, W., Yoshino, A., Ishida, H., Moriizumi, T.: Gas sensor network for air-pollution monitoring. Sensors and Actuators B: Chemical 110(2), 304–311 (2005)
6. Leonard, N.E., Paley, D., Lekien, F., Sepulchre, R., Fratantoni, D., Davis, R.: Collective motion, sensor networks, and ocean sampling. Proceedings of the IEEE, Special Issue on the Emerging Technology of Networked Control Systems (95), 48–74 (2007)

7. Jiang, X., Dawson-Haggerty, S., Dutta, P., Culler, D.: Design and implementation of a high-fidelity ac metering network. In: Proceedings of the 2009 International Conference on Information Processing in Sensor Networks, IPSN 2009, pp. 253–264. IEEE Computer Society, Washington, DC (2009)
8. Basha, E.A., Ravela, S., Rus, D.: Model-based monitoring for early warning flood detection. In: Proceedings of the 6th ACM Conference on Embedded Network Sensor Systems, SenSys 2008, pp. 295–308. ACM, New York (2008)
9. Lee, U., Magistretti, E., Zhou, B., Gerla, M., Bellavista, P., Corradi, A.: Mobeyes: Smart mobs for urban monitoring with vehicular sensor networks. IEEE Wireless Communications 13(5) (2006)
10. Marques, L., Casimiro, A.: Lightweight dependable adaptation for wireless sensor networks. In: Proceedings of the 30th IEEE International Symposium on Reliable Distributed Systems Workshops, 4th International Workshop on Dependable Network Computing and Mobile Systems (DNCMS 2011), Madrid, Spain (2011)
11. Marques, L., Casimiro, A.: Evaluating lightweight dependable adaptation in 802.15.4 wireless sensor networks. Technical report, TR-2012-04, Dep. of Informatics, Univ. of Lisboa, http://docs.di.fc.ul.pt/handle/10455/6873
12. Zug, S., Dietrich, A., Kaiser, J.: An architecture for a dependable distributed sensor system. IEEE T. Instrumentation and Measurement 60(2), 408–419 (2011)
13. Chen, C., Brown, D., Sconyers, C., Zhang, B., Vachtsevanos, G., Orchard, M.E.: An integrated architecture for fault diagnosis and failure prognosis of complex engineering systems. Expert Syst. Appl. 39(10), 9031–9040 (2012)
14. Marzullo, K.: Tolerating failures of continuous-valued sensors. ACM Trans. Comput. Syst. 8(4), 284–304 (1990)
15. Koushanfar, F., Potkonjak, M., Sangiovanni-Vincentelli, A.: On-line fault detection of sensor measurements. In: IEEE Sensors, pp. 974–980 (2003)
16. Isermann, R.: Model-based fault detection and diagnosis: status and applications. In: Proceedings of the 16th IFAC Symposium on Automatic Control in Aerospace, St., pp. 71–85 (2004)
17. Doebling, S.W., Farrar, C.R., Prime, M.B.: A summary review of vibration-based damage identification methods. The Shock and Vibration Digest 30, 91–105 (1998)
18. Makarenko, A., Durrant-whyte, H.: Decentralized data fusion and control in active sensor networks. In: Proceedings of the Seventh International Conference on Information Fusion (2004)
19. Zug, S., Kaiser, J.: An approach towards smart fault-tolerant sensors. In: Proceedings of IEEE International Workshop on Robotic and Sensors Environments (ROSE 2009), Lecco, Italy (November 2009)
20. Rufino, J., Veríssimo, P., Almeida, C., Arroz, G.: Integrating inaccessibility control and timer management in canely. In: ETFA, pp. 348–355. IEEE (2006)
21. Souza, J.L.R., Rufino, J.: An approach to enhance the timeliness of wireless communications. In: The Fifth International Conference on Mobile Ubiquitous Computing, Systems, Services and Technologies (UBICOMM), Lisbon (November 2011)
22. Li, Q., Rus, D.: Global clock synchronization in sensor networks. IEEE Transactions on Computers 55(2), 214–226 (2006)
23. Yoon, S., Veerarittiphan, C., Sichitiu, M.L.: Tiny-sync: Tight time synchronization for wireless sensor networks. ACM Trans. Sen. Netw. 3(2) (June 2007)
24. Liang, C.J.M.: Interference characterization and mitigation in large-scale wireless sensor networks (2011)

An Approach Supporting Fault-Propagation Analysis for Smart Sensor Systems

Sebastian Zug, Tino Brade, Jörg Kaiser, and Sasanka Potluri

Otto-von-Guericke Universität Magdeburg
Department for Distributed Systems
Universitätsplatz 2,
39106 Magdeburg
{zug,brade,kaiser,sasanka}@ivs.cs.uni-magdeburg.de

Abstract. Distributed sensor-actuator-systems in automotive or avionic applications have to fulfill safety requirements strictly. Those implementation has to be monitored during the development process and on runtime. For this purpose we presented a data centric fault categorization, fault representation and measurement validation concept.

In this paper we enhance our approach and describe a fault propagation mechanism suitable for a permanent evaluation of tolerable fault level. Based on a common fault representation each component is characterized by its effects on the signal validity. As shown in an exemplary scenario the proposed matrix notation provides a flexible and powerful method to implement and monitor the fault propagation.

1 Introduction

Many mobile embedded systems rely on the reliable perception of their environment as the basis for moving and actuating safely. They recently have been addressed as cyber-physical systems emphasizing the tight links and loops between electronic intelligent devices and the physical world. Because more and more vehicles like smart cars, autonomous transportation systems, service robots for cleaning, mowing and other housekeeping tasks start sharing the same space with other such vehicles and humans, the proof for safety has become a decisive requirement for allowing such artifacts to leave their so far well defined and segregated operational space. Communication opens many desirable but challenging opportunities. On the perception side, communication offers access to a rich spectrum of sensors in the environment and on other smart vehicles. Distributed sensing allows extending the range of perception, the modalities, and potentially the precision. However, at the same time, it becomes more difficult to assess the quality of sensor information. For local sensors, the control algorithms can safely assume a certain precision, a sampling rate and an error model. These assumptions including well-known margins of uncertainty are reflected in the control loop of the vehicle. A robust control loop tolerates some degree of

F. Ortmeier and P. Daniel (Eds.): SAFECOMP 2012 Workshops, LNCS 7613, pp. 162–173, 2012.

uncertainty. Sensors may have a very subtle behavior in case of a failure. Providing checks for local sensors or hardening the control algorithm against such failures is difficult [1]. However for external sensors, this is impossible without an intimate knowledge of the sensor that is not available a priori in the general case. Additionally, latencies and omissions of the wireless network put a new class of uncertainties to sensor information. Therefore we provide an estimate of the sensor data quality in terms of a validity value together with the sensor data itself.

The nature of sensor faults and particularly the impact they have on generated sensor readings is very complex. Ni et. all [2] make a very useful distinction between a data centric and a system centric perspective on sensor faults. The data centric view largely ignores the root cause of a fault and analyses the sensor data according to an anticipated signal behavior, statistical analysis or assumptions about the environment. In terms of accepted dependability notions, this approach provides checks against a well-defined sensor error model. This is also the prevalent approach in control engineering where a robust control algorithm resists some of these erroneous sensor data. A systematic way dealing with sensor data faults is the FDI approach (Fault detection and isolation). The system-centric view on the other side tries to identify a root cause of a failure and forecasts the impact on the respective sensor data. The fault-tolerance community traditionally takes a system-oriented view on handling faults. Faults are anticipated, the respective measures for predicting the effects of faults like fault-trees and Failure Modes and Effects Analysis (FMEA) are performed and fault handling schemes on the system level are introduced. It should be noted, that the system-centric analysis is largely an off-line analysis in which the effects and the propagation of a fault originating from a well-defined root cause is in the focus of interest. In contrast, the data-centric approach is interested in the validity of an individual sensor reading and tries to identify faulty data without any knowledge of the root cause on the basis of the perceived signal properties only. This perspective is particularly attractive for sensor faults because identification of the cause of a failure may be very difficult.

As emphasized by Ni et al. these two perspectives are by no means disjoint. It is a matter of perspective. E.g. an expressive error model may well be derived from thorough root cause analysis. Faulty behavior however, is analyzed solely on the basis of the produced data. Additionally, the system centric approach can be used to build more reliable sensors by dealing with the root cause of failures.

In our paper we take a data centric view. However, we are less interested in deriving test and analysis methods for sensor data than in the question how we can exploit the knowledge about test outcomes on the system level. In contrast to the binary decisions "good" or "bad" in the system centric view, the data centric view rather provides a continuum of usefulness or trustworthiness in sensor data within some bounds. E.g. sensor readings are typically affected by noise, offsets, drift and other specific environmental perturbations. However, this does not mean that they are completely useless. Respective filters and error detection methods are able to suppress such effects to a large extent. Thus we strive for deriving validity measures for sensor data that are provided with the respective value itself. This validity estimates can be exploited by remote nodes that fuse multiple sensor sources for assessment and selection. The validity estimate is derived from the quality and extent, to which the sensor data is checked for errors. This issue is discussed in more detail in Sec. 2.

Estimating the validity of a single sensor reading however is only one, although an important part towards assessing the overall impact of failures to the system. We consider systems that combine and fuse individual sensor data to generate higher level, application relevant information. Thus, there is a chain of filters, estimators, and fusion components which finally produce the desired output to the control functions. It is therefore important to analyze how errors (and validity estimates) will propagate through this chain of processing elements and influence perception quality. Thus the first objective of our paper is to present a concept providing expressive validity information for sensor data to be used in a distributed sensor-actuator system. To the best of our knowledge this is not provided so far elsewhere. Secondly, we try to experimentally verify the usefulness of the scheme. Because of the many failures possibilities and all their combination that have to be considered, analytical models seem not appropriate to derive a deep understanding of the impact of individual failures. Therefore, we propose an approach based on simulating error propagation. This will require maintaining information about the checks that were applied to the individual sensor inputs together with some normalized validity estimation. In our paper we will discuss the assessment of sensor data validity based on a well-defined fault and error model. The basic idea is to map the complex behavior of a sensor failure to a normalized model of sensor data validity. We call this failure semantics following the ideas of Christian [3] defining a classification for distributed system failures. Subsequently we discuss the refinement of the model with respect to simulate error propagation through a chain of processing stages.

2   State of the Art

For a comprehensible handling of the expected different faults we need a uniform representation of the error. Because we take a data centric view, the error level represents the deviation from the correct data value.. Such an abstraction has to consider two opposing requirements. On one hand, the fault representation has to provide all relevant information (occurrence probability, effect on the signal, duration) necessary for a fault effect analysis and fault propagation estimation. On the other hand, the abstraction should encapsulate the individual fault characteristic as far as possible and provide a generic representation.

The established concepts for expressing possible faults and confidence levels are focused on a compact fault representation. For instance, the Failure Modes and Effects Analysis (FMEA) [4] implements a classification scheme that analyzes the processing capabilities and expected fault characteristic. As a result the user gets a single validity value called

Risk Priority Number (RPN). The RPN value maps the multiple aspects as occurrence, detection probability and amplitude of errors handled by multiple detection mechanisms to a single number between 1 and 1000. Different application areas (automotive, avionics, automation industries) develop individual standards that contain a fault description and effect analysis. The ISO 26262 for instance provides a process model for fault identification and validation [5,6]. The degree of abstraction is high. ISO 26262 defines four Automotive Safety Integrity Levels (ASIL). An ASIL determines the level of integrity in which a critical function should be executed. In a transformation step this has to be mapped to the respective requirements for the architectural components.

In addition to these design-time oriented approaches there exists a number of fault abstractions for run-time validations. The authors of [7] map all occurring faults to three meta-models: "Short" indicates a temporal, sudden change of the measurement signal, "Noise", encapsulates all stochastic faults and "Constant" covers all offset variants. Due to the missing specification of the fault amplitude and occurrence probability, the approach does not provide a detailed fault propagation analysis. More detailed representations are presented in [8,9]. The author developed an evaluation scheme that maps the current fault state of a node on a data validity value. The fault characteristic of a measurement is condensed into a single value validity estimation (16 categories, integer values between 0 and 100). The evaluation value is assigned to each data set. Due to the missing information about the implemented detection methods those single values are difficult to interpret and to compare. Does a high validity value indicates the result of a simple detection method, that is probably unable to recognize a certain fault or can we assume a set of detectors coverage all expectable faults?

Beside these problems the existing concepts of both domains (run-time, design-time) do not support a hierarchical or component oriented system view. Due to the high level abstraction, the values are determined for one specific hardware/software implementation. If the structure is changed, the whole determination procedure has to be passed once again. In the same way the results are not reusable on a higher level of system representation. The individual RPNs of a sensor, controller and actuator system cannot be mixed up to calculate a common validity value.

3   Concept

As a consequence of the gaps in established fault representation methods we developed a new fault semantic, combining a system and an event validity [1]. The first one characterizes the expected fault levels and their effect on the system output. Its definition is based on the comparison of the node characteristics (sensors, processor, periphery) with the assigned detection and fault-tolerance capabilities. At the end, the system validity is to be determined based on the design-time and it indicates the trustworthiness of a node. In addition to this hardware oriented view, the event validity summarizes the results of the individual detection methods. On runtime all fault detection methods generate normalized output that are combined in the event validity. This information is attached to each measurement. Only in combination of both information an objective evaluation of each data set is provided [10]. The system validity provides an evaluation of the event validity and it can be used to identify the detection methods applied to a measurement. The output of high performance sensor can be distinguished from a low level sensor with limited fault detection capabilities, although a similar event validity were generated.

Up to now we determine the system validity with an adapted FMEA-scheme as a single value. As mentioned in the Chapter 2 such a high level abstraction do not well support the further processing of the sensor data and particularly, is not suited for tracing the effects of a fault. In this paper we describe a refined fault representation and develop a vector representation maintaining the effects of individual faults. In addition to the sensor data validity assessment it enables the analysis of fault propagation in a distributed system. This extension allows a flexible estimation of the system confidence level based on a continuously automated fault propagation concept. Hence, the developer can monitor the effect of a new filter, fusion algorithm, improved sensor, etc. immediately.

3.1   Fault Categorization

Every sensor signal suffers from multiple sources of external disturbances and inherent internal errors resulting in a difference between the observed physical unit and the captured value [11,12]. The deviation depends on the physical principles of the perception process, possible external disturbances and on the hardware characteristics of the sensor node. In a distributed scenario the need of (wireless) communication causes probably an additional delays, omissions, missed links, etc. In contrast to other fault definitions, we define each difference between digital representation and real physical value as a fault. This concept covers deviations caused by outliers, spikes, offsets, etc. as well as effects of the processing chain and system specification like saturation, discretization or constant noise. We need this comprehensive data centric view for generating a notion of system validity that reflects the impact of all these errors, their dependencies and inter-relationship.

In Tab. 1 we structure the most relevant (sensor) fault types with respect to their characteristics into five major divisions (A-E). Within these categories, a fine grain of classification may still be possible, e.g. an offset may be constant or a bad calibration or varying over time like temperature dependent offsets. These differences and the respective detection schemes are however outside the scope of this paper. For a more detailed discussion of sensor faults the reader is referred to [1].

Based on this investigation we deduce two generic parameters necessary to identify the effect of certain fault model:

- The occurrence probability p is a stochastic representation of the frequency of derivation. For fault models in the last column (E) p becomes 1 related to the permanent effect of the fault. Fault models assigned in one of the other columns have a value in between 0 and 1.

– Similar to the FMEA or its variants, a maximum deviation d indicates the level of the disturbance. We assume d as the absolute difference between correct and measured value.

Table 1. Classification of sensor faults according to occurrence characteristics and knowledge of signal parameter

		occurrence pattern		
		sporadic	periodic	static
temporal extension	short	A1 omission A2 outliers A3 spikes ⋮	B1 time-correlated glitches ⋮	N.A.
	long	C1 stuck-at C2 node crashes C3 permanent network failures ⋮	D1 periodic perturbation ⋮	E1 drift E2 noise E3 delay E4 offset ⋮

Each fault model (A1-E4) is defined by a tuple $[p, d]_i$. For further processing we organize these 12 parameter sets in two separate vectors p and d whereby the position index is associated with a concrete fault model (A1=1 ...E4=12 element). If a certain fault model is not relevant for a sensor, the corresponding entry is set to 0 in the p vector. Accordingly, the size of both vectors is constant.

Table 2. Shortened representation of an exemplary set of vectorized faul parameters

Fault models		Sensor faults		Requirements	
		Occurrence probability p_S	Maximum deviation d_S	Occurrence probability p_R	Maximum deviation d_R
	⋮	⋮		⋮	
A2	Outlier	0.037	16 cm	0.01	3 cm
	⋮	⋮		⋮	
E2	Constant noise	1.0	1.6 cm	1.0	0.3 cm
E4	Constant delay	1.0	40 ms	1.0	5 ms
	⋮	⋮		⋮	

The white columns of Tab. 2 illustrate the utilization of the vector fault representation in a concrete case. They contain the set of fault parameters defined for the popular IR distance sensor GPD120[13] that, although popular suffers from a number of deficiencies (precision, noise, energy consumption, sensitivity to external light, etc.). Related to a previous careful investigation of this sensor type we experimentally obtained values for the entries of the occurrence probability p_S and maximum deviation d_S vector. The subscripted "S" indicates the fault vectors as assigned to a sensor output. Fault model A2 (outliers) occurs in 3.7 % of all measurements. The maximum deviation is quite high with 18 cm. Beside the temporary outliers two fault models effects the perception process permanently, the constant measurement noise and a constant delay (E2, B3). It is remarkable, that for the last entry the deviation d contains a time value and not a distance. The other elements of the vectors are set to zero. All parameter sets of a sensor can be stored in a electronic data sheet that accompanies the development process [14].

3.2   Fault Propagation

Each application component demands a certain validity level (maximum deviation, noise, delay, etc.) for its inputs. If a measurement or a signal does not meet these requirements, the system is not able to fulfill its tasks. In control applications for instance the algorithms expect a certain range of measuring age and noise level. A data set out of the specification range cannot be tolerated and the system could result in an uncertain state. For this reason, the developer has to integrate a number of appropriate methods to close the gap between the quality level of a component and the requirements of the other one. In case of the mentioned control loop, the developer has to implement filters and an estimator to provide smooth and approximated measurements without a delay. The knowledge about the requirements and the appropriate algorithms has to be realized by the developer. A proof that the measurement quality meets the request has to be done in an elaborate evaluation.

The systematic adjustment of measurement quality and tolerable faults needs an abstract specification of the requirements. Our detailed description of the fault characteristics in a vectorized representation is very well suited for these requirements. The gray columns of Tab. 2 depict an example of a characteristic set of parameters. These concrete values are derived from a distributed robotic scenario, where the measurements of a GP2D120 sensor node are used for a robot trajectory control. If the distance measurements do not follow the definitions in Tab. 2, the robot shows quite abrupt moves that disturbs other sensors systems (odometry, acceleration sensors, gyroscopes). Comparing the white columns (sensor specification) and gray columns (control requirements) in Tab. 2 it becomes clear, that the cheap distance sensor cannot fulfill the quality demands without appropriate filter mechanisms. The amplitude of outliers for instance has to be reduced by a factor of 5. Consequently, the vectors p_S and d_S represents the starting point and the entries of p_R and d_R the intended fault characteristic at the end point of the processing chain.

According to this idea, the changes of the signal characteristic by filters, fusion algorithms, communication, etc. has to be monitored permanently. With such fault propagation the influence of a component on the common fault characteristic can be analyzed and evaluated. The propagation concept has to fulfill two tasks. Firstly, it has to provide the mapping of an input with an output fault vector. Secondly, a metrics is needed for a comparison of the output fault vector of the last component with the requirement vector. Both aspects are discussed in the following paragraphs.

The mathematical mapping of an input fault vectors p_{old} and d_{old} with output fault vectors p_{new} and d_{new} can be applied in different ways. Related to the vectorized fault representation we choose a matrix multiplication based on homogeneous coordinates. Such a transformation is used in projective geometry and allows especially a scaling and shifting of a vector entry in one operation. Following this idea each component is characterized by a set of two matrices $[M_p, M_d]$. Each of them has a size of 13x13 elements related to 12 fault models. One additional column and row is necessary to provide an additional bias for the resulting value. For instance, if the processing duration of a calculation increases the age of a measurement, the additional delay can be considered in the matrix M_d.

The output fault vectors are calculated by $p_{old}^T \cdot M_p = p_{new}$ and $d_{old}^T \cdot M_d = d_{new}$. For a chain of multiple components the equation can be extended to

$$p_{old}^T \cdot M_p^1 \cdot M_p^2 \cdot \ldots \cdot M_p^n = p_{new} \qquad (1)$$
$$d_{old}^T \cdot M_d^1 \cdot M_d^2 \cdot \ldots \cdot M_d^n = d_{new}$$

The following paragraphs illustrate the different mapping situations using the developed concept. For a comprehensible representation we reduce the fault vectors $p_{old}, d_{old}, p_{new}$ and d_{new} to the fault models – outlier, constant noise and constant delay – shown in Tab. 2. Accordingly, the example-transformations matrices M_p and M_d contain 4x4 instead of 13x13 entries:

No effect. The component does not influences the occurrence probability or deviation of a fault model. This relation is indicated by a single 1 on the main diagonal in the assigned matrix column. As shown in Equ. (2) the new entry for p_{noise} in the fault probability vector is calculated by $p_{outlier} \cdot 0 + p_{noise} \cdot 1 + p_{delay} \cdot 0 + 1 \cdot 0 = p_{noise}$. The concrete transformation matrix M_p represents probably a gradient filter that detects outliers but do not smooth the measurement signal.

Proportional transformation. This effect is visible in the first column of the transition matrix in Equ. (2). The single value of 0.1 in M_p shows the reduction of the occurrence probability for outliers by a factor of ten.

$$\begin{bmatrix} p_{outlier} \\ p_{noise} \\ p_{delay} \\ 1 \end{bmatrix}_{old}^T \cdot \begin{bmatrix} 0.1 & 0 & 0 & 0 \\ 0 & 1 & 0 & 0 \\ 0 & 0 & 1 & 0 \\ 0 & 0 & 0 & 1 \end{bmatrix} = \begin{bmatrix} p_{outlier} \\ p_{noise} \\ p_{delay} \\ 1 \end{bmatrix}_{new} \qquad (2)$$

Elimination. If a filter works perfectly, it provides the complete elimination of a fault model. In this case the hole column of the matrix is set to zero.

Static offset. Beside a proportional relations between input and output independent additional offsets can be quantified in homogeneous coordinates. Equ. (3) gives an example for the transformation of a derivation vector d. The old delay entry d_{delay} is increased by a constant value $d_{delay} \cdot 1 + 1 + 0.2ms$. The bias of $0.2ms$ is just an example and can be caused by the runtime of the algorithm, communication delays, etc.

If the proportional parts of the transformation are set to zero, the output fault vector shows a constant entry for this fault model. Related to the delay such a behaviour is needed in case of an estimation filter using "old" measurements to approximate a current value.

$$\begin{bmatrix} p_{outlier} \\ p_{noise} \\ p_{delay} \\ 1 \end{bmatrix}_{old}^T \cdot \begin{bmatrix} 1 & 0 & 0 & 0 \\ 0 & 1 & 0 & 0 \\ 0 & 0 & 1 & 0 \\ 0 & 0 & 0.2ms & 1 \end{bmatrix} = \begin{bmatrix} p_{outlier} \\ p_{noise} \\ p_{delay} \\ 1 \end{bmatrix}_{new} \tag{3}$$

Interference. The last transformation category addresses the mutual interference between different fault models. Following our sensor example we assume now another outlier filter with a smaller trustworthiness. The limited detection capabilities are visible by the proportional ratio of 0.3 in Equ. (4). Additionally, the detection result is influenced by another fault model, the measurement noise made a correct evaluation difficult. Hence, the new outlier probability is calculated by $p_{outlier} \cdot 0.3 + p_{noise} \cdot 0.1 = p_{outlier}$.

$$\begin{bmatrix} p_{outlier} \\ p_{noise} \\ p_{delay} \\ 1 \end{bmatrix}_{old}^T \cdot \begin{bmatrix} 0.3 & 0 & 0 & 0 \\ 0.1 & 1 & 0 & 0 \\ 0 & 0 & 1 & 0 \\ 0 & 0 & 0 & 1 \end{bmatrix} = \begin{bmatrix} p_{outlier} \\ p_{noise} \\ p_{delay} \\ 1 \end{bmatrix}_{new} \tag{4}$$

The examples mentioned above contain single transitions only. If more than one component are integrated in a processing chain, the transition mechanisms of Equ. (2)-4 have to used as shown in Equ. (1).

The resulting fault vectors (p, d) should be continuously compared to the requirement vectors (p_R, d_R). At the moment we assess a system configuration as valid if all entries of p and d are smaller than p_R and d_R. Future research will focus on more elaborate metrics for the evaluation process.

4   Example

In this section we want to apply the mechanisms described in the previous section on a concrete implementation integrating a GP2D120 distance sensor. As already mentioned, the measurement quality of this sensor type does not meet the requirements of the control application. The related fault vectors (p_S, d_S) and (p_R, d_R) are visible in Fig. 1 on the left and right side. For practical reasons, the vectors contain only the relevant entries. The example scenario includes a

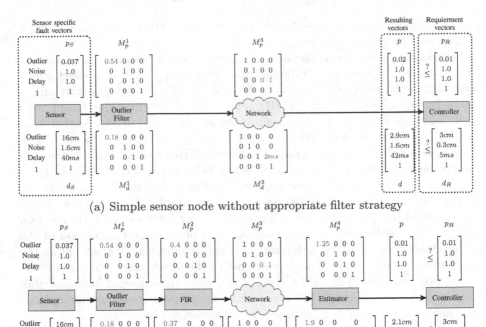

(a) Simple sensor node without appropriate filter strategy

(b) Sensor node with suitable measurement quality

Fig. 1. Application example of the fault-propagation concerning different variants of a sensor-filter-controller chain

communication component beside the filter and detection methods. The behavior of the network is represented with the homogeneous coordinates.

The mismatching contents of p, d, p_R and d_R make an additional effort in signal conditioning and filtering necessary. Fig. 1 illustrates two different processing chains for this scenario. In Fig. 1(a) the sensor measurements are locally filtered for outliers, communicated via a network and used as an input for the control algorithm. We determine the transition matrices (M_p, M_d) of these steps – gradient based outlier detection and network communication – based on a Matlab/Simulink implementation. The fault effects and the corresponding matrix entries are investigated using a set of recorded distance measurements. The outlier filter cuts the respective outlier probability nearly to halve of the original value. Additionally, it reduces the maximum deviation significantly. The network related transformation has an effect only on the delay entry. Due to the fact that a constant communication delay is assumed, those probability is set to fixed to "1". The delay entry in the deviation vector increases by 2 ms as visible in M_d^3. The fault vectors of the network output (p, d) can be calculated according to Equ. (1) by $p_S^T \cdot M_p^1 \cdot M_p^3 = p$ and $d_S^T \cdot M_d^1 \cdot M_d^3 = d$. Obviously, the fault level of possible outliers meets the controller requirements but the amplitude of the measurement noise is too large. Accordingly, the age of the measurements cannot be tolerated from the application.

Consequently, the developer designs a second implementation as shown in Fig. 1(b). He integrates an additional smoothing filter on the embedded sensor node and implements an estimator in front of the controller. The first one, a Finite Impulse Response Filter (FIR) is responsible for the reduction of noise level. Additionally, it effects the remained outliers as visible in M_d^2. At this stage the deviation level is decreased by $d_{outlier} \cdot 0.18 \cdot 0.37 = d_{outlier}$. The maximum noise level is reduced by the factor 0.11 after the FIR filter. The communication component shows the application independent behavior as described in the paragraph before. The new estimator applies a mathematical model to predict the measurement results to minimize the age of the samples. Due to uncertainties in the model the probability of outliers (and other fault categories) increases, but the delay is limited by tenth with a small offset. The comparison of the output fault vectors of the estimator with the requirement vectors shows the applicability of the intended processing chain. The developer made a good job.

The presented fault propagation helps to evaluate the expected fault probability and deviation systematically. If one or more components should be replaced by a new one, we are able to monitor the consequences immediately.

In case of a missing transition matrix set, it has to be determined in a first step. For this purpose we add the fault characteristic in our data sheet concept embedded in Matlab/Simulink [14]. The combination of an abstract fault representation with the simulation capabilities of Matlab/Simulink will provide an automated calculation of the transition matrices.

5   Conclusion

The fault propagation analysis presented in this paper complements and extends the fault handling strategies for distributed sensor-based applications. The data-centric concept of system and event validity developed for run-time assessment of sensor faults is now exploited for design-time evaluation of a specific system configuration. The development process can be monitored according to a requirement vector set that defines the fault-tolerance level of a certain component.

For large applications a multitude of requirement vectors can be embedded on different layers. The concept provides a multi-level evaluation of the assigned output fault vectors. Future work will strive for developing a respective framework in Matlab/Simulink.

Acknowledgment. This work has partially supported by the EU under the FP7-ICT Programme, through project 288195 "Kernel-based ARchitecture for safetY-critical cONtrol" (KARYON).

References

1. Zug, S., Dietrich, A., Kaiser, J.: Fault-Handling in Networked Sensor Systems. Concept Press Ltd., St. Franklin (2012)

2. Ni, K., Ramanathan, N., Chehade, M., Balzano, L., Nair, S., Zahedi, S., Kohler, E., Pottie, G., Hansen, M., Srivastava, M.: Sensor network data fault types. ACM Transactions on Sensor Networks (TOSN) 5(3), 1–29 (2009)
3. Cristian, F.: Understanding fault-tolerant distributed systems. Communications of the ACM 34, 56–78 (1991)
4. Stamatis, D.H.: Failure Mode and Effect Analysis: FMEA from Theory to Execution, 2nd edn. ASQ Quality Press (April 2003)
5. ISO 26262-3: Draft International Standard Road vehicles – Functional safety - Part 3: Concept phase. ISO, International Organization for Standardization (2009)
6. Hillenbrand, M., Heinz, M., Adler, N., Matheis, J., Muller-Glaser, K.: Failure mode and effect analysis based on electric and electronic architectures of vehicles to support the safety lifecycle ISO/DIS 26262. In: 21st International Symposium on Rapid System Prototyping (RSP 2010), pp. 1–7. IEEE (June 2010)
7. Sharma, A., Golubchik, L., Govindan, R.: On the prevalence of sensor faults in real-world deployments. In: 4. Conference on Sensor, Mesh and Ad Hoc Communications and Networks, SECON 2007, pp. 213–222. IEEE (2007)
8. Sukumar, S., Bozdogan, H., Page, D., Koschan, A., Abidi, M.: Sensor selection using information complexity for multi-sensor mobile robot localization. In: International Conference on Robotics and Automation, pp. 4158–4163. IEEE
9. Elmenreich, W., Pitzek, S., Schlager, M.: Modeling Distributed Embedded Applications on an Interface File System. In: Proceedings of the Seventh IEEE International Symposium on Object-Oriented Real-Time Distributed Computing (ISORC 2004), Vienna, Austria, pp. 175–182 (2004)
10. Kaiser, J., Zug, S.: A fault-aware sensor architecture for cooperative mobile applications. In: 17th IEEE Workshop on Dependable Parallel, Distributed and Network-Centric Systems, Shanghai (May 2012)
11. Kopetz, H.: Real-Time Systems: Design Principles for Distributed Embedded Applications. Springer (April 1997)
12. Dietrich, A., Zug, S., Kaiser, J.: Detecting External Measurement Disturbances Based on Statistical Analysis for Smart Sensors. In: Procedings of the IEEE International Symposium on Industrial Electronics (ISIE), pp. 2067–2072 (July 2010)
13. Sharp Cooperation: GP2D120 Data Sheet (2007),
   http://sharp-world.com/products/device/lineup/data/pdf/datasheet/gp2y0a21yk_e.pdf
14. Brade, T., Schulze, M., Zug, S., Kaiser, J.: Model-Driven Development of Embedded Systems. In: 12th Brazilian Workshop on Real-Time and Embedded Systems (WTR). Brazilian Computer Society, Gramado (2010)

Use of Quality Metrics for Functional Safety in Systems of Cooperative Vehicles

Kenneth Östberg and Rolf Johansson

SP Technical Research Institute of Sweden, Borås, Sweden
{kenneth.ostberg,rolf.johansson}@sp.se

Abstract. Looking at functional safety of vehicles, we have seen an evolution from federated to integrated E/E architectures. When extending the way of specifying and analysing functional safety to also address cooperative functionality, it is not possible to keep a static view of the boundaries of the system for which to ensure safety. This is because the set of vehicles realizing a cooperative function may change a lot during the execution of the cooperative function. In this work in progress paper we suggest to move part of the task to show safety, from design time to run time. This implies that it will become necessary to monitor the system at run time, continuously calculate its quality and share that information between the individual vehicles to assert that the system is safe. In order to accomplish this, appropriate metrics are needed, both during design time and run time. Inspired by information theory, this paper sketches some common properties for metrics, and indicates how that can be beneficial.

Keywords: Safety, Redundancy, Quality, Software metrics.

1   Introduction

It is foreseen that in the near feature autonomous functionality in vehicles will allow the dynamic formation of collective groups for collaboration and the realization of services beyond the ability of isolated vehicles, e.g. group vehicles into a road train (platoon). Also in the aircraft domain different kinds of cooperative functionality are currently investigated. The problem discussed in this paper is the safe implementation of this kind of cooperative functionality, while still fulfilling commercial constraints.

When claiming functional safety, it is important to understand from where the underlying evidence and arguments have to be found. Di Natale and Sangiovanni-Vincetelli elaborates in [5] on the trend from federative to integrated architectures. In the former a number of control units realize "mostly independent or loosely interconnected functions". This means that when constructing a safety case for a functionality, most (all) of the needed pieces of evidence and arguments can be found in the realization of a dedicated system of sensors, control unit, and actuators. In the integrated architecture, the functionalities can all be distributed and share resources with one another. This means that pieces of evidence and arguments are shared, and that there might be complicated dependencies between the separate efforts to prove the safety of

F. Ortmeier and P. Daniel (Eds.): SAFECOMP 2012 Workshops, LNCS 7613, pp. 174–179, 2012.
© Springer-Verlag Berlin Heidelberg 2012

the different functionalities realized by the same architecture. As pointed out the advantages of integrated architectures are extensibility, flexibility and modularity. But they also require more when it comes to functional safety, for example in regard to: semantics of component models, and new methods and tools for analysing results of composition. In the avionics domain the driver for the integrated architecture is IMA, and in the automotive domain it is AUTOSAR.

From a functional safety perspective, it is critical to distribute safety requirements among suppliers (in several tiers), and also to collect evidence and arguments from the different organizations, in order to be able to build a safety case. [3] describes a pattern for how to model safety requirements for this purpose. This expands the general modelling support for functional safety of complex automotive designs that are presented in [2]. The pattern of distributing responsibilities for enabling safety-critical complex systems has been discussed in many papers. Bate et al [1] described this as design and safety contracts, putting the thoughts of Meyer [4] into a safety context.

Building vehicles for cooperative functionality is yet one step further beyond the integrated architecture, and this also requires more than when realizing an integrated architecture. The design problem for cooperative functionalities is a system-of-systems problem, where the set of systems may change a lot during run time. Nevertheless, all existing standards for functional safety require a complete safety case at design time. But for cooperative functions, the set of parts may change at any time, since the set of systems (vehicles) may change at any time.

One way to prove the safety for one cooperative functionality, would be to build one complete safety case at design time valid for every possible run time scenario. This might lead to designs that are commercially unattractive. Another approach would be to take into account the possibility of graceful degradation of each functionality, and view each step of degradation as a safety case of its own. Then we could move from design time to run time, part of the task of showing that all safety requirements always are met. This implies, however, that we can express which properties of the parts of the system-of-systems that are of importance for fulfilling this during run time. What is proposed in this paper is that traditional design time methods have to be complemented by run time methods. An enabler for run time methods would be to introduce quality metrics that can be used for arguing which levels of safety integrity that are achieved (and how they change) during run time.

2   Basic Concept of Information Theory

Information theory is a mathematical theory about communication, focusing on source coding and channel coding (and decoding) i. e how to code information efficiently when it is sent over a noisy communication channel. Source coding is about data compression and channel coding is about error coding. To be able to make these calculations it is necessary to quantify the concept of information in some way. In IT the word information is a measurable quantity and is related to events and their probability. There are two aspects of information. Mutual information is related to the communication between a sender and a receiver and includes aspects of redundancy.

Self-information is related to the probability of a single event X. By starting with the concept of self-information and extending its scope, there is hope that the concept of mutual information will later on be useful to express redundancy in a system. IT can, at least, serve as an inspirational source and give a deeper understanding of how information quality, redundancy and probability can be treated in a uniform way.

In IT, self-information is described with a simple formula (1) where I (X) denotes self-information for event X. It has no unit and its domain is [0, 1] and a range of [infinity, 0].

$$I(X) = -\log 2 \ \text{Probability\_of} (X) \tag{1}$$

If the probability of X is 100 % the self-information becomes:

$$I(X) = -\log 2 \ 1 = 0 \tag{2}$$

If the probability is approaching 0% self-information approaches infinity. Self-information can be interpreted as how surprised one becomes when event X happens or how much information one can obtain from the event. If event X has a probability of 100% to happen then there should be no surprise about it, thus its self-information is 0. The more unsure one becomes about the event, the more information can be gained from it. In [6] Kaiser and Zug elaborate on ideas about quality metrics and self-assessment for sensor data. Our idea is to extend the scope of self-assessment to denote all types of metrics dealing with quality measurements related to a single object, both during design time and run time.

We believe that (1) has interesting properties that can be applied to quality metrics in general. To get a better understanding of (1), let us look at information from two different aspects: a spatial view and a temporal view, fig 1.

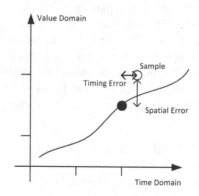

Fig. 1. Spatial and temporal noise

In general, when information is sampled by a sensor we get a quantizing error or quantizing noise. There is also some form of noise in the temporal domain, e.g. phase noise due to an imperfect clock signal. The terms information and sensor are to be taken very broadly. A lower quantizing noise means better quality. The same goes for the temporal domain. If these two error sources or noises were absent the information would be of the "highest quality". These two sources of noise are part of the probability function for failure in a communication channel. Low noise increases the probability of correct transmission, which in turn can be viewed as high quality. Quality can be measured as "the absence of bad", or the relation between what is considered good in a measurement and what is considered fault, annoyance, disturbance, missing or noise. If two quality metrics are independent as the case above with quantizing noise and phase noise, it can make sense to combine them into a single metric. From these arguments it seems reasonable to have zero to indicate the highest quality, or absence of bad, and infinity to indicate the lowest quality, or absence of good for a metric. The operation of addition to combine metrics will then preserve the notion of highest quality as well as lowest quality. It will also be simple to weight the metrics before addition with multiplication of scaling factors. From this point of view we suggest to extend the use of formula (1) to not only be a quantity of probability but any relative quality measure of something good (3).

$$M(X) = -\log 2 \; \text{Probability\_or\_ Percentage\_of\_something\_good} \; (X) \qquad (3)$$

Formula (3) and (1) are indeed the same. The only difference is that its domain is not restricted to the probability of an event, but rather any metric related to quality is expressed in a uniform way. This will put zero as the common reference value for "highest quality". The value is unit less and can thus be mixed freely if needed. Selecting a good common reference point is important since it can impact the simplicity of calculations and give better semantics to standard operators. Defining quality as "absence of bad" turns quality metrics into being additive in same way as noise is additive in a communication channel.

The use of quality metrics is not only useful during run time in regard to the safety aspect, but it is also useful in the design and verification process. To argue that a system is safe, it may not be sufficient in the future to rely only on good design practice. Using relevant metrics during design time will improve quality and this practice has the potential to be reused during run time. In general, any process or function that operates on information will at best preserve the quality of incoming information, but it can never improve the quality unless redundancy is introduced.

3   Functional Safety and Quality Calculations

The concept of functional safety can be described in different ways depending on the application and on the related safety standard. Most of the standards are elaborating on the theme "absence of unacceptable risk" where the risk is examined via risk analysis. Allowing vehicles to cooperate introduces additional risk, but it also provides means to reduce risk. Cooperative vehicles are likely to have overlapping (redundant) information. As redundancy is a means to reduce risk, the fact that vehicles are cooperating is an enabler for risk reduction. However, in reality the degree of redundancy may vary a lot during operation (run time) mainly because of the varying availability of reliable vehicle-to-vehicle communication, and of reliable sensor data.

When building a safe cooperative system, there are in principle two strategies to follow. The first one is to make a complete analysis beforehand in which is shown that the necessary risk reduction is always achieved for the entire mission of the system. The second one is to let the system itself calculate the actual available risk reduction continuously at run time, and adjust the mission in such a way that the achieved risk reduction is sufficient. This strategy can be seen as graceful degradation, where the mode of operation is adjusted so that the needed risk reduction always is fulfilled.

The process to determine the needed risk reduction is different between the different safety standards, but in principle there is a common idea of required levels of "safety integrity". The idea is that the higher level of safety integrity, the surer we are that there will be no safety-critical failure. In IEC 61508 these are called SIL (Safety Integrity Level), with SIL4 denoting the highest level. In ISO 26262 they are called ASIL (Automotive Safety Integrity Levels) with ASILD denoting the highest level.

When applying redundancy in a safety-critical system design, the safety standards tells you how the required safety integrity of the redundant parts may be lower than for the required safety integrity of the entire system. In the ISO26262 standard this is called ASIL decomposition, and there is a defined set of rules (an "ASIL algebra") telling possible ways to determine the required safety integrity of redundant architectural elements.

These kinds of rules assume that the redundancy itself can be guaranteed. This guarantee is required to have at least an integrity level as of the redundant system itself. If for example there is a requirement on ASILD that is realized by ASILA+ASILC, the guarantee of the redundancy still have to be ASILD.

In a scenario with cooperative vehicles, it is most likely never the case that the nominal redundancy pattern can be guaranteed valid for the entire operation with a high level of integrity. In order to be able to take benefit from such redundancy in the safety argumentation, it is thus necessary to measure it continuously during run time. This requires however that what can be measured by the system itself during run time, can be transformed into a metrics for safety integrity level according to the applicable safety standard.

Our hypothesis is that different quality metrics measured during run time can be used for estimating the achieved level of safety integrity. We can say that we are in a quest for "an algebra of quality".

In the end what is relevant is how much we can trust, or be confident, about the information in the system. Attributes such as standard deviation, degree of redundancy and probabilities of correct values are important quality attributes. Looking closer at information theory, IT, one realizes that these attributes are what IT is about. So our view of (3) is that it transforms a product of probabilities into addition of quality attributes when producing evidence according to a safety argument.

4   Conclusion

This paper describes work in progress related to enable the extension of safety standards to deal with cooperative functionalities. To argue the safety of a system consisting of collaborative vehicles, appropriate metrics is needed; both during design time and during run time. The run time metrics will be used to assert the integrity of the system continuously during operation and for comparison with the, at design time identified, required safety integrity levels. These metrics will be shared, compared and processed in different ways. At the moment, all kinds of metrics that will be needed for different domains and services cannot be foreseen, but it is possible to assert that they share some common properties and can be handled in a uniform way. Standard operators as multiplication and addition will then have simple semantic meaning when scaling and combining quality indexes. Information theory is based on probability and has sound theoretical ground. Its definition of self-information has properties that are wanted. Safety is also related to probability so it seems natural to try to extend the scope of self-information to also be about quality metrics.

This paper has focused on quality metrics for safety on a technical ground. Focusing more on quality metrics also has other merits. There exist efforts like ISO/IEC 15504 to evaluate and improve a design process, but their analysis is more based on manual inspection than processing quality metrics. The work to understand how to measure and process quality metrics during run time based on design time quality metrics can hopefully also aid such efforts.

Acknowledgment. This work as been supported by the EU under the FP7-ICT programme, through project 288195 "Kernel-based ARchitecture for safetY-critical cONtrol" (KARYON).

References

1. Bate, I., et al.: A Contract-Based Approach to Designing Safe Systems. In: 8th Australian Workshop on Safety-Critical Systems and Software, SCS 2003 (2003)
2. Chen, D., Johansson, R., Lönn, H., Papadopoulos, Y., Sandberg, A., Törner, F., Törngren, M.: Modelling Support for Design of Safety-Critical Automotive Embedded Systems. In: Harrison, M.D., Sujan, M.-A. (eds.) SAFECOMP 2008. LNCS, vol. 5219, pp. 72–85. Springer, Heidelberg (2008)
3. Johansson, R., et al.: A Road-Map for Enabling System Analysis of AUTOSAR Based Systems. In: Proceedings of Critical Automotive applications: Robustness & Safety, CARS (2010)
4. Meyer, B.: Object-Oriented software Construction. Prentice Hall (1988)
5. Di Natale, M., Sangiovanni-Vincentelli, A.L.: Moving From federated to Integrated Architechtures in Automotive: The Role of Standards, Methods and Tools. Proceedings of the IEEE 98, 603–620 (2010)
6. Kaiser, J., Zug, S.: A fault-aware sensor architecture for cooperative mobile applications. In: Proc. 17th IEEE Workshop on Dependable Parallel, Distributed and Network-Centric Systems (DPDNS 2012), Shanghai, China, May 25 (2012)

From Autonomous Vehicles to Safer Cars: Selected Challenges for the Software Engineering

Christian Berger

Department of Computer Science and Engineering
Chalmers, University of Gothenburg, Sweden
christian.berger@chalmers.se

Abstract. In November 2007, the DARPA Urban Challenge took place on the former George Airforce base in Victorville, California. Within that competition, teams from all-over the world had to demonstrate the autonomous driving capabilities from their robot cars in an urban-like environment. From initially 89 competitors, only eleven qualified for the final event wherein "Boss" from Carnegie Mellon finally won the race. In this article, a short overview over European's best team "CarOLO" and its vehicle "Caroline" within that competition is outlined. Based on the experiences from that competition, remaining challenges for the software engineering are described to realize safer cars in the future.

Keywords: autonomous driving, automotive safety functions, software engineering.

1 Introduction

The 2007 DARPA Urban Challenge was the third major challenge for autonomously driving vehicles within the last decade. That competition was the successor of the 2004 & 2005 DARPA Grand Challenges series wherein robot cars had to drive safely within stationary surroundings. However, that last competition increased the requirements to these robot cars significantly because they had to deal safely within moving traffic while they had to obey the Californian traffic regulations at the same time.

In Fig. 1(a), the robot vehicle "Caroline" from team "CarOLO" of the Technische Universität Braunschweig is depicted. "Caroline" based on a 2006 Volkswagen Passat station wagon, which was modified to meet the requirements of the DARPA Urban Challenge [3]. The main idea behind its sensor setup was to rely on redundant and overlapping viewing areas on the one hand; on the other hand, different measuring principles were used to avoid a sensor's individual weaknesses.

To detected moving traffic, "Caroline" used two IBEA Alasca XT sensors together with one Hella IDIS Lidar and one SMS UMRR radar, which were mounted at the vehicle's front; on the rear side, one IBEO ML, one Hella IDIS Lidar, and two SMS Blind Spot detectors were used to back out safely from

F. Ortmeier and P. Daniel (Eds.): SAFECOMP 2012 Workshops, LNCS 7613, pp. 180–189, 2012.
© Springer-Verlag Berlin Heidelberg 2012

(a) Sensor setup of the autonomously driving robot vehicle "Caroline".

(b) Computers in the vehicle's trunk, which were used to process the mass data to derive driving decisions.

Fig. 1. The autonomously driving vehicle "Caroline"–the contribution from the Technische Universität Braunschweig, which competed in the 2007 DARPA Urban Challenge as the best European entry ([1,2])

a parking spot. For detecting the lanemarkings, four Point Grey Flea2 firewire cameras were used [4]. The drivable area in front of the robot vehicle was detected with an IDS μEye monocular color-camera together with two Sick LMS 291 single layer laser scanners [5]. All data was processed in the vehicle's trunk by several computers, which were running with Debian Linux (cf. Fig. 1(b)).

As shown in Fig. 2, incoming sensors' data was processed by the *pipes and filters* architectural design pattern [7]: The perception layer gathers all data from the sensors, which includes not only online data that is read from all mounted sensors, but also a priori available offline data like annotated digital maps. That

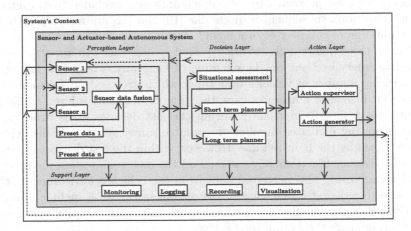

Fig. 2. System architecture, which consists of a data perception layer, a decision layer, and an action layer; the support layer is used to inspect non-reactively the data flows (according to [6]).

layer creates and updates continuously an environmental model, which is the input for the following decision layer. Within that layer, the model of the surroundings is interpreted and evaluated to derive driving decisions. Therefore, a short-term planner reacts on the current traffic situation while the long-term planner tries to achieve the overall goal like reaching the final destination point. From that layer, set points for the action layer are derived to be driven by control algorithms. A more detailed description of "Caroline" can be found at [1] and [2]. While the depicted system architecture shows the specific realization of "Caroline", a similar architecture can be found in recent projects like [8], which was enhanced by an HMI layer and a state model for the driver's actions; however, those aspects were not part of the 2007 DARPA Urban Challenge competition for driverless robots.

However, the 2007 DARPA Urban Challenge excluded the at least protected traffic participants: Pedestrians and bicyclists [3]. To provide autonomously driving vehicles for daily usage, it is necessary to increase their reliability significantly so that they act safely in various and even unpredictable traffic situations [9]. In this contribution, selected challenges for the software engineering are described, which arise from the goal to avoid casualties and fatalities, to reduce energy consumption, and to increase the overall traffic flow on our roads. The paper is structured as follows: First, a short overview over related work is provided, followed by a description of selected challenges for the software engineering. Finally, the paper summarizes the open issues and provides a short outlook.

2   Related Work

The 2007 DARPA Urban Challenge fostered the research and development of robot vehicles especially for urban and rural environments. However as already mentioned, the least protected traffic participants were excluded from that competition. Therefore, subsequent projects like [10] and [11] address explicitly this extended and more complex environment.

In Fig. 3, three different charts are depicted to illustrate the impact of recent automotive safety systems on the example of Germany. The green line shows the increasing number of vehicles over time, which are used on German roads. Despite that increased number of cars, the number of fatally injured traffic participants has dropped significantly during the last decades. This drop can be deduced from the increased number of available safety systems in the vehicles, which is shown by the light red line. However, within the last decade, more and more vehicle safety functions rely not only on the own vehicle data anymore; instead, they are using also perceived data from the vehicle's environment. Thus, it can be deduced that an increase in the overall safety must include also data from a vehicle's surroundings. Therefore, more and more complex systems are required to improve the overall road safety.

These increasingly complex systems can be regarded as so-called *cyber-physical systems* (CPS) [12], which enable further possibilities on the one hand [13]; on the other hand, new methods are required to safely and reliably develop

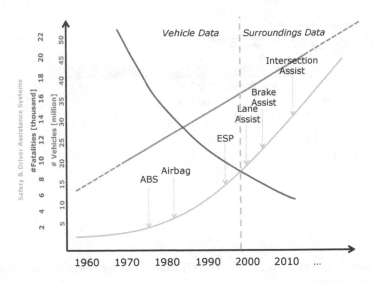

Fig. 3. Green line: Increasing number of vehicles in Germany (based on *Statistisches Bundesamt, www.destatis.de*); dark red line: Decreasing number of fatally injured traffic participants (based on *Bundesanstalt für Straßenwesen, www.bast.de*); light red line: Increasing number of safety & driver assistance systems (based on *ADAC e.V., www.adac.de)*. The recent assistance systems rely additionally on the vehicle's surroundings data.

and test these more and more interconnected safety-critical systems [14]. Therefore, in [6] and [15], an approach is outlined, which enables a virtualized testing environment for autonomously driving vehicles. Furthermore, formal methods could be successfully applied to focus on the *correct* implementation of the *right* requirements [16] during the requirements elicitation at a large German automotive OEM. However, there are still open issues for today's software engineering during the development and the lifecycle of these CPS, which are discussed in the following section.

3   Selected Challenges for Software Engineering

In Fig. 4, the lifecycle of a vehicle is shown. According to [17], the development of these nowadays more and more complex and software-intense systems lasts approximately 3.5 years, which is followed by a production cycle of roughly 7 years. However, the estimated usage duration of the vehicles is on average about 8 years. Therefore, decisions, which were met at development time must be valid for approximately 18 years in the worst case. Thus, today's software engineering is faced with questions regarding the product's long-term usage, which arise during the entire lifecycle of complex and software-intense CPS, which perceive the surroundings for interactions. Solutions to these questions are important especially for safety-critical automotive functions. Selected open issues are discussed

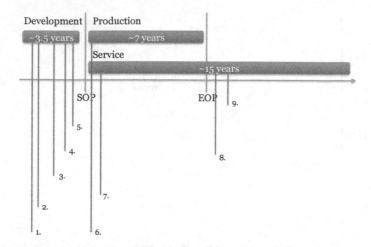

Fig. 4. Automotive lifecycle according to [17] annotated by selected challenges for today's software engineering

in the following, which are related to the design of embedded vehicle functions that rely on data from the surroundings for a proper functioning.

1. How can we effectively apply formal methods for modeling requirements to increase our confidence in the later implementation?

Today's vehicles assist passengers not only with comfort functions but even more with safety-critical vehicle functions in dynamically critical driving situations. For example, the vehicle can initiate a braking maneuver due to a predicted collision, which is deduced from the gathered sensor data. Since November 2011, the ISO 26262 is in effect to provide guidelines for the development of functions with a certain automotive safety integrity level (A-SIL). However, formal methods are suggested to be "recommended" and only semi-formal methods are suggested to be "highly recommended"; nevertheless, there are also first success stories from the pre-development stage for safety-critical vehicle functions, which applied formal methods even for the requirements specification during the requirement [16]. Thus, the aforementioned question also includes aspects how new standards can be implemented effectively.

2. How can we identify and derive necessary parameters and their interrelations (e.g. sensor setup and mounting positions) already very early during the development to find the optimal design of a context-aware embedded function?

As shown in Fig. 3, recent automotive software functions rely more and more on data, which is perceived from the vehicle's surroundings. However, parameters and their interrelations like mounting positions or opening angles, which significantly influence design decisions and the resulting vehicle function's quality, are hardly to estimate in a correct and complete manner already at the beginning of the development. However, the development of first prototypes consume considerable resources on the one hand; on the other hand, sensors' data from traffic situations, in which the vehicle function shall operate, must be available very early to develop a stable concept, which consists of both a hardware and a software architecture.

3. How can we predict the impact of design decisions alongside the development process (e.g. sensor type & position, viewing angles, logical software architecture, resulting distribution among ECUs, economic boundaries, ...) regarding the quality of the resulting implementation?

This issue is related to the previous one and requires the extensive usage of complex simulations. Especially for software functions, which base on environmental data, a high responsiveness to a developer's questions can be achieved by appropriate simulation environments. Thus, experiments with these complex systems could be carried out in such a virtualized environment to pose the right questions during the development.

4. Which simulations must be repeated (for example by automated regression simulations) in case of changes in the requirements or in the implementation and why?

However, while simulations can provide valuable answers, they are also time- and resource-consuming. Therefore, models are required to derive figures for guiding computationally intense simulation runs. Furthermore, when simulations are used as a part of the software construction process as outlined in [18,1,6], these models shall provide information to decide which simulation runs are necessarily required when requirements and/or the implementation changes.

5. Which real test-drives must be carried out to confirm results from previous simulation runs and which real test-drives can be omitted without difficulty and why?

Right before the start of production (SOP), vehicle functions must be formally released to meet this fixed date. Therefore, simulations, which were a vital part during the development, shall provide information to decide which real test-drives must be carried out to confirm previously derived simulative results. Furthermore, this information can also be used to plan long-term robustness test-drives effectively by providing information about traffic situations, which were difficult to handle within the simulation.

6. How can results from simulations and real test-drives be adapted and predicted for software variants from a software product line?

Even more, these simulations must play a major role in today's diverse vehicle projects, which often only differ slightly. However, they are even more important for the outlined systems, which also rely on data from the vehicle's surroundings. For example, a collision detection system in a premium car could rely on a more expensive sensor compared to a system for a low-cost vehicle; however in the end, the expected behavior from the customer's point of view is identical regardless of the underlying technology. Thus, simulations must be designed and carried out to achieve synergies for different real CPS with similar behavior.

7. How can we use statistical vehicle data (e.g. maintenance, ...) from the field to improve the development process and to predict the software quality for future vehicle projects?

For example, maintenance data from the field could be analyzed to find an erroneous behavior pattern of a software function. This pattern could be modeled in a centralized simulation environment as a specific traffic situation to improve further variants of the software function and to realize a "lessons learnt" for the software development of oncoming vehicle projects. Furthermore, data from vehicle flows is nowadays already used to predict traffic jams or to estimate bottle-necks in the road infrastructure for example [19]. In the future, vehicle-to-X data could also be used in an online manner during the journey to adapt driving profiles according to the current traffic situation for example. However, models from this highly volatile data are necessary to improve future vehicle functions based on insights, which are deduced from a fleet's field data.

8. How do we maintain our long-term software quality when e.g. sensors and V2X protocols evolve?

However, the most challenging points arise from the long-term usage of these software-intense and complex vehicle functions. Due to the traditional development of automotive systems, vehicle functions are often separated and deployed to their specific ECUs. However, this development model was rethought with the development and introduction of AUTOSAR, which enables the OEMs to separate vehicle functions from the hardware. But the concepts of AUTOSAR must be enhanced when reconfiguration during the functions life-time is required by changes in the surroundings as described by [20] for example. This change can be caused simply by an exchange of existing sensors or even by evolving communication protocols. Furthermore, another aspect is to tackle such a reconfiguration with proper design-time models according to the aforementioned safety standards.

9. How can we predict and ensure reliability of our vehicle functions in a long-term manner regarding mixed traffic, which consists of vehicles with different levels of "intelligence"?

Nowadays, vehicle systems realize functions, which are related to the own vehicle and to the directly visible surroundings. However, when vehicle-to-X communication is a vital part of a comfort or perhaps a safety system, simulations must be significantly improved to include data about mixed traffic. This traffic consists of vehicles with different "intelligence" levels ranging from none to high. Furthermore, the structure of this mixed traffic will change and evolve over time. Therefore, models for this mixed traffic will be mandatory and crucial in the future the ensure the quality of interconnected and interrelated automotive functions.

However, how can the aforementioned challenges be successfully addressed? A possible solution was already pointed out in some of the aforementioned questions: Simulations must play a larger role within the software engineering. Contrary to other engineering disciplines, simulations are nearly mandatory during the design of control algorithms for example or for the analysis of physical phenomena. In those areas, they are an essential method during the development. Furthermore and already 1999, [21] pointed out that simulative approaches are not only helpful for the analysis of the technical and physical context but they can also assist to analyze processes in software engineering.

Regarding CPS, simulative approaches must be used more intensively to increase the confidence in the resulting implementation because of its complex surroundings. Real world tests will still play an important role in the foreseeable future but simulations will additionally provide valuable insights and feedback already at earlier stages during the development process where real prototypes of there interconnected CPS are not yet available. Thus, a methodical incorporation of these simulative approaches in software engineering processes will become increasingly important.

4   Conclusion

The 2007 DARPA Urban Challenge was a showcase that fostered significantly the research and development for autonomously driving vehicles. Recent prototypes proved long-term usability with ranges over more than 140,000mi [22]. Furthermore, first initiatives are successful to permit the usage of such vehicles in public traffic in some states in the US.

However, as shown along the lifecycle of a vehicle, there still remain several open issues to manage the development and maintenance of such a complex and software-intense CPS from a software engineer's point of view. The major challenge is that more and more safety-critical vehicle functions rely on data from the vehicle's context, which is very volatile due to mixed traffic or evolution in vehicle-to-X communication protocols for example. However, in contrast to the avionics sector, which demands a software development according to DO 178C, or the railway sector, which relies on a development that follows EN 50128, function development according to ISO 26262 for safety-critical automotive functions is very young because the standard was released in November 2011 first. Thus, industrial success stories from development projects, which implement the ISO 26262, will arise primal in the upcoming years to show the practical benefit.

In this contribution, selected challenges for the software engineering for these complex CPS were discussed. For many of these exemplary questions, simulative approaches, which include explicitly the system's context, could provide the means for developers to analyze these interconnected and interrelated systems already at early development stages. However, a further elaborated methodology for their usages within the software engineering is required, which outlines how and to which extent these simulations could be successfully used–especially for more than only one project to achieve synergies.

References

1. Rauskolb, F.W., Berger, K., Lipski, C., Magnor, M., Cornelsen, K., Effertz, J., Form, T., Graefe, F., Ohl, S., Schumacher, W., Wille, J.M., Hecker, P., Nothdurft, T., Doering, M., Homeier, K., Morgenroth, J., Wolf, L., Basarke, C., Berger, C., Gülke, T., Klose, F., Rumpe, B.: Caroline: An Autonomously Driving Vehicle for Urban Environments. Journal of Field Robotics 25(9), 674–724 (2008)

2. Basarke, C., Berger, C., Berger, K., Cornelsen, K., Doering, M., Effertz, J., Form, T., Gülke, T., Graefe, F., Hecker, P., Homeier, K., Klose, F., Lipski, C., Magnor, M., Morgenroth, J., Nothdurft, T., Ohl, S., Rauskolb, F.W., Rumpe, B., Schumacher, W., Wille, J.M., Wolf, L.: Team CarOLO - Technical Paper. Informatik-Bericht 2008-07, Technische Universität Braunschweig, Braunschweig, Germany (October 2008)

3. DARPA: Urban Challenge Technical Evaluation Criteria. Technical report, DARPA, Arlington, VA, USA (2006)

4. Lipski, C., Scholz, B., Berger, K., Linz, C., Stich, T., Magnor, M.: A Fast and Robust Approach to Lane Marking Detection and Lane Tracking. In: Proceedings of the IEEE Southwest Symposium on Image Analysis and Interpretation, pp. 57–60. IEEE (2008)

5. Berger, K., Lipski, C., Linz, C., Stich, T., Magnor, M.: The Area Processing Unit of Caroline - Finding the Way through DARPA's Urban Challenge. In: Sommer, G., Klette, R. (eds.) RobVis 2008. LNCS, vol. 4931, pp. 260–274. Springer, Heidelberg (2008)

6. Berger, C.: Automating Acceptance Tests for Sensor- and Actuator-based Systems on the Example of Autonomous Vehicles. Shaker Verlag, Aachener Informatik-Berichte, Software Engineering Band 6, Aachen, Germany (2010)

7. Raymond, E.S.: The Art of Unix Programming. Addison-Wesley, Boston (2003)

8. Flemisch, F., Nashashibi, F., Rauch, N., Schieben, A., Glaser, S., Gerald, T., Resende, P., Vanholme, B., Löper, C., Thomaidis, G., Mosebach, H., Schomerus, J., Hima, S., Kaussner, A.: Towards Highly Automated Driving: Intermediate report on the HAVEit-Joint System. In: Proceedings of the 3rd European Road Transport Research Arena, Brussels, Belgium, pp. 1–12 (November 2010)

9. Berger, C., Rumpe, B.: Autonomous Driving - 5 Years after the Urban Challenge: The Anticipatory Vehicle as a Cyber-Physical System. In: Goltz, U., Magnor, M., Appelrath, H.J., Matthies, H.K., Balke, W.T., Wolf, L. (eds.) Proceedings of the INFORMATIK 2012, Braunschweig, Germany (September 2012)

10. Nothdurft, T., Hecker, P., Ohl, S., Saust, F., Maurer, M., Reschka, A., Böhmer, J.R.: Stadtpilot: First Fully Autonomous Test Drives in Urban Traffic. In: Proceedings of the International IEEE Conference on Intelligent Transportation Systems, Washington, DC, USA, pp. 919–924 (October 2011)

11. Wang, M., Ganjineh, T., Rojas, R.: Action Annotated Trajectory Generation for Autonomous Maneuvers on Structured Road Networks. In: Proceedings of the 5th International Conference on Automation, Robotics and Applications, Wellington, New Zealand, pp. 67–72 (December 2011)

12. Lee, E.A.: Computing Foundations and Practice for Cyber-Physical Systems: A Preliminary Report. Technical Report UCB/EECS-2007-72, University of California, Berkeley, CA, USA (2007)

13. Geisberger, E., Broy, M. (eds.): agendaCPS - Integrierte Forschungsagenda Cyber-Physical Systems (acatech STUDIE). Springer, Heidelberg (2012)

14. Giese, H., Rumpe, B., Schätz, B., Sztipanovits, J.: Science and Engineering of Cyber-Physical Systems. Dagstuhl Reports 1(11), 1–22 (2012)

15. Berger, C., Rumpe, B.: Engineering Autonomous Driving Software. In: Rouff, C., Hinchey, M. (eds.) Experience from the DARPA Urban Challenge, pp. 243–271. Springer, London (2012)

16. Siegl, S., Hielscher, K.S., German, R., Berger, C.: Automated Testing of Embedded Automotive Systems from Requirement Specification Models. In: Proceedings of the 12th IEEE Latin-American Test Workshop, Porto de Galinhas, Brazil, pp. 1–6 (March 2011)

17. Schäuffele, J., Zurawka, T.: Automotive Software Engineering. Friedr. Vieweg & Sohn Verlag, Wiesbaden, Germany (2003)
18. Basarke, C., Berger, C., Rumpe, B.: Software & Systems Engineering Process and Tools for the Development of Autonomous Driving Intelligence. Journal of Aerospace Computing, Information, and Communication 4(12), 1158–1174 (2007)
19. Jiang, R., Hu, M.B., Jia, B., Wang, R., Wu, Q.S.: Effect of Adaptive Cruise Control Vehicles on Phase Transition in a Mixture with Manual Vehicles. In: Appert-Rolland, C., Chevoir, F., Gondret, P., Lassarre, S., Lebacque, J.P., Schreckenberg, M. (eds.) Traffic and Granular Flow 2007, pp. 105–115. Springer, Heidelberg (2009)
20. Weiss, G., Zeller, M., Eilers, D., Knorr, R.: Towards Self-organization in Automotive Embedded Systems. In: González Nieto, J., Reif, W., Wang, G., Indulska, J. (eds.) ATC 2009. LNCS, vol. 5586, pp. 32–46. Springer, Heidelberg (2009)
21. Christie, A.M.: Simulation: An Enabling Technology in Software Engineering. CROSSTALK - The Journal of Defense Software Engineering 12(4), 25–30 (1999)
22. Thrun, S.: What we're driving at (2010)

Modelling of Safety-Related Timing Constraints for Automotive Embedded Systems

Oscar Ljungkrantz, Henrik Lönn, Hans Blom, Cecilia Ekelin, and Daniel Karlsson

Advanced Technology & Research
Volvo Group Trucks Technology
Gothenburg, Sweden
{oscar.ljungkrantz,henrik.lonn,hans.blom,cecilia.ekelin,
daniel.b.karlsson}@volvo.com

Abstract. Timing and functional safety are important aspects when developing automotive embedded systems. The two aspects have however mostly been studied as separate aspects, up to now. This paper presents an investigation of safety-related timing constraints within the functional safety standard ISO 26262. Although the standard defines several such timing constraints it also leaves room for interpretation, which is discussed in the paper. Clear interpretations are needed to support current trends towards model-based development. A few extensions are proposed to the state-of-the-art modelling languages EAST-ADL and TADL to specify the timing constraints.

Keywords: Automotive embedded systems, fault/failure modelling, functional safety, ISO 26262, timing, EAST-ADL.

1 Introduction

The embedded systems in motor vehicles are getting increasingly complex. Drive-by-wire solutions, diagnostic services, safety systems, infotainment systems and hybrid electric vehicles all add to the complexity. This challenge has in part been addressed by the automotive industry in different collaboration and standardisation initiatives. The *AUTOSAR* architecture addresses software standardization and enables a common market for automotive software components, see [1]. AUTOSAR was presented in 2004 [2] and can now be considered a de facto standard. EAST-ADL [3] complements AUTOSAR with descriptions at higher level of abstractions. *EAST-ADL* is an architectural description language (ADL) supporting model-based development of automotive embedded systems.

When developing automotive embedded systems, not only the functionality must be handled but also other aspects such as safety, timing, variability and cost. *Safety* and *timing* are two challenging aspects that have gained a lot of interest in recent years, manifested in for instance the *ISO 26262* standard [4][5] and the *Timing Augmented Description Language (TADL)* [6].

The ISO 26262 standard addresses functional safety of electrical/electronic (E/E) systems in road vehicles. The aim of the standard is absence of unacceptable risk by

F. Ortmeier and P. Daniel (Eds.): SAFECOMP 2012 Workshops, LNCS 7613, pp. 190–201, 2012.

avoiding malfunctions of the system. EAST-ADL provides several language constructs to model safety-related properties and requirements of ISO 26262 [7].

TADL was introduced to extend the modelling of EAST-ADL and AUTOSAR with time constraints that relates to events and event chains. The main concepts have been included in EAST-ADL and AUTOSAR (since Release 4.0.1), but the TADL has been further improved, see [8].

Although timing and safety have been much investigated, they have typically been studied as separate aspects. Nonetheless, the two aspects overlap. For instance a *safety requirement* can mandate the system to protect against harm or hazards with a certain probability, see [9], and thus the required timing of the mitigation, the *safety mechanism*, is a crucial part. Also other timing requirements and properties of the system may be safety-critical, such as the reaction time of the brakes. These properties and requirements are here denoted *safety-related timing constraints*.

This paper presents the work-in-progress of the *TimeSafe* project regarding modelling of safety-related timing constraints of ISO 26262. The ISO 26262 has been scrutinized looking for timing constraints, and the suitability of the EAST-ADL and TADL languages to model these timing constraints has been investigated. In the authors' knowledge no similar study has been performed before. The contribution of this paper is the analysis of seven safety-related timing constraints and the proposed guidelines and new language constructs to specify the constraints.

The next section briefly describes the EAST-ADL modelling language. Section 3 gives an overview of the safety-related timing constraints. Section 4 presents the proposed language additions and thereon Section 5 and Section 6 discuss two constraints in detail. Finally, the work is concluded in Section 7.

2   Modelling Language

The purpose of EAST-ADL is to capture engineering information related to automotive E/E system development, from early phase to final implementation. The EAST-ADL model has a core part representing the E/E system, which interfaces to an Environment model for near and far environment. Extensions for variability, dependability, etc., annotate the core elements with additional aspects. One of the extensions concerns dependability and captures information related to safety. Another extension captures system timing using events, event chains and timing constraints, as defined in TADL.

The EAST-ADL system model is organized in 4 abstraction levels, see Fig. 1, from the *Vehicle Level* (*VL*) abstract and solution-independent feature models over the *Analysis Level* (*AL*) hardware independent functional models and the *Design Level* (*DL*) hardware-allocated functional architecture to the *Implementation Level* (*IL*) AUTOSAR software and hardware architecture.

The ISO 26262 defines phases for the design of E/E systems. Fig. 1 also shows how these phases relate to the EAST-ADL abstraction levels. In the *concept phase*, safety goals with a certain Automotive Safety Integrity Level (ASIL) are defined on VL based on a solution-independent risk assessment. The safety goal is refined to functional safety requirements allocated to elements of a preliminary architecture on AL. Technical safety requirements are allocated to system elements on DL in the *product development phase - system*. In the *product development phase – HW and SW*, requirements are allocated to HW and SW components on IL.

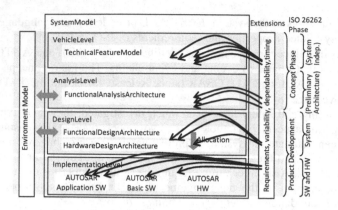

Fig. 1. EAST-ADL organization and ISO 26262 Phases

3   Overview of the Safety-Related Timing Constraints

The following seven timing constraints have been identified as explicitly mentioned in part 3–6 of ISO 26262. The first five are also defined in the vocabulary, part 1.

1. Fault tolerant time interval
2. Emergency operation interval
3. Fault reaction time
4. Multiple-point fault detection interval
5. Diagnostic test interval
6. Fault detection time
7. Exposure duration

The timing constraints are mentioned in several parts of the standard and can be interpreted differently at different abstraction levels of the related solution. The first four constraint are defined in the vocabulary of ISO 26262 using *solution-neutral* concepts such as fault, failure, hazard and transition to safe state. In part 3–6, the seven timing constraints are stated to be specified or analysed relating to solutions, such as safety mechanisms, as part of the functional-, technical-, hardware- or software safety requirements or concepts. Timing constraints referring directly to elements of the architectural solution can be viewed as *solution-specific* constraints derived from the solution-neutral constraints. Nevertheless, the distinction is not absolute, since the concepts of the solution-neutral constraints, such as faults, may refer to specific solutions. The seven different constraints are described below.

Five of the timing constraints are introduced in Fig. 2, relating to solution-neutral concepts. This figure is based on the figure in 1-1.44[1] of ISO 26262 and extended with the two timing constraints that are put in parentheses. The *Fault Tolerant Time Interval* (*FTTI*) acts as an upper bound for safety mechanisms, relating a fault to the possible

---

[1] Specific clauses of ISO 262626 are indicated as "m-n" within this paper, where "m" represents the number of the particular part and "n" represents the number of the clause within that part.

hazard that may be caused if not handled by a safety mechanism. FTTI is further discussed in Section 5. The *emergency operation interval* is the time between the occurrence of a fault and the transition to a safe state. An emergency operation shall be specified when a safe state cannot be reached within an acceptable time interval. The emergency operation interval is further discussed in Section 6. The *fault detection time* and the *fault reaction time* naturally refers to the detection and reaction upon the fault, respectively. The concept of fault detection time is not defined by ISO 26262, but several clauses in part 5 (hardware level) of ISO 26262 concern analysis of the fault detection time associated with dual-point failures. It is included in the figure to clarify the relations. The *diagnostic test interval* is specified in ISO 26262 though, as the "amount of time between the executions of online diagnostic test by a safety mechanism". It can thus be viewed as the worst case fault detection time, since the actual fault detection time may be shorter in some occasions.

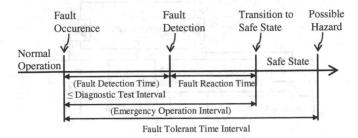

Fig. 2. Some basic concepts and timing constraints of ISO 26262 [4]

The *multiple-point fault detection interval* is the time to detect a multiple-point fault "before it can contribute to a multiple-point failure". It relates to two (dual-point) or more faults that only if all are present contribute to the violation of safety goals, for instance a fault in a safety-related sensor and a fault in the corresponding safety mechanism. Each of these individual faults is denoted multiple-point fault. Finally, the *exposure duration* shall be considered in the analysis of dual-point faults and may include the multiple-point fault detection interval, the maximum duration of a trip and the average time to vehicle repair. It is not defined in ISO 26262 vocabulary but introduced and explained in relation to the hardware analysis in 5-9.4.2.1.

The constraints are further explained using an abstract view of a safety mechanism, that detects and reacts upon the fault, in Fig. 3. This safety mechanism is assumed to be *periodically* executed and having a certain *response time* to reach the safe state. As seen, both times can be modelled using TADL. At this abstract view, the diagnostic test interval is the same as the periodic interval, which in turn is approximately the worst case fault detection time. Likewise, the fault reaction time is the same as the response time. The sum of the fault detection time and the fault reaction time shall not be longer than the FTTI. Since the actual fault detection time may vary, a rational requirement mentioned in part 5 of ISO 26262, is that the diagnostic test interval plus the fault reaction shall not be longer than the fault tolerant time interval.

Fig. 4 shows a possible, general design of the safety mechanism. The elements have the corresponding response times (RT) and are potentially periodically executed with corresponding periodic intervals (PI). These times can be modelled the same way as in Fig. 3.

In general, the sum of PI_A, RT_A, PI_B and RT_B represents the worst case fault detection time. This sum may be considered to be the diagnostic test interval but note that this does not conform to the wordings of the definition. Likewise, the sum of PI_C, RT_C, PI_D and RT_D represents the worst case fault reaction time. Also note that the time until the transition to safe state, and hence the fault reaction time, can be longer than this sum for some safety mechanisms as specified by the emergency operation. Typically, several executions of the safety controller could be needed. The timing constraints may also be further broken down and detailed in later design steps taking for instance communication times and scheduling into account.

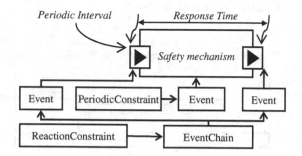

Fig. 3. An abstract view of a safety mechanism system, which is recurrently/periodically executed. The periodic interval and response time are indicated in italic and formalized using TADL.

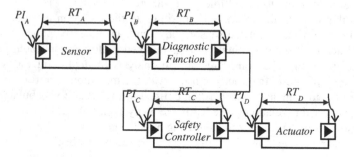

Fig. 4. A possible design of a safety mechanism consisting of four elements, which are all potentially periodically executed with corresponding periodic intervals (PI) and response times (RT). These times/intervals can be modelled the same way as in Fig. 3.

4   Proposed Modelling Language Extensions

This section presents the proposed language extensions to enable to specify the seven timing constraints introduced in the previous section. For brevity reasons all seven timing constraints cannot be discussed in detail, but the fault tolerant time interval and emergency operation interval are chosen as representative examples and are discussed in Section 5 and Section 6, respectively.

Although the TADL language can be satisfactorily used to specify timing constraints referring directly to elements of the architectural solution, it can currently *not* be used to refer to concepts such as fault, failure, hazard and transition to safe state. For this reason the authors of this paper proposes to extend the TADL event model with four new events, as seen in Fig. 8.

The *EventFaultFailure* represents the occurrence of a fault or failure. The FaultFailure element contains a faultFailureValue that defines the specific value among the possible faults or failures that the FaultFailure represents. The FaultFailure element can in turn refer to an in-port or out-port of an error model. This is utilized in the examples of the next two sections. Likewise, the *EventFeatureFlaw* represents the occurrence of a feature flaw. A feature flaw is an inability to fulfil one or several of the requirements, and can be seen as an abstract failure already considered during the vehicle phase. The *EventState* and *EventMode* represent the entrance or the exit (as specified by the *EventStateKind* attribute) of a mode/state. This can be used to refer to the transition to the safe state, e.g., as is done in Section 6.

5   Fault Tolerant Time Interval (FTTI)

This section discusses the fault tolerant time interval (FTTI) and how it can be modelled. Since the ISO 26262 leaves room for interpretation, this is first discussed. Three different examples are then used to support the discussions.

The FTTI is defined as the "time-span in which a **fault** (1.42) or faults can be present in a **system** (1.129) before a **hazardous** (1.57) event occurs" (1-1.45). On the other hand, the figure in 1-1.44 relates the FTTI to a fault and a *possible hazard*, see also Fig. 2 in this document. The difference between a hazard and a hazardous event is that the latter also includes an *operational situation*. This difference can have significant impact on the time, as will be evident from the airbag example in Section 5.2 below. The fact that the word "hazardous" alone, not "hazardous event", is emphasised in the definition adds to the confusion as well.

The FTTI is mentioned several times in ISO 26262. Part 3 states that the FTTI *shall be considered* (3-8.4.2.3) when specifying the functional safety requirements. Already the safety goal *can include* FTTI (3-7.4.4.6). Furthermore, part 4 states that the FTTI *shall be specified*, for relevant safety mechanisms, as part of the technical safety requirements (4-6.4.2.3). The FTTI is also mentioned several times in part 5, regarding compliance/consistency of the safety mechanisms with the FTTI.

5.1   Interpretation

The authors' interpretation is that the *operational situations must be considered* when determining the FTTI. The rationale is that 1) the actual definition of FTTI in 1-1.45 refers to hazardous event, and 2) it may take time before the system is in such a situation, where the failure can cause any harm and thus it's reasonable to include this time.

When determining the FTTI, a judgment must hence be made regarding the probability over time of the considered situation. Moreover, several hazardous events may be considered together, since the concept of fault tolerance includes being able to handle the different situations. This can be compared with the combination of similar safety goals into one, where hazardous events of different ASILs are mitigated by a safety goal with highest ASIL. An FTTI is therefore specified for each relevant combination of fault and a group of hazardous events, related by a common safety goal, where an *assessment* regarding the related hazardous events and their probability is needed.

The FTTI assessment is a nontrivial task to be performed in accordance with good engineering practice. ISO 26262 is not clear about this though and do not describe how the assessment shall be made. Stochastic calculations could be made, for instance assuming a constant rate per time for the occurrence of each hazardous event as in Fig. 5, if such data is available. The ASILs of the hazardous events must also be considered. In particular this can be challenging when several hazardous events with different ASILs and different probability for occurrence are considered. Nonetheless, an FTTI assessment could result in a time limit anticipating that *the probability that a hazardous event occurs before this time has passed since the fault occurred, is acceptably low.*

Moreover, the authors' experience and the examples below suggest that only a part of the operational situations must be included in the FTTI measure. The time until a specific situation depends on the probability of the traffic or environmental situation but this is captured by the *exposure* when determining the ASIL. The difference in time for the driver to react upon the failure in different situations is captured by the *controllability* part of the ASIL. However, the failure of a system can in some situations not cause any harm until the system is actually *requested*. This time is important to capture in the FTTI measure. The difference between different parts of the situations is particularly important when modelling the FTTI and precise events are pointed out.

As discussed, the FTTI can be specified at different abstraction levels. In the authors' experience it's often too early to determine FTTI as part of the safety goal. Technical solutions are not known at this stage and therefore faults and the system's tolerance against faults cannot be considered. The FTTI can naturally be introduced as part of the functional safety concept, when abstract technical solutions are considered, and as part of the technical safety concept, when safety mechanisms shall be specified.

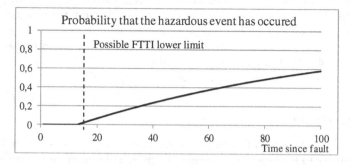

Fig. 5. Example of an exponential distribution function, relating the probability of a hazardous event to the time since the fault occurred

5.2   Examples

EPS: Imagine an *Electric Power Steering* system (EPS), where a fault in the torque sensor, such as a short-cut, may cause the failure that an unreasonable torque is suddenly applied to the steering column. This failure represents a hazard since it can cause harm in different situations. It is likely that there will be a hazardous event when the failure occurs, since basically all driving situations are hazardous in combination with this failure. The faster the vehicle moves, the shorter is the time for the driver to react upon the failure, which will result in that the corresponding hazardous event has the highest ASIL. It's necessary also to consider the physical system in which the EPS acts; for instance the response time of the electrical motor may act as a filter of the sudden torque change suggested by the controller. The FTTI should hence be larger than the time from fault to failure due to dynamics of the system, in the limiting high-speed situation, and is rather short, possibly in order of hundreds of milliseconds.

BBW: The second example is a *Brake-By-Wire* (BBW) system, where a fault in the primary electric energy source can cause an inability to brake (E/E failure and hazard). The operational situations that must be considered are the situations in which the driver must use the brake. The faster the vehicle is driven and the shorter the distance to an obstacle, the shorter the time to react. For example, driving at a highway, the speed is higher but the brakes used less frequently compared to driving in the city. This time can be captured as the time until the brake is actually *requested* but there is an inability to brake, which can be considered a vehicle failure. A restrictive but unlikely situation is when the vehicle is driven at high speed but must be stopped immediately, for instance due to an accident in front of the vehicle, and the fault occurs just when the driver hits the brake. If the vehicle speed is 100 km/h it takes about 100 ms to drive 3 meters. These figures could also be compared with the response time of the driver, which typically is in the order of seconds and with the normal braking distance, which is some tens of meters; possibly the FTTI is in order of hundreds of milliseconds or even seconds.

Airbag: A different example is an airbag in which a broken sensor (fault) may cause the airbag to not be able to deploy in case of a crash (E/E failure and hazard). The time between fault and failure is very small, but the airbag is not needed until a crash occurs (hazardous event). Such a crash could occur at the same time as the failure, but this is very unlikely. Again, this time can be captured as the time until the airbag is *requested* but unable to deploy, which can be considered a vehicle failure. Having analysed the situation probabilities, the FTTI could for instance be one vehicle trip or the time until the vehicle is planned for maintenance so that the airbag can be repaired.

5.3   Modelling

When developing the functional or technical safety concept, an ErrorModelType with an ErrorBehavior can be used to represent the fault and the failure of the E/E system. Likewise, an error model can be used to represent the fault propagation of the plant. FaultFailure elements denote the value representing the fault or failure at the respective fault/failure port. This way an EventFaultFailure at the fault input of the E/E error model represents the occurrence of the fault and an EventFaultFailure at the failure output of the plant error model represents the inability to fulfil the functionality of the vehicle, when it's requested. As seen by the examples above, the request of the functionality captures the relevant part of the operational situation. This request can be made explicit as an input to the plant error model. The EventFaultFailure at the failure output of the plant error model also realizes the abstract FeatureFlaw from the vehicle abstraction level, which is connected to the hazard. A Rationale can also be provided to explain the assessment.

The relations of the error models and their ports to the architectural elements and their ports may be different in different examples. Fig. 6 represents the examples where the safety mechanism monitors a sensor and uses the same actuator as the ordinary controller, for instance to mitigate unreasonable values. The lower limit of the reaction constraint should be interpreted such as it can be assumed that a hazard is present and the related functionality requested first when this time has passed, if the fault is not taken care of by a safety mechanism. This corresponds well to the view that the probability that a hazardous event occurs before this time has passed is acceptably low.

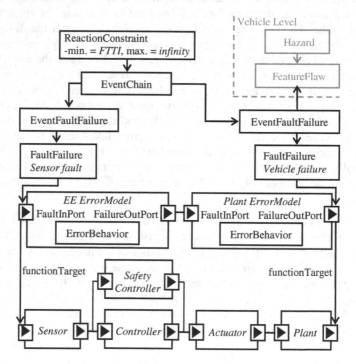

Fig. 6. Example modelling of the fault tolerant time interval (FTTI) from a specific fault occurs until a hazardous event possibly occurs

6   Emergency Operation Interval (EOI)

The definition in 1-1.35 states that emergency operation interval (EOI) is the specified time-span that emergency operation is needed to support the warning and degradation concept and 1-1.34 specifies emergency operation as degraded functionality from the state in which a fault occurred until the transition to a safe state is achieved.

The EOI is mentioned in part 3 and 4 of ISO 26262. EOI *shall be considered* (3-8.4.2.3) when specifying the functional safety requirements and an emergency operation shall be specified if a safe state cannot be reached by a transition within an acceptable time interval (3-8.4.2.4). Furthermore, EOI *shall be specified* for relevant safety mechanisms, as part of the technical safety requirements, if the safe state cannot be reached immediately (4-6.4.2.3).

6.1   Interpretation

Typically the EOI is relevant when the transition to a safe state is *not possible* to do immediately, due to for instance response time in actuators, or is *not desired* to do immediately, for instance deactivation of applied servo-systems. In the former type of examples, the EOI should be as short as possible and is restricted by the time for the safety mechanisms to detect and react upon the fault, see Fig. 2. In the latter type of examples, the EOI could be a balance between the desire to reach the safe state and the controllability by the operator to handle the situation.

6.2   Examples

EPS: If an EPS that applies a supporting torque to the steering column, for instance in a curve, needs to be turned off due to a faulty torque sensor, it could be hazardous to turn it off immediately. A smooth deactivation is desired. Since there is a reason for the EPS to be turned off, the EOI should not be too long, but it should be long enough to allow the driver to manage the situation.

BBW: For the brake-by-wire example, the EOI should be no more than the FTTI and consists of the time to detect the fault and to activate a secondary electric power supply. In this example it might be sufficient to explicitly specify the FTTI, the fault detection time and the fault reaction time.

6.3   Modelling

Modelling that the fault occurs can be done using an EventFaultFailure pointing to a FaultFailure, just as for the FTTI. However, the error model is not necessarily needed here, since the EOI does not refer to the failure and since the FaultFailure is typically already created and pointed out by the SafetyConstraint that defines the ASIL level of the corresponding functional or technical safety Requirement. The safe state is represented by a Mode or State element, which refers to the safe state Mode element created as part of the corresponding SafetyGoal at the vehicle abstraction level. Fig. 7 represents the example that the EPS is smoothly turned off during approximately ten seconds.

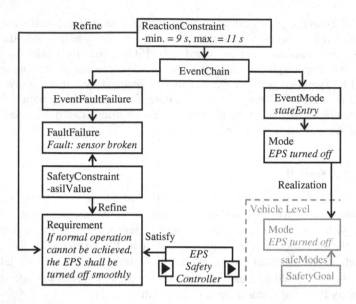

Fig. 7. Example modelling of the emergency operation interval (EOI) from a specific fault occurs until the transition to a safe state is achieved. In this example the electric power steering (EPS) shall be turned off smoothly

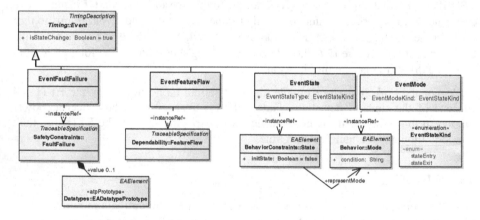

Fig. 8. The four shown Event types are proposed as an extension of TADL to enable to specify timing constraints relating to fault, failure and transition to a safe state

7   Conclusions and Further Work

This paper presents seven different safety-related timing constraints from ISO 26262. These are important constraints of the safety mechanisms that should detect faults and mitigate or hinder failures. Clear definitions are important to be able to model the times accurately. This paper discusses the interpretation of these times, in particular the fault tolerant time interval, which is currently unclearly defined.

This paper also proposes a few language extensions so that the modelling languages EAST-ADL and TADL can be used to specify the timing constraints. Further work includes investigating other timing-related aspects of ISO 26262.

Acknowledgment. The TimeSafe project is sponsored by the Swedish Governmental Agency for Innovation Systems (VINNOVA), within the FFI program. Thanks to the MEANAD and TIMMO-2-USE projects for helping out with language issues. Thanks also to Fredrik Törner at Volvo Car Corporation for interesting discussions.

References

[1] AUTOSAR, http://www.autosar.org
[2] Heinecke, H., Schnelle, K.-P., Fennel, H., Bortolazzi, J., Lundh, L., Leflour, J., et al.: AUTomotive Open System ARchitecture - An industry-wide initiative to manage the complexity of emerging automotive E/E-architectures. In: Proc. Convergence Int. Congress & Exposition on Transportation Electronics, Detroit, MI, USA (2004)
[3] Cuenot, P., Frey, P., Johansson, R., Lönn, H., Papadopoulos, Y., Reiser, M.-O., et al.: The EAST-ADL Architecture Description Language for Automotive Embedded Software. In: Giese, H., Karsai, G., Lee, E., Rumpe, B., Schätz, B. (eds.) MBEERTS. LNCS, vol. 6100, pp. 297–307. Springer, Heidelberg (2010)
[4] ISO 26262, Road vehicles – Functional safety, Part 1-9, 1st edn. International Organization for Standardization (November 2011)
[5] ISO/FDIS 26262-10, Road vehicles – Functional safety – Part 10: Guideline on ISO 26262, International Organization for Standardization (March 2012)
[6] Blom, H., Johansson, R., Lönn, H.: Annotation with timing constraints in the context of EAST-ADL2 and AUTOSAR – the timing augmented description language. In: Proc. Workshop on the Definition, Evaluation, and Exploitation of Modelling and Computing Standards for Real-Time Embedded Systems, Dublin, Ireland, pp. 2–5 (June 2009)
[7] Chen, D., Johansson, R., Lönn, H., Blom, H., Walker, M., Papadopoulos, Y., et al.: Integrated safety and architecture modeling for automotive embedded systems. E & I Elektrotechnik und Informationstechnik 128(6), 196–202 (2011)
[8] Peraldi-Frati, M.-A., Blom, H., Karlsson, D., Kuntz, S.: Timing modeling with AUTOSAR - Current state and future directions. In: Proc. Design, Automation & Test in Europe, Dresden, Germany, pp. 805–809 (March 2012)
[9] Firesmith, D.: Engineering safety requirements, safety constraints, and safety-critical requirements. Journal of Object Technology 3(3), 27–42 (2004)

Workshop on Dependable
and Secure Computing for Large-scale
Complex Critical Infrastructures
(DESEC4LCCI 2012)

Introduction to DESEC4LCCI 2012

Christian Esposito[1], Marco Platania[2], and Francesco Brancati[3]

[1] ICAR - CNR,
Via Pietro Castellino, 111 - 80131 Napoli, Italy
[2] Dipartimento di Ingegneria Informatica Automatica e Gestionale "A. Ruberti",
University of Roma La Sapienza,
Via Ariosto, 25 - 00185 Roma, Italy
[3] Resiltech,
Piazza Iotti, 25 - 56025 Pontedera (PI), Italy
`christian.esposito@na.icar.cnr.it`, `platania@dis.uniroma1.it`,
`francesco.brancati@resiltech.com`

Introduction

This DESEC4LCCI '12 workshop aims at providing a forum for researchers and engineers in academia and industry to foster an exchange of research results, experiences, and products in the area of dependable and secure computing in large-scale critical systems both from a theoretical and practical perspective. Large-scale Complex Critical Infrastructures (LCCIs), such as water and power supply plants, or transport infrastructures (*e.g.*, airports and seaports), play a key role into several fundamental human activities. It is easy to think about their economic and social impact: the consequences of an outage can be catastrophic in terms of efficiency, economical losses, consumer dissatisfaction, and even indirect harm to people and deaths. Currently, LCCIs make extensive usage of Information and Communications Technology (ICT) (*e.g.*, computing systems, communication networks, and sensing hardware), and especially software systems for LCCI interconnection, control, and management, in charge of providing support for advanced monitoring and control facilities. These systems have to be highly resilient in order to reduce the risk of LCCI catastrophic failures. Nevertheless, the resiliency of future LCCI is compromised by several factors, which can be intentional and unintentional. First, these systems are more and more conceived as the composition of several Off-The-Shelf (OTS) items and/or legacy subsystems, increasing the probability of failure occurrences, due to unexpected or erroneous modes of operation. Second, they have been designed without considering that their size would have significantly grown, crossing national boundaries, and that their operational environment, originally planned to be "closed", would become "open" to the world to allow interoperability among LCCIs and remote access and control. This implies that the both accidental events and malicious attacks should be taken into account.

A workshop on dependable and secure computing for LCCI is motivated by the unsuitability of the current approaches due to the novel challenges imposed by LCCI. In fact, several works exist in the literature about these research themes.

F. Ortmeier and P. Daniel (Eds.): SAFECOMP 2012 Workshops, LNCS 7613, pp. 205–208, 2012.
© Springer-Verlag Berlin Heidelberg 2012

However, existing solutions are usually applied to simpler and closed system. The innovative and challenging aspect is to apply these strategies, or to define novel ones, in the context of complex, evolvable, and extremely heterogeneous systems, which will compose future LCCI systems. It is needed to define novel middleware technologies, models, and methods to assure and assess the resiliency level of current and future OTS-based LCCIs, to diagnose faults in real time, and to tolerate them by means of dynamic reconfiguration. Assuring the resiliency level of LCCIs is crucial to reduce, with known probabilities, the occurrence of catastrophic failures, and consequently, to adopt proper diagnosis and reconfiguration strategies.

The ultimate goal of this workshop is to envision new trends and ideas about theoretical and practical aspects of designing, implementing, and evaluating dependable and secure solutions for the next generation critical networked infrastructures. In particular, the workshop aims at presenting the advancement of the state of art in the fields of distributed systems, hardware and software diagnosis, and software engineering, crucial for improving trustworthiness on ICT facilities, and spreading their adoption in very critical scenarios involving main infrastructures for modern society.

Program

The program of DESEC4LCCI '12 consists of 11 high-quality papers, covering the above-mentioned topics. In particular, we can group them in two main classes according to their topic:

- Security in Critical Infrastructures:
  1. "Quantitative Security Evaluation of a Multi-Biometric Authentication System" by Leonardo Montecchi, Paolo Lollini, Andrea Bondavalli and Ernesto La Mattina;
  2. "Protecting the WSN zones of a Critical Infrastructure via enhanced SIEM technology" by Valerio Formicola, Salvatore D'Antonio, Luigi Romano and Luigi Coppolino;
  3. "On Securing Communications among Federated Health Information Systems" by Mario Ciampi, Giuseppe De Pietro, Christian Esposito, Mario Sicuranza, Paolo Mori, Abraham Gebrehiwot and Paolo Donzelli;
  4. "How secure is ERTMS?" Robert Stroud, Ilir Gashi, Robin Bloomfield and Richard Bloomfield.
- Dependable Systems and Practical Experience:
  1. "International Cooperation Experiences: Results Achieved, Lessons Learned, and Way Ahead" by Salvatore D'Antonio, Luigi Romano, Craig Gibson and Matteo Melideo;
  2. "A Federated Simulation Framework with ATN Fault Injection Module for Reliability Analysis of UAVs in Non-controlled Airspace" by Magali Andreia Rossi, Jorge Rady Almeida Junior, Andrea Bondavalli and Paolo Lollini;

3. "WSDM-based autonomic augmentation of classic multiple-version software fault-tolerance mechanisms" by Roeland Dillen, Jonas Buys, Vincenzo De Florio and Chris Blondia;
4. "HSIENA: a hybrid publish/subscribe system" by Fabio Petroni and Leonardo Querzoni.
- Methodologies and Analysis:
  1. "Formal Verification of a Safety Argumentation and Application to a Complex UAV System" by Julien Brunel and Jacques Cazin;
  2. "Electronic Reliability Estimation: How reliable are the results?" by Nuno Silva and Rui Lopes;
  3. "Model-based assessment of multi-region Electric Power Systems showing heterogeneous characteristics" by Silvano Chiaradonna, Felicita Di Giandomenico and Nicola Nostro.

They are focused on several heterogeneous application domains, spanning from Health Information Systems and Electric Power Systems to Complex UAV Systems and Railway Control Systems (just to cite some of them). Each paper was selected according to at least two reviews produced mainly by Program Committee members and a little percentage of external reviewers. Selected papers come from several countries around the world, with a good balance between academic and industrial research. In addition, we are glad to open the workshop with a remarkable keynote speech by Andrea Bondavalli, distinguished professor at the University of Florence, Italy. Finally, the workshop is followed by a panel to discuss the presented topics and to indicate possible future avenues of exploration for this challenging research area.

Thanks

We would like to thank the SAFECOMP organization committee and collaborators for their precious help in handling all the issues related to the workshop. Our next thanks go to all the authors of the submitted papers who manifested their interest in the workshop. With their participation the First SAFECOMP Workshop on Dependable and Secure Computing for Large-scale Complex Critical Infrastructures becomes a real success and an inspiration for future workshops on this new and exciting area of research. In addition, we thank Resiltech for financially sponsoring this workshop.

Special thanks are finally due to Program Committee members and additional reviewers for the high quality and objective reviews they provided.

Acknowledgement. This workshop has been supported by the following research projects:

- Dependable Off-The-Shelf based middleware systems for Large-scale Complex Critical Infrastructures (DOTS-LCCI, dots-lcci.prin.dis.unina.it), a project financed by Italian Ministry for Education, University, and Research (MIUR) in the framework of the Project of National Research Interest (PRIN) DOTS-LCCI aims at investigating middleware solutions to realize large-scale complex critical infrastructures, which are defined as the federation of heterogeneous, maybe already-existent, systems.

− CRITICAL Software Technology for an Evolutionary Partnership (CSTEP, www.critical-step.eu), a project financed by European Commission (contract number 230672) as Marie-Curie action within the framework of the 7th Work Programme (FP7) CSTEP aims at establishing the basis for a long term strategic research collaboration between partners involved in this project in the growing and challenging domain of software for large-scale Safety-Critical Systems (SCSs) based on the use of Off-The-Shelf (OTS) software components for the control of complex distributed infrastructures such as Air Traffic Management (ATM) systems, complex industrial plants, etc.

− Blending Technologies for Ubiquitous Real-Time Data Access (BLEND), a project financed by the European Union within the context of EuroStar financing scheme BLEND addresses the need of next-generation mission and business critical system-of-systems, such as Air Traffic Control, Multi-Exchange Trading, and Border Surveillance, for ubiquitous access to real-time data over a multitude of communication technologies and over an ultra-large scale.

− A railway automatic track warning system based on distributed personal mobile terminals (ALARP, www.alarp.eu), a project financed by the European Commission within the context of FP7 Transport (including Aeronautics) programme The objective of the ALARP project is to study, design and develop an innovative more efficient Automatic Track Warning System (ATWS) to improve the safety of railway trackside workers.

Quantitative Security Evaluation
of a Multi-biometric Authentication System

Leonardo Montecchi[1], Paolo Lollini[1], Andrea Bondavalli[1], and Ernesto La Mattina[2]

[1] University of Florence, 50134 Firenze, Italy
{lmontecchi,lollini,bondavalli}@unifi.it
[2] Engineering Ingegneria Informatica S.p.A., 90146 Palermo, Italy
ernesto.lamattina@eng.it

Abstract. Biometric authentication systems verify the identity of users by relying on their distinctive traits, like fingerprint, face, iris, signature, voice, etc. Biometrics is commonly perceived as a strong authentication method; in practice several well-known vulnerabilities exist, and security aspects should be carefully considered, especially when it is adopted to secure the access to applications controlling critical systems and infrastructures. In this paper we perform a quantitative security evaluation of the CASHMA multi-biometric authentication system, assessing the security provided by different system configurations against attackers with different capabilities. The analysis is performed using the ADVISE modeling formalism, a formalism for security evaluation that extends attack graphs; it allows to combine information on the system, the attacker, and the metrics of interest to produce quantitative results. The obtained results provide useful insight on the security offered by the different system configurations, and demonstrate the feasibility of the approach to model security threats and countermeasures in real scenarios.

Keywords: quantitative security evaluation, multimodal biometric authentication, modeling, ADVISE, CASHMA.

1 Introduction

Biometric authentication systems verify the identity of users by relying on their distinctivetraits like fingerprint, face, iris, signature, voice, etc. Even though biometrics is commonly perceived as a strong authentication technique, several well-known vulnerabilities exist in practice, potentially allowing attackers to substitute themselves to legitimate users of the system. As the adoption of biometric systems is spreading in real world applications, multi-biometric systems are starting to receive considerable attention. Such kind of systems combine multiple biometric traits to verify user identities, trying to overcome some of the limitations of unimodal systems, such as noisy data, intraclass variation, non-universality, and susceptibility to spoofing attacks [1]. Security aspects are of major importance in such systems, especially when biometric authentication is adopted to secure the access to applications controlling critical systems or infrastructures. The recent "Stuxnet" worm attack [2] shows that facing modern attackers requires to take into

F. Ortmeier and P. Daniel (Eds.): SAFECOMP 2012 Workshops, LNCS 7613, pp. 209–221, 2012.
© Springer-Verlag Berlin Heidelberg 2012

account several aspects during security analysis, including skills and motivation of attackers, system knowledge, and human factors.

In this paper we perform a quantitative security evaluation of the multi-biometric authentication system defined within the CASHMA project [3], assessing the security provided by different system configurations against different attackers. The analysis is performed using the recently introduced ADVISE modeling formalism [4], which is especially tailored to quantitative security evaluation. The contribution of this work is twofold: on one hand we evaluate quantitative metrics that allow to compare different security configurations of the target system; on the other hand we describe one of the first applications of ADVISE for the analysis of a more comprehensive system, with the aim to assess its capabilities to represent security aspects in a real scenario.

The paper is organized as follows. Section 2 reviews related work, while Section 3 describes the CASHMA system and the scenario under analysis, discussing some of the major security threats. Section 4 provides a brief description of the ADVISE formalism, and then describes the model that will be used for evaluations. Evaluations and results are discussed in Section 5. Finally, conclusions are drawn in Section 6.

2   Related Work

Many works on the evaluation of biometric systems focus on the performance of the matching process, which compares the data acquired from sensors with reference samples associated with enrolled users. Two main quantities are usually considered: the rate of wrongly accepted matches (False Accept Rate, FAR), and the rate of wrongly rejected matches (False Reject Rate, FRR) [1,5]. Since the first measure provides a quantification of potentially unauthorized accesses, it is often used to quantify the security of the overall system. It is however believed that such simple indicators are no longer appropriate, and that more comprehensive evaluation frameworks taking into account the security of the system as a whole are needed [6].

Our approach uses model-based analysis to evaluate security measures of an overall biometric system. Model-based analysis has been extensively used for dependability analysis, and it has been later adopted in security analysis as well [7]. An abstraction of the system is created and then used to evaluate measures, verify properties, or identify possible issues on the system. One of the first formal models introduced for security analysis is the Dolev-Yao model [8], which is commonly used to verify properties of cryptographic protocols through semi-automatic tools like CASPER [9]. Attack trees [10] allow to describe the possible ways in which an attacker can compromise the system, and they are extensively used to model the security of the system as a whole; however they do not have the notion of time, and cannot be used to express complex dependencies between events. Attack graphs [11] extend attack trees by introducing the notion of state, thus allowing to describe more complex interactions between events and attacks. Other approaches use classic formalism borrowed from reliability analysis such as Stochastic Petri Nets and their extensions [12].

The ADVISE formalism, which has been recently introduced in [4,13], extends the attack graph concept, taking into account the attack behavior and capabilities of different kind of attackers. Support for the formalism is going to be provided by future versions of the Möbius multi-formalism modeling framework [14]; currently, support is provided by an "alpha" (i.e., in development) version of the tool. To the best of our knowledge, the only case study that applies the ADVISE method is described in [4,13], where a SCADA system is analyzed.

3   Targeted System and Scenario

The purpose of the CASHMA system is to provide an authentication service, which operates as a bridge between users that need to access to a given application, and applications that require secure access control. The core elements of the CASHMA architecture are the authentication server and the template database, in which samples of biometric data ("templates") are stored. Different kind of biometric sensors, located on the client, are used to acquire user biometric data. When users need to access to a certain application, their biometric traits are acquired and transmitted to the authentication service, which compares them with the templates stored in the database. If authentication is successful, the user is provided with a certificate that can be used to access the application(s). The CASHMA authentication service supports very different kind of applications, including those with high security constraints (e.g., kiosks securing the access to critical infrastructures management facilities), but also entertainment and informational applications. The main assumption on client devices is that they have the only role of acquiring biometric data, while all the processing and comparison tasks are performed server-side.

3.1   Security Threats to Biometric Authentication Systems

Although common sense would suggest that biometrics provides a very high degree of security, there are actually several means for attackers to compromise a biometric system. For example, data acquired from biometric sensors during the authentication of a legitimate user can be logged and later reused by the attacker, in a similar way as logging keystrokes allows to obtain passwords typed at a terminal. Another option is to create an artificial biometric sample, which is actually feasible with common materials even for those considered strong biometric traits, like fingerprint [15] or even iris [16]. In the following we list some of the vulnerabilities that have been identified for the CASHMA authentication service, briefly discussing how they could be exploited by an attacker and which are the possible countermeasures. Such list has been used as a basis in the construction of the analysis model.

Denial of service (DoS) attacks are designed to corrupt or incapacitate the biometric sensors, and can consist in physical damage, power loss, or introducing adverse environmental conditions to degrade the quality of the acquired data. Using *fake physical biometric*, also known as *sensor spoofing*, consists in using counterfeit physical biometrics to circumvent the biometric system. This is one of the most convenient attacks to this kind of systems: little system knowledge is required, involved materials are usually common and cheap, and most digital countermeasures (e.g., data encryption) are bypassed. Copies of legitimate biometrics can be obtained with relatively low effort: fingerprints are left on many things we touch; face and voice are easily recorded. Countermeasures to this kind of attack are "liveness detection" mechanisms [1], i.e., mechanisms looking for life indicators, like heartbeat or eye movement.

Reuse of residuals exploits the fact that some biometric devices may hold the last few acquired samples in some kind of local memory. If an attacker gains access to this data, he may be able to reuse it to provide a valid biometric sample. Countermeasures to this attack include clearing memory and forbidding perfectly identical biometric samples. *Replay attacks* involve the communication between the sensor and the processing resource that performs the comparison. A replay attack is composed of at least two stages: first an authentic communication is intercepted (*eavesdropping*), then it is replayed when needed, possibly modifying its content in accordance with the objectives of the attacker. Data encryption and digital signatures offer significant protection against this kind of attack. Finally, *template modification* consists in directly altering the template database, and it is one of the most serious threats to biometric systems: it potentially allows an attacker to obtain unauthorized access by simply presenting its real biometrics, and substituting to any of the legitimate users of the system. Countermeasures to this kind of attack include strict access policies to the template database, as well as encryption and digital signature for database content.

The attacks that an adversary may attempt obviously depend on the system architecture; a more comprehensive list of threats to biometric systems can be found in [1] and [17]. Finally, it should be noted that one of the most valuable resources for an attacker is the collaboration, or the coercion, of a legitimate user of the system.

3.2   Scenario Description and Analysis Objectives

The scenario that we consider in our analysis is an instance of the CASHMA system, supporting three biometric traits: voice, face, and fingerprint. The authentication server and the template database reside on a private network, protected from the Internet by a firewall. Communication between the client and the authentication server uses an encrypted logical channel (e.g., the SSL/TLS protocol [18]).

No assumptions are made on the kind of application(s) to which the authentication service provides access. Consequences of unauthorized access depend on the actual application, and potentially include catastrophic events in case of critical infrastructures control systems. Therefore, we focus on security attributes of the authentication service, and consider the time that it takes for an attacker to obtain unauthorized access as the main indicator of system security. In particular, we evaluate:

- $P_E(t)$: Probability that, at time t, the attacker has been successfully authenticated.
- T_E: Mean time required to the attacker to obtain authentication.

In our analysis we will compare three different system configurations, which have been identified as representative alternatives within the project:

1. User authentication requires only two of the three supported biometric traits. This configuration allows to trade security for broader client support: the absence of one sensor (e.g., fingerprint reader on mobile phones) or bad environment conditions (e.g., low light or noise) will still allow authentication by using the remaining sensors. The acquired biometric data is transmitted using a single encryption key.
2. User authentication requires all the supported biometric traits. The acquired biometric data is transmitted using a single encryption key.
3. User authentication requires all the supported biometric traits, and the biometric data is transmitted using three separate encryption keys.

The three above configuration variants are intended for systems having different security requirements, and aim to provide an increasing level of security, with #1 being the least secure configuration, and #3 being the most secure. It is assumed that the system is subject to different kind of attackers, distinguished by the knowledge they have of the system, the elements they can access, and their skills. Our objective is to assess the ability of above configuration to contrast the different attackers.

A realistic characterization of attackers is a challenging task for system-level security analysis; a common technique for network-based systems is the use of "honeypots", i.e. intentionally low protected machines exposed on public networks to attract attackers and analyze their actions (e.g., see [19]). This approach is however less practical when non-network-based attacks are considered. In our analysis we consider a representative set of attackers, covering different abilities, knowledge, and accesses. The detailed definition of the different attacker profiles is provided in Section 4.2.

4   Modeling Approach

This section describes how the system has been modeled using ADVISE. Section 4.1 briefly introduces the formalism, while Section 4.2 describes the model itself.

4.1   The ADVISE Formalism

The analysis method supported by the ADVISE [4,13] formalism relies on creating executable security models that can be solved using discrete-event simulation to provide quantitative metrics. One of the most significant features introduced by this formalism is the precise characterization of the attacker (the "adversary") and the influence of its decisions on the final measures of interest. In fact, the overall security of a system is influenced not only by its actual strength in contrasting intrusion attempts, but also by its strength as *perceived* by attackers.

The specification of an ADVISE model is composed of two parts: an Attack Execution Graph (AEG), describing how the adversary can attack the system, and an adversary profile, describing the characteristics of the attacker. The AEG is a particular kind of attack graph comprising different kinds of nodes: *attack steps, access domains, knowledge items, attack skills,* and *attack goals.* Similarly as in attack graphs, attack steps describe the possible attacks that the adversary may attempt. Access domains describe what the attacker needs to possess (e.g., intranet access), while knowledge items describe what it needs to know (e.g., admin passwords); attack skills describe the proficiency of the adversary in certain abilities; attack goals describe its objectives. Each attack step requires a certain combination of items to be held by the adversary. The set of what has been achieved by the adversary defines the current state of the model. Differently from other attach graphs, ADVISE attack steps have also additional properties, which allow creating executable models for quantitative analysis. Each attack step has an associated stochastic duration, a cost, and a set of different outcomes, each one modifying the state of the model in a different way. A probability of occurrence and a probability of being detected (as perceived by the adversary) are associated with each outcome.

The adversary profile defines the set of access items and knowledge items that are initially owned by the adversary (i.e., the initial state of the model), as well as his proficiency in attack skills. The adversary starts without having reached any goal, and works towards them. To each attack goal it is assigned a *payoff* value, which specifies the value that the adversary assigns to reaching that goal. Three weights define the relative preference of the adversary in: i) maximizing the payoff, ii) minimizing costs, or iii) minimizing the probability of being detected. Finally, the *planning horizon* defines the number of steps in the future that the adversary is able to take into account for his decisions; this value can be thought to model the "smartness" of the adversary.

The ADVISE execution algorithm [4] evaluates the reachable states based on enabled attack steps, and selects the most appealing to the adversary based on the above described weights. The execution of the attack is then simulated, leading the model to a new state. Metrics of interest are defined using reward structures [7].

4.2   ADVISE Model

Due to space limitations, in this section we only provide a high-level description of the model. The full details of the model can be found as a technical report in [20].

Attack Execution Graph. The AEG for configurations variant #2 (see Section 3.2) consists of 1 attack goal, 10 access domains, 5 knowledge items, 5 attack skills, and 18 attack steps; the AEGs for the other two variants have only slight differences. Its graphical representation is shown in Fig. 1, using the graphical notation introduced in [4]: attack goals are represented by ovals, access domains by squares, knowledge items by circles, attack skills by triangles, and attack steps by rectangles.

The description of the AEG in Fig. 1 is carried out in the following, in a bottom-up fashion. The model has only one attack goal, "Open Session", representing the objective of obtaining authentication. In configuration #2, to accomplish its goal the attacker should be authenticated by each unimodal biometric subsystems. Successful authentication with each of the three biometric traits is represented by the three access domains "VoiceAuth_Ok", "FaceAuth_OK", and "FingerprintAuth_OK", which enable the "WaitResponse" attack step. In this step the attacker simply waits the response from the authentication service. The adversary has basically two ways to reach the three access domains: he can perform a combined spoofing attack on biometric sensors, or he can compromise the template database.

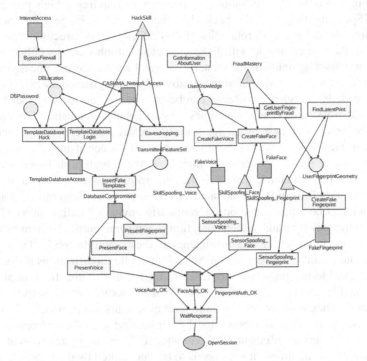

Fig. 1. The structure of the ADVISE attack execution graph for variant #2

The modification of the template database is represented by the "InsertFakeTemplate" attack step. However, to successfully accomplish that, he needs a high score in the "HackSkill" attack skill, access to the template database ("TemplateDatabaseAccess" access domain) and knowledge of previously transmitted feature sets ("TransmittedFeatureSet" knowledge item). If this attack is successful he can then use his real biometrics to obtain authentication ("PresentVoice", "PresentFace", "PresentFingerPrint" attack steps). Access to the template database can be obtained by knowing its location and credentials ("DBLocation" and "DBPassword" knowledge items) and having access to the private network ("CASHMA_Network_Access"), which enables the "TemplateDatabaseLogin" attack step. Another way to access the database is performing the "TemplateDatabaseHack" attack step, which requires knowing the location of the database, having access to the CASHMA internal network, and a high proficiency in the "HackSkill" attack skill. If the location of the database is not known to the attacker, he can obtain it with the "Eavesdropping" attack step, i.e., observing network communication on the CASHMA internal network. The same attack may also provide information on transmitted biometric data ("TransmittedFeatureSet"); however it requires access to the internal network, and the "HackSkill" attack skill.

Obtaining the three access domains through sensor spoofing techniquesis represented by the "SensorSpoofing_Voice", "SensorSpoofing_Face", and "SensorSpoofing_Fingerprint" attack steps, each one requiring a specific attack skill and access domain. For example, "SensorSpoofing_Fingerprint" requires a high proficiency in the "SkillSpoofing_Fingerprint" attack skill, and the "FakeFingerprint" access domain. Moreover, the success probability of this attack step is directly proportional to the score in the related attack skill. Fake biometric samples can be either owned by the attacker at the beginning of the scenario, or can be obtained in a sneaky way from legitimate users, but it is required to have knowledge of registered users of the system ("UsersKnowledge"). Such knowledge can be obtained by performing the "GetInformationAboutUsers" attack step, which has no particular prerequisites. Obtaining fake samples for voice and face biometric traits ("CreateFakeVoice" and "CreateFakeFace" attack steps) does not require additional items, since it may be as simple as taking a picture or recording a conversation; however, a high probability of detection is associated with such attack steps. For the fingerprint biometry, instead, it is necessary to have the fingerprint of an authorized user ("UserFingerprint" knowledge item), which can be either found on the biometric device ("FindLatentPrint"), or obtained from the user by fraud, e.g., having him touch some particular item or material. The latter option however requires proficiency in the "FraudMastery" attack skill".

To evaluate the other two configuration variants, little modifications are required to the AEG. Considering only two biometric traits for user authentication simply requires to modify the prerequisites for the "WaitResponse" attack step, in order to enable it even when only two out of three biometric traits are provided. Having three different encryption keys is represented by replicating the "Eavesdropping" attack step and the "TransmittedFeatureSet" knowledge item, to represent that the tree communications using different keys needs to be intercepted by the attacker.

Adversary Profiles. A summary of parameters used for the definition of the four adversary profiles is shown in Table 1. The table is divided in five blocks which describe, from top to bottom: the proficiency in attack skills, access domains, knowledge items, preference weights, and planning horizon of the four adversaries. Access domains and knowledge items that are not mentioned in the table are not owned by any adversary at the beginning of the scenario.

Table 1. Definition of the four adversary profiles

	Malicious user (voice)	Malicious user (voice+face)	Hacker	Terrorist organization
SkillSpoofing_Voice	1000	1000	200	600
SkillSpoofing_Face	200	900	200	600
SkillSpoofing_Fingerprint	200	200	200	600
FraudMastery	200	200	200	600
HackSkill	200	200	800	600
FakeVoice	Y	Y	N	N
FakeFace	N	Y	N	N
FakeFingerprint	N	N	N	N
DatabaseLocation	N	N	Y	N
WeightCost	0.3	0.3	0.25	0.05
WeightDetection	0.3	0.3	0.25	0.05
WeightPayoff	0.4	0.4	0.5	0.9
PlanningHorizon	7	7	7	7

The *malicious user (voice)* attacker represents a malicious user of the system trying to authenticate on behalf of someone else. He owns a fake biometric sample of the victim's voice, which could have been obtained for example by simply recording a conversation, but he does not have other particular skills. The *mailicious user (voice+face)* is also able to provide a fake sample of the victims' face biometry, e.g. a high resolution picture. The *hacker* attacker has an high skill in the "HackSkill" ability, allowing him to perform advanced cyber-attacks to the system, and he has some additional knowledge on system configuration. Finally, the *terrorist organization* attacker is characterized by a high motivation in reaching the intended goal ("WeightPayoff") and pays little attention to needed costs and to the possibility of being detected. It has average proficiency in several skills, but he does not have fake biometric samples to use for sensor spoofing.

The planning horizon parameter has been set to 7 for all the adversaries, as a good compromise between solution time and accuracy of results: by further increasing it we experienced a great increase in computation time, without significant differences in the evaluated measures of interest. For all the adversaries a payoff of 1000 has been set for the "SessionOpen" attack goal; measures of interest are however not affected by this value, since it is the only attack goal available to attackers.

5   Evaluation and Results

In this section we describe the results obtained by evaluating the model defined in Section 4.1. The model has been solved using the simulator included in the Möbius framework. The probability that the attacker has been successfully authenticated at time t, $P_E(t)$, is obtained by evaluating the probability that, at time t, the adversary owns the "SessionOpen" attack goal. All the measures have been evaluated using a relative confidence interval of 0.1, a confidence level of 99%, and collecting at least 100 and at most 10000 samples.

5.1   Variant #1: Two Biometric Traits, Single Encryption Key

Fig. 2 shows the results obtained for the default system configuration, for each of the four attackers. In this configuration three of the four considered attackers are able to reach the goal. The "terrorist organization" attacker is the fastest to compromise the system, since it is able to obtain authentication in 1/5 the time required to the other two successful attackers. This is due to the great ability of this attacker to perform sensor spoofing attacks on the system [20]; moreover, since only two of them are required for authentication, he is allowed to select the ones that require less effort for him (both in time and costs). The "malicious user (voice+face)" and "hacker" attackers are both able to obtain authentication, with the former spending on the average 25% additional time (about 150 minutes) with respect to the latter.

5.2   Variant #2: Three Biometric Traits, Single Encryption Key

In this section we evaluate the impact of using three biometric traits for authentication; results are shown in Fig. 3. This configuration variant has two main effects on system security. The first is a considerable increasing of the time required to the "terrorist organization" attacker to obtain authentication, which has increased by 4 times with respect to variant #1. The second effect is that only two of the four adversaries are able to obtain authentication: the "malicious user (voice+face)", which was able to obtain authentication in Variant #1, is now unable to compromise the system, since he has no means to bypass fingerprint authentication. Finally, this modification has little effect on the "hacker" adversary, which is still able to compromise the system using the same amount of time as in variant #1. This attacker spends the greatest part of the time in accessing the database and eavesdropping the communications [20], steps that

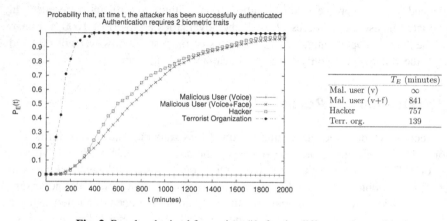

Fig. 2. Results obtained for variant #1, for the different adversaries

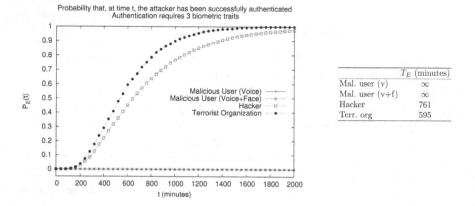

Fig. 3. Results obtained for variant #2, for the different adversaries

require the same amount of timein this configuration as well. As expected, using additional biometric traits results in a considerable increase of security against certain kind of attackers. However, it is also highlighted that such solution provides a security improvement only if the template database is well-protected: against the "hacker" attacker this configuration is no more secure than variant #1.

5.3 Variant #3: Three Biometric Traits, Three Encryption Keys

In the third configuration variant, biometric data acquired from sensors is transmitted to the server using three different encryption keys, one for each biometric trait. This modification only affects the "hacker" attacker, which is the only one able to obtain authentication by compromising the template database [20]. Fig. 4 compares how $P_E(t)$ and T_E change for the "hacker" adversary when introducing this modification. Introducing different encryption keys does not prevent the "hacker" adversary to obtain authentication from the system; however he will need more time to succeed, since he will have to perform additional attack steps to obtain all the data required to modify the template database. Moreover, results show that security is not simply improved by a factor of 3: the mean time required to obtain authentication is in fact only doubled with respect to variants #1 and #2.

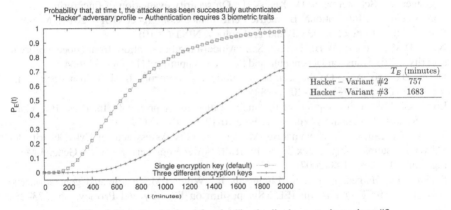

	T_E (minutes)
Hacker – Variant #2	757
Hacker – Variant #3	1683

Fig. 4. Results obtained for the "hacker" adversary in variant #3

6   Conclusions

In this paper we have performed a quantitative security evaluation of the CASHMA multi-biometric authentication system, using the recently introduced ADVISE formalism. We successfully modeled the threats to biometric authentication systems, taking into accountaspects related to human factors (e.g., cheat on users to obtain biometric samples), system knowledge, and skills of attackers. Taking into account these aspects in assessing the security of critical infrastructures control systems is of primary importance in understanding and contrasting modern cyberattacks. However, some aspects need to be further investigated; in particular, setting model parameters is challenging; for example, defining the duration and cost of each attack step introduces several assumptions that are hard to verify. Another interesting aspect concerns model solution, which is currently carried out by discrete-event simulation; analytical solution techniques, when applicable, could improve the accuracy of results.

Acknowledgments. This work has been partially supported by the Italian Ministry for Education, University, and Research (MIUR) through the FIRB project CASHMA: Context Aware Security by Hierarchical Multilevel Architectures [3].

References

1. Li, S.Z. (ed.): Encyclopedia of Biometrics, 1st edn. Springer Reference (2009)
2. Chen, T., Abu-Nimeh, S.: Lessons from Stuxnet. IEEE Computer 44(4), 91–93 (2011)
3. FIRB – Fondo per gli Investimenti della Ricerca di Base, CASHMA: Context Aware Security by Hierarchical Multilevel Architectures (2008)
4. LeMay, E., Ford, M., Keefe, K., Sanders, W., Muehrcke, C.: Model-based Security Metrics Using ADversary VIew Security Evaluation (ADVISE). In: 8th International Conference on Quantitative Evaluation of Systems (QEST 2011), pp. 191–200 (2011)
5. Phillips, P.J., Martin, A., Wilson, C.L., Przybocki, M.: An introduction evaluating biometric systems. IEEE Computer 33(2), 56–63 (2000)
6. Henniger, O., Scheuermann, D., Kniess, T.: On security evaluation of fingerprint recognition systems. In: International Biometric Performance Conference (IBPC 2010), March 1-5. National Institute of Standards and Technology, NIST (2010)
7. Nicol, D.M., Sanders, W.H., Trivedi, K.S.: Model-based evaluation: from dependability to security. IEEE Trans. on Dependable and Secure Computing 1(1), 48–65 (2004)
8. Dolev, D., Yao, A.C.: On the security of public-key protocols. IEEE Transactions on Information Theory 29(8), 198–208 (1983)
9. Lowe, G.: Casper: a compiler for the analysis of security protocols. In: Proc. 10th Computer Security Foundations Workshop, June 10-12, pp. 18–30 (1997)
10. Ten, C.-W., Liu, C.-C., Govindarasu, M.: Vulnerability Assessment of Cybersecurity for SCADA Systems Using Attack Trees. In: IEEE Power Engineering Society General Meeting, June 24-28, pp. 1–8 (2007)
11. Sheyner, O., Haines, J., Jha, S., Lippmann, R., Wing, J.M.: Automated generation and analysis of attack graphs. In: IEEE Symposium on Security and Privacy, pp. 273–284 (2002)
12. Beccuti, M., et al.: Quantification of dependencies in electrical and information infrastructures: The CRUTIAL approach. In: 4th International Conference on Critical Infrastructures (CRIS 2009), pp. 1–8 (2009)
13. LeMay, E., Unkenholz, W., Parks, D., Muehrcke, C., Keefe, K., Sanders, W.H.: Adversary-Driven State-Based System Security Evaluation. In: Proceedings of the 6th International Workshop on Security Measurements and Metrics, MetriSec 2010 (2010)
14. Courtney, T., Gaonkar, S., Keefe, K., Rozier, E.W.D., Sanders, W.H.: Möbius 2.3: An Extensible Tool for Dependability, Security, and Performance Evaluation of Large and Complex System Models. In: DSN 2009, Estoril, Lisbon, Portugal, pp. 353–358 (2009)
15. Matsumoto, T., Matsumoto, H., Yamada, K., Hoshino, S.: Impact of artificial 'gummy' fingers on fingerprint systems. In: Proc. SPIE, vol. 4677, pp. 275–289 (2002)
16. Pacut, A., Czajka, A.: A liveness Detection for IRIS Biometrics. In: Proc. of the 40th Int. Carnahan Conference on Security Technology (ICCST 2006), pp. 122–129 (October 2006)

17. Roberts, C.: Biometric attack vectors and defences. Computers & Security 26(1), 14–25 (2007)
18. Dierks, T., Rescorla, E.: The Transport Layer Security (TLS) Protocol – Version 1.2, RFC 5246, IETF Network Working Group (August 2008)
19. Salles-Loustau, G., Berthier, R., Collange, E., Sobesto, B., Cukier, M.: Characterizing Attackers and Attacks: An Empirical Study. In: IEEE 17th Pacific Rim International Symposium on Dependable Computing (PRDC), pp. 174–183 (2011)
20. Montecchi, L., Lollini, P., Bondavalli, A.: ADVISE model for the security evaluation of the CASHMA multi-biometric authentication system, University of Florence, RCL Group, Technical Report RCL120301 (2012),
http://rcl.dsi.unifi.it/publications

Protecting the WSN Zones of a Critical Infrastructure via Enhanced SIEM Technology

Luigi Romano[1], Salvatore D'Antonio[1], Valerio Formicola[1], and Luigi Coppolino[2]

[1] University of Naples "Parthenope", Department of Technology, Naples, Italy
{luigi.romano, salvatore.dantonio,
valerio.formicola}@uniparthenope.it
[2] Epsilon S.r.l., Naples, Italy
luigi.coppolino@epsilonline.com

Abstract. Attacks on Critical Infrastructures are increasing and becoming more sophisticated. In addition to security issues of Supervisory Control And Data Acquisition systems, new threats come from the recent adoption of Wireless Sensor Network (WSN) technologies. Traditional security solutions for solely Information Technology (IT) based infrastructures, such as the Security Information and Events Management (SIEM) systems, can be strongly enchanced to address such issues. In this paper we analyze limits of current SIEMs to protect CIs and propose a framework developed in the MASSIF Project to enhance services for data treatment. We present the Generic Event Translation and introduce the Resilient Storage modules to collect data from heterogeneous sources, improve the intelligence of the SIEM periphery, reliably store information of security breaches. Particularly, by focusing on the first two features, we illustrate how they can improve the detection of attacks targeting the WSN of a dam monitoring and control system.

Keywords: Security Information and Event Management (SIEM), Supervisory Control and Data Acquisition (SCADA), Wireless Sensor Networks.

1 Rationale and Contribution

Coordinated and targeted cyber-attacks to Critical Infrastructures (CIs) are increasing and becoming more sophisticated [1][2]. Mostly, such infrastructures rely on legacy Supervisory Control And Data Acquisition (SCADA) systems that have been designed without having security in mind, as they were originally isolated and based on proprietary protocols. Moreover, the recent and increasing trend of critical infrastructure monitoring is based on Wireless Sensor Network (WSN) technology, which introduces new security threats in addition to a number of advantages, such as dramatically reduction of deployment costs, possibility for deploying a proper level of redundancy, effective monitoring in several scenarios [3][4][5].

According to the National Institute of Standards and Technology (NIST) [6], securing a Critical Infrastructure is very different from protecting solely Information Technology-based infrastructures, hence traditional solutions, such as the Security

F. Ortmeier and P. Daniel (Eds.): SAFECOMP 2012 Workshops, LNCS 7613, pp. 222–234, 2012.
© Springer-Verlag Berlin Heidelberg 2012

Information and Event Management (SIEM) systems are often ineffective for CIs protection. In order to overcome such issues, the European Commission funded project MASSIF [7] proposes an enhanced SIEM for the protection of Critical Infrastructures. In this paper we analyze the main limits of current SIEM solutions when applied to protecting CIs and design and implement a framework to overcome the identified limits by enhancing data collection and storage services of a SIEM. The solution is composed of several modules that we named Generic Event Translation (GET) and Resilient Storage (RS) which allow to: i) increase the heterogeneity and number of data sources; ii) move part of the data processing toward the edge of the distributed IT system managing the CI; iii) provide post-accidental support allowing a precise and reliable reconstruction of the happening of a security breach and forensic evidence of such a circumstance. A final contribution of this paper is the application of the proposed solution to protect a real CI, namely a dam, monitored by means of WSN technology. To the best of our knowledge, no works in literature discuss the adoption of SIEM technology to protect the WSN zones of a CI. Most of the related work faces security issues in WSN technology by means of Intrusion Detection Systems (IDS) and improved routing protocols. For instance, in [8] a reputation based approach combined with clustering algorithms is used to detect attacks to the WSN routing protocols. In [9] an hybrid agent based IDS detects routing protocol attacks, such as sinkhole and sleep deprivation. In [10] intrusion detection algorithm based on neighbor nodes' power is applied to WSN with static nodes.

In Section 2, the paper discusses the main limits of current SIEM technologies when applied to protect Critical Infrastructures and excerpts a list of features for an enhanced SIEM for CIs. Section 3 introduces the data service components in the context of the MASSIF framework. Section 4 presents the implementation of such solutions and their usage to protect a dam monitoring and control system. Section 5 closes the paper with final remarks and an overview of future plans.

2   Enhanced SIEMs for CIs

MASSIF project has analyzed four real world scenarios and has identified the main limits of current State of the Art (SotA) technology [8] when deployed to protect CIs. Such limits may invalidate the effectiveness of SIEM operation, which, primarily, has to avoid security-induced safety issues impacting society and environment. In Table 1 we shortly summarize them and excerpt a list of features for an enhanced SIEM for CIs.

Besides such capabilities, MASSIF project has identified additional services which can be offered on the top of the SIEM (e.g. attack modeling and simulation, decision support and reaction/countermeasure systems, advanced visualization, etc.); however, these topics are out of the scope of this paper. In the following we will present our solution to address issues presented in Table 1, with the exception of resilient data dissemination, faced in MASSIF and partially discussed in [17]. Moreover the RS module is briefly introduced, but no more details are provided in this work.

Table 1. Features for an enhanced SIEM for Critical Infrastructures

Enhanced SIEM capability	Rationale
Data collectors should be able to integrate legacy and novel information sources in an effective and flexible way, by interpreting multi-layer and multi-domain data formats, typically characterized by heterogeneous syntax and semantics.	Traditionally, SIEMs focus on IT infrastructure events [12][13][14][15], but some security occurrences may not produce evidence at this level. Enhanced SIEMs should have a more comprehensive view of security-aware processes.
SIEMs should limit the consumption of shared resources as much as possible (e.g. bandwidth, central server processing).	SCADA and SIEMs are deployed together in the same environment, thus they compete for the same resources, which are often very constrained.
SIEM should provide mechanisms to treat and pre-correlate data at the edge of the (SIEM) architecture, very close to the field devices.	i)Correlation may be more effectively operated when the security information is contextualized, detailed data can be retrieved on-demand and analysis can exploit knowledge of the specific application domain. ii)Traditional SIEMs disseminate information through intermediate communication nodes and towards remote correlation servers, by exposing sensitive data to third parties.
SIEMs should be capable of high data volume performance at the edge of the network, specifically in data treatment components, such as data collectors, data parsers and event correlators.	Field devices are even more capable to generate massive physical data and perform very complex operations. This may result in overwhelming the SIEM for CIs with huge amounts of security related patterns and alerts.
SIEM storage systems should provide high capabilities in terms of: data authenticity of event sources; fault and intrusion tolerance; control of data access by authorized parties. Forensic events, and only such events, must be kept, while unnecessary details must be deleted or made anonymous ("least persistence principle").	CIs are very attractive to malicious actions, so security events may be used for forensic purposes. In order to use SIEM reports as forensic proof, digital evidence (e-evidence) properties like Authentication, Admissibility and Best-evidence should be granted [16].
SIEM should be able to disseminate events in a reliable manner by means of resilient architectures.	Data channels of SIEMs are vulnerable to faults and malicious activities which may impact correct and timely dissemination of events from data sources to central engines and may invalidate SIEM analysis.

3   Data Treatment Framework of MASSIF SIEM

MASSIF project proposes a SIEM with enhanced capabilities such as those exposed above. Specifically, the SIEM is deployed as a logical overlay on the monitored infrastructure. The GET is the MASSIF module that collects data from the "Payload Machinery" of the CI, which is typically composed of heterogeneous and multi-layer event sources - legacy IT and SCADA components, security applications and appliances – and performs preliminary security analysis of the data at the edge side of the SIEM architecture. The Resilient Storage (RS) implements a set of techniques which allow to reliably store data containing information of relevant security breaches.

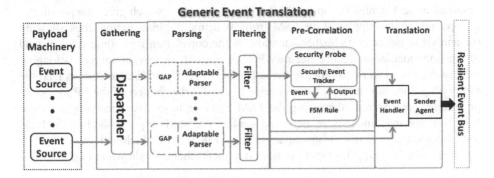

Fig. 1. Architecture of Generic Event Translation (GET) module

Cross-layer Data Collection

The GET is the module of the SIEM in charge of cross-layer event collection, which in turns requires gathering, parsing, filtering and translating data generated by the Payload Machinery. GET is made of several components located at the edge-side of the MASSIF SIEM architecture. Each one is assigned to a single subtask. Moreover, the GET can be interfaced very closely to the field systems and can sign information as soon as it is generated. Follows a list of the GET components, shown in Fig 1.

Dispatcher gathers raw data from event sources by means of textual based protocols, such as Syslog [18], which is by far the most widely used transport protocol to send event logs. *Adaptable Parsers (APs)* extracts information from the flow of raw data (e.g., a stream of characters) previously collected (*parsing*). APs adopt Compiler-compiler technology to automatically manipulate formally specified documents [19]. This approach retains a number of associated advantages including: a very large degree of expressiveness, the availability of well-known tools for the automatic processing of grammar-based artifacts, a high level of generality and technology-independence, which decouples the format definition from the underlying technology used for data processing. Each AP is joined to the *GET Access Point (GAP)*, which supports the Dispatcher by associating a data source stream with the related parser. *Event Filters* selectively discard events generated by the event sources to avoid the propagation of useless data to SIEM analysis. *Event Handler (EH)* translates the message format into a common and generic event format, in order to be effectively processed by SIEM core engines. *Sender Agent* sends SIEM-formatted events to the dissemination layer of the enhanced SIEM, namely the Resilient Event Bus of MASSIF.

Edge-Side Data Analysis

The part of the GET in charge of cross-layer event correlation, aggregation and abstraction is the Security Probe (SP). The SP introduces a novel level of intelligence into SIEM analysis and contextualizes it to the specific application domain. Particularly, SP is a Finite State Machine (FSM)-based event pattern detector which reduces the burden of processing the whole data at the core of the SIEM. Specifically, SPs are based on State Machine Compiler (SMC) [20] technology, which gives the possibility to separate the description of the FSM from its actual implementation, thus allowing the analyst to concentrate his/her attention on the correlation logic (and rule) instead of the implementation details. Security Probes operate with event sources belonging to very different layers: in order to make FSMs "evolve", Adaptable Parsers feed the SPs with proper information. The Security Event Tracker is part of the SP in charge of getting input events, identifying the FSM instance to evolve, receiving the feedback from the machine (e.g. an alert) and sending the FSM output to the EH; the FSM logic (states, transitions, ...) is maintained in the Finite State Machine Rule.

An SP which aggregates input events and related schema in shown in Fig. 2.

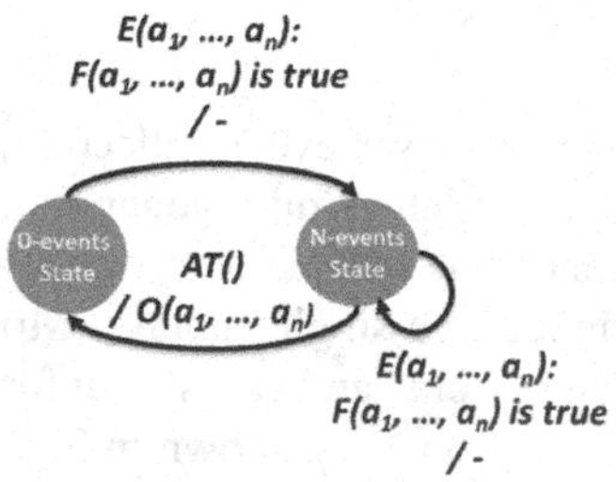

Function/ Parameter	Meaning
$a_1, ..., a_n$	(parsed) data fields of the input event
$E(a_1, ..., a_n)$	input event with n data fields
$O(x)$	output event computed from x
$AT()$	aggregation trigger which activates the output: e.g. timer, counter, threshold *(Output Condition)*
$F(a_1, ..., a_n)$	boolean condition to evolve the machine *(Aggregation Condition)*

Fig. 2. Security Probe: aggregation schema

a_1: timestamp variable; T: first event timestamp; K: time window
$a_2...a_j$: new input fields $\underline{a_2}...\underline{a_j}$: first event input fields
a_i: field to be summed
$F(a_1, a_2,..., a_j,..., a_n)$: $(T < a_1 < T + K)$ AND $(a_2...a_j == \underline{a_2}...\underline{a_j})$
AT:(counter >= N) OR (timer >= t)
$O(a_1, ..., a_n)$: $E(T, a_2...a_j, sum(a_i))$

Fig. 3. Time based aggregation on input data

For instance, consider a time-reference based aggregation, which consolidates a certain number of events sharing same values of the first event arrived (or part of it) and generated in the same time window. Given the formalism expressed above, we can configure the FSM as follows:

The schema in Fig. 3 generates an aggregate output if the number of events arrived overcomes the threshold N or the timer associated with the Aggregator expires. The output message creates a new event, which contains: the Timestamp of the first message, the invariant of data fields, a new data field obtained by summing the events aggregated. Overcoming this example, we prefigure the possibility to create aggregated events by providing several operations on data fields: for instance we could disseminate the first and the last timestamps in order to identify the time window extent of aggregated events, or link the identity fields of aggregated events.

As GET framework functionalities are distributed among several (edge-side) components, load distribution policies and mechanisms, such as load balancing, can be implemented: this would allow handling load peaks in different phases of the edge-side data processing and reconfiguring the usage of computational resources. Moreover, SotA security technologies have been adopted to protect data channels among GET components, such as SSL/TLS protocols. Indeed, in this way, as new data arrive at the Dispatcher, they are signed and encrypted.

Data Storage for Forensic Purposes

The Resilient Storage (RS) is the MASSIF module in charge of supporting reliable storage of information related to security incidents. Key mechanism adopted to design the RS is the threshold cryptography [21] combined to diversity and replication techniques and hardened with Write-Once-Read-Many (WORM) storage devices [22]. RS is particularly useful to criminal/civil prosecution of attackers in the post-security breach stage: in this case the main component feeding the RS is the SIEM Correlation/Rule Engine at core-side.

4   Protecting the WSN Zones of a Dam Infrastructure

In the following we present our solution applied to the case study of a dam monitoring and control system which adopts the WSN technology. Dams are complex infrastructures conceived for a multitude of purposes and, typically, a huge number of physical parameters are monitored to guarantee safety and security. Monitoring and control systems are based on geotechnical instrumentation combined with SCADA systems. Such systems are increasingly becoming automated and remotely controlled and this fact paves the way for a new class of security induced safety issues that is for the possibility that cyber-attacks against the IT layer of the dam, ultimately result in damage to people and environment.

Case Study. In our case study we consider a dam feeding a hydroelectric power station, as depicted in Fig. 4. The *Intake* Gate of the dam is controlled to release the basin water and activate the Turbine in the power plant. Normally, water flow in the

Penstock is controlled to not exceed an alert threshold. Indeed, high turbine speed may result in electric overload and in power plant facility failure due to excessive vibrations. The deployment of our case study is based on three water flow sensors placed at different points of the penstock (WF1, WF2, WF3). Moreover, other sensors are placed in the seepage channels under the dam wall. Indeed, parameters of seepage waters (turbidity, water levels, etc.) are continuously monitored to foresee dangerous events such as erosion and piping phenomena (sensors WL1 and WL2). A Tilt sensor is placed on the dam gate and measures gate opening levels (inclination). A Vibration sensor is placed on the Turbine. All the sensors constitute the nodes of a WSN and, at regular intervals, send their measurements to a WSN Base Station (BS) located at the dam surveillance office. The BS acts as a wireless Remote Terminal Unit (RTU), which forwards the measurements to the Remote SCADA server. Finally, opening commands are issued by the remote SCADA facility toward the gate actuator. The SCADA allows to open the gate only if safety conditions are verified in the turbine, i.e. if the penstock water flow is under the safety threshold.

The IT security deployment of our case study includes a Network-based Intrusion Detection System (N-IDS) in the remote SCADA server facility, a Host-based Intrusion Detection System (H-IDS) in the dam local facility, a SIEM with the correlation engine located in a remote warehouse.

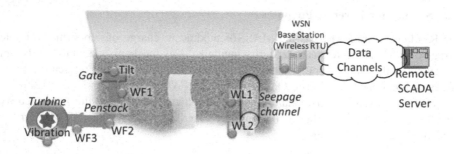

Fig. 4. WSN-based monitoring of a dam

In order to extend the analysis of the SIEM from a multi-layer security perspective, we feed the SIEM correlation engine with the evidence of physical incoherencies in the parameters measured by the WSN nodes. This is only possible if we have specific knowledge of the critical infrastructure under control. It's worth noting that to do this with a traditional SIEM, we should disseminate physical data to the central correlation engines, resulting in several issues, such as: difficulty in gathering and translating physical data from sensor devices into the SIEM format; unsuitability of SIEM correlation engines to describe and detect physical anomalies; wasting of computational and bandwidth resources to propagate and elaborate data into the SIEM correlation engine.

Misuse Case. In order to present the effectiveness of our framework, we considered a storyboard that closely mimics Stuxnet behavior [23]. The attack target is the failure of the turbine facility. The attacker alters the water flow measurements to hide their actual values and solicit excessive gate opening. Precondition to the attack is that the attacker has access to some hosts in remote station and can execute tools to hack the SCADA machines and the BS host (e.g. by plugging a USB device in). The attack is perpetrated in a chain of malicious activities, which we summarize as follows: usage of malicious software to locate and exploit SCADA server vulnerabilities; creation of a backdoor on the SCADA server; gathering of information about RTU devices and facilities (i.e. IP address of BS host); scanning and violation of the BS host; access to the BS host and execution of a malicious Over-The-Air (OTA) programming with a rogue code. In particular, we point out that the attacker can install the rogue code both as privileged user of the BS device or by executing a WSN injection tool, such as those indicated in [24] [25]: for instance he/she can perform a sinkhole attack by violating one of the seepage channel sensors or manually reprogramming the routes of the wireless data paths. Finally, the gate command is issued by the attacker self (e.g. by the compromised SCADA host) or is further executed by the authorized personnel.

Security Probes for WSN Zones

In the following we describe the Security Probes deployed for our case study. They will be used to support the detection of the misuse case presented above. The state machines are depicted in Fig. 5.

Triple Modular Redundancy. As the three water flow sensors are related to the same physical event (water discharge), physical values outside the same range can be highlighted and reported to the SIEM. In order to do so, we designed a Security Probe implementing a Triple Modular Redundancy (TMR) system. TMRs generate a single output from several independent processes by adopting majority voting decision (Fig. 5(a)). The TMR SP aggregates the three measurements and reports the number of sensors falling in the same physical range. Disagreeing sensors are indicated in the output. Sample logs are reported in Fig. 6 (TMR SP).

Gate command-Water Flow Incoherence. This SP generates warnings if low water flow levels are measured after a gate opening command has been issued.

Gate command-Gate Tilt Incoherence. This SP (Fig. 5 (b)) generates warnings if the Tilt sensor doesn't reveal variations after a gate opening command.

Gate command-Turbine Vibration Incoherence. This SP generates warnings if the Vibration sensor doesn't reveal variations after a gate opening command.

Experimental Set-Up

In order to test our solution we deployed an experimental testbed composed of: 1) an application configured for monitoring of dams, namely DaMon (Dam Monitor) - developed by Epsilon R&D department together with the University of Naples Parthenope FITNESS research group - realized by using a powerful web-based, AJAX enabled framework for SCADA design, namely Mango [26]; 2) a set of WSN Libelium Waspmote ZigBee devices with Digimesh communication protocol to measure

Tilt, Vibration, Water Levels, Water Flows [27]; 3) a Linux-based BS host; 4) an RTU (based on Datataker DT85G) communicating via Modbus protocol. The Gate actuator is controlled by the DaMon HMI through the RTU.

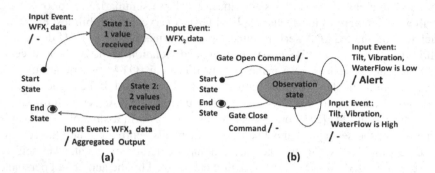

Fig. 5. WSN Security Probes: TMR (a) – Gate-Sensors Incoherence (b)

```
<directive id="500001" name="WSN zone warning" priority="5">
        <rule type="detector" name="Snort Portscan" reliability="2"
            occurrence="1" from="ANY" to="ANY" port_from="ANY" port_to="ANY"
            plugin_id="1100" plugin_sid="21">
            <rules>
                <rule type="detector" name="Last log"
                    reliability="3" occurrence="1"
                    from="1:DST_IP" to="10.0.0.1"
                    port_from="ANY" time_out="100000" port_to="ANY"
                    plugin_id="1010" plugin_sid="1" userdata1="!reboot"/>
                <rule type="detector" name="TMR Security Probe"
                    reliability="2" occurrence="2"
                    from="ANY" to="ANY"
                    port_from="ANY" time_out="100000" port_to="ANY"
                    plugin_id="1011" plugin_sid="1"/>
                <rule type="detector" name="Gate-Tilt incoherence"
                    reliability="1" occurrence="1"
                    from="ANY" to="ANY"
                    port_from="ANY" time_out="100000" port_to="ANY"
                    plugin_id="1012" plugin_sid="1"/>
                <rule type="detector" name="Gate-Vibration incoherence"
                    reliability="1" occurrence="1"
                    from="ANY" to="ANY"
                    port_from="ANY" time_out="100000" port_to="ANY"
                    plugin_id="1012" plugin_sid="2"/>
                <rule type="detector" name="Gate-Flow incoherence"
                    reliability="1" occurrence="1"
                    from="ANY" to="ANY"
                    port_from="ANY" time_out="100000" port_to="ANY"
                    plugin_id="1012" plugin_sid="3"/>
            </rules>
        </rule>
</directive>
```

Fig. 6. OSSIM directive of a WSN attack

Security tools installed are: Snort NIDS [28], Linux shell monitor (Last), the OSSIM SIEM by AlienVault [29] integrated with the GET modules and the RS system.

The attack has been performed by executing an OTA code on the Seepage Channel sensors. The OTA forces the routes from the penstock sensors to pass through the seepage channel sensors (destination address and maximum hops are reprogrammed). The seepage sensors alter the water flow values transiting through them.

The warning events generated by the system are: i) a network scan by Snort; ii) a shell activity in the Linux BS host; iii) a TMR warning; iv) a number of warnings from the Gate-Tilt/Vibration/Flow Security Probes.

The misuse case model presented above is used to configure an OSSIM *Directive* as in Fig. 6. The rule triggers alerts with a total reliability (i.e. alert confidence) of 10. Actually, observe that the Vibration and Tilt warnings are not necessarily generated (this only happens if the violated node of the WSN modifies all the data through it). Even if the Directive may generate lower level alerts – in case of few physical evidence – we may identify additional conditions related to other physical parameters.

The GET modules are able to gather, parse and process the data format shown in Fig. 7, such as Libeium Waspmote data, Gate commands reported by DaMon HMI (text based reports) and Syslog reports by Snort and "Last" utility. The SPs show three capabilities: they treat physical data from a security perspective; they place SIEM intelligence at the periphery and avoid irrelevant data to be propagated to the central system; they exploit specific knowledge of the application domain (redundancy and physical incoherence).

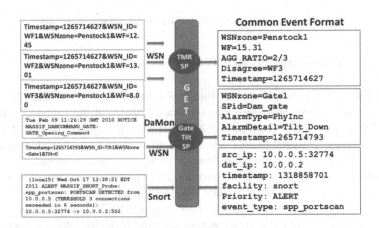

Fig. 7. GET processing at the edge of MASSIF SIEM

Fig. 8 shows DaMon interface and in particular the gate monitoring and control mimics. This interface allows users to change the gate openess levels; each actuator command generates notification messages, such as in Fig. 7.

Fig. 9 shows an OSSIM Alarms, which includes the events that generated the alerts (Fig. 8).

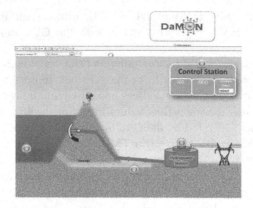

Fig. 8. DaMon interface showing gate and penstock details

#	Id	Alarm	Risk	Date	Source	Destination	Correlation Level
1	15	WSN zone warning	6	2011-03-30 14:01:15	ANY	ANY	6
		Alarm Summary [Total Events: 6 - Unique Dst IPAddr: 2 - Unique Types: 2 - Unique Dst Ports: 1]					
1	15	Gate-Flow Incohe	1	2011-03-30 13:59:29	ANY	ANY	6
2	14	Gate-Vibration In	1	2011-03-30 13:59:26	ANY	ANY	5
3	12	Gate-Tilt Incohe	1	2011-03-30 13:59:25	ANY	ANY	4
4	8	TMR Security Probe	1	2011-03-30 13:59:24	ANY	ANY	3
5	5	Last log	1	2011-03-30 13:54:12	ANY	ANY	2
6	2	Snort Portscan	1	2011-03-30 13:49:10	ANY	ANY	1

Fig. 9. OSSIM alarm and related events (addresses are obfuscated)

5   Conclusions and Future Work

In this paper we have discussed main limits of current SIEM technology when deployed to secure CIs. We have described the main features of the enhanced SIEM for CIs developed in the EC-funded project MASSIF [7], mainly focusing on the framework of the system assigned to data collection and storage, namely the Generic Event Translation (GET) and the Resilient Storage (RS). We have proposed them in the challenging case study of a dam monitoring and control system which uses WSN technologies. We have presented an attack model aimed at tampering the WSN data from a remote facility and have indicated how to support SIEM detection of the attack with a number of Security Probes triggering warning revealing physical incoherence in the measurements. In the future we plan to produce quantitative evidence of the benefits due to the adoption of the enhanced SIEM, against traditional solutions.

Acknowledgments. The research leading to these results has received funding from the European Commission within the context of the Seventh Framework Programme (FP7/2007-2013) under Grant Agreement No. 257644 (MAnagement of Security information and events in Service Infrastructures, MASSIF Project).

References

1. Seung, H.K., Qiu-Hong, W., Johannes, B.U.: A comparative study of cyberattacks. Commun. ACM 55(3), 66–73 (2012), doi:10.1145/2093548.2093568
2. Symantec ® Applied Research: Symantec 2010 Critical Infrastructure Protection Study (Global Results) (October 2010)
3. Buttyan, L., Gessner, D., Hessler, A., Langendoerfer, P.: Application of wireless sensor networks in critical infrastructure protection: challenges and design options. Security and Privacy in Emerging Wireless Networks. IEEE Wireless Communications 17(5), 44–49 (2010), doi:10.1109/MWC.2010.5601957
4. Bai, X., Meng, X., Du, Z., Gong, M., Hu, Z.: Design of Wireless Sensor Network in SCADA System for Wind Power Plant. In: Proceedings of the IEEE International Conference on Automation and Logistics, Qingdao, China (2008)
5. Minteos DamWatch (2011),
   http://www.minteos.com/wp-content/uploads/2011/02/
   Microsoft-Word-minteos-damwatch_ita.pdf
6. Stouffer, K., Falco, J., Scarfone, K.: Guide to Industrial Control Systems (ICS) Security. National Institute of Standards and Technology (NIST), SP 800-82 (2011)
7. MASSIF project, http://www.massif-project.eu/
8. Bankovic, Z., Vallejo, J.C., Malagon, P., Araujo, I., Moya, J.M.: Eliminating routing protocol anomalies in wireless sensor networks using AI techniques. In: Proceedings of the 3rd ACM Workshop on Artificial Intelligence and Security (AISec 2010), pp. 8–13. ACM, New York (2010), doi:10.1145/1866423.1866426
9. Coppolino, L., D'Antonio, S., Romano, L., Spagnuolo, G.: An Intrusion Detection System for Critical Information Infrastructures using Wireless Sensor Network technologies. In: 5th International Conference on Critical Infrastructure (CRIS), pp. 1–8 (2010)
10. Wang, Q., Wang, S., Meng, Z.: Applying an Intrusion Detection Algorithm to Wireless Sensor Networks. In: Second International Workshop on Knowledge Discovery and Data Mining, WKDD 2009, pp. 284–287 (2009)
11. MASSIF project. Scenario requirements Deliverable D2.1.1, Project MASSIF (April 2011)
12. RSA™ Security: RSA enVision™ Universal Device Support Guide (2008)
13. AlienVault™: Available OSSIM Plugin List (2010)
14. ArcSight™: ArcSight™ Smartconnector (2009)
15. Q1Labs™: Supported devices,
   http://q1labs.com/products/supported-devices.aspx
16. The Committee on the Judiciary House of Representatives: Federal Rules of Evidence (December 2010),
   http://judiciary.house.gov/hearings/printers/111th/evid2010.
   pdf
17. Sousa, P., Bessani, A., Correia, M., Neves, N., Verissimo, P.: Highly available intrusion-tolerant services with proactive-reactive recovery. IEEE Transactions on Parallel and Distributed Systems 21(4) (2010)
18. BSD Syslog Protocol, RFC 3164, http://www.ietf.org/rfc/rfc3164.txt
19. Campanile, F., Cilardo, A., Coppolino, L., Romano, L.: Adaptable Parsing of Real-Time Data Streams. In: Proceedings of the 15th Euromicro International Conference on Parallel, Distributed and Network-Based Processing (PDP 2007), pp. 412–418. IEEE Computer Society, Washington, DC (2007), doi:10.1109/PDP.2007.16
20. Home of SMC: the State Machine Compiler, http://smc.sourceforge.net/

21. Shoup, V.: Practical Threshold Signatures. In: Preneel, B. (ed.) EUROCRYPT 2000. LNCS, vol. 1807, pp. 207–220. Springer, Heidelberg (2000)
22. Zhu, Q., Hsu, W.W.: Fossilized Index: The Linchpin of Trustworthy Non-Alterable Electronic Records. In: Proceedings of the ACM International Conference on Management of Data, Baltimore, Maryland, pp. 395–406 (June 2005)
23. Langner, R.: Stuxnet: Dissecting a Cyberwarfare Weapon. IEEE Security and Privacy 9(3), 49–51 (2011), doi:10.1109/MSP.2011.67
24. Parthasarathy, R., Peterson, N., Song, W.Z., Hurson, A., Behrooz Shirazi, A.: Over the Air Programming on Imote2-Based Sensor Networks. In: 43rd Hawaii International Conference on System Sciences, pp. 1–9 (2010)
25. McNabb, J.: Vulnerabilities of Wireless Water Meter Networks. In: DEF.CON Hacking Conference (2011)
26. Mango, Open Surce M2M, http://mango.serotoninsoftware.com/
27. Libelium™ Waspmote, http://www.libelium.com/products/waspmote
28. Snort™, Network IDS/IPS, http://www.snort.org/
29. OSSIM AlienVault™, http://www.alienvault.com/

On Securing Communications
among Federated Health Information Systems

Mario Ciampi[1], Giuseppe De Pietro[1], Christian Esposito[1], Mario Sicuranza[1],
Paolo Mori[2], Abraham Gebrehiwot[2], and Paolo Donzelli[3]

[1] ICAR - CNR,
Via Pietro Castellino, 111 - 80131 Napoli - Italy
[2] IIT-CNR,
Via Giuseppe Moruzzi, 1- 56124 Pisa - Italy
[3] DDI - Presidency of the Council of Ministers,
via Po, 14 - 00198 Roma - Italy
{mario.ciampi,giuseppe.depietro,christian.esposito,
mario.sicuranza}@na.icar.cnr.it,
{paolo.mori,abraham.gebrehiwot}@iit.cnr.it, p.donzelli@governo.it

Abstract. The current trend in designing Health Information Systems
is to apply federated architectures by integrating existing systems. This
exacerbates the security guarantees that such systems are required to satisfy and demands the introduction of advanced methods for dealing with
security. This paper aims at describing how federated Health Information
Systems can offer security properties by adopting proper mechanisms to
protect exchanged data and provided functionalities from malicious manipulations.

Keywords: Security, Access Control, Health Information Systems.

1 Introduction

A *Health Information System* [1] is the application of ICT technologies for storing and distributing medical data, with the aim of contributing to a high-quality
and efficient healthcare. The traditional vision of a HIS is a system to manage
the digitalized form of medical documents, such as images or reports, created
by means of editing programs within a certain department or hospital. Practical examples are the *Radiology Information System* (RIS) [2], to store and to
retrieve radiological images or the *Picture Archiving and Communication System* (PACS) [2], for the management and communication of images from several
different departments within the hospital. Nowadays, the emerging need to orchestrate the healthcare offered to patients by different providers, which can
be located within the same region or even spaning different regions within the
given country or among different countries, has imposed a radical rethink of HIS.
Such an evolution consists in the integration of all the hospital-size HIS so as
to form regional HIS, and federating all the regional HIS so to have national
and trans-national HIS, referred in this paper as *Wide-Area HIS* (WAHIS).

F. Ortmeier and P. Daniel (Eds.): SAFECOMP 2012 Workshops, LNCS 7613, pp. 235–246, 2012.
© Springer-Verlag Berlin Heidelberg 2012

A practical example is the WAHIS under development within the context of the epSOS project[1], funded by the European Commission. The scope is the progressive interconnection of health systems and health policies across the European Union, and the application also to healthcare of the central principle within the European Union of freedom of movement for people, goods and services. This has recently received a further boost with the European Commission Directive 2011/24/EU on patient rights in cross-border healthcare[2]. Similar initiatives are currently running in the European countries, to integrate their regional HIS into a seamless WAHIS, such as the OpenInFSE project[3] under development in Italy.

Security is a critical issue for HIS, since the data stored or exchanged may contain very sensitive information. Any HIS design should encompass a series of mechanisms to protect its data and functionalities from any unauthorized access or misuse, but at the same time to make them available to authorized users such as general practitioners or hospital-based physicians. Achieving security for traditional HIS limited within a certain department or hospital is a simple task since (i) dedicated networks are used, (ii) data are stored in trusted and managed repositories, and (iii) there are limited access points for users to interact with the HIS. The evolution from hospital-size HIS to regional and trans-regional HIS has contributed to pushing HIS into a more challenging environment by increasing the complexity of the security issues to be addressed: (i) data are conveyed by wide area networks, (ii) clinical data of a patient can be stored in different repositories belonging to several distinct HIS, each with given security assurances, and (iii) a large number of users can interact with the infrastructure. Therefore, the need to protect patient data and to keep them available when required is no longer a trivial concern, and more advanced security mechanisms are needed than the ones commonly used in traditional HIS.

This paper aims at describing how to ensure that the security requirements of HIS are satisfied by adopting the most suitable solution among the ones available within the current literature. In particular, we present in Section 2 the security requirements that a WAHIS must satisfy. Section 3 describes the solutions we propose to meet the described requirements, and how we have implemented them within the context of a concrete WAHIS, i.e., the one under development by the mentioned OpenInFSE project, whose architecture of reference is depicted in Figure 1 and described in detail in [3]. In particular, the contribution of this paper is to have combined well-established methods and widely-recognized standards within an holistic framework for secure clinical dissemination, so as to easily adopt it within the context of the Italian national healthcare system and to integrated in the already existing regional HIS. Next, Section 4 analyses the available related work on securing communications within WAHIS and compares it with our solutions. Last, we conclude with some final remarks and plans for future work in Section 5.

---

[1] http://www.epsos.eu/
[2] Available at
   http://ec.europa.eu/health/cross_border_care/ policy/index_en.htm
[3] http://ehealth.icar.cnr.it/

2   Security Requirements

There is a common agreement about the security requirements of HIS and of the communications among their composing entities. The first three security aspects are driven directly by the *CIA Triad*, which is well-established within the current literature:

- Confidentiality: Clinical data of patients are not made available to unauthorized individuals, and patients can have control on where their data are stored and who may have access to them. The only exception to this is during an emergency when the patient is not able to give its consent. In this case, the HIS has to give doctor access to the patient clinical data.
- Integrity: Manipulations of data and overall infrastructure functionalities only happen in a standard and authorized manner.
- Availability: Medical data are not denied to authorized consumers.

Such aspects alone are not felt to be sufficient to define all the properties that a HIS has to provide in order to be considered secure. In fact, security professionals felt that the focus on only confidentiality, integrity and availability alone is not enough for satisfying the requirements of protecting sensitive clinical information. For this reason, in addition to the CIA Triad, we have found other aspects to better characterize a secure HIS:

- Authenticity: The identity of users has to be checked and validated;
- Authorization: The rights to access certain pieces of clinical data or even to use certain system functionalities are granted to given users depending either on their identities or on their role within a given healthcare provider;
- Non-Repudiation: It should be possible to obtain an evidence of the origin of any change to certain pieces of clinical data;
- Accountability: Each activity triggered by users on HIS has to be persistently traced so as to allow later forensic analysis and to map a security threat to a responsible party.

3   Proposed Solution

In [3], we have presented the architecture for a federation of HIS called InFSE, which is under development within the context of the previously mentioned OpenInFSE project, and depicted in Figure 1. Such an architecture is based on the Web Service technology, and data are exchanged as SOAP messages in accordance with the Health Level 7 Clinical Document Architecture (HL7 CDA) standard[4], which specifies a common syntactic model for structuring medical data for clinical documents. As described in [3], the web services composing InFSE can be easily integrated within the already-existing HIS of a given region, and used to define a federation of HIS to manage medical documents, to define an index registry on them and to notify clinical data. Each of these functionalities

---

[4] http://www.hl7.org/

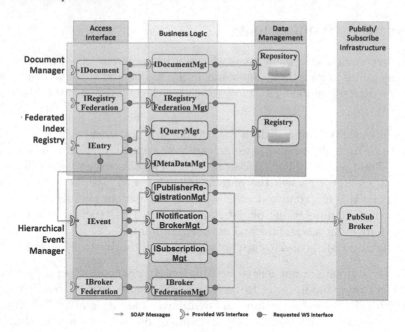

Fig. 1. Overview of the InFSE architecture

is provided by a proper business component of InFSE as shown in the figure. The highest level of the InFSE architecture, named *Access Interface*, is a set of five web services that represent access points from the rest of the world to the functionalities provided by InFSE. Below such a level, we can find the web services that implement the application logic of InFSE, and each component has at least one web service at this level, which is accessible by users from one of the web services within the access interface. The lower level is constituted by a *Data Management* layer to store the medical data in a proper repository and the relative metadata in a registry, to be used to allow users to search for data of interest, and also a Publish/Subscribe Infrastructure to realize event notification of clinical data. The usage of such services and exchanged data is protected by an additional component called *Access Policy Manager*, which is not shown in Figure 1. The scope of this paper is to describe how the last component has been implemented to support security in the federation of HIS[5].

3.1 State of the Art in Securing Web Services

Since the key technology of our federation solution is represented by web services, we have drawn from the research made to secure them. In particular, we have followed the principles of WS-Security [6], which is the specification of

---

[5] We refer interested readers to [3] and [4] for more details on the mentioned business components of InFSE.

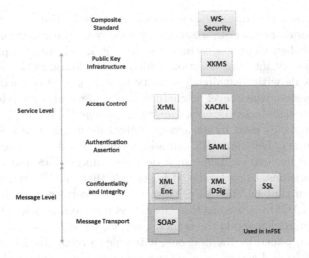

Fig. 2. Overview of the WS-Security specification, adapted from [5]

reference when addressing security for web services. WS-Security is a composite standard made by combining other different specifications and methods, and specifies two different levels of mechanisms to enforce the provided security level, as shown in Figure 2. The first is implemented at the message level by defining a SOAP header that carries out extensions to security. The second is realized at service level to perform higher-level security mechanisms such as access control or authentication. In particular, at the message level we can find two main XML security standard techniques that can be introduced in the SOAP header extensions: *XML Signature* (XML DSig in the figure) and *XML Encryption* (XML Enc in the figure). The former aims at having a small portion of the XML content digitally signed (such element is called digest) so as to provide integrity and non-repudiation for the overall XML content. On the other hand, the latter has the goal to encrypt a part of the overall XML content by using a certain key, which can be public or private according to the chosen encryption strategy. In the case of WS-Security, the SOAP header has a given field, called Digest-Value, to contain the digest with indications of the adopted signature method. If XML Enc is used, the SOAP header has to contain the adopted encryption key, which is itself encrypted by using a proper public key. Besides these two important message-level methods, we have an additional one: Secure Socket Layer (SSL), which realizes a secure form of the TCP transport protocol, by offering mechanisms for the key agreement, encryption and authentication of the endpoints of a connection-oriented communication. On top of these message-level mechanisms, we can find service-level ones. *Security Assertion Markup Language* (SAML) is a framework to exchange authentication and authorization information in a request/respond manner when the communication participants do not share the same platform or belong to the same system. The core of this framework is the *assertion*, expressed as XML constructs, containing the identity of the requestor, and the authorization decisions or credentials. Therefore, SAML conveys the result of an authorization process, with the assertion assumed to be a security token to access secured services, granted only by processing the information present into the assertion, which can be found in the SOAP header. SAML only deals with formalizing security tokens, and is teamed up with the above mentioned message-level mechanisms to achieve also confidentiality, and integrity. *Extensible Access Control Markup Language* (XACML) is used to specify roles and policies used by an access control mechanism to infer the access decisions for users. Different HIS can adopt their own access roles and grants, and XACML is used to exchange such decisions among HIS and to orchestrate their access decisions. In particular, it is possible that an HIS returns to the user a security token that he/she can use also to access services and data hosted by another HIS. XACML is used so that the access roles and policies of the first HIS can be disseminated towards the second one. So, when the second HIS receives a security token issued by the first one, it is able to recognize it and to take the right access decision. Last, we can find two other specifications: *Extensible Rights Markup Language* (XrML) and *XML Key Management Specification* (XKMS). The first is used to express rights and conditions related to the access control (such as expiration times); while the second defines interfaces for the distribution of keys used in XML DSig and XML Enc.

3.2 Securing Web Services in InFSE

In InFSE, we have chosen not to adopt all the specifications composing the WS-Security standard, but a certain sub-set, as clearly illustrated in Figure 2. First of all, we have not used XML Enc to encrypt the body of the exchanged SOAP Messages, but only the signatures of XML DSig. Therefore, we do not need XKMS. The reason is due to the fact that exchanged SOAP messages, when they are carrying sensitive medical information are made anonymous so as to implicitly protect patient privacy [7]. In fact, national and international regulations demand the elimination of the personal nature of healthcare data by separating patient personal information and clinical data (*i.e.*, these two elements should not be present in the same message or the same data repository). The so-called "Identifier Control Facility" (ICF) is used to give pseudonyms to patients, which are attached to all the exchanged and stored clinical data. Such pseudonyms univocally identify patients and also track where patient personal data can be retrieved. On the other hand, we protect the communications by using *HyperText Transfer Protocol over Secure Socket Layer* (HTTPS), which layers HTTP on top of the SSL. Incoming SOAP messages contain assertions defined by means of SAML, which are evaluated before being passed to their web service of interest. Figure 3 illustrates how the web services to perform a query are executed when security is applied. The given web services are contained between a PreHandler and a PostHandler, provided by the JAX-WS platform used to develop InFSE[6]. The first hijacks a SOAP message before it is delivered

---

[6] A specification of Java API for XML Web Services; in particular we have used Metro as implementation of JAX-WS (http://jax-ws.java.net/).

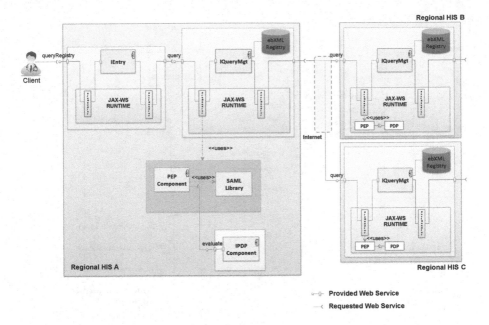

Fig. 3. Architectural Overview of the dependancies among the software components used for performing a query operation in a federated setting

to its target web service to store and to evaluate the security assertions contained in its header. If such evaluation is verified, *i.e.*, an access right can be grated to the given SOAP message based on the contained assertion, then the body of such a message is passed to the web service. Otherwise, the message is discarded. On the other hand, the PostHandler attaches to the SOAP message outgoing from the target web service the security assertion stored by the PreHandler. The PostHandler is crucial when several web services are composed, otherwise the security assertion will be lost after the execution of the first web service, *i.e.*, the one belonging to the Access Interface. Not only received assertions are stored, but also the taken access decisions, so to trace all the operations performed by the security components. While we use the simple implementation of the PostHandler, for the PreHandler we have implemented a Java class called *PEPComponent* and an additional web service named as *IPDPComponent*. Using a SAML Library, the first has the following duties:

- Analyze the correctness of the received assertions contained in the header of the incoming SOAP message;
- Verify the digital signature contained in each assertion;
- Check the correctness of the role assigned to the physician who sent the SOAP message and its purpose of use;
- Interact with a regional management system of the patient consent to access its clinical data, so to control the access rights granted to the physician.

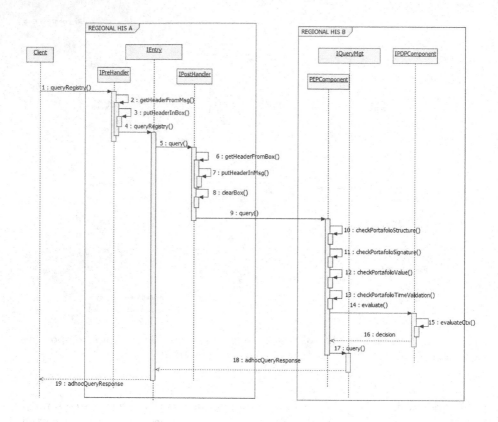

Fig. 4. Execution of a query directed to IQueryMgt service

On the other hand, the second is invoked by the PEPComponent for granting access to the target web service depending on the proper regional XACML access policies and on the role of the physician within the regional healthcare provider. In addition, despite of using keys for XML DSig, we do not need XKMS since the used keys are private, decided and provided to healthcare providers by each region.

3.3   Use Cases

To practically describe how security is realized in InFSE, let us consider two concrete usage scenarios: the first one aims at finding a given medical document within the federation, while the second one consists of retrieving a medical document from a given regional HIS. National and international regulations impose that a clinical document has to be stored in the repository of the healthcare provider that has produced it, and it is not allows to be moved in another repository.

To issue a query, the user has to invoke a query operation on the IEntry web service, which will redirect the request to the local IQueryMgt service or to remote ones. To retrieve a document, the user has to invoke a retrieve operation on the IDocument web service, which will pass it to IDocumentMgt that accesses the data repository looking for the requested document. Figure 4 contains a sequence diagram that shows the interactions among the components in Figure 3 to perform a query operation (the registry in Figure 1 has been realized according to the ebXML specification[7] so to have more flexible and interoperable registries). As mentioned, the client sends a SOAP message to IEntry to invoke a query. Such a message is passed to the PreHandler before reaching IEntry. PreHandler is implemented in a simple manner with the only scope to store the assertions contained in the received SOAP message. The message is then received by the IEntry, which forwards it to a given instance of the IQueryMgt, such as the one managed by the same regional HIS or the one of another regional HIS (as in the figure). Right after leaving IEntry, the message is given to the PostHandler, which only attaches the stored assertions. Also before reaching the IQueryMgt instance, the message is given to the PreHandler, which in this case is realized by the PEPComponent. Such component does the basic string operations of a PreHandler, but in addition it checks the assertions as mentioned before. A query request SOAP message contains three different assertions in its header:

- Identity Assertion, which contains the identifier of the physician requesting the query operation. A regional HIS has its own system giving identifiers to physicians (named Issuer), who is also the guarantor of the level of assurance and responsible of what contained in this assertion. In fact, such assertion is signed by the issuer and may be contained in a smart card that the physician uses for authentication.
- Role Assertion, which states the role of the physician within the regional healthcare provider, who has signed the assertion.
- Context Assertion, which grants or not access to a given requested service. A regional HIS has its own system giving access grants to physicians and signing the access assertions.

In addition, the query request requires a parameter indicating a purpose of use for the requested data, which can assume a particular value, *i.e.*, *emergency*, to represent that the request is performed during an emergency. In the this case, the doctor has access to patient data even if he/she has not granted it. As shown in Figure 5, such assertions are validated by the IPDPComponent, which verifies their syntactical and logical correctness. Only if this check is passed, the message can reach the IQueryMgt service. This service can look for the requested document within the registry by considering a given query statement. If such statement is satisfied, the service returns to the user the identifiers of the documents that has verified the provided query statement, and an Access Assertion for granting access to those documents returned by the query. Otherwise, the

---

[7] https://www.oasis-open.org/committees/regrep/

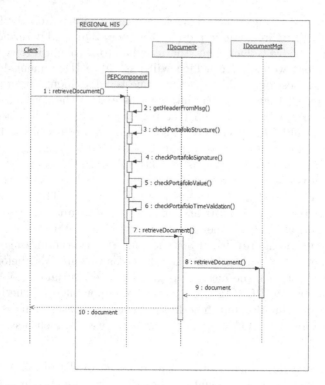

Fig. 5. Execution of a retrieve directed to a given instance of IDocument

service can decide to turn the request towards another IQueryMgt instance running in a different regional HIS. In this last case, the PostHandler is executed so to attach the stored assertions to the outgoing SOAP message.

In the second usage scenario, depicted in Figure 5, the scope of the user is to retrieve a document given a proper identifier, e.g., after the return of a query operation. So, the client invokes the retrieve operation of IDocument web service. In this case, the PreHandler is implemented as a PEPComponent, which checks the assertions in the header (the designer is free to select a particular implementation of the PreHandler). In this case, the only assertion is the Access Assertion, which has been returned after the execution of a query. In fact, it is reasonable that a retrieval is invoked after a query since the user may not know the identifier of a given document. Only the access assertion is required for a retrieval since such operation is always resolved within a given regional HIS, while a query operation is likely to be distributed among the members of the federation. In the last case, the access assertion of a regional HIS has no validity outside of its issuer, so the Identity and Role Assertions are required to take an access decision based on well defined XACML policies. If the assertion verification is successful, then the request is passed to IDocument, which redirects the request to IDocumentMgt. The last one accesses the data repository, takes the request document, if exists, and returns it to the user.

3.4   Summary

Concluding, the presented solution is able to guarantee all the security requirements listed in Section 2:

- Anonymization of clinical data and the use of SSL provide Confidentiality.
- XML DSig assures data integrity and non-repudiation, and the implemented access control mechanism allows the overall infrastructure functionalities to be only used in an authorized manner.
- Security assertions expressed in SAML support Single-Sign-On so that credentials issued by a given regional HIS can be utilized also in other federated regional HIS. This assures that medical data are also available for the physicians that do not belong to the healthcare provider where the data reside.
- Authenticity is realized by means of proper handlers.
- Authorization is regulated by proper XACML policies and implemented by a Role-Based Access Control [8], which is known to be effective to manage complex access control policies charactering a typical healthcare provider.
- Accountability is supported by persistently storing all incoming requests and access decisions so to be used in post-mortem analysis to detect the root causes of a security issue and to resolve it.

4   Related Work

Security in healthcare has been an active research topic in the last decades, and the review in [9] provides a complete view of the research efforts spent and achievements obtained so far. As noticeable from the Appendix 1 of this review, less attention has been spent on architectures and frameworks, but more focus has been given to qualitative research, modeling and economic studies. Based on these research activities, few prototypes have been realized. Our work has not only an academic value since it investigates security with a theoretical perspective, but also a very practical added value, since we have realized a prototype that we are integrating in the existing regional HIS. In addition, all the existing efforts to enforce security were limited to systems with limited size, such as within an hospital or even a clinical department. Our work differs from those since we are addressing the more challenging issue of securing operations for an HIS within a region, but also within a federation among heterogeneous regions, which differ among each other not only from the technological point of view, but also from an organizational one (such as different specification of security requirements and policies). The work closer to ours is the one presented in [10], which proposes a security architecture for interconnecting HIS. Similar to us, this work is designed to satisfy the main security requirements, and the proposed solutions are quite similar to ours. However, only an architecture is presented without any implementation. In addition, our solution is more flexible since it is based on the specifications composing WS-Security.

5 Final Remarks and Future Work

This paper has presented a solution to secure the communications and functionalities of a federation of HIS. In particular, we have described the part of WS-Security specification that can be used for this scope. We have provided a qualitative assessment of our solution with respect to the security requirements of a HIS. As a future work, we are investigating the performance overhead related to the introduction of security, and the possible integration of other security mechanisms, such as Intrusion Detection Systems as in [11].

Acknowledgment. This work has been partially supported by the project named OpenInFSE, a Convention between the Department for the digitization of public administration and technological innovation (DDI) and the ICT Department of the Italian National Research Council (CNR).

References

1. Hauxe, R.: Health information systems. International Journal of Medical Informatics 75(3), 268–281 (2006)
2. Huang, H.K.: PACS and Imaging Informatics: Basic Principles and Applications. Wiley-Liss (April 2004)
3. Ciampi, M., Pietro, G.D., Esposito, C., Sicuranza, M., Donzelli, P.: On Federating Health Information Systems. In: Proceedings of the International Conference Healthcare Informatics and Biomedical Engineering, HiBES (July 2012)
4. Esposito, C., Ciampi, M., Pietro, G.D., Donzelli, P.: Notifying Medical Data in Health Information Systems. In: Proceedings of the 6th ACM International Conference on Distributed Event-Based Systems, DEBS (July 2012)
5. Naedele, M.: Standards for XML and Web services security. IEEE Computer Magazine 11(3), 4–21 (2009)
6. Nordbotten, N.A.: XML and Web Services Security Standards. IEEE Communications Surveys & Tutorials 36(4), 96–98 (2003)
7. Brannigan, V.M., Beier, B.R.: Patient privacy in the era of medical computer networks: a new paradigm for a new technology. Medinfo 8(pt. I), 640–643 (1995)
8. Park, J., Sandhu, R., Ahn, G.-J.: Role-based access control on the web. ACM Transactions on Information and System Security 4(1), 37–71 (2001)
9. Appari, A., Johnson, M.: Information security and privacy in healthcare: current state of research. International Journal of Internet and Enterprise Management 6(4), 279–314 (2010)
10. Gritzalis, D., Lambrinoudakis, C.: A security architecture for interconnecting health information systems. International Journal of Medical Informatics 73(3), 305–309 (2004)
11. Ficco, M.: Achieving security by intrusion-tolerance based on event correlation. International Journal of Network Protocols and Algorithms (NPA) 2(3), 70–84 (2010)

How Secure Is ERTMS?

Richard Bloomfield[1], Robin Bloomfield[2,3], Ilir Gashi[2], and Robert Stroud[3]

[1] Independent Consultant, UK
richardbloomfield52@yahoo.co.uk
[2] Centre for Software Reliability, City University London, London, UK
{reb,i.gashi}@csr.city.ac.uk
[3] Adelard LLP, London, UK
rjs@adelard.com

Abstract. This paper reports on the results of a security analysis of the European Railway Traffic Management System (ERTMS) specifications. ERTMS is designed to be fail-safe and the general philosophy of 'if in doubt, stop the train' makes it difficult to engineer a train accident. However, it is possible to exploit the fail-safe behaviour of ERTMS and create a situation that causes a train to halt. Thus, denial of service attacks are possible, and could be launched at a time and place of the attacker's choosing, perhaps designed to cause maximum disruption or passenger discomfort. Causing an accident is more difficult but not impossible.

Keywords: Security assessment, safety-critical systems, ERTMS, railway signaling systems, safety and security interactions.

1 Introduction

This paper reports on the results of a security analysis of the European Railway Traffic Management System (ERTMS) specifications that was commissioned on behalf of key UK railway stakeholders and UK government. ERTMS is a major industrial project that aims at replacing the many different national train control and command systems in Europe with a standardised system. In the UK, Network Rail are preparing to introduce ERTMS as part of the upgrade of the signalling and communications systems running on Britain's rail infrastructure. This upgrade has the potential to increase the risk of an electronic attack on the rail infrastructure, as it brings more systems under centralised control. Consequently, the railway industry and government identified a need to understand the security implications of the new technology, and we were asked to conduct a security audit of ERTMS to identify potential vulnerabilities and suggest mitigations.

In this paper, we discuss the ERTMS/ETCS specifications from a security perspective and identify areas where there are potential vulnerabilities. We also explain our methodology of using attack scenarios to assess the impact of these vulnerabilities and present our overall assessment of the scenarios we analysed. However, because the results of our analysis are sensitive, we do not provide details of specific vulnerabilities or attack scenarios, which can be found in our detailed reports [1,2]. Although

F. Ortmeier and P. Daniel (Eds.): SAFECOMP 2012 Workshops, LNCS 7613, pp. 247–258, 2012.
© Springer-Verlag Berlin Heidelberg 2012

these reports are currently not publicly available, copies can be made available on request, subject to the approval of the key stakeholders.

The rest of the paper is organised as follows: section 2 gives an overview of ERTMS; section 3 explains the scope of our analysis; section 4 discusses our threat model; section 5 describes our methodology; section 6 discusses the trust relationships between the components of the ERTMS architecture; section 7 presents a summary of the weaknesses and vulnerabilities that we found in each part of the ERTMS specifications; section 8 explains our use of attack scenarios to assess the impact of these vulnerabilities and our scenario analysis technique; section 9 discusses related work on ERTMS security; and finally section 10 provides a discussion, conclusions and areas for further work.

2   Overview of ERTMS

ERTMS consists of two major components:

- **ETCS** is the European Train Control System, an automatic train protection system that is intended to replace existing legacy train protection systems;
- **GSM-R** is a radio system for providing voice and data communication between the track and the train. It is based on GSM technology but uses a different frequency range and has some special features for railway applications.

ERTMS is implemented using a number of trackside and on-board sub-systems, and the ERTMS/ETCS specifications describe the interfaces by which these various sub-systems interact. The ERTMS/ETCS System Requirements Specification (SRS) [3] provides a technical specification of the overall system, and details of specific protocols can be found in related standards. However, it is important to understand that ERTMS is an interoperability standard, and only deals with the interaction between trains and trackside devices. The interfaces that are used by each national railway to control and manage its own infrastructure are outside the scope of the standard.

This is illustrated in Figure 1, which shows the relationship between ERTMS and a national railway implementation. Green arrows denote interfaces and protocols that are covered by the ERTMS specifications, whilst red arrows denote interfaces that are considered to be part of the national implementation.

The SRS defines four different ERTMS application levels, which cover different operational relationships between the track and the train. Our review focused on Level 2, which is the application level currently being considered for deployment in Britain. At ERTMS/ETCS Level 2, traditional trackside signals are replaced by movement authorities, which are sent to the train over the GSM-R radio link from a control centre. Movement authorities provide safety-critical information about the track conditions ahead, and how far and how fast the train can go. The train also gets location references from devices called balises that are mounted in the track. An on-board computer uses this information to give a display to the driver (via the Driver Machine Interface (DMI)) and to monitor the speed that the train is being driven at, in order to ensure that the train stays within the limits of its movement authority; if not, the on-board computer (not the DMI) applies the brakes automatically.

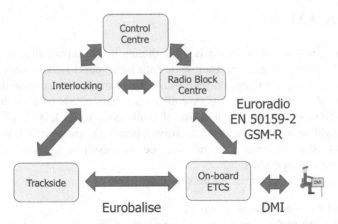

Fig. 1. Relationship between ERTMS and national railway implementation

3   Scope of Analysis

The aim of the study was to examine the ERTMS specifications for potential security vulnerabilities and identify systemic weaknesses in the ERTMS specifications. This was a paper-based study and we were concerned with conceptual problems with the specifications rather than vulnerabilities introduced by design flaws and bugs in implementations of ERTMS technology. Nor did we consider vulnerabilities that might be caused during the operation or maintenance of an ERTMS system. Such vulnerabilities are important but were outside the scope of our study.

Our analysis was holistic and considered whether a national deployment of ERTMS might introduce vulnerabilities into the national rail infrastructure. Our review focused on ERTMS Application Level 2, which made it possible to restrict attention to a number of core specifications, and ignore specifications for interacting with legacy train protection systems and trackside signalling equipment. We also considered the security of GSM-R and analysed how GSM security impacts on GSM-R security. We were particularly interested in electronic attacks that could be launched remotely and would cause widespread disruption.

However, it is important to note that the ERTMS/ETCS specifications only deal with the interoperability requirements of a European Railway Traffic Management System, and therefore do not cover the interfaces that are used by each national railway to control and manage its own infrastructure. This limits the scope of any security or safety analysis to interactions between the various components of the ERTMS/ETCS architecture. For example, although the Radio Block Centres (RBCs) need to interact with the existing rail infrastructure, these interfaces are not required for interoperability and are typically proprietary. This is problematical from the perspective of a security review because it means that these interfaces cannot be reviewed, even though they are critical to the safety and security of the overall system.

4   Threat Model

Traditionally, computer security deals with threats to confidentiality, integrity, and availability, but here we are concerned with train movements rather than information, so our primary concern is integrity, then availability, and finally confidentiality. Loss of integrity could result in accidents or collisions, whereas loss of availability would bring the railway system to a halt. Loss of confidentiality is less of an immediate threat, but might result in the leak of sensitive operational information. Reliability is also important, since an unreliable train service will result in a loss of public confidence in the railway operators.

Thus, the hazards or potential failures or undesirable outcomes to be avoided are:

- a collision involving multiple trains;
- an accident such as derailment involving a single train;
- widespread disruption of train service over a large area;
- disruption to individual trains, or trains within a local area;
- creation of a situation that leads to panic and potential loss of life (e.g., an emergency stop and uncontrolled evacuation onto the track);
- creation of a situation that leads to passenger discomfort and dissatisfaction, (e.g., stopping a train indefinitely in a tunnel);
- loss of public confidence in the railway system due to intermittent low-level problems affecting the reliability of the service;
- leak of sensitive information (e.g., movements of hazardous cargoes or VIPs).

The ERTMS safety analysis considers the effect of potentially catastrophic events on the integrity of the system. Faults that could result in an accident need to be considered in both a safety and security analysis, regardless of the underlying cause of the fault (accidental, deliberate or malicious).

A security analysis also needs to consider the capabilities of the attacker. It is usual to make a distinction between an insider and an outsider. An insider is someone with legitimate access to a system that abuses their position and privileges, either willingly or under duress, whereas an outsider is someone outside the system with limited access, who seeks to break into the system out of curiosity, malice, or for personal gain. Historically, railway systems have relied on highly specialised, proprietary technology, and there has been a relatively small community with the necessary knowledge to exploit vulnerabilities. However, the widespread adoption of open standards like ERTMS that are designed to promote interoperability and the commoditisation of technology could result in both the necessary knowledge and the necessary tools becoming more readily available to potential attackers who are sufficiently motivated to gain the necessary skills.

5   Methodology

We started by considering the trust relationships between the various components of the overall architecture and analysing the consequence of a breach of trust. This enabled us to identify a set of potential weaknesses and vulnerabilities in the specifications. We then developed scenarios that showed how these weaknesses could be exploited by an attacker. These scenarios were refined and validated in discussion with railway stakeholders, and proved to be a very effective way of communicating the risks of an ERTMS implementation being compromised.

6   Trust Relationships

ERTMS is implemented using a number of trackside and on-board sub-systems, and the ERTMS/ETCS specifications describe the interfaces by which these various sub-systems interact to ensure that trains move safely without exceeding their movement authority. Our approach to the security analysis was to consider the trust relationships between the various components of the overall system and analyse the consequences of a breach of trust.

Messages are transmitted between the ERTMS/ETCS sub-systems over various channels, so a security analysis needs to consider:

- whether there are safeguards built into the system that protect against messages being corrupted or deleted in transmission by the input channel;
- whether these safeguards protect against all possible threats to the input channel (for example, deliberate attacks on the channel, as opposed to random failures);
- whether the source of the input is trustworthy, or whether it is possible for the input source to have been compromised;
- whether there is adequate protection at the application level to guard against malicious messages generated by an attacker who controls the input source.

With this approach in mind, we performed a systematic analysis of the ERTMS/ETCS specifications from a security perspective by examining the on-board ETCS application, and considering its interfaces and trust relationships with other components of the ERTMS/ETCS system, both trackside and on-board the train.

7   Weaknesses and Vulnerabilities

Based on our analysis of the trust relationships, we identified a set of potential weaknesses and vulnerabilities in the ERTMS interoperability specifications, which we outline here. The details can be found in our full report [1].

7.1   General Observations

Safety is always paramount in railway systems, and ERTMS/ETCS is designed to be a safe system. Thus, the general philosophy is 'if in doubt, stop the train', which means that it is very difficult for an attacker to engineer a train accident. However, it is possible for an attacker to exploit the 'fail-safe' behaviour of ERTMS, and create a situation that causes a train to halt. Thus, denial of service attacks are possible, and could be launched at a time and place of the attacker's choosing, perhaps designed to cause maximum disruption or passenger discomfort, for example, by arranging for a train to halt in a tunnel.

Nevertheless, most attacks exploiting ERTMS/ETCS would require the attacker to have physical access to the railway line and are therefore localised in their impact; attacks that cause disruption over a wide area depend on compromising the GSM-R network. The threats and vulnerabilities posed by GSM-R depend very much on the national implementation of GSM-R and its supporting telecommunications network.

Moreover, some of the most critical elements of the ERTMS/ETCS system, for example, the interfaces between the control centres and the RBCs, are outside the scope of the ERTMS/ETCS specifications, which are only concerned with interoperability and do not address implementation issues within a single ERTMS/ETCS system. However, it is important to ensure that these interfaces remain logically separate and secure during the migration of existing control systems towards ERTMS, because this process will involve the integration of installations that are currently separate, and the use of multi-purpose transmission networks that carry messages for different applications with varying degrees of criticality.

One of the major vulnerabilities of ERTMS/ETCS is that it is a data-driven system, and therefore any compromise to the data held by the RBCs could cause a serious accident. However, the procedures for managing and updating this data fall outside the scope of the ERTMS/ETCS specifications.

Similarly, the security of the Euroradio protocol [4] used to safely transmit movement authorities depends on the security of the key management and key distribution process. There is a specification for off-line key management between key management domains [5], but the procedures for key management within a key management domain are a matter for the national or local implementation.

Nevertheless, the specification for off-line key management [5] defines a set of security requirements that must be met by the operational key management systems in each key management domain. These requirements, together with compliance with the off-line key management specification, provide a basis for secure key management between key management domains.

Ideally, the ERTMS/ETCS specifications would impose a similar set of requirements on other parts of the system that are managed by national authorities, for example, the interface between control centres and RBCs.

7.2   Specific Observations

The on-board ETCS system needs to interact with a number of other systems, and it is therefore possible to draw conclusions about the security of ERTMS/ETCS with respect to each of these interfaces.

Driver/Train. The driver and train interfaces are only specified at a functional level, but the interfaces to these systems are fairly narrow and limited. However, clearly both the driver and the train itself are trusted components of the system: the driver because he could override the entire ERTMS/ETCS system, and the train because it could have been sabotaged in other ways, such as compromising the braking system. In the present specifications, there is no authentication on the communication channels that are used for these interfaces. This is only acceptable as long as these driver and train interfaces remain part of a closed network that is only connected to the on-board ETCS system. If the ETCS system were ever to be connected to an on-board network that also carried non-critical messages, for example, passenger access to the Internet, then there would be a very real possibility of ETCS being compromised by a virus or deliberate intervention.

Balises. Messages from balises are protected against accidental transmission errors and interference from outside the immediate area of the track. However, the interface does not address the possibility that an attacker might have subverted existing balises, or placed a new balise on the track at a strategic location. Although various levels of data consistency checks are built into the ERTMS/ETCS, balises provide no authentication guarantees, which opens up the possibility of malicious attacks via the balise interface, since the data received from a balise is effectively trusted by the system.

In particular, the ERTMS specifications make a distinction between linked and unlinked balises. Trains are informed about the locations of linked balises in advance as part of their movement authorities, which are transmitted by radio over a secure channel; failure to encounter a linked balise in the expected location will cause the train to halt. However, trains must also be prepared to react to unlinked balises, which can be encountered anywhere. Although trains will only accept a limited number of commands from an unlinked balise, an attacker can exploit almost all of these commands to a greater or lesser extent. Most of these attacks would result in some form of denial of service, but some commands can be used to create a hazardous situation.

Euroradio. The Euroradio protocol [4] uses a shared secret key to establish a secure communications channel. The protocol guarantees authenticity and integrity of messages, but does not guarantee confidentiality. Thus, if the underlying GSM-R network were to be compromised, it would be possible for an attacker to eavesdrop on ERTMS messages and perhaps learn sensitive information. In particular, the ability to eavesdrop on messages also makes it easier for an attacker to intercept communications using a 'man in the middle' attack.

Otherwise, the Euroradio protocol appears to be sound from a security perspective, although we are not aware of it ever having been subjected to a formal cryptographic analysis. However, the specification prescribes the use of Triple DES (Data Encryption Standard) as the underlying cryptographic algorithm rather than a more modern algorithm such as AES (Advanced Encryption Standard). Triple DES is no longer recommended for use in new cryptographic systems and the Euroradio specification should be upgraded accordingly, but for ERTMS, a bigger problem is managing key distribution on the scale of an international railway network.

The ERTMS/ETCS interoperability specifications only deal with secure key management between different key management domains [5], leaving key distribution within a key management domain to the national implementation. A new specification has recently been published that deals with the distribution of keys to ETCS entities (trains and trackside devices) within a key management domain [6], but the current standards mandate an off-line key management solution, which is not practical, particularly if there is a requirement to refresh or revoke keys. For example, in the UK, depending on the key allocation policy, there could be as many as 400,000 keys to manage.

Voice. GSM-R extends the basic GSM network services with some special services that are required for railway operations. Standardised numbers are used to address onboard functions, and an attacker with access to the GSM-R network and an authorized SIM (Subscriber Identity Module) card could cause considerable disruption.

GSM-R. GSM-R is built on top of GSM, which is known to be fundamentally insecure [7]. In particular, GSM uses weak encryption algorithms and does not provide any form of network authentication, which means that GSM networks are vulnerable to a 'man in the middle' attack. Also, an attack on the GSM-R network could bring down the ERTMS/ETCS system over a large area, creating a wide area denial of service attack. The engineering of the GSM-R network is critical to addressing these risks.

8   Scenario Analysis

Having identified some potential vulnerabilities in the ERTMS specifications, we devised attack scenarios to explore the ways in which an attacker could exploit these potential weaknesses and vulnerabilities to achieve one of the undesirable outcomes listed in section 4. In this section, we explain our methodology for constructing these scenarios and summarise our overall assessment. Full details can be found in our report [2].

We devised seven attack scenarios and then analysed each scenario in detail by considering the following questions:

- **How** is the attack performed?
- **What** vulnerabilities does the attack exploit?
- **Where** can the attack be launched from?
- **What** are the possible mitigations?

We then graded each attack according to a range of criteria:

- The **type of access** required to exploit a vulnerability;
- The **level of technical sophistication** required to exploit a vulnerability;
- The **type of failure** caused by a successful attack;
- The **scale of effect** for a successful attack;
- The **scalability of the attack** from the attacker's perspective;

- The **type of impact** caused by a successful attack;
- The **types of mitigation strategy** that are possible;
- The **level of difficulty** for implementing each mitigation.

Our analysis and grading methodology was partially based on a technique for scenario analysis that was devised by a NATO Research Task Group for a study on the Dual Use of High Assurance Technologies [8].

We considered several different categorisations but chose these particular categories because we thought they were the most informative and provided a good summary of the issues raised by each scenario. We deliberately did not attempt to rank the various attack scenarios using a weighted average of the category scores because we believe that such a ranking would be too simplistic – the relative weighting of the various categories and the ranking of the scenarios is a matter for government and industry stakeholders. Similarly, we did not attempt to estimate the likelihood of attacks being successful because this would depend on the national implementation of ERTMS and is therefore best left to the domain experts. Instead, we used colour coding (HIGH, MEDIUM, Low) to highlight the issues, as shown in Table 1.

Table 1. Grading of the issues

Minimum access required	Technical sophistication	Type of failure	Scale of effect	Scalability of the attack	Type of impact	Mitigation strategies	Ease of mitigation
REMOTE ACCESS ACCESS TO INFRASTRUCTURE, BUT NOT THE TRACK SUPPLY CHAIN ACCESS Physical access to the track	LOW MEDIUM High	LOSS OF LIFE DENIAL OF SERVICE	GLOBAL NATIONAL REGIONAL Local	HIGH MEDIUM Low	SAFETY-CRITICAL ECONOMIC POLITICAL Psychological	REACTIVE Preventive	HARD MEDIUM Easy

Using this colour coding, we summarise our grading of each attack scenario in Table 2 to enable the scenarios to be easily compared.

Broadly speaking, attacks that can be launched remotely do not require a high level of sophistication and are highly scalable – however, such attacks are relatively easy to mitigate. Conversely, attacks that require local access are less scalable but also more difficult to mitigate. Hence important trade-offs need to be made by the relevant decision makers and risk managers. The advantage of the analysis and grading approach presented here is that it identifies these trade-offs and helps decision makers to make more informed decisions.

Table 2. Grading of the issues

	Minimum access required	Technical sophistication	Type of failure observed	Scale of effect	Scalability of the attack	Type of impact	Mitigation strategies	Ease of mitigation
Scenario 1	REMOTE ACCESS	LOW	DENIAL OF SERVICE AND LOSS OF LIFE.	LOCAL/ GLOBA L	HIGH	SAFETY-CRITICAL AND/OR PSYCHOL OGICAL	Preventive and reactive	Easy
Scenario 2	REMOTE ACCESS	LOW	DENIAL OF SERVICE	LOCAL/ GLOBA L	HIGH	ECONOMIC, POLITICAL	Preventive and reactive	Easy
Scenario 3	REMOTE ACCESS	LOW	DENIAL OF SERVICE	LOCAL/ GLOBA L	HIGH	ECONOMIC, POLITICAL	Preventive and reactive	Easy
Scenario 4	REQUIRES ACCESS TO WIRELESS CELL.	High	DENIAL OF SERVICE	Local	MEDIUM	ECONOMIC, POLITICAL	REACTIVE	MEDI UM
Scenario 5	REQUIRES ACCESS TO WIRELESS CELL.	High	DENIAL OF SERVICE AND LOSS OF LIFE	Local	Low	SAFETY-CRITICAL AND/OR PSYCHOL OGICAL	Preventive and reactive	MEDI UM
Scenario 6	Physical access to track	LOW	DENIAL OF SERVICE AND LOSS OF LIFE	Local	Low	SAFETY-CRITICAL AND/OR PSYCHOL OGICAL	REACTIVE	HARD
Scenario 7	Physical access to track	MEDIUM	DENIAL OF SERVICE AND LOSS OF LIFE	Local	Low	SAFETY-CRITICAL AND/OR PSYCHOL OGICAL	REACTIVE	MEDI UM

9   Related Work

We are aware of some related work, but to the best of our knowledge, this is the first holistic study that analyses the security of ERTMS at the level of a national infrastructure and considers the potential impact of an ERTMS implementation being compromised. In a paper published around the time of the development of the Euroradio protocol, one of the authors of the specification discusses the safety and security requirements for the technology [9]. More recently, ERTMS has attracted the attention of security researchers and we are aware of two presentations in German [10,11] that touch on some of the issues identified in our more detailed and extensive study, which pre-dates this German work. One of these presentations was to the Chaos Communication Congress in Berlin and attracted a lot of media attention [12], although the media reports were rather confused and made little sense to rail engineers familiar with the technology [13].

10   Discussion and Conclusions

Safety and security are both forms of dependability and use similar techniques to assess the impact of possible failures on the overall behaviour of a system. In general, a safety assessment assumes that failures have accidental causes rather than deliberate causes. In contrast, a security analysis tends to assume a worse case scenario in which all failures are possible.

Nevertheless, safe systems need to be secure – if they are not secure, then they are not safe. A safety analysis that does not consider hazards that could be caused by underlying security vulnerabilities is deficient.

In practice there may be conflicts between security requirements and safety requirements. For example, in an emergency situation, a timely response may be more important than a secure response. Moreover, safety concerns are rather different from security concerns: confidentiality is not usually a safety concern, and in fail-safe systems such as ERTMS, availability is considered to be a reliability issue rather than a safety issue. In contrast, security is traditionally concerned with confidentiality, integrity and availability. A failure of confidentiality would not be considered a safety concern, but would definitely be a security concern. Similarly, fail-safe behaviour is important from a safety perspective but conflicts with the security requirement to maintain availability.

In this paper we presented the results of a security audit of the ERTMS interoperability specifications. ERTMS is designed to be a safe system and the general philosophy is 'if in doubt, stop the train'. This 'fail-safe' behaviour makes it relatively easy for an attacker to bring trains to a halt. Causing an accident is more difficult but not impossible – it is important to remember that ERTMS does not drive the train and it is the driver who is ultimately responsible for the safety of the train. However, as the speed and number of trains increases, the ability of the driver to react to critical issues in a timely fashion may become limited, forcing the system to become more dependent on automated control.

Some of the vulnerabilities we identified depend very much on the specific details of the national implementation of ERTMS and GSM-R. Moreover, some of the most critical parts of an ERTMS implementation (e.g., the interface between the control centre and the RBCs) are outside the scope of the ERTMS/ETCS specifications, which are only concerned with interoperability and do not address implementation issues within a national implementation. Thus, a complete security analysis would need to consider the whole of the national railway infrastructure.

More generally, our work has highlighted the need to ensure that security issues are taken into account when preparing safety cases [14], and we plan to do more work on "security-informed" safety cases, particularly in the context of the Artemis-JU project on Security and Safety Modelling for Embedded Systems (SESAMO) [15].

Acknowledgments. Our original research was commissioned on behalf of the UK railway industry and UK government and we are grateful to our sponsors who commissioned the research and facilitated discussions with key railway stakeholders that were invaluable to us in developing our scenarios and validating our work. Our current research is partially funded by Artemis-JU as part of SESAMO (project number 295354).

References

1. Bloomfield, R., Stroud, R., Gashi, I., Bloomfield, R.: Information Security Audit of ERTMS, Technical Report (2010)
2. Stroud, R., Gashi, I., Bloomfield, R., Bloomfield, R.: ERTMS Specification Security Audit – Analysis of Attack Scenarios, Technical Report (2011)
3. UNISIG SUBSET-026, System Requirement Specification, Version 2.3.0, http://www.era.europa.eu/Document-Register/Pages/UNISIGSUBSET-026.aspx
4. UNISIG SUBSET-037, Euroradio FIS, Version 2.3.0, http://www.era.europa.eu/Document-Register/Pages/UNISIGSUBSET-037.aspx
5. UNISIG SUBSET-038, Offline Key management FIS, Version 2.3.0, http://www.era.europa.eu/Document-Register/Pages/UNISIGSUBSET-038.aspx
6. UNISIG SUBSET-114, KMC-ETCS Entity Off-line KM FIS, Version 1.0.0, http://www.era.europa.eu/Document-Register/Pages/UNISIGSUBSET-114.aspx
7. Quirke, J.: Security in the GSM system (2004)
8. Bloomfield, R., Craigen, D., Miller, A.: Dual Use of High Assurance Technologies, Technical Report (2009), http://www.rto.nato.int/Pubs/rdp.asp?RDP=RTO-TR-IST-048
9. Braband, J.: Safety and Security Requirements for an Advanced Train Control System. In: Proc. 16th International Conference on Computer Safety, Reliability and Security (SAFECOMP 1997). Springer, York (1997)
10. Stump, F.: Datenübertragung über öffentliche Netze im Bahnverkehr – Fluch oder Segen?!, Safetronic 2010 (2010)
11. Katzenbeisser, S.: Can trains be hacked? Die Technik der Eisenbahnsicherungsanlagen. In: 28th Chaos Communication Congress, Behind Enemy Lines (December 2011)
12. BBC News, Train-switching technology 'poses hacking threat' (December 2011), http://www.bbc.co.uk/news/technology-16347248
13. RailUK Forum, BBC News: Hackers could delay trains (December 2011), http://www.railforums.co.uk/showthread.php?t=57565
14. Bloomfield, R.E., Guerra, S., Miller, A., Masera, M., Weinstock, C.B.: International Working Group on Assurance Cases (for Security). IEEE Security and Privacy 4(3), 66–68 (2006)
15. SESAMO – Security and Safety Modelling, ARTEMIS Embedded Computing Systems Initiative 2011, Project Number 295354 (May 2012)

International Cooperation Experiences: Results Achieved, Lessons Learned, and Way Ahead

Craig Gibson[1], Matteo Melideo[2], Luigi Romano[3], and Salvatore D'Antonio[3]

[1] BCE and Bell Group of Companies, Canada
craig.gibson@bell.ca
[2] Engineering Ingegneria Informatica, Italy
matteo.melideo@eng.it
[3] Consorzio Interuniversitario Nazionale per l'Informatica (CINI), Italy
{salvatore.dantonio,luigi.romano}@uniparthenope.it

Abstract. In this paper we discuss the experience we had with international co-operation initiatives with respect to three projects, funded by the European Commission within the context of FP6 and FP7. We provide a summary of the main technical achievements which were directly related to international cooperation, and present the workplan for future research, specifically related to international cooperation. Besides the technical aspects, we discuss the pros and cons of the specific funding tools on which international cooperation was based at the time of these projects, and compile a wish list for upcoming funding initiatives for International Cooperation.

Keywords: Open Source Software, Software Quality, Critical Infrastructure Protection, Synchrophasors, Security Information and Event Monitoring, Global Positioning System.

1 Rationale and Contribution

We claim that international collaboration is highly beneficial, in that research greatly benefits from diverse cultural and scientific backgrounds, and problem domain contexts. To support our claim, we provide tangible evidence of remarkable technical achievements that international cooperation has brought about. More specifically, we discuss the experience we had with international cooperation initiatives within the context of three projects, namely: QualiPSo, INSPIRE (and its accompanying action INSPIRE-INCO), and MASSIF. The main contribution of this paper is thus an overview of the main technical achievements which were directly related to international cooperation. In a nutshell: QualiPSo demonstrated that in the software development domain, international cooperation favours the creation of consensus around common practices, to guarantee higher quality of the final product; INSPIRE demonstrated that Critical Infrastructure Protection must rely on techniques that are compatible, and scalable; MASSIF demonstrated that sharing experience and factorizing interests may widen the scope of individual research plans. While QualiPSo and INSPIRE are now over, MASSIF is an ongoing project. For it, besides commenting the results achieved

F. Ortmeier and P. Daniel (Eds.): SAFECOMP 2012 Workshops, LNCS 7613, pp. 259–270, 2012.

so far, we also present the workplan for future research, with respect to international cooperation. The technical details are in sections II, III and IV with reference to QualiPSo, INSPIRE, and MASSIF, respectively.

Another important contribution of the paper is a discussion of the pros and cons of the specific funding tools on which international cooperation was based at the time of these projects (as well as an analysis of the opportunities for international cooperation that were provided by "Call 9: Objective ICT-2011.10.3: International partnership building and support to dialogues"), and the consequent wish list for upcoming funding initiatives with respect to International Cooperation.   This is detailed in section V.

2   The QualiPSo Experience

2.1   Short Description of the Project

QualiPSo [1] was a project funded by the European Commission (EC) under the FP6, which ended in January 2011. When it was conceived, Open Source was making the transition from a mere development approach (as well as a paradigm, a life style, and a philosophy just for hackers or hobbyists) to a novel and efficient business approach. In fact, at that time the ICT economy was undergoing a deep transformation, moving from a product-oriented to a service-oriented business, with the Web playing a leading role and Open Source identified as a key enabler of this paradigm shift (it is worth mentioning that an article from BBC, dated 21 Jan 2009, claimed that "The secret to a more secure and cost effective government is through open source technologies and products.") [2]. In this new paradigm for the IT domain, where the economy is based on services, interoperability among provided and consumed services becomes essential for the survival of the business model itself, which mandates for open and interoperable technological standards. Open Source facilitates and supports the definition of open standards, thus favouring the development of interoperable systems, and ultimately avoiding vendor lock-in. However, while Open Source has a deep penetration in the academic domain and in some market niches, several industrial domains are still reluctant to use Open Source software products or services or to adopt an Open Source process as their own software production environment. There were (and there are) many persistent myths and yet unsolved drawbacks that made the industry sceptical about Open Source real benefits. One of the objectives of the QualiPSo project was to prove (and demonstrate) the quality of Open Source software and of the processes used for producing it, in order to demolish with facts the false myths about lack of support and maintenance, or about the low quality of Open Source software. Another important objective of the QualiPSo project was to address some of the main open issues of Open Source software, and in particular: (i) the intellectual property issues that require a clarification and simplification of the licensing matters, (ii) the lack of a qualified and specialized educational program in high education about Open Source, and (iii) the fragmentation of the Open Source community. In order to overcome the above mentioned issues and benefiting from the favourable economic context, the QualiPSo initiative was conceived. QualiPSo aimed at making a major contribution to the state of the art and to the practice of Open Source Software. The goal was to define and implement technologies, procedures, and policies to leverage the Open Source Software development current practices to sound and well recognized and established industrial operations. Eighteen international companies and research groups (from Europe, Brazil, and China) worked together in the project for fifty-one months. The project brought together software companies, application solution developers, and research institutions. It was driven by the need of having for Open Source software the appropriate level of trust which would make Open Source development an industrial and wide accepted practice.

2.2   Specific Results Achieved

QualiPSo intended to address in a comprehensive way the main research aspects affecting the adoption of Open Source solutions in an industrial business context. This means to address aspects concerning legal issues, business models, interoperability (at the organizational and at the technical level), data and information management, quality and trustworthiness (of the products and processes), and - last but not least - collaborative development environments more suited for an industrial adoption. Specifically, the main technical and scientific results achieved were [3]:

- An IPR Tracking Methodology, a Licence Compatibility methodology (with a supporting prototype), and a framework for an International Legal Issue web portal;
- A set of strategies for Industries and SMEs to move towards an Open Source paradigm, and the business models for its adoption and sustainability;
- A set of methods, specifications, and proof-of-concepts to handle technical, semantic, and organizational interoperability;
- Prototypes to perform conceptual and semantic searches on heterogeneous sources of information available within a specific forge, supported by advanced and innovative navigation systems to manage query results;
- Two methods (namely: Model of Open Source Software Trustworthiness – MOSST, and Open Source Maturity Model - OMM), and a supporting quality software suite for the measurement of the quality of OSS products and processes;
- The prototype of an innovative forge (named QualiPSo Factory) with novel functionality, a modular and lightweight architecture, new services, and a new user friendly and usable User Interface.

In addition to the above mentioned technical and scientific results, the QualiPSo project fostered and supported the creation of a network of Open Source Competence Centres (CC) to sustain and promote QualiPSo results using them as a leverage for a wider and more conscious adoption of Open Source worldwide. The original plan was to open CCs only in Brazil, Spain, Germany, Italy and China, but in the end CCs were also opened in Japan and Poland [4]. The idea was to create these CCs in different regions of the world, to complement and support the already existing local initiatives in the education and awareness on the benefits of the Open Source paradigm thanks to the new knowledge, expertise, and technologies deriving from the QualiPSo experience. Most of these CCs were built in the wake of already existing initiatives (i.e. Berlios in Germany and Morfeo in Spain), while others started from scratch exploiting the strategic programs (running or planned) defined by the respective Governments for the massive adoption of Open Source solutions in the Public Administration (both local and central). Each QualiPSo CC has to be a physical place which operates and provides more congenial services to its operative context but, to be recognised as a QualiPSo Competence Centre, it must reuse technologies, procedures, and policies produced by QualiPSo and should be part of the QualiPSo Network. To be part of the Network each CC must sign an agreement once its request of joining is accepted by the other members [5]. This agreement is the "Table of Law" which works like a framework to ensure coherency within the network and providing rules and regulations needed by the QualiPSo Network to accomplish its mission and guaranteeing uniformity, transparency, and efficiency in the relations amongst CCs and between individual CCs and the QualiPSo Network as a whole. This organization also allows dealing with diversity. Each competence centre can become part of the network but at the same time this partnership does not preclude the adoption of different legal frameworks and different business models. The Brazilian, Spanish, German, Italian and Chinese CCs were born under the umbrella of the QualiPSo contractual commitment, but the quality and novelty of the QualiPSo results together with the idea of the network encouraged two new competence centres to join: one in Japan and one in Poland. While the Polish CC was opened by one of the partners of the QualiPSo project, the Japanese one (part of the Information-Technology Promotion Agency - IPA [29]) had no relationships with QualiPSo but contacted the Network to join since they were interested in part of the QualiPSo results. Specifically, in Japan the Government was pushing and investing for the adoption of Open Source solutions and IPA wanted to offer services for the measurement of the quality of Open Source solutions to be used. IPA identified those offered by QualiPSo as possible candidates for use. In addition, IPA identified in the participation to the network the possibility to rely on the support of the other CCs for testing and adapting the identified QualiPSo solutions. It is worth emphasizing that the QualiPSo approach made the following innovative contributions: (i) a new way to sustain project results - by interconnecting Industries, Academia, Public Administrations, and Open Source Communities - driven respectively by the their needs, their inputs, and their support; (ii) the federated organization of the network of CCs, that allowed individual centers to act locally (exploiting the characteristics and needs of specific countries), while cooperating globally (exploiting the expertise and skills of other competence centres belonging to the network).

3   The INSPIRE + INSPIRE-INCO Experience

3.1   Short Description of the Project

INSPIRE (INcreasing Security and Protection through Infrastructure Resilience) was a STREP targeting Objective ICT-SEC-2007.1.7: Critical Infrastructure Protection[6]. Since the key enabling technology of Critical Infrastructures is SCADA (Supervisory

Control And Data Acquisition) systems, INSPIRE focused on enhancing the security of such systems. In the recent years coordinated and targeted cyber-attacks have been conducted against critical infrastructures rising to an unprecedented level of sophistication. Simple experiments are now turning into sophisticated activities carried out for profit or political reasons. The core idea of the INSPIRE project was to protect Critical Infrastructures by appropriately configuring, managing, and securing the communication network which interconnects distributed process control systems. To increase the resilience of such systems INSPIRE developed traffic engineering algorithms, self-reconfigurable architectures, and intrusion diagnosis and recovery techniques.

The INSPIRE thread of research was augmented by means of an additional action, namely the INSPIRE-INCO (INSPIRE-International Cooperation) Project, within the context of call ICT-2009.9.2: Supplements to Support International Cooperation between Ongoing Projects [7]. The INSPIRE-International cooperation project specifically aimed at supporting the international cooperation between the INSPIRE project and the US GridStat project [28], by fostering the collaboration between INSPIRE researchers and GridStat researchers in the field of power grid protection. This collaboration aimed at the following objectives: 1) Making US power grid data available to INSPIRE, and 2) Establishing relationships with US partners, and exchanging US-EC experiences and demonstration activities.

3.2   Specific Results Achieved

INSPIRE mainly focused on how to increase the protection level of SCADA systems, the key component of most legacy, contemporary, and future Critical Infrastructures. In this section, we present the conceptual architecture of the diagnostic and reconfiguration scheme which was developed within the context of the INSPIRE project, and then extended to the US context, thanks to the additional funding provided by the INSPIRE-INCO project.

The INSPIRE architectural framework for SCADA systems resilience and security comprised three main functional blocks, namely: (i) Monitoring, (ii) Diagnosis, and (iii) Reconfiguration. Monitoring aims at gathering and aggregating status data from diverse parts of a SCADA system: communication network, Remote Terminal Units, wireless sensors, wired sensors, and supervisory stations. In order to cope with the heterogeneity of the formats of diagnostic data, grammar-based parsers were employed to translate raw events to an intermediate format. The INSPIRE monitoring sub-system built on our previous experience [8], specializing it to the context of SCADA systems. After parsing, data collected by individual probes is merged in a single stream, which feeds a set of diagnostic systems, implementing diverse diagnosis approaches. Based on diagnosis outputs, the most suitable reconfiguration technique (to treat the specific intrusion/fault) is selected. An example of reconfiguration is to implement routing mechanisms that make the communication infrastructure of a SCADA system resilient to both node/link failures and attacks, by guaranteeing timeliness and reliability of data delivery.

Special attention was paid to the vulnerability of power grids. The widespread use of SCADA systems for control of power grids is providing increasing ability to cause serious damage and disruption by means of cyber-attacks. In order to improve the accuracy and coherency of SCADA systems, utilities are more and more integrating Phasor Measurement Unit (also known as synchrophasors) into existing SCADA/EMS (Energy Management Systems). We performed a thorough security analysis of two key technologies which enable data collection in Power Grids, namely synchrophasor devices and Phasor Data Concentrators (PDCs). We emphasize that the study was conducted on a commercial product by a major vendor (as far as the synchrophasor is concerned), and on a widely used open source product (as far as the PDC is concerned). We set up a simplified - yet realistic - testbed, and we conducted a penetration testing campaign against the two aforementioned components. As a result of the testing sessions, we exposed several vulnerabilities, some of which can be easily exploited for conducting attacks to current smart grid data collection infrastructures if proper measures are not taken and additional protection devices are not integrated in the system.

Fig. 1 shows the testbed we used for our security analysis. Even though the testbed architecture is a simplified version of a real set-up (which would typically consist of multiple hierarchal levels of PDCs, and also include additional components with the capability of enforcing specific protection mechanisms), we emphasize that our testbed is based on components which are actually used in current Smart Grid deployments. Thus, many of the vulnerabilities that we expose in our study may well be present in real set-ups, especially those - which are not rare indeed - where security-related best practices have been disregarded. Commercial products and/or best practices that provide answers to some of the problems which we have pointed out include: [10, 11, 12, 13, 14, 15, 16, 17, 18].

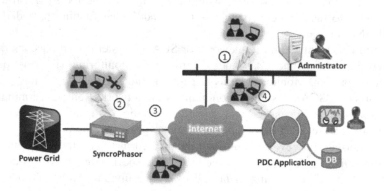

Fig. 1. Schematic representation of the experimental testbed

In the following, we provide a short summary of the key findings of the study. A more detailed treatment is available in [19].

The password management and maintenance subsystem has several security weaknesses, and in particular: (i) the default passwords are very common and consist of simple alphabetic strings, which are vulnerable to dictionary attacks, (ii) passwords are editable but no constraints is given for the strength of new passwords, (iii) multiple levels can share a common password, and (iv) passwords can be totally disabled via hardware intervention, by tampering with the front panel and setting a jumper off.

The system is vulnerable to man-in-the-middle attacks. A malicious eavesdropper can intercept the messages exchanged between one of the synchrophasors and the PDC and modify parameter values or even impersonate the synchrophasor.

The PDC application receives data streams from many different synchrophasors deployed across the monitored smart grid, using the C37.118 protocol [20]. We have demonstrated that by carefully crafting C37.118 protocol messages, it is possible to inject malicious SQL code to the back-end database.

Another important achievement of this international cooperation was access to real large scale and varied power grid data. The North American grid provides data from US electricity providers (including: AREVA, BBN, ABB-USA, and Siemens-USA), on a scale which is not achievable on the currently (relatively) limited EU grid size. The INSPIRE-INCO action contributed to overcome this limitation in the current EU grid data availability. An experimental testbed for power grid data collection was set-up, and is still operational at the time of this writing. Two synchrophasor devices (specifically, Frequency Disturbance Recorders) were installed, one in Naples (Italy) and one in Darmstadt (Germany), which are connected to the US network of the FNET group of the University of Tennessee, Knoxville [9].

4   The Massif Experience

4.1   Short Description of the Project

Security Information and Event Management (SIEM) solutions have become the backbone of virtually all security infrastructures. They collect data on events from different security elements, such as sensors, firewalls, routers or servers, analyze the data, and provide a suitable response to threats and attacks based on predefined security rules and policies. Despite the existence of highly regarded commercial products, their technical capabilities show a number of constraints in terms of scalability, resilience, and interoperability. The MASSIF project aims at achieving a significant advance in the area of SIEMs by integrating and relating events from different system layers and various domains into a more comprehensive view of security-aware processes and by increasing the scalability of the underlying event processing technology. The main challenge that MASSIF will face is to bring its enhancements and extensions to the business layer with a minimal impact on the end-user.

4.2   Specific Results Achieved and Expected

Two representatives of the MASSIF project (namely: Luigi Romano and Salvatore D'Antonio) participated in the First Canada EU Workshop on the "Future Internet", which was held in Waterloo, Ontario, Canada from 23 to 25 March, 2011. The major objective of the workshop was to explore prospects for deeper exchange and collaboration between the Canadian and European research communities in the area of "Future Internet (FI)" in Europe. With this workshop, EU and Canadian researchers were offered an opportunity to directly interact, to be updated on the respective research status, and to explore areas for potential cooperation. The event was designed to address industry interests and to provide prospective Canadian partners with an opportunity to participate in EU research related to the Future Internet. At the Waterloo workshop Luigi Romano and Salvatore D'Antonio had technical discussions with Craig Gibson on the possibility of addressing research issues related to Global Positioning System (GPS) spoofing attacks on synchrophasor networks. The basic idea is to use satellite simulator devices to perform an attack to synchrophasor networks by providing an altered time reference to the measurements acquired by synchrophasors deployed in a specific area. Synchrophasor devices rely on civilian GPS to acquire a synchronized time reference for their phase and frequency measurements. It has been proven that civilian GPS, unlike its military version, is inherently not secure [21], as it does not provide any encryption [22]. For this and other reasons the spoofing of the GPS signal is relatively easy to implement [22] and GPS satellite simulators are available on the market for the testing of navigation and other GPS based applications [24, 25, 26]. The effects a successful attack based on these technologies could range from the invalidation of the acquired phasor measurements to the injection of a false phase shift detection. We explicitly note that the detection of a phase shift is a high priority alarm, since it predicts a major failure of the power grid. An actual example is provided by the Aug. 14th, 2003 Blackout in the US (Fig. 2).

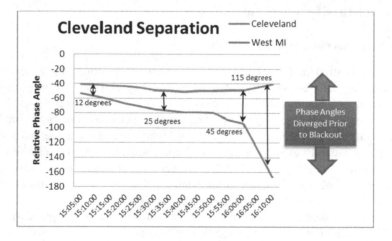

Fig. 2. Phase shift prior the black-out

According to NERC: "A valuable lesson from the August 14 blackout is the importance of having time-synchronized system data recorders. NERC investigators labored over thousands of data items to synchronize the sequence of events. ... That process would have been significantly improved ... if there had been a sufficient number of synchronized data recording devices." [27].

A preliminary research work plan was defined, which was then improved and extended in the months which followed the event. The finalized research plan was presented in the International Cooperation Working Group session at the Internet of Services 2011 Collaboration Meeting for FP7 Projects, which was held in Brussels, from 28 to 29 September 2011. The presentation raised significant interest in the audience, and we do believe we have identified a relevant research path, which we are willing to explore in depth. Our plan is to investigate the feasibility and possible consequences of GPS Spoofing based attacks on synchrophasor networks. In order to do so, the first step has been the definition of the main attack scenarios to be investigated. Based on the results of this activity, the requirements for the testbed have been specified. The testbed reproduces in a laboratory environment a realistic set up for a synchrophasor network, and allows the implementation of the attack scenarios of interest. The testbed - as illustrated in Fig. 3 - includes the core components of a synchrophasor network (specifically: synchrophasor devices, a communication network, and a Phasor Data Concentrator application, the visualization and monitoring point), and the GPS spoofing equipment (i.e. the GPS satellite signal simulator and the control and attack software). Additional components (such as the power line controlled by the synchrophasor) will be integrated in the testbed using software mock-ups, which will mimic the behaviour of the corresponding real objects, based on the specifications set out in the attack scenario definition. The use of mock-ups has the important advantage of allowing us to evaluate the effects of the attacks in detail while keeping the cost of the testbed (and of the experiments) acceptable.

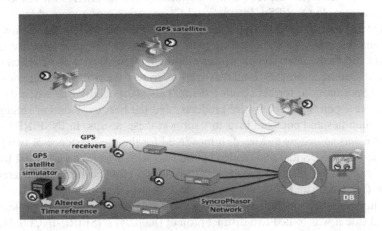

Fig. 3. GPS Spoofing attack experimental testbed for a synchrophasor network

At the time of this writing, the architecture of the testbed has been designed, and all the hardware and software components are already available in our lab in Naples. The testbed has been deployed and configured, and correct operation of all system subparts has been tested. We are now in the process of starting the experiments, i.e. implementing the attack scenarios defined in the first phase and collecting the results. In the experimental campaign we will use a GPS spoofing system to generate fake

GPS signals, and monitor the synchrophasor network to analyze the actual consequences of the injection of false GPS data in the system. The campaign will consist of multiple phases, which will be repeated iteratively. At each iteration, we will observe the results, and use them to fine tune the attacks in the next iteration. For each attack scenario, a report will be produced that will describe the most significant intrusions which have been observed and, most importantly, analyze the severity of the consequences on the synchrophasor network. Finally, an attempt will be made to come up with possible countermeasures for limiting the effects of the attacks.

5   Conclusions and Wish List

In this paper, we have provided tangible evidence of remarkable technical achievements that international cooperation has brought about. The QualiPSo project demonstrated that in the software development domain, international cooperation favours the creation of consensus around common practices, to guarantee higher quality of the final product, which ultimately results in the establishment of trust, the key enabler of technology take up. The INSPIRE (and INSPIRE-INCO) project demonstrated that Critical Infrastructure Protection, given the ever increasing interconnections between national and continental set-ups, must rely on techniques that are compatible, and scalable. The MASSIF project demonstrated that sharing experience and factorizing interests may widen the scope of individual research plans.

Besides the technical aspects, a few comments are in order with respect to the funding schemes. In QualiPSo, International Cooperation was a main characteristic of the project since its inception. This resulted in efficient and smooth interaction among international partners. To create an international network of centres dedicated to the promotion and to the adoption of project outputs is the easiest way to efficiently exploit and disseminate project results, as well as to test them in real scenarios and to offer the opportunity to further develop them. This is especially true when the results produced are Open Source software products, and the best exploitation strategy is to have communities and potential investors support these results. In INSPIRE the funding scheme was somehow awkward. It mandated for the pre-existence of two projects (one funded by the US and one funded by the EC) with significant potential for cooperation. Specifically, the two projects were GridStat (funded by an NSF grant) and INSPIRE (funded by an EC grant). On the US side the additional funding for supporting the international cooperation was pumped directly into the GridStat project, while on the EU side it was routed to a distinct project (namely, INSPIRE-INCO). Handling two distinct flows of funding, one only for research and one only for mobility, resulted in a number of (unnecessary) difficulties. We have shared this experience at the International Cooperation Working Group session at the Internet of Services 2011 Collaboration Meeting for FP7 Projects, which was held in Brussels, from 28 to 29 September 2011 and we were assured by EC representatives that the INSPIRE + INSPIRE-INCO scheme was indeed an exception, with the rule being much more effective and seamless solutions. We were glad to learn that, and we are keen on finding a joint research avenue/process which can provide additional support for the new thread of research on GPS spoofing that we have started within the context of the MASSIF project. We look forward to a funding tool which can provide additional stamina to this promising collaborative research. We emphasize that the power grid desynchronization research shown here describes the mechanism by which legacy design issues relying on unauthenticated transmission can result in (at a very fundamental level) denial of service to critical infrastructures. Some opportunities for continuing this cooperation seemed to be provided by Call 9, specifically Objective ICT-2011.10.3: International partnership building and support to dialogues. Specifically, the target outcome of this action was: "support to dialogues and cooperation with strategic partner countries and regions, to create cooperative research links between European organisations and partners in third countries". Regrettably, this initiative - with respect to High Income Countries (such as Canada) - aimed at supporting dialogues, and at increasing cooperation, but it did not provide explicit funding for doing research. While we look with interest at the opportunities provided by initiatives for the organisation of events and the strengthening of cooperative research links between European organisations and relevant organisations in Canada, what we really look for is a funding tool providing direct support to research activities. Thus, we look with interest at upcoming initiatives, particularly Security Research Call 6 (FP7-SEC-2013-1).

Acknowledgments. The research leading to these results has received funding from the European Community's Sixth Framework Programme (FP6/2002-2006) under Grant Agreement No. 034763 (QualiPSo) and Seventh Framework Programme (FP7/2007-2013) under Grant Agreement No. 225553 (INSPIRE Project), Grant Agreement No. 248737 (INSPIRE-INCO Project), and Grant Agreement No. 257475 (MAnagement of Security information and events in Service Infrastructures, MASSIF Project).

References

1. QualiPSo project website, http://www.qualipso.org
2. Shiels, M.: Calls for open source government, BBC news, http://news.bbc.co.uk/2/hi/7841486.stm
3. Detailed list of the QualiPSo results, http://www.qualipso.org/documents
4. QualiPSo Competence Centres Presentation, http://www.qualipso.org/competence_centres
5. QualiPSo Network Agreement, http://www.qualipso.org/sites/default/files/Qualipso%20D8.2%20Network%20Agreement%20V2.pdf
6. INSPIRE project website, http://www.inspire-strep.eu
7. INSPIRE-INCO project website, http://www.inspire-inco.eu
8. Campanile, F., Coppolino, L., Giordano, S., Romano, L.: A Business Process Monitor for a Mobile Phone Recharging System. Journal of Systems Architecture (2008)
9. Power Information Technology Lab in the Department of Electrical Engineering and Computer Science at the University of Tennessee, http://powerit.utk.edu/
10. Secure Communications, Schweitzer Engineering Laboratories, Inc., http://www.selinc.com/securecommunications/

11. Cybersecurity, Schweitzer Engineering Laboratories, Inc.,
    http://www.selinc.com/cybersecurity/
12. Stewart, J., Maufer, T., Smith, R., Anderson, C., Ersonmez, E.: Synchrophasor Security
    Practices. Schweitzer Engineering Laboratories, Inc.,
    http://www.selinc.com/WorkArea/DownloadAsset.aspx?id=8502
13. Smith, R.: Cryptography Concepts and Effects on Control System Communications.
    Schweitzer Engineering Laboratories, Inc.,
    http://www.selinc.com/WorkArea/DownloadAsset.aspx?id=5200
14. Hurd, S., Smith, R., Leischner, G.: Tutorial: "Security in Electric Utility Control Systems".
    Schweitzer Engineering Laboratories, Inc.,
    http://www.selinc.com/WorkArea/DownloadAsset.aspx?id=3491
15. Mix, S.: Primer Discussion on Cyber Security: "What do the CIP Standards Mean for Syn-
    chroPhasors in the future?" North American Electric Reliability Corporation (NERC),
    http://www.naspi.org/meetings/workgroup/2009_february/presen
    tations/nerc_cyber_security_mix_20090205.pdf
16. Introduction to NISTIR 7628, Guidelines for Smart Grid Cyber Security, The Smart Grid
    Interoperability Panel Cyber Security Working Group,
    http://www.nist.gov/smartgrid/upload/nistir-7628_total.pdf
17. Braendle, M.: Cyber security - effectively and efficiently tackling the challenges ahead.
    ABB, http://www.abb.com/cawp/seitp202/
    a6a42387602e838285257842000766310.aspx
18. Hadley, M.D., McBride, J.B., Edgar, T.W., O'Neil, L.R., Johnson, J.D.: Securing Wide
    Area Measurement System. Pacific Northwest National Laboratory,
    http://www.oe.energy.gov/DocumentsandMedia/Securing_WAMS.pdf
19. Coppolino, L., D'Antonio, S., Elia, I.A., Romano, L.: Security Analysis of Smart Grid Da-
    ta Collection Technologies. In: Flammini, F., Bologna, S., Vittorini, V. (eds.) SAFECOMP
    2011. LNCS, vol. 6894, pp. 143–156. Springer, Heidelberg (2011)
20. IEEE Standard for Synchrophasors for Power Systems, IEEE Std C37.118-2005 (Revision
    of IEEE Std 1344-1995), pp. 1–57 (2006)
21. Vulnerability Assessment of the Transportation Infrastructure (2001),
    http://www.fas.org/spp/military/program/asat/gpstrans.pdf
22. GPS Fact Sheet. Global Positioning Systems Directorate,
    http://www.losangeles.af.mil/library/factsheets/factsheet.as
    p?id=5311
23. Warner, J.S., Johnston, R.G.: A Simple Demonstration That the Global Positioning System
    Is Vulnerable to Spoofing. Journal of Security Administration (2003)
24. CAST Navigation GPS Satellite Simulators,
    http://www.castnav.com/products/
25. Spectracom GPS Satellite Simulators,
    http://www.spectracomcorp.com/ProductsServices/
    TestandMeasurement/GPSSimulators/tabid/1268/Default.aspx
26. Aeroflex, GPS Satellite Simulators,
    http://www.aeroflex.com/ats/products/category/Avionics/GPS_S
    imulators.html
27. Brown, S.: Thoughts on the Florida Blackout,
    http://www.elp.com/index/display/elp-article-tool-
    template/_saveArticle/articles/utility-automation-
    engineering-td/volume-13/issue-4/departments/from-the-
    editor/thoughts-on-the-florida-blackout.html
28. Gridstat project website, http://www.gridstat.net/
29. Information Technology Promotion Agency, Japan,
    http://www.ipa.go.jp/index-e.html

A Federated Simulation Framework
with ATN Fault Injection Module for Reliablity Analysis
of UAVs in Non-controlled Airspace

Magali Andreia Rossi[1,2], Jorge Rady de Almeida Junior[1],
Andrea Bondavalli[3], and Paolo Lollini[3]

[1] University of São Paulo, School of Engineering (Poli-USP), Brasil
[2] Technical College FATEC Carapicuíba, Brasil
mandreiarossi@gmail.com, jorge.almeida@poli.usp.br
[3] University of Florence, Systems and Computer Science dept, Italy
{bondavalli,lollini}@unifi.it

Abstract. This work presents a federated simulation framework for safety and reliability analysis in Aeronautical Communications Networking (ATN) considering the insertion of Unmanned Aircraft Vehicles (UAV) in the airspace control. The main objective is to quantitatively assess the impact of ATN faults on the risk collision probability between manned and unmanned aircraft. The paper first presents the framework that simulates the communication systems used in a non-controlled airspace. Then it is described the ATN fault injection module, which is then used to evaluate the impact of network-level faults on the risk of collisions probability considering a representative simulation scenario comprising 1500 aircraft in flight.

Keywords: Safety, Reliability, Simulation Framework, UAV, ATN, Fault Injection.

1   Introduction

A Unmanned Aerial Vehicle (UAV) is an autonomous aircraft, remotely controlled, currently used for specific missions such as flights and military operations in segregated areas, i.e., in a monitoring operation it is determined the area size to be monitored, for example, in square kilometers and its geographical coordinates. The current state of research on UAVs, throughout the world, indicates that technological factors will be the factor that restricts, in the near future, the development of UAV really smart.

However, much development in this area is focused on the actual design of the aircraft, its maneuverability and its flight dynamics. There is still a wide technological gap, considering the use of techniques that allow UAVs to act in a way almost totally autonomous in their context, including, for example, the ability to assess its operational status and the environment around them, the mission progress and especially the ability to fly in a non-controlled airspace. This condition can jeopardize the missions for which UAVs are assigned, causing financial loss or credibility.

F. Ortmeier and P. Daniel (Eds.): SAFECOMP 2012 Workshops, LNCS 7613, pp. 271–281, 2012.
© Springer-Verlag Berlin Heidelberg 2012

Excepting military operations, many of today's UAVs flights around the world are performed with airspace segregation. It is still a consensus among authorities that the lack of effective standards for these aircrafts flights represents a potential risk to other airspace users [1].

Considering such safety issues, the current legislation restricts the UAV operation to places far enough away from densely populated areas, aerodrome zones and noise sensitive areas such as schools, parks, hospitals, churches, and others. Another important point is that, unless specifically authorized by an aviation authority with jurisdiction over the area, the operation should be performed at a maximum height of 400 feet above the surface and in the event of traffic conflict with manned aircraft, the UAV must give way immediately, even with the risk to be damaged or even destroyed [2].

This paper proposes a simulation framework for safety and reliability analysis considering the insertion of UAVs in non-controlled airspace, providing conditions for evaluation of the decision-making control organisms. The framework contains several modules that provide different information, enabling the air traffic control authority to obtain real-time information about manned and unmanned aircrafts [3]. Using this information the framework proposes a single control authority for both aircraft, ensuring that communication with the control unit is performed

It allows the integration of external flight simulators (e.g., Flight Gear, MS Flight Simulator), ADS-B (Automatic Dependent Surveillance-Broadcast), and the use of messages via CPDLC (Controller-Pilot Data Link Communications) using IPv6 (Internet Protocol version 6) for data transfer within the Aeronautical Communications Network (ATN).

The framework allows assessing the impact of network faults on the risk collision probability between manned and unmanned aircrafts in non-controlled airspace. As such, it can be used as an effective support for decision making process by the responsible authorities as response to emergency events, as well as to standards development.

This work is structured as follows. Section II presents the related works. Section III presents details about the simulation framework and the description of the environment characteristics in which the simulation is used. Section IV presents the structure of the fault injection module in ATN and the structure of the Bayesian Network it is based on. Section V presents the simulation results considering a representative scenario, while conclusions are finally drawn in Section VI.

2   Related Works

There are only few related works in the literature, typically addressing specific aspects of the communication network. For example, in [4] there is a comparison about the congestion control employing an ATN network and an IP network environment. However, network faults are not considered at all. In [5], it is presented a simulation model for mobile communication using VDL (VHF Digital Link Mode 3). It is described the use of ground stations that provide VHF (Very High

Frequency) so that communication is established between the aircraft and the land controls. In [6], it is presented the communication model for UAV using wireless network. It is analyzed the communication channel modeling for packet dropout, not considering any network fault. In [7], it is presented an analysis of quality in performance of high bandwidth communication UAV link, considering contextual events. However, the context-controlled system uses the communication radio link and segregate airspace of the flights. The simulation framework proposed in this paper allows the reliability and safety analysis of UAV in non- controlled airspace, also considering the impact faults within ATN. As such, it constitutes a clear advancement of the state-of-the-art.

3   ATN Environment and Simulation Framework

3.1   ATN

ATN defines by the standards established by ICAO (International Civil Aviation Organization), all interconnections to digital data transmission between ground-ground and air-ground systems [8]. The routing service for the messages is offered over ATN routers, which perform dynamic routing, allowing the updating of tables with the aircraft movements information and changing in the network topology due to possible faults [3], [9].

The ICAO Annex 15 defines the importance of control and routing data that passes under the ATN and the effects caused by corrupt or incorrect data, as follows [10]:

"The object of the aeronautical information service is to ensure the flow of information necessary for the safety, regularity and efficiency of international air navigation. The role and importance of aeronautical information/data changed significantly with the implementation of area navigation (RNAV), required navigation performance (RNP) and airborne computer-based navigation systems. Corrupt or erroneous aeronautical information/data can potentially affect the safety of air navigation."

With the purpose to guarantee the desired safety level for data transmission, ATN design is based on the concepts and technologies adopted in CNS / ATM (Communications, Navigation and Surveillance / Air Traffic Management) [11], [12] by manned aviation, which aim to ensure a higher level of flight safety.

However, using the same technologies for unmanned and manned aircrafts is still a very big challenge. Unmanned aircrafts have high-level technology in embedded systems [13] which include, for example, satellite communications and digital data transmissions. However, the main difficulty lies in its inclusion in non-controlled airspace, which requires, for example, their immediate identification in control systems.

In this work we are considering a non-controlled airspace in which the air traffic control agencies have the information about manned aircraft, and need to register in the system the entry of civil or military unmanned aircraft.

3.2   The Federated Simulation Framework

This paper proposes a simulation framework that allows considering the impact of ATN faults as message delays and losses on the collision risk probability between aircrafts. The challenge presented by the framework is the definition of a single control authority for manned and unmanned aircrafts ensuring safety in data communication. Thus, through the ATN Fault Module is feasible to provide the possible communication failures of both aircraft from this single control

We developed the fault injection module integrated into the aircraft simulator platform PIpE-SEC (Integrated Platform for Critical Test for Embedded Systems), which meets the standards required by the control organisms to simulate this environment. This module is called ATN Fault Module in Figure 1.

The PIpE-SEC is a set of applications and libraries that allow the execution of experiments by integrating the network IVAO (International Virtual Aviation Organization) and flight simulators, such as Flight Simulator and Flight Gear, and also algorithms that implement CNS/ATM technologies, developed in the GAS – Safety Analysis Group [14], [3]. Figure 1 illustrates the set of modules with their links.

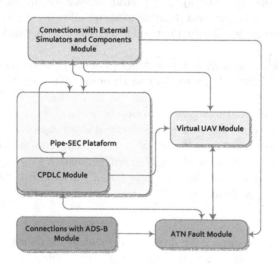

Fig. 1. Links between the Simulation Framework Modules

The CPDLC Module simulates the sending and receiving coded messages between the pilot and ground control. The Virtual UAV Module simulates flight conditions of an unmanned aircraft. The Connections with External Simulators and Components Module helps the platform providing information on aircraft in flight. The Connections with ADS-B Module simulates the surveillance information of the aircraft.

The links between the modules represent messages transmissions using the communications between ground control systems and aircraft embedded systems.

The ATN Fault Module has links with all other modules of the platform. The link to CPDLC Module allows the establishment of the air-ground communication.

The ATN Fault Module uses the information of the messages exchanged between the other modules to inject faults in the communication environment, injecting the faults directly into the established communication between the Virtual UAV Module and the control ground systems.

The link between the Virtual UAV Module and the CPDLC Module is used to automatically receive control messages that must be recognized by the on-board embedded systems. We consider the great automation level of the aircraft, since it does not have any human interference in the communications between the aircraft and the ground control.

The links with Connections with External Simulators and Components Module provide real-time information of the virtual network IVAO (International Virtual Aviation Organization) where the UAVs are inserted, using the same space and air control. Important information of the aircraft is received for the simulation, such as altitude, latitude, flaps movements, ailerons, spoilers and others. This information is used by other modules and represents the aircraft stability in flight.

The link with the Connections with ADS-B Module allows sending surveillance information of the aircrafts, and it is primarily used in conjunction with the CPDLC system.

4   Fault Injection

A key point in the development of a resilient and safe computer system is the validation of its fault handling mechanisms, as ineffective or unintended operations of these mechanisms can significantly impair the dependability of a computer system. Fault injection is an important experimental technique for assessment and verification of fault-handling mechanisms, as it allows how to analyze computer systems react and behave in the presence of faults.

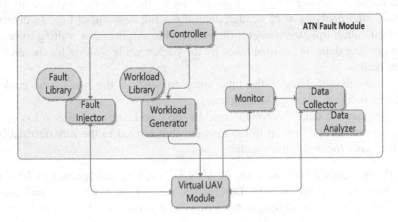

Fig. 2. Components within the ATN Fault Module

Figure 2 illustrates the components belonging to the developed software simulation-based fault injection module. Each component has a specific function in the simulation environment and can be implemented separately in relation to their use and implementation of the services provided [15].

In this environment, the fault injector injects faults in the target system, executing commands sent by the load generator.

The fault injector has the function of simulating various types of faults, such as temporal, hardware or software faults. The monitor performs continuous monitoring of the commands executed and makes data collection. The data collector performs the data collection online, while the analyzer data performs processing for data analysis. However, the environmental control is performed by the controller, which can run directly in the Virtual UAV Module or in a separate hardware. The load library is set to allow greater portability and flexibility in the environment.

4.1   Fault Injection in ATN

Currently, in many cases, a computer network environment may be characterized by its complexity, involving various physical mechanisms to establish communication between ES (End Systems).

In ATN these End Systems are commonly known as computer applications, which are responsible for implementing services of various types and purposes, such as ATC (Air Traffic Control) database FIS (Flight Information System), Weather Database, Aeronautical Operations Control.

During the packet transmission process, the ability to send data between End Systems can be decreased, causing delays in sending data. The most significant delays related to network performance are: processing delay, nodal processing delay, queuing delay, transmission delay and propagation delay, as detailed below [16]:

- The processing delay is determined by the time taken for analysis in the packet header.
- The nodal processing delay is characterized by the arrival of a packet to a router, which, after analysis of its header, determines the best output link. In determining the best output link, the packet is directed to this output and is waiting to be sent.
- The queuing delay is the time taken by the packet while waiting for its sending to a specific link.
- The transmission delay is the time taken to send all the bits of the packet to a specific link (i.e., message sending time).
- The propagation delay is characterized by the time taken a bit after it has started its transmission in the link up to the moment that arrived to the link destination, that is, it reaches the destination router.

Thus, the process of fault injection in ATN is based on the concept of IP networks faults. However, ICAO, through DOC 9705, defines the time delay and maximum acceptable sizes for the messages transmission in aeronautical applications based on ATN.

The messages sent through the CPDLC (Controller-Pilot Data Link Communications) system, have a size of 1 octet used for simple messages and responses, reaching a size of 1607 octets in case of messages with the aim of investigating complex instructions. The downlink messages have a size of 13 octets and the uplink messages around 45 octets [17], [18].

The maximum delay time defined by the ICAO for the CPDLC messaging is 8 seconds for terminal area and 15 seconds en route [17], [18]. This time represents the maximum time for preventing aircrafts collision.

Thus, we analyze the impact of ATN network faults affecting the delay times for sending messages on the probability of collisions between aircrafts.

4.2   Network Faults

The ATN Fault Module is used to inject faults in the ATN communication environment, considering the routing environment characteristics of air-ground messages, and right times for message transmission (the messages are transmitted using the IPv6 protocol with specific routing for the ATN) [17].

Using the ATN Fault Module, the faults are injected according to the communication degradation possibilities between the aircraft and the ground control systems.

The injected faults have different occurrence probabilities. These injected faults affect each aircraft according to its message processing capability, which can compromise the aircraft stability.

Hazards probability calculation caused by a fault in the ATN communications environment is based on a Bayesian Network representing the faults model.

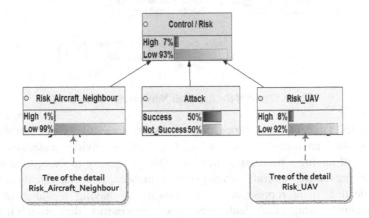

Fig. 3. Bayesian Network representing the faults model (within ATN Fault Module)

Figure 3 presents a part of the Bayesian Network representing the adopted network fault model (ATN Fault Module in the Figure 1). It represents a unique structure of airspace shared between manned aircraft (Risk_Aircraft_Neighbor node) and autonomous aircraft (Risk_UAV node). We considered a single control system (Control/Risk node), which is represented on the highest level of the tree [3].

The manned and autonomous (unmanned) aircrafts are represented in the two branches of the tree. In each node there are some percentage values that establish the probability of occurrence of the corresponding node, and the fault occurrence probabilities propagate from the leafs to the root.

Figure 4 contains the details of the branch of the tree Risk_UAV. The faults can affect the information processing time, the message sending time, the aircraft performance and the response automation, and they can be injected at any level of the network. Therefore, any faults occurred in a given level of the tree will be observed directly by the control system (Control/Risk node) [3].

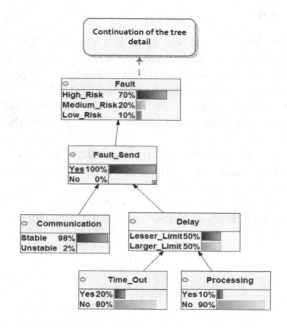

Fig. 4. Detail of the Bayesian Network for Risk_UAV

The nodes Time_Out and Processing represent, respectively, the probability of exceeding the maximum delays in sending and receiving messages, and the probability of having a processing problem. The probability to exceed the maximum delay for preventing aircrafts collision is represented in the Delay node. The Communication node represents the probability of having a stable or unstable communication, while the Fault_Send node represents the probability that a (Communication or Delay) fault is propagated to the upper nodes of the tree.

Basing on these probability values, the risk classification of a fault can be computed to be low, medium or high (node Fault), which propagates up to the root to determine the overall risk of aircraft collisions.

The set of the data represents the probability values related to the collision risk between aircrafts and the time limits for communication in ATN. The sets of values used are determined by the ICAO ANNEXES 10 and 11 [19].

5   Safety Evaluation

The fault injection module has been used to evaluate the possible occurrence of a collision between manned and unmanned aircrafts.

We simulate this environment from the fault risk level, automation level of the aircraft (not present in Figures 3 and 4), and their exposure risk to the collision (Risk UAV node). The complete fault tree can be found in [3]. The tests were performed with 1500 records, which represent the amount of the aircrafts in the environment.

For the simulations we considered three levels of fault risks (node "Fault" of Figure 4): low, medium and high. These levels are characterized by the hazard intensity degree that the communication fault can cause to the aircraft using the ATN.

In addition, we consider the aircraft automation degree through the communication architecture of embedded systems, which is intended to prevent collisions between aircrafts. Their design considers the use of same technology employed in embedded systems currently used in manned aircraft.

Figure 5 presents the simulation results obtained considering the occurrence of a fault with low, medium and high risk level. Specifically, in Figure 5 we show the number of aircrafts that have satisfactorily answered (Satisfactory Response plot) and the number of aircrafts that have not satisfactorily answered (Non Satisfactory Response plot), thus having a higher exposition to collision risks. The Satisfactory Response and Non Satisfactory Response are related to the aircraft capacity in the use of communication embedded systems to exchange messages with the authority control.

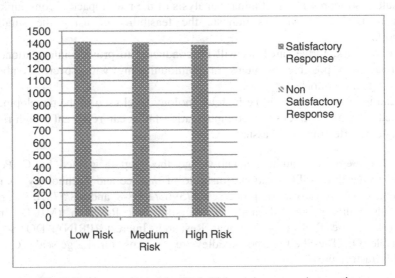

Fig. 5. Representation of the Fault Risk vs. Assurance Automation

Considering the Low Risk, 1414 aircraft had satisfactory response to a fault communication and 86 aircraft had non satisfactory response (5,73% of the total number of aircraft). Considering the Medium Risk, 1408 aircraft had satisfactory response to a fault communication and 92 had not successful. With respect to the Low Risk case, there was a significant increase of 6% in the probability of exposing the aircraft to an accident.

Considering the High Risk, the results were satisfactory for 1386 aircraft and non satisfactory for 114 aircraft (7,6% of the total number of aircraft). With respect to the Low Risk case, there was an increase of aircraft that cannot answer satisfactorily to faults injected of about 28%, which can be considered a relatively high increase rate.

6   Conclusion

The embedded systems in UAVs are considered complex and with a complex architecture. The tests in UAV systems need high resources, professional expertise and high amount of working hours. Thus, the simulation represents an accessible way to overcome such problems.

This work presented a framework for the integration of communications and surveillance modules jointly with a specific module (ATN Fault Module) for fault injection in ATN environment. The module uses simulation to assess the UAVs communication dependability in non-controlled airspace. The presented results show that the classification level of injected faults interferes significantly in the communication with the aircraft, even if it has high automation level.

In particular the results demonstrate that, despite the high level of automation, in some cases a faulty communication directly affects the safety level of UAV flights. The results also represent a preliminary analysis of the real impact of communication failures in UAVs, as well as indicate the feasibility of using the simulation framework.

In future work, further analysis will be conducted to provide information, such faults related to possible problems in communicating with specific embedded systems, e.g., auto-pilot

We can infer that even with the high technology level used in the development of embedded systems for UAVs, the communication faults can represent a high risk for these systems, affecting safety assurance.

Acknowledgment. The authors acknowledge the support granted by CNPq and FAPESP to the INCT-SEC (National Institute of Science and Technology – Critical Embedded Systems – Brazil), processes 573963/2008-8 and 08/57870-9, and by the Italian Ministry for Education, University, and Research (MIUR) in the framework of the Project of National Research Interest (PRIN) "DOTS-LCCI: Dependable Off-The-Shelf based middleware systems for Large-scale Complex Critical Infrastructures".

References

1. Rossi, M.A., De Almeida Jr., J.R., Corrêa, M.: Sistemas de Apoio à Tomada de Decisão Para Aplicações VANT em Rede de Telecomunicação Aeronáutica. In: IX SITRAER - Simposio de Transporte Aéreo. SBTA, Manaus (2010)
2. Corrêa, M., Camargo Jr., J.B., Gimenes, R.A., De Almeida Jr., J.R.: Integration UAV in to controlated air space using cooperative multiagent negotiation. In: V SITRAER - Simpósio de Transporte Aéreo, pp. 315–324. EDUSP, Brasilia (2006)
3. Rossi, M.A., Lollini, P., Bondavalli, A., De Almeida Jr., J.R.: 2011 30th IEEE Symposium on Reliable Distributed Systems Workshops, pp. 67–71 (2011)
4. Gao, S., Liu, K., Zhu, Y., Zhang, Y.: A Model and Mapping Algorithm of Explicit Congestion Notification in Tunnel for ATN over IP Scheme. In: 14th Asia-Pacific Conference on Communications, pp. 1–5. IEEE (2008)
5. Hung, B., Hong, Y.: Modeling and simulation of the VDL mode 3 subnetwork in the ATN environment. In: 19th DASC, 19th Digital Avionics Systems Conference, pp. 7A7/1–7A7/7. IEEE (2000)
6. Zhou, Y., Li, J., Lamont, L., Rabbath, C.: Modeling of Packet Dropout for UAV Wireless Communications. In: International Conference on Computing, Networking and Communications, pp. 677–682. IEEE (2012)
7. dos Santos Moreira, E., Vanni, R.M.P., Função, D.L., Marcondes, C.A.C.: A Context-Aware Communication Link for Unmanned Aerial Vehicles. In: 2010 Sixth Advanced International Conference on Telecommunications, pp. 497–502. IEEE (2010)
8. Feighery, P., Hanson, T., Lehman, T., Mondrus, A., Scott, D., Signore, T., et al.: The Aeronautical Telecommunications Network (ATN) testbed. In: 15th DASC. AIAA/IEEE Digital Avionics Systems Conference, pp. 117–122. IEEE (2002)
9. ICAO. Aeronautical Telecommunications Network (ATN) - Comprehensive ATN Manual, CAMAL (1999)
10. ICAO. Aeronautical Information Services - Annex 15 (1997)
11. Crow, R.P.: Civil aviation's next generation global CNS/ATM system. In: Position Location and Navigation Symposium, pp. 66–73. IEEE (2000)
12. Smith, A., Baldwin, J.: Application of CNS/ATM technologies to airport management. In: 22nd Digital Avionics Systems Conference, pp. 4.A.1–4.1-8. IEEE (2003)
13. Jiakun, S., Hongxing, L., Shixianjun: Hardware-in-the-loop Simulation Framework Design For a UAV Embedded Control System. In: Control Conference - CCC 2006, pp. 1890–1894. IEEE (2006)
14. Gil, F., Aldecôa, V.M.: Pipe-SEC: Relatório geral dos módulos implementados (2010)
15. Hsueh, M.-C., Tsai, T.K., Iyer, R.K.: Fault injection techniques and tools. Computer 30(4), 75–82 (1997)
16. Gallo, M.A., Hancock, W.M.: Comunicação entre Computadores e Tecnologias de Rede. Pioneira Thomson Learning, São Paulo (2003)
17. ICAO. Manual of Technical Provisions for the Aeronautical Telecommunications Network (ATN) (1999)
18. de Oliveira Gil, F., Vismari, L.F., Camargo Jr., J.B.: Analysis of the CPDLC Real Time Characteristics and the MODE S Data Link Capacity. In: SITRAER VII - Simpósio de Transporte Aéreo, pp. 92–99. SBTA (2008)
19. Rossi, M.A., Lollini, P., De Almeida Jr., J.R., Bondavalli, A.: Reliability Evoluation of UAV Communication in non-controlled Airspace. University of São Paulo and University of Florence, Technical report. São Paulo (2012)

HSIENA: A Hybrid Publish/Subscribe System*

Fabio Petroni and Leonardo Querzoni

Department of Computer, Control, and Management Engineering Antonio Ruberti
Sapienza University of Rome – Rome, Italy
fabio.petroni.1986@gmail.com, querzoni@dis.uniroma1.it

Abstract. The SIENA publish/subscribe system represents a prototypical design for a distributed event notification service implementing the content-based publish/subscribe communication paradigm. A clear shortcoming of SIENA is represented by its static configuration that must be managed and updated by human administrators every time one of its internal processes (brokers) needs to be added or repaired (e.g. due to a crash failure). This problem limits the applicability of SIENA in large complex critical infrastructures where self-adaptation and -configuration are crucial requirements. In this paper we propose HSIENA, a hybrid architecture that complements SIENA by adding the ability to self-reconfigure after broker additions and removals. The architecture has a novel design that mixes the classic SIENA's distributed architecture with a highly available cloud-based storage service.

1 Introduction

The widespread adoption of the clients/server interaction paradigm has led in the past to the development of distributed applications with a rigid structure, constrained by the lack of flexibility of point-to-point and synchronous interactions. The evolution of the Internet, pushed in the last years by the huge growth of large-scale systems in the form of peer-to-peer and social applications, is clearly marking the limits of this approach to communication, and raising the demand for more flexible interactions schemes. The publish/subscribe interaction paradigm [3] has been introduced in the past as an alternative to the clients/server sibling, with the aim of providing a form of communication where interacting parties are decoupled. This paradigm is today witnessing a wide adoption thanks to its ability to support large scale applications [8,2,5,13] and represents a preferred choice for communication in large complex critical infrastructures (LCCI).

In a publish/subscribe interaction participants to the communication can act both as producers (*publishers*) or consumers (*subscribers*) of information that takes the form of *events*. Subscribers can express which events they want to receive issuing *subscriptions* that express conditions on the content of events (*content-based subscription model*) or just on a category they belong to (*topic-based subscription model*). The paradigm states that once an event is published,

---

* This work has been partially funded by the DOTS-LCCI Italian project.

F. Ortmeier and P. Daniel (Eds.): SAFECOMP 2012 Workshops, LNCS 7613, pp. 282–293, 2012.
© Springer-Verlag Berlin Heidelberg 2012

for each subscription whose conditions are satisfied by the event (i.e., the event matches the subscription), the corresponding subscriber must be notified. The basic building block of systems implementing the publish/subscribe paradigm is an *event notification service* (ENS) whose goal is to diffuse any published event from the publisher to the set of matched subscribers. The complete decoupling offered by this form of interaction makes it appealing for modern distributed applications characterized by very large scale and variable loads.

The SIENA publish/subscribe system [6,7] is widely recognized as a representative example of a distributed ENS adopting the content-based subscription model. However, its adoption in LCCI scenarios has been hindered by the lack of adequate support to system reconfiguration. In particular the addition of a new broker to the ENS infrastructure, due for example to a load surge that cannot be adequately managed by the existing brokers, requires a manual intervention of the administrators that would bring the system to a full halt, with a strong impact on service availability and continuity. Similarly, node failures are not tolerated by the current SIENA design, and their correct management requires again manual intervention by system administrators. Both these characteristics are fundamental in LCCIs where unexpected load surges or failures must be quickly tackled with, thus raising the demand for communication infrastructures able to self-adapt and configure.

In this paper we propose HSIENA, a hybrid architecture that complements SIENA by adding the ability to self-reconfigure after broker additions and removals. The architecture has a novel design that mixes the classic SIENA's distributed architecture based on managed brokers with a highly available cloud-based storage service (hence the *hybrid* adjective). Brokers use this storage service as a shared memory space they can rely-on to adapt at runtime the ENS application-level network without service disruption. This shared memory space will contain all the information needed to build the internal state of each broker (with the exclusion of content-based addresses) and will be updated every time a new broker joins the system or as soon as a broker failure is detected. Due to costs associated with accesses (read and write) to the cloud-based storage service (both in terms of access latency and economical costs), HSIENA is designed to limit its usage only to broker additions and removals, that should be considered as "rare" events.

The rest of this paper is organized as follows: Section 2 provides fundamental background knowledge on the publish/subscribe paradigm, on the SIENA system and on the current state of the art related to this work; Section 3 introduces the HSIENA system describing its architecture, the data structures it uses, the fundamental functionalities it provides and how it manages concurrency and event diffusion. Finally, Section 4 concludes the paper.

2   Background

The publish/subscribe interaction paradigm provides users of a system with an alternative communication model with respect to the classical client/server model. In a publish/subscribe system users interact playing one of two roles: publishers that produce information and inject (publish) it into the system in the form of events, and subscribers that consume events received from the system. A third component, the event notification service, has the role of receiving the events injected by the publishers and notify all the subscribers that can be interested in those events. The ENS plays in the system a role of a mediator between publishers and subscribers, decoupling the interactions among them in time, space and flow.

Subscribers can define the set of events they are interested in by issuing subscriptions. Each subscription works as a filter on the set of events injected in the system: the subscriber will be notified only about events that satisfy (match) the conditions expressed by its subscriptions. Subscriptions can be expressed in various ways depending on the subscription model adopted by the system. Currently, two models have been widely accepted by the community working on publish/subscribe: the topic-based and the content-based models.

The content-based model provides users with an expressive subscription syntax. This model requires the definition of a global event space represented by a collection of attributes each characterized by a name and a type (integer, floating-point, strings, etc.). Given a specific event space, an event is a collection of values, one for each attribute. The greater flexibility of this model comes from the possibility of defining each subscription as a complex expression constituted by constraints expressed on the attributes defined by the event space. A subscriber will by notified by the event notification service about an event only if it satisfies the expression contained in one of the node's subscriptions. Examples of systems that adopt the content-based subscription model are SIENA [6,7], JEDI [9] and Gryphon [14].

2.1 SIENA Pub/Sub System

The SIENA publish/subscribe system [7] is based on a distributed architecture where the ENS is made up of several machines, named *event brokers*. Brokers act as access points for clients (publishers and subscribers) that want to access the system and, furthermore, they are in charge of routing events among them in order to correctly notify published events to the intended recipients. SIENA's ENS is designed as a layered architecture:

- at the bottom layer stands an application-level *overlay network* represented by a generic graph interconnecting all the brokers. SIENA does not define how this overlay networks should be built and maintained, but only assumes that it is always connected;
- just above it a *broadcast layer* defines multiple spanning-trees (one for each broker as a possible source of events) that are used to diffuse published events toward all brokers where target subscribers are attached; spanning trees are defined with broadcast function $B : N \times I \to I^*$ that is supposed to be statically configured by a system administrator;

– at the top a *content based layer* is used to prune branches of spanning-trees that do not lead to potential target subscribers in order to reduce the amount of network traffic generated during event diffusion. Pruning is done on a per-event basis using information collected from previously issued subscriptions. Such information is maintained by each broker in a *content-based forwarding table* whose content is updated on the basis of two complementary proto-cols called *receiver advertisements (RA)* and *sender request/update replies (SR/UR)*.

Note that the two lowermost layers defined in SIENA are *static*, i.e. the authors assume that they are managed by system administrators and do not provide any algorithms for their maintenance. However, the correctness of event routing mechanism working on top of the layered architecture is based on the assumption that the spanning-trees defined in the broadcast function B are always connected.

2.2   Related Work

A few works in the literature has tackled the problem of making the SIENA pub/sub system more autonomous and adaptable by allowing automatic re-configurations and fault tolerance at the overlay and broadcast layers. Among these we can cite XSIENA [10] that adopts a strategy based on soft-state and lease timeouts to maintain up-to-date routing information within the system and thus tolerate possible reconfigurations. The complexities of readapting the application-level network topology after failures have been explored in [12] where the authors also proposed an enhancement to the "strawman approach". Finally, self-organization and reconfiguration of the application-network has also been exploited in [4] with a different goal, i.e. performance optimization.

The idea of using a cloud-based services for building more reliable pub-lish/subscribe system has only been recently applied Hedwig [2] that leverages the Zookeeper service for configuration storage (e.g. locations of ledgers, sub-scriber information), topic leader election and system membership. However, it should be noted that Hedwig has been designed as a system completely inte-grated within the cloud provider architecture, while our solution uses a cloud based storage service as a completely external service and can thus be deployed *outside* of the cloud provider architectural boundaries.

From this point of view our approach closely follows what has been proposed in [11]. Also in that paper a hybrid architecture is proposed, but, differently from HSIENA, a cloud-based storage service is only used to maintain simple loosely structured information.

3   HSIENA Architecture and Algorithms

The following section introduces HSIENA a hybrid architecture that comple-ments SIENA by adding the ability to self-reconfigure to manage broker ad-ditions and removals. We will first give an overview of HSIENA architecture together with the principles we adopted in its design; then we will detail the data structures it uses and the algorithms that support broker additions and removals.

3.1   Overview and Design Principles

The main issues that must be faced to add self-reconfiguration capabilities are: (i) reconfigure the overlay network, (ii) recalculate the broadcast function B, (iii) diffuse information about the new B in the ENS and (iv) update the content based forwarding tables.

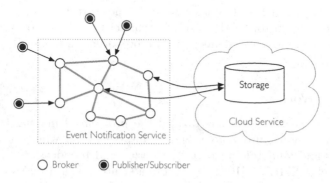

Fig. 1. HSIENA hybrid architecture

These operations must be conducted by managing issues related to concurrency among brokers and trying to reduce the possible loss of events published in the system while reconfigurations are ongoing. To fulfill its goals, the HSIENA system employs an hybrid architecture where the classical SIENA distributed ENS is paired with a cloud-based storage service (see Figure 1). The storage service is used by brokers as a *shared memory* where some of the global system state can be maintained, to be retrieved and updated every time a new broker needs to join the system or an existing one leaves or fails. The usage of a cloud-based storage service provides guarantees on availability and reliability of stored data, does not impose a limit on the system scalability and provides basic concurrency control features. However, accessing such service has a non negligible impact on performance (due to latencies induced by remote read/write operations) and overall cost (the cloud service provider applies specific billing policies for each operation).

Brokers entering the system first creates links toward other brokers. We here assume that these links are initialized as the result of a call to an external bootstrap service whose details are out of the scope of this paper. Then, the broker reads from the storage service the current state of the system and uses a variation of the classic Floyd-Warshall algorithm to build its broadcast spanning-tree and update the global B function. When the system state is updated, the broker starts a procedure to inform other brokers in the system that the global state has been updated and that they should access the storage service to update their local data structure. During this last phase content-based forwarding tables are updated in accordance with the new B function. Broker removals follow a similar approach.

Transitions from a system state to the next one, due to a broker addition or removal, are marked by an *epoch number*. States relative to old epochs are maintained in the storage service until all events published during that epoch has been correctly notified to the intended recipients.

3.2 Data Structures

The cloud-based storage service is used to maintain three main data structures. The first (and most important) is a list of couples of matrices. Each couple is associated to a specific *epoch* i and is constituted by D^i and $Pred^i$ matrices. The size of both matrices is $|N^i| \times |N^i|$ integer values, where N^i is the set of brokers in the system for epoch i and their content is calculated using the Floyd-Warshall algorithm (further details are given in Section 3.3). The D^i matrix contains in position $d[x, y]$ the length of the path connecting broker b_x to b_y in the spanning tree routed on b_x (the matrix is symmetrical as the B^i function must respect the *All-pairs path symmetry* condition as is defined in [7]). The $Pred^i$ matrix contains in position $p[x, y]$ the id of the broker that precedes b_y in the path that connects b_x to b_y. The $Pred^i$ matrix describes the broadcast functions of every node $x \in N^i$. In fact, let V_x^i be the set of neighbors of x (its interfaces set) at epoch i:

$$v \in B_x^i(y, \cdot) \leftrightarrow p[y, v] = x \ \forall v \in V_x^i \ \forall x, y \in N^i \tag{1}$$

The second data structure is a single integer variable whose value represents the current epoch.

Finally a list of ongoing operations Ops is used to manage concurrent access from various brokers to the previous data structures. This list is managed as a queue and brokers willing to execute some operations on the global state (i.e. write updated D_i and $Pred_i$ tables and/or update the current epoch) must first enqueue here their operations and act only after previous modification have been concluded and the corresponding entries removed from the list (see Section 3.5 for further details).

Such data structures can be easily stored in any cloud-based storage service. In the following, we will consider a concrete example where Amazon SimpleDB [1] is used for this purpose. More specifically the HSIENA system access its global state stored on SimpleDB using the *CreateDomain, DeleteDomain, BatchPutAttributes, ConditionalPut* and *Select* commands offered by the SimpleDB API.

Brokers locally maintain a copy of the B function and the content based forwarding table for several epochs i. A *garbage collection* mechanism can be employed to remove old data structures both from brokers and from the storage service. Data structures relative to epoch i can be removed as soon as all the brokers made their transition to some epoch $j > i$.

3.3 Broadcast Layer Reconfiguration Protocol

When a broker k must be added or removed from the system the first step to be performed is a reconfiguration of the broadcast layer whose goal is to update the B function on all brokers. This reconfiguration is performed by HSIENA using a protocol whose internal functioning is tailored to the specific operation that is going to be performed: insertion or removal. While node insertion are always voluntary, a broker can leave the system either voluntarily (i.e. a controlled shutdown or reboot) or due to a crash failure. In the latter case we assume that the reconfiguration protocol is executed on behalf of the crashed broker by one of its former neighbors. Note that, for the sake of clarity, here we will omit details related to concurrency management. Such details will be added in section 3.5.

Broker k executes the following protocol:

1. reads the current epoch number i from the storage service;
2. reads D^i and $Pred^i$;
3. executes the specific *insertion* or *removal algorithm*;
4. stores D^{i+1} and $Pred^{i+1}$ on the storage service and updates the current epoch to $i + 1$;
5. floods the system with an *Epoch Update* (EU) message containing (i) its id, (ii) a bit representing the fact that the update has been caused by the insertion or the removal of a broker and (iii) the current epoch number $i + 1$. The message flooding is realized directly on the overlay network connecting all brokers and we assume that k is the first broker to receive the message.

When a broker y receives an EU message related to the insertion or removal of broker k that moved the system to epoch $i + 1$ it follows these steps:

1. discards it if the same message was previously received and halt the protocol;
2. forwards the message on the overlay network to continue the flooding operation;
3. for each $s \in N^{i+1}$, $B(s, \cdot) = \emptyset$;
4. performs a *select* operation on the storage over D^{i+1} in order to know which rows have the element at column y equal to 1. This set represents the new set of neighbors V_y^{i+1}. Interfaces are added or removed accordingly;
5. for each $x \in V_y^{i+1}$ performs a *select* operation on the storage over $Pred^{i+1}$ in order to know which rows have the element at column x equal to y. Let R be the set of ids (rows) in which this occur. It sets $\forall s \in R, B^{i+1}(s, \cdot) = B^{i+1}(s, \cdot) \cup \{I_x\}$

If the operation is an insertion, in order to avoid event loss during reconfiguration, the node reads the row y from $Pred^{i+1}$. If in this line the id k is present, then it changes the predicate associated with interface I_{out} to ALL (i.e. the predicate is matched by any content based address), where I_{out} is the interface through which y reaches k in the spanning tree routed at y. Note that executing the same operation in case of a broker removal cannot prevent event loss, and can thus be skipped.

The insertion and removal algorithms (step 3 of the *reconfiguration protocol*) both work locally on the basis of D^i and $Pred^i$ matrices in order to produce D^{i+1} and $Pred^{i+1}$.

Broker insertion algorithm

1. Broker k builds its set of neighbors V_k^{i+1} resorting to an external bootstrap service[1];
2. adds a new line and a new column, both labelled with its id k, to D^i and $Pred^i$ obtaining locally the matrices D^{i+1} and $Pred^{i+1}$;
3. fills line k of matrix D^{i+1} using the following rule:

$$\forall y \in N^i, y \neq k, d[k, y] = min\{d[x, y] : x \in V_k^{i+1}\} + 1 \qquad (2)$$

   The addition of a single unit is due to the fact that we consider the weights of links connecting brokers all equal to 1. Column k is filled with the same values as D is symmetric;
4. every time an entry $d[k, y]$ is updated in D^{i+1} it checks which is the neighbor x (i.e. $x \in V_k^{i+1}$) that minimizes $d[x, y]$ and then updates $Pred^{i+1}$ using the following rule:

$$\forall y \in N, p[k, y] = p[x, y]$$
$$p[y, k] = x$$

5. loops on every $x, y \in N^{i+1}$ with $x, y \neq k$: if $d[x, y] > d[x, k] + d[k, y]$ then it sets $d[x, y] = d[x, k] + d[k, y]$ and $p[x, y] = p[k, y]$.

Broker removal algorithm

The removal algorithm is constituted by a recursive routine that takes as input a set X of row ids, a set Y of column ids and a set V of visited broker ids. The first call is executed using $X = \{1, \cdots, k-1, k+1, \cdots, n\}$, $Y = V_k^i$ and $V = \{k\}$.

1. for each $y \in Y$
   (a) defines $X' = \{x \in X : p[x, y] \in V\}$;
   (b) defines $Y' = V_y^i / V$;
   (c) if $Y' = \emptyset \wedge X' \neq \emptyset$ the overlay network is disconnected and the procedure halts as the manual intervention of a system administrator is needed[2];

---

[1] This bootstrap service, although not precisely defined in this paper, could be easily designed using the cloud based storage service where a list of ids and IP addresses of brokers currently in the system can be maintained.

[2] Note that spanning trees defining B are built by the insertion procedures using minimum paths among any pair of brokers in the system. Therefore, if we consider the union of all the spanning trees, we obtain the graph representing the overlay network connecting all brokers. As a consequence, the crash of a broker disconnects the system if and only if this broker did not appear in any spanning tree as a leaf. This property gives us a good methodology to understand if a disconnection has occurred just knowing the id of the failed broker and the *Pred* matrix.

(d) if $X' \neq \emptyset$ executes a recursive call using X', Y' and $V \cup \{y\}$ as input parameters;

(e) for each $x \in X'$:
   - sets $d[x, y] = min(d[x, z], z \in Y') + 1$ in D^{i+1};
   - every time an entry $d[x, y]$ is updated it checks which is the neighbor z (i.e. $z \in Y'$) that minimizes $d[x, z]$ and then updates $Pred^{i+1}$ with $p[x, y] = z$;

2. returns from the recursive call.

3.4   Content Based Layer Reconfiguration Protocol

The insertion or removal of a broker can easily disrupts the correctness of information stored on several content based forwarding tables. Therefore, after the conclusion of the broadcast layer reconfiguration protocol, broker k must take care of starting a new phase where content based forwarding tables, whose information could have become stale, are updated accordingly with the new system configuration.

If the phase is started after an insertion procedure, k executes the following protocol:

1. for each interface I_a it builds an *ad-Hoc Sender Request* (HSR) message that, beside all the information included in a standard *Sender Request* message, includes a set of brokers S_a such that $\forall s \in S_a, B_k^{i+1}(s, \cdot) \supseteq I_a$, and forwards it through I_a;
2. waits for a corresponding *ad-Hoc Update Reply* (HUR) message from the same interface I_a and uses its content to update the predicate associated to I_a in the content based forwarding table.

HSR messages are treated by a brokers y receiving it almost like a normal *Sender Request* messages. The only exception being that for any id $s \in S_a$ included in the HSR y checks if $B_y^{i+1}(s, \cdot) = \emptyset$. If the condition is satisfied it removes s from S_a and locally stores a triple $< HSRnumber, s, P_y >$ (where P_y is y's predicate).

Also HUR messages are treated similarly to standard *update replies*. When a broker y receives an HUR message for each triple $< HSRnumber, s, P_y >$ previously stored it adds to the body an *Extended Update Reply* EUR message containing a tuple $< s, P_y, \emptyset >$. For each EUR message $< s, P_x, \emptyset >$ already contained in the HUR it adds to the predicate its own predicate P_y (i.e. the EUR message become $< s, P_x \cup P_y, \emptyset >$). Finally, multiple EUR messages targeted to the same broker s are collapsed in a single EUR message containing the union of the respective predicates.

When k receives the expected HUR messages, it knows each of them will contain as many EUR messages as the number of broker ids included within S was. Also in this case multiple EUR messages targeted to the same broker s are collapsed in a single EUR message containing the union of the respective predicates. For each EUR message $< s, P, \emptyset >$, k calculates the route the message will follow on the overlay network in order to reach s. This route is obtained by looking at paths defined within $Pred^{i+1}$ and is then included in the EUR message as a list of brokers, i.e. $< s, P, \{k, \cdots, s\} >$. The message is then forwarded by brokers in the ENS simply following the path included in it. When a broker y receives an EUR message targeted to it, it updates the predicate associated in its content based forwarding table to the interface the message was received from by performing an union of the existing predicate with the one contained in the message.

In the case of a broker removal procedure HSIENA simply requires brokers receiving an EU message to reissue their predicate through a standard *receiver advertisement* procedure.

Note that after both these procedures brokers in the overlay have content based forwarding tables containing predicates that are correct (i.e. events are notified to all the intended recipients) but not exact (i.e. some events could be routed on some edges of the overlay without reaching any matched subscription). This behavior is consistent with the *inflation* phenomenon that already affects SIENA and can thus be mitigated using the standard SIENA mechanisms.

3.5   Concurrency Management

Broker insertions and removals can happen concurrently in HSIENA as their actions are not coordinated by a central administration. Consequently, multiple brokers can concurrently execute the previous procedures, while the coherence of information stored both on the brokers and in the storage service must be preserved. To this aim, a concurrency management strategy is needed such that concurrent operations will always leave at least the information stored on the storage service in a coherent state.

To reach this goal we assume that the storage service provides a *test-and-set* primitive that can be used to write data without ignoring previous updates. In SimpleDB this primitive is called *ConditionalPut*.

The list of ongoing operations Ops is the core of our concurrency management solution. Each element in the list is a tuple $< i, [INS/REM], y, V >$ indicating the broker y is performing a $[INS/REM]$ operation that will bring the system to epoch i. V is a set of broker ids used only for INS operations. The list Ops is managed by brokers as a queue, so insertion operations only happens at the tail. When a broker y starts an insertion (removal respectively) operation:

1. it reads Ops from the storage service;
2. reads the last epoch number i (the epoch number of the last element in the queue or the current epoch number, if the queue is empty) and the current epoch number e;
3. adds an item $< i + 1, INS, y, V_y^{i+1} >$ ($< i + 1, REM, y, \emptyset >$ resp.) in the queue;
4. tries a *test-and-set* operation to store the new version of the list on the cloud; if the operation fails (i.e. some other broker is concurrently executing the same operation), it re-executes the procedure from point 1;

5. executes the insertion or removal procedures as described in Section 3.3 for every element in *Ops* with the exception of those for which the epoch number is less or equal to e (these operations have been already concluded);
6. reads again the current epoch number e' from the storage service; if $e' > i+1$ it skips the *epoch update* procedure and proceeds to the last step;
7. tries a *test-and-set* operation in order to update current epoch number to $i + 1$, if it fails, it re-executes from the previous point;
8. deletes its entry from *Ops* and tries to write it on the storage service, using again the *test-and-set* procedure.

Such procedure guarantees that, in the worst case, the same insertion/removal operations will be executed multiple times by different nodes. However, these operations, thanks to their deterministic evolution, will always bring the system in the same final state.

3.6   Event Routing

Event routing in HSIENA is performed using the same mechanism employed in SIENA with the only exception that messages containing events must include the epoch in which each event was published. In principle, an event published in epoch i should be diffused on one of the spanning trees defined in B^i. However, epoch transitions can impose updates on B and this clearly impacts event diffusion. Suppose an event e is published in epoch i while the system is transitioning to epoch $i + 1$ (generally an epoch $i' > i$). This case can arise due to the fact the publish operations and epoch changes happen concurrently, and the broker where the event is published possibly did not receive the EU message before the event publication time. To this respect we must distinguish two cases: if the epoch update has been caused by the insertion of a new broker the event diffusion could continue using the old B^i function (with the obvious drawback that the newly inserted broker will not receive the event) as none of the broker present in the spanning tree used for routing it within the ENS disappeared. Contrarily, if the epoch update has been caused by the removal of a broker there is a possibility that the spanning tree has been disconnected by such removal and that the event diffusion will not be completed correctly.

To overcome these issues we propose a straightforward solution that sacrifices some efficiency in favor of better robustness: every time a broker receives an event published in an epoch i older than the epoch i' it knows, it stops the diffusion in i and republish the event in epoch i'. In this way the event will be diffused using updated spanning trees that will take into account possible broker removals. The dual case where a broker receives an event published in an epoch i newer than the epoch i'' it knows, is easily solved by forcing an epoch update on the broker.

The drawback of this approach is that it can cause brokers to receive the same event multiple times (in different epochs); this issue can be mitigated by locally keeping trace of received events in order to avoid local notifications, while waste of network resources cannot be avoided.

4 Conclusions

This paper introduced HSIENA, a hybrid architecture that complements the SIENA publish/subscribe system by adding the ability to self-reconfigure after broker additions and removals. HSIENA has a novel design that mixes the classic SIENA's distributed architecture based on managed brokers with a highly available cloud-based storage service that brokers use as a shared memory space they can rely-on to adapt at runtime the ENS application-level network without service disruption. Currently we are implementing a prototype of HSIENA to test its behaviour under various realistic loads. Our purpose is to asses both its ability to support insertion and deletions while providing service continuity (i.e. continuing to notify events also during reconfiguration phases) and to study the tradeoff existing between the level of service HSIENA can guarantee and the cost incurred for maintaining state information stored on a cloud service.

References

1. Amazon SimpleDB, http://aws.amazon.com/simpledb/
2. Hedwig, https://cwiki.apache.org/confluence/display/BOOKKEEPER/HedWig
3. Baldoni, R., Querzoni, L., Tarkoma, S., Virgillito, A.: Distributed Event Routing in Publish/Subscribe Communication Systems. Springer (2009)
4. Baldoni, R., Beraldi, R., Querzoni, L., Virgillito, A.: Efficient publish/subscribe through a self-organizing broker overlay and its application to siena. Comput. J. 50(4), 444–459 (2007)
5. Bharambe, A.R., Rao, S., Seshan, S.: Mercury: a scalable publish-subscribe system for internet games. In: Proceedings of the 1st Workshop on Network and System Support for Games, pp. 3–9 (2002)
6. Carzaniga, A., Rosenblum, D., Wolf, A.L.: Design and evaluation of a wide-area notification service. ACM Transactions on Computer Systems 3(19), 332–383 (2001)
7. Carzaniga, A., Rutherford, M.J., Wolf, A.L.: A routing scheme for content-based networking. In: INFOCOM (2004)
8. Cooper, B., Ramakrishnan, R., Srivastava, U., Silberstein, A., Bohannon, P., Jacobsen, H., Puz, N., Weaver, D., Yerneni, R.: Pnuts: Yahoo!'s hosted data serving platform. Proceedings of the VLDB Endowment 1(2), 1277–1288 (2008)
9. Cugola, G., Nitto, E.D., Fuggetta, A.: The jedi event-based infrastructure and its application to the development of the opss wfms. IEEE Transactions on Software Engineering 27(9), 827–850 (2001)
10. Jerzak, Z., Fetzer, C.: Soft state in publish/subscribe. In: Gokhale, A.S., Schmidt, D.C. (eds.) DEBS. ACM (2009)
11. Montresor, A., Abeni, L.: Cloudy weather for p2p, with a chance of gossip. In: Asami, T., Higashino, T. (eds.) Peer-to-Peer Computing, pp. 250–259. IEEE (2011)
12. Picco, G.P., Cugola, G., Murphy, A.L.: Efficient content-based event dispatching in the presence of topological reconfiguration. In: ICDCS, pp. 234–243. IEEE Computer Society (2003)
13. Pietzuch, P., Shand, B., Bacon, J.: Composite event detection as a generic middleware extension. IEEE Network 18(1), 44–55 (2004)
14. The Gryphon Team: Achieving Scalability and Throughput in a Publish/Subscribe System. Tech. rep., IBM Research Report RC23103 (2004)

WSDM-Enabled Autonomic Augmentation of Classical Multi-version Software Fault-Tolerance Mechanisms

Roeland Dillen, Jonas Buys, Vincenzo De Florio, and Chris Blondia

University of Antwerp
Department of Mathematics and Computer Science
Performance Analysis of Telecommunication Systems
1 Middelheimlaan, B-2020 Antwerp, Belgium
Interdisciplinary Institute for Broadband Technology
8 Gaston Crommenlaan, B-9050 Ghent-Ledeberg, Belgium

Abstract. Web services are increasingly deployed in many enterprise applications. For this type of applications, dependability issues are usually resolved by introducing some form of redundancy in the system. Whereas hardware redundancy schemes have traditionally been defined through static configurations based on worst-case analysis, the enhanced flexibility and interoperability of web services allows for dynamic (self-) management of redundancy at the application layer. Combining this advantage with service-oriented platforms such as OSGi facilitates the replication of software components and their integration within redundancy schemes. The application of such redundancy schemes inevitably comes at a price though — primarily due to the allocation of additional system resources. It is often unknown to the service provider how much redundancy and management complexity is required. Furthermore, the degree of redundancy and the dependability strategy to be employed may be restricted by the budget and requirements of the client, both of which may vary. In this paper, we propose a solution to allow the client to express a trade-off between its dependability requirements and its available budget at request level. A dedicated service provider will then attempt to honour these objectives — failing to do so would obviously result in failure from the client point of view. Furthermore, we show how classical multi-version software fault-tolerance techniques can be augmented with advanced redundancy management leveraging the Web Services Distributed Management standard.

1 Introduction

When constructing complex software systems, dependability issues will eventually unfold. In [1], Laprie defines dependability as the combination of reliability, availability, safety, security and maintainability. Amongst the available techniques to achieve dependability, and improve the reliability and availability in particular, a great deal of attention has been paid in the literature to

F. Ortmeier and P. Daniel (Eds.): SAFECOMP 2012 Workshops, LNCS 7613, pp. 294–306, 2012.

fault-tolerant redundancy schemes leveraging design diversity. Two prevalent examples of multi-version software fault-tolerance strategies are recovery blocks and n-version programming [2,3]. Recovery blocks subject the response of a call to a replica to an acceptance test, trying each replica in sequence until the output passes the acceptance test or until there are no more replicas left to try. In an n-version programming redundancy scheme, however, replicas are queried in parallel and a decision algorithm is responsible for adjudicating the correct result. Many different types of decision algorithms have been developed, which are usually implemented as generic voters [4]. One example of such voting approaches is plurality voting: for each invocation of the scheme, the replicas will be partitioned based on the equivalence of their results, and the result associated to the largest cluster will be accepted as the correct result.

These classical fault-tolerant strategies have traditionally been applied with a predetermined degree of redundancy on an immutable set of replicas. As such, they are context-agnostic, i.e. they do not take account of changes in the operational status of any of the components contained within the redundancy scheme. It was shown in [5] that this lack in flexibility may jeopardise the effectiveness of the fault-tolerant unit from a dependability, timeliness as well as a resource expenditure perspective. All dependability originating from the use of redundancy inevitably comes at a price, which is primarily due to the additional expenditure ensuing from the allocation of additional system resources. While a fixed amount of redundancy is applicable to hardware systems, applying fault-tolerance strategies at the application layer allows to incorporate advanced redundancy management capable of choosing the amount of redundancy autonomously.

In this paper, we formulate an approach to leverage the flexibility of service-oriented architectures to show how classical multi-version software fault-tolerance techniques can be augmented with advanced redundancy management. Firstly, we propose a solution to allow the client to express a trade-off between its dependability requirements and its available budget at request level. Accordingly, the system will autonomously select the appropriate amount of redundancy, honouring the budgetary constraints stated. Secondly, the system is responsible for maintaining a pool of instances — replicas — of a specific web service and is capable of autonomously deploying additional replicas (if needed), or removing or rejuvinating existing, poorly performing replicas.

The remainder of this paper is structured as follows: Section 2 provides an overview of the technologies used for our service-oriented solution. The design and architecture of the solution is then described in section 3. Next, the performance of the system will be analysed in section 4, after which we conclude this paper by a discussion and future work.

2   Key Technologies and Standards

In order to achieve its design goals, our solution relies on several key technologies. The first employed technology is web services. A web service is defined by the W3C as "a software system designed to support interoperable machine-to-machine interaction over a network" [6, Sect. 1.4]. XML-based web services in particular offer a high degree of interoperability, which mainly stems from the use of the Simple Object Access Protocol (SOAP) protocol to envelop messages to be exchanged, and from the numerous standardisation initiatives.

One such standard is the Web Services Distributed Management [7] (WSDM) family of specifications, which defines how networked resources can be managed by exposing their capabilities and properties by means of a web service interface. The constituent Management of Web Services (MoWS) specification describes how web services themselves can be considered as resources, and require manageability features as well [7, WSDM-MOWS]. More specifically, it defines a number of metrics to expose information regarding the operational status of a web service, which are of particular intrest within the scope of this paper.

Finally, the Java-based Open Services Gateway initiative (OSGi) framework allows bundled applications and services to be remotely and dynamically deployed, without necessitating a reboot of the system. This characteristic will be exploited to automatically deploy new instances of a specific web services (i.e. replicas) should the available amount of system resources prove to be insufficient.

3   Basic Principles and Components

In this section, we provide an overview of the architecture of our service-oriented solution and elaborate on its design aiming to improve the effectiveness of traditional recovery strategies from the following three angles.

Firstly, our solution enables the dynamic and autonomic management of the degree of redundancy of the system. The rationale for this objective is that a predetermined degree of redundancy has traditionally been hardwired within classical software fault-tolerance strategies. Changes in the operational status of the system (i.e. its context) may result in the over- or undershooting of the required degree of redundancy needed to sustain a certain level of dependability [8,5]. It is also likely that the optimal degree of redundancy changes in time.

Secondly, the reliability of the fault-tolerant composite is largely dependent on the quality of the constituent replicas [9]. Our architecture therefore includes a monitor component, which was designed to observe changes in the operational status of the available replicas. As such, replicas that consistently perform poorly may be removed and replaced if necessary, which may further improve the reliability of the composite.

Thirdly, for individual requests issued on the fault-tolerant composite, the system will intelligently determine an appropriate degree and selection of replicas honouring the dependability requirements expressed by the client, i.c. the redundancy strategy to be used and timing as well as budgetary constraints. The anticipated cost of invoking a redundancy scheme is primarily determined by the resource allocation expenditure model and the operational status of the available system resources maintained by the service provider though. We have therefore chosen to implement the service provider as a WSDM-enabled resource, exposing the expected cost for the various redundancy strategies it supports by means of resource properties [10, WSRF-RP]. This allows the client to judiciously select a service provider capable of delivering the requested service level.

An overview of the system architecture is shown in Fig. 1. The architecture includes four dedicated components: a replicator, a dispatcher, a monitor and a context data repository (CDR), each of which have been implemented as WSDM-enabled web services. Any web service that will serve as version to be replicated is required to expose a WSDM manageability interface.

In line with our second objective described hereabove, the replicator component is responsible for maintaining a given amount of instances (replicas, that is) of a specific web service (version). Deploying multiple instances of a particular software component in a distributed system has proved successful in lowering the risk of a complete system failure as the result of hardware failures [5]. It is assumed that an increased degree of redundancy results in an increase of the dependability, provided that badly performing replicas are removed. In order to support the dynamic replication of a web service, the replicator will manage of a number of agents. Such utility application web services are deployed on different network hosts and will periodically broadcast a heartbeat to the replicator. When the replicator issues a command to replicate a web service, one or more agents will be instructed to locally deploy a new instance of the service. The replicator exposes a manageability interface for the manipulation of replicas: new instances can be created, the amount of replicas for a given version can be adjusted, and individual replicas can be disabled. Note how the replicator maintains a registry of the system resources, federating different service groups, each exposing the deployed instances of a specific web service [10, WSRF-SG]. This design permits WSDM advertisement messages to be broadcast upon service creation or destruction, such that the monitor and the CDR components can acquire the relevant context information.

The monitor component serves the purpose of monitoring the operational status of the replicas in the system. It was implemented to automatically enrol for participation in a publish-and-subscribe model, so as to receive notifications issued by the WSDM framework on behalf of a replica whenever the value of some MoWS metric changes [11,7]. Notification messages reporting on the change of the value of these metrics need to comply to the format as defined in [10, WSRF-RP]. For instance, a replica that returns faulty responses all too frequently, as can be deduced from the value of the `mows:NumberOfFailedRequests`

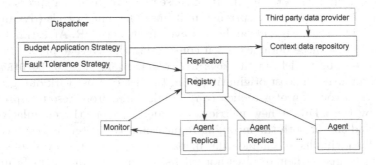

Fig. 1. Overview of the overall system architecture

metric, can be eliminated from the system and replaced by another. In this capacity, the monitor will use the replicator's manageability interface.

Client transparency is attained by means of the dispatcher component that exposes the redundancy scheme as a single web service, shielding the intricacies of the redundancy management. The dispatcher exposes a manageability capability to deploy an OSGi bundle in the system that creates replicas as well as the composite service. Moreover, it can be fitted with support for different fault-tolerance strategies. The dispatcher will select an appropriate degree and selection of resources and integrate them within an appropriate fault-tolerant redundancy scheme, attempting to honour the constraints and preferences expressed by the client. For instance, the client could specify that the dispatcher should use a recovery block strategy, selecting an adequate selection of replicas that does not exceed the budget, or that is guaranteed to return a result within a given time span. We will explain this approach in further detail in Sect. 3.1.

The CDR can be set up acting as a receiver for third party metrics of particular interest, each of which are identified by the QName of the corresponding resource property exposed through the WSDM manageability interface. By default, it will attempt to issue a subscription request so as to enrol in a publish-and-subscribe scheme and receive notifications whenever the value of the relevant metrics change [11,7]. Again, the payload of these messages is formatted as defined in [10, WSRF-RP]. The system will attempt to establish such subscriptions for all replicas registered within the system, driven by the WSDM advertisement messages issued by the replication mechanism.

3.1   Budget Application Strategy (BAS)

We will now elaborate on the redundancy management provided by the dispatcher and how it was designed to determine an adequate selection of replicas matching the requirements stated by the client. An overview of the overall process can be found in Fig. 2.

The cost resulting from the invocation of a redundancy scheme is modelled by two components: the cost to transfer the request message from the dispatcher to the selected replicas and have the response returned accordingly, and the processing cost charged for the use of an invoked replica. We will use an abstract model to quantify the cost resulting from these two components, expressed in currency_unit/byte, respectively currency_unit/ms. The unit price is (dynamically) set for individual replicas and can be retrieved from the CDR. An estimate of the processing cost can be obtained when considering the average processing time, which can be obtained from the mows:ServiceTime and mows:NumberOfRequests metrics. Similarly, the cost originating from the use of a network datagram service for the invocation of a replica can be calculated from resource properties exposed by the CDR. A new metric was added to store the cumulative message payload size of both the incoming request and the outgoing response. This model, albeit simplistic, enables the dispatcher to rank the available system replicas in terms of their total estimated usage cost, sorting them from cheap to expensive. A subset is then iteratively chosen until the available budget has been exhausted. Note that the budget is not necessarily entirely spent, for it is not always necessary to actually use all the replicas selected — *cf.* recovery blocks *vs.* *n*-version programming. Having determined an adequate selection of system replicas, the dispatcher will then initialise the selected redundancy strategy, integrating the selected replicas. Our dispatcher implementation currently supports the following strategies:

1. Plain recovery block strategy: the selected replicas are queried in turn until one of them has returned a response that passes the acceptance test.
2. Replicating recovery block strategy: similar to the plain recovery block strategy. If the budget has not been entirely exhausted and all active replicas have been tried, additional replicas will be created and invoked until a valid response is obtained, or until the budget has been spent.
3. Active voting strategy: *n*-version programming scheme in which all replicas are queried simultaneously; the first response acquired will be returned.
4. Plurality voting strategy: *n*-version programming scheme in which all replicas are queried simultaneously. If the decision algorithm can establish the existence of a consensus block that constitutes a plurality in the generated partition based on the equivalence of the responses returned, the corresponding response is returned.

```
<soap:Header xmlns:wsa="http://www.w3.org/2005/08/addressing">
    <wsa:To>http://localhost:8888/dispatcher/services/service</wsa:To>
    <wsa:Action>http://adss.pats.ua.ac.be/service/version</wsa:Action>
    ...
    <wsp:Policy xmlns:wsp="http://schemas.xmlsoap.org/ws/2004/09/policy"
                xmlns:rcfg="http://adss.pats.ua.ac.be/dispatcher"
                xmlns:ba="http://adss.pats.ua.ac.be/service">
        <ba:BudgetAssertion>
            <ba:budget>
                <ba:value>0.05</ba:value>
                <ba:unit>ct</ba:unit>
            </ba:budget>
        </ba:BudgetAssertion>
        <rcfg:RecoveryConfig>
            <rcfg:RecoveryStrategy>
                http://adss.pats.ua.ac.be/strategies/PlainRecoveryBlockStrategy
            </rcfg:RecoveryStrategy>
            <rcfg:parameters>
                <rcfg:parameter>
                    <rcfg:name>timeout</rcfg:name>
                    <rcfg:value>1000</rcfg:value>
                </rcfg:parameter>
            </rcfg:parameters>
        </rcfg:RecoveryConfig>
        <rcfg:AcceptanceTest>
            contains(//versionResponse/text(),'i carry correct result')
        </rcfg:AcceptanceTest>
    </wsp:Policy>
</soap:Header>
```

Listing 1.1. The dependability, timing and budgetary requirements of the client are relayed by means of a WS-Policy element embedded in the SOAP header.

Which of the aforementioned fault-tolerance strategies will be employed is at the behest of the client, a choice which will be conveyed to the dispatcher by means of a special WS-Policy element embedded within a SOAP header block attached to the issued request message, as is shown in List. 1.1 [12]. This WS-Policy element contains a set of assertions, including the mandatory parameterised assertion `rcfg:RecoveryConfig`. Its purpose is to identify the redundancy strategy by means of a predefined Uniform Resource Identifier (URI), and to provide any additional parameters the chosen strategy may require. An optional `ba:BudgetAssertion` can be included to state the available budget. Observe how the acceptance test to be used for the recovery block strategies is relayed through the parameterised `rcfg:AcceptanceTest` assertion, holding an XPath expression that will be used to assess the validity of the response returned by each of the probed replicas. Furthermore, an optional `rcfg:parameter` element can be set by the client to hold a timeout parameter. It is, however, entirely up to the dispatcher's implementation of the redundancy scheme to honour this constraint.

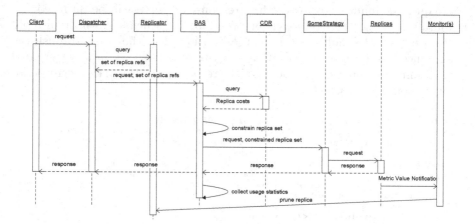

Fig. 2. Request handling overview: sequence diagram

It makes no use to squander the available budget on replicas that do not significantly contribute to the effectiveness of the redundancy scheme. As an additional measure to increase the overall availability of the requested service, the monitor component is configured so as to automatically replace replicas with a high degree of failed requests. In this capacity, the monitor will observe changes in the values of the metrics defined in the MoWS specification so as to assess the health of a replica. It does so by considering the relative number of requests for which a given replica failed to return a valid response, i.e. for which a SOAP fault was returned. When the ratio between the `mows:NumberOfFailedRequests` and the `mows:NumberOfRequests` metrics is found to exceed a certain threshold, the affected replica is considered to be unhealthy and the monitor will instruct the replicator to remove the replica from the system. Note that this process is fully transparent to the client and is driven by the monitor component. The dispatcher allows the plain and replicating recovery block and plurality voting strategies to be enhanced with this replica pruning procedure.

4   Performance Analysis

In this section, we will analyse the performance of each of the proposed strategies in Sect. 3.1, assuming they are operating in an environment subject to transient faults. Failures are injected into the system by means of a special service that will affect the outcome of an acceptance test for strategies built on the recovery block procedure, or that will affect the generated partition for voting-based strategies.

For a given replica, it is assumed the number of requests in between any two successive failures is geometrically distributed with a constant parameter p. This failure probability p is drawn from an exponential distribution with $\lambda = 3.33$. As random variates drawn from an exponential distribution do not necessarily generate values within $[0, 1]$, all the mass above is truncated to 1. The rationale behind the use of the exponential for sampling values for p as described is that a replica is assumed to be affected by transient faults and will therefore only fail periodically. Lower failure rates approaching 0 are more likely, as opposed to permanent faults for which $p = 1$. The choice of λ will result in the generation of probabilities high enough to be visualised easily but not excessively so. By analogy with the findings in [13], variations in the response times of replica invocations are simulated utilising a gamma distribution. In what follows, we will analyse the performance for the following redundancy strategies when subject to the failure model just described:

1. Simplex system: a single replica which obviously is not tolerant of failures.
2. Plain recovery block strategy: classical recovery block, as defined in Sect. 3.1.
3. Replicating recovery block strategy: extends the logic of the plain recovery block in that additional replicas are automatically created if the initial set of replicas to be used is exhausted and a sufficient share of the budget is left.
4. Plurality voting strategy: n-version programming scheme combined with plurality voting, as defined in Sect. 3.1.

Furthermore, some of these strategies have been tested in combination with the replica pruning feature introduced in Sect. 3.1. Replicas are judged unhealthy if more than 20% of the requests previously handled have failed. The monitor will instruct the replicator to remove such replicas from the system.

5. Plain recovery block with replica pruning, extending scenario 2.
6. Replicating recovery block with replica pruning, extending scenario 3.
7. Plurality voting strategy with replica pruning, extending scenario 4.

4.1   Results

We will now provide an overview of the performance of the strategies mentioned. Each of the graphs below compares the basic scenario, without and with replica pruning by the monitor component. Figures 3, 4 and 5 show the same metrics, measuring the (in)effectiveness of a given redundancy strategy:

- Errors (plusses and crosses in the graphs at the right): indicative of the percentage of the total number k of invocations of the composite that resulted in failure ($k = 4000$).

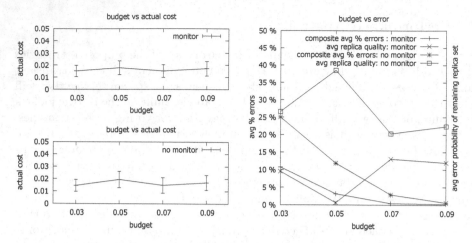

Fig. 3. Scenarios 2 and 5: Plain recovery block strategies

- Costs (shown in the graphs at the left): indicative of the average, actual cost for all requests. Graphs show average and standard deviation.
- Average replica quality (squares and asterisks): at the end of a run, all remaining replicas in the system that were not pruned by the monitor are asked for the probability with which they were struck by a failure. The corresponding average is shown.

There is no need to actually simulate the first scenario, i.e. the simplex system, as one can directly derive the percentage of the k invocations of the system that will result in failure. As the error degree for each replica is chosen from an exponential distribution with $\lambda = 3.33$, the mean failure probability is $\mu = 0.3$. One can then surmise that the Bernouilli process that describes the probability of a failure affecting a request has probability parameter $p = \mu$.

Figure 3 shows the results of scenarios 2 and 5. The percentage of failed invocations is below 30%, for both scenarios with and without the monitor, and thus an improvement compared to the simplex system. A growing degree redundancy because of a bigger budget results in less failures of the scheme. Furthermore, the advantage that the replica pruning appears to deliver diminishes as the budget increases. The effect of the replica pruning is also visible on the average replica quality. The quality of the replicas is distinctly less without replica pruning. The actual cost of the recovery block strategy appears to be, on average, much lower than the actual budget. The cost, however, appears to vary significantly, although not to a degree that it will likely exceed the budget.

Figure 4 shows the results for the replicating recovery block, in which the classical recovery block scheme is augmented with the possibility to create further replicas. The error rate is well below the 30% benchmark for the simplex system. Furthermore, it can be observed that a small advantage is gained from utilising the monitor component. With respect to the cost, the same discrepancy between the actual cost and the budget is noted, including a significant degree

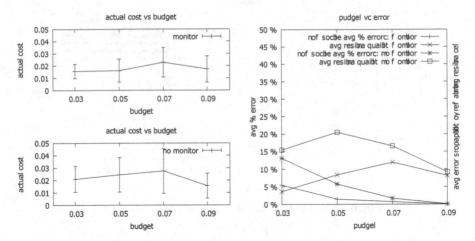

Fig. 4. Scenarios 3 and 6: Replicating recovery block strategies

of variability. The same diminishing returns of the replica pruning mechanism can be observed as in the previous experiment. As the budget and therefore the number of replicas increases, their average quality worsens. This may be an effect of the abundance of replicas causing not all replicas to be queried frequently enough for the monitor to confidently decide to prune a replica.

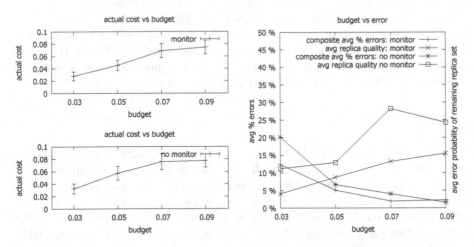

Fig. 5. Scenarios 4 and 7: Voting strategies, with and without replica pruning

Figure 5 shows the classical voting strategy augmented by the measures mentioned in Sect. 3.1. The voting strategy also performs better than the 30% benchmark set by a single service. It also benefits from the replica pruning by about

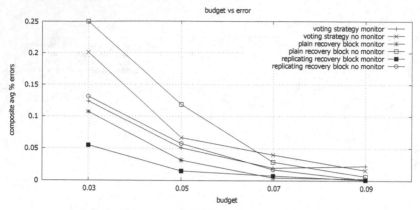

Fig. 6. Percentage of failed composite invocations

10% points in the lower budgets. As more budget becomes available — and therefore more replicas — this advantage diminishes as is also the case for scenarios 5 and 6 based on recovery blocks. This strategy seems to have an effect on the overall replica quality: even in the higher budgets the average replica quality is better in the monitor case. This is most likely caused by the fact that all selected replicas that fit within the budget are actually invoked. This causes the monitor to reach a good confidence about the health of the replica much faster.

Figure 6 shows a comparison of the ratio of invocations resulting in failure of all transient scenarios. It shows that all the strategies provide the best results when fitted with a replica pruning monitor. Of all the pruning strategies the addition of direct replication capabilities in combination with replica pruning as done by the replicating recovery block yields the best result for the smallest budget. We have determined that the use of some simple MoWS features like the `mows:NumberOfFailedRequests` metric already can provide some meaningful improvement on the classical multi-version fault-tolerance strategies.

4.2   Discussion

The replicating recovery block strategy with replica pruning clearly yields the best results. It must be noted though that devising a proper acceptance test is usually very application-specific and may not always be possible due to the limited information exposed in the service interface. Improving the applicability of the recovery block mechanism, our system has been designed so that the acceptance test can be configured at runtime, and is no longer hardwired within the fault-tolerant unit.

The voting strategy can be more widely applied, as it employs a generic plurality voter. The primary disadvantage of the voting system though stems from the fact that all selected replicas will be invoked in parallel, incurring greater actual cost. In this regard, the sequential iterative invocation of individual replicas by the recovery block mechanisms show that, on average, not all replicas are actually used. At the risk of sporadically overstepping the budget, much greater redundancy — and therefore dependability — can be provided.

Because of the monitoring component and its ability to remove poorly performing replicas, an increase in replicas will result in an increase in dependability, provided that the replicas are used sufficiently; it takes a number of requests to achieve sufficient confidence about the health of a replica.

5   Conclusions and Future Work

In this paper, we have shown how software fault-tolerance strategies can be applied to XML-based web services, aiming to increase the dependability, and in particular the availability of the overall service the system seeks to provide. Furthermore, the design of dedicated WSDM-based web services can augment these classical fault-tolerance strategies in that they can accommodate for advanced redundancy management. We have argued that poorly behaving replicas can easily be detected leveraging some simple metrics provided by the MoWS specification. Moreover, it was apparent from our experimentation that it is advantageous to prune such replicas and have them replaced by newly initialised ones. A service-oriented architecture was introduced that builds on top of the OSGi and Apache MUSE frameworks encompassing a monitor component that keeps track of the operational status of the available system resources, and a replicator utility service to ease the dynamic deployment of additional replicas.

The flexibility offered by the service-oriented architecture presented allows to adaptively reconfigure the amount of redundancy and, accordingly, the selection of resources for individual requests. Moreover, our experiments suggest that, on average, combining the devised replica pruning and replacement features with a classical recovery block strategy outperforms the other fault-tolerance mechanisms tested, both in terms of cost and availability.

As part of future work, we envisage investigating more advanced detection mechanisms for the monitor component, encompassing additional metrics extending beyond the set of metrics defined in MoWS. Furthermore, additional experimentation is required to obtain a more general view on the performance of the system using a wide range of failure injection models.

References

1. Laprie, J.C., Avižienis, A., Kopetz, H. (eds.): Dependability: Basic Concepts and Terminology. Springer (1992)
2. Randell, B.: System structure for software fault tolerance. In: Proceedings of the 1st ACM International Conference on Reliable Software, pp. 437–449 (1975)
3. Avižienis, A.: The N-version approach to fault-tolerant software. IEEE Transactions on Software Engineering 11(12), 1491–1501 (1985)
4. Lorczak, P., et al.: A theoretical investigation of generalized voters for redundant systems. In: IEEE Digest of Papers on the 19th International Symposium on Fault-Tolerant Computing (1989)

5. Buys, J., et al.: Towards Context-Aware Adaptive Fault Tolerance in SOA Applications. In: Proceedings of the 5th ACM International Conference on Distributed Event-Based Systems, pp. 63–74 (2011)
6. W3C: Web Services Architecture (2004),
   http://www.w3.org/TR/2004/NOTE-ws-arch-20040211/
7. OASIS: Web Services Distributed Management (WSDM) 1.1 (2006),
   http://www.oasis-open.org/committees/wsdm
8. De Florio, V.: Robust-and-evolvable resilient software systems: Open problems and lessons learned. In: Proceedings of the 8th ACM Workshop on Assurances for Self-Adaptive Systems, pp. 10–17 (2011)
9. De Florio, V., et al.: Software tool combining fault masking with user-defined recovery strategies. IEE Proceedings – Software 145(6), 203–211 (1998)
10. OASIS: Web Services Resource Framework (WSRF) 1.2(2006),
    http://www.oasis-open.org/committees/wsrf/
11. OASIS: Web Services Base Notification 1.3 (2006),
    http://www.oasis-open.org/committees/wsn/
12. W3C: Web Services Policy 1.5 - Framework (2007),
    http://www.w3.org/TR/ws-policy/
13. Gorbenko, A., et al.: Real Distribution of Response Time Instability in Service-oriented Architecture. In: IEEE Symposium on Reliable Distributed Systems, pp. 92–99 (2010)

Formal Verification of a Safety Argumentation and Application to a Complex UAV System

Julien Brunel and Jacques Cazin

ONERA-DTIM
2 Av Edouard Belin, BP 74025, F-31055 Toulouse Cedex, France
{Julien.Brunel,Jacques.Cazin}@onera.fr

Abstract. In the context of safety-critical systems, arguing that the system is acceptably safe is a major issue, in particular when facing a certification process. We are developing an approach which aims at providing assurance that safety objectives are met by a system under development. We propose a language to express a safety argumentation together with a semantic definition on which an implementation is based. The ultimate objective is to have means to decide, at the level of requirements, the correctness of an argumentation using a formal and tool supported approach. In this paper, we illustrate our argumentation framework on the problem of safe insertion of Unmanned Aerial Vehicle (UAV) into the air traffic. The system we consider is a socio-technical organization, which consists of the UAV control systems, and the air traffic management. The support environment built upon existing tools is briefly described.

Keywords: argumentation language, safety validation, requirement analysis, formal verification, UAV system.

1 Introduction

In the context of safety-critical systems, arguing that the system is acceptably safe is a major issue, in particular when facing a certification process. The presentation of arguments that a system meets such acceptable levels of safety is typically referred to as a "safety case". A safety case [1], [4] presents the general safety objectives, and arguments that justify how evidence, such as safety assessments, allow to ensure the safety objectives. However, in practice, safety cases often focus on the evidence, presenting detailed safety assessment, and neglect the relation between evidence and safety objective that explains how the former allow to ensure the latter. Interesting academic propositions define languages, *e.g.* Goal Structuring Notation (GSN) [6], [16], dedicated to safety cases, with a focus on the link between the safety objectives and the evidence that support it, *i.e.*, the argument itself. But they do not define, for these argumentation languages, a formal semantics that could be used as a basis for automatic verification.

Nevertheless, the requirement engineering community introduces models that have similarities with argumentation frameworks. Indeed, some of the most convincing academic methodologies propose to structure requirements from more

F. Ortmeier and P. Daniel (Eds.): SAFECOMP 2012 Workshops, LNCS 7613, pp. 307–318, 2012.

abstract goals to the most detailed requirements in a tree-like AND-OR decomposition. Their objective is to help the statement of clear and coherent requirements, and to ensure that a pre-specification of the system meets these requirements. Although they do not represent all the concepts that are necessary to model an argumentation (such as evidence) they define a partially formalised semantics. In particular, i^*-Tropos [2] and Kaos [7] methods define a formalisation based on propositional logic and temporal logic respectively. The framework we propose in this article takes inspiration from Kaos method and use temporal logic to define a formal semantics.

In this article, we present

- a framework to represent an argumentation;
- a mathematical foundation (formal semantics) that allows automatic validation of the argumentation;
- a pragmatic approach based on this framework to easily edit and validate a safety argumentation;
- an illustration of our approach on the study of a safe insertion of an Unmanned Aerial Vehicule (UAV) into the air traffic.

The central aspect of our approach, illustrated by Fig. 1, is an argumentation model. The aim of this model is to help the representation of a clear, structured, and rigourous safety argumentation. The basic elements of an argumentation are the safety *claims* to guarantee. Each claim is refined into more precise sub-claims, which are sufficient conditions to ensure it. The process of *claim refinement*, also called decomposition, is guided by well identified *strategies*. The obtained tree-like structure describes an argument allowing one to conclude the top safety claims from elementary sub-claims that can be inferred directly from evidence, also called *witnesses*.

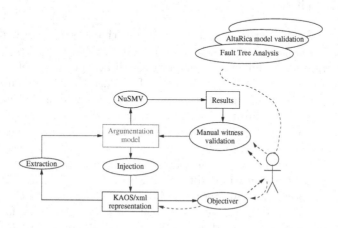

Fig. 1. Argumentation based verification approach

We propose to support the process of validating an argumentation. An argumentation is correct if the refinements (or decompositions) that link the top claims to the elementary leaf claims are correct, and if the evidence are correct (they effectively allow to infer elementary claims). A claim refinement is correct if the claim can be deduced from its sub-claims. This can be formally and automatically verified provided that the claim and its sub-claims have been formalised, in our approach in Linear Temporal Logic (LTL). As the other automatic verifications in our approach, this is performed by the model checker NuSMV [3].

An evidence can be either the result of a safety analysis which is conducted outside our framework (a fault tree analysis, a failure mode and effects analysis, etc.) or an operation of the system that can be specified in our framework (a software collision avoidance operation, as we will consider in our case study). In the former case, the correctness of the evidence must be manually validated by the engineer in charge of the argumentation, in collaboration with the safety engineer that performed the corresponding safety analysis. In the latter case, the correctness can be expressed in LTL and the validation can be performed automatically.

In order to ease the process of validating the argumentation, the evidence and the claims have a status (*validated* or *not validated*) indicating whether they have already been proved (or manually confirmed) correct. In case a refinement is formally proved (or manually confirmed) the propagation of the status from the sub-claims to a claim is performed by our tool.

In order to have a graphical representation of our argumentation model, we use the tool Objectiver [11] , which supports KAOS method. All the concepts of an argumentation model that are not KAOS concepts are represented here as textual annotations. We use specific conventions so that our tool can interpret these annotations as meaningful concepts.

We illustrate our approach on the study of safe insertion of a UAV into the air traffic. The highest level claim states that *the insertion of the UAV into the air traffic is safe*. This claim is refined into more precise sub-claims, according to some refinement *strategies*. We continue the refinement process until we come to elementary claims that may be ensured by evidences.

This article is organized as follows. Sect. 2 presents our argumentation language and its semantics. In Sect. 3, we illustrate our framework on our case study, which deals with safe insertion of UAV into the air traffic. Sect. 4 describes our prototype environment, which supports the approach. And Sect. 5 relates our approach to other works.

2   The ForSALE Language

ForSALE stands for Formal Safety Argumentation Language and Environment. In the following sections, we give an overview of the main supported concepts and the way they interact with each other, propose a concrete syntax and provide some elements of the formal semantics.

2.1 ForSALE Basic Concepts

In our approach, an argumentation is a formal object which is based on the following elements and considerations:

Claims: a claim is an assertion stating that something is correct. *The function F is implemented, F has been verified, F has been tested* or *The implementation of F has been formally proved* are several examples of claims. A claim is defined in a given **Context** in which, for example, the definitions used in this claim are given;

Compound Claims: a claim may be elementary or composed of several sub-claims. For example *The system S provides the functionality F* may be decomposed into the claims previously mentioned; these ones may be combined using conjunction and disjunction. For example *The function F is implemented* AND *(F has been tested* OR *The implementation of F has been formally proved)*;

Witnesses: a witness is an elementary fact. *The source code of F has been versioned* and *Test cases of F have been successfully passed* are example of witnesses;

Rules: a rule allows to associate a witness to a claim. This association may be considered as an argument. For example, *To assess the acceptability of a function failure, the results of hazard analysis must be at disposal* may be a rule used to link the claim *Risks of loss of F are acceptable* to the witness *Report on the Preliminary System Safety Assessment (PSSA)*. Rules may be used either in a *prescriptive* way (to reach the goal you should do that...) or in an *evidential* way (the goal is reached due to the fact that ...);

Strategies: a strategy describes the (pragmatic) way a type of goals may be split into sub-goals which can be reached independently from each other. An example of that is the strategy *Strat:Functional/Safety* which will be used in the following examples. It states that to reach a goal *G*, a corresponding function *F has been developed* and that *The risks of losing F are acceptable*. Here also strategy may be used either in a *prescriptive* or in an *evidential* way.

These elements are the main ingredients of ForSALE meta-model as represented on Fig. 2 in an entity association style. C-leaf and C-node are the two varieties of claims, either elementary or compound. Alternatives are possible ways of combining several Claims to set up a more global one. A Stategy is used to produce only one Alternative for a given Claim; although restrictive, this has not revealed to be so much of a constraint in our approach.

So, to summarize, an argumentation is composed of several alternate conjunctions of arguments which can be compound or elementary; the latter are justification that a claim is correct due to the fact that a given rule may be applied to assert it and that a witness exists to certify that the rule has effectively been applied.

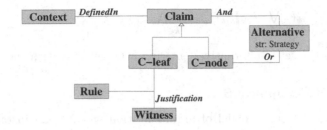

Fig. 2. ForSALE meta-model

2.2 Semantics

To define the semantics of ForSALE we will use an interpretation of each term of the meta-model in logic. We use linear temporal logic LTL mainly for two reasons:

- LTL is widely used to express prescriptive statements on a system behaviour; in particular, it is used in KAOS to express goals and to give the semantics of operationalisation (the fact operations ensure a requirement) [9];
- as it will be argued in the perspectives, we plan to introduce in ForSALE precedence operators to provide the arguments with an order relation, and in this context, temporal operators will be useful.

So each element of the language will be interpreted using the following semantic functions:

$$[\![\cdot]\!]_{clm} : Claim \quad\quad \to F$$
$$[\![\cdot]\!]_{alt} : Alternative \to F$$
$$[\![\cdot]\!]_{ctx} : Context \quad\quad \to F$$

where F is the set of LTL formulas;

This is not the aim of the present paper to give a complete and detailed semantics of ForSALE. To illustrate it we can give the following excerpt which is the definition of the semantics of an Alternative:

$$[\![a]\!]_{alt} \equiv \bigwedge_{c \in \mathcal{C}(a)} ((\bigwedge_{k \in \mathcal{K}(c)} [\![k]\!]_{ctx}) \to [\![c]\!]_{clm})$$

where $\mathcal{C}(a)$ and $\mathcal{K}(c)$ are respectively defined as the set of Claims entering a *And* relation with a given Alternative a and the set of Contexts entering a *DefinedIn* relation with a given Claim c.

This can be informally read as: the semantics of an Alternative is the formula made of the conjunction of a set of implications, each of which relates a Claim entering the alternative with the conjunction of the Definitions it uses.

So to express that the refinement of a Claim which is composed of several C-node is correct, we use the formula made of the disjunction of the semantics of its constituting Alternatives and prove that it entails the formula of the Claim in its context, that is:

$$(\bigvee_{a \in \mathcal{A}(c)} (\llbracket a \rrbracket_{alt})) \rightarrow ((\bigwedge_{k \in \mathcal{K}(c)} \llbracket k \rrbracket_{ctx}) \rightarrow \llbracket c \rrbracket_{clm})$$

where $\mathcal{A}(c)$ is the set of alternatives entering a *Or* relation with the Claim c.

2.3 Concrete Graphical Syntax

To describe a particular model of argumentation which is an instance of the aforementioned meta-model, we use a graphical syntax which is totally compatible with the KAOS approach and its support tool. The conventional symbols we use (Claim as a parallelogram, Context in a round ended rectangle, Witness in an ellipse etc.) are detailed on Fig. 3. The example of the next sections will follow this graphical syntax. It is worth noting that, as it will be illustrated later, a formal definition, using LTL formulas, may be associated to each Claim, Context or Witness.

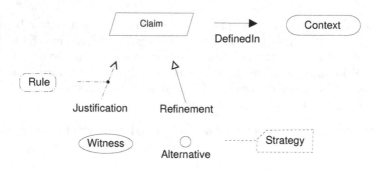

Fig. 3. ForSALE graphical syntax

3 The UAV Insertion Case Study

The IDEAS project ("Insertion des Drones dans l'Espace Aérien et Sécurité") is an ONERA internal project started in 2009. Its concern is to study the feasibility of a safe insertion of UAVs into the civil air traffic. Specific engineering methods (process, guides, tools) are proposed for defining and proving safety requirements for UAVs. This conceptual work is validated thanks to ONERA experimental facilities, in particular three UAV helicopters on which sensors and autonomous capacities are embedded and evaluated.

In this context, we propose to represent, in our ForSALE environment, a global argumentation that an UAV can perform safely a mission in the civil air traffic. The system under reasoning is a complex socio-technical system involving the UAV itself (with its embedded systems), the pilot, the ground station, and the Air Traffic Management. We argue and we want to show that a *UAV will complete its mission safely*. In our example we do not examine all safety cases. We will consider that the mission is "safe" if major identified risks (collision, loss of critical functions) for the UAV are managed.

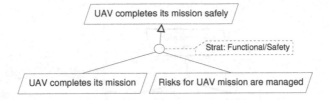

Fig. 4. Decomposition of the first claim according to the Functional/Safety strategy

So, the first claim decomposition (see Fig. 4) which follows a strategy we call *Functional/Safety strategy*, gives two sub-claims: a functional one (*UAV completes its mission*) and a safety one (*Risks for UAV mission are managed*). If we continue the decomposition of the latter claim, we list the identified risks that will be considered in the argumentation. In our case, the risks of collision and the risks to lose a critical capacity (communication, computer, inertial measurement unit ...).

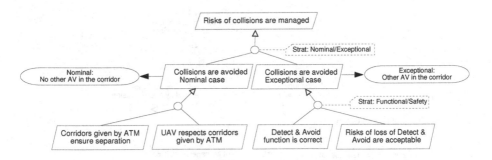

Fig. 5. Decomposition of the risks of collisions claim

The risks of collision, for instance, can again be decomposed following the different ways to prevent collision depending on the context, as illustrated by Fig. 5. Here, we follow a strategy we call *Nominal/Exceptional* that allows to distinguish between the nominal collision avoidance guaranteed by the aerial corridors (given by Air Traffic Management), and the exceptional collision avoidance, ensured by a specific emergency procedure (based on the so-called *Detect & Avoid function*). We apply the Functional/Safety strategy on the emergency avoidance, which means the risks of loss of the function must be managed.

To illustrate a formal decomposition of claims, we can consider the claim *Detect and Avoid function is correct*, as illustrated by Fig. 6. The formal definition of the claim is given by the LTL formula:

$$[C] \qquad G(d_{obstacle} < d_{min}) \rightarrow ((d_{obstacle} \neq 0) \; U \; (d_{obstacle} > d_{min}))$$

where $d_{obstacle}$ represents the distance to an obstacle, d_{min}, is the threshold of emergency avoidance, G (respectively U) is the always (respectively until) LTL operator.

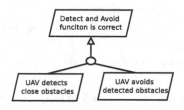

Fig. 6. Decomposition of Detect and Avoid function

The formal definition of the two sub-claims is given by the two following LTL formulas:

[C1] $G((d_{obstacle} < d_{min}) \rightarrow detect)$

[C2] $G(detect \rightarrow ((d_{obstacle} \neq 0) \ U \ (d_{obstacle} > d_{min})))$

In order to validate the refinement, we have to prove that $C1 \wedge C2 \rightarrow C$, which is obviously true.

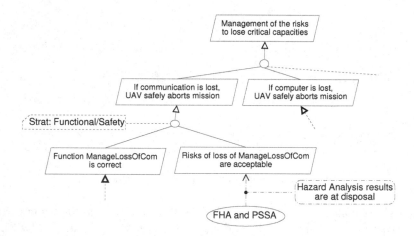

Fig. 7. Decomposition of the risks of loss of communications

The management of the risks to lose critical capacities are decomposed according to the identified critical capacities. Fig. 7 shows an excerpt of the corresponding claim decomposition diagram: we consider two sub-claims dealing with the communication between the pilot or the ground station, and the computer. In the context of our in-house experimental system embedded on board of Onera's UAV, we identified a function `ManageLossOfCom`, the role of which is to safely abort the mission in the case of loss of communication with the pilot or the ground station. The application of the *Functional/Safety* strategy to the claim concerning the loss of communication gives two sub-claims: a functional one stating that the function `ManageLossOfCom` is correct, and a safety one claiming that the risks of loss of this function are acceptable. The Functional

Hazard Assessment (FHA) of our experimental system identified a severity for each failure mode of this function, and each flight mode (automatic or manual) of the UAV [15]. Safety requirements were then derived and assessed using the formal modeling language AltaRica and associated tools, as part of the Preliminary System Safety Assessment (PSSA). These analyses are referred to in the argumentation as a witness which validates that the risks of loss of `ManageLossOfCom` are acceptable.

4 ForSALE Support Environment

To experiment our argumentation approach, we have developed the ForSALE environment as sketched on figure 8. It has been built up by a smooth integration of two main tools which are:

- the Objectiver requirement editor supporting the KAOS approach. It is used to edit and display AND/OR argumentation trees;
- the model-checker NuSMV which is used both to check the validity of formal refinement operations if any, and to check the correctness of the developed argumentations.

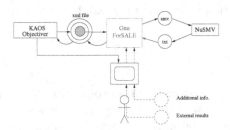

Fig. 8. ForSALE support environment

The integration is made on the basis of a communication by file between the internal/external data representations used by Objectiver and NuSMV. This requires some conversions between these representations and a command interface. All of these has been developed using Gnu EMACS-LISP which is distributed with a very rich text manipulation library.

- Objectiver uses a xml internal representation. A part of it is used to implement the argumentation model and have it displayed "for free" by the tool;
- the input interface of the NuSMV checker is text files following the SMV syntax;
- the output of NuSMV are pure text files that are analyzed by ForSALE. The results are communicated to the end user, and, if he agrees, they are introduced as enrichments of the xml internal representation.

ForSALE environment is open which means that it can be used to integrate results produced by various tools. It is continuously under the control of the end user, and a usual way to proceed is to check and/or introduce a result of an elementary verification, and to check its propagation upwards in the argumentation model. So she may use ForSALE to experiment various argumentation scenarios:

- from a given refinement level (*i.e.*, a given claim and all its subclaims until the leaf claims) all the claims are formalised (by means of LTL formulas). In this case, the NuSMV part of ForSALE is used to check the validity of the refinement for the corresponding sub-tree of the argumentation (laying on the semantics of refinement presented in [9]). The result (either success or failure of the verification) is stored in the KAOS argumentation model to be used later in the verification of the argumentation;
- a safety verification result has been obtained by using an external tool. The end user may decide to introduce it as a valid argument in the model;
- the argumentation tree may be globally checked. If each final goal is a valid argument, and if the refinement semantics is respected, then the global argumentation is verified. If some final arguments are missing then the global argumentation is valid provided that these missing arguments can be proved valid. If the refinement relation between arguments is not followed then the global argumentation is definitely not valid.

5   Related Work

The work presented in this paper is at the crossroads of several technical domains which are rather intensively explored: requirement specification and analysis, safety cases development and analysis, formal methods. In our approach, all of those aim at feeding or supporting argumentation.

Our argumentation framework has been partially inspired by the seminal work on this topic by Toulmin [14]. The notion of claim, reason, evidence and warrant are indeed used as such in our approach. Nevertheless, due to the safety target domain and its constraints, we do not need the most general concepts like qualifier, stating the strength of an argument or rebuttal which introduces controversial arguments.

Existing works already try to combine results coming from several of the mentioned domains, for example:

- the developments around the Goal Structuring Notation GSN. It is clear (see for example [5]) that the community around this notation is very active and becomes numerous. Even though the notation was an initial motivation (see [16] for example), the very design of systems and related safety concerns are major topics and motivate the development of notation based and properties oriented tools. Our work aims at extending these approaches in the direction of argumentation engineering;

- requirement expression and formal analysis [8], [9], [12]; unlike in the GSN approaches, the refinement operations may be formally verified. The difference with our work is that their approach is mainly focused on the functional correctness of the developed system itself, whereas we address the problem of the correctness of the argumentation about the properties of such a system;
- safety cases formal evaluation. John Rushby clearly address the problem of formal safety evaluation [13] using higher order logic and PVS as support tool. But, even though the argumentation is formally checked, it must be re-built from the sequence of interaction with the user and is not a formal object on which various verification operation can apply;
- arguments manipulation and computation. In [10], the authors focus on the way arguments may be computed to assist the elaboration of a decision. The approach is formally supported by predicates logic. Nevertheless, it is totally unrelated with any system development approach.

6 Conclusion and Future Work

The work we have presented in this paper is totally driven by the objective of developing a clear, convincing, formal, and verifiable argumentation. Our concern is not to propose novative concepts or solutions in the area of system requirement engineering or safety assessment which are matters of specialists. It is instead to exploit results obtained in these domains to feed the development of an argumentation which is, for us, a first class object. A meta-model has been proposed to support the many aspects of this object. Moreover a formal semantics, based on LTL, has been developed to found a calculus allowing to tackle the problems of validity and completion of an argumentation.

One important goal is to relate the development of an argumentation with the other activities taking place in the engineering of a system. Our claim is that this link must be done as soon as possible in the development process, viz. during the requirement phase, even if the data which are to be processed (the so-called witnesses, the justification of elementary arguments) will be obtained at the other end of the cycle. Supporting this idea, we elaborate around the notion of a development strategy which entails the construction of an argumentation.

Several directions are still open for future works. Concerning strategies for example, it will be interesting to consider the way the structure of an argumentation part can be obtained "for free" as a consequence of applying a development strategy. What we have observed also is that we need sometimes to express some dependencies between claims that are stronger than pure compositional one. For example a claim may be set *before* another one. So we are considering the introduction of a precedence relation between claims in our meta-model. "Pretty" presentation of an argumentation should be also a major concern as we must keep in mind that the ultimate objective is to convince, not a specialist of temporal logic, but a certification authority instead, that the properties of a system are met. And finally, our approach must be validated by addressing significant case studies as we started to do with a part of the UAV insertion problem.

References

1. Bishop, P., Bloomfield, R.: A Methodology for Safety Case Development. In: The Sixth Safety-critical Systems Symposium, Birmingham, UK (1998)
2. Bresciani, R., Perini, A., Giorgini, P., Giunchiglia, F., Mylopoulos, J.: Tropos: An agent-oriented software development methodology. Autonomous Agents and Multi-Agent Systems 8, 203–236 (2004)
3. Cavada, R., Cimatti, A., Jochim, C.A., Keighren, G., Olivetti, E., Pistore, M., Roveri, M., Tchaltsev, A.: NuSMV User Manual. FBK-irst (2006), http://nusmv.fbk.eu/NuSMV
4. Safety case development manual. Technical Report, Eurocontrol, DAP/SSH/091 (2006)
5. The Goal Structuring Notation Website - University of York, http://www.goalstructuringnotation.info
6. Kelly, T., Weaver, R.: The Goal Structuring Notation – A Safety Argument Notation. In: Dependable Systems and Networks 2004 Workshop on Assurance (2004)
7. van Lamswerde, A.: Requirements engineering, From System Goals to UML Models to Software Specifications. Wiley (2009)
8. Letier, E., Kramer, J., Magee, J., Uchitel, S.: Fluent Temporal Logic for Discrete-Time Event-Based Models. In: ESEC/FSE 2005 - 5th Joint Meeting of the the European Software Engineering Conference and the ACM SIGSOFT Symposium on the Foundations of Software Engineering (2005)
9. Letier, E., van Lamsweerde, A.: Deriving Operational Software Specifications from System Goals. In: FSE 2002 - 10th International Symposium on the Foundation of Software Engineering (2002)
10. Morge, M., Mancarella, P.: Modèle d'argumentation concret pour le raisonnement pratique. Actes des Journées Francophones Planification Décision Apprentissage pour la Conduite des Systèmes, JFPDA 2007 (2007)
11. Objectiver, a power tool to engineer your Technical and Business Requirements, http://www.objectiver.com
12. Rifaut, A., Massonet, P., Molderez, J.-F., Ponsard, C., Stadnik, P., van Lamsweerde, A., Van Hung, T.: FAUST: formal analysis using specification tools. In: Proceedings of 11th IEEE International Requirements Engineering Conference (2003)
13. Rushby, J.: A safety-case approach for certifying adaptive systems. In: AIAA Infotech@Aerospace Conference (2009)
14. Toulmin, S.: The Uses of Argument. Cambridge University Press (1969)
15. Toussaint, B.: Safety analysis of a U.A.V helicopter, by modelling, simulation, and formal methods. Master's thesis, ONERA/ISAE (2010)
16. Weaver, R., Fenn, J., Kelly, T.: A pragmatic approach to reasoning about the assurance of safety arguments. In: 8th Australian Workshop on Safety Critical Systems and Software, SCS 2003 (2003)

Electronic Reliability Estimation:
How Reliable Are the Results?

Nuno Silva and Rui Lopes

Critical Software S.A, Parque Industrial de Taveiro, Lote 48, 3045-504, Coimbra, Portugal
{nsilva,rmlopes}@criticalsoftware.com

Abstract. The development of Safety Critical Systems requires the compliance to several safety standards and regulations. Since, most of the times, human life is at stake, it is crucial to fully understand the behaviour of the system being developed in order to predict and avoid any potential deadly failures. The system shall be therefore resilient and reliable.

The understanding of such systems is not an easy task. Safety Critical Systems are, nowadays, large-scale and complex systems that require a methodological approach in order to fully comprehend all its functionalities and interactions. Several reliability analyses are performed in the development of such systems. The reliability analysis of all electronic equipment is one of them. The ability to predict the failure profile of electronic components is essential to design the system and plan maintenance activities.

This paper presents the preliminary reliability estimation activities of an electronic system designed for a large-scale and complex safety critical system. The standards and methodologies followed are described as well as the tools used to support the activities. Finally, the estimation results and a list of considerations regarding the activities performed are presented.

Keywords: Reliability, Estimation, MIL-Hdbk-217F, MTTF.

1 Introduction

The preliminary reliability activities subject of this paper aimed to estimate the mean time to failure (MTTF) of three Printed Circuit Boards (PCBs) still at design phase in order to provide feedback to the engineering design team. The three PCBs are a completely new design for a Safety Critical System and there are no old PCBs with historical failure data that can be used as a baseline to perform the reliability estimates. Furthermore, since the PCBs are still at design phase, no accelerated life testing is yet possible at this stage. The estimation performed has been based in the military standard MIL-Hdbk-217F [1], with the support of Reliasoft™ tool "Lambda Predict" [2] and its associated database "PartLibraries.org". The outcomes of this activity provided the design team valuable information about their design decisions and will trigger corrective actions that might be required to increase the boards' reliability and achieve the reliability requirements. Given that the PCBs will be integrated in a large complex system, the reliability results may trigger modifications in the overall system

F. Ortmeier and P. Daniel (Eds.): SAFECOMP 2012 Workshops, LNCS 7613, pp. 319–327, 2012.
© Springer-Verlag Berlin Heidelberg 2012

architecture such as equipment redundancy or implementation of fault tolerance mechanisms. The reliability concepts definition used in this paper are aligned with the ones presented in [3].

2   Reliability Estimation – Methodology, Case Study and Tools

The most important factor for a valuable Reliability Estimation is the source of input data. The input data may be acquired or generated using several methods. An overview of some of the possibilities that shall be considered is presented hereafter:

- Field data: One can estimate the reliability of a new electronic board based on the field data collected of a similar board already operating under similar conditions. According to industry experts, this is one of the best approaches to estimate reliability. This is only possible if a correct maintenance process has been followed throughout the years of operation of the boards. This implies a correct identification and logging of every failure, time and operation conditions.
- Accelerated Life Testing: This method applies stress testing to several units of the system being analysed and records all the failures detected from these tests. This method is usually performed at a later design phase where units have already being built and target tests can be performed. Accelerated Life Testing usually requires proper equipment (e.g. test chambers) that allows creating the necessary conditions for the stress tests (e.g. temperature variations, moisture and humidity variations, vibrations, etc).
- Reliability standards: Whenever the design of the system is at an early stage and no previous similar systems exist, the preliminary reliability estimation shall be conducted following a specific reliability standard that provides guidance with respect to the factors that influence reliability as well as standard failure rates that can be used with a certain degree of confidence.

Given the characteristics of the system in question and the project lifecycle, the reliability estimation performed has been based in one of the most common standards used in the industry: the military standard MIL-Hdbk-217F.

2.1   Reliability Estimation Methodology

The methodology followed to perform the preliminary Reliability Estimation was based in the "Part Count" method described in the MIL-Hdbk-217F.

The electronic reliability estimation allows predicting the mean time to failure (MTTF) of the system being analysed. The MTTF represents the actual Failure Rate (λ), which is considered constant throughout the time, of each component and is given by:

$$\lambda = \frac{1}{MTTF} \tag{1}$$

In fact, the failure rate value is not constant throughout the components life time as it can be shown by the typical Bathtub curve (see **Fig. 1**) that represents the actual variation of this variable ($h(t)$):

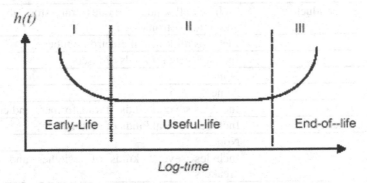

Fig. 1. Typical bathtub curve[1]

However, manufacturers usually use Accelerated Stress Testing (AST) to ensure that when the component leaves the factory it is already in Section II of the Bathtub Curve, in which the failure rate is constant and therefore also the MTTF. The reliability analysis is then performed based on the constant MTTF ($h(SectionII) = \lambda$) provided by the manufacturers and do not extrapolate into Section I and III of the component life time.

Note also that the term MTTF and mean time between failures (MTBF) are two distinct metrics. In fact, MTBF only becomes meaningful in reparable systems because, by definition, it measures the time between two failures, which necessarily include the mean time to repair (MTTR) the system. Most of manufacturers inaccurately provide the equipment MTTF labelled as MTBF, adding some confusion to the actual definition of the two metrics. Taking in consideration a reparable system with a constant failure rate, the two metrics are related according the following expression:

$$MTBF = MTTF + MTTR \qquad (2)$$

At this stage of the project, the MTTR is not a concern and, therefore, is not part of the estimation process. This paper will only address the MTTF estimation.

Military Handbook: Reliability Prediction of Electronic Equipment (MIL-Hdbk-217F). The military standard MIL-Hdbk-217F [1] was created by the US Department of Defence in order to provide a guideline for electronic reliability estimation. The latest issue of this standard is "Notice 2" (N2) from February 1995. For completeness purposes, the types of components considered by this standard are presented hereafter.

---

[1] Figure presented in [**Error! Reference source not found.**].

Table 1. Type of electronic components considered in MIL-Hdbk-217F

Component	Comments
Microcircuits	Includes all kinds of gates, microcontrollers, memories and integrated circuits
Discrete Semiconductors	Includes all kinds of diodes, transistors, thyristors and optoelectronics
Tubes	Includes all kinds of electronic tubes
Lasers	Includes several kinds of lasers
Resistors	None
Capacitors	None
Inductive Devices	Includes several kinds of transformers and coils
Rotating Devices	Includes several kinds of motors
Relays	None
Switches	Includes several kinds of switches and circuit breakers
Connectors	None
Interconnection assemblies	None
Connections	None
Meters	Includes several kinds of meters and panels
Quartz Crystals	None
Lamps	None
Electronic Filters	None
Fuses	None
Miscellaneous Parts	Includes other components that are not categorised as any of the previous types

The standard also defines sub-types for each type of component whenever found necessary but, for clarification purposes, are not presented here. As can be observed, the types of components are somehow outdated with respect to the evolution of electronics in the latest years. Some considerations regarding this list are presented in chapter4.

Parts Count. This method is defined in the MIL-Hdbk-217F and defines the physical and application factors that influence the reliability of electronic components. The mathematical expressions that correlate the referred factors are also provided.

The input for applying this method is the "Bill Of Materials" (BOM) of a specific electronic board or system. Once the list of components is set, one can estimate the failure rate of each component by:

- Categorising the component in one of the categories presented in Table 1;
- Characterising the component with respect to the several factors that are applicable to the selected category (Table 2 presents some of the considered factors).

After estimating the failure rate of each component, the failure rate of the complete electronic board or system is computed by adding the failure rates of all its components.

For completeness purposes, some of the factors considered by the standard to estimate reliability are presented hereafter. This is not an exhaustive list but allows presenting a representative subset of the factors that are in question.

Table 2. Factors that influence electronic components reliability

Type of factor	Factor	Comments
Physical factor	Number of pins	None
	Quality	Related to manufacturing process
	Rated Voltage/Power	None
	Construction or Package type	None
	Technology	TTL, Bipolar CMOS, etc
Application factor	Environment	Ground, Airborne, etc
	Ambient Temperature	Used to calculate Junction Temperature
	Case Temperature	Used to calculate Junction Temperature
	Power Dissipation	None
	Power Stress	None

2.2   Case Study

This paper is based on a Preliminary Reliability Analysis activity performed on three electronic boards (hereafter referred as "Board A", "Board B" and "Board C") that will be part of a large-scale system for the railway industry, that must comply with the appropriate safety critical standards (e.g. [4]). The complete infrastructure will be constituted by several other boards, which are also being designed at this stage. Boards A, B and C implement safety critical functions and are therefore subject of an initial preliminary reliability analysis. These boards are also at design phase and the analysis aims to provide an initial assessment of their reliability. The design team shall use the results to assess if any design changes are required or advisable before concluding the design phase. Hereafter is presented a summary of the case study:

- Number of electronic boards: 3 (Board A, Board B and Board C);
- Domain: Railway;
- Environment: Closed facilities, compatible with the MIL-Hdbk-217F "Ground, Fixed" definition;
- System: Large-scale and complex system, which interacts with other systems and operates safety critical functionalities;
- Design: The complete system is being designed at this stage with little or no legacy components or sub-systems.

In order to understand the complexity of the electronic boards that are part of this case study, the following table presents the number of total components and unique components of each board. The "unique components" count is made by the component reference. If one specific component (e.g. analog gate) is present in three different locations of the board, the "# of components" is incremented by three but the "# of unique components" is incremented by only one.

Table 3. Boards components metrics

Metrics	Board A	Board B	Board C
Total number of components	860	1100	650
Total number of Unique components	171	202	137

2.3 Tools

The reliability activity has been performed with the support of the following Reliasoft™ tools:

- Lambda Predict 3
- PartLibraries.org

The "Lambda Predict" tool supports the MIL-Hdbok-217F standard, allowing saving considerable effort by performing the required reliability calculations. The entire list of component types (Table 1) and sub-types is available as well as their respective modelling options (Table 2).

The "PartLibraries.org" is a database that integrates with "Lambda Predict" that provides the reliability of several electronic components currently at the market (including the following databases: EPRD-97, NPRD-95 and MIL-M-38510). The usage of such databases provides two main advantages: saves the effort of modelling a "generic component" and provides a more accurate failure rate than the one that would be obtained via the modelling of a generic component.

3 Results

Hereafter are presented the results of the reliability analysis for Board A, Board B and Board C, with the support of Reliasoft™ tools. As described in previous sections, the MTTF was the only metric estimated in this activity.

Given the methodology used (Parts Count, from MIL-Hdbk-217F), the total number of components has a considerable weight in the overall reliability. Nonetheless note that despite the fact that Board B is constituted by significantly more components than Board A, its MTTF is higher than the first. This indicates that the selection of the components has an impact on the reliability estimates. Table 5 presents the relationship between the total number of components and the number of unique components observed for each board.

Table 4. Reliability results

Board	# of components	MTTF (hours)	Average MTTF per component (hours)
A	860	39360	33,88E+6
B	1100	41620	45,78E+6
C	650	57100	37,12E+6

Table 5. Total components and unique components relationship

Board	# of components per # of unique components	Average
A	5,03	
B	5,45	5,25
C	4,74	

The accuracy of the reliability estimation is difficult to evaluate. To perform such evaluation, it is essential to identify indicators that contribute (or not) to the accuracy of the results. The following indicators might be used for this purpose:

- Number of assumptions made during the components modelling task;
- Ratio between generic components modelled and database components used.

The number of assumptions made in the electronic components modelling task provides a good indicator on the accuracy of the model with respect to reality. As previously referred, the usage of database (DB) components also provides an added confidence in the model since the data required to model the electronic component has already been confirmed, collected and stored. Table 6 presents the two indicators. Further considerations regarding this subject are presented in section4.

Table 6. Accuracy indicators

Board	# of assumptions	# of unique DB components used	# of unique DB components used per # of unique components (%)	# of DB components used per total # of components (%)
A	19	24	14,0%	10,8%
B	24	36	17,8%	13,4%
C	25	14	10,2%	19,4%
TOTAL	68	74	14,5%	14,0%

4   Limitations and Lessons Learned

A list of considerations has been identified during the execution of the Preliminary Reliability Estimation and is presented hereafter:

- Parts Count method does not consider the possibility of electronic redundancy: The reliability of a system is calculated based on the premise that the system fails if any of its constituting components fails, i.e. the system is always modelled as a serial system. This may not be correct since an electronic board may have redundant electronic blocks to increase its fault tolerance and reliability. Whenever this happens, the reliability engineer must deviate from the standard method by calculating the reliability of the parallel sub-system and including the resultant system as "one part" in the Parts Count method.
- Types of components are outdated: The MIL-Hdbk-217F is based on previous standards developed by the US Department of Defence. Although several types and sub-types of components are considered, the list is outdated with respect with the state-of-the-art electronics (e.g. ASICs, FPGAs). This becomes a potential source of deviation between the estimated reliability and reality.
- Parameters required to correctly model the components are difficult to obtain: This is more relevant in a preliminary analysis. Nominal parameters must be used too often, which represents a potential source of deviation between the estimated reliability and reality.
- Databases of component models have a limited number of components: The aim in using databases is to provide more accurate component models than the ones obtained manually and reducing effort. As shown in **Table 6**, only around 16% of the components have been identified in the components database. Therefore, the benefit of using the database was reduced.

5   Conclusions

MIL-Hdbk-217F parameters required to model components are questionable. The reliability of the components is deeply affected by environment parameters such as temperature. Although this is not questionable, the lack of parameters related to other environmental factors (e.g. moisture, humidity) may represent an important deviation between the estimation and reality.

Reliability estimations based on MIL-Hdbk-217F are rather conservative. Field data from previous electronic boards present higher reliability figures. With newer and more modern electronic components, the expectation was that the reliability of the boards should be higher. More recent standards have been developed to address this gap between reliability estimations and field data such as the RIAC 217Plus [5]. Although several modifications have been performed (type of components, physical and application characteristics), field data is still the most reliable source of data reliability estimation.

The effort required to model electronic components based on the MIL-Hdbk-217F standard is also high. More recent standards such as the RIAC 217Plus [5] tackle this issue by reducing the amount of parameters to be filled by the reliability engineer.

Based on the presented conclusions, the results from a preliminary reliability estimation activity must be always analysed with a critical view. Several experts consider that the difference between what is obtained via MIL-Hdbk-217F and the data collected from the field is so significant that the estimation exercise has very low value (see [6]). Although the reliability figure obtained via MIL-Hdbk-217F may not be as accurate as desired, it provides a good guideline to the design team, especially when deciding between more than one design or alternative components. Also, more recent standards should be considered instead of the somehow outdated MIL-Hdbk-217F. The reliability estimation shall be revisited in later project phases when data from accelerated life testing activities becomes available.

6 Future Work

New Reliability Estimation projects are currently being executed. For these projects, the RIAC 217Plus [5] has been selected instead of the MIL-Hdbk-217F. A similar study to the one presented in this paper will be performed, highlighting the advantages and disadvantages, similarities and differences of using each standard from the reliability engineer point of view.

Another activity is to extend the study to more than two domain areas and to a larger amount of boards studied. Currently, we used data from railway and aeronautics studies and these domains have their own specificities, in terms of environmental factors and certification requirements for example, that other domains might deal in a different way.

Acknowledgement. This work has been partially supported by the project CRITICAL Software Technology for an Evolutionary Partnership (CRITICAL-STEP, http://www.critical-step.eu), Marie Curie Industry-Academia Partnerships and Pathways (IAPP) number 230672, within the context of the EU Seventh Framework Programme (FP7).

References

1. Military Handbook: Reliability Prediction of Electronic Equipment – Notice 2, MIL-Hdbk-217F-N2 (February 1995)
2. Lambda Predict User's Manual, Reliasoft (2009)
3. O'Connor, P., Kleyner, A.: Practical Reliability Engineering, 5th edn. John Wiley (2012)
4. CENELEC EN 50126: Railway applications — The specification and demonstration of Reliability, Availability, Maintainability and Safety (RAMS) (1999-2007)
5. Handbook of 217Plus^{TM} Reliability Prediction Model, RIAC-HDBK-217Plus, RIAC (May 26, 2006)
6. Why you cannot predict Electronic Product Reliability, Lambda Consulting, 2012 ARS – Europe (March 2012)
7. Pattavina, J.S., Harris Corporation: Tutorial of Analyzing High Reliability: Part 1 (October 2004)

Model-Based Assessment
of Multi-region Electric Power Systems
Showing Heterogeneous Characteristics

Silvano Chiaradonna[1], Felicita Di Giandomenico[1], and Nicola Nostro[1,2,*]

[1] ISTI-CNR, Pisa, Italy
{silvano.chiaradonna,felicita.digiandomenico,nicola.nostro}@isti.cnr.it
[2] Università degli Studi di Firenze, Firenze, Italy
nicola.nostro@unifi.it

Abstract. Analysis of complex systems, as critical infrastructures are especially because of interdependent structure and behavior of their composing parts, is typically tackled in a number of refinements steps. Simplistic models of the system under analysis are initially set-up, then gradually extended to encompass more and more sophisticated phenomena and behavior which lead the model to be more adherent to reality. This was the process followed in a series of studies, conducted by (part of) the authors of this paper, targeting the analysis of Electric Power Systems (EPS) to understand the impact of interdependencies between the electric power grid and of the cyber control infrastructure in critical scenarios. Specifically, from the original model accounting only for a regional EPS, we moved to a more sophisticated and realistic multi-region organization, first characterized by homogeneous conditions of the network parameters and of the cost associated to power losses and to power generation and subsequently enriched with some aspects of heterogeneity. Here, we go further with exploring other aspects of heterogeneity and related impact on black-outs indicators, to both prove the feasibility of the developed modeling framework and to assess the relevance of accounting for such heterogeneity.

Keywords: Stochastic Modeling, Electric Power System, Infrastructures Dependencies, Blackout-size Assessment.

1 Introduction

Electric power utilities are among the most critical infrastructures providing services highly impacting on everyday life of modern and future society. Therefore, understanding the vulnerabilities and threats they are exposed to, as well as their impact on the offered services, is a priority in order to take appropriate measures to mitigate their effects. After major black-outs in Europe and North America occurred at the beginning of years 2000s, several research initiatives

---

* Corresponding author.

F. Ortmeier and P. Daniel (Eds.): SAFECOMP 2012 Workshops, LNCS 7613, pp. 328–339, 2012.

have been started, also as International level efforts, to investigate practical methodologies, tools and measurement metrics to analyze Electric Power Systems (EPS) [3]. One research direction is focusing on understanding the impact of dependencies between the electrical grid and the cyber infrastructure controlling the electrical grid in EPS, since they have proved to be responsible of many cascading, escalating and common mode failures.

The authors of this paper have contributed to such research on the analysis of interdependencies in the last few years, starting with activities conducted in the context of the EU project CRUTIAL [9]. An innovative, modular EPS modeling approach, that considers separately the two constituting EPS infrastructures, but takes into account their interdependencies and allows to assess the impact of reciprocal failures, has been developed [8,4,5]. The study evolved from the modeling of a single EPS region to a more complex and realistic model addressing EPS organized as a set of interacting regions [6]. A variety of critical scenarios have been exercised as case-studies to demonstrate the applicability and usability of the developed modeling framework. Although the models were developed as much as possible in a parametric and general form, so as to be able to account for a variety of real EPS scenarios, the applications of the modeling framework initially addressed only homogeneous scenarios, from the point of view of the entities of the power grid, and considering uniformly distributed random failures affecting such elements. Only recently, in [7], some aspects of heterogeneity have been accounted for in the analyzed scenarios, namely in two forms: the presence of loads of different criticality (from the point of view of consequences of power loss) and the option of different failure rates for the power lines. However, the choice of which loads had different criticality, as well as which power lines had different failure rate, was made randomly. Although relevant to get measures representative of average trends of the power delivered by EPS in scenarios of interest for the user and/or for the service provider, the random choice is not appropriate when the interest is on phenomena affecting specific components of the grid. This is what we have pursued in this paper, where we conducted analyses considering aspects of heterogeneity characterizing specific components of the grid topology, as well as failure of specific power lines, and not resorting to random choices. We therefore extended and enriched the analyses performed in previous studies and showed the applicability of our EPS modeling framework to deal with heterogeneous load criticality and failure events affecting a number of specific grid elements.

The paper is organized as follows. In Section 2, a brief summary of the multi-region EPS modeling framework, the analyses conducted in this paper are based on, is provided. This section constitutes the background to understand the developed analyses, covering also the related work. The next Section 3 introduces the grid topology used for experimenting the modeling framework under heterogeneous conditions, the measures evaluated and the scenarios considered in terms of loads criticality and failed power lines. Then, the analysis results are shown and commented in Section 4. Finally, conclusions and indications for future work are sketched in Section 5.

2   Overview of the Multi-region EPS Model

The multi-region EPS modeling framework used in this study has been presented in [6], as an evolution of the previously developed regional solution to deal with electrical grid topologies organized and controlled as a set of interacting regions. To better understand the analyses conducted in this paper, we briefly recall it.

As already mentioned in the Introduction, EPS systems are composed by two major parts: the electrical infrastructure (EI) and its control information infrastructure (ITCS).

EI includes all the electrical elements that, for the purpose of modeling, are logically distinguished in: *generators*, which produce the energy, the *power lines*, through which the produced energy is conveyed to reach *loads*, which are different types of end-users using the produced energy. Some simplifying assumptions have been made to represent the power flow through the transmission grid, following the same approach used in [1,2,11]. Therefore, the state and the evolution of the transmission grid are described by the active power flow F on the lines and the active power P at the nodes (generators, loads or substations), which satisfy linear equations for a direct current (DC) load flow approximation of the alternate current (AC) system.

The ITCS control has been modeled through the two subsystems hierarchically composing the teleoperation system: i) LCS (Local Control System) which guarantees the correct operation of a node equipment and reconfigures the node in case of breakdown of some apparatus, and ii) RTS (Regional Telecontrol System), which monitors all the electrical components of its assigned region and takes reconfiguration actions to restore the functionality of the grid in case of breakdowns suitable involving the whole region and possibly also RTS of neighboring regions, if necessary. The two considered reconfiguration strategies, performed by LCS and RTS respectively, are:

- $\mathcal{RS}_1()$, to represent the effect of the reactions of ITCS to an event that has compromised the electrical equilibrium of EI when only the state local to the involved EI components is considered. Given the limited information required by this reconfiguration, performed by the LCS controlling the electrical apparatus affected by the failure, it is considered very fast (actually, instantaneous) in the model.
- $\mathcal{RS}_2()$, to represent the effect of the reactions of ITCS to an event that has compromised the electrical equilibrium in EI when the state global to all the EI system under the control of ITCS is considered. This reconfiguration, performed by the RTS of the affected region, requires knowledge of the global state of the region and therefore reacts in a longer time.

The output values of $\mathcal{RS}_1()$ and $\mathcal{RS}_2()$ (i.e., the new values for F and P) are derived by solving different Linear Programming (LP) problems, based on the overall grid.

The EPS organization in multi regions requires a coordination among them when computing a reconfiguration spanning a number of regions. A reconfiguration algorithm considering multiple regions has been developed, based on the principle that first a new electrical equilibrium is attempted inside the region where the failure occurred and, only in case this is not possible, neighbor regions are called to contribute. In this second case, a number of steps are performed, possibly limited by some constraints tied to costs of keeping the electric grid under unstable equilibrium. If more than one step is allowed, at each step after the first one (where only a minimum set of regions is considered based on the current configuration and on the involved reconfiguration function, $\mathcal{RS}_1()$ or $\mathcal{RS}_2()$), additional regions of the grid are involved according to the results of the LP problem applied on the set of regions considered at the previous step. Details on the algorithms implemented by $\mathcal{RS}_1()$ and $\mathcal{RS}_2()$ are in [6], where a few cost functions the LP problem is based on are also described. Typically, $\mathcal{RS}_1()$ is based on the grid configuration immediately before the occurrence of the disruption and $\mathcal{RS}_2()$ is based on the nominal grid configuration, the initial configuration at time 0 (e.g. if the power demand is constant).

The implementation of the EPS framework just recalled has been carried out using the SAN formalism [14] and the Möbius tool [10]. Atomic models for each of the main EI and ITCS components, also accounting for interdependencies and propagation of failure phenomena, have been developed and connected (*Join* and *Rep* operators) through some shared places of the SAN model, that represent part of the states of the EPS. This modular approach makes the modeling framework general and flexible to accommodate the characteristics of various EPS, theoretically allowing the modeling and analysis of any possible EPS configurations. Details about the developed SAN models are omitted for lack of space, since they are fully described in the publications previously referred.

3   The EPS Configuration under Analysis, Measures of Interest and Scenarios

The IEEE Reliability Test System - 1996 (RTS-96) (described in [12,13]) was created by a commitee of power system experts in order to provide a standardized test grid for different power system reliability evaluation methodologies. The test grid can include many diffreent configurations and it was already chosen as representative power grid topology in our previous papers to demonstrate the features of the modeling frameworks we have incrementally developed. Therefore, to maintain continuity with such studies, also in view of possible comparisons of the obtained results, the RTS-96 in the configuration shown in Figure 1 has been chosen to derive the analysis results shown in the next section. It is composed of 42 nodes (of which 10 are generators and 17 are loads) and 56 lines. It has been structured into four interconnected regions, without following any specific criterion, but in a rather arbitrary way just for the purpose of exercising a multi-regional power grid. In the figure, each region is enclosed into a dashed box.

In the figure, the label "P_i/P_i^{max}" associated to the generators (circles) represents the initial (active) power P_i and the maximum power that the generator i can supply P_i^{max}. The label "D_i" associated to the loads (squares) represents the power demand (constant over time) of the load i. The label "F_{ij}/F_{ij}^{max}"

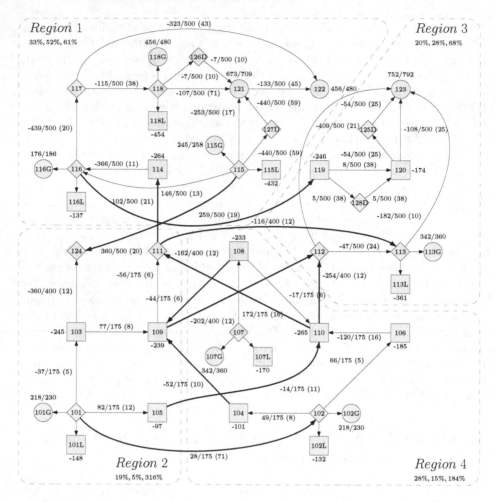

Fig. 1. Diagram of the EI grid corresponding to the RTS96 test grid

associated to the lines represents the initial power flow F_{ij} through the line (i, j) and the maximum power flow that a transmission line can carry F_{ij}^{max}. A negative F_{ij} value means that the current is flowing in the opposite direction of the corresponding arrow. Also, in brackets it is shown the susceptance of each line. The percentages under the region name represent, in the order, the percentage of the (active) power demand of the region with respect to power demand of the overall grid, the percentage of power provided by the region with respect to power demand of the overall grid, and the percentage of the maximum power of the region needed to satisfy the power demand of the region (i.e., the ratio between the whole power demand of the region and the maximum power that can be supplied by the region itself).

Concerning the measures assessed in the evaluation as indicators of the blackout size, they are: $P_{UD}(0, l)$ and $P_{UD_h}(0, l)$, defined as the mean of the percentage of power demand $UD(0, l)$ that is not met in the interval $(0, l)$ for the whole grid and for load h, respectively. In the following analyses, we considered the interval of 1 day, indicated as $(0, 1d)$.

Several scenarios have been considered based on the grid topology in Figure 1, each focusing on specific combinations of loads criticality and power lines failures. The heterogeneity aspect that has been addressed in the analysis pertains the loads. Specifically, we have considered that one or more loads may have different criticality with respect to the others, where criticality is defined in terms of the cost associated with undelivered power demand with respect to the requested one, which leads shedding operations to be performed on the critical loads only after the shedding of the non critical loads involved in the reconfiguration has been performed without resulting in an electrical equilibrium. Concerning power lines, we have assumed the failure of one or more power lines. The heterogeneity dimension accounted here was already taken into account in [7], but the choice of how to allocate the heterogeneity is different. In fact, in [7], randomness was the principle followed in assigning the criticality to loads and to select the failed power lines. Here, instead, the loads heterogeneity and the failure of power lines are applied to specific power grid elements, to investigate on power loss in presence of well identified circumstances, useful e.g. to electric operators to understand the robustness of their grid when affected by malfunctions in specific areas of the topology, or to set-up appropriate contractual policies with users requiring specific service conditions. Moreover, as a novel contribution with respect to previous analyses, we have studied the effect of the failure of clusters of power lines, formed by one selected power line in conjunction with neighbor ones, to resemble real situations where a failure propagates along adjacent lines, affecting all of them.

The results have been obtained using the simulator engine of the Möbius tool. The failure event triggering the intervention of the ITCS reconfiguration is a disruption of power lines. Therefore, in the experiments performed, the simulation starts just after the failure of one (or more) power line(s), and lasts one day (the length of the time window of our transient analysis). Each result is obtained by executing 80000 simulation runs (batches). The confidence level was set to 0.95. The confidence intervals obtained for the results are shown in the plots, although, for some values, they are very small (similar to points).

4   Analysis Results

This section concentrates on the analyses we conducted, applying aspects of heterogeneity on the different scenarios briefly sketched in the previous section. As a general note, to improve readability only a subset of the power lines or of the loads are shown in the following figures, selected among those that have a significant impact on the assessed measure of interest. Moreover, the case of no critical load is always included, for comparison purposes.

Figure 2 shows the results of the mean percentage of undelivered load at varying the (single) power line (i, j) that fails (on the x axis). In particular,

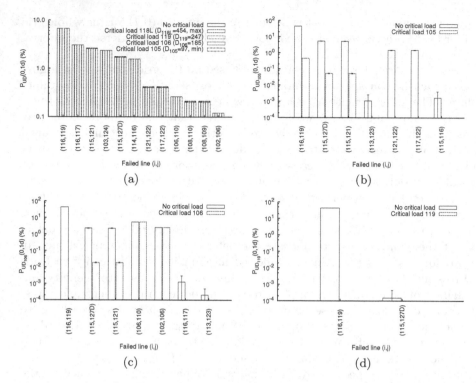

Fig. 2. $P_{UD}(0, 1d)$, at varying the single failed power line, for different critical loads (a). $P_{UD_{105}}(0, 1d)$ (b), $P_{UD_{106}}(0, 1d)$ (c) and $P_{UD_{119}}(0, 1d)$ (d), at varying the single failed power line.

Figure 2(a) illustrates the trend of $P_{UD}(0, 1d)$ for the overall grid, in presence of different critical loads. The loads have been chosen so as to include: the one requesting the highest demand (load *118L*), the one requesting the lowest demand (load *105*) and two representative of a medium demand request (loads *119* and *106*). The other three Figures 2(b), 2(c), and 2(d) show the results of $P_{UD_h}(0, 1d)$, for the critical load h (where h assumes respectively the value of *105*, *106*, and *119*). A corresponding figure relative to load *118L* is not shown, since its $P_{UD_{118L}}(0, 1d)$ is always zero, either when it is considered critical or not and whichever be the failed power line.

Figure 2(a) shows that, whatever be the failed power line, considering a different criticality for a specified load does not impact on the percentage of undelivered power demand of the overall electrical grid, whether the load has a maximum, intermediate, or minimal demand. Instead, looking at the Figures 2(b), 2(c) and 2(d), where the measure of interest is relative to the single load considered critical, it can be observed how the failure of the specific power line impacts differently on the different critical load. As expected, when a load is critical its undelivered demand is in general lower (sometimes zero) with respect to the case when it is not critical. However, there are cases where the loss remains the same when, given the location of the failed power line and the critical load, a new equilibrium cannot be restored without affecting the power demand of that critical load. For example, in Figure 2(c) when the load *106* is critical, the failure of the power lines $(106, 110)$ or $(102, 106)$, does not lead to improve its $P_{UD_{106}}(0, 1d)$ with respect to the case when this load is not critical.

Figure 3 shows how the only failure of the power line $(116, 119)$ has impact on $P_{UD_h}(0, 1d)$, for each load h, both in the case where load h is assumed to be the only critical load in the grid and in the opposite case where all the loads are critical except load h. The same analysis has been performed also focusing on the specific load *119* and showing how the $P_{UD_h}(0, 1d)$ of the other loads changes when the load *119* is the only critical one or the only not critical one; the results are shown in Figure 4. We selected line $(116, 119)$ as the failed power line since, from Figure 2(a), it is the one causing the greatest load loss.

Figure 3 displays the two extremes power losses incurred by each load h when the power line $(116, 119)$ fails, for the two extreme criticality conditions of the load itself. Not surprisingly, when load h is the only non critical one, its demand is always fully undelivered, while in the opposite case its loss significantly decreases.

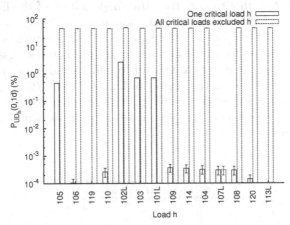

Fig. 3. $P_{UD_h}(0, 1d)$, at varying the load h, when h is the only critical load and when it is the only non-critical load, in case of failure of power line $(116, 119)$ only

Figure 4 shows how the criticality or non criticality of load *119* impacts on the undelivered demand $P_{UD_h}(0, 1d)$ suffered by all the other loads h: it can be observed that for some loads there is almost no influence, but for others (like loads *109* and *114*) the impact is significant.

In order to move towards more realistic scenarios, the next two figures show the results of the analyses performed to evaluate the impact of the failure of a cluster of power lines.

Figure 5 shows the $P_{UD_h}(0, 1d)$, when load h is the critical one or the specific load *119* is the critical one, in presence of the failure of the whole set of power lines directly connected with $(116, 117)$, including $(116, 117)$ itself. The results are compared, in the figure, with the simplest case in which only the line

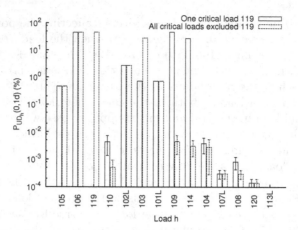

Fig. 4. $P_{UD_h}(0, 1d)$, at varying the load h, when *119* is the only critical load and when it is the only non-critical load, in case of failure of the power line $(116, 119)$ only

$(116, 117)$ fails, to better appreciate the effects of the failure of the cluster of power lines. It is interesting to note that the single failure of the line $(116, 117)$ never impacts on the $P_{UD_h}(0, 1d)$ of each load h when it is critical, while the failure of the power line and of all its neighboring one determines in general a significant loss (leading to total loss for some loads, in some cases). Although the trend is not surprising, the results are useful to understand some characteristics of the grid. For instance, when the cluster of lines fails, the $P_{UD_{101L}}(0, 1d)$ relative to load *101L* is the same both if the load is critical and if it is not critical. This implies that no shedding of the other loads helps in reducing the power loss of the node *101L* when it is critical.

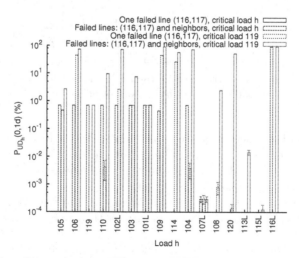

Fig. 5. $P_{UD_h}(0, 1d)$, at varying the load h, for each critical load h, or critical load *119*, in case of failure of one specified single power line $(116, 117)$ only, or of the power line $(116, 117)$ and all its neighboring power lines

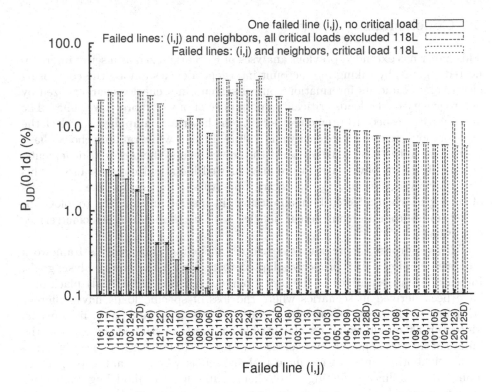

Fig. 6. $P_{UD}(0, 1d)$, at varying the failure of power line (i, j), on the x axis, together with the failure of its neighboring lines, for different criticality conditions of the loads

Figure 6 shows $P_{UD}(0, 1d)$, at varying the failure of power line (i, j), on the x axis, together with its neighboring power lines (e.g., the neighbors of power line $(110, 106)$ are: $(110, 112)$, $(108, 110)$, $(110, 111)$, $(105, 110)$, $(102, 106)$). The analyses have been performed considering three cases: i) the grid has no critical loads and only the power line (i, j) fails; ii) the only critical load is the load *118L* (chosen since, as a result of the analysis illustrated in Figure 2, no single failure of power lines has effect on this load); iii) all the loads are critical except the load *118L*. The last two cases are in presence of simultaneous failure of the power line (i, j) and its neighboring lines.

The first immediate result from this analysis is that the impact of a single power line on the mean power loss $P_{UD}(0, 1d)$ is limited to a small set of power lines only (12 out of the 56 power lines included in the grid), while the failure of clusters of power lines has always a relevant effect. The second comment is that the failure of cluster of power lines (whose dimension varies depending on the number of neighbors of each power line) has, in the great majority of the cases, an impact that is independent from the number of critical loads considered. This is due to the fact that the damages caused by the failed power lines are so substantial that the criticality dimension of the loads becomes almost irrelevant.

5   Conclusions

This paper has extended previous analyses of EPS organized as a set of interconnected regions, by taking into account interdependencies among the composing electrical grid and its information control system, in scenarios characterized by heterogeneity of the loads criticality and failure of one or more power lines. The novelty with respect to previous studies is in the criterion applied to select the grid components for heterogeneity and failure. In fact, while random choices have been made in the past, here we direct the choice on specific power grid elements, to investigate on power loss in presence of well identified circumstances. This kind of analysis is useful, e.g., to electric operators to understand the robustness of their grid when affected by malfunctions in specific areas of the topology, or to set-up appropriate contractual policies with users requiring specific service conditions.

To this purpose, a previously developed modeling and analysis framework has been employed and properly adapted to deal with the new analysis goals. Indicators representatives of the user's perceived forms of (partial) black-outs have been derived in scenarios where the loss of specific loads have different criticality levels, as well as scenarios where failures of specific power lines occur. Moreover, as an additional novel contribution, we have studied the effect of the failure of clusters of power lines, formed by one selected power line in conjunction with neighboring ones, to resemble real situations where a failure propagates along adjacent lines, affecting all of them. Although the modeling framework already included this feature, it has been never exercised on concrete scenarios in previous work. The performed analyses, although limited to the considered scenarios, are successful in showing: i) the ability of the framework to account for heterogeneous characteristics and failure phenomena affecting specific grid elements, and ii) the importance of accounting for these aspects to get accurate results in specific EPS conditions.

Further explorations would be interesting, e.g. in terms of additional heterogeneity aspects to address and indicators of quality of service perceived by users. Actually, we plan extensions of our investigations in these directions.

References

1. Anghel, M., Werley, K.A., Motter, A.E.: Stochastic model for power grid dynamics. In: 40th IEEE Hawaii Int. Conf. on System Sciences (CD-ROM), Waikoloa, Big Island, Hawaii, pp. 113–122 (January 2007)
2. Chen, J., Thorp, J.S., Dobson, I.: Cascading dynamics and mitigation assessment in power system disturbances via a hidden failure model. Int. J. Electr. Power Energy Syst. 27(4), 318–326 (2005)
3. Chiaradonna, S., Di Giandomenico, F., Lollini, P.: Evaluation of Critical Infrastructures: Challenges and Viable Approaches. In: de Lemos, R., Di Giandomenico, F., Gacek, C., Muccini, H., Vieira, M. (eds.) Architecting Dependable Systems V. LNCS, vol. 5135, pp. 52–77. Springer, Heidelberg (2008), http://dx.doi.org/10.1007/978-3-540-85571-2_3

4. Chiaradonna, S., Di Giandomenico, F., Lollini, P.: Assessing the impact of inter-dependencies in electric power systems. International J. System of Systems Engineering 1(3), 367–386 (2009)
5. Chiaradonna, S., Di Giandomenico, F., Lollini, P.: Definition, implementation and application of a model-based framework for analyzing interdependencies in electric power systems. International Journal of Critical Infrastructure Protection 4(1), 24–40 (2011)
6. Chiaradonna, S., Di Giandomenico, F., Nostro, N.: Modeling and analysis of the impact of failures in electric power systems organized in interconnected regions. In: IEEE/IFIP 41st Int. Conf. on Dependable Systems and Networks (DSN 2011), pp. 442–453 (June 2011)
7. Chiaradonna, S., Di Giandomenico, F., Nostro, N.: Analysis of electric power systems accounting for interdependencies in heterogeneous scenarios. In: Ninth European Dependable Computing Conference (EDCC 2012) (May 2012)
8. Chiaradonna, S., Lollini, P., Di Giandomenico, F.: On a modeling framework for the analysis of interdependencies in electric power systems. In: IEEE/IFIP 37th Int. Conf. on Dependable Systems and Networks (DSN 2007), pp. 185–195 (June 2007)
9. CRUTIAL: European Project CRUTIAL - Critical utility infrastructural resilience, http://crutial.erse-web.it
10. Daly, D., Deavours, D.D., Doyle, J.M., Webster, P.G., Sanders, W.H.: Möbius: An Extensible Tool for Performance and Dependability Modeling. In: Haverkort, B.R., Bohnenkamp, H.C., Smith, C.U. (eds.) TOOLS 2000. LNCS, vol. 1786, pp. 332–336. Springer, Heidelberg (2000)
11. Dobson, I., Carreras, B.A., Lynch, V., Newman, D.E.: An initial model for complex dynamics in electric power system blackouts. In: 34th IEEE Hawaii Int. Conf. on System Sciences (CD-ROM), Maui, Hawaii, 9 pages (January 2001)
12. IEEE RTS Task Force of the APM Subcommittee: IEEE reliability test system. IEEE Trans. Power App. Syst. PAS-98(6), 2047–2054 (November 1979)
13. IEEE RTS Task Force of the APM Subcommittee: The IEEE reliability test system - 1996. IEEE Trans. Power Syst. 14(3), 1010–1020 (1999)
14. Sanders, W.H., Meyer, J.F.: Stochastic Activity Networks: Formal Definitions and Concepts. In: Brinksma, E., Hermanns, H., Katoen, J.-P. (eds.) FMPA 2000. LNCS, vol. 2090, pp. 315–343. Springer, Heidelberg (2001)

ERCIM/EWICS/Cyberphysical Systems Workshop

Introduction to the ERCIM/EWICS
Cyberphysical Systems Workshop 2012

Erwin Schoitsch[1] and Amund Skavhaug[2]

[1] AIT Austrian Institute of Technology, Safety & Security Department
Donau-City-Straße 1, TechGate
A-1220 Vienna, Austria
Erwin.schoitsch@ait.ac.at
[2] The Norwegian Univ. of Science and Technology,
Department of Engineering Cybernetics
Trondheim, Norway
amund.skavhaug@ntnu.no

Dear Participant,

Computers are everywhere – may they be visible or integrated into every day equipment, devices, and environment, outside and inside us, mobile or fixed, smart, interconnected and communicating. Comfort, health, services, safety and security of people depend more and more on these "cyber-physical systems". They combine software, sensors and physics, acting independently, co-operative or as "systems-of-systems" composed of interconnected autonomous systems originally independently developed to fulfil dedicated tasks. The impact on society as a whole is tremendous - thus dependability in a holistic manner becomes an important issue, covering safety, reliability, availability, security, maintainability, robustness and resilience, despite emergent behaviours and interdependencies.

Technology is developing very fast. Demanding challenges have to be met by research, engineering and education. Smart (embedded) systems are regarded as the most important business driver for European industry. They are a targeted research area for European Research Programmes in Framework 7, in the ARTEMIS Joint Undertaking, and in several other dedicated Programmes and European Technology Platforms (ARTEMIS, EPoSS). Their application is not only in the traditional areas of aerospace, railways, automotive, or process industry and manufacturing, but also in robotics and services of all kind, in home appliances (smart environments, smart homes, ambient assisted living) and health care.

This workshop at SAFECOMP follows already its own tradition since 2006. It started as a co-operation between EWICS TC7, the European Workshop on Industrial Computer Systems, the founder and main sponsor of SAFECOMP as an International Conference on Computer Safety, Reliability and Security, and the ERCIM Working Group on Dependable Embedded Systems, ERCIM being the European Research Consortium for Informatics and Mathematics. The topics are covering aspects from design, development, verification and validation, certification, maintenance, standardization and education & training in the area of dependable (embedded) systems. This is a workshop, and to be distinct from the SAFECOMP conference

F. Ortmeier and P. Daniel (Eds.): SAFECOMP 2012 Workshops, LNCS 7613, pp. 343–346, 2012.
© Springer-Verlag Berlin Heidelberg 2012

mainstream, allows reports on "work in progress" aiming at hopefully fruitful discussions and experience exchange. Reports on European or national research projects (as part of the required dissemination) as well as industrial experience reports are welcome.

This year the workshop is co-hosted by the ARTEMIS projects R3-COP ("Resilient Reasoning Robotic Co-operating Systems", http://www.r3-cop.eu), MBAT ("Combined Model-based Analysis and Testing of Embedded Systems", http://www.mbat-artemis.eu) and pSafeCer/nSafeCer ("Safety Certification of Software-intensive Systems with Reusable Components", http://www.safecer.eu). ARTEMIS (Advanced Research and Technology for Embedded Intelligence and Systems) is a European, industry-driven research initiative (so-called "Joint Technology Initiative" comprised of the EC, the ARTEMIS Industrial Association and the Public Authorities of the ARTEMIS member states) aiming at helping European industry consolidate and reinforce its world leadership in embedded computing technologies and to overcome the fragmentation of the embedded systems industries. The economic impact in terms of jobs and growth is expected to exceed € 100 billion over ten years. As a Joint Undertaking it is funding mainly a set of rather big projects, following the ARTEMIS Strategic Research Agenda in its work program and conducting each year a separate call for proposals based on its work program. Funding is shared between the EC and the national funding authorities.

ARTEMIS is the major European Embedded Systems Initiative, and therefore the three co-hosting ARTEMIS projects will be described briefly:

As an example may be taken R3-COP, which aims at providing European industry with new leading-edge innovations, that will enable the production of advanced robust and safe cognitive, reasoning autonomous and co-operative robotic systems at reduced cost. The major objective is to achieve cross-sector reusability of building blocks, collected in a knowledge base, by developing and implementing a generic framework and platform with domain-specific instantiation, and use of a multi-purpose computing platform. About the concepts to follow towards a future European Technology Reference Platform a paper will be presented in the workshop.

MBAT will achieve better results by combining test and analysis methods. A new leading-edge Reference Technology Platform (RTP) for effective and cost-reducing validation and verification of Embedded Systems will be developed. MBAT project will strongly foster the development of high-quality embedded systems within transportation products at reduced costs, or in short: higher quality embedded systems at lower price. Higher quality embedded systems within transportation products will in turn increase the overall quality and market value of the transportation products. This will be of high value for the European industry and future projects, and contribute to the overarching ARTEMIS Goal of a Common Technology Reference Platform. Therefore close co-operation with related projects is envisaged, especially with those of the ARTEMIS Safety & High-reliability Cluster (e.g. CESAR, MBAT, SafeCer, iFEST, R3-COP).

SafeCer aims at increased efficiency and reduced time-to-market together with increased quality and reduced risk through composable certification of Safety-relevant embedded systems in the industrial domains of automotive and construction equipment, avionics, and rail. SafeCer will also develop certification guidelines for other domains, including cross-domain qualification and the application of the pSafeCer Certification framework in new domains. SafeCer will provide support for efficient reuse of safety certification arguments and prequalified components within and across industrial domains. This addresses the overarching goal of the ARTEMIS JU strategy to overcome fragmentation in the embedded systems markets.

This year, the dependable embedded (Cyberphysical) systems workshop has sessions on:

- Dependable Embedded Systems Applications
- Secure Systems –Systems Security
- Validation, Verification and Qualification
- Systems Safety and Trust
- Ambient Assisted Living

The applications presented in the workshop are three: one paper discusses the elaboration of safety requirements in the avionic domain (by EADS, an industrial paper), the second one presents the before mentioned robotics/ autonomous systems research project R3-COP, focussing on the knowledge-based approach to compose robotic applications and tool chains for V&V from a collection of building blocks in ontology-driven data bases, which is considered as basis for a reference technology platform for robotics and autonomous systems, as developed by AIT Austrian Institute of Technology, DTI Danish Technology Institute, tecnalia Spain, TU Brno, Czech Republic (paper authors) and other R3-COP partners. In the last session of the day, a third application and implementation is presented by NTNU (Norwegian University of Technology), an AAL monitoring system to enable elderly people a longer and safer stay at home, with some demonstration and video clips.

The session on system security includes three presentations, looking at different aspects of secure system. "On the Design of Secure Time-Triggered Systems" focusses on a novel joint safety and security architecture for dependable time-triggered systems, adding the security aspects to the already well-studied and proven time-triggered system architecture (by AIT, TU Vienna, Austrian Academy of Sciences and TTTech).

Todays' and evolving cyber-physical systems (CPS) have as typical feature wide-spread distribution of nodes. In the presentation of the work of pSHIELD, another ARTEMIS project, by SESM (Italy) and the Polytechnic Institute of Coimbra (Portugal), is demonstrated an architecture framework supporting security, privacy and dependability as built-in feature in a network of embedded nodes, improving also re-use of already verified embedded components and systems. The "Cyber-Physical Attacker", developed by Technical University of Denmark (DTU), models attacker scenarios which addresses the peculiarities of a cyber-physical adversary, which allows to study security properties of a CPS.

Validation, verification and qualification are issues of great importance when trying to prove trust in CPS. The NuSMV model checker is well known in the formal methods community. The first paper in this session presents an interesting extension to NuSMV, Parallel NuSMV, which is presented by ALES S.r.l. from Italy as part of the FormalSpecs Verifier Framework for the formal verification of complex embedded systems, using Simulink/Stateflow models.

One of the ideas to considerably improve and speed up development of safety-critical embedded systems is the use of tool chains, which implies seamless integration of different tools to cover significant parts of the development life cycle. Safety standards require qualification of tools, but are not looking in-depth into the issue of integration of pre-qualified tools into tool-chains. The paper on "Automated Qualification of Tool Chain Design" from KTH (Sweden) presents a promising approach to reduce effort in qualifying tool chains by automatically analysing a tool chain model for safety issues. The last paper of this session is on a model-based development approach for the design and validation of electronic control systems by simulation, using a Data Time Flow Simulator, developed by AIT in context of the ARTEMIS project POLLUX which tackles problems on the design of the next generation of electric cars.

A topic always crucial in context of safety-critical systems is how to achieve and prove trust in such a system. One issue in such systems is predictability, essentially in the time domain. Compiling for time predictability is one approach to generate code which has a predictable timing behaviour even in case of complex processors. Within the T-CREST project, the University of Technology of Vienna and the University of Hertfordshire (and others) worked on HW/SW architectures and code-generation strategies to achieve time-predictability, explaining the single-path code generation process in their paper. In the NOR-STA project, the University of Gdansk addressed development, maintenance and assessment of structured, evidence-based arguments to support trust assurance in CPS, using the TRUST-IT methodology and presenting the adequate tool support in the NOR-STA platform of software services available on internet.

The workshop will hopefully provide some insight into the topics, and enable fruitful discussions during the meeting and afterwards. The mixture of topics is well balanced, as is the distribution over Europe and European projects. Authors are from research, academia as well as from industry, which is a good mixture as we believe.

As chairpersons of the workshop we want to thank all authors and contributors who submitted their work, and want to express our thanks to the SAFECOMP organizers who provided us the opportunity to organize the workshop at SAFECOMP 2012 in Magdeburg. Particularily we want to thank the EC and national public and funding authorities who made the work in the research projects possible, and we want not to forget the continued support of our companies and organizations, and of ERCIM and EWICS who always helped us to learn from their networks.

We hope that all participants will benefit from the workshop, enjoy the conference and accompanying programmes and will join us again in the future!

The Cyber-Physical Attacker

Roberto Vigo

DTU Informatics, Technical University of Denmark, Kongens Lyngby, Denmark
rvig@imm.dtu.dk

Abstract. The world of Cyber-Physical Systems ranges from industrial to national interest applications. Even though these systems are pervading our everyday life, we are still far from fully understanding their security properties. Devising a suitable attacker model is a crucial element when studying the security properties of CPSs, as a system cannot be secured without defining the threats it is subject to. In this work an attacker scenario is presented which addresses the peculiarities of a cyber-physical adversary, and we discuss how this scenario relates to other attacker models popular in the security protocol literature.

Keywords: attacker model, cyber-physical threats, cyber-physical systems, security protocol verification.

1 Introduction

Cyber-Physical Systems (CPSs) have been drawing the attention of the scientific community since the early 2000s, due to the increasing exploitation of these systems in the realization of critical infrastructures (e.g. power grid, healthcare, traffic control, defence) as well as general-purpose personal applications (e.g. home automation, entertainment). As a consequence of the proliferation of these systems, their nature and properties must be thoroughly investigated; efforts are still needed in order to tackle the diverse issues addressed in the literature. Among the questions about CPSs that remain partially unanswered, is the question of security, as compromising such a system (e.g. the power grid or a military network) could lead to economic, social, and political damages. A great many works call for a scientific investigation of cyber-physical security properties [1,10,11,19]; specific facets of the problem have been addressed (e.g. in [2,15,16]), but the characterization of a suitable adversary model is far from being complete.

In this work we present a model which encompasses the attacks a CPS is exposed to, stressing the novelties which arise when considering an adversary that is able to physically tamper with system components. Moreover, we compare the expressiveness of existing well-known frameworks, like the Dolev-Yao model [14] and a version of the computational model [17], with the peculiarities of a cyber-physical attacker. This comparison is enabled by the definition of a simple framework in which the outcomes of both physical and cyber actions are expressed in a common language.

F. Ortmeier and P. Daniel (Eds.): SAFECOMP 2012 Workshops, LNCS 7613, pp. 347–356, 2012.

The benefit of this investigation is two-fold: first of all, we show to what extent a cyber-physical attacker can be described using notions that stem from models developed in the security protocol literature; and secondly, we highlight the novelties of such an adversary on the basis of behaviours that are not encompassed by those frameworks. Finally, as there are a number of tools that can perform automated verification of the security properties of communication protocols within those frameworks, our comparison identifies the limits of these tools when dealing with a cyber-physical adversary.

Outline. In Section 2 we give a brief introduction to CPSs, as well as outline the model we refer to throughout the paper. Based on this model, the attacks a CPS suffers are explained in Section 3, leading to the formulation of the cyber-physical attacker. Section 4 presents a perspective unifying cyber and physical actions, which is leveraged for comparing the cyber-physical attacker with other models in Section 5. Finally, Section 6 draws a conclusion and sketches a line for future work.

Related Work. The definition of an attacker scenario for CPSs is a poorly-addressed topic, regardless of this, the need for such an investigation is often claimed in the literature. Benenson et al. studied an attacker model for Wireless Sensor Networks (WSNs) in [5,6], focusing on physical attacks. Di Mauro et al. expand on those works and consider new security issues introduced by Energy-Harvesting WSNs [12]. In [9], the authors exploit the Byzantine model [13] to characterise a cyber-physical attacker, but their model addresses high-level behaviours and they do not discuss the adversary's capabilities in detail. Finally, [2] addresses the importance of a quantitative approach to the security of CPSs, by studying an eavesdropping adversary under this perspective.

2   CPS Essentials

It is worth noting that given the many different fields in which CPSs are employed, it is almost impossible to provide a detailed definition; nonetheless some general common characteristics recur: CPSs are complex systems which monitor physical processes by means of interconnected networks of sensors, whose measures are exploited for acting on the sensed environment in order to optimise an operational goal [18,21,20]. Thus, CPSs can be logically organised in two coupled layers:

- a *physical* layer, consisting of sensors and actuators that interact with given properties of the environment of interest (e.g. physical parameters like temperature, humidity, etc.),
- and a *cyber* layer, in charge of transforming the sensed data into information, to be exploited for driving the environment toward a given goal, possibly by means of the actuators.

Typically such a system consists of a significant number of devices (up to tens of thousands of nodes), each one capable of sensing and/or actuating, computing, and transmitting data. In the following, we assume that we are dealing with CPSs that rely on WSNs for exchanging information among nodes. While such a network can be considered a CPS, in general a CPS might rely on a different infrastructure for communications. Notwithstanding this specific point, we will examine WSN-based CPSs; due to the broadcasting nature of the ether, this is a conservative assumption, as a wireless medium is exposed to the same threats as a wired medium, and possibly even more.

Finally, it is relevant to point to some characteristics of CPSs which have a deep impact on their security [2,19]:

- such systems get inputs from the physical environment, thus we must consider communication channels that have not yet been investigated in the literature about computer security, which need to be secured: *an attacker does not need to break into the system in order to affect its behaviour*, the attacker can act on the environment monitored by the system;
- a CPS is generally widely distributed, and some components lie in locations where there is a lack of physical security: nodes are exposed to be physically captured by an attacker;
- physically capturing a node is made easier by the fact that, for financial reasons, they are usually not equipped with tamper-proof chips.

The possibility to physically capture a node is a distinguishing trait of such systems, and this introduces new threats that we will present after having defined the reference model.

Reference Model. A CPS can be formally defined as a pair $S = (\mathcal{N}, M)$, being $\mathcal{N} = \{n_1, \ldots, n_m\}$ the set of components of the system (nodes), and M the topology of the system, represented as a matrix $m \times m$. For the sake of simplicity, we consider a bi-dimensional evenly-spaced grid.

We assume nodes in $\mathcal{N}$ to exhibit a similar structure, displayed in Fig. 1. A generic node $n \in \mathcal{N}$ consists of interfaces towards the environment (e.g. a node-to-host interface H_n) and towards other nodes (e.g. a wireless transceiver T_n), a computational section, consisting of an EEPROM chip M_n for logging sensed data and a micro-controller P_n for storing and executing the control program (note that P_n contains cryptographic material K_n, if any), batteries providing power and possibly some energy scavenging unit E_n that can recharge the batteries using energy from the environment.

We assume that communication channels are not private, that is, the attacker can always eavesdrop messages if he is in the range of the involved transceivers.

3   Attacker Model

The threats to which a CPS is exposed can be easily grouped into *physical* and *cyber* menaces, depending on whether these threats are directed against physical devices or against the messages the components exchange. Physical threats require that the adversary has physical access to the node in order to

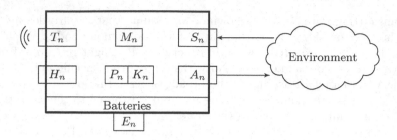

Fig. 1. Abstract model of a CPS component n

be able to attack it, while cyber menaces require that the adversary is in the proximity of the node (according to the range of the transceivers). Nevertheless, it is relevant to observe that every physical attack has some cyber effects, which are the only aspects with which an automated verification technique can cope. Some significant work has been devoted to studying the physical attacks a WSN node is exposed to (e.g. see [5]). These attacks are directly related to the structure of a component n of the system, and the basic actions they involve can be summarised as follows:

- **remove** - removing n from the network, temporarily or permanently, e.g. by destroying the node or removing its batteries;
- **read/write** - obtaining/modifying the content of the memory M_n;
- **reveal** - reading the content of the local control program P_n (obtain cryptographic material);
- **reprogram** - modifying the local control program P_n, thus making the node execute an arbitrary algorithm;
- **starve** - preventing the energy scavenging unit E_n from collecting energy (e.g. by casting a shadow on a solar panel).

Observe that all these attacks (except the last one) require the adversary to physically tamper with a device, removing it from the network for a period of time, which may vary from between few minutes and one day, depending on the sort of attack and the skills of the intruder. Finally, there is another possibility for the attacker to physically tamper with the whole system by inserting new nodes into the network (**insert**). In general, an adversary able to insert nodes in a network is more powerful than one who cannot (e.g. he can alter the result of a given voting mechanism on which the network is based).

Cyber attacks concern standard communication-related actions that can be categorised as follows: **block**, blocking messages (e.g. by jamming the communication channel); **eavesdrop**, obtaining messages communicated over the network; **inject**, sending messages over the network. An attack is performed as a combination of these actions with internal computations (e.g. elaboration of stolen messages to produce a new message to be injected).

As we have mentioned above, both physical and cyber attacks depend on the position of the adversary with respect to the target device. Given a CPS

$S = (\mathcal{N}, M)$, we can model the attacker as a set $\mathcal{A}$ of pairs $(l, \mathcal{C})$, being l a location in the network where the attacker lies, and $\mathcal{C}$ a set of cyber-physical capabilities, each one being a tuple (a, c, r), where a is an attack/action, c its cost in terms of energy/time, r the range of the attack expressed as a set of locations in M that could be affected.

According to this model, the attacker can be composed of various profiles $\mathcal{A}_1, \ldots, \mathcal{A}_k$ describing his capabilities in relationship with the locations where he lies. Note that in case of `insert`, r identifies locations where new nodes can be deployed; moreover, as a consequence of inserting a node, a new profile is generated if it is deployed in a location where the adversary was not present before, thus extending his area of influence.

4 A Protocol Perspective

Automated verification of security protocols is an active research area, where a number of approaches have been studied for formally defining protocols, security properties, and verification procedures. In the following, we propose a conceptual map that describes the attacker's capabilities as discussed above with terminology used in the protocol world. The contribution of such a map is two-fold: it enables us to formulate security questions about CPSs in a well-known domain, facilitating the comparison with existing models, and it helps highlight the novelties CPSs bring to computer security, identified as behaviours that classic adversary models do not encompass.

From Nodes to Agents. We can simply rethink nodes in $\mathcal{N}$ as communicating principals of a security protocol P. Given a node $n \in \mathcal{N}$, its memory M_n, and the memory local to its control program P_n, the corresponding principal p has a knowledge K_p which consists of

- initial knowledge IK_p (e.g. trusted third parties' identities);
- knowledge RK_p gained through running the protocol (received messages);
- long-term keys LK_p;
- knowledge DK_p derived combining all of the above (e.g. a message obtained decrypting a received cipher-text with a known key), among which we distinguish session keys SK_p established in some sessions of the protocol.

Finally, the local software P_n controlling the node is the role R_p played by the corresponding principal in the protocol, which describes the steps a principal goes through during one execution of the protocol (a session). Figure 2 summarises this relationship.

As a CPS generally interacts with the physical environment it is deployed across, we also need to represent the environment as a communicating principal, designing sensing operations as messages from the environment to principals, and actuating operations as messages from principals to the environment, making it acting as a standard agent. On the other hand, the environment is a special principal as it can communicate with all the other participants, without spatial

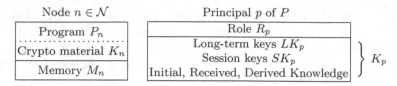

Fig. 2. From CPS nodes to protocol agents

restrictions. Nonetheless, when we deal with a geographically constrained adversary, we would like to model the fact that such an adversary can compromise only a limited portion of the environment, depending on his presence. In order to describe such a scenario without introducing new entities, we could partition the environment into $m \times m$ principals, each one representing the environment related to a single position of the network.

Referring to this conceptual map, in the remainder of this section we reformulate the cyber-physical attacks described in Section 3 in accordance with this new terminology, thus expressing the attacker's capabilities from a unified perspective.

Bridging Physical and Cyber Worlds. In order to relate physical and cyber attacks we leverage the mapping introduced above between a node n and a corresponding principal p, which leads to translating the attacks into basic get and set actions on the knowledge of a principal:

- get IK_p, get RK_p, get DK_p, get SK_p, get LK_p - by eavesdropping communications on the network the attacker obtains some received messages RK_p, which he can combine with other stolen information, thereby obtaining a subset of DK_p. Moreover, by physically accessing a node, he can extract IK_p, SK_p, LK_p from the memories where this information is stored. For the sake of generality a different get action is suggested for each subset of a principal's knowledge;
- set RK_p, set DK_p - injecting messages, the attacker is able to change the knowledge of the target principal with respect to received messages. As an example, assume that the attacker is changing some parameters of the environment that a given node is sensing: sending fake messages about the environment, the attacker modifies RK_p and a subset (possibly empty) of the derived knowledge DK_p. Setting received messages, the attacker is implicitly able to inhibit a principal from participating to a protocol.

These actions are sufficient in order to mount all the attacks mentioned in Section 3, except for starve which cannot be expressed without introducing a notion of the energy-level of a principal.

The ability of obtaining a principal's long-term and session keys, together with the capability of eavesdropping and sending messages, allows the adversary to impersonate the attacked principal. Thereby the adversary achieves the same effect as if he reprogrammed the node, but with much less effort. If the attacker knows everything a legal principal p knows, indeed, he can make p play an arbitrary role since he is able to send and receive messages on the network on behalf of p. We can conclude that get $\{RK_p \cup SK_p \cup LK_p\}$ and set RK_p imply reprogram. As reprogramming a node is the most powerful achievement the attacker can hope for, the actions above include only the minimal attacks that can be performed with the aim of reprogramming a node. The list could be extended to include, for instance, keys modification, but as writing can generally be assumed more difficult than reading, and reading already leads to reprogramming, we do not consider those actions. Observe that set RK_p can be implemented as a cyber attack (no physical tampering) by message injection, a capability within the range of any wireless device. Hence, the only *physical* attack we need to consider is get $\{SK_p \cup LK_p\}$, as this is the only basic action that introduce new security issues with respect to pure cyber attacks, and combining it with message injection we can achieve the outcome of more complex physical attacks. In the literature on security protocol verification, the capability of obtaining part of a principal's private knowledge is generally referred to as *agent compromise* or *corruption*.

The ability of the attacker to insert new nodes can also be reduced to a combination get and set actions. In the event that the adversary can forge new terms, he could forge a new agent's identity and the corresponding keys. It is worth noting that inserted principals must be new, otherwise insertion and honest agents corruption coincide.

5   Expressiveness of Existing Frameworks

In the following we compare the cyber-physical attacker, in the light of the previous discussion, to other models that are documented in the literature about security protocol verification, with the aim of highlighting existing frameworks which model the elements we need to formalise the security aspects of CPSs.

The Dolev-Yao Model. The Dolev-Yao model [14] is the most addressed attacker framework in the literature on security protocol verification, and numerous tools have been built based on some of its variations (see for instance [7,8]). The model is based on the following assumptions: (i) perfect cryptography (cryptographic primitives are unbreakable), (ii) the attacker controls the communication medium, and (iii) the attacker is a legitimate user.

With respect to the cyber-physical attacker, the presence of a Dolev-Yao adversary is always global (assumption (ii)), whereas the former could be spatially limited. Secondly, the capabilities of a Dolev-Yao adversary are: get $\{RK_p \cup D\}$ with $D \subseteq DK_p$ (i.e. eavesdrop), and set $\{RK_p \cup D\}$ (i.e. inject), that is, a Dolev-Yao adversary cannot obtain LK_p or SK_p unless these can be derived from outputted messages, and this is unlikely to happen in a smart security protocol. In contrast to this, a cyber-physical attacker does not need this condition to be met, as he can physically access the memory of a node.

An Educated Adversary. In [3] Basin et al. present a physics-aware attacker, in order to formally reason about the properties of the physical environment (e.g.

proximity) that, in some applications, are required to be established in a secure way. The authors propose an operational semantics of traces which captures the basic physical properties of space and time, that constrain any real attacker (e.g. the time it takes a message to flow from one node to another). The network and the agents are precisely modelled: each agent has a set of transceivers, lies in a particular location, and has some initial knowledge; the network is then formalised as an adjacency matrix representing the connectivity between agents: for each entry a lower bound on the signal propagation time is given. On the intruder side, the authors formalise a Dolev-Yao attacker which is restricted both by spatial and temporal constraints: the adversary can intercept and inject messages only at given locations (where a compromised node, i.e. the attacker, lies), and the exchange of information between nodes (even if compromised) is not instantaneous, but is determined by the network topology.

With respect to our cyber-physical attacker, this framework successfully expresses spatial limitations, but it is still incomplete with respect to the adversary's capabilities since it lacks an agent compromise mechanism.

A Compromising Adversary. One of the main novelties introduced by the cyber-physical attacker with respect to a Dolev-Yao adversary is the ability to selectively compromise honest agents: when he has obtained the knowledge of a principal p, the attacker is able to impersonate p, making him play an arbitrary role. Thus, at a given time, an agent within the range of the attacker may become dishonest. Basin and Cremers directly address this issue in [4], presenting an attacker model where agents can be compromised dynamically: the adversary can obtain the long-term keys of a principal or session-related data.

A key point of this work is that the semantics explicitly inhibits the adversary from obtaining any session key, because "revealing it trivially violates the protocols' security" [4, Sec. 2.4]. In the usual interpretation of security protocols no communication would indeed be secure with respect to a fully-compromising adversary, as messages cannot be protected against disclosure if the attacker can obtain every cryptographic key.

Besides a fully-compromising ability, this attacker lacks a reference to the spatial dimension. Moreover, we deem that the concept of compromise should be intertwined more strictly with temporal conditions, up to consider time-limited compromise. In regular WSNs, indeed, nodes are often replaced by new devices, for example when the old ones run out of power: the situation may arise in which new nodes do not share information with old ones.

6 Conclusion and Future Work

We have presented an attacker that is able to exploit both physical and cyber weaknesses of CPSs. The model captures two essential features of the adversary: his capabilities and spatial distribution. On the basis of a reference model for CPSs, a simple framework has been devised which serves as a common ground for comparing physical and cyber attacks. This framework highlights that the main novelty introduced by physical attacks corresponds to agent corruption, in protocol terminology: an attacker who controls the communication and can obtain cryptographic keys of legal principals is able to reprogram them. Moreover, this model enabled us to make a direct comparison between the cyber-physical attacker, the Dolev-Yao model, and two recent adversary models, showing that these models describe weaker attackers.

This investigation has led to highlighting behaviours that attacker models tailored to security protocols verification do not encompass, like a fully-compromising adversary. No protocol is secure with respect to the cyber-physical attacker, but his omnipotence is hampered by spatial and temporal constraints that must be considered when addressing an automated verification procedure. Analysing a CPS, indeed, we cannot depart from phrasing questions in a quantitative way, asking for instance how much time it takes to carry out an attack, the amount of energy that the attacker must consume in order to complete it, the number of locations from which the attack must be carried out, and so on. This is an active research topic, and complementing the cyber-physical attacker we have described with a suitable execution model, in which quantitative questions may be raised about time and energy, is a point open for future examination. Once this model has been provided, more sophisticated notions of compromise should be investigated, as this is the main tool the cyber-physical adversary possesses to break CPSs.

Acknowledgments. This work was supported by the IDEA4CPS project granted by the Danish Research Foundations for Basic Research.

The author would like to thank Flemming Nielson and Hanne Riis Nielson for they stimulated this investigation, and Sebastian Mödersheim for valuable comments.

References

1. Anand, M., Cronin, E., Sherr, M., Blaze, M., Ives, Z., Lee, I.: Security Challenges in Next Generation Cyber Physical Systems. In: Beyond SCADA: Cyber Physical Systems Meeting, HCSS-NEC4CPS (2006)
2. Anand, M., Ives, Z., Lee, I.: Quantifying Eavesdropping Vulnerability in Sensor Networks. In: 2nd VLDB Workshop on Data Management for Sensor Networks, DMSN (2005)
3. Basin, D., Capkun, S., Schaller, P., Schmidt, B.: Formal Reasoning about Physical Properties of Security Protocols. ACM Transactions on Information and System Security (TISSEC) 14(2), 16 (2011)
4. Basin, D., Cremers, C.: Degrees of Security: Protocol Guarantees in the Face of Compromising Adversaries. In: Dawar, A., Veith, H. (eds.) CSL 2010. LNCS, vol. 6247, pp. 1–18. Springer, Heidelberg (2010)
5. Benenson, Z., Cholewinski, P., Freiling, F.: Vulnerabilities and attacks in wireless sensor networks. In: Lopez, J., Zhou, J. (eds.) Wireless Sensors Networks Security. IOS Press (2007)
6. Benenson, Z., Dewald, A., Freiling, F.: Presence, Intervention, Insertion: Unifying Attack and Failure Models in Wireless Sensor Networks. Technical report, University of Mannheim (2009)

7. Blanchet, B.: Automatic verification of correspondences for security protocols. Journal of Computer Security 17(4), 363–434 (2009)
8. Buchholtz, M., Nielson, H.R., Nielson, F.: A Calculus for Control Flow Analysis of Security Protocols. International Journal of Information Security 2(3-4), 145–167 (2004)
9. Burmester, M., Magkos, E.: Modeling Security in Cyber-Physical Systems. In: Sixth Annual IFIP Working Group 11.10 International Conference on Critical Infrastructure Protection (2012)
10. Cárdenas, A., Amin, S., Sastry, S.: Secure Control: Towards Survivable Cyber-Physical Systems. In: 28th International Conference on Distributed Computing Systems, ICDCS 2008 Workshops (2008)
11. Cárdenas, A., Amin, S., Sinopoli, B., Giani, A., Perrig, A., Sastry, S.: Challenges for Securing Cyber Physical Systems. In: Workshop on Future Directions in Cyberphysical Systems Security (2009)
12. Di Mauro, A., Papini, D., Vigo, R., Dragoni, N.: Toward a Threat Model for Energy-Harvesting Wireless Sensor Networks. In: Benlamri, R. (ed.) NDT 2012, Part II. CCIS, vol. 294, pp. 289–301. Springer, Heidelberg (2012)
13. Dolev, D.: The Byzantine generals strike again. Journal of Algorithms 30, 14–30 (1982)
14. Dolev, D., Yao, A.: On the security of public key protocols. IEEE Transactions on Information Theory 29(2), 198–208 (1983)
15. Gamage, T.T., McMillin, B.M., Roth, T.P.: Enforcing Information Flow Security Properties in Cyber-Physical Systems: A Generalized Framework Based on Compensation. In: 34th Annual Computer Software and Applications Conference Workshops, IEEE COMPSACW 2010 (2010)
16. Gamage, T.T., Roth, T.P., McMillin, B.M.: Confidentiality Preserving Security Properties for Cyber-Physical Systems. In: 35th IEEE Annual Computer Software and Applications Conference (2011)
17. Goldwasser, S., Micali, S., Rivest, R.L.: A Digital Signature Scheme Secure Against Adaptive Chosen-Message Attacks. SIAM J. Comput. 17(2) (1988)
18. Lee, E.A.: Cyber Physical Systems: Design Challenges. In: International Symposium on Object/Component/Service-Oriented Real-Time Distributed Computing, ISORC (2008)
19. Neuman, C.: Challenges in Security for Cyber-Physical Systems. In: DHS Workshop on Future Directions in Cyber-Physical Systems Security (2009)
20. Shi, J., Wan, J., Yan, H., Suo, H.: A Survey of Cyber Physical Systems. In: International Conference on Wireless Communications and Signal Processing, WSCP 2011 (2011)
21. Xiao, K., Ren, S., Kwiat, K.: Retrofitting Cyber Physical Systems for Survivability through External Coordination. In: 41st Hawaii International Conference on System Sciences (2008)

Dependable and Secure Embedded Node Demonstrator

Przemysław Osocha[1], João Carlos Cunha[2], and Fabio Giovagnini[1]

[1] SESM s.c.a.r.l., Naples, Italy
{p.osocha,fabio.giovagnini}@gmail.com
[2] Polytechnic Institute of Coimbra / CISUC, Coimbra, Portugal
jcunha@isec.pt

Abstract. The European industry competitiveness in the embedded devices market is threatened by challenges such as cost-effectiveness, interoperability, reliability, and re-usability. This is particularly important now, when the value of embedded electronics components share in the final products is increasing, especially in ICT and health/medical equipment domains.

To address these challenges, the pSHIELD project, co-funded by ARTEMIS JU, was aimed at developing an architecture framework supporting security, privacy and dependability (SPD) as built-in features in a network of embedded nodes. That approach will provide industry with the key improvements such as a faster design, standardized development of SPD solutions and a flexible way to reuse already verified embedded systems.

This paper reports the architecture of an FPGA-based intrusion detection embedded device for a freight train, built to validate the pSHIELD concept at a node level. The use case demonstrates the legacy components integration, dependability, security, self-reconfiguration and the node-level composability.

Keywords: security, dependability, embedded system, FPGA, partial reconfiguration.

1 Introduction

In the modern world, embedded devices are present anytime and anywhere. They are distributed ubiquitously, pervasively and unobtrusively in everyday environments in many different forms: small or large, visible or invisible, simple or complex, wired or wireless and so on.

The massive deployment of networked embedded systems, seamlessly interconnected with each other, dealing with sensitive information and acting in critical environments is posing new challenges to developers. Dependability and security of embedded systems cannot be any longer analyzed for separated devices, but rather in a distributed context as systems of systems.

The contemporary market of embedded systems requires a built-in approach where security, privacy and dependability (SPD) functionalities are natively addressed from the design through the entire system life-cycle in contrast with an SPD add-on approach, which is in use today. In particular, the industry needs an approach to SPD

F. Ortmeier and P. Daniel (Eds.): SAFECOMP 2012 Workshops, LNCS 7613, pp. 357–364, 2012.

which will provide the key improvements such as a faster design, a flexible way to reuse already validated systems and the standardized development of SPD solutions.

To meet these ambitious requirements, ARTEMIS JU [1] co-funded the pSHIELD project [2], addressing the reusability of previously designed solutions and the standardization and interoperability of advanced SPD technologies. This project aims to build a reference model for all the security, privacy and dependability aspects involving networked embedded systems [3]. In fact, the provided architecture will pursue the design and development of a multi-layer/multi-technology framework able to guarantee the composability of SPD functionalities. The project concept development is continued under the new ARTEMIS JU project nSHIELD. To validate the pSHIELD project concept, a global use case scenario based on the monitoring of hazardous materials transported by train has been proposed. This paper presents the architecture and scenarios built to demonstrate the pSHIELD SPD capabilities at the Node level.

2   Embedded Node Architecture

The pSHIELD framework [3] is composed of four layers: Node, Network, Middleware and Overlay. The Node layer implements intelligent hardware and firmware SPD functionalities and services; the Network layer is responsible for the secure, trusted, dependable and efficient data transfer based on self-configuration, self-management, self-supervision and self-recovery; the Middleware layer assures secure and efficient resource management and inter-operation among heterogeneous Embedded Systems' (ES) networks; the Overlay layer guarantees that different SPD modules belonging to the node, network and middleware layers can be *composed* in a proper way in order to solve any SPD issue globally. The output of each layer is available at the upper level which will take advantage of SPD features developed at a lower level empowering SPD features of the whole pSHIELD architecture in a transparent but manageable way.

At the Node level there may be distinguished three different kinds of Intelligent ES Nodes: Nano Node, Micro/Personal Node and Power Node. These three types of nodes, which can be considered as three node levels of increasing complexity, represent the basic components of the lower part of the SPD pervasive system and cover the possible requirements of several market areas: from the field data acquisition to transportation, personal space, home environment and to public infrastructures, etc.

Figure 1 provides a conceptual model of a pSHIELD Node Layer. This generic SPD Node architecture is composed of several functional blocks, where each block can implement features of various complexity. These nodes can be built using miscellaneous hardware architectures, they can also provide diverse functionalities and capabilities and assure different SPD compliance levels, depending on the type of a node and on the application field. For example, a typical Nano Node does not include capabilities such as Security and Privacy, Power Management and Reconfiguration.

The pSHIELD SPD Node Layer has two interfaces: one providing the pSHIELD Node Capabilities (pS-NC) to the pSHIELD Middleware Layer offering, for example, the necessary means for composing different nodes in an SPD system; and another interface with legacy, technology-dependent Node Capabilities (NC). The Legacy Node Capabilities are the capabilities already available for any embedded device provided by the Node Legacy Device Components such as CPU, I/O interfaces, memory, battery, etc. These capabilities are extended with SPD functionalities by the Node pSHIELD Specific Components which provide innovative SPD functionalities, such as the checkpoint-recovery, status and metrics. The translation between the technology-independent commands, configurations and decisions coming from the pS-NC interface into the technology-dependent ones is assured by the pSHIELD Node Adapter.

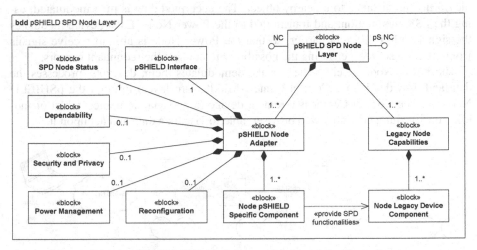

Fig. 1. pSHIELD SPD Node Layer Conceptual Architecture

Then, some innovative SPD components have been grouped into proper modules, such as: the pSHIELD Interface, which provides a proper interface for the pSHIELD Network; the SPD Node Status responsible for collecting the status of each individual component and providing SPD-relevant parameters and measurements to the Middleware Layer, and also responsible for checking the system health status for self-recovery, self-reconfiguration and self-adaptation; Reconfiguration, which performs the module or system reconfiguration by demand of the system SPD Node Status or the Middleware; Dependability responsible both for applying self-dependability at a node layer by detecting problems related to the system health status and for starting recovery; Security and Privacy, which enforces the system security and privacy at a node level by providing hardware or software encryption, decryption, key generation, firmware protection, etc.; and Power Management for managing power sources, and providing protection against blackouts, etc. The rationale behind the choice of these modules comes from the pSHIELD requirements, where a node should be built with extended dependability, security, privacy, composability, self-reconfiguration, self-adaptation and power management. Further details are available in the public deliverables of the pSHIELD project [3].

3   Power Node Demonstrator

Some of the pSHIELD Node capabilities were demonstrated by building a prototype for a test scenario. It consisted in the use of the FSK modulation to transmit the data between intrusion detection sensors placed in different cars of a freight train and an SPD Power Node, which in turn processes the signals and sends information to a Control Center through the pSHIELD network.

The intrusion detection systems are embedded devices which include a remote proximity sensor and a data encryptor. The remote proximity sensor is continuously measuring the distance to a nearby object. The encrypted data is then modulated, using the FSK modulation, and transmitted to the Power Node. Each device modulates the signal with a different carrier, so that the Power Node is able to receive signals from different sources, ensuring the possibility to connect the redundant sensors.

The Power Node receives the signals, demodulates them, decrypts, processes the data and provides it to a Control Center (Middleware layer) through the pSHIELD Network. The Control Center is a remote device (a personal computer, tablet or mobile phone) equipped with a web browser, able to visualize data and act upon it.

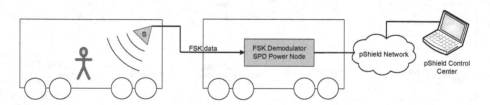

Fig. 2. Power Node demonstrator context

Figure 2 presents the demonstrator context: the SPD Power Node is located in a central car of the freight train. It receives the FSK modulated and encrypted data from other cars and delivers the plain information to the Control Center through the pSHIELD network. In our demonstrator, however, we have used a single sensor with two distinct carriers emulating sensor redundancy.

Based on the pSHIELD architecture framework (Fig. 1) and the demonstrator context (Fig. 2), a system has been developed, as presented in Figure 3. It consists of two different devices: the Intrusion detector and the FSK Demodulator SPD Power Node. The first one receives the data from an intrusion data generator and is connected to a push button, which makes it possible to request it to switch between the two carriers that are used for the FSK modulation. This system then sends the encrypted and FSK modulated data to the second system, the FSK Demodulator SPD Power Node. This system is also connected to a push button, which allows an injection of an internal fault into the node. Finally, the FSK Demodulator SPD Power Node is connected through the Ethernet to the pSHIELD Network, from where a Control Center can receive data and control this node.

The Intrusion detector is implemented on an EP3C120F780 Cyclone III Altera FPGA board. It is composed of three basic blocks corresponding to:

- a proximity sensor, consisting of an intrusion data generator which is based on a data file with emulated distances to the nearest object;
- a data encryptor, encrypting the sensor data, based on a blowfish algorithm with a 64 bit length fixed key;
- an FSK modulator, consisting of a hardware module (IP Core programmed on the FPGA), and using one of the two predefined carriers: 1 kHz and 2 kHz. If the carrier is 1 kHz, then the "Space" frequency is 968 Hz and the "Mark" frequency is 1031 Hz. If the carrier is 2 kHz, the "Space" frequency is 1937 Hz and the "Mark" frequency is 2062 Hz.

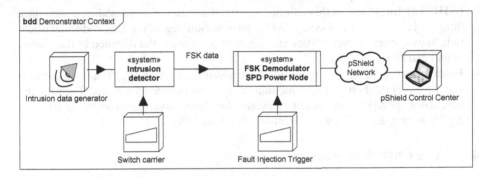

Fig. 3. Block diagram of the demonstrator context

The SPD Power Node is based on a Xilinx ML507 Evaluation Platform with a Virtex-5 FPGA. The modules composing this Power Node correspond to the pSHIELD SPD blocks depicted in Figure 1. These modules, with the exception of the Power Management, are the following:

- **Node Legacy Device Component**, which in the demonstrator is a legacy FSK demodulator module, implemented as an IP Core of a digital demodulator working with a clock of 32 kHz and demodulating 12 bits modulated data into 8 bits demodulated one.
- **Node pSHIELD Specific Component**, which is an SPD specific demodulator, providing the legacy demodulator with SPD capabilities, such as metrics and discovery. The system has several metrics values (dependability level, number of failures occurred, number of successful recoveries occurred, etc.) and it answers over the IP protocol to any discovery request incoming from the network layer. It is able to communicate the class it belongs to, the subclass specific features, the kind of demodulation, the carrier, the sampling rate and other information useful to identify the node.

- **Dependability** module, containing error detection and recovery. The system can recognize a fault condition (with a hardware based detection subsystem) and use a plausibility evaluation subsystem. If a fault is recognized, the system tries to restore the damaged feature by reconfiguring the appropriate part of the FPGA using for that the partial reconfiguration feature (see below, the Reconfiguration).
- **Security and Privacy** module, performing data decryption using a 64 bit fixed key blowfish algorithm. It is not the most flexible solution but it represents a very good compromise between robustness, liability and resources consumption.
- **Reconfiguration**, using the dynamic partial reconfiguration [4] of FPGA to instantiate a new demodulation core, with a different carrier frequency. The partial reconfiguration is also used for the dynamic adjustment of the system. If the modulator switches for any reason from one carrier frequency to another, the system automatically recognizes this fact and adjusts itself by reconfiguring the part of an FPGA containing demodulator logic with a new partial bitstream that implements the new required frequency demodulator.
- **pSHIELD Interface**, in this case it consists of a web server providing a web page through HTTP, with embedded XML information regarding the node identification, status, metrics, capabilities and function responses (the distance to the nearest object and alarms).
- **Fault Injector Trigger** is represented by a simple push button. When an external agent presses the button, the demodulator stops its proper operations. Then the demodulator specific component recognizes this faulty condition and triggers recovery by writing a new copy of the bitstream on the FPGA.

4   Use Case Scenarios

Several scenarios have been designed in order to demonstrate these SPD Power Node capabilities. Every scenario validates one or more innovative capabilities of the proposed node architecture, as presented in previous sections. These use case scenarios cover the demonstration of all the SPD blocks (see Fig. 1), except for the Power Management.

1. **Node Discovery and Legacy Component Integration** - This first scenario demonstrates the basic functions of the SPD Power Node and the Control Center (Fig. 2). It also demonstrates how a node can provide discovery information used for composability and how a legacy device was integrated in the SPD Power Node context: (a) The SPD Power Node runs a web server and thus provides the Control Center with a web page containing the information about the node identification, capabilities and status of the device. (b) The Control Center accesses this web page through an HTTP protocol by means of a web browser. (c) The Control Center displays the SPD Node identification, status and capabilities, including those related to the FSK Demodulator (a legacy device component).
2. **Metrics and High Performance** - The next scenario demonstrates the ability of the SPD Power Node to demodulate and decrypt the received data in real-time. (a) The intrusion detecting sensor in the first coach (Fig. 2) provides the generated data simulating a distance to an object. This data is encrypted, modulated and sent to the SPD Power Node. (b) The SPD Power Node demodulates the signal,

decrypts it and stores in a local database (requires high performance). (c) Metrics data is continuously collected and stored in a local database of the SPD Power Node. (d) The Control Center requests and displays SPD Power Node metrics, including distance to the intruding object; the information is continuously updated.

3. **Self-reconfiguration** - The SPD Power Node demonstrates its ability for self-reconfiguration to adapt to environmental changes. (a) The modulator in the intrusion detecting sensor switches to a different carrier. (b) The SPD Power Node detects a demodulation error and the demodulator is automatically reconfigured to the new carrier by a partial reconfiguration of the FPGA. (c) In the Control Center, the displayed sensor data is still valid. The metrics reveal that a self-reconfiguration has been performed. (d) The Control Center operator then may request another reconfiguration to the other carrier. The SPD Power Node reconfigures to the other configuration and then goes back to the previous one, as it does not match the carrier of the modulated signal. These switches can be noted from the changes in status and metrics readings.

4. **Dependability** - The SPD Power Node device autonomously recovers from a failure. (a) A fault is injected into the demodulator by pressing a pushbutton of a fault-injector prepared for the demonstrator. (b) An error is detected and recovered through the software and hardware (FPGA reconfiguration) recovery. (c) The correct data is still presented to the Control Center. The metrics reveal that an error has occurred and the recovery was successful.

5. **Security** - This last scenario demonstrates how encryption is used for a secure connection between the sensor devices and the SPD Power Node. (a) The encryptor in the intrusion detecting sensor switches to a different encryption key. (b) The SPD Power Node detects a decryption error. (c) The Control Center displays invalid sensor data. The metrics reveal that an error occurred.

All the scenarios have been successfully executed.

Fig. 4. pSHIELD SPD Node demonstrator

Figure 4 partially shows the demonstrator setup: the Xilinx ML507 board (the FSK Demodulator SPD Power Node), a network router and a mobile phone acting as the Control Center and presenting some data received from the SPD Node.

5   Conclusion

Security and dependability are the emerging topics in the design of embedded systems [5], and as such, they arouse both industry and researchers' interest. In this paper we presented an embedded node prototype with the integrated security, privacy and dependability (SPD) technologies which could be incorporated into an embedded network of SPD nodes, commanded by a control center.

This SPD node has been validated in an application scenario, which successfully demonstrated the legacy component integration, dependability, security, self-reconfiguration and the node-level composability.

The aim of the pSHIELD was to define an architecture framework for the development of the standardized nodes with built-in SPD capabilities, seamlessly composable in a network. The setup of an application with such nodes would be easier and faster; moreover, it would lower production costs and prolong active lifetime of developed systems. The demonstrator presented in this paper constitutes a step forward to validate the pSHIELD concept.

Acknowledgements. The authors acknowledge the support of the Critical Step project in their collaboration concerning the work presented in this paper.

References

1. ARTEMIS Joint Undertaking, the public private partnership for R&D in embedded systems, http://www.artemis-ju.eu/
2. pSHIELD project co-funded by the ARTEMIS Joint Undertaking (GA no.: 100204). Research of Security, Privacy and Dependability in context of Embedded Systems, http://www.pshield.eu/
3. pSHIELD project deliverables D2.3.2, D3.3, D5.3, http://pshield.unik.no/wiki/PublicDeliverables (accessed May 2012)
4. Rana, V., Santambrogio, M., Sciuto, D.: Dynamic Reconfigurability in Embedded System Design. In: IEEE International Symposium on Circuits and Systems, ISCAS 2007, New Orleans (2007)
5. Schoitsch, E.: Design for Safety and Security of Complex Embedded Systems: A Unified Approach. In: Kowalik, J.S., Gorski, J., Sachenko, A. (eds.) Cyberspace Security and Defense: Research Issues. NATO Science Series II - Mathematics, Physics and Chemistry, vol. 196, pp. 161–174 (2005)

Towards Secure Time-Triggered Systems

Florian Skopik[1], Albert Treytl[2], Arjan Geven[3], Bernd Hirschler[2],
Thomas Bleier[1], Andreas Eckel[3], Christian El-Salloum[4], and Armin Wasicek[4]

[1] AIT Austrian Institute of Technology, Safety and Security Department
`firstname.lastname@ait.ac.at`
[2] Austrian Academy of Sciences, Institute for Integrated Sensor Systems
`firstname.lastname@oeaw.ac.at`
[3] TTTech Computertechnik AG
`firstname.lastname@tttech.com`
[4] Vienna University of Technology, Institute of Computer Engineering
`firstname.lastname@tuwien.ac.at`

Abstract. This paper presents the development of a novel joint safety
and security architecture for dependable embedded time-triggered systems. While fault-tolerance properties of time-triggered protocols have
been very well studied, research on security aspects for time-triggered
systems have hardly been covered. Therefore, we explore system design
principles which efficiently realize security mechanisms for time-triggered
architectures. A particular focus is on synergistic effects of security and
safety-related functions, thereby supporting the roll-out of safety-critical
embedded systems even in 'untrusted' environments. As a main contribution, we present the Secure COmmunication in Time-Triggered sYstems
(SCOTTY) approach to build secure time-triggered systems.

Keywords: time-triggered systems, security challenges, safety-criticality.

1 Introduction

It is widely acknowledged that security is gaining significant importance in the
area of embedded systems and in particular in safety-critical systems. An important aspect of these emerging security requirements is that traditional embedded
systems were operated in physically secured environments like within a nuclear
power plant. The trend towards ubiquitous and pervasive computing creates
open environments that do not offer this physical security anymore. In some
environments even the owners of a system can be potential attackers. Successful
attacks could lead to catastrophic events like mechanical damage on the equipment, financial loss, or - in the worst case - the loss of human lives. It is of utmost
importance that **safety** *and* **security** is seen in an integral way [10], because an
attacker could target the whole sphere of control of the embedded system that
also encompasses its physical environment.

The predefined time-triggered schedule can be used as a basis to introduce
a synergetic security concept for time-triggered communication protocols. The
bus guardian supervising the correct execution of the schedule can serve as the

F. Ortmeier and P. Daniel (Eds.): SAFECOMP 2012 Workshops, LNCS 7613, pp. 365–372, 2012.
© Springer-Verlag Berlin Heidelberg 2012

core for a firewall component protecting the network infrastructure and the application traffic using the network. However, this direct use of the bus guardian requires assumptions hardly to be met in practical implementations, especially, if distributed systems are considered: (i) First core assumption is that an attacker has no physical access to the switches and the connected devices (e.g., the system has to be located in a locked room). An attacker having physical access to the system could simply change the wiring on the switch, or physically bypass the bus guardian. (ii) Secure (initial) authentication of devices during startup is required to prevent the insertion of malicious devices. An attacker can - intentionally or unintentionally - insert malicious devices, e.g., as replacement of defect devices. (iii) Third core assumption is that no man-in-the-middle attack [1] is possible. If an attacker can modify the content of messages during transmission, confidentiality and integrity of the message content is endangered.

Thus, the natively provided properties, implemented in a time-triggered protocol are not sufficient. The major objective of our approach is to extend the features of time-triggered protocols to a full security architecture that can deal with threat models, including 'physical access' of attackers. The isolation in the time domain is the basis for a novel security architecture that in a synergetic way extends safety functionality by security functionality to counteract malicious attacks. Additionally, the following challenges need to be addressed: (i) *Scalability from small-scale closed networks to large-scale integrated networks.* At the point, when a system becomes larger (i.e. system of systems, large-scale time-triggered networks), the possibility and the interest in unauthorized access to such systems also increases. (ii) *Protection from intended and unintended modifications.* In addition to increased scale there are also possibilities that are brought up by the mere availability of a technology, where the owner of a system can achieve access and accidentally or intentionally modify parts of the system behavior, thereby altering important dependability properties.

The contributions in this paper are: (i) *Security Challenges and Design Aspects.* We discuss the fundamental requirements for hardening time-triggered systems in order to reach an appropriate level of security. (ii) *Security Architecture for Time-triggered Communication.* We highlight promising approaches and propose basic architectural models to meet the aforementioned requirements.

The remainder of the paper is organized as follows. Section 2 discusses background and related work, Sect. 3 introduces the SCOTTY design principles and basic models, and Sect. 4 sums up our work and concludes the paper.

2   Basic Concepts and Related Work

Dependable embedded computer systems [2] are a well-accepted solution for many applications in the fields of transportation, automation, and medicine [6]. The dependable-computing community has made a tremendous progress in the past decades building ultra-dependable systems out of less reliable components. Further, a multitude of practical techniques with respect to fault masking, error detection, fault diagnosis, and recovery has evolved to improve the reliability of a safety-critical system. Yet, almost all of these approaches put a focus on the safety aspect and assumes that the system is not under active malicious attack. The SCOTTY approach has the aim to introduce a security architecture allowing operation of these systems in non-isolated environments and withstanding malicious attacks [1] - a trend that needs to be addressed [15].

The communication system which interconnects single components is crucial for the safety *and* security properties of the final system [16]. When designing real-time systems, the time-triggered communication paradigm [7] proves to be particularly promising, because of its determinism and predictability facilitating validation and verification efforts for accordingly built systems [9]. A multitude of time-triggered protocols (e.g., FlexRay, TTP, TTEthernet) [4] has already been successfully deployed in many application domains. However, none is known dealing with security services. Within SCOTTY, the TTEthernet system is used as a representative of time-triggered protocols, mainly because of its broad industry acceptance, e.g., by the NASA [5]. Highly dependable time-triggered communication protocols like TTEthernet, FlexRay or TTP/C provide timeslots statically assigned to unique nodes according to a pre-defined time-triggered schedule. Each node is allowed to transmit data on the physical communication medium exclusively during its assigned time slots. This policy is usually enforced by special encapsulation mechanisms, called bus guardians, which prevent any misbehaving node from disrupting the communication among other nodes by transmitting outside of its allocated time slots thereby preventing message collisions. Whereas there exist generic solutions for dependable embedded computing [3] and security for event-triggered protocols has been very well researched and applied (e.g., in wireless sensor networks [8]), research on security in the time-triggered domain is still in its infancy [13]. The core of time-triggered protocols is a common knowledge and usage of time itself. Security research needs to focus on providing a common knowledge of time to implement security features.

Security for clock synchronization is essential, since the domain of clock synchronization for industrial communication systems and sensor networks is becoming a vital aspect for system operation. The synchronized clocks are building the foundation for many critical application domains. A variety of services is enabled by synchronized, distributed clocks, ranging from the application layer (timestamping of measurement data) down to the network layers where clock synchronization is used to schedule media arbitration (e.g., TTEthernet, Flexray) or location determination of sensor nodes. Due to the increasing interconnection of networks, security is of growing interest for industrial networks. Field level devices are connected to external networks and assumptions based on restricted physical access do not apply any more. Clock synchronization and security have to be carefully thought about when they are used together [11,12]. Two considerations have to be taken into account. Firstly, security mechanisms often make use of distributed synchronized time bases. Secondly, clock synchronization in general and timestamp information in particular, which is exchanged over the network to achieve synchronization, are assets that need to be protected by appropriate security mechanisms.

3   The SCOTTY Approach

The SCOTTY security architecture is realized on top of an existing time-triggered real-time communication system. It provides a highly flexible, adaptable, and applicable security layer, which closely integrates with the safety functionality of the system and facilitates existing fault tolerance mechanisms.

3.1   A Security Architecture for Time-Triggered Communication

The fault-tolerance mechanisms and dependability properties of time-triggered communication protocols already provide mechanisms to separate traffic and manage access control. The security part of a time-triggered system can benefit from its fault tolerance mechanism, because both require similar properties [6,13]. Yet, whenever an attacker is able to physically modify parts of the system, like replacing components with malicious components or changing the wiring, the safety properties of today's system cannot be guaranteed anymore.

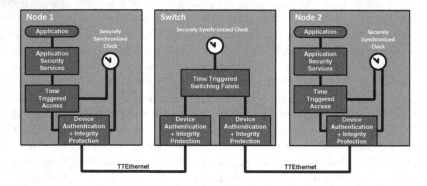

Fig. 1. Functional overview of a secured SCOTTY time-triggered system

Figure 1 shows a schematic overview of the system. Core element is the time-triggered switch and its predefined timeslot scheduling module (Time Triggered Access), which facilitates the access control and traffic separation in the safety domain of the time triggered protocol. To be able to gain synergies for the security system subsystems for (i) device authentication, (ii) secure clock synchronization and (iii) application level security have to be added.

Device Authentication Subsystem. One of the main prerequisites for security is that devices properly mutually authenticate themselves to prevent insertion of malicious devices or messages in case of a man-in-the middle attack. Physical device security is not in the primary scope of our work. Nevertheless, the design of the security protocol foresees these important requirements by allowing the integration in security modules such as smart cards or trusted platform modules. The main challenge in the design and implementation of device authentication mechanisms is to retain the temporal properties of a real-time system, i.e., the designer has to take care that introducing an authentication scheme in the real-time communication does not spoil the original real-time properties of the time-triggered system [14]. Any additional and unpredictable delay in the communication path is critical for the communication and consequently for the access control and traffic separation based on the time-triggered protocol.

Secure Clock Synchronization. A major objective of the security architecture is to protect the temporal properties of the system in the presence of malicious attacks. In a time-triggered system, the accurate temporal coordination of distributed activities is controlled by a consistent global time base. TTEthernet already provides fault-tolerant clock synchronization mechanisms that harden the global time against accidental faults like single-event upsets (SEUs). In order to harden the global time against malicious attacks within SCOTTY a secure clock synchronization protocol is developed on top of the existing clock synchronization protocol. The targeted security goal is to maintain the integrity of the global time base, even under attack, which is a service for communication and application layer security. The main goal is that any node should either be in trusted synchrony with the global time base or reliably detect that it has lost synchronization. Malicious message delay needs to be detected and compensated even considering an attacker model where every message can be potentially created, forged, replicated, deleted, delayed or accelerated by the attacker. This scenario is totally different from the fault hypotheses of classical clock synchronization algorithms targeted on accidental faults (e.g., as used in FlexRay or TTP), which are always based on an upper bound of faulty nodes or messages. The trusted global time base is realized based on mutual checking of signed clock synchronization messages. Additionally, measures need to counteract the modification of messages. These measures are in particular important during the start-up phase. In this respect, authentication and message integrity are the two major issues. Although security systems exists to protect these properties the challenges in SCOTTY lie in the fact that on the one hand high real time requirements need to be met and that on the other hand in opposite to many other real-time security protocols time cannot be used as a base. In particular execution time and jitter need to be considered. Possible solutions are based on a very close integration of security in the time slot scheme to avoid jitter and dedicated algorithms to detect delay.

Application Level Security. Applications on the one hand demand that the communication infrastructure is secure, yet on the other hand they also need additional application specific security service to protect data on an end-to-end basis. The envisioned application level security provides the following secure communication services on top of TTEthernet in order to guarantee real end-to-end security: (i) Authenticated unicast and broadcast; (ii) Application authentication; (iii) Confidential message delivery and integrity protection. The security layer establishes authenticity, integrity and confidentiality even if the attacker has physical access to the system. Since the secure clock-synchronization developed in SCOTTY already protects the global time, time itself can be used to efficiently establish other security properties with low computational and communication overhead. Examples for security-related benefits of a trusted global time are replay prevention of messages containing application data, or broadcast authentication via efficient symmetric protocols like TESLA [5,14].

3.2 Scalability and Legacy Support of the Security Architecture

The security components described before protect the communication infrastructure of and the application data exchanged via a single time-triggered system. Coverage of applications in a cross-domain approach demands the scalability and the support to integrate security-unaware devices. The SCOTTY concept foresees native support for these features.

Scalable Extension of Secure Time-Triggered Networks. Figure 2, shows a simple scenario, where all physical elements that are associated with a link (i.e., the devices, switches and the cabling) are attached to a single switch. This example corresponds to the scenario with a physically secured wiring within a single cabinet. In TTEthernet multiple security-unaware virtual communication channels can coexist on a single shared physical communication infrastructure. The encapsulation mechanisms of TTEthernet ensure that faults cannot cause any influence between virtual communication channels. With the SCOTTY security architecture these channels are also protected against malicious attacks. Hence, the different virtual communication channels (orange and green channels in Figure 2) are also security domains protected against each other. The security services add the following additional properties to normal TTEthernet channels (i) Malicious or bogus devices cannot connect or send messages; (ii) Man in the middle modification of messages is not possible. If application layer confidentiality is used also eavesdropping can be prevented; (iii) Clock synchronization is protected.

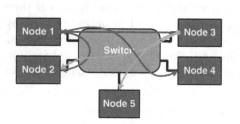
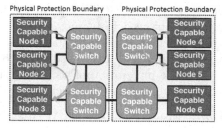

Fig. 2. Single communication cell with secured virtual communication channels

Fig. 3. Cascaded communication cells with secured virtual communication channels

The security domains can be extended by cascaded switches where the interconnection between the cascaded switches occurs transparently (Figure 3). Each link is separately authenticated, i.e. to connect additional switches only the link between the switches has to be added to the security system. The concept of time-triggered scheduling already supports such cascaded switches and therefore can be used as it is. For the SCOTTY security architecture it is irrelevant whether these connections are within a single switch (e.g. a cabinet) between switches within a single physical protection boundary, or even between different physical protection boundaries (e.g. multiple buildings).

Inclusion of Security-Unaware Devices. To support existing security-unaware devices the SCOTTY security architecture also foresees the bridging of two network segments via a secure tunnel established by security gateways. In this scenario, the security layer only has to be installed in both security gateways. The other devices do not have to be modified and are relieved from computational intensive calculation of cryptographic operations. As shown in Figure 4, such a tunnel allows to interconnect two existing networks that do not support security. On the left side (physical protection boundary A) an implementation with a firewall-like security gateway is depicted. This security gateway has two ports and includes all security functionality. This concept is preferred from a security and validation point of view, since there is a single component maintaining the security. On the right side (physical protection boundary B) a security-capable switch and a detached security gateway managing the tunnel(s) is used. Given the traffic separation properties of the security-capable switch no security breach occurs. This solution has advantages in the safety concept since multiple parallel tunnels can be used to connect two boundaries.

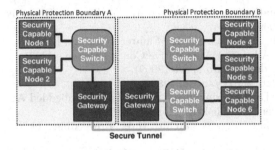
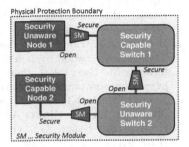

Fig. 4. Secure tunnels between security unaware networks

Fig. 5. Interconnection of security-unaware devices

The concept of the security gateway is also scalable in a way that it can be used to interconnect single security-unaware devices. Figure 5 shows different examples how end-devices and switches can be connected. In this case not the complete aspect of the tunnel functionality is used but the gateway rather serves as a translator. The SCOTTY approach pays special attention to this aspect to develop versatile and re-usable security components that are in particular needed to offer a migration path for existing installations.

4   Discussion and Conclusion

In this paper, we introduced the SCOTTY approach, enabling secure communication in time-triggered systems. The key assumption is to relax the requirement of 'no physical access' of former safety-critical systems. To sum up, the advantages compared to existing solutions are:

- Full protection inside the time-triggered system that allows secure communications beyond physical protection boundaries.
- Synergetic use of safety and security components by reuse of functional modules and integration in existing safety-related design concepts and tool approaches.
- Protection of temporal properties of a real-time system in addition to the standard security attributes, authenticity, integrity and confidentiality.

Future work includes the implementation and evaluation of the introduced concepts under realistic conditions. Special focus will be set on the real-time behavior, attack analysis and versatility of the developed concepts and components to cope with existing and emerging threats and to allow use in numerous application areas.

References

1. Anderson, R.J.: Security engineering - a guide to building dependable distributed systems, 2nd edn. Wiley (2008)
2. Avizienis, A., Laprie, J.C., Randell, B., Landwehr, C.E.: Basic concepts and taxonomy of dependable and secure computing. IEEE Trans. Dependable Sec. Comput. 1(1), 11–33 (2004)
3. Bar-El, H.: Intra-vehicle information security framework. Tech. rep., Discretix Technologies Ltd. (September 2009)
4. Berwanger, J., Ebner, C., Schedl, A., Belschner, R., Fluhrer, S., et al.: FlexRay – The Communication System for Advanced Automotive Control Systems (2001)
5. Cooney, M.: Nasa takes ethernet deeper into space (2009), http://www.networkworld.com/community/node/40899
6. Kopetz, H.: Real-Time Systems: Design Principles for Distributed Embedded Applications, 1st edn. Kluwer Academic Publishers, Norwell (1997)
7. Kopetz, H., Bauer, G.: The time-triggered architecture. Proceedings of the IEEE 91(1), 112–126 (2003)
8. Perrig, A., Szewczyk, R., Tygar, J.D., Wen, V., Culler, D.E.: Spins: Security protocols for sensor networks. Wireless Networks 8(5), 521–534 (2002)
9. Rushby, J.: A comparison of bus architectures for safety-critical embedded systems. Research Report NASA/CR-2003-212161, pp. 112–126 (2003)
10. Schoitsch, E.: Design for safety and security of complex embedded systems: a unified approach. In: Proceedings of the NATO Advanced Research Workshop on Cyberspace Security and Defense: Research Issues, pp. 161–174. Springer (2004)
11. Treytl, A., Gaderer, G., Hirschler, B., Cohen, R.: Traps and pitfalls in secure clock synchronization. In: ISPCS, pp. 18–24 (2007)
12. Treytl, A., Hirschler, B.: Securing IEEE 1588 by ipsec tunnels - an analysis. In: ISPCS, pp. 83–90 (2010)
13. Wasicek, A.: Security in Time-Triggered Systems. Ph.D. thesis, Vienna University of Technology (2012)
14. Wasicek, A., Salloum, C.E., Kopetz, H.: Authentication in time-triggered systems using time-delayed release of keys. In: ISORC, pp. 31–39 (2011)
15. Wolf, M., Weimerskirch, A., Paar, C.: Embedded security in cars: Securing current and future automotive it applications (2006)
16. Wood, A.D., Stankovic, J.A.: Denial of service in sensor networks. IEEE Computer 35(10), 54–62 (2002)

Towards a Framework for Simulation Based Design, Validation and Performance Analysis of Electronic Control Systems

Alexander Hanzlik and Erwin Kristen

AIT Austrian Institute of Technology, Vienna, Austria
{alexander.hanzlik.fl,erwin.kristen}@ait.ac.at

Abstract. This paper presents a model based development approach for the design and validation of electronic control systems, the DTF Data Time Flow Simulator. The DTF is developed at the AIT in the course of the EU ARTEMIS project POLLUX, which is related to the design of embedded systems for the next generation of electric cars. One application of the DTF is the design of vehicle electronic control systems. The automotive industry operates in a very competitive market, where it is hard to get detailed technical information from manufacturers and suppliers. To raise the acceptance for development tools in such a market, the challenge for tool developers is to provide tools that the customers can use without the need to share corporate know-how with third parties. This challenge is addressed in this paper. We present a generic framework for the design of electronic control systems and an application example for performance analysis of such a control system for use in an electric car.

Keywords: Model Based Design, Simulation, Electronic Control Systems, Automotive, Performance Analysis.

1 Introduction

Overcoming the problem of steadily increasing system complexity is an engineering challenge today and it can be expected that it will remain to be a challenge in the future. This is especially true for vehicle electronic control systems. The trend in the development of such systems shows that mechanical and hydraulic components will be more and more replaced by electronic components. A good example for this evolution are the emerging brake-by-wire and steer-by-wire technologies that aim on the mechanical de-coupling of driver actions and the physical reaction of the vehicle. By-wire technologies are already state-of-the-art in avionics, where the control systems have to fulfill stringent requirements to ensure passenger safety. Introducing these technologies in vehicle control systems will not only increase system complexity, but will also increase the demands on functional safety for vehicles. The recently released norm ISO 26262 "Road vehicles - Functional safety" [1] defines, among others, functional safety aspects of the entire development process and provides requirements for

F. Ortmeier and P. Daniel (Eds.): SAFECOMP 2012 Workshops, LNCS 7613, pp. 373–381, 2012.

validation and confirmation measures. This norm has been released at the end of the year 2011 and it can be expected to become a de-facto standard for the automotive industry.

On the one hand, steadily increasing system complexity and safety requirements raise the need for regulations and standards for the development process of safety-relevant systems. Such standards are already well established in avionics, like the DO-178B released in 1992 that deals with the safety of software used in airborne systems.

On the other hand, development time is costly and the automotive industry is a very competitive market. Moreover, it is a market of mass production. Products are released in large quantities, and car manufacturers and suppliers are very ambitious to keep the costs per piece as low as possible. In this area of tension between system complexity, quality considerations, safety requirements and time constraints it may become hard to maintain product quality and safety at affordable costs unless there are appropriate tools at hand for support of system design processes. Although good engineering skills, practice and know-how will always be the most important factors, it seems reasonable to support engineers with tools that facilitate the design process and that help to avoid costly re-design activities caused by the detection of substantial design weaknesses in later phases of product development.

1.1   Motivation and Objectives

From this situation, the following objectives for the DTF have been derived:

- **Early validation of system design concepts.** The aim is to make all relevant design decisions in a very early phase of development, ideally before any hardware and software has been built. Based on the system requirements, a simulation model of the system is created. This simulation model is iteratively refined until all requirements are fulfilled. On the base of this model, the system is implemented.

  Such an approach reduces the probability that substantial design weakness emerge in a later phase of development, like in the test and integration phase. As a consequence, such an approach also helps to reduce the number of costly re-design activities in the development process.

- **Identification of an optimal system design.** „Optimal“ means a design that is as simple as possible and as complex as necessary to fulfill all requirements. A clear and mean design facilitates implementation and test and supports functional safety. Further, it reduces the costs of the final hardware implementation, which is an important commercial aspect in a market of mass production like the automotive industry.

- **Complete vehicle simulation.** This is the notion of a virtual vehicle where the DTF is embedded into a co-simulation environment together with external simulators like MATLAB. These external simulators cover the simulation of mechanic, electrical or hydraulic systems, the DTF serves as the electronic control system of this virtual vehicle.

- **Generic approach for vehicle control system design.** The automotive industry operates in a very competitive market, where detailed technical information is hard to get from manufacturers. To raise the acceptance of development tools in such a market, it is essential to provide something that allows manufacturers to develop their systems without sharing corporate know-how with third parties, like tool developers.

1.2   System Model

Modern vehicle control systems are distributed systems, built from spatially separated electronic control units (ECUs) interconnected via shared communication resources [2]. ECUs are embedded systems that control one or more of the electrical or mechanical systems in a vehicle.

For the following considerations, we assume that a vehicle electronic control system can be built by repetitive use of the following components:

- **ECU.** An Electronic Control Unit ECU is an embedded system that controls one or more of the electrical systems or subsystems in a vehicle. An ECU receives state signals from sensors and/or other ECUs and issues control signals to actuators and/or other ECUs. Different ECUs are assigned different control tasks, like engine control, damping control or transmission control.
- **Communication medium.** A shared communication resource interconnects different ECUs. For communication, dedicated communication protocols are used, like CAN [3], FlexRay [4], LIN [5] or MOST [6].
- **Segment.** ECUs are grouped into segments, which are sets of ECUs that execute a distributed control task concurrently. The ECUs in a segment are linked via a communication medium. Typical segments in a vehicle are the powertrain, the body electronics or the infotainment segment.
- **Gateway.** A gateway links different segments and allows for communication between these segments. Further, gateways are used for gathering diagnostic information from each segment.
- **Transceiver.** Transceivers are the interfaces between the vehicle electronic control system and the environment. *Sensors* are used to deliver signals for further computation, like the brake pedal position or the current lateral speed. *Actuators* are used to control mechanical or electrical components, like the brakes or the motor rotational speed.

Figure 1 shows a vehicle control system architecture providing four segments (Powertrain, Chassis, Body and Infotainment), four gateways and connections to the dashboard and the on-board diagnostics interface of the car.

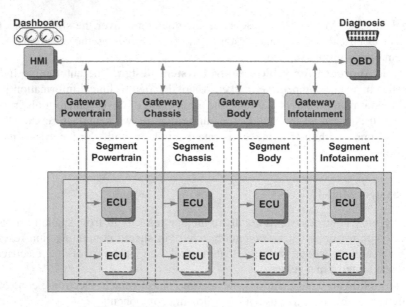

Fig. 1. Vehicle Control System Architecture

2 The Data Time Flow Simulator

The Data Time Flow Simulator DTF is a simulation environment that is currently under development at the Austrian Institute of Technology AIT. The vision of the DTF simulator is to improve the design process of distributed electronic control systems by continuous performance analysis and assessment using virtual prototypes of the target system, integrating different physical domains during an overall system simulation. Performance analysis and assessment are based on the monitoring of action chains from sensors to actuators.

The DTF simulator is a discrete-event simulation [7] environment for the design and validation of electronic control systems. It is based on a modular assembly system that provides a set of primitive building blocks, the *elements*. Elements can be grouped together to form more complex structures, like ECUs. Each element has an input buffer, one output and a propagation delay. When an element receives data in its input buffer, the data is processed and, with the propagation delay defined for this element, the processed value is sent to the output.

Elements are linked together to form so-called *action chains*. An action chain is a directed path from a source element (e.g. a sensor) to a destination element (e.g. an actuator). Figure 2 shows a simple electronic control system consisting of two sensors S1 and S2, two actuators A1 and A2, ECUs A, B C and D and a communication network BUS. The ECUs and the BUS are constituted by elements from the DTF modular assembly system. For example, the ECUs contain a Processor element *Proc* and a Controller element *CC*. The control system has four possible action chains: one from sensor S1 to actuator A1, one from sensor S1 to actuator A2, one from sensor S2 to actuator A1 and finally one from sensor S2 to actuator A2.

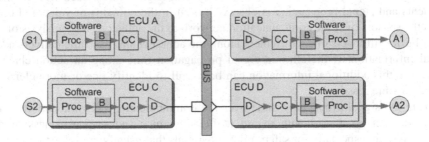

Fig. 2. Simple electronic control system

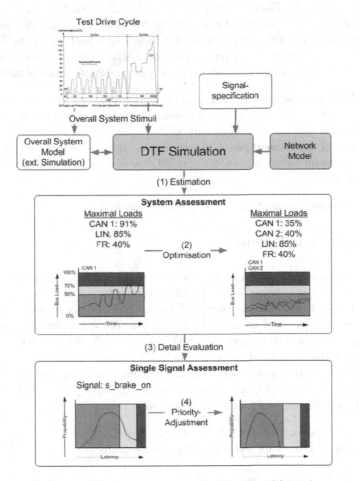

Fig. 3. System Performance Analysis – Principle of Operation

To analyze the performance of the control system, signals are issued to the sensor elements and signal propagation is observed, both in the domains of value and time, from the sensors over the communication network to the actuators. The analysis of the input buffer fill levels of each element along the action chain over time delivers additional information. If the allowed signal propagation time along an action chain is exceeded, this additional information can be useful to identify one or more elements as the possible reasons.

From the signal propagation time over the communication network important information can be gained with regard to the dynamics and responsiveness of the control system, especially for safety-relevant signals that usually are subjected to real-time constraints, like e.g. the brake pedal position.

Figure 3 shows the workflow for a system performance analysis with the DTF based on a drive cycle. The drive cycle consists of a set of events that are issued to the sensor elements of the system and that contain typical driving scenarios like the brake pedal positions or the different positions of the steering wheel during the drive cycle. Using this set of events, the system is put under stress and the system behavior is observed. The assessment of the system performance consists of two phases:

- In the **System Assessment** phase, the maximum loads of different network segments during the drive cycle are determined. If a given maximum network load is exceeded, the network model is modified.
- In the **Signal Assessment** phase, single control signal latencies are examined. If a given maximum signal latency is exceeded, the network communication schedule is modified.

This process is iterated until all requirements are fulfilled.

3   Application Example

A simple application example shall illustrate the system performance assessment described in the last section. We will analyze the performance of a single segment, shown in Figure 4. It consists of twelve ECUs, a CAN bus, six sensors and six actuators. For the simulation of the drive cycle, we use four burst control signals with a constant period issued to sensors S02, S03, S04 and S05. Sensors S00 and S01 are triggered with chirp signals of varying period.

For the performance assessment, we consider the maximum network load of the CAN bus and the control signal latency of signal s_brake_front which is issued to sensor S04. The requirements for this application example are

- Maximum network load for CAN bus < 70%
- Control signal latency for signal s_brake_front < 28ms

3.1   System Assessment Phase

For the defined drive cycle, the single segment network model shown in Figure 4 does not fulfill the maximum network load requirement. The load of the CAN bus exceeds 70%.

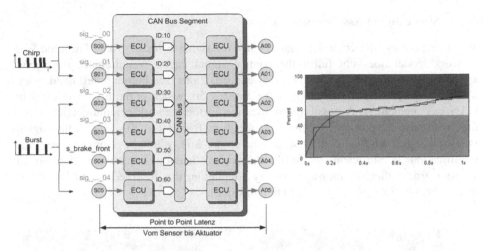

Fig. 4. Single Segment Network Model

A possible modification of the network model is to split the single segment into two segments and to connect them via a gateway. The refined network model is shown in Figure 5.

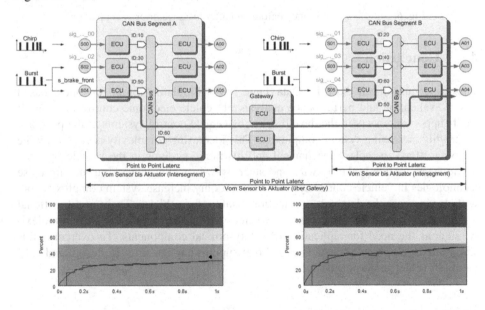

Fig. 5. Two Segment Network Model

For the defined drive cycle, the two segment network model fulfills the maximum network load requirement for both CAN segments, because in both segments the maximum network load is clearly below 70%.

3.2   Single Signal Assessment Phase

We now examine the control signal latency for signal *s_brake_front*. The modified network model does not fulfill the control signal latency requirement for signal *s_brake_front*, because the signal latency exceeds 28ms (see Figure 6, left hand side). The message priority of signal *s_brake_front* is 50, which is the lowest priority in CAN bus segment A. A possible modification of the network communication schedule is to raise the priority of signal *s_brake_front* from 50 to 20 such that this signal is not pre-empted by the control signals of sensor S02, which have priority 30. This modification is sufficient to fulfill the signal latency requirement for signal *s_brake_front*: after the message priority adaptation, the observed signal latency is clearly below 28ms (see Figure 6, right hand side).

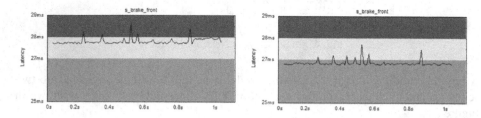

Fig. 6. Control signal latency before and after message priority adaptation

4   Conclusion

This paper introduced the DTF Data Time Flow Simulator, a tool for model based design, validation and performance analysis of vehicle electronic control systems. It shall support engineers in the development of vehicle control systems in the presence of steadily increasing system complexity. This increasing complexity is caused by the ongoing efforts to replace mechanical and hydraulic systems in the vehicle by electronic systems, like brake-by-wire and steer-by-wire technologies. Introducing these technologies in vehicle control systems will not only increase system complexity, but will also increase the demands on functional safety for vehicles. These non-functional requirements that shall ensure passenger safety will further increase system complexity, such as the need for replication of safety-critical components. To overcome this situation, development tools are needed that support engineers in the design and validation of vehicle control systems.

References

1. ISO 26262. Road vehicles – Functional safety, http://www.iso.org
2. Zimmermann, W., Schmidgall, R.: Bussysteme in der Fahrzeugtechnik – Protokolle, Standards und Softwarearchitektur. Vieweg+Teubner, 4. Auflage (2010)

3. Etschberger, K. (Hrsg.): CAN Controller Area Network – Grundlagen, Protokolle, Bausteine, Anwendungen. Hanser Fachbuchverlag, Deutschland (2001)
4. FlexRay Communications System Protocol Specification Version 3.0.1, http://www.flexray.com
5. Grzemba, A., Von der Wense, H.: LIN-Bus. Franzis, Deutschland (2005)
6. Grzemba, A.: MOST. The Automotive Multimedia Network. From MOST25 to MOST150. Franzis (2011)
7. Banks, J., Carson, J., Nelson, B.: Discrete-Event System Simulation. Prentice Hall (2000)

Compiling for Time Predictability*

Peter Puschner[1], Raimund Kirner[2], Benedikt Huber[1], and Daniel Prokesch[1]

[1] Institute of Computer Engineering
Vienna University of Technology, Austria
{peter,benedikt,daniel}@vmars.tuwien.ac.at
[2] Department of Computer Science
University of Hertfordshire, United Kingdom
r.kirner@herts.ac.uk

Abstract. Within the T-CREST project we work on hardware/software architectures and code-generation strategies for time-predictable embedded and cyber-physical systems.

In this paper we present the single-path code generation approach that we plan to explore and implement in a compiler prototype for a time-predictable processor. Single-path code generation produces code that forces every execution to follow the same trace of instructions, thus supporting time predictability and simplifying the worst-case execution-time analysis of code. The idea of the single-path generation and details about the code-generation rules of the compiler can be found in this work.

Keywords: real-time systems, compilers, time predictability, worst-case execution-time analysis.

1 Introduction

Many embedded and cyber-physical systems need safe and tight predictions about the timing of the hard real-time software that controls safety-critical parts of the application. The problem of current systems is that planning application timing and obtaining reliable information about the timing behaviour of applications is getting more and more difficult, the reason being that the complexity of hardware and software is growing without limits. This, in turn, has the effect that efforts and costs of both the construction and the validation of safety-critical real-time applications are steadily increasing and becoming unacceptably high.

Within the T-CREST project we are developing a novel processor architecture and new software and code-generation strategies to make real-time systems more time-predictable and reduce the complexity of temporal planning and timing analysis. The strategy is to use simpler hardware that can be controlled by software and to generate code that behaves in a more predictable manner than traditional code.

---

* This research was partially funded under the European Union's 7th Framework Programme under grant agreement no. 288008: Time-Predictable Multi-Core Architecture for Embedded Systems (T-CREST).

F. Ortmeier and P. Daniel (Eds.): SAFECOMP 2012 Workshops, LNCS 7613, pp. 382–391, 2012.

Within this paper we present the code-generation strategy of the T-CREST approach. The ideas for the single-path code generation, that is at the core of our code generation, have been published in [1] – In the single-path approach input-dependent code alternatives are translated into sequential pieces of predicated code of the same functional behaviour. In this paper we now present the rationale for the single-path code transformation and provide details about the code-generation rules used in this approach.

The advantages of the proposed code generation strategy are that it yields predictable, compositional and stable code execution times. These properties make it easy to argue about code timing. Further, they support a structured or hierarchical design and analysis of systems with respect to timing properties.

2 Desirable Code-Timing Properties

When compiling code for time-predictable embedded systems we should strive for the following properties:

- *Composability:* The execution times of generated code should not be dependent of the software context in which the code is executed, i.e., adding, changing, or removing one part of some software must not change the worst-case timing of the other code sections. This is necessary to make timing an integral (though platform specific) property of a code piece or software component, which is a prerequisite for a hierarchical software development process for real-time applications.
- *Compositionality:* Given the timing of some pieces of code, the timing of a composite should be derivable by a simple timing formula from the timing of its constituent code pieces.
- *Analyzability:* The code structure should allow for an accurate timing analysis at reasonable cost. In particular, the overestimation of the worst-case execution time should be low, in the order of a few percent.
- *Stability:* The generated code should run with constant execution time or with small execution-time jitter (variability). This greatly simplifies both timing analysis and the argumentation about the temporal behaviour of real-time application software.
- *Simplicity:* The execution-time analysis of the resulting code should be of low complexity. Simplicity also fosters analyzability.

3 How to Make Execution Times Predictable

The execution time of a piece of code is determined by three factors: (1) the hardware on which the code is to run, (2) the sequence of actions defined by the code (depending on the algorithm chosen to solve a computing problem and the compiler that transforms the source code into machine code that the processor can execute), and (3) the context in which the code is executed [2]. The latter depends on the hardware state resulting from the execution history and the application-specific context (e.g., the possible value assignments of variables) in which the code is executed.

Each of the listed factors influences time predictability. Within the T-CREST project we aim at creating an environment in which time predictability is supported by all three factors.

In the hardware domain, the architecture of the Patmos processor [3], which is developed in the T-CREST project, provides means to make the processor timing independent of the execution context. It features a fully predicated instruction set (cf. Section 4.1), where every instruction is conditionally executed depending on the value of one of the eight predicate registers. The VLIW nature of the in-order execution dual-issue pipeline demands that hazards are resolved during compile time instead of stalling the pipeline implicitly at runtime. The memory architecture, which provides a predictable function cache and a software-managed scratchpad area, ensures that timing of memory accesses is controllable by software.

As for the software, coding guidelines and specific code-generation strategies ensure that the sequence of instructions executed during a program execution are insensitive to the values of input variables. The sequence of instructions executed by the resulting code is easy to analyse, and, again, independent of the context in which the software is run.

Within this paper we focus on code generation.

Enforcing Equal Timing for All Inputs

Regarding software, the central question in this paper is: How can the software help to make code timing predictable?

Software contributes to variable timing by executing different instruction traces for different inputs. These different traces, in general, have different timing. So, if we want software to help make code timing predictable, we must find a way to make alternative code sections execute with equal time consumption. This can be addressed in two ways: either find ways to *make the timing of alternative traces equal* or *eliminate alternatives*.

Enforcing Equal Timing for Alternatives. Assuming that the processor provides constant instruction execution times and memory access times, an input-data dependent execution time can be traced back to some control-flow branch where different alternatives take a different amount of time. This difference can be eliminated by inserting so many single-cycle NOP instructions into the shorter (less time-consuming) alternative that the execution times of the alternatives become equal. A similar strategy can be applied to every loop with a non-constant but bounded number of iterations — insert another loop of identical iteration timing but empty functionality to compensate for non-taken iterations in the original loop. So the number of iterations of both loops taken together is always the same. The same goal could be achieved by substituting the NOP sequences by a DELAY instruction, parametrised to stall execution for the equivalent amount of time the NOPs would take.

This strategy is related to the approach of timing instructions, so-called *deadline instructions*, as provided in the implementation of the PRET architecture of Lickly et al. [4]. A deadline instruction sets the execution time limit for subsequent instructions until the next deadline instruction is encountered, which then stalls the execution until the specified time has elapsed. If the execution takes longer, an exception is raised which could be handled by the application, although it is desirable to verify the absence of such events.

There are some drawbacks with the NOP or DELAY insertion approach: First, the insertion of NOP respectively DELAY instructions increases code size. Second, the NOP-insertion approach can only be used in architectures that do not suffer from hardware-state dependent execution times. E.g., in architectures with instruction caches one cannot assign a fixed execution time to a set of instructions, because access times of instructions differ for hits and misses (see Fig. 1). Even in architectures whose instruction execution times are not state dependent, NOP insertion requires detailed knowledge about the hardware timing in order to determine the correct number of NOP instructions that need to be placed in different code locations. Similarly, the insertion of DELAY instructions needs a detailed analysis of the worst-case timing of code sections to set timers correctly, thus confronting us with the whole set of problems of a highly complex WCET analysis.

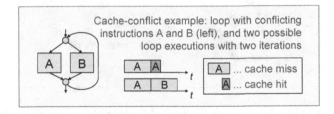

Fig. 1. Example Illustrating that There is Nothing Like a Fixed Execution Time for a Branch

Eliminating Alternatives. If we manage to generate code that follows the same execution trace for whatever input data it receives then obtaining composable and stable timing becomes almost trivial. This is the idea behind the single-path transformation [1]. The single-path transformation is a code generation strategy that extends the idea of if-conversion [5] to transform branching code into code with a single trace. Instead of using conditional branches to react to different input data, the transformed code uses predicated instructions – comparable to instructions that hide the branches within – to control the semantics of the executed code. Code generation for loops follows a similar idea. Loops with input-dependent iteration conditions are transformed into loops for which the number of iterations is known at compile time. Input-data dependent iterations are again removed by if-conversion.

The execution of single-path code requires a little hardware support (see Section 4.3). Single-path code generation is however a purely software-based approach, meaning that it does not need any information about the timing of hardware operations. This independence from hardware timing makes the single-path approach the preferable code-generation strategy among the discussed solutions.

4   Generating Single-Path Code

4.1   If-Conversion

As said before, the single-path transformation builds upon *If-Conversion* [5]. If-conversion removes branches in the control flow of a piece of code by using predicated instructions. Predicated instructions are instructions whose semantics are controlled by a predicate, where the predicate can be implemented by the condition code flag(s) or specific predicate flags of the processor. If the predicate is true the instruction realises the function associated with its op-code. If the predicate evaluates to false, the instruction behaves like a NOP instruction.

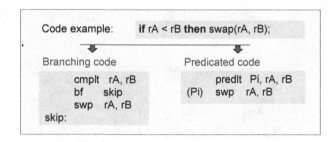

Fig. 2. Branching Code (left) versus Predicated Code (right) Generated from the Same Source-Code Example

Figure 2 shows an if-conversion example. In this example the values of two variables, rA and rB are swapped if the value of rA is less than the value rB. On the left side of the figure we see the branching code generated for the example, assuming the two variables are held in registers. The right side displays the code after if-conversion. The code on the right side is semantically equivalent, but uses a predicated swap instruction instead of the conditional branch.

Let us for the moment assume that we have a processor that supports a fully predicated instruction set, i.e., the processor provides a predicated version of each of its op-codes. Building on this instruction set we can use if conversion to transform arbitrary conditional code branches resulting from *if-then-else* constructs into predicated code.

Figure 3 illustrates the single-path transformation of an *if-then-else* construct. The original – branching – version uses a conditional branch to control which

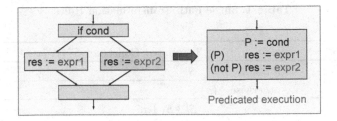

Fig. 3. Using If-conversion to Eliminate Alternatives

alternative should be effective. The single-path version computes a predicate, P, and executes both alternatives with predicates P and *not P*, respectively, to implement the same semantics without branching.

4.2   The Single-Path Transformation

We will now explain how we can use the if-conversion of conditionals to build a set of rules that allows us to transform more complex programs, i.e., programs that include sequences of constructs, loops, and procedure calls. These rules can then be applied to any piece of WCET-boundable code[1] to transform it into a single-path equivalent.

Preparing for the Single-Path Transformation. Recall that only those conditional branches whose branching decision depends on the program inputs create different paths of program execution. Therefore, the single-path transformation only has to eliminate these input-data dependent branches. Conditional branches whose behaviour is not influenced by program inputs should not be affected by the transformation.

To make sure that only input-dependent conditionals are transformed, the actual single-path transformation and code generation is preceded by a data-flow analysis [6]. This data-flow analysis traverses the entire program code and marks all parts of the code as either input-data dependent or input-data independent.

The Actual Transformation. After the data-flow analysis the actual single-path transformation and code generation are performed. Although the single-path transformation is conducted on an intermediate representation of the code, we will demonstrate it here for programming language constructs represented at the source-language level. We think that this makes the performed steps easier to comprehend.

To transform a program given in high-language source, we first construct its syntax tree. We then recursively traverse the syntax tree and use the appropriate rules from Table 1 to perform the single-path transformation for the constructs represented by the nodes of the syntax tree.

---

[1] The maximum number of iterations can be bounded for all loops.

Table 1. Single-Path Transformation Rules

Construct S		Translated Construct $\mathcal{SP}[\![\,S\,]\!]\,\sigma\delta$
S	if $\sigma = T$	S
	otherwise	$(\sigma)\,S$
$S_1 ; S_2$		$\mathcal{SP}[\![\,S_1\,]\!]\,\sigma\delta ;$ $\mathcal{SP}[\![\,S_2\,]\!]\,\sigma\delta$
if $cond$ then S_1 else S_2	if $ID(cond)$	$guard_\delta := \sigma ;$ $\mathcal{SP}[\![\,S_1\,]\!]\langle\sigma \wedge \ \ guard_\delta\rangle\langle\delta + 1\rangle ;$ $\mathcal{SP}[\![\,S_2\,]\!]\langle\sigma \wedge \neg guard_\delta\rangle\langle\delta + 1\rangle$
	otherwise	if $cond$ then $\mathcal{SP}[\![\,S_1\,]\!]\,\sigma\delta$ else $\mathcal{SP}[\![\,S_2\,]\!]\,\sigma\delta$
while $cond$ max N times do S	if $ID(cond)$	$end_\delta := $ false for $count_\delta := 1$ to N do begin $\quad \mathcal{SP}[\![$ if $\neg cond$ then $end_\delta := $ true $]\!]\,\sigma\langle\delta + 1\rangle ;$ $\quad \mathcal{SP}[\![$ if $\neg end_\delta$ then $S\,]\!]\,\sigma\langle\delta + 1\rangle$ end
	otherwise	while $cond$ do $\mathcal{SP}[\![\,S\,]\!]\,\sigma\delta$
call proc $p\,(pars)$	if $\sigma = T$	call proc $p\,(pars)$
	otherwise	call proc p-sip$(\sigma, pars)$
def proc $p\,(pars)$ S		def proc $p\,(pars)\ S;$ def proc p-sip $(pcnd, pars)$ $\mathcal{SP}[\![\,S\,]\!]\langle pcnd\rangle\langle 0\rangle$

Table 1 shows the single-path transformation rules for the basic control constructs used in a high-level language – simple constructs, sequences, alternatives, loops, and procedures[2]. We assume that conditions controlling the execution of alternatives and loops are boolean variables, and thus side-effect free expressions. Besides the statement type, each rule has two parameters, σ and δ. The first parameter, σ, is a boolean value that represents the *precondition* under which the statement under transformation is executed. The second parameter, δ, is used to pass the value of a counter to the code transformation rule. Some rules use this counter value to generate unique variable names in the context of the rule. The details of the rules are as follows:

Simple Statement. For a simple statement S we distinguish two cases. If the precondition evaluates to *true* then the statement will be executed in every execution. Therefore the transformation generates S. Otherwise S will be executed conditionally depending on the value of σ. Therefore the transformation generates code for the predicated execution of S with predicate σ.

---

[2] To keep the paper short we demonstrate the transformation for one representative of alternative statements (*if–then–else*) and loop statements (*while*) only. The rules for other variations of these statement types are similar.

Statement Sequence. For a statement sequence, the generated code is the result of the sequence of its transformed constituents.

Conditional Statement. For a conditional statement, as represented by the *if–then-else* construct, we distinguish two cases. If the outcome of the branching condition depends on the program inputs (*ID(cond)* is *true*), then we generate a code sequence that consists of the serialisation of the two single-path transformed alternatives S_1 and S_2, where the precondition parameters of the alternatives are the conjunction of the old precondition (σ) and the evaluation result of *cond* (for S_1) respectively *not cond* (for S_2). If the branching condition does not depend on the program inputs then the transformation conserves the *if–then–else* structure and only transforms S_1 and S_2.

Loop. In order to eliminate input-dependent control flow from a loop, the transformation replaces the original loop by a *for–loop* with constant execution count — as we are transforming hard real-time code we assume that there is an input-data independent expression N bounding the maximum number of loop iterations. The termination of the new *for–loop* is controlled by a new counter variable $count_\delta$. Further, we introduce an end_δ flag to enforce that the transformed loop has the same semantics as the original. This flag is initialised to *true* and assumes the value *false* as soon as the termination condition of the original loop evaluates to *true* for the first time. In the new loop the original loop body S is only effective as long as the end flag has not been set. Thus S in the end executes under the same condition as in the original loop.

Procedures. The last two rules illustrate code generation for procedures. If the precondition of a call is always *true*, then the generated code calls the procedure unconditionally. Otherwise, i.e., σ will only be known at runtime, we have to generate code that ensures that the procedure is called in every execution, but that the procedure execution respects the call's precondition. To facilitate the latter, we generate code for a new, single-path version of the procedures (with suffix `-sip`) that has an additional parameter *pcnd*. In the code generation for the definition of the single-path version of the procedure, *pcnd* is incorporated as a precondition that controls the predicated execution of the procedure body S. In the code generation for the call of the single-path version of the procedure, *pcnd* accepts the actual value of the precondition passed to the procedure.

4.3   Single-Path Transformation and Partial Predication

So far we assumed that our processor provides support for full predication. While this is the case for the processor being developed in T-CREST it seems noteworthy that the single-path transformation can be easily adapted for architectures that support only partial predication. In fact, work published in [7] gives an excellent guide on how to apply if-conversion for such architectures.

The idea behind code generation for partially predicated architectures is to compute intermediate results of both alternatives of an *if–then–else* statement,

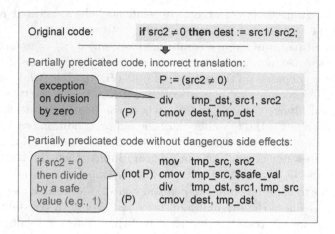

Fig. 4. If-Conversion for Partial-Predication Support

but only use the results from that one alternative for which the condition evaluates to *true*. *Predicated Move* instructions are used to control that the correct temporary results are moved to the variables that store the final results of the translated code.

An if-conversion example for an architecture with partial predication is shown in Figure 4. The example also demonstrates how the if-conversion avoids adverse side effects when generating code with partial predication.

5   Conclusion and Outlook

As the architectures of both hardware and software used in embedded and cyber-physical systems get more and more complex, the temporal predictability of code gets lost. This predictability loss brings about a number of unpleasant effects for the design and analysis of time critical systems: the absence of timing composability and compositionality impedes a meaningful argumentation about timing properties when designing, implementing, or re-using software components. The multitude of parameters determining hardware timing and execution paths make code timing unstable and difficult to analyse, thus resulting in great timing variability of execution times and pessimistic results in worst-case execution time analysis and global timing analysis, both leading to an overestimation of resource needs and thereby higher than necessary expenses for computing resources.

The goal of T-CREST is to build a hardware/software platform for time predictable computing. With simpler and controllable hardware and single-path software we want to eliminate the above-mentioned problems.

The single-path conversion described in this paper allows us to produce code that executes on the same execution path for all possible inputs. The resulting code behaviour is insensitive to the values of input variables, which makes the analysis easy and supports stability from the software side. Together with time-predictable hardware the proposed code-transformation strategy also provides the composability and compositionality of code timing that is desirable for real-time applications. The latter has been highlighted in [8].

So far the proposed single-path transformation has been explored in small experiments that incorporated the manual transformation of branches into conditionals [9]. Within T-CREST we are now implementing a compiler that performs the code transformation automatically. A first compiler prototype is expected to be available in a few months. This will allow us to conduct further experiments (including experiments with larger code) and gain insights into the practical aspects of the automated single-path generation of code.

References

1. Puschner, P., Burns, A.: Writing temporally predictable code. In: Proc. 7th IEEE International Workshop on Object-Oriented Real-Time Dependable Systems, pp. 85–91 (January 2002)
2. Wilhelm, R., Engblom, J., Ermedahl, A., Holsti, N., Thesing, S., Whalley, D., Bernat, G., Ferdinand, C., Heckmann, R., Mitra, T., Mueller, F., Puaut, I., Puschner, P., Staschulat, J., Stenström, P.: The worst-case execution-time problem – overview of methods and survey of tools. ACM Transactions on Embedded Computing Systems 7(3) (2008)
3. Schoeberl, M., Schleuniger, P., Puffitsch, W., Brandner, F., Probst, C.W., Karlsson, S., Thorn, T.: Towards a time-predictable dual-issue microprocessor: The Patmos approach. In: First Workshop on Bringing Theory to Practice: Predictability and Performance in Embedded Systems (PPES 2011), pp. 11–20 (March 2011)
4. Lickly, B., Liu, I., Kim, S., Patel, H.D., Edwards, S.A., Lee, E.A.: Predictable programming on a precision timed architecture. In: Proceedings of the 2008 International Conference on Compilers, Architectures and Synthesis for Embedded Systems, CASES 2008, pp. 137–146. ACM, New York (2008)
5. Allen, J., Kennedy, K., Porterfield, C., Warren, J.: Conversion of Control Dependence to Data Dependence. In: Proc. 10th ACM Symposium on Principles of Programming Languages, pp. 177–189 (January 1983)
6. Gustafsson, J., Lisper, B., Kirner, R., Puschner, P.: Code analysis for temporal predictability. Real-Time Syst. 32(3), 253–277 (2006)
7. Mahlke, S., Hank, R., McCormick, J., August, D., Hwu, W.: A Comparison of Full and Partial Predicated Execution Support for ILP Processors. In: Proc. 22nd International Symposium on Computer Architecture, pp. 138–150 (June 1995)
8. Schellekens, M.: A Modular Calculus for the Average Cost of Data Structuring. Springer (2008)
9. Puschner, P.: Experiments with wcet-oriented programming and the single-path architecture. In: Proc. 10th IEEE International Workshop on Object-Oriented Real-Time Dependable Systems, pp. 205–210 (February 2005)

Towards the Automated Qualification
of Tool Chain Design

Fredrik Asplund, Matthias Biehl, and Frédéric Loiret

Embedded Control Systems
Royal Institute of Technology
Stockholm, Sweden
{biehl,fasplund,floiret}@kth.se

Abstract. The development of safety-critical embedded systems is supported by a number of development tools, which are increasingly integrated into automated tool chains. Safety standards require these tool chains to be qualified, which is costly and requires a large effort. To reduce cost and effort tool chains can be composed of pre-qualified tools and then themselves pre-qualified by identifying the parts of tool chain software that have an impact on safety more exactly. In this paper we propose the use of a modeling language to describe this tool chain composition. This allows us to reduce effort even further by automatically analyzing the tool chain model for safety issues. It also promises to reduce the effort and cost of later steps in the deployment of the tool chain by formalizing the communication of safety issues and automating the generation of code for tool chain software.

Keywords: Tool Integration, Qualification, Safety.

1 Introduction

We are surrounded by a growing number of increasingly complex safety-critical embedded systems, such as advanced driver assistance systems in cars and autopilots in airplanes. We study two trends in the development of such embedded systems: (1) the need for qualification of software and (2) the automation and size of the tool chains and development environments. While these aspects are typically studied independently, we believe that there are critical interdependencies.

(1) For a number of embedded systems domains there are safety standards that stipulate both restrictions for the development process and require software tool qualification. Examples include IEC 61508:2010 [4], ISO26262:2011 [11] for the automotive industry and DO-178C/DO-330 [12,13] for the aviation industry.

(2) Tool chains grow in size and complexity, as the development of an embedded system typically requires collaboration between a large number of experts. The use of sophisticated software tools joined together by automation has increased in an attempt to increase productivity.

F. Ortmeier and P. Daniel (Eds.): SAFECOMP 2012 Workshops, LNCS 7613, pp. 392–399, 2012.

The implication of (1) is that *all* software that has implications on safety should be qualified. Together with (2) this leads to the conclusion that not only isolated tools, but also the integration of tool chains should be qualified [5]. However, as shown in [8], there is a reluctance of practitioners to use a one-size-fits-all solution for tool chains. Tool chains are therefore typically tailored to the specific development process(es) and the set of tools used in a project.

This means that there is a clash of objectives between the need to qualify a potentially large part of a development environment and the need to provide a customized tool chain for each individual project. This conflict can be solved by stipulating safety goals for different parts of each tool chain at hand, safety goals which allow the qualification to be limited to the parts of a development environment that have the potential to influence the safety of end products. In this way the risks introduced due to tool integration can be mitigated, while the qualification effort and cost is kept at a manageable level.

In this paper we report on our work in progress. In section 2 we describe our overall approach, limiting ourselves to the second step of a method defined in an earlier publication. We divide this step into two parts. The first part, detailed in section 3, is the use of a modeling language to model reference workflows and tool chains. The second part, detailed in section 4, is to analyze the models for safety issues related to tool integration. Thereafter we describe related work in section 5 and summarize the paper in section 6.

2   Approach

We use an approach for tool chain qualification in four steps, namely (step 1) pre-qualification of engineering tools, (step 2) pre-qualification at the tool chain level, (step 3) qualification of the tool chain and (step 4) qualification at the tool level [5]. This approach lets us separate the parts required by modern safety standards in regard to software tool qualification from the extra effort suggested by us to identify safety issues related to tool integration.

This paper deals with the second step, the pre-qualification at the tool chain level, which is concerned with identifying the required safety goals due to tool integration. The output from this step is a description of a reference workflow and tool chain with the relevant parts annotated with the mitigating efforts required due to tool integration. The tools mentioned throughout the paper are assumed to already be pre-qualified to the requirements of a relevant safety standard (a similar approach is used by other works, such as [9,10]).

As a format for the description we propose to use the Tool Integration Language (TIL) [6], a modeling language for systematically describing the composition of tools into tool chains. In contrast to other work [9,10], we can therefore explicitly describe the tool chain in the form of models. The activities for qualifying the composition can then be formalized, since the tool chain is described systematically and in a structured form. This formalized description of the qualification activity can be the basis for partly automated qualification. Additionally, the same models can be used as a basis for realizing the tool chain as a software solution through automated code generation and as a formal way of communicating safety-relevant requirements on the tool chain. The use of TIL should therefore help reduce effort and cost even further. TIL is relatively mature, as it has been used for modeling industrial tool chains [2] and generate code from these models [7].

To make use of TIL we divide the second step of our approach into two separate parts, which are detailed in the following sections:

- Section 3 describes the tailoring of the tool chain by composition of pre-qualified tools, in which tool chains are composed by selecting pre-qualified components and describing the connections between them.
- Section 4 describes the analysis of the composition, in which the composition is analyzed and annotated with information on which parts require mitigating efforts to handle safety issues due to tool integration.

3   Tailoring of the Tool Chain

In this part of the second step we compose pre-qualified tools into tool chains. This consists of creating an early TIL design model. Below we give a short overview of TIL, by referring to a simple example model in Figure 1.

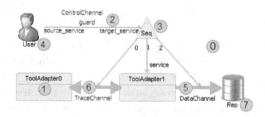

Fig. 1. A Simple TIL Model Illustrating the Graphical Syntax

In TIL a tool chain is described in terms of a number of *ToolAdapters* ① and the relation between then. A *ToolAdapter* exposes data and functionality of a tool. The relation between the *ToolAdapters* is realized as any of the following *Channels*: a *ControlChannel* ② describes a service call, a *DataChannel* ⑤ describes data exchange and a *TraceChannel* ⑥ describes the creation of trace links. A *Sequencer* ③ describes sequential control flow; it executes a sequence of services in a defined order. A *User* ④ is a representative for a real tool chain user. It is used to describe and limit the possible interactions of the real users with the tool chain. Outgoing control channels from the user denote services invoked by the user, incoming control channels to a user denote a notification sent to the user. A *Repository* ⑦ provides storage and version management of tool data.

Each ToolAdapter has an associated *ToolAdapterMetamodel,* which specifies
the structure of the data and the signature of the functionality exposed by the
tool adapter. An important design decision taken during the specification of the
tool adapter is the scope and granularity of the exposed data. This decision depends on the role of the tool within the tool chain. Our experiments on specifying
ToolAdapterMetamodels of different granularity can be used as a guideline [7] for
creating an adequate tool adapter metamodel. Each DataChannel has an associated model transformation, which resolves structural heterogeneities between
the data of the ToolAdapters, which is structured according to the ToolAdapter-
Metamodels. The source and target metamodels of the model transformation are
thus the respective ToolAdapterMetamodels.

4   Analysis of the Composition

After a tool chain has been modeled in TIL, the risks related to tool integration
can be identified from the model. If such a risk is identified, an associated safety
goal [5] can be required to be fulfilled for that part of the tool chain. Such a safety
goal will point to certain types of mitigating actions that need to be shown to
be in place in later steps of our approach.

Below we describe three different types of risk associated with tool integration,
the analysis of TIL models required to identify these types of risk and the safety
goals that can mitigate them. The discussion is based on a small part of a
tool chain described in Figure 2. In this example requirements are written by a
requirements engineer utilizing the IRQA requirements tool. The requirements
are then persisted to a repository before a designer utilizing Enterprise Architect
uses them to build an UML model of the end product. After the UML model has
been reviewed it is subsequently transferred manually into a Simulink model by
a developer. As seen in the minimal TIL model in Figure 2, the tool integration
in this example is mainly handled manually. This is not uncommon, even if it is
becoming rarer, in state of the practice tool chains.

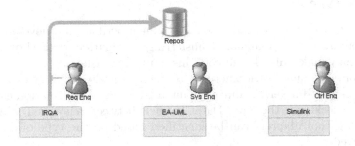

Fig. 2. Tool Chain of the Running Example Modeled in TIL

4.1   Risk Type 1

Risk Type 1: A developer creates a development artifact. Later during development another developer, who uses information from the previously developed artifact, develops another, more refined artifact. This refined artifact is not complete in regard to or not consistent with the previous artifact, but this can not be detected by the developers. The undetected inconsistencies or incompleteness can lead to hazards in the end product.

Detection: The qualification activity to detect whether there is no possibility to detect inconsistencies and incompleteness can be formalized by checking if there are TraceChannels between the ToolAdapters (these provide the ability to create traces).

Safety Goal: If this type of risk is detected, it can be mitigated by the safety goal that tracing needs to be enabled by the relevant parts of the tool chain, developers trained in this functionality and processes established to ensure that the functionality is used. The example shown in Figure 2 does not contain any trace channels. After this is detected the analyst can require traceability to be enabled between all ToolAdapters, as shown in Figure 3.

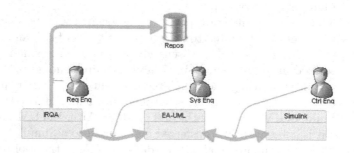

Fig. 3. Traceability Added to the TIL Model

4.2   Risk Type 2

Risk Type 2: A developer studies a development artifact and develops another development artifact by manually transferring information. A tired or untrained developer may make mistakes during this manual transfer.

Detection: The qualification activity to detect whether tired or untrained developers can introduce errors during manual transfers of information can be formalized by checking if there are DataChannels between relevant ToolAdapters. The *relevant* ToolAdapters can be identified based on the type of engineering tools involved.

Safety Goal: If this type of risk is detected, it can be mitigated by the safety goal that automatic transformation of development artifacts needs to be enabled by the tool chain, tool chain developers trained in the domain knowledge of the developers and processes established to ensure that the functionality is used. The example shown in Figure 2 does not contain a DataChannel between Enterprise Architect and Simulink, even though it is tedious work to manually transform models from UML to Simulink. After this is detected the analyst can require a DataChannel to be enabled between these tools, as shown in Figure 4.

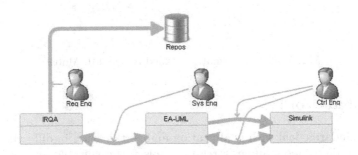

Fig. 4. Transformation Added to the TIL Model

4.3   Risk Type 3

Risk Type 3: A project manager retrieves a project report, supposedly extracted from the most recent data on the project status. Unfortunately the new report has been delayed, the manager reads through obsolete information and fails to take mitigating action regarding project issues that may affect safety.

Detection: The qualification activity to detect whether the use of obsolete information can not be detected can be formalized by checking if each relevant ToolAdapter has a DataChannel to a Repository/CMSystem (these are, by definition, required to support timestamps or similar [1]). The *relevant* ToolAdapters can be identified based on which data is used for decision support.

Safety Goal: If this type of risk is detected, it can be mitigated by the safety goal that relevant development artifacts need to be time stamped according to a global clock and project managers trained in correctly identifying the time information. For the sake of the example we can assume that a new, complete Simulink model is of interest to project managers. Simulink is not connected to a Repository/CMSystem in the example shown in Figure 2. After this is detected the analyst can require Simulink to be connected to the Repository/CMSystem, as shown in Figure 5.

This last model, shown in Figure 5, can be annotated to highlight the required changes in the tool chain, but also with requirements outside the technical domain (such as the training and processes mentioned above). In this way what needs to be supported by the deployed tool chain to mitigate the risks due to tool integration can be communicated and the qualification focused on a more limited part of the development environment.

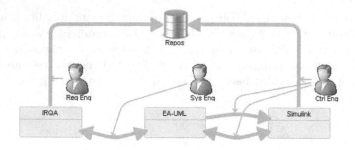

Fig. 5. Time Information Added to the TIL Model

5   Related Work

Existing standards deal with qualification and certification in different ways, as discussed in [5]. Some standards require tools to be suitable and of a certain quality [3], while some are stricter and require the development of relevant tools to fulfill the same objectives as the development of the products handled by the standard itself [12]. However, the approach of these standards or the related state of the practice discussion is mostly to limit any software qualification effort to engineering tools and their immediate environment. This means that modern safety standards do not address all hazards that occur due to the integration of tools into tool chains in modern development environments. An example is the introduction of an automated transformation of data between two tools. If this is at all dealt with in the context of the current standards, it will most likely be viewed as some kind of error-reducing mechanism that lowers the qualification effort required for the tool that delivers data to the transformation (in the way IEC 61508:2010 views all integration as only positive [4]). However, ideally the transformation itself should also be subject to qualification and its effects on developers identified (if it for instance lowers the possibility for developers to detect errors in output).

Apart from the approach to qualify everything in a development environment, only a few proposals for how to approach tool chain qualification exists today ([10] suggests to only qualify the first and the last tools in a tool chain). Little effort has however been spent on identifying the actual implications on safety due to tool integration.

6   Summary and Future Work

In this paper we propose the use of a modeling language for tool chains, TIL, to tailor and analyze tool chains for developing safety-critical embedded systems. This supports a pre-qualification effort of tool chains consisting of pre-qualified tools, aimed at identifying the risks related to tool integration. These risks point out the safety goals that need to be supported by the tool chain after it is deployed to ensure the safety of the end product.

Through this approach the qualification effort is reduced to only those parts relevant to ensure safety. It also allows for a formal way of communicating these parts and the requirements on them, or even automatically generating code for them. These benefits should both increase the confidence in catching safety issues due to software used in the development of safety-critical products and reduce the cost of attaining this confidence. The next steps include:

- Extending the annotations of the TIL models to include issues like the granularity of traces, the skill level of operators, etc.
- Formalizing additional patterns and providing automated analysis.
- Making use of the existing code generation from TIL models.
- Performing a case study to compare the result of our automated qualification with that of a manual process and determine the efficiency gain.

Acknowledgement. The research leading to these results has received partial funding from the ARTEMIS Joint Undertaking under grant agreement n° 269335 and from the Swedish Vinnova funding authority.

References

1. Biehl, M.: Tool Integration Language. Technical Report ISRN/KTH/MMK/R-11/16-SE, Royal Institute of Technology (KTH) (September 2011)
2. Biehl, M.: Early Automated Verification of Tool Chain Design. In: Murgante, B., Gervasi, O., Misra, S., Nedjah, N., Rocha, A.M.A.C., Taniar, D., Apduhan, B.O. (eds.) ICCSA 2012, Part IV. LNCS, vol. 7336, pp. 40–50. Springer, Heidelberg (2012)
3. CENELEC. BS/EN 50128:2001, railway applications - communications, signalling and processing systems - software for railway control and protection systems (2001)
4. International Electrotechnical Commission. BS/IEC 61508:2010, functional safety of electrical/electronic/programmable electronic safety-related systems
5. Asplund, F., El-khoury, J., Törngren, M.: Qualifying Software Tools, a Systems Approach. In: Ortmeier, F., Daniel, P. (eds.) SAFECOMP 2012. LNCS, vol. 7612, pp. 340–351. Springer, Heidelberg (2012)
6. Biehl, et al.: A Domain Specific Language for Generating Tool Integration Solutions. In: 4th Workshop on Model-Driven Tool & Process Integration at the European Conference on Modelling Foundations and Applications (June 2011)
7. Biehl, et al.: High-Level Specification and Code Generation for Service-Oriented Tool Adapters. In: Proceedings of ICCSA 2012 (June 2012)
8. Christie, et al.: Software Process Automation: Interviews, Survey, and Workshop Results. Technical report, SEI (1997)
9. Conrad, et al.: Qualifying software tools according to ISO 26262. In: Proceedings of MBEES 2010 (February 2010)
10. Hamann, et al.: ISO 26262 release just ahead - remaining problems and proposals for solutions. In: SAE 2011 World Congress & Exhibition (April 2011)
11. International Organization for Standardization. ISO 26262:2011, road vehicles - functional safety (2011)
12. Special Committee 205 of RTCA. DO-178C, software considerations in airborne systems and equipment certification (2011)
13. Special Committee 205 of RTCA. DO-330, software tool qualification considerations (2011)

A Systematic Elaboration of Safety Requirements in the Avionic Domain

Antoaneta Kondeva, Martin Wassmuth, and Andreas Mitschke

EADS Deutschland GmbH, EADS Innovation Works
Willy-Messerschmitt-Str. 1, 85521 Ottobrunn, Germany
{antoaneta.kondeva,andreas.mitschke,martin.wassmuth}@eads.net

Abstract. Avionic safety standards such as ARP4754A, DO-178B, and DO-254 specifying the development, validation and verification processes do not provide an unambiguous guideline for system developers, refining ARP4754A system requirements down to DO-178B or DO-254 specific items. Consequently, tracing the high-level system safety requirements down to safety item requirements of the individual system components is extremely difficult and error-prone. Today, the refinement of system safety requirements and their allocation to items, that shall realize them, is done mostly ad-hoc. This utilized ad-hoc approach is due to a lack of systematic elaboration methodologies. In this paper we advocate an approach that explicitly specifies the transition from abstract system requirements to concrete item requirements.

Keywords: safety requirements, seamless and explicit refinement, ARP4754A, domain knowledge.

1 Introduction

Over time, the design of aircraft systems has experienced rapid increase of complexity. Throughout different domains, more and more functions are realized by electronics and software, which significantly increases the challenge for system designers to maintain the safety of systems. This is among other things due to lack of a comprehensive method supporting the specification of safety requirements and their refinement throughout the system development process.

Industry safety standards such as ARP4754A [2] for system development, DO-178B [3] for software development and DO-254 [4] for hardware mandate the results that shall be provided to ensure that the system under development is acceptably safe. However, these standards do not provide detailed information on how these results can be achieved. With respect to safety requirements management, these standards are still considered as vague and ambiguous [1]. In essence, there is no clear answer to the following questions:

– What are the relationships between system requirements, derived requirements, safety requirements, system architecture, and high- and low-level software requirements?

F. Ortmeier and P. Daniel (Eds.): SAFECOMP 2012 Workshops, LNCS 7613, pp. 400–408, 2012.
© Springer-Verlag Berlin Heidelberg 2012

- How can high-level safety requirements be split in concrete safety properties of the components building the system?
- How does the system architecture on one development level influence safety requirements at the next level?

To summarize, the explicit and systematic specification of system safety properties and how they evolve during the system development process is not clear. Therefore, this paper introduces a seamless and systematic process for safety requirements evolution while being conform to existing safety standards. Section 2 will present a technique for explicit specification and transition of abstract system safety requirements to concrete item requirements. Section 3 describes our approach integrated into the ARP4754A development process. Section 4 demonstrates the application of the systematic safety requirements refinement on a real use case (Doors Management System). Finally, Section 5 concludes this paper and presents some possible areas for future work.

2 From System Safety Requirements to Item Safety Requirements

ARP4754A specifies system as "a combination of inter-related items arranged to perform a specific function(s)". An item is : "hardware or software element having bounded and well-defined interfaces". Referring to these specifications system refinement concerns the decomposition of a system into subsystems until the system properties can be allocated to properties of the concrete hardware or software elements.

System level safety requirements can be seen as constraints on the system functionality. In other words, specification of conditions that shall not hold. In this section, we discuss, how system safety requirements can be refined into requirements for the system items.

2.1 Safety Requirements Specification and Refinement

Our approach for specification and refinement of system safety requirements relies on the work of Jackson [5,6]. We distinguish between system requirements, domain knowledge, and item requirements. *System requirements* specify the relation between environment phenomena, desired to be fulfilled by the system. *Item requirements* state the intended item behaviour that is sufficient to realize the system requirement. Often it is difficult to directly associate a particular item property to environment phenomena without making some assumptions about how the environment behaves. We need to determine the *domain knowledge* representing facts and assumptions about the environment. *Domain properties* specify the facts about the application domain i.e physical laws. *Domain assumptions* are descriptive statements about the application domain, which are believed to be needed for the realization of the environment property. They serve as intermediate step between the system requirements and the item requirements. In fact, the domain knowledge specifies the translation of the environmental phenomena in concrete properties of the system. To illustrate these concepts, consider as example the A320 breaking logic introduced in [7]. The system safety requirement for the system is: To prevent engagement of reverse thrust while the aircraft is in flight. The related environment phenomena in the requirements are *InFlight(Aircraft)* and *Enabled(ReveseThrust)*, respectively. The system designers shall give a technical meaning for these abstract phenomena. They take the design decision that the turning of the wheels of the landing gear indicates that the aircraft is moving on the runway and is not in flight. The requirement to sense when the wheels are turning is allocated to a sensor.

$$SysR : InFlight(Aircraft) \Rightarrow \neg Enabled(ReverseThrust)$$
$$DP1 : MovingOn(Aircraft, Runway) \Leftrightarrow \neg InFlight(Aircraft)$$
$$DA1 : MovingOn(Aircraft, Runway) \Leftrightarrow Turning(Wheels, Runway)$$
$$ItemR(Sensor)\ 1 : Turning(Wheels, Runway) \Rightarrow PulsOn(Sensor)$$
$$ItemR(Controller)\ 2 : PulsOn(Sensor) \Rightarrow Enable(ReverseThrust)$$

According to the described concepts we can explicitly specify the relationship between system safety requirements, derived requirements and item requirements. "If an item whose behaviour satisfy ItemR is in the environment, and the environment has the properties described in D, then the environment will exhibit the properties specified in SysR" (according to [6]).

$$D, ItemR \models SysR$$

The considerations so far have a conventional refinement character. Conventional means, we refine the system safety requirements in the same way as functional requirements. In essence, we have described how to translate the abstract system phenomena into technical item properties. But considering the safety aspect, we have to analyse if the specified domain knowledge will hold in all possible circumstances or whether scenarios exist which violate the domain assumptions. In fact, we have to show the completeness according safety.

2.2 Safety Analysis

From a safety point of view, the designer has to demonstrate that the domain assumptions and the item requirements will hold under the intended circumstances. If no particular circumstances are specified, then evidence shall be given for all possible circumstances. Thus, it should be proven that there are no scenarios that will violate the assumptions. Considering the domain assumption from the example above:

$$MovingOn(Aircraft, Runway) \Leftrightarrow Turning(Wheels, Runway)$$

This domain assumption is general in its nature. We have to check if the wheels will turn under all possible circumstances, for example under all environment conditions. Is the above statement always true? What if we take into account the possible conditions of the runway: $condition(Runway) = (wet, dry)$ and check the statement with the variable value: $condition(Runway) = wet$?

A serious incident during an A320 landing on a rainy day at Warsaw airport shows that incomplete and implicit domain assumptions (the plane wheels will not turn in case of aquaplaning) result in incomplete derived requirements for the system components.

3   The Safety Requirements Elaboration and the ARP4754 System Development Process

In the previous section, we have described a technique for the specification of system requirements, item requirements and how to explicitly specify the relation between them. In this section, we show how this technique can be applied to the system development process specified in ARP4754A so that the questions stated in the introduction of the paper can be clarified.

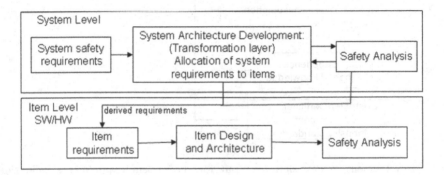

Fig. 1. Safety requirement elaboration process

Figure 1 shows the safety requirements elaboration based on the system development process specified in ARP4754A. The input for the process are the system safety requirements, which are specified as a relation of environment phenomena. During the system architecture development the abstract system safety requirements are transformed into item requirements. Here, the system designers make assumptions about how the desired environment phenomena can be technically realized (specifying the domain assumptions). Depending on the assumptions, the environment phenomena are related to the behaviour of the items. Thereafter, the designer analyses if the item behaviour will hold under the particular circumstances (safety analysis), to determine if the system requirement can be allocated under the responsibility of the selected item. The outcome of the system architecture development is the system architecture. The system architecture and the rationale for the design decisions are explicitly specified as domain assumptions and domain properties. Item requirements are derived from the system architecture. ARP4754A specifies this step as: Allocation of system requirements to Items. It states that: "In practice, the system architecture development and the allocation of system requirements to item requirements are tightly-coupled, iterative processes...., the identification and understanding of derived requirements increases and the rational for the allocation of system-level requirements to hardware or software at the item level becomes clearer".

The derived requirements are the item requirements, which are deduced from the domain knowledge specified during the system development architecture and the safety analysis. By using this methodology we can explicitly specify all the information needed for the validation process of the system requirements as required by the ARP4754A (Figure 2).

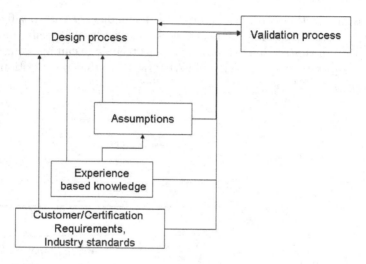

Fig. 2. Development process data as input for the system requirements validation process (adapted from ARP4754A, [2])

4   Case Study

To demonstrate the systematic elaboration of safety requirements we choose the safety-critical system Aircraft Doors Management System (DMS). In the past, there were a few aircraft accidents and incidents [8] caused by failure of this system, for example: incorrect closing operation by the operator, unreliable latches, and unexpected reaction by the pilot.

4.1   Case Study Description

The DMS has two main objectives (functions allocated to this system):

1. Manage Door Operation
2. Provide safe operation

Consider the doors management system as part of the aircraft. The system-level aircraft hazards related to the aircraft doors include: aircraft decompression, resulting from door opening during flight, a person being hit from a closing door, person opening a door and being blown out of the aircraft due to significant difference between the pressure outside and inside of the plane, passengers being unable to escape from the plane in a dangerous situation in the aircraft compartment.

4.2 Applying the Requirements Elaboration Process on the DMS

Tracing the system hazard `Aircraft decompression` into the hazardous behaviour of the DMS, we get the system hazard `Door opens while aircraft in flight` and the resulting safety requirement `Prevent door opening during flight`. We will demonstrate the safety requirements refinement process by refining the above stated system requirement.

Refining System Requirement: $InFlight(Aircraft) \Rightarrow \neg Openable$ **(Door).** The system requirement has an abstract notion and cannot be verified. The requirement shall be refined to be able to be allocated to items of the system. We have to specify the domain assumptions. That is, the environment phenomenon: $\neg Openable(Door)$ shall be specified. $\neg Openable(Door)$ means, that the aircraft door must remain in the compartment frame during the aircraft is in flight. It shall be impossible to take the door out of the door frame. There are two possible solutions: by appropriate design of the door (plug-in door design) or by using structural element preventing the door from opening. Considering the first solution (using inward door), it is physically impossible to open the door during flight because of the high differential pressure. An aircraft has two types of doors: passenger and cargo doors. Cargo doors are typically outward, because of the requirement `Fast cargo loading and high cargo capacity`. Therefore, the second possible solution to use (interlock) latches is preferred. Latches are movable mechanical elements which, ones engaged, prevent the door from opening. The new system element responsible to keep the door in the "closed" position is the latch. The latches can be engaged (latched) or not engaged (unlatched). The behaviour of the latch can be specified as follows: when the latch is in state "latched" and power is resolved, the latch goes in state "unlatched". When the latch is in state "unlatched" and power is resolved, the latch goes in state "latched". If the latch is latched, the door cannot be opened. Thus, the door is in state "fully closed". Otherwise, the door state becomes the value "closed". The design assumptions and the item requirement resulting from the taken design decision are shown in Figure 3.

The next step is to prove that the latches can guarantee to keep the door in the closed position under the intended circumstances (inFlight). The question is: Can we allocate the requirement under the responsibility of the latch? We analyse the following scenario: What can lead to unlatching latches during flight and establish that latches only are insufficient to fulfil the system requirement. One possible

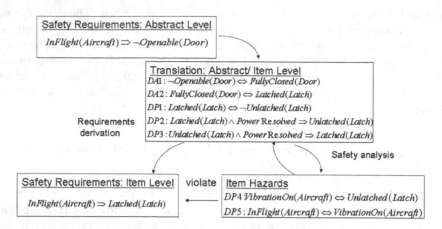

Fig. 3. System requirement refinement and allocation analysis for the latch item

scenario of unlatching the latches during flight is when power is resolved during flight. To prevent this item related hazard a new requirements is defined: Sources of power that could initiate unlatching of any door must be automatically isolated from the latches prior to flight and it must not be possible to restore power to the door during flight. Depending on the type of latches (electrical, hydraulic, and pneumatic) this requirement will be refined differently. Let us assume, the design decision is to use electrical latches. Therefore, the resulting (derived) requirement for the controller, controlling the latch operations, is as follows: The controller shall be set to ''inactive'' prior to fly. Another possible cause of unlatching the latches during flight is because of specific environment conditions. Due to their nature, the latches (structural elements) are subject to vibration, structural loads and deflections, positive and negative loads, and aerodynamic loads. Under specific values of the above listed environment conditions, the latches can get unlatched. In fact, such environment conditions emerge, when the aircraft is in flight. Consequently, the system requirement: keep the door in the fully closed position during flight cannot be realized only by the latch component. In other words, the expression for the satisfaction of the system requirement: $DA1, DA2, DP1, DP4, DP5, ItemR \models SysR$ is false.

To prevent the event of unlatching during flight, an additional interlock (lock) is added to the system architecture. Locks are mechanical elements, in addition to the latch operating mechanism, that monitor the latch positions and when engaged, prevent the latches from becoming disengaged. The new system element responsible to keep the door in the "closed" position is the lock (DA2 is modified). If the lock is engaged, the door cannot be opened. Thus, the door is in state "fully closed". Otherwise, the door state becomes the value "latched". The lock can be engaged (locked) or not engaged (unlocked). The behaviour of the lock can be specified as follow: when the latch is in state "latched" and power is resolved to the lock, the lock goes in state "locked". The behaviour of the latch is also modified (DP2), respectively. It goes in the unlatched state only if the

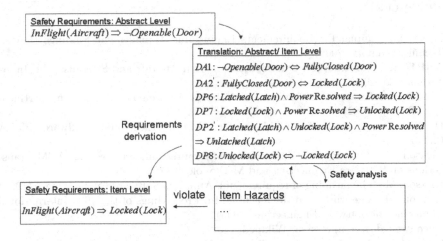

Fig. 4. System requirement refinement and allocation analysis for the lock item

state of the lock is unlocked and power is resolved on the latch. The resulting domain knowledge and the modified item requirement are shown in Figure 4.

Now we have to prove that the added elements (locks) can guarantee to keep the door close under the intended circumstances or whether they add new hazards that can lead to opening of the door.

5   Conclusion and Future Work

This paper illustrates an approach for systematic refinement of system safety requirements into item safety requirements. First, we adopt the mature technique of Jackson [5,6] to be applied for cyber-physical systems. Hence, the requirements, the design and the safety aspects are integrated into one model and the different artefacts (system requirement, design decision and domain property, and item requirement and item hazards) and their relations to each other are explicitly specified. To be conform to the industry safety standard ARP4754A we showed how our approach can be concretely applied for the system development process.

For future work, we intend to specify the system requirements, the design knowledge and the item requirements in LTL or CTL to automatically (using a model checker) evaluate if the system requirements are satisfied by the derived item requirements. To provide a more realistic use case for our investigations, we will extend the use case specifying all system safety requirements for the Doors Management System that have not been fully addressed in this paper.

Acknowledgement. We would like to thank Prof. Manfred Broy, Stephan Stilkerich for helpful comments and feedback.

References

1. Miller, S., Lempia, D.: Requirements Engineering Management Findings Report. Technical Report (2009)
2. ARP4754A. Guidelines for Development of Civil Aircraft and Systems. SAE International (2010)
3. DO-178B. Software Considerations in Airborne Systems and Equipment Certification. RTCA (1992)
4. DO-254. Design Assurance Guidance for Airborne Electronic Hardware. RTCA (2000)
5. Jackson, M., Zave, P.: Four dark corners of requirements engineering. ACM Transactions on Software Engineering and Methodology (1997)
6. Jackson, M.: The meaning of requirements. Annals of Software Engineering 3 (1997)
7. Jackson, M.: The world and the machine. In: Proceedings of the 1995 International Conference of Software Engineering (1995)
8. Uncontrolled decompression: Wikipedia,
   http://en.wikipedia.org/wiki/Uncontrolled_decompression

Parallel NuSMV: A NuSMV Extension for the Verification of Complex Embedded Systems

Orlando Ferrante, Luca Benvenuti, Leonardo Mangeruca, Christos Sofronis, and Alberto Ferrari

ALES S.r.l., Rome, Italy
firstname.surname@ales.eu.com

Abstract. In this paper we present Parallel NuSMV, a tool based on the NuSMV model checker that integrates the ManySAT parallel SAT solver. The PNuSMV is part of the FormalSpecs Verifier framework for the formal verification of Simulink/Stateflow models. The experiments we performed show that the use of a parallel SAT solver allows for an average speedup of an order of magnitude or more on industry-level size models. The main contributions of the papers are (1) the description of the PNuSMV model checker (2) the description of the verification time speedup w.r.t. the NuSMV tool for the verification of industrial-sized embedded systems and (3) the integration of the tool in the FormalSpecs Verifier framework for the verification of Simulink/Stateflow models with the application to a cruise control case study.

Keywords: model checking, embedded systems, contract-based design, formal verification.

1 Introduction

Model checking has reached a high maturity level that allows applying this technique to the verification of complex embedded systems. Several techniques and tools have been proposed to tackle industrial-sized models. In [1] the authors describe the verification of a Flight Control System modeled in MATLAB Simulink using the NuSMV model checker. In [2] the verification of avionics embedded software is performed using three different model checkers (namely NuSMV [3], SAL [4] and PROVER [5]). In addition, model checkers have been successfully applied to the verification of software using both static and dynamic analysis [6] [7] [8]. During last decades several techniques have been developed in order to tackle the state explosion problem that limit the application of formal methods. The use of binary decision diagrams allowed the application of model checking to industrial case studies [9]. Bounded model checking [10] introduced the use of SAT solvers in the context of symbolic model checking and provided the basis for its extension to the unbounded case. During last decade increased research and industrial efforts have been spent on the area of Satisfiability Modulo Theories (SMT) [11] trying to improve formal verification tools efficiency exploiting the integration of SAT-based reasoning methods with specific theories

F. Ortmeier and P. Daniel (Eds.): SAFECOMP 2012 Workshops, LNCS 7613, pp. 409–416, 2012.
© Springer-Verlag Berlin Heidelberg 2012

obtaining promising results in particular in the field of software model checking. However, the application of such theories to complex industrial embedded systems that usually expose nonlinear dynamics and complex numeric control algorithms is still an open point. In this paper we present a tool called Parallel NuSMV (PNuSMV) that is a modified version of the NuSMV model checker that integrates the ManySAT parallel SAT solver [12]. The PNuSMV is part of the FormalSpecs Verifier framework for the formal verification of Simulink/Stateflow models. The experimental results have been collected using a rich set of industrial use cases and they show the existence of an exponential speedup of the verification time when the bounded model checking technique is used to check model's invariants. The PNuSMV allows for exploiting last advances in SAT solver techinques with the strength of the FormalSpecs Verifier environment and the NuSMV model checking tool. In this paper we present the application of PNuSMV to a cruise control system and an additional set of logic model of industrial size. The main contributions of the papers are (1) the description of the PNuSMV model checker (2) the description of experimental results that shows the exponential speedup for the verification of invariant properties of industrial sized embedded systems compared to the NuSMV model checker using the bounded-model checking technique and (3) the integration of the tool with the FormalSpecs Verifier framework for the verification of Simulink/Stateflow models and the application to a cruise control case study.

2   FormalSpecs Verifier Verification Framework

The PNuSMV tool is part of the FormalSpecs Verifier (FSV) framework for the verification of discrete systems for the MATLAB Simulink environment [13]. The framework supports several operative modes. In this paper we focus on the capability of verifying properties described as invariant or temporal logic formulae. The FSV tool can be seen as a translator from a Simulink model and specification to the NuSMV tool native language. The transformation process produces a semantically equivalent NuSMV representation of the input model taking into account the non-determinism resolution that may be introduced during the transformation step. In Figure 1 the flow is described in details. As a first step the Simulink textual file is parsed. Then the parsed Simulink model is processed generating a semantically equivalent NuSMV model that is used to generate the concrete NuSMV artifact with a model to text step.

The technology used to perform the model transformation step is an internally developed Java embodiment of the OMG Query/View/Transformation (QVT) language called JQVT. The JQVT library aims at providing an industry-level operational implementation of the QVT language. It supports the definition of QVT mappings and the definition of mappings inheritance, disjunction and merging. JQVT allows capturing the mapping relation that links a source model element to a target model element and it supports the resolve and resolveIn operators to retrieve the set of mapping source model elements from a given mapped target model element. JQVT does not support the entire

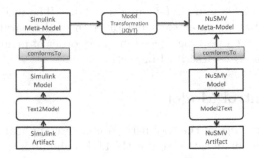

Fig. 1. FormalSpecs Verifier transformation flow

QVT specification. However, it has been extensively used as translation infrastructure of different tools for the translation of industry-level sized models [14].

3   Parallel NuSMV Tool

The Parallel NuSMV (PNuSMV) tool is a modification of the open source NuSMV2 symbolic model checker. The structure of the tool is represented in Figure 2.

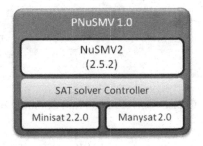

Fig. 2. Parallel NuSMV layered structure

The top layer is an unmodified version of the NuSMV 2.5.2 open source model checker that is a state-of-the art tool for the formal verification of discrete systems. NuSMV2 supports several verification techniques such as binary decision diagrams and SAT-based bounded model checking using different SAT solvers (such as Minisat [15] and Z-Chaff [16]. A new component (the SAT Solver Controller) has been implemented as intermediate layer between the model checker and the underline SAT solver. The role of the controller is to correctly support the instantiation of (possibly several) SAT solvers providing a common interface to the NuSMV2. Currently we successfully integrated the MiniSat v2.2.0 and the ManySAT 2.0. The latter is the last iteration of the parallel SAT solver that won the SAT-Race 2008 and SAT-Competion 2009. The availability of multi-core platforms allows for an efficient exploitation of the parallel nature of the solver easily obtaining an average speed up of an order of magnitude for several industrial level models as described in Section 5.

4   Cruise Control Model

To show the performance of the tool using a concrete application we describe a cruise control system modeled using the MATLAB Simulink and translated with the FormalSpecs Verifier tool. Cruise control is the term used to describe a control system that regulates the speed of an automobile. The basic operation of a cruise controller is to sense the speed of the vehicle, compare this speed to a desired reference, and then accelerate or decelerate the car as required. A simple control algorithm for controlling the speed is to use a "proportional plus integral" feedback based on the error between the current and the desired speed. The model of the truck is based of a force balance for the body, see Figure 3. For a detailed description of the example please refer to [17]. Let v be the speed of the truck, m the total mass , F_T the traction force related to the wheels, and F_d the force related to additional elements (such as gravity and aerodynamic drag). The mathematical model

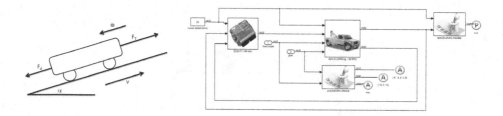

Fig. 3. Cruise control model and Simulink model

of the system is given by the equation $m dv/dt = F_T - F_d$ where $m = 3450kg$ and F_T is the force of the engine. Force F_d is composed by gravity (F_g), rolling friction (F_r) and aerodynamic drag (F_a) forces. $F_g = mg\sin(a)$ with a road slope and g gravitational constant. Rolling friction is $F_r = mgC_r sign(v)$ with C_r friction coefficient. Finally $F_a = 1/2\rho C_x A(v + w)^2$ where ρ is air density, C_x is the aerodynamic drag coefficient, A is the area of the truck and ω models the wind gusts. In our model the values of the equations parameters are $\rho = 1.228kg/m^3$, $C_x = 0.55$ and $A = 2.4m^2$. The control algorithm regulates the traction force F_T on the basis of the error $e = v_{REF} - v$ between the desired speed v_{REF} and the current speed v of the car. The algorithm consits of a proportional-integral control as follows: $F_T(kT) = k_p e(kT) + k_I \sum_{h=0}^{k} e(hT)$ where $T = 40ms$ and k_P, k_I are the proportional and integral gains.

The cruise control system has been modeled in MATLAB Simulink (Fig. 3) implementing a conservative discrete-time abstraction of the plant. The model has two inputs of type signed 32 bit integers representing the road slope percentage value and the wind gusts value. The model represents the system in steady state with cruise speed of $22m/s$. The specification of the property to be checked has been captured using the FormalSpecs Verifier properties toolbox following the contract-based methodology ([18], [19], [20]) that allows for the specification of requirements in terms of contracts $C = (A, G)$ where A is the assumption and G the guarantee (or promise). Intuitively a contract is a requirement of the form $A \to G$ where the promise represents the set of possible system behaviors under the hypothesis that the environment behaves as described in the assumption (i.e. A represents the set of acceptable environments). The contract-based theory and its application to the verification of complex distributed embedded systems is investigated by the authors in the context of the SPRINT EU project [21]. In the case of the cruise control system the assumption has been formalized as the conjunction of the following assertions: the road slope is constrained to assume value in the set $\{-8, -4, 0, 4, 8\}$, the wind gusts value is constrained to be in the set $\{-15, 0, 15\}$ m/s) and its derivative can have a maximum absolute value of 15 m/s (to take into account that the wind gust cannot change its value arbitrarily faster). The contract promise requires that the effective speed must be within 95% and 105% of the reference speed value.

5   Experimental Results

In this section we describe the performance results obtained executing the PNuSMV 1.0 and NuSMV 2.5 tools. The host machines used for the execution of the experiments are an Intel iCore 7@1.87 Ghz with 8 GB RAM platform hosting a Linux 64 bit Ubuntu 10.04 operating system (platform A) and an Intel(R) Xeon(R) CPU X5550 @ 2.67GHz with 50 GB RAM platform hosting an Ubuntu Linux 10.04 64 bit operating system (platform B).

5.1   Cruise Control Model

For the cruise control we developed several experiments trying to exercise the verification tools in different ways. The model has been designed to falsify the property previously described after 33 execution steps. The translated NuSMV model has size 88 bits that is small compared to the size of the other models used in another set of experiments (thousands of bits). However, the model represents a good benchmark for automotive applications models that usually contains 32-bit signals, complex arithmetic operators and multiple feedback control loops. In addition, the model is hard to verify and the NuSMV tool is not capable of finding a counter-example even after several days of computation and it represents an interesting benchmark for the quantitative evaluation of PNuSMV performance speedup.

Bounded Model Checking Verification with Incremental Bounds as a first experiment we execute a bounded model checking verification of the property using different bound lengths. The verification has been performed using the

Table 1. First experiment results

Steps	PNuSMV (s)	NuSMV (s)	AV. SP.	Plat
8	6.53 ± 0.65	34.47 ± 7.01	5.28	A
15	40.02 ± 5.92	856.41 ± 275.07	21.19	A
20	121.86 ± 119.72	6220.72 ± 2127.13	51.05	B
25	516.89 ± 118.37	49149.79 ± 219.51	95.09	B
33	5446.32 ± 456.08	N/A	N/A	B

check_invar_bmc_inc command with the forward strategy. The average execution time of each set of runs is summarized in Table 1. For each length bound a set of executions have been performed using both NuSMV and PNuSMV and the average value and standard deviation of execution times have been computed. Collected data give us the opportunity to propose some comments. The speedup factor (computed as NuSMV execution time/PNuSMV execution time) is always greater than one and it increases with the dimension of the bound length. This is in line with the ManySAT solver expected performances. In particular we noticed that the PNuSMV fully exploits the available CPUs taking advantage of the parallel nature of the SAT solver. A noticeable drawback of the use of the ManySAT solver is the increasing consumption of memory that, however, did not explode exponentially making the approach usable for industrial applications.

Bounded Model Checking Verification with Fixed Bound Value as a second experiment we performed a bounded model checking verification of the property trying to reach its violation. The PNuSMV software found a valid counter example in average time of 5446 seconds (approximately 1 hour and 30 minutes). The same model has been processed using the NuSMV software but a valid counter example has not been found within 11000 minutes (approximately 7 days) of computation (considered as a time-out limit for our experiments). In Figure 4 we represented the execution time for both NuSMV and PNuSMV and we extrapolate an approximate exponential trend function between the number K of BMC step performed and the average execution time. We can notice how the speedup gain is approximately of the form ae^{bK} with $b \simeq 0.16$.

5.2   Additional Experiments

The cruise control model is an open-source model developed for the evaluation of the PNuSMV performance for automotive domain applications and we collected promising results in terms of verification speedup. In order to better evaluate the tool performance for a larger set of applications we performed additional experiments using another set of models based on synthetic logic systems. These models in contrast with the cruise control contains mainly logical operators and the reduced number of arithmetic blocks allows for the efficient verification of

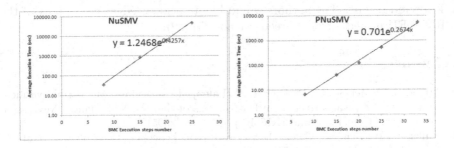

Fig. 4. PNuSMV and NuSMV performance graph

Table 2. logic-based tests execution results

Model	PNuSMV (s)	NuSMV (s)	AV. SP.
I	440 ± 75	3094 ± 925	7
II	639 ± 208	14074 ± 12629	20

thousands of bit sized models in few hours (in contrast with the cruise control that is two order of magnitudes smaller in size but it requires two orders of magnitude more time to verify the property). In our experiments, two models were analyzed both of the size of thousands of bit and we performed a BMC incremental verification of an invariant property falsified in fixed amount of steps using both NuSMV and PNuSMV. The value of the speedup factors are summarized in Table 2 (all experiments have been executed on platform B). For this class of models we noticed a significant variability of the speedup factor. This is in line with the reported behavior of the ManySAT engine w.r.t. the reproducibility of the performances. As a final remark let us observe that the average speedup value grows with a factor of 3 (from 7 to 20) with an increase of the size of the model. This is in line with what we experienced in the first set of experiments.

6   Conclusions and Future Works

In this paper we described PNuSMV a tool that integrates the NuSMV2 open source model checker with the ManySAT 2.0 parallel SAT solver. The experimental results report a promising speedup for both control-based models, such as the cruise control model described in this paper, and logic-based models. Several extensions of this work are possible. At first we aim at supporting different parallel SAT solvers to analyze the performances of the different back-ends. In addition we are working at a deeper integration of the ManySAT solver with the NuSMV engine in order to obtain higher performance gains. Finally, we want to apply the PNuSMV to additional industrial models in order to estimate the performance gain for a broader set of application scenarios.

Acknowledgment. The authors would like to acknowledge the support of the SPRINT EU project (grant agreement no: 257909).

References

1. Miller, S., Anderson, E., Wagner, L., Whalen, M., Heimdahl, M.: Formal verification of flight critical software. In: Proceedings of the AIAA Guidance, Navigation and Control Conference and Exhibit, pp. 15–18 (2005)
2. Miller, S., Whalen, M., Cofer, D.: Software model checking takes off. Communications of the ACM 53(2), 58–64 (2010)
3. Cimatti, A., Clarke, E., Giunchiglia, E., Giunchiglia, F., Pistore, M., Roveri, M., Sebastiani, R., Tacchella, A.: NuSMV 2: An OpenSource Tool for Symbolic Model Checking. In: Brinksma, E., Larsen, K.G. (eds.) CAV 2002. LNCS, vol. 2404, pp. 359–364. Springer, Heidelberg (2002)
4. http://sal.csl.sri.com/
5. http://www.prover.com/
6. Ball, T., Levin, V., Rajamani, S.K.: A decade of software model checking with slam
7. Ball, T., Cook, B., Levin, V., Rajamani, S.K.: SLAM and Static Driver Verifier: Technology Transfer of Formal Methods inside Microsoft. In: Boiten, E.A., Derrick, J., Smith, G.P. (eds.) IFM 2004. LNCS, vol. 2999, pp. 1–20. Springer, Heidelberg (2004)
8. Godefroid, P.: Compositional dynamic test generation (extended abstract)
9. Burch, J.R., Clarke, E.M., Mcmillan, K.L., Dill, D.L., Hwang, L.J.: Symbolic model checking: 10 20 states and beyond (1990)
10. Biere, A., Cimatti, A., Clarke, E., Zhu, Y.: Symbolic Model Checking without BDDs. In: Cleaveland, W.R. (ed.) TACAS 1999. LNCS, vol. 1579, pp. 193–207. Springer, Heidelberg (1999)
11. Barrett, C., Sebastiani, R., Seshia, S., Tinelli, C.: Satisfiability modulo theories. In: Handbook of Satisfiability, vol. 4 (2009)
12. Hamadi, Y., Sais, L.: Manysat: a parallel sat solver. Journal on Satisfiability, Boolean Modeling and Computation, JSAT (2009)
13. http://www.mathworks.com/products/simulink/
14. Ferrari, A., Mangeruca, L., Ferrante, O., Mignogna, A.: Desyreml: a sysml profile for heterogeneous embedded systems. In: Embedded Real Time Software and Systems, ERTS (2012)
15. Een, N., Sörensson, N.: An extensible sat-solver (ver 1.2) (2003)
16. Herbstritt, M.: zchaff: Modifications and extensions (2001)
17. Murray, R.M., et al.: Feedback Systems An Introduction for Scientists and Engineers. Princeton University Press (2009)
18. Benvenuti, L., Ferrari, A., Mangeruca, L., Mazzi, E., Passerone, R., Sofronis, C.: A contract-based formalism for the specification of heterogeneous systems (invited). In: FDL, pp. 142–147. IEEE (2008)
19. Ferrante, O., Codella, G., Sofronis, C., Mangeruca, L., Ferrari, A.: Verify contract-based designed discrete systems by simulation. In: INCOSE, EuSEC (2010)
20. Ferrante, O., Mignogna, A., Sofronis, C., Mangeruca, L., Ferrari, A.: Contract based design chain integration: An automotive domain case study. In: Applied Simulation and Modelling. ACTA Press (2011)
21. http://www.sprint-iot.eu/

Supporting Assurance by Evidence-Based Argument Services

Janusz Górski[1,2], Aleksander Jarzębowicz[1,2], Jakub Miler[1,2], Michał Witkowicz[2],
Jakub Czyżnikiewicz[2], and Patryk Jar[2]

[1] Department of Software Engineering, Gdansk University of Technology, Poland
[2] NOR-STA Project, Gdansk University of Technology, Poland
www.nor-sta.eu
{jango,olek,jakubm,miwi,jakubc,patryk.jar}@eti.pg.gda.pl

Abstract. Structured arguments based on evidence are used in many domains, including systems engineering, quality assurance and standards conformance. Development, maintenance and assessment of such arguments is addressed by TRUST-IT methodology outlined in this paper. The effective usage of TRUST-IT requires an adequate tool support. We present a platform of software services, called NOR-STA, available in the Internet, supporting key activities related to argument editing, communication and assessment and demonstrate an example of its application based on real case study focusing on analyzing safety of an innovative IT system.

Keywords: evidence-based argument, standard conformance, safety case, TRUST-IT methodology, NOR-STA services.

1 Introduction

Evidence-based arguments are widely recognized in the domain of systems engineering as means to demonstrate (required) system properties, for instance safety of critical applications like medical, avionic, military and others. In many cases it is required by the regulations that a *safety case* is explicitly presented, which in its essence is an argument supported by sufficient evidence [1]. Dedicated methods of developing and presenting safety cases are in use, e.g. [2, 3].

However, safety is not the only quality aspect to be argued for in an explicit way. Other properties, like security or reliability are also considered important in some application contexts which leads to the notions of *security case* or *reliability case*, or in more general terms, *assurance case* [4]. In even more general terms, a *trust case* can be considered, as an evidence-based argument that is used to strengthen trust in any postulated claim, not necessarily related to an IT system property [5]. An example of application of trust cases is demonstrating conformance to standards. In such situation, an evidence-based argument is used to justify the claim about standard conformance and such argument can then be assessed by independent auditors.

In this paper we first introduce a methodology of editing, assessing and presenting evidence-based arguments, called TRUST-IT, then describe a set of NOR-STA

F. Ortmeier and P. Daniel (Eds.): SAFECOMP 2012 Workshops, LNCS 7613, pp. 417–426, 2012.

services which support application of this methodology in different contexts, and next present a demonstration scenario where the services are used to represent and improve a safety argument related to a WSN based application supporting a patient in his/her home environment.

The argument model of TRUST-IT is based on [6] and its underlying concepts are similar to these of Claim-Argument-Evidence (CAE) [2] and Goal Structuring Notation (GSN) [3]. TRUST-IT distinguishes from other approaches by its argument assessment mechanism [7] and by the concept of conformance argument template which is presently used to support implementation of different standards [8]. The existing tools, commercial (e.g. ASCE [9] and ISCaDE [10]) and resulting from research projects (e.g. Visio add-on by University of York [11] and ACCESS by University of Virginia [12]) do not support group work and remote access. The tools [9], [11] and [12] are desktop applications and provide little, if any, support for sharing arguments and sharing the supporting evidence. The tool [10] is based on IBM Telelogic DOORS environment and provides a limited multi-user work mode using thick-client. Each of these tools require an installation process dedicated for each user. NOR-STA services supporting TRUST-IT are offered in a cloud accessible for any Internet user and can be used without any prior investment in infrastructure. The services provide full support for argument creation and maintenance, for argument assessment and for integration of the supporting evidence residing in user chosen repositories.

The paper is structured as follows. Section 2 introduces TRUST-IT methodology and explains the underlying argument model. Section 3 describes how the methodology is implemented by NOR-STA services. Section 4 presents a demonstration scenario of applying TRUST-IT and NOR-STA in developing a safety argument for a WSN-based system. Other areas of application are outlined in Section 5. The paper is concluded in Section 6, which also provides directions of future work.

2   Evidence Based Arguments – The TRUST-IT Model

TRUST-IT [5, 13, 14] is a method of representing arguments based on the generic Toulmin's argument model [6]. An argument includes: a *conclusion* to be justified, *premises* the conclusion is reasoned from and a *warrant* which establishes the relationship between the premises and the conclusion.

In TRUST-IT, an evidence-based argument is a tree-like structure and is composed of different types of nodes which define the language for representing arguments. The model of an argument (including node types and their relationships) is shown in Fig. 1, where an arrow represents the *can-be-child-of* relationship.

Argument conclusion is represented by a *claim* node. A node of type *argument* links the *claim* to the corresponding premises and uses the *warrant* to explain how the premises justify the *claim*. A premise can be of the following type: an *assumption* represents a premise which is not further justified; a *claim* represents a premise to be further justified by its own premises; and a *fact* represents a premise which is supported by some evidence. The evidence is provided in external documents which are pointed to by nodes of type *reference*. As *claim* can represent both, the conclusion

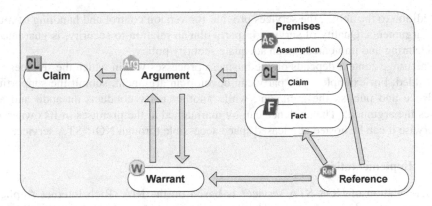

Fig. 1. The TRUST-IT argument model

and a premise, the model allows to represent complex tree-like structures (in our experience up to several thousands of elements).

An argument represented in accordance with TRUST-IT explicitly shows how the topmost conclusion is justified by the evidence through a possibly long chain of reasoning. The 'compelling power' of such argument can be assessed by a human who can analyze and assess both, the support given by the evidence and the validity of the reasoning included in the argument. In [7] an argument assessment method based on Dempster-Shafer theory of belief functions [15] and its application to TRUST-IT type arguments is presented. In addition to this method, other more specific assessment schemes can be applied, for instance in some applications we use a simple scale of three values: *accept*, *partially accept*, *reject* to assess the support given by the evidence to a fact and the support given by the premises to the related conclusion.

3   Tool Support – NOR-STA Services

In this section, we present the functional scope of the NOR-STA services, the architecture and technology of their implementation, and finally their quality assurance.

3.1   Scope

The scope of functionalities of NOR-STA services include:

- argument representation and editing using the graphical symbols shown in Fig. 1;
- integration (through references) of various types evidence, including textual documents, graphics, images, web pages, video and so on;
- argument assessment and visualization of the assessment results;
- publishing of an argument;
- evidence hosting in protected repositories.

In addition to the above, the services provide for version control and handling of multiple arguments. Quality of service, in particular in relation to security, is guaranteed by declaring and implementing an adequate security policy.

The usage context depends on the business processes within which the services are embedded. For example - one party can develop an argument, submit the supporting evidence and publish the argument, while another party conducts an audit and assesses the argument. The evidence can by maintained at the premises of its owner, or otherwise it can be hosted at a leased space accessible through NOR-STA service.

3.2   Implementation

Implementation of NOR-STA services is based on the RIA (Rich Internet Application) concept and uses modern technologies, in particular AJAX, FLOSS, VMware and others. The main screen interfacing to NOR-STA services is shown in Fig. 2.

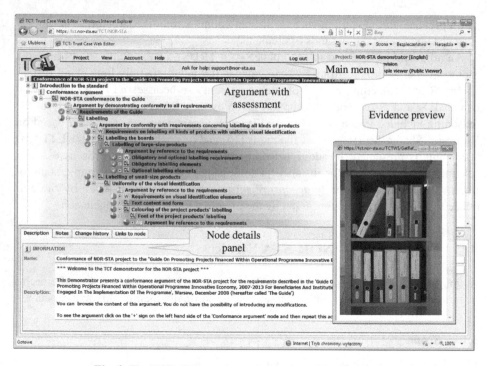

Fig. 2. The NOR-STA services window in an Internet browser

The architecture of NOR-STA services follows the rich client-server model which is illustrated in Fig. 3. The model includes three layers: database server PostgreSQL, application server JBoss and a client written in JavaScript in accordance with AJAX (Asynchronous JavaScript and XML). The lowest layer (the database) implements the business logic as a set of stored procedures. The intermediate layer is based on JEE and links the database with the client. Communication between these layers is based on RESTful Web Services and JSON (JavaScript Object Notation).

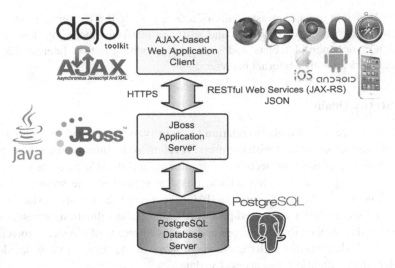

Fig. 3. The architecture of NOR-STA services

The services are deployed in a cloud in accordance with the Software-as-a-Service model. Due to this model they can be used as needed, without any prior investment in a specialized IT infrastructure. End users do not need to install any software and simply access the services with a standard Internet browser. SaaS model was chosen because it provides for high accessibility and maintainability of the services, straightforward integration with other Internet services, low distribution costs and flexible charging.

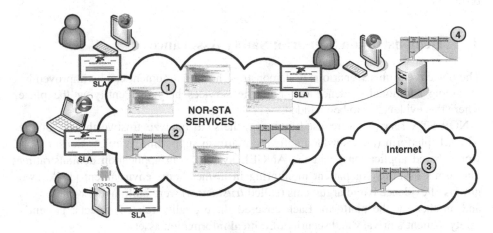

Fig. 4. NOR-STA services as a cloud

Fig. 4. explains the NOR-STA services deployment model where the key architectural elements are marked with numbers in circles. It is possible to integrate the argument (1) with both, internal (i.e. being a part of NOR-STA services - 2) or external repositories where the evidence is stored. An external repository can be located in the

Internet (3) or in a private infrastructure of a user (4). NOR-STA services are available from a wide variety of hardware and software platforms including desktop PCs, laptops, iOS or Android tablets and smartphones with Firefox, Internet Explorer, Chrome, Opera and other Internet browsers.

3.3   Service Quality

Quality of service, in particular in relation to security, is guaranteed by signing a Service Level Agreement (SLA) with the users. It refers to the Information Security Policy (ISP) which explains how security of arguments and the related evidence is being guaranteed by organizational, logical and physical measures. The security measures include Role Based Access Control (RBAC), encrypted data transmission between browser and server (SSL), encrypted passwords, input data validation, intrusion detection system, data replication techniques and advanced means of physical protection of servers. User's data remain under exclusive control of the user who can decide who and under which conditions can access the data.

Virtualization technologies provide for delivering a reliable, scalable and highly available platform of services. Service availability is continuously monitored by on-line tools. The measurements show that the availability of NOR-STA services was at the level 99.7% over a period of six months [8].

The services are under continuous development for more than five years, following the incremental and evolutionary software development model. The testing strategy applied in this process is described in [16]. A new release of NOR-STA services will provide enhanced cross-browser compatibility which includes support for mobile web browsers.

4   Demonstration Scenario: Safety Assurance

The objective of this scenario is to demonstrate how an argument can be improved by providing additional evidence and how the services help in identifying the place where this evidence is to be included.

NOR-STA services were used, among others, to analyze trustworthiness of the ANGEL platform (an embedded software platform supporting Wireless Sensor Networks based applications) and the ANGEL system – an application demonstrating platform's usability for patient monitoring in his/her home environment [17][1]. Two groups of evidence based arguments (called *trust cases*) were built, one for the system and another for the platform. Each covered three quality related aspects: patient's safety, patient's privacy and security of critical information assets.

In this demonstration scenario we focus on the safety aspect of ANGEL system. The argument focuses on the safety hazards that were identified by analyzing possible system usage scenarios. All identified hazards were then assessed with respect to their

---

[1] 6th FR STREP Project ANGEL (Advanced Networked embedded platform as a Gateway to Enhance quality of Life) Contract number IST-033506.

severity and likelihood of occurrence. An example of a hazard together with the re-sulting safety requirement is given below:

Hazard: Alarm message is not correctly and timely delivered
Requirement: ANGEL system has to assure that in case of unexpected event (e.g. health state deterioration or smoke detected in the apartment), the related alarm message is correctly delivered to the recipient (*Correctness of alarms*).

The identified safety requirements were documented as argument claims and sub-jected to further analysis investigating their possible design solutions leading to im-plementation of the requirement (documented as sub-claims). Actual implementation of such solution provided the evidence that was referred to while arguing a fact that a given hazard has been successfully mitigated.

The completed safety argument was evaluated by an auditor who assessed the sup-port given by the evidence to the facts listed in the argument. The assessment of the claims was then calculated automatically following the algorithm based on Dempster-Shaffer belief functions presented in [7]. A part of the evaluated argument is shown in Fig. 5. The colors represent the result of argument evaluation: red color shows the parts which are weakly supported by the available evidence whereas these parts which are strongly supported are shown in green color. [2]

As can be seen in Fig. 5, the fact *Alarm management system reliably handles alarms in ANGEL application* is (in the eyes of the auditor) weakly supported by the evidence item *D5.5 Integration of the demonstrator components (section 2.3.4)* being an extract from the system design report. This weak support was then propagated to all higher level claims presented in Fig. 5.

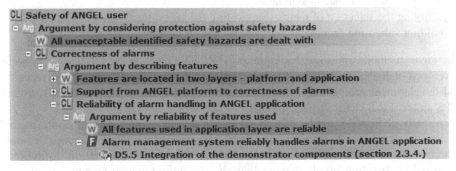

Fig. 5. Initial assessment of *Safety of ANGEL user* argument

The weakness indicated in Fig. 5 resulted in the decision to strengthen safety assur-ance by carrying additional tests aiming at validation of the safety alarm mechanism present in the system. The resulting evidence (test plans and test results) was added to the argument to better support the *Alarm management system reliably handles alarms in ANGEL application* fact. The result is presented in Fig. 6, where an additional piece of evidence *Experimental validation of the safety alarm* is included to support

---

[2] Figures 4 and 5 are extracts from the screens presenting the argument in the browser window.

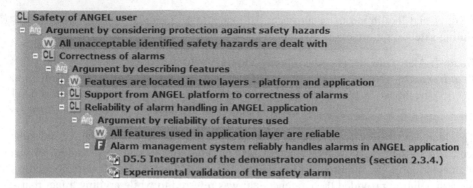

Fig. 6. Safety *of ANGEL user* argument strengthened with additional evidence

the fact. Fig. 6 also shows the result of the argument re-assessment: in this case sufficient support is given to the fact and this positive appraisal is propagated to all higher level claims.

5   Present Experience

TRUST-IT methodology and the NOR-STA services were already used to build arguments in many different applications contexts, such as:

- analyzing trustworthiness of systems and services, including safety, security and privacy claims,
- analyzing conformance to standards,
- justifying the selection of metrics supporting the stated measurement objective,
- building validation arguments for systems and services.

The ideas, methods and tools underpinning TRUST-IT and NOR-STA services were developed over the last few years while participating in three 5th and 6th FR research and development projects: 5th FR STREP Project DRIVE, 6th FR Integrated Project PIPS and 6th FR STREP Project ANGEL.

Presently NOR-STA services are being applied to develop standards conformance arguments, in relation to standards in healthcare, standards related to security of outsourcing and standards related to self-assessment of public administration institutions. A formal cooperation involves more than 30 institutions which signed formal contracts as NOR-STA services users. The services are also experimented with in relation to monitoring of implementation of Regulation (EU) No 994/2010 of the European Parliament and of the Council concerning measures to safeguard security of gas supply Member States.

6   Conclusions

Our services for evidence based arguments were successfully applied to build, assess and communicate very large and complex arguments in various application contexts.

In relation to standards conformance, NOR-STA services are highly evaluated by their users for both, their quality and business value [8]. The users particularly appreciate improvement in evidence management, better preparation to the audit, better visibility of conformance status, easier conformance maintenance as well as high availability and reliability of the services.

Future work is directed towards researching new application areas, identification of suitable business models as well as further extension of the scope of services and improvement of their quality. In particular, a new version of the services is planned for release in mid-2012, which will particularly focus on usability, personalization, flexibility, effective interaction, and browser and platform compatibility. The progress, user assessment and development plans are constantly presented at the NOR-STA portal www.nor-sta.eu/en. Among the main directions of future research and development are comparative conformance cases (e.g. for monitoring implementation of common regulations at different sites), domain specific argument patterns, dynamic arguments for automatic monitoring of changing evidence, automatic detection of events (e.g. ageing evidence, evidence changes requiring re-evaluation of the argument, and so on) and full support for version control and reporting.

Acknowledgments. This work was partially supported by the NOR-STA project co-financed by the European Union under the European Regional Development Fund within the Operational Programme Innovative Economy (grant no. UDA-POIG.01.03.01-22-142/09-03).

References

1. Ministry of Defence, Defence Standard 00-56 Issue 4: Safety Management Requirements for Defence Systems (2007)
2. Emmet, L., Guerra, S.: Application of a Commercial Assurance Case Tool to Support Software Certification Services. In: Proceedings of the 2005 Automated Software Engineering Workshop on Software Certificate Management, SoftCeMent 2005. ACM, New York (2005)
3. Kelly, T., Weaver, R.: The Goal Structuring Notation - A Safety Argument Notation. In: Proceedings of the Dependable Systems and Networks Workshop on Assurance Cases (2004)
4. Rhodes, T., Boland, F., Fong, E., Kass, M.: Software Assurance Using Structured Assurance Case Models, NIST Interagency Report 7608, US Department of Commerce (2009)
5. Górski, J.: Trust Case – a case for trustworthiness of IT infrastructures. In: Cyberspace Security and Defense: Research Issues. NATO Science Series II: Mathematics, Physics and Chemistry, vol. 196, pp. 125–142. Springer (2005)
6. Toulmin, S.: The Uses of Argument. Cambridge University Press (1958)
7. Cyra, Ł., Górski, J.: Support for argument structures review and assessment. Reliability Engineering and System Safety 96, 26–37 (2011)
8. Górski, J., Jarzębowicz, A., Miler, J.: Validation of services supporting healthcare standards conformance. Metrology and Measurements Systems 19(2), 269–282 (2012)
9. ASCE home page, http://www.adelard.com/asce/ (visited June 27, 2012)
10. ISCaDE home page, http://www.iscade.co.uk/ (visited June 27, 2012)

11. GSN add-on for Visio home page,
    http://www-users.cs.york.ac.uk/~tpk/gsn/ (visited June 27, 2012)
12. Steele, P., Collins, K., Knight, J.: ACCESS: A Toolset for Safety Case Creation and Management. In: Proc. of 29th International Systems Safety Conference, Las Vegas, NV (2011)
13. Górski, J.: Trust-IT – a framework for trust cases. In: Workshop on Assurance Cases for Security - The Metrics Challenge, Proc. of DSN 2007, Edinburgh, UK, pp. 204–209 (2007)
14. Górski, J., Jarzebowicz, A., Leszczyna, R., Miler, J., Olszewski, M.: Trust case: justifying trust in IT solution. Reliability Engineering and System Safety 89(1), 33–47 (2005)
15. Shafer, G.: Mathematical Theory of Evidence. Princeton University Press (1976)
16. Górski, J., Witkowicz, M.: Experience with instantiating an automated testing process in the context of incremental and evolutionary software development. E-informatica: Software Engineering Journal 5(1), 51–63 (2011)
17. Górski, J., Jarzębowicz, A., Miler, J., Gołaszewski, G., Cyra, Ł., Witkowicz, M.: Deliverable D5.4: Trust Case for ANGEL platform demonstrator, ANGEL STREP Project deliverable, project no. IST-5-033506-STP (2008)

Towards Composable Robotics: The R3-COP Knowledge-Base Driven Technology Platform

Erwin Schoitsch[1], Wolfgang Herzner[1], Carmen Alonso-Montes[2], P. Chmelar[3], and Lars Dalgaard[4]

[1] AIT, Austria
[2] Tecnalia, Spain
[3] TU Brno, Czech Republic
[4] DTI, Denmark

{erwin.schoitsch,wolfgang.herzner}@ait.ac.at,
carmen.alonso@tecnalia.com, chmelarp@fit.vutbr.cz,
ldd@teknologisk.dk

Abstract. The ARTEMIS project R3-COP (Resilient Reasoning Robotic Co-operating Systems) aims at providing European industry with leading-edge innovation that will enable the production of advanced robust and safe cognitive, reasoning autonomous and co-operative robotic systems at reduced cost. This is achieved by cross-sector reusability of building blocks, collected in a knowledge base, within a generic framework and platform with domain-specific instantiations.

The R3-COP Framework is targeting at becoming basis for a European RTP (Reference Technology Platform) for robust autonomous systems by embodying methodologies, methods, and tools for safety-critical hard-real-time system development and verification supported by European tool vendors. To enable this, interoperability issues have to be resolved at several levels, including meta-models, models, tool interfaces and component descriptions. The link is established by the knowledge base described in more detail in this paper to allow composition of robotic applications from building blocks, guiding design & development as well as validation & verification (supporting certification in the end). The concept of the knowledge base could be re-used in the planned ARTEMIS Common Reference Technology Platform for critical systems engineering.

Keywords: robotics, autonomous systems, co-operative systems, composability, building blocks, ontology-based knowledge base, reference technology framework, safety, cognitive systems, robotic vision, testing, certification.

1 Introduction

R3-COP (Resilient Reasoning Robotic Co-operating Systems) aims at developing and implementing a generic framework and platform with domain-specific instantiations which will facilitate the production of advanced robust and safe cognitive, reasoning

F. Ortmeier and P. Daniel (Eds.): SAFECOMP 2012 Workshops, LNCS 7613, pp. 427–435, 2012.

autonomous and co-operative robotic systems (mobile and immobile) at reduced cost. This will be achieved by enabling cross-sector reusability of building blocks, collected in a knowledge base, which is part of a technology platform and framework and contains the required information on how ARS (Autonomous Robotic Systems) methods, components, subsystems and systems work and interact with each other and what characteristics they have. This addresses the interoperability issues of building blocks (meta-models, models, components and interfaces) and tools to be provided within the R3-COP framework.

The framework is targeting at a European RTP for robust autonomous systems embodying meta-models, technologies, methods, and tools for safety-critical hard-real-time system development supported by European tool vendors. In the long term, this European robotics RTP should become an on-line resource which anyone in the autonomous systems community can contribute to and benefit from.

Besides creating the knowledge data base (structure, description of characteristics of building blocks, interfaces), R3-COP creates a *portfolio of methodologies* to be used and a *tool box* of architectural frameworks, guidelines and tools necessary to apply the information from the knowledge base in specific design contexts in order to arrive at a viable solution for an autonomous robotic systems problem. The primary goal within the project will be to provide a solution that can be applied directly to the projects' use cases (ground-based, airborne and underwater, including applications from manufacturing, home appliances, surveillance, inspection, manipulation, transport etc.). Generalisation and flexibility are considered as secondary goals. The knowledge base is for reasons of practicability and parallel development of methods and tools for design & development (1) as well as for validation & verification (2) split in two parts accordingly.

2   The R3-COP Concept: Framework and Interoperability

The overall goal of R3-COP is to improve the quality of robotic systems and to increase trust in the systems by composable design and by developing new test strategies for mobile and adaptive (co-operating) systems with complex sensor input (e.g. stereo vision) and autonomous behavior, with measurable coverage of sensorial information and behavioral aspects, based on in-depth domain analysis. In detail, the target research areas are:

- **Design and development:** model-driven process for the compositional development of safety critical (mobile) systems
- **Analysis Methods:** System analysis and evaluation are addressed in context of safety cases
- **V&V (Validation & Verification):** new test strategies, methods and tools for vision-based perception and (co-operative) behavior of (mobile) autonomous systems

- **European Standard Reference Technology Platform (Framework)**: utilizing results and experiences of recent European projects, the framework is targeting at a European RTP for robust autonomous systems
- **Qualification, standardization and certification** support issues
- **Cross domain applicability:** The framework knowledge base covers all domains and enabling technologies for autonomous systems (transport, automation, surveillance, co-operation, emergency services on ground, underwater and air)

R3-COP focuses, in particular, on design & development level in providing components as building blocks for robotic autonomous systems (compositional design), including positioning, navigation and communication, as well as on very specific problems of assessing correctness, safety and robustness of autonomous robotic systems in developing new V&V methods and tools (analysis and test) for complex sensors and perception modules, and co-operative behaviour. These artifacts are collected in a Knowledge Base in a standardized manner (see Fig. 1), which requires a common interoperability definition with respect to interfaces and attributes. R3-COP will achieve its goals by

1) developing a design methodology (reference architecture) with means for tailoring it for specific applications. It will be substantiated in a number of domain-specific platforms and demonstrators, including cross-domain co-operating systems,

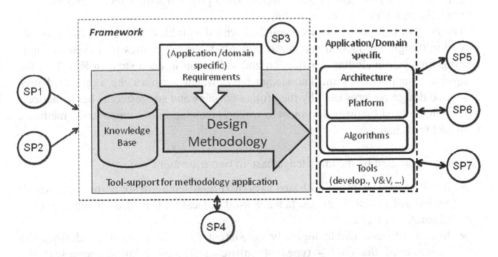

Fig. 1. The R3-COP Framework concept: The knowledge base enabling composition of robotic applications (SP1, SP2 provide foundations and new specific robotic/autonomous systems features, SP3 and SP4 are developing the D&D and V&V methods & tools,. SP5-SP7 are applications/domains)

2) developing innovative system components for the robust perception of the environment including sensor fusion, and for reasoning and reliable action control,
3) developing a fault-tolerant high-performance processing platform, based on a multi-core architecture.

An important goal of R3-COP is the establishment of a "knowledge base" for autonomous and robotic systems, using ontology for knowledge description and taxonomy, consisting of two parts:

- "design & development" (DDKB): supports the Design &Development (DD) methodology by providing information about hard- and software components, their purpose, costs, strength and limits, possible combinations or conflicts etc.
- "validation and verification": supports the V&V process by providing information about analysis and test tools applicable for robotic components, their purpose, costs, strength and limits, possible combinations or conflicts etc.

3   The Knowledge Base for Design and Development (DDKB)

Briefly, an *Autonomous Robotic System* (ARS) is made for the purpose of performing some *task* (e.g. surveillance, vacuum cleaning or some kind of a mission) within the operating *environment* (e.g. ground, underwater or airborne) under given set of *requirements* (both functional and non-functional). Thus, the ARS *design process* can be expressed as a *process* to find a solution for a problem with a set of *"robots"* performing the task under some conditions.

The ARS design process is accomplished with the problem statement, analysis, engineering design, production and some post production activities in a systems engineering life-cycle including verification and validation in each step. In R3-COP, the designs are supported by the knowledge base, which includes the aggregated use-cases and design patterns used by the project partners and suggested as best practices. These can be used by other designers as a recommendation of components, methods, tools and tool chains.

This is supported by the knowledge base in two equivalent ways:

- In a human-readable Wiki-based hypertext representation supported by a search engine and a classification scheme is used to locate information in the system as illustrated in Fig. 2.
- In a machine-readable logically consistent form. The ontology defines the structure of the data – types of entities and their relations represent the knowledge necessary to apply automated deductive reasoning (see Fig. 3). This is important for interoperability – to have a standardized format for description of entities (components) and their relations. The ontology browser uses WebProtégé.

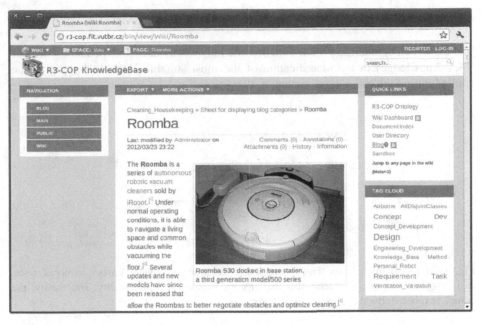

Fig. 2. The R3-COP knowledge base Wiki including the tag cloud classification scheme

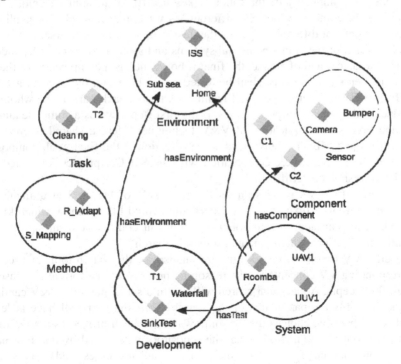

Fig. 3. The R3-COP ontology illustration of individual entities organized in sets – classes and connectors using property relations

4   The Knowledge Base for V&V (VVKB)

The main idea behind the VVKB is to provide help to any user (independently of their V&V knowledge) in the identification of the most suitable V&V technique to be applied during the robot development or afterwards.

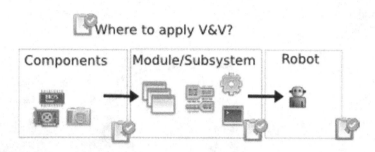

Fig. 4. The V&V techniques shall be applied to components (touch sensors, cameras, laser, etc), SW modules or subsystems that implements an specific functionality, and finally, the complete robot (formed by the previous elements)

The inherent complexity of the robot makes it difficult to apply a unique V&V technique for the complete robot. So, different V&V techniques need to be applied for different elements, at different stages of the design phase, and of course, to the complete robot. Each of the components, subsystems and systems shall be independently tested and validated, and of course, the final robot, which is a composition of the previous components and systems, shall be tested as a whole. So, the need of a Knowledge Base (KB) to describe potential techniques to test each part or the whole system, reducing the number of possibilities, is the first step towards a complete automation in the process of application of V&V techniques. Here a shared interest with ARTEMIS project MBAT is envisaged; if certification is the final goal, composable certification is an issue where co-operation with the SafeCer project is planned (e.g. via a joint workshop on certification).

The general strategy can be seen on the right side of Fig. 5. The ultimate goal would be that any user (expert or non-expert) that would like to know which kind of V&V techniques can apply to his robot development could search through the R3-COP ontologies with an "intelligent and semantic search".

A specific VV ontology provides the mechanism of the search tool for accessing the corresponding VV concepts, so the reasoning process will be formalized based on ontological concepts. A particular search will return a set of possible V&V candidate techniques that fits the parameters of the search. Thus the user will have at least a reduced set of possible choices that in some way have been proved as a good option for that particular problem. Notice that the repository will be fed by the information provided from the analysis done for the domains and use cases, and some specific content can be inferred from concepts of the VV ontology. Hence, the information

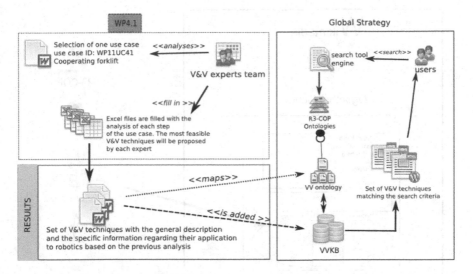

Fig. 5. Relationship among the results of V&V WP and the global strategy behind the ontology proposal (the mentioned use case is taken as an example)

returned to the users will be twofold enriched: general information coming from human expert analysis and other inferred information, taken from the VV ontology.

Each candidate technique is shown to the end user following a predefined structure, containing general information, human analysis information and inferred information from the ontology. The candidates have to be described in a comparable manner, so again interoperability is a key issue. For this purpose, a preliminary form has been defined in order to unify the presentation to the users. Each individual V&V technique is described in this standardized format and stored in the VVKB. The general parts can be split up into several sections: general, human expert analysis and inferred information. The general information corresponds to the general descriptions of the technique: name, description, type, category, benefits and limits. The human expert analysis will be added in two sections: relationship with challenges of ARS, and others. Initially, this content is influenced by the analysis of the current R3-COP use cases, but will be growing with new usages in other scenarios, following the collaborative way of working in Wikipedia. This was already indicated before as the RTP was referred to as an on-line resource for the autonomous systems community in the future.

Some additional information can be directly inferred from the concepts stored within the particular ontology for VV and the others used in R3-COP. This information is automatically generated from the information in the form ("inferred elements from the ontology"-section). In this section is shown in which types of "robot tasks" (navigation, grasping, movement, etc.) a particular V&V technique has been used. The same reasoning process can be applied to "features" and "environment". In Fig. 6, the relationship among the contents of the Wikimedia document and both the ontology and the VVKB are shown.

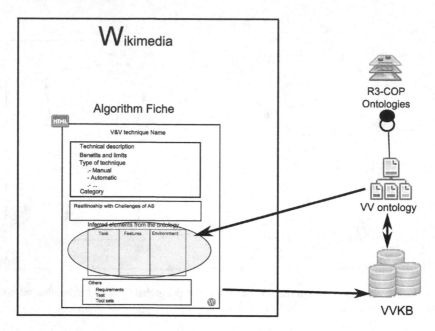

Fig. 6. Relationship between wiki, ontology and the fields of the individual algorithm form

5   Conclusions

Composability, re-use and interoperability are main targets for R3-COP to create robust, safe robotic autonomous systems from building blocks. A knowledge base for design & development as well as for validation & verification with ontology-based and human-readable (Wiki-) standardized descriptions for methods, tools and components are key to this approach. Developing new test strategies for moving and adaptive (co-operating) systems with complex sensor input (e.g. stereo vision) and autonomous behavior, with measurable coverage, based on in-depth domain analysis, is one of the innovative contributions, which may be added together with the Knowledge Base concept to the ARTEMIS CRTP (Common Reference Technology Platform) to address these issues most relevant not only for cognitive robotic systems, which have not been addressed systematically until now, but also to critical systems engineering in general.

The ARTEMIS CRTP is aimed at by a cluster of ARTEMIS projects in the safety & high reliability area (e.g. CESAR, MBAT, SafeCer, iFEST, see references). Therefore, in the last phase of R3-COP, where the robotic RTP is addressed, closer information- and experience exchange with the other High-Rel Cluster projects is planned

Acknowledgements. The work is partially funded by the EC (ARTEMIS Joint Undertaking) and the partners' national funding authorities under grant agreement 100233 (R3-COP project).

References

1. ARTEMIS Joint Undertaking, the public private partnership for R&D in embedded systems, http://www.artemis-ju.eu/
2. Related ARTEMIS-projects of the Safety/High-reliability cluster of projects:
    a. R3-COP project "Resilient Reasoning Robotic Co-operating Systems", http://www.r3-cop.eu
    b. CESAR project "Cost-efficient methods and processes for safety relevant embedded systems", http://www.cesarproject.eu
    c. MBAT project "Combined Model-based Analysis and Testing of Embedded Systems", http://www.mbat-artemis.eu
    d. pSafeCer/nSafeCer projects "Safety Certification of Software-intensive Systems with Reusable Components", http://www.safecer.eu
    e. iFEST project "Industrial Framework for Embedded Systems Tools", http://www.artemis-ifest.eu
3. Benini, A., Mancini, A., Minutolo, R., Longhi, S., Montanari, M.: A modular framework for fast prototyping of cooperative unmanned aerial vehicles. Journal of Intelligent & Robotic Systems 65, 507–520 (2012), doi:10.1007/s10846-011-9577-1
4. Dalgaard, L.: Rational System-level Design Methodology for Autonomous Robotic Systems, Ph.D. Thesis. Odense (2011)
5. Lill, R., Saglietti, F.: Model-based Testing of Autonomous Systems based on Coloured Petri Nets. In: Proc. Workshops ARCS 2012, February 28. Lecture Notes in Informatics, vol. P-200. GI, TU Munich (2012)
6. Micskei, Z., Szatmári, Z., Oláh, J., Majzik, I.: A Concept for Testing Robustness and Safety of the Context-Aware Behaviour of Autonomous Systems. In: Jezic, G., Kusek, M., Nguyen, N.-T., Howlett, R.J., Jain, L.C. (eds.) KES-AMSTA 2012. LNCS, vol. 7327, pp. 504–513. Springer, Heidelberg (2012)
7. Saglietti, F., Söhnlein, S., Lill, R.: Evolution of Verification Techniques by Increasing Autonomy of Cooperating Agents. In: Unger, H., Kyamaky, K., Kacprzyk, J. (eds.) Autonomous Systems: Developments and Trends. SCI, vol. 391, pp. 353–362. Springer, Heidelberg (2012)
8. Szatmári, Z., Oláh, J., Majzik, I.: Ontology-based Test Data Generation using Metaheuristics. In: Proc. of the 8th International Conference on Informatics in Control, Automation and Robotics (ICINCO 2011), July 28-31 (2011)

Addressing the Needs of an Aging Population: An Experiment for Monitoring Behaviour in a Domestic Environment

Marte E.B. Skjønsfjell[1], Aslak R. Normann[1], Dag Sjong[2], and Amund Skavhaug[1]

[1] Department of Engineering Cybernetics, NTNU
[2] Norsk Automatisering as
{marte.skjonsfjell,aslakrin}@gmail.com,
dag@norskautomatisering.no, skavhaug@itk.ntnu.no

Abstract. An increasingly aging population will challenge the current organization of society and will require new technological solutions for assisting as well as maintaining the health of this demographic. In this article, results from an experiment on remote monitoring of a domestic environment implemented in the home of an elderly citizen, are presented.

A system comprised of several types of both stationary and body-worn sensors together with a framework for collecting, interpreting and presenting the gathered data in a useful manner was developed, and a pilot-study was conducted. It is demonstrated that one can get useful information via remote monitoring, even implemented as a low cost monitoring system using off-the-shelf components. It is shown that such a system could have significance in assisting health personnel.

Keywords: Welfare, aging, population, monitoring, wireless, iPad, Android, BlueTooth LE, Linux.

1 Introduction

As the population ages, we are now facing a shift in demographics where more people enter their golden years, live longer, and are entitled to their due welfare benefits. With this shift, the neo-traditional institutionalization of elderly is no longer tenable on the scale we will need in a few years. Welfare technology is an emerging field of research which therefore is becoming increasingly important. One of the key areas of application for welfare technology is to assist elderly living at home longer, in safety and comfort, as well as assisting primary caregivers in identifying potential health issues, both developing trends and acute illness. Signs of deteriorating health can include appetite loss, insomnia and reduced activity level. Remote activity monitoring can give health personnel indicators on the condition of the patients and give an objective overview of how their days have been. As health personnel often may only come by once a day or less, it is beneficial to be able to supervise the patients' condition when they are alone.

F. Ortmeier and P. Daniel (Eds.): SAFECOMP 2012 Workshops, LNCS 7613, pp. 436–446, 2012.

There are many ailments specific to elderly, such as dementia, chronic obstructive pulmonary disease, heart conditions, Parkinson's, restricted movement, generally poor constitution and others. Each of these has their own set of parameters which may need monitoring and assessment.

In [11], a body-worn sensor platform for monitoring a few such parameters was developed and integrated with a mobile device for display. As mentioned in [11] many types of sensors are of interest for monitoring the condition of a subject under

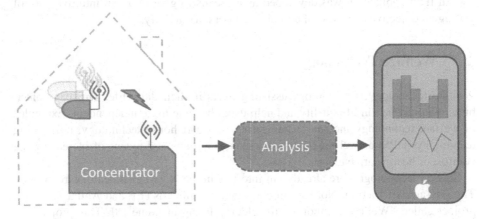

Fig. 1. Simplified overview of the developed system. Analysis can be performed on-site to increase privacy.

observation, and a combination of heterogeneous sensor data may be required to assess a subject's condition. Our aim in this work was therefore to show how information from various sources may be handled and combined, to develop a framework for collecting, interpreting and presenting heterogeneous data and finally to realize and test such a system. An entire monitoring system, as opposed to focusing on smaller details, has been realized to get a broad insight into the different aspects of creating a platform for welfare monitoring, as well as a more overall picture of how a monitored environment can be used and developed further.

Body-worn sensors must necessarily be wireless if they are to give a live feed of the wearer's condition without restricting movement or otherwise demanding undue mental effort. Stationary sensors also benefit from communicating wirelessly, the main advantages being modularity and cost savings both for installation and for maintenance throughout the lifetime of a sensor network.

A subject's condition may be sensed either directly via e.g. a cardio-pulmonary monitor, or indirectly via the subject's activity level, mobility and interaction with the environment. The advent of "Smart Houses" as ever more mature commercial products, which by their nature monitor activity in a home, makes the latter indirect method a promising venue for exploiting synergies, lowering costs and risks. Both an ambulant and a stationary platform were implemented here. The system was implemented in a domestic environment and monitored a volunteered test subject. Only some details of the implemented system are presented. More of the test-environment, deployment of the stationary sensor nodes used for "Smart House" location- and activity tracking, and the development of a body-worn sensor is found in [11]. The total system is illustrated in Fig. 1.

Presentation of the aggregated data is a crucial part of making the implemented system available for health personnel, relatives or others without them needing to know the particularities of the system. The presentation must be easy to comprehend and an iPad application was developed as a means to give users an intuitive way of getting an objective overview of a monitored person's activity.

2   Welfare Technology

Welfare technology is technology assisting users in their daily life. This can contribute to an increase in life quality and help users become more independent. Examples of welfare technology include cleaning robots, smart house technology, positioning technology (GPS) as well as body-worn sensor systems and means of increasing the comfort of health care patients.

Several technologies are already put into use in the Norwegian health care system. The city-area of Bærum, Norway, in cooperation with SINTEF and Abilia AS has a project called "Welfare technology for elderly living at home"[8]. This project has created a showroom apartment [9] with technical solutions to enable elderly to live at home as long as possible. The solutions include aid to help the user remember dates, appointments and medicines, keep in contact with family and health personnel as well as automatic lighting and alarms. A few nursing homes use a robotic seal for social stimulation of patients with dementia [10] and "Hjelpemiddelsentralen" distributes fall sensors with GPS [3].

Ambient Assisted Living (AAL) is the form of welfare technology focusing only on the elderly part of the population. The European Union has a project called Ambient Assistant Living Joint Program (AAL JP) that focuses on technological solutions for enhancing the life quality of elderly in Europe. Focus of the project in spring 2012 is "ICT-based Solutions for (Self-) Management of Daily Life Activities of Older Adults at Home"[1]. Earlier, three other focuses have resulted in funding of several projects under development:

- ICT based solutions for Prevention and Management of Chronic Conditions of Elderly People
- ICT based solutions for Advancement of Social Interaction of Elderly People
- ICT-based Solutions for Advancement of Older Persons Independence and Participation in the Self-Serve Society

A few of these projects are presented below:

The H@H Health at Home [4] project focuses on elderly with Chronic Heart Failure by remotely monitoring cardiovascular and respiratory parameters by automatic systems as well as health personnel. The aim is to reduce re-hospitalization by detecting situations that might become critical at an early stage.

The HOPE Smart Home for Elderly People [5] project is focusing on giving elderly with Alzheimer's disease a more independent life. This is achieved through a smart home solution with functionality for fall detection, security and communication.

CARE Safe Private Homes for Elderly Persons [2] aims to realize an intelligent monitoring and alarming system for independent living of elderly persons. This is to be accomplished by automatically detecting critical situations such as a fall or immobility, by using stationary sensors.

One of the main concerns when it comes to ICT solutions in health care is the issue of privacy and safety of patients. It is illegal for handlers of personal data to distribute or use this in a way not approved by the individual source of the data. The Norwegian law of personal data (*Personopplysningsloven*[6]) states how personal data should be handled and has as an objective to protect the individual right to privacy. Information about a persons' health condition is considered to be sensitive, and Information and Communication Technology is subject to strict regulation when it comes to harvesting and use of data. One cannot gather sensitive personal data without the knowledge and approval of the affected person. Considering these rules and regulations, it is clear that the collecting and storing of personal data needs to be thoroughly evaluated to make sure the data is secure regarding unauthorized access. Concerns regarding the protection of privacy of individuals have proven to be legitimate. An example was when two university students working on electronic journal software was given access to 110,000 journals from their professor [7] without the approval or knowledge of the involved patients. Another example is of health personnel having accessed electronic journals of patients just out of curiosity.

3   Overview of the Implemented System

The system was installed at the house of the test subject. The test subject is an 86 year old male, living alone in his own house. The test subject is in good health, and is able to do everyday chores by himself.

Fig. 3 shows an overview of the structure and data flow in the system. The leftmost box shows that in the house used as test-environment, there is a processor board running Linux which works as a concentrator for various wireless sensor data. This data is stored in a database and can be processed locally at the user's home, or can be sent via a gateway to an interpreting process running on a remote machine. The presentation platform for the data was an Apple iOS application we developed during the project.

Magnetic sensors were placed on most doors, including the refrigerator and microwave oven. Passive-infrared-sensors were installed to create zones for detection in all rooms. Additionally, a body-worn Blue-tooth LE device was programmed to transfer acceleration data to measure activity this way. A wireless energy metering device was attached to the electric wires of the Coffee-machine.

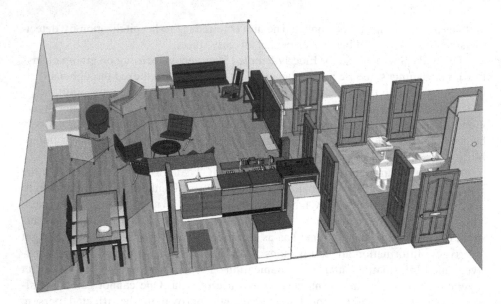

Fig. 2. 3D model of test subject's house, showing the field of view of one of the living room sensors

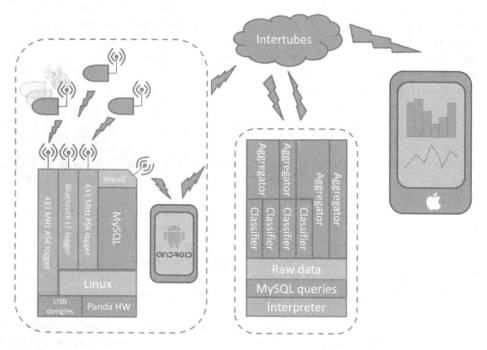

Fig. 3. General structure of data flow from sensor nodes through a concentrator, through an internet gateway, through an interpreting mechanism to a presentation platform

Using a database server locally for persistent storage made attaching different logger-processes storing data simultaneously easy, while at the same time giving an arbitrary number of processes access to historical data. Sending real-time sensor data directly to interpreting and displaying processes is a possible improvement, but considering the relatively slow dynamics of human behaviour this was not considered worth the increased complexity.

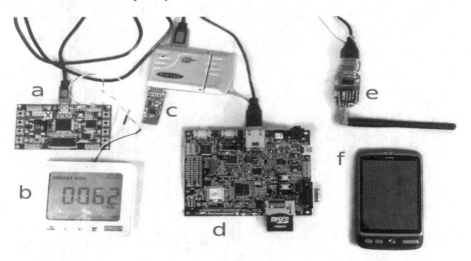

Fig. 4. The data concentrator as deployed:. (a) Xplain board connected to a test pad on the (b) Efergy display module, (c) BLE dongle, (d) PandaBoard, (e) MultiTRX transceiver, (f) Mobile Wifi-Hotspot

4 Some Results

4.1 Zone Occupancy

From Fig. 5 we can see how the location classification performed. In general all lost events lead to some deviance from the truth, but as the zones with PIR (passive infrared) sensors will receive events throughout a stay, some loss can be tolerated while maintaining an adequate degree of accuracy. The same is not true for lost door events for doors leading to zones without PIR sensors, as they are responsible for most of the obvious errors.

4.2 Orientation and Pedometer Data

Before the subject goes outside in the morning it's quite clear when the subject is sitting or standing up. We can also see that the subject reattaches the sensor and lies down on the side or back. If we look at stable periods with medium tilt it's safe to assume that the subject is sitting down, because a belt (where the sensor was attached) is naturally tilted at an angle when sitting, and an absence of activity can often be

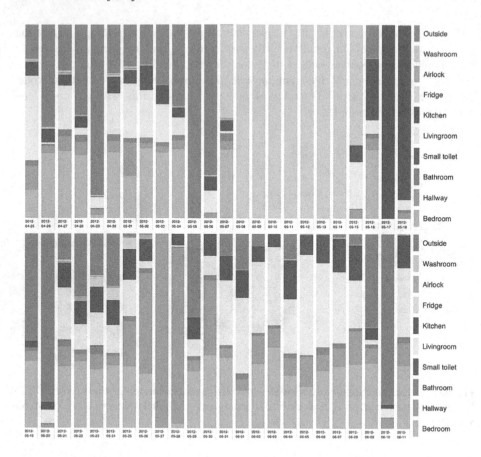

Fig. 5. iPad screenshots. Location summary per day for May 25th until June 11th.

observed. We note that the degree of tilt varies wildly between the assumed sitting periods. Whether this is a result of varied sitting positions or a shift in sensor position is difficult to determine. The subject has a wide variety of chair and sofa types, and there are a number of ways to sit, so a combination is likely.

4.3   Presentation

The iPad application gave a fairly clear overview of the subject's movements and history. For health personnel, this can be used to manually get an indication of past and present activity of a subject. Looking at the amount of time the subject spent in the bedroom, outside and in the bathroom it is clear that the time spent outside, as well as time spent in the bathrooms varies unpredictably and are somewhat inversely correlated. The time spent asleep is much more stable, and here it is easier to see and draw conclusions from deviations from the norm. For example: In the period of May 28th till June 6th the test subject came down with pneumonia, and had to get medical treatment. On the 1st of June it can be seen that the test subject slept less than the days before and after.

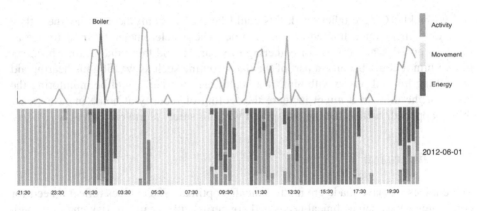

Fig. 6. Detailed overview of June 1st

In Fig. 6, the specifics of this day are shown. We see that the test subject went to bed before 21:30, and that he had a short bathroom break around 00:15. Then, the test subject got up again close to 01:45, and this time he turns on the boiler and starts his day. On June 4th and 5th it was seen that the test subject slept for a very limited amount of time. This is not completely accurate, as examining the days more carefully, showed that there were breaks in the bedroom stays both nights for approximately 30 minutes. The sleep classifier as implemented considers any break for more 10 minutes as a sign of the sleep being finished, and any stays in the bedroom after this are regarded normal day activity and thus not added to the sleep. This means that days with very little sleep can be detected, when it is just a sleep that is more disturbed.

The main trend is that the more time spent outside, the less activity from the indoor sensors. This is to be expected, but it can also be seen that this varies a lot, especially when much time is spent inside. This could be a result of visitors in the house. Normalizing the measured activity level against the amount of time spent in the sensors' field of view by some mechanism makes sense intuitively, and a deviance from the prediction could give us an indication of a subject's general condition. For activity sensed with infra-red sensors, this may hold only if activity goes down because activity from visitors can mask inactivity on the part of the subject under observation.

4.4   Experience of the Test Subject

The test subject was asked a few questions about his experience and how he perceived the monitoring. He claimed that he did not feel uncomfortable being monitored, and that his activity level had not been reduced or increased due to the sensors in the house. We did particularly ask about how he felt regarding the sensors in private areas such as bathroom and bedroom, and he said that he had no hesitations to these, as he was well aware that the sensors only detected movement. He did mention that others might be more sensitive to this, as the sensors can resemble cameras. When it came to the sensors, he said that he didn't mind them being in the house, and that the only time he paid any special interest to them was when some of them fell down from time to time. The sensors were not perceived as unsightly either, and he got used to them pretty quickly. On the other hand, this could be the case only because he knew they were only there for a limited period of time. The accelerometer he tried to use as much as possible and it was not bothering to wear. He did think that in time bringing it with him it could become a part of the daily routine such as wearing his hearing aid and taking his cell phone with him. If a health care worker would be monitoring the behavior, he thought it might increase the feeling of security at home in case something happened, such as feeling indisposed with his safety alarm out of reach.

5   Discussion

The choices we have made are not technically optimal. The choices reflect a need for compromise between technical needs and concerns with regards to risk and cost, with the goal being to get enough nodes of enough types running soon enough to evaluate the entirety of the solution. We recommend more robust wireless protocols for further work. While there can be a significant amount of slack with regards to timing and precision without degrading the quality of the data, the data reported to health personnel or caregivers should not be inaccurate, i.e. reporting something that is completely false, such as an observed staying for days in a laundry room.

The local concentrator node had a high percentage of uptime. One unexplained reset occurred, but remote access was reestablished automatically. It is therefore in our opinion, a good choice to rely on tried and tested platforms such as Linux running on relatively cheap hardware for future implementations and even full scale deployment.

As has been observed in the public debate surrounding electronic patient journals, privacy and security are paramount in gaining and keeping the trust of users. We believe that the use of restricted local access and public-key encrypted end-to-end remote connections as used in our implementation is sufficient regardless of the possible low security of the (wireless) local network.

Technically, securing stored data and restricting access is quite straight forward. The challenges in this regard are probably more of an administrative nature.

The event routing and interpretation framework are perhaps the most important design decisions to make, except for how data is presented to the user, as it will greatly affect development and maintenance cost, as well as runtime performance. Our experience is that an emphasis on weak coupling between components and layers and a separation of concerns indeed made it easier to develop and test each component separately. The effect of abstracting sensor data as context cues enabled us to develop higher order interpreting routines, but this effect was perhaps not fully utilized as time constraints required the development to stop before more classifiers could be implemented. Although letting each context classifier process data independently means it takes some minutes to classify a month of raw data on a modern computer, we find the performance acceptable considering the reduction in complexity. The interpretation of sensor data is intended to run continuously and to persistently store generated information, making the achieved performance more than adequate in a deployed system.

A thorough evaluation is needed to decide which rooms should be presented as graphs with statistics. The amount of sleep, time spent in the bathroom and time spent outdoors all seem as good indicators of a subject's health condition, but these need to be classified into groups of similar days to give a clearer view of possible abnormalities. With a larger data set, it would be interesting to compare a recent time interval with the same time interval the previous year, as this can give a better indication of e.g. sleep routines having changed over this period. Human behavior is as previously mentioned unpredictable, and this is clearly seen from the results. This means better algorithms need to be implemented to detect abnormalities, as simple statistics isn't necessarily enough.

A thorough examination in cooperation with health personnel or relatives is required to determine the benefits in a health context with the system as it is. Having a system for seeing what a patient has done since the last visit from health personnel might help detect loss of appetite or sleep at an earlier stage. Incipient dementia or similar diseases could also be captured by health personnel by seeing small signs of a patient being disorientated e.g. by cooking or wandering outside at unseemly times. These are symptoms that may not normally be seen before the disease is more developed, but by knowing that one can pick these up at an earlier stage, the medical treatment of the patient could be accommodated to allow the patient to stay safely at home as long as possible. The sensor types we have looked at in the experiment record parameters related to behaviour and activity. While this can be interesting both for emergencies and as a diagnostic tool, more targeted sensor types such as for instance blood sugar measurements or lung capacity could also be integrated to perhaps avoid hospital visits simply for routine monitoring.

6   Conclusion

A platform for monitoring elderly in a domestic environment has been developed. A full system has been implemented, presented and evaluated, from choosing and placing sensors, to receiving, interpreting and presenting the data to an end-user. The system presented is directly reusable in any home environment by modifying metadata, it is built upon cited design concepts and can serve as a firm foundation for further work in various directions. Different areas of applications of remote monitoring in a health context have been demonstrated as plausible. It has been shown that it is possible to develop such a system with low-cost simple sensors, and that useful information can be extracted from the system and presented in a meaningful way to users.

We believe the presented platform as-is could benefit health personnel and caregivers in a diagnostic capacity as a tool for assessing objective data. With further work aimed at identifying abnormal behavior or targeting specific health parameters, such a system could increase comfort and security, identify deterioration of health at an early stage and potentially save lives by detection of critical situations in time.

References

1. Ambient Assistant Living Joint Programme, `http://www.aal-europe.eu` (retrieved March 3, 2012)
2. CARE - Safe Private Homes for Elderly Persons, `http://care-aal.eu/` (retrieved March 3, 2012)
3. COGNITA FALLOFON, fall sensor with GPS, `http://www.hjelpemiddeldatabasen.no/r11x.asp?linkinfo=21482/` (retrieved June 1, 2012)
4. H@H - Health at Home, `http://www.health-at-home.eu/` (retrieved March 3, 2012)
5. HOPE - Smart Home for Elderly People, `http://www.hope-project.eu/` (retrieved March 3, 2012)
6. Lov 2000-04-14 nr 31: Lov om behandling av personopplysninger (personopplysningsloven), `http://www.lovdata.no/all/nl-20000414-031.html/` (retrieved March 3, 2012)
7. Studenter fikk ulovlig tilgang p pasientjournaler, `http://www.vg.no/helse/artikkel.php?artid=560054` (retrieved March 14, 2012)
8. Velferdsteknologi for hjemmeboende - Bærum kommune, `https://www.baerum.kommune.no/Organisasjonen/Pleie-og-omsorg/Velferdsteknologi/` (retrieved June 1, 2012)
9. Hjemme hos fru Paulsen. NHO magasinet (2011)
10. Indreiten, A.B.: Robotselen Paro kjenner igjen Sverre (2011), `http://www.nrk.no/nyheter/distrikt/ostafjells/vestfold/1.7769505` (retrieved June 1, 2012)
11. Normann, A.R., Skjønsfjell, M.E.B.: An Approach to Networked Welfare Sensing (December 2011)
12. Normann, A.R., Skjønsfjell, M.E.B.: Monitoring Behaviour in a Domestic Environment. Master's thesis. Department of engineering Cybernetics. NTNU (June 2012)

International Workshop
on Digital Engineering (IWDE 2012)

Introduction to IWDE 2012

Veit Köppen[1] and Gunter Saake[2]

[1] Center for Digital Engineering, Magdeburg, Germany
veit.koeppen@ovgu.de
http://www.cde.ovgu.de
[2] Otto-von-Guericke University Magdeburg,
Institute for Technical and Business Information Systems,
Magdeburg, Germany

Abstract. Digital Engineering is an emerging trend that brings together different experts to develop new products and processes or to enhance existing ones. Functionalities are often non-visible in the development process. Virtual reality is a promising technology to visualize aspects such as quality, security, or safety. Due to the increasing amount of software that is inherited in products or used to control processes different domain experts have to collaborate with software engineers. With the help of Digital Engineering methods and tools, system properties such as reliability and safety can be early included in the development.

Keywords: Digital Engineering, Virtual Reality, Software Engineering, System Properties.

1 Overview

Software-intensive systems are becoming more and more important in an increasing number of traditional engineering domains. Digital Engineering is an emerging trend that meets the challenge to bring together traditional engineering and modern approaches in software and systems Engineering. Engineers in the traditional domains are confronted with both, the usage of software systems in a growing amount and also with the development of software-intensive systems. Therefore, software- and systems-engineering play a growing role in many engineering domains. Although, functional properties of software systems are often included in the development process, non-functional properties of safety and security and their early inclusion in the development process are not respected sufficiently.

We introduced the workshop series in 2010 [4]. The first focus was set on emerging trends that combine mechanical and software engineering with the help of Virtual Reality. We see Digital Engineering as a necessary extension of virtual engineering and a consequence to support a holistic approach for product and process life cycle management [3].

In 2011, the Second International Workshop on Digital Engineering brought domain experts and scientists together [5]. A focus of this workshop was the usage

F. Ortmeier and P. Daniel (Eds.): SAFECOMP 2012 Workshops, LNCS 7613, pp. 449–453, 2012.

of Virtual Reality. Therefore, visualization as well as software intensive systems were in focus. Engineers in traditional domains and software developers are confronted the usage of software systems and the development of software intensive systems in a growing amount. Therefore, software- and systems-engineering play a growing role in all engineering domains.

Interdisciplinary plays an growing role in the development and improvement of products and processes. Virtual Reality enables a cost-efficient test and development environment that has to include different experts from divertive domains, such as mechanics, electrics, and software. Furthermore, organization structures, techniques, tools, and methodologies have to be considered and developed for this cooperation. Digital Engineering is the discipline that enables a shortened development cycle, observes quality requirements, and reduces cost.

2   Objectives

The aim of the 3rd International Workshop on Digital Engineering 2012 is to bring together experts, researchers, and practitioners, from different communities, such as software engineering, mechanical engineering, and safety and security.

The 3rd International Workshop on Digital Engineering (IWDE) at the Center for Digital Engineering is held in conjunction with SAFECOMP 2012 in Magdeburg, Germany. This workshop focuses on new methods and applications in the domain of digital-, software- and systems-engineering. Scientific contributions to the domain of development and management using digital technologies are addressed as well as evaluations of current trends in research. An explicit goal is to foster a future research agenda and to establish cooperation of the workshop participants in joint activities.

3   Topics

The specific topics of the workshop include, but are not limited to:

- Systems- and Software Engineering Approaches to Digital Engineering
- Architectures and Implementations of Real-Time Simulation
- Interoperability of Embedded Devices and VR Systems for Safety Critical Systems
- Interaction of VR / AR and Simulation Models
- VR-Simulation for Safety and Security Engineering
- Quality and Requirements for Sensor Networks and Embedded Systems
- Cyber Mobility & Cyber Threats
- Compliance in Eternal Systems
- Security and Privacy in Digital Engineering
- Privacy and Trustworthiness in Virtual Engineering
- Security Aspects of Service-oriented Architectures and Middlewares
- Secure and Trustworthy Man-Machine Interaction
- Secured RFID Sensor Network Technologies
- Cryptographic Methods and Algorithms

4   Workshop Contributions

In the paper *Modeling the Effects of Software on Safety and Reliability in Complex Embedded Systems* by Steiner, Keller, and Liggesmeyer [9] the development of autonomous vehicle systems underlines an increased usage of software based control mechanisms. A high complexity is the result and an accurate analysis is required. This paper investigates potential effects of software issues on safety, reliability, and availability of complex embedded autonomous systems. A mapping of integrated behavior-based control networks to State-Event Fault Tree models is presented.

Dietrich, Zug, and Kaiser [1] focus in their paper *Towards Artificial Perception* on adaptability to changing environments and environmental conditions as a key concern for future smart applications. Autonomous systems need to extend the local view on environment. In such a case, external sensors, fixed or mobile, are very useful, because, they support the acquisition of information that is described as "Internet of Things", "Intelligent Environments", "Industrial or Building Automation", "Ambient Intelligence", or "Ubiquitous Pervasive Computing". Information is ubiquitously available. However, interpretation and integration into single-points-of-truth architectures is a challenging task. The authors propose a new type of distributed middleware for the environmental perception, abstracting the environment from different available sensor systems. They use three steps to describe adaptive functionalities that can be extracted from a control application to support artificial perception and environment modeling.

In *A Case Study of Radio-based Monitoring System for Enhanced Safety of Logistics Processes* [8] Soffner et al. discuss the inclusion of transport units in logistics processes that have an important influence on safety at the workplace of a logistics hub. These units often cause serious accidents. Tracking systems can be used to reduce the risk of collisions. Special dynamic challenges, such as weather conditions and limited visibilities, arise in such a scenario. The authors describe a collision detection system based on an industrial radio-based real-time location system. Furthermore, they evaluate accuracy and usability of their system in an application scenario.

Yang, Keller, and Liggesmeyer present in *Visual Approach Facilitating the Importance Analysis of Component Fault Trees* [10] a safety analysis technique for embedded systems: Component fault tree analysis. This technique estimates respective contributions of potential basic failures and set them into ratio to an overall system failure. In such an analysis, results are typically represented in an aggregated form. The authors propose a visualization approach to integrate importance analysis results with structures of component fault trees. Their approach facilitates identification of critical components. Furthermore, it supports an analysis of basic failures.

In [6] Kuhlmann et al. describe an important issue in the cooperation of networked embedded systems and possibilities of their simulation. Potential impacts of IT security incidents and security protective measures are addressed without an explicit prototype. Dependency structures and structural effects of complex embedded networks have to be recognized and possible visualized. An increasing number of control units, sensors, and actuators, make it impossible to test all system components and their dependencies. Therefore, the authors describe a simulation model that represents possible interactions. This is evaluated by a simulation case study in the automotive domain.

The paper *From Discrete event simulation to virtual reality environments* from Nielebock et al. [7] present a concept that uses Virtual Reality to understand system dynamics. Due to complex technical systems and the prediction of system dynamics, it is hard to understand system behavior. However, this is a crucial part in Digital Engineering. Virtual simulations enable an opportunity to cope with this problem. Virtual reality simulations are a possibility to experience a system in a cost-efficient manner. The authors describe a mixed simulation environment, based on a discrete event simulator (DES) which is coupled in a virtual reality environment. Technical and conceptual challenges as well as user interaction are investigated in a case study. A prototype based is used to evaluate the approach.

Feigenspan et al. investigate in their paper *Program Comprehension in Pre-processor-Based Software* [2] how to support a programmer for customizable embedded software. Customization is a technique to cope with heterogeneous hardware, software of embedded systems provides customization capacities. Typically, this customization is achieved using conditional compilation with preprocessors. However, preprocessor usage can lead to obfuscated source code that can be difficult to comprehend, which in turn cause increased maintenance costs, bugs, and security vulnerabilities. To profit from the benefit of preprocessors usage, program comprehensibility has to be improved. How to get into control of comprehensibility with measurements is developed and this can improve maintainability, reliability, and security of source code.

5   Program Committee

For the 3rd International Workshop on Digital Engineering we want to thank all contributors and reviewers. The Program committee consists of:

- G. Saake, OvGU Magdeburg, Germany (Program Chair)
- R. Dachselt, TU Dresden, Germany
- M. Güdemann, INRIA Rhône-Alpes, France
- A. Brenke, University of Applied Science Niederrhein, Germany
- V. Köppen, OvGU Magdeburg, Germany (Local Organizing Chair)
- F. Ortmeier, GI Regional Group "Sachsen-Anhalt", Germany
- M. Schenk, OvGU & IFF Magdeburg, Germany
- D. Reiners. University of Louisiana at Lafayette, USA
- A.-B. M. Salem, Ain Shams University, Egypt
- H. Rohling, TU Hamburg-Harburg

Acknowledgment. We would like to thank Heike Luka for her support in organizing the workshop. Furthermore, this work is partially supported by the German Ministry of Education and Science (BMBF) within the ViERforES-II project, contract no. 01IM10002B.

References

1. Dietrich, A., Zug, S., Kaiser, J.: Towards Artificial Perception. In: Ortmeier, F., Daniel, P. (eds.) SAFECOMP 2012 Workshops. LNCS, vol. 7613, pp. 466–476. Springer, Heidelberg (2012)
2. Feigenspan, J., Siegmund, N., Fruth, J., Kuhlmann, S., Dittmann, J., Saake, G.: Program Comprehension in Preprocessor-Based Software. In: Ortmeier, F., Daniel, P. (eds.) SAFECOMP 2012 Workshops. LNCS, vol. 7613, pp. 517–528. Springer, Heidelberg (2012)
3. Köppen, V., Saake, G.: Einsatz von Virtueller Realität im Prozessmanagement. Industrie Management 26(2), 49–53 (2010)
4. Köppen, V., Saake, G. (eds.): IWDE 2010: Proceedings of the First International Workshop on Digital Engineering. ACM, New York (2010)
5. Köppen, V., Saake, G. (eds.): Proceedings of the Second International Workshop on Digital Engineering. Faculty of Computer Science, Otto-von-Guericke-University (November 2011)
6. Kuhlmann, S., Fruth, J., Hoppe, T., Dittmann, J.: Simulation of Structural Effects in Embedded Systems and Visualization of Dependencies According to an Intended Attack or Manipulation. In: Ortmeier, F., Daniel, P. (eds.) SAFECOMP 2012 Workshops. LNCS, vol. 7613, pp. 498–507. Springer, Heidelberg (2012)
7. Nielebock, S., Ortmeier, F., Schumann, M., Winge, A.: From Discrete Event Simulation to Virtual Reality Environments. In: Ortmeier, F., Daniel, P. (eds.) SAFECOMP 2012 Workshops. LNCS, vol. 7613, pp. 508–516. Springer, Heidelberg (2012)
8. Soffner, M., Nykolaychuk, M., Adler, F., Richter, K.: A Case Study of Radio-Based Monitoring System for Enhanced Safety of Logistics Processes. In: Ortmeier, F., Daniel, P. (eds.) SAFECOMP 2012 Workshops. LNCS, vol. 7613, pp. 477–485. Springer, Heidelberg (2012)
9. Steiner, M., Keller, P., Liggesmeyer, P.: Modeling the Effects of Software on Safety and Reliability in Complex Embedded Systems. In: Ortmeier, F., Daniel, P. (eds.) SAFECOMP 2012 Workshops. LNCS, vol. 7613, pp. 454–465. Springer, Heidelberg (2012)
10. Yang, Y., Keller, P., Liggesmeyer, P.: Visual Approach Facilitating the Importance Analysis of Component Fault Trees. In: Ortmeier, F., Daniel, P. (eds.) SAFECOMP 2012 Workshops. LNCS, vol. 7613, pp. 486–497. Springer, Heidelberg (2012)

Modeling the Effects of Software on Safety and Reliability in Complex Embedded Systems

Max Steiner, Patric Keller, and Peter Liggesmeyer

AG Software Engineering: Dependability, TU Kaiserslautern
{steiner,pkeller,liggesmeyer}@cs.uni-kl.de

Abstract. The development of autonomous vehicle systems demands the increased usage of software based control mechanisms. Generally, this leads to very complex systems, whose proper functioning has to be ensured. In our work we aim at investigating and assessing the potential effects of software issues on the safety, reliability and availability of complex embedded autonomous systems. One of the key aspects of the research concerns the mapping of functional descriptions in form of integrated behavior-based control networks to State-Event Fault Tree models.

Keywords: safety analysis, reliability analysis, state-event fault trees.

1 Introduction

Recent trends concerning the automation of high-tech products like cars, airplanes and trains lead to embedded systems of tremendous size and complexity. This development particularly affects the quality of those systems. Important (non-functional) quality characteristics often related to in this context are safety, reliability and availability. The compliance with predefined quality goals is ensured by the increased usage of software-based mechanisms. Depending on the nature of the considered systems, this may be crucial. Especially, in cases where software is applied to fulfill certain safety requirements.

The way software affects safety-critical systems is manifold. But not only safety is a factor influencing the final quality of a product. Faults introduced due to misinterpretation, wrong design decisions, or implementation errors may lead to unreliable services, or to reduced functionalities, which might affect the availability of the whole system. The other way around, unreliable or non-available services may again end up in safety critical events, e.g., the failure of anti-blocking systems of cars in emergency cases. In this regards, important questions focus on determining the impact of software faults on safety, reliability and availability of complex software-intensive embedded systems.

In general, the range of the considered systems only differs slightly with respect to its principle composition and its mission profiles: Data generated from sensors, responsible for the acquisition of environmental information, is collected and prepared for further processing. Based on the provided data, decisions are

F. Ortmeier and P. Daniel (Eds.): SAFECOMP 2012 Workshops, LNCS 7613, pp. 454–465, 2012.

inferred determining the behavior of the system, e.g., whether or not a collision detection system should trigger an alarm in case of an imminent collision with other objects. Depending on the sort of system, the decision may also control actuators like engines and steering devices, as it is the case in autonomous vehicles.

Our efforts center on finding a way to draw conclusions about influences of software on quality characteristics like reliability, safety and availability of complex software-intensive embedded systems of autonomous vehicles. The main focus lies on how to map corresponding relations of software-artifacts of functional descriptions of integrated Behavior-Based Control (iB2C) networks [9] to safety and reliability analysis models using State Event Fault Trees (SEFT) [3]. Analyzing these mappings shall facilitate answering questions like:

- How do software-artifacts react on corrupted input data?
- At which point do software components fail?
- Given assumptions about the reliability of the input data, how imminent is the occurrence of certain unwanted/critical system-level events with respect to safety, reliability and/or availability?

Our research relies on the description of an autonomous vehicle demonstrator system called RAVON (Robust Autonomous Vehicle for Off-Road Navigation), which has been developed by the Robotics Research Lab at the University of Kaiserslautern.

The remainder is structured as follows. In Sect. 2 we provide an overview about the type of the demonstrator system used to conduct the studies. In Sect. 3 we review some of the related modeling techniques. Subject of Sect. 4 is the discussion of how to use the modeling elements of State-Event Fault Trees to map the interrelations between reliability and safety. Sect. 5 describes the way of using the technique to assess the overall system safety based on the information about interference to sensor (data) failure. In Sect. 6 we provide the results of an analysis of safety subsystems of our demonstrator system. We conclude with Sect. 7 and provide a short outlook of future work.

2 Demonstrator: RAVON

RAVON is a mobile robot developed by the Robotics Research Lab at the University of Kaiserslautern to research off-road navigation of autonomous vehicles [11]. It uses several different sensor systems to perceive its environment. Laser scanners are used for front and back distance measuring and obstacle detection. Additional information about the environment is added with cameras. Pressure sensitive bumper systems at the front and the back of the robot cause an emergency stop if triggered. All sensor systems are processed by the software part of the system, which then generates control values for the actuators. The control software is realized using the behavior-based control architecture iB2C [9]. RAVON has four electric wheel hub motors bringing it to a maximum velocity of 10 km/h. Its total weight of 750 kg brings up a potential risk of serious damage to itself and the environment including injuries in collisions with humans. It is therefore imperative that the system is analyzed for residual risks despite of the built-in safeguards. Unfavorable environmental conditions could lead to a non-detection of an obstacle by one or more sensors. In a safety analysis it has to be examined how such a fault affects the driving behavior and if it leads to an accident.

2.1 Behavior-Based Network Description

In RAVON a behavior-based control framework named iB2C [9] is used. The control architecture is a layer-based network consisting of several behavior modules. An iB2C behavior has several behavior-specific input and output signals to determine its influence on the behavior network. In addition to the behavior signals a behavior module has an input and output vector for values controlled by the behavior.

Interaction between behavior modules is realized by fusion behaviors, which combine outputs from different modules to one single output. Two different kinds of fusions are used in RAVON: maximum fusion and weighted fusion. The maximum fusion forwards the output vector of the behavior with the highest activity. The weighed fusion merges the output vectors of the input behaviors, which are weighted with their corresponding activity. All driving motions can be altered by safety behaviors by slowing down or changing direction.

In [9] some more complex design patterns for iB2C are described. As they are used frequently, it is planned to implement direct translations or at least translation templates for SEFT generation. The most important and most frequently used pattern is the behavioral group pattern. A behavioral group is a hierarchical abstraction of several behaviors, which manipulate the same output values. They are combined into a group, which looks like a behavior from the outside.

3   Related Work

Cheung et al. [1] provided a framework for reliability prediction of software components at the architectural level. Their model consists of three phases: First, determine system states including normal and abnormal behavior. Second, determine transitions with help of hidden Markov models and other sources of information, which is still a challenge. Third, solve the model and compute reliability via steady state analysis and the calculation of the probability of being in a failure state. They only consider reliability in their analysis. It might be possible to extend the technique to analyze safety and availability. We did not use this approach, because with SEFTs we can model everything Markov-models can describe, and additionally SEFTs can be used to analyze safety. Also, we have a tool, with which we can create and analyze SEFTs.

Min et al. [7] propose template software fault trees for Ada95 code for safety analysis on a very low abstraction level. They use standard fault trees, which do not take into account the component structure of larger systems. Only implementation errors are analyzed, and McDermid states in [6] "that many safety problems relate to requirements faults, not mistakes in coding". As a consequence, additional analyses are needed to check for faults in earlier development stages.

Lano et al. [5] propose HAZOP (hazard and operability study) guide words for the analysis of object-oriented models in UML. They provide new guide word interpretations for state transition, class and sequence diagrams. HAZOP is used to find system failures, which themselves have to be analyzed further. It can be used before a fault tree analysis to determine possible top events.

Förster and Trapp [2] developed a Fault Tree based method to cope with the problem of few or no information about failures early in the development. They base the analysis on Component Fault Trees (CFT) [4] to model system composition. The uncertainty of (software) safety probabilities for basic events is modeled with the help of probability distributions over intervals instead of single probabilities. For calculating an overall probability distribution, every interval is sampled many times and the overall probability per sample is calculated. CFTs offer the possibility to model big systems with many components in a structured way. In embedded systems the state of the system changes as a reaction on events. Therefore a reliability or safety analysis has to be able to consider states as well as events. CFTs do not support the distinction of states and events, which is possible in Petri-nets.

Sacha proposes in [10] an analysis called Transnet using structure Petri-nets. The analysis based on Petri-nets is similar to ours as we also conduct a reachability analysis. One drawback with Petri-nets is that the nets are considerably large, even for relatively small systems. SEFTs combine the ability to model states and events of Petri-nets with the ability to model component-wise like CFTs.

4   State-Event Fault Trees

In our approach we use State-Event Fault Trees (SEFT) [3] to analyze safety and reliability from a functional system description. SEFTs are a combination of deterministic state machines, Markov chains and Fault Trees [14], and can model system states as well as timing constraints. Quantitative evaluation is done by translating SEFTs into deterministic and stochastic Petri-nets (DSPN [8]). DSPNs are an extension of Generalized Stochastic Petri-nets (GSPN) to additionally model deterministic delay. A DSPN is a timed variant of Petri-nets, which means the time a transition waits, before it fires, is specified.

In [3] a SEFT-to-DSPN translation algorithm, which we use, is described. A SEFT has a finite state space, and a component is in exact one state at a time – the active state – and stays in that state for some time. The state of a component is described as a state expression: "component c is in state s at time t". A probability can be assigned to a state expression for each point in time. Contrary to a state, an event has no duration. State transitions are events, but additional events are possible. As in DSPNs events can occur after a deterministic or exponentially distributed probabilistic delay. They can also be triggered by other events. In addition to the standard boolean gates used in Fault Trees (AND, OR), several new gates are introduced. For example `History-AND` remembers events that have occurred in the past, and `Priority-AND` additionally remembers if they have occurred in a given order.

As a result, one receives a directed acyclic graph (one cause can trigger multiple effects). In the graph causal loops are forbidden, except if some explicit delay is introduced into the cycle. Event ports allow triggering relations across component borders. SEFTs are constructed like Fault Trees: start with an undesired state or event, and find influences or causes. Basic events of FTs correspond to solitary exponentially distributed events in SEFTs. Subcomponents can be modeled by other means like Markov chains and easily included into the SEFT.

5   Modeling Approach

In this Section, the approach to apply SEFTs on functional system models is described on the example of RAVON. Starting with the general process chain, a description of all steps from iB2C behavior modules to failure probabilities is given.

5.1   Process Chain

Fig. 1 shows the different steps of our approach to analyze the safety and reliability of a functional model. First, a SEFT of the behavior network is developed describing how failures are propagated through the system hierarchy. After modeling the structure, probabilities for basic events are entered. This is done using the tool ESSaRel [13]. The SEFT can not be analyzed directly, so it is converted into a DSPN via an export function to the TimeNET [12] format. TimeNET is a tool for analyzing DSPNs. Now, interesting places have to be identified, for which a reachability analysis will be done. Usually, such places are the failure states of the topmost component in the model. In TimeNET probabilities for system states can be calculated. It can be expressed if a desired system state is reached with a certain probability, or an undesired state (failure state) is reached with a certain probability. This probability can be compared to a threshold to see if predefined constraints are met.

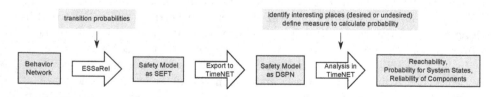

Fig. 1. Process chain

5.2   Translation from iB2C to SEFT

Before an analysis can be done, the system has to be modeled with regard to failure propagation. In ESSaRel a system can be modeled component-wise. Single iB2C behavior modules, fusion behaviors, whole behavior groups or behavior patterns can be seen as components. In the following, two architectural components seen in iB2C are briefly described with a translation scheme into a SEFT. More detailed descriptions of iB2C components can be found in [9].

Behavior Modules. A behavior usually controls one or more control values like a velocity or a joint angle. These values have to be within certain boundaries in certain situations for the system to be in a state, in which no safety condition is violated. Additionally, the activity of a behavior module is closely related to the environmental situation. A model of such a behavior observes deviations from desired values of control values and activities.

Some modeling rules can be formulated: First, determine possible states of control values and/or activity. Possible states are one or more failure states and a state for normal operation. Next, determine causes for state transitions and model them as events. Events that are caused by the environment of the system should be modeled with a failure rate (either deterministic or exponentially distributed events). Events that are triggered by other events from other components are of the type "Triggered Event".

In Fig. 2 an example SEFT of a simple behavior module is shown. It consists of one OK state (out_vel_ok) and one failure state (out_vel_high). The init event is pointed at the OK state. Two events (no_obstacle_detected and sensors_working) switch between the states. The events are connected to event outports (black triangles), which are used to connect this component to others.

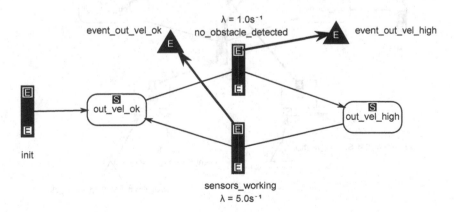

Fig. 2. Example SEFT for a simple behavior

Fusion Behaviors. As stated in Sect. 2.1, behaviors that influence the same control values are merged with fusion behaviors. The failure modes of a fusion behavior result from the failure modes of its input behaviors. For a maximum fusion only the failure modes of the behavior with the highest activity are propagated. The maximum fusion results in an "OR" gate for the failure modes and an "History-AND" gate for the normal modes. That means if at least one of the behaviors is in the failure mode, the output of the fusion behavior is also in the failure mode. On the other hand, if both input behaviors are in normal mode, the fusion behavior is also in normal mode.

For the weighted fusion there are a few ideas that still have to be implemented: As for the maximum fusion the failure modes of the weighted fusion depend on the ones from the input behaviors. In contrast to the maximum fusion the weighted fusion has an infinite number of states. To be able to model these with a SEFT, they have to be classified. For the first modeling attempt, the weighted fusion can be abstracted as a maximum fusion.

In Fig. 3 an example SEFT of a maximum fusion behavior with two input behaviors is shown. The states are determined by the merged behaviors. At least one OK state and one failure state is needed. Events are triggered events in contrast to the exponentially distributed events of behavior modules. State changes depend on the inputs of this component (white triangles are event inports). Inputs of failure events are merged with an OR gate (≤ 1), inputs of OK events with a History-AND (H&). Like in the previous example, the events are also connected to event outports (black triangles).

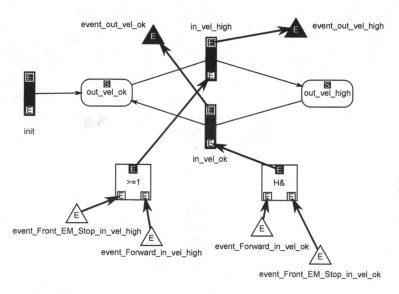

Fig. 3. Example SEFT for a maximum fusion with two input behaviors (Front_EM_Stop and Forward)

5.3   Translation from SEFT to DSPN

The translation from SEFT to DSPN is done using the translation rules described in [3], which are implemented as an export function in ESSaRel. SEFT models are translated component-wise, events become transitions and states become places. The init node transforms into an initial marking of the place corresponding to the state, to which the init node is connected. Gates are translated according to a dictionary in [3]. Component ports also have a special translation.

At the bottom of Fig. 4 an example SEFT and its corresponding DSPN are shown. The SEFT model depicts one component with two states, two events and two event outports to connect the component to others. This SEFT is translated into the DSPN shown below the SEFT. The states are directly translated into places. Same names indicate corresponding states and places. The places have an additional prefix indicating the component. This is needed to distinguish places with the same name that come from different components. The same holds for events and transitions. The exponentially distributed trigger rates of the events in this example are translated into exponentially distributed delays of the DSPN transitions. The two event outports are translated to one place and one transition each. Other components can be attached to these transitions.

5.4   Analysis in TimeNET

When the SEFT is translated into a DSPN, it can be analyzed with TimeNET. The translation is done, because with DSPNs it is possible to calculate the reachability of states and the probability for the system to end up in a certain state. It is possible to draw conclusions about system reliability by calculating the probability that the system is in the OK state. If there exists a repair transition to leave each of the failure states, availability can be measured by calculating the probability of the system to be in the OK state at the top component at a given time. Also, safety can be analyzed by calculating the probability for the system to be in a safety-critical failure state. The same can be done for each single component, if desired.

Before the analysis can be done, a separate measure has to be defined for each observed state. An example measure `result = P{#P1=1};` would result in the probability that place `#P1` contains one token. TimeNET then calculates the probabilities for the system to be in the defined states during runtime.

6   Results

As an example a small part of the RAVON system is modeled. The modeled part controls the forward velocity of RAVON. Two different behaviors can slow down the robot by overwriting the velocity value. Fig. 4 shows the translation of the whole example. In the top-left part the SEFT model is shown consisting of five components, which are connected via their component ports. Two components are connected via a fusion behavior (second component to the top). On the

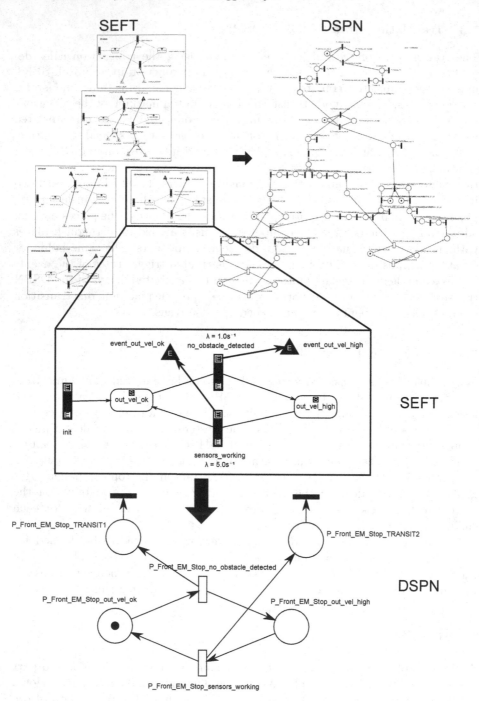

Fig. 4. Top-left: the SEFT model of the example system, consisting of five components. Top-right: the corresponding DSPN. Middle: one enlarged component of the SEFT. Bottom: the enlarged translation to DSPN of the SEFT

right, the corresponding DSPN can be seen. Below, one component is enlarged to depict the translation in more detail:

(G) Front Emergency Stop is a behavior group, abstracted as a module, which could be modeled in more detail later on. It uses the bumper sensors to detect obstacles by touch and reduces the output velocity down to zero if an obstacle is detected. We identified "output velocity too high" as the only failure mode of this behavior at this abstraction level, making this one failure state in the SEFT model. With the OK state (out_vel_ok), we need events, which enable the transitions between the failure state and the OK state. As initial state, the OK state is selected, because it is assumed that the system is OK at the beginning.

In the SEFT model of (G) Front Emergency Stop each event has a trigger rate (λ) assigned, which indicates how often the events are happening per second. At the moment, this rate has been arbitrarily chosen, because it is not yet interesting to have accurate values for this small example. In case of the event "no obstacle detected", it is the failure rate of the obstacle detection, the rate of the other event is the rate, with which the system detects obstacles, depending on sensor speed.

At the bottom of Fig. 4 the enlarged translation of the previous SEFT is shown. States are translated to places, events to transitions, the init event to an initial marking, and the component ports to transit structures consisting of places and triggered events. The trigger rate of the modeled events is translated into a transition with an exponentially distributed delay.

With this model, the probability, that the modeled components end up in a failure state, can be determined. For example, the reliability of the component (G) Front Emergency Stop depends on the probability, that it is in the OK state. This probability depends on the failure and repair rates given in the model and can be determined by an analysis with TimeNET. TimeNET can do a reachability analysis and calculate probabilities for the system to be in certain states.

Using this method, it is possible to analyze safety, reliability and availability of complex behavior-based systems. The propagation of failures from sensors through the control software can be modeled and quantitatively analyzed, provided reliability data for the sensors is available. The same could be achieved with DSPNs, but with greater modeling effort for larger systems.

The advantage of the proposed method is, that is possible to model software-intensive embedded systems with system states and externally triggered events (sensor inputs). The modeling in SEFT is easier than with Petri-nets, because complex systems can be modeled component-wise, instead of building one large net. Also, system states and events, that contribute to a failure, can be combined using logic gates like in fault trees.

7 Conclusion

We proposed a method to apply State-Event Fault Trees on functional descriptions of hardware and software to analyze safety, reliability and availability.

The main contribution are translation rules from the functional description of behavior-based systems to an SEFT model. In this SEFT model desired and undesired system states are selected. The analysis of the SEFT is done via transformation into a DSPN. The results are probabilities that the system or system components are in previously selected states. From this probabilities the system reliability, availability or, in case of safety related components, the system safety can be measured.

The next steps will be to develop translation schemes for all of the patterns, and to expand the existing translations.

Acknowledgement. This work was funded by the German Ministry of Education and Research (BMBF) in the context of the "Virtuelle und Erweiterte Realität für höchste Sicherheit und Zuverlässigkeit Eingebetteter Systeme – Zweite Phase" (ViERforES II) project. We also thank our colleagues from the Robotics Research Lab of the University of Kaiserslautern for providing us with the input data.

References

1. Cheung, L., Roshandel, R., Medvidovic, N., Golubchik, L.: Early prediction of software component reliability. In: Proceedings of the 30th International Conference on Software Engineering, ICSE 2008, pp. 111–120. ACM, New York (2008)
2. Förster, M., Trapp, M.: Fault tree analysis of software-controlled component systems based on second-order probabilities. In: ISSRE 2009 Proceedings (2009)
3. Kaiser, B., Gramlich, C., Förster, M.: State-event-fault-trees – A safety analysis model for software controlled systems. Reliability Engineering & System Safety 92(11), 1521–1537 (2007); In: Heisel, M., Liggesmeyer, P., Wittmann, S. (eds.) SAFECOMP 2004. LNCS, vol. 3219, pp. 195–209. Springer, Heidelberg (2004)
4. Kaiser, B., Liggesmeyer, P., Mäckel, O.: A new component concept for fault trees. In: 8th Australian Workshop on Safety Critical Systems and Software, Canberra (October 2003)
5. Lano, K., Clark, D., Androutsopoulos, K.: Safety and Security Analysis of Object-Oriented Models. In: Anderson, S., Bologna, S., Felici, M. (eds.) SAFECOMP 2002. LNCS, vol. 2434, pp. 82–93. Springer, Heidelberg (2002)
6. McDermid, J.: Software Hazard and Safety Analysis. In: Damm, W., Olderog, E.-R. (eds.) FTRTFT 2002. LNCS, vol. 2469, pp. 23–34. Springer, Heidelberg (2002)
7. Min, S.-Y., Jan, Y.-K., Cha, S.-D., Kwon, Y.-R., Bae, D.-H.: Safety Verification of Ada95 Programs Using Software Fault Trees. In: Felici, M., Kanoun, K., Pasquini, A. (eds.) SAFECOMP 1999. LNCS, vol. 1698, pp. 226–238. Springer, Heidelberg (1999)
8. Priese, L., Wimmel, H.: Petri-Netze. Springer (2008)
9. Proetzsch, M., Luksch, T., Berns, K.: Development of complex robotic systems using the behavior-based control architecture iB2C. Robotics and Autonomous Systems 58(1), 46–67 (2010)
10. Sacha, K.: Safety Verification of Software Using Structured Petri Nets. In: Ehrenberger, W. (ed.) SAFECOMP 1998. LNCS, vol. 1516, pp. 329–342. Springer, Heidelberg (1998)

11. Schäfer, B.H.: Robot Control Design Schemata and their Application in Off-road Robotics. Ph.D. thesis, TU Kaiserslautern (2011)
12. TU Berlin, Real-Time Systems and Robotics group: TimeNET 4.0 (2007), www.tu-ilmenau.de/TimeNET
13. TU Kaiserslautern, AG seda and Fraunhofer IESE: Embedded system safety and reliability analyzer (ESSaRel) (2009), http://www.essarel.de
14. Vesely, W., Goldberg, F., Roberts, N., Haasl, D.: Fault Tree Handbook. U.S. Nuclear Regulatory Commission (1981)

Towards Artificial Perception

André Dietrich, Sebastian Zug, and Jörg Kaiser

Otto-von-Guericke-Universität Magdeburg
Department of Distributed Systems (IVS)
Universitätsplatz 2, 39106 Magdeburg, Germany
{dietrich,zug,kaiser}@ivs.cs.uni-magdeburg.de
http://www-ivs.cs.uni-magdeburg.de

Abstract. Adaptability to changing environments and environmental conditions is a key concern for future smart applications. Therefore, for autonomous systems it will be necessary to extend the local view on the environment with external sensors, either fixed or mobile ones. New evolving technologies support the acquisition of a myriad of information, described as "Internet of Things", "Intelligent Environments", "Industrial or Building Automation", "Ambient Intelligence", or "Ubiquitous/Pervasive Computing", etc. Thus, information is always available, but its interpretation and integration into the own view remains an open problem. We therefore propose the development of a new type of distributed middleware for the environmental perception, that abstracts the environment from the diversity of available sensor systems. In three steps we describe how more and more functionalities can be extracted from the control application to support artificial perception and environment modelling.

Keywords: artificial perception, middleware, environment model.

1 Introduction and Motivation

With the rapid evolving development in the area of robotic assistance that directly interacts with humans, a change occurs in many fields of scientific research. Future autonomous or partial-autonomous robotic systems will have to cope with highly complex and dynamically changing environments in contrast to today's industrial robots, build and programmed for one purpose only. Adaptability to changing environments and environmental conditions is a key concern for many smart/robotic applications like service-, healthcare-, or search-and-rescue-robotics. Furthermore, there is a new trend in manufacturing towards flexible production lines; more and more products (e.g., in automotive industry) are produced according to specific customer demands.

The growing number of distributed entities – sensors, actors, and controllers – offers new opportunities, but entail some fundamental problems. The classical perception-control-loop approach is no longer applicable to solve complex tasks in such environments. New types of control applications are developed which incorporate supervision, coordination and planning, situation awareness,

F. Ortmeier and P. Daniel (Eds.): SAFECOMP 2012 Workshops, LNCS 7613, pp. 466–476, 2012.

diagnostics, etc. Practical examples for this are hierarchically structured controllers (vehicles), dynamically reconfigurable controllers (UAVs), or deliberative/reactive controllers (robotics). A yet unsolved problem concerns the perception in changing intelligent environments. External heterogeneous sensors (building and home automation, sensor networks, sensor vision of other robots, mobile devices, etc.) can be used to extend the view on the environment. Receiving foreign information is quite simple in contrast to an aggregation, selection, validation, and interpretation. Even adding a single sensor or actor is a huge problem and requires a manual modification of the application code.

As a good example to illustrate the ideas behind our approach can serve an automatic parking assistant. The controller requires a distinct view on the environment (external model), generated with the help of local sensors. We assume a multi-modal sensor system for this purpose. Furthermore, knowledge about the car, like the size, geometry, or axis distance (internal model) is necessary to control the car. Supervision is a crucial precondition to react propperly on changing environmental parameters (size of the parking lot, geometry of neighboring cars, width of the road). Additionally, the system itself can be changed, for instance by attaching a trailer. These changes cause a lot of problems, while the task stays the same "parking":

1. Adaption of the environment perception, by incorporating the trailers sensor systems.
2. Selection of usable sensors due to possible occultations caused by the trailer.
3. New car-dimensions cause adapted decisions about the parking lot.
4. Furthermore, the controller has to change its parking strategy[1], due to the trailer and possible cargo.

Furthermore it would be helpfull to enhance the environmental perception by external sensors from other cars. Related to possible faults, occultations, relevance, monitored area, etc. appropriate and adaptive selection methods are required.

A separation of application logic and perception could remedy such general problems. As mentioned before, every control application requires a distinct view on the environment. Such a view can be some basic parameters (position, distances, states, etc.), 2D or 3D representations, graphs, many more and a combination of them. Thus, before building systems that can subsist in complex environments we need to build systems that can perceive these environments. Imagine an environmental abstraction by a perception middleware layer, which hides recurrent sensory tasks, like interpretation, validation, fusion, etc., comparable with a communication middleware that abstracts the network. A control application could define the required type of abstraction while the middleware is responsible for its generation.

---

[1] The parking stategy incorporates a change of the kinematics and trajectory planning. The automated calculation of the inverse and direct kinematics by using a solver and a description of the system is commonly used for robot manipulators [1], but also possible for basic vehicles (see [2] and [3]).

1.1   Contributions

The aim of our current research lies in the development of a new kind of middleware, see Fig. 1. Our previous projects coped with the abstraction of the network. Therefore we developed a middleware called FAMOUSO (Family of Adaptive Middleware for autonomOUs Sentient Objects) [4],[5]. FAMOUSO provides a real-time event-based communication even between highly integrated systems like 8-bit-microcontroller across different networks (e.g., CAN, Ethernet, Wifi, etc.).

The MOSAIC-Framework (fraMework for fault-tOlerant Sensor dAta processIng in dynamiC environments) provides fault-tolerant data-acquisition and a processing architecture with focus on dynamic scenarios [6], [7], [8]. XML data sheets are used to enable a seamless data-integration and -interpretation, which characterizes the configuration of the node and all transmitted data like physical units, possible faults, their occurrence probabilities and their impact on the sensor-measurement.

The beneficial combination of both MOSAIC and FAMOUSO has already been described in [9].

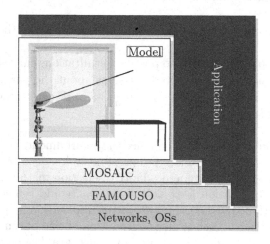

Fig. 1. Threefold system architecture with FAMOUSO (network abstraction), MOSAIC (sensor/actuator abstraction), and the environment abstraction

However, the original two layered approach fails of using complex sensors, in complex environments, or for complex tasks. A third abstraction is therfore required to put the heterogenous sensor measurements, the actuators and other objects of the environment into a context. Therefore, we are currently developing the basis for a perception middleware, with focus on the spatial perception, while for the sake of complexity reduction chemical, thermal, and mechanical issues are left out for the moment.

1.2 Outline

Other projects meet only partial aspects of an environmental abstraction or show highly specialized solutions for special-purpose applications. An overview on the related work in the area of environment perception and modeling is given in the next section. Afterwards we present our three step approach. Beginning from basic and fixed scenarios we will extract more and more functionalities from the control application and end up in highly dynamic environments. In addition to every step, we give an overview of our current and future developments, which also deals with middleware integration, introduced in Section 3.3.

The main emphasis of our ongoing work lays in Sec. 3.1 and 3.2. While most of the parts described in Section 3.1 are already implemented, other components (e.g., distributed data-management, positioning, generation of views) are under construction.

2 Related Work

A strict separation of perception and consciousness, as a general concept for mechatronic systems, was firstly presented in [10] (motivated by the psychological model). However, the perception is always artificial, just a model of the environment, constructed out of available sensory information, prior knowledge, and assumptions. Consciousness exists on multiple layers, defined by goals, assessment, planning, and predictions as well as machine learning.

Such a separation is more or less implemented in some specialized applications like for example in reconfigurable control systems for UAVs [11] or the VerUM-Project for distributed data storage and analysis in vehicles [12]. The advantage of such specialized implementations is, that only local sensor systems are used, the number of possible situations is well known, and a situation is described in both cases as a simple feature vector. Sensor analysis and fusions are hand coded and are not transferable to other applications. Thus, the dynamic integration and interpretation of additional sensors (internal or external) is not possible. Nevertheless, these systems could be used for task oriented sensor selection, as it was also proposed in [13] by applying middleware concepts.

2D and 3D representation offer more complex abstraction of the environment, easy to understand for humans, but hardly to interpret for machines. Many sensor systems enable the generation of complex 2D and 3D structures that can be used for navigation, localization, or obstacle avoidance for indoor and outdoor scenarios, see [14] and [15]. By using object recognition methods, complex geometrical objects can be identified in 3D point clouds and/or camera streams. This links additional attributes to some specific objects, and thus enables more complex environment descriptions like it was described in [16] and [17] for kitchen environments. Additional physical properties were used in [18], this allowed more complex simulations to derive future states. Furthermore, it was shown that even more complex representations (including color or mass) are essential for human-machine interaction. To follow commands like "Give me the blue screw driver on my left!", a system must be able change its own viewpoint [19]. These examples of highly specialized applications solve predefined tasks by using fixed models of the environment. There are currently no interfaces to connect or share different environmental models of different entities. A robotic vacuum cleaner cannot share its knowledge of the environment with a Wakamaru although both would benefit from it, due to their intersecting working areas.

In contrast to these specialized applications, smart environments should support a seamless integration and segregation of divers entities (a good overview on this topic is given in [20]). The PEIS-Ecology Project [21] shows the strongest relation to our approach. It follows the philosophy of a distributed robot, where every sensor, actuator, or other RFID-tagged entities represent PEIS objects, that share their functionalities among each other. In contrast to our strategy, it describes a top-down approach, where perception is not considered in detail, everything is covered by fixed services. For example the service "localization", that is offerd by a camera-system, does not incorporate other sensor systems or even dynamically appearing and disappering ones, to get an enhanced position estimation.

3   Roadmap

3.0   Initial Situation

Fig. 2 depicts the classical approach that is widely used nowadays, where the sensory abstraction of the environment is an inherent part of the control application. To be able to react appropriately on changes in the environments, all inputs, outputs, and possible disturbances have to be known during the phase of implementation.

Fig. 2. Generell concept of a perception-control-loop. The sensors S perceive the environment and deliver the inputs to the *Controller*. It aggregates the sensor measurements according to an internal *Model*, processes them and generates commands to the actuators A. The actuators change the state of the environment, that is monitored by the sensors.

3.1   Spatial Arrangement

The first step serves basic spatial and geometrical arrangement in fixed scenarios, see Fig. 3, while the "geometry" describes the shape of an object and "spatial"

their relative position to each other. The handling of sensory inputs is still a part
of the control application (using MOSAIC). With the help of different XML notations we are able to build basic geometrical models, including representation
of the area, immobile objects like tables, chairs, etc. and the representations of
sensors and actuators, like depicted in Fig. 1. Depending on the kind of entity, we
use different description methods. Basic geometries are described with ode-XML
(Open Dynamics Engine [22]). More complex robots and actuators are described
in URDF (Unified Robot Description Format [23]), including a kinematic and
dynamic description of the robot, a visual representation, and a simplified collision model. Sensors are described with a mixture of the sensor description format
of MOSAIC and OpenRAVE (Open Robotics Automation Virtual Environment
[24]). This combines the sensor simulation capabilities of OpenRAVE with the
more realistic and comprehensive description format of MOSAIC. Furthermore,
MOSAIC enables to access and interpret the sensor measurements of real sensors, while OpenRAVE is used to genarate virtual measurements in the virtual
environment.

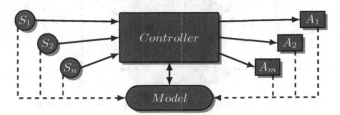

Fig. 3. Extraction of spatial and geometrical properties

This type of modeling is enough to solve different problems like:

- Calculate the translations and rotations of objects relative to each other
  automatically.
- Next to signal based fault detection methods for sensors (presented in [25])
  or combined test methods [6], we applied these models for plausibility checks,
  by comparing real measurements with their counterparts in the virtual environment, see [26].
- Task oriented sensor selection, based on the sensor position, coverage and
  monitoring area, like proposed in [27], is an important supplement to the
  pure signal based selection, as presented in [28].
- The loss of real measurements can shortly be bypassed with virtual measurements.

That means for automatic parking assistant, the dimensions of the car, the trail
and the parking space can be extracted from the virtual representation as well
as the positions and orientations of the locally used sensor system. This allows
additionally to detect hidden sensors and thus allows an enhanced sensor filtering
(see Fig. 6a).

3.2   Dealing with the Dynamically Changing Environments

So far we can cope with single and fixed scenarios, but it should be possible to share these XML-descriptions among interested entities. Thus, by interpreting XML-descriptions of foreign systems it is possible to include their sensory vision into the own local view. Like in dynamically changing environments, nodes can appear and disappear, see Fig. 4. But these descriptions have to be extended by the name of the topics under which data is published, the services that are offered, and the transformation relative to another entity. This has the advantage that the effect of control messages of other components can be directly interpreted within the virtual representation.

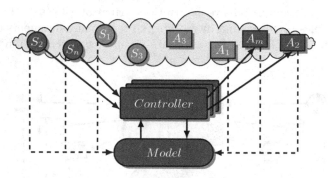

Fig. 4. Extension for distributed smart environments

Furthermore, the required transformations can no more be derived from static XML-documents, presented in the previous section, and thus, have to be calculated dynamically, mostly over a sequence of known transformations. In reality, every single transformation is aditionally affected by an uncertainty.

To be able to deal with these uncertainties, we are going to extend the ROS (RobotOperatingSystem [29]) transformation packet [30] with functionalities described in [31], building on a graph-based transformations instead of tree-based structures. The usage of additional uncertainty information in combination with sensor descriptions and the MOSAIC validity values allows extended task oriented sensor selections, fusion and validation strategies in comparison to those described in [7].

Every entity has its own view on its local environment that is updated in its own manner. Therefore, the identification of and the connection to foreign entities, to share knowledge about the environment, requires a distributed data management. Besides the development of an interface for this purpose, the focus lays on an appropriate organization and structuring of the distributed knowledge (models, parameters, sensor measurements, states, services, etc.).

Considering the automatic parking assistant again, it would now be able to integrate and interpret the external sensor measurements (gray) as well as the geometries of these cars within its own view on the environment. Furthermore, state information (like "door is open") can be easily interpreted within the model as well as their influence on real sensor measurements (see Fig. 6a).

3.3   Middleware Integration

This last step covers the development of a distributed middleware that separates environmental perception from the application development, depicted in Fig. 5. Tasks or problems that were formerly part of the control application are integrated as services within the middleware (i.e., localization, tracking, mapping, obstacle or object recognition, anchoring, etc.). The control application defines its required type of environment abstraction, including the area, the validity, currentness, and format. The middleware is then responsible for the generation of the requested view.

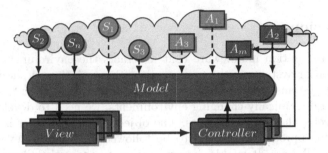

Fig. 5. Decoupling of perception and control application

A view in this case defines the type of abstraction; it can be a map, a graph, a 3D-representation or basic feature vectors. For example, if the automatic parking assistant would require an occupancy grid map, like depicted in Fig. 6b, the middleware should select the appropriate sensors for the position estimation according to the requirements of the application.

A dedicated view on the environment as well as on the included systems is the basis for human-machine-interaction, like demonstrated in [32]. The current and/or future states of the robot and its sensors were visualized with AR-techniques (Augmented Reality). According to different user roles we could identify different requirements for the visualization. An engineer requires a very detailed view on the robot, including the robot's state, sensor states and measurements, etc. In contrast to this, an operator for example, which interacts with the robot, needs to have a notion of the robots intention like future trajectories, working pieces, current and future working places, etc.

The validity of a view can be derived as a combined measure from the single sensor validities (contributed by MOSAIC), their coverage areas, and update rates. Thus, the application could request for the required amount of validity, depending on the task, and if this validity value cannot be achieved, the application has to be notified about the maximum validity.

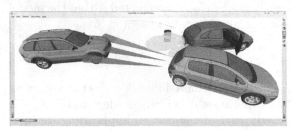
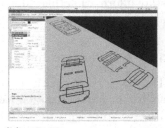

(a) Implementation of an automatic parking assistant using OpenRAVE

(b) 2D-View as occupancy grid map in *rviz*

Fig. 6. Environmental representations on different layers. (a) shows the general environment representation, including all entities (non-functional objects, actuators and sensors), while (b) represents a very specific view, derived from (a) by using filters.

4   Conclusion

An artificial perception middleware that abstracts the environment from heterogeneous sensor systems is the next step on the evolutionary ladder. Before we can build systems that are able to subsist and solve different tasks in an uncertain and dynamically changing environments, we need to develop systems that can perceive these environments. The objective of this paper is to present a step by step approach, that need to be followed in order to develop such a perception middleware. It enables smart entities to share their knowledge and their experiences about the environment, independently from the used sensor systems and type of environmental abstraction.

Acknowledgments. This work is (partly) funded by the German Ministry of Education and Research within the project ViERforES-II (grant no. 01IM10002B).

References

1. Ikfast: The robot kinematics compiler (2012),
   http://openrave.org/docs/latest_stable/openravepy/ikfast/
2. Wang, Y., Linnett, J., Roberts, J.: A unified approach to inverse and direct kinematics for four kinds of wheeled mobile robots and its applications. In: Proceedings of the 1996 IEEE International Conference on Robotics and Automation, vol. 4, pp. 3458–3465. IEEE (1996)
3. Şucan, I.A., Moll, M., Kavraki, L.E.: The Open Motion Planning Library. IEEE Robotics & Automation Magazine (to appear, 2012), http://ompl.kavrakilab.org
4. Schulze, M., Zug, S.: Exploiting the FAMOUSO Middleware in Multi-Robot Application Development with Matlab/Simulink. In: Proceedings of the ACM/IFIP/USENIX Middleware 2008 Conference Companion, Leuven, Belgium, pp. 74–77. ACM, New York (2008), http://doi.acm.org/10.1145/1462735.1462753

5. Schulze, M.: Adaptierbare ereignisbasierte Middleware für ressourcenbeschränkte Systeme. Doktorarbeit, Fakultät für Informatik, Otto-von-Guericke Universität Magdeburg (2011)
6. Zug, S., Dietrich, A., Kaiser, J.: Fault-Handling in Networked Sensor Systems. Concept Press Ltd., St. Franklin (2012)
7. Zug, S., Dietrich, A.: Examination of Fusion Result Feedback for Fault-Tolerant and Distributed Sensor Systems. In: IEEE International Workshop on Robotic and Sensors Environments (ROSE 2010), Phoenix, AZ, USA (2010)
8. Zug, S.: Architektur für verteilte, fehlertolerante Sensor-Aktor-Systeme. Doktorarbeit, Fakultät für Informatik, Otto-von-Guericke Universität Magdeburg (2011)
9. Zug, S., Schulze, M., Dietrich, A., Kaiser, J.: Programming abstractions and middleware for building control systems as networks of smart sensors and actuators. In: Proceedings of Emerging Technologies in Factory Automation (ETFA 2010), Bilbao, Spain (September 2010)
10. Caulfield, H., Johnson, J.: Artificial perception and consciousness. In: Sixth International Conference on Education and Training in Optics and Photonics, Cancún, Mexico, July 28-30 1999, p. 112. Society of Photo Optical (2000)
11. Wills, L., Kannan, S., Sander, S., Guler, M., Heck, B., Prasad, J., Schrage, D., Vachtsevanos, G.: An open platform for reconfigurable control. IEEE Control Systems Magazine 21(3), 49–64 (2001)
12. Hermann, A., Desel, J.: Driving situation analysis in automotive environment. In: IEEE International Conference on Vehicular Electronics and Safety, ICVES 2008, pp. 216–221. IEEE (2008)
13. Rotenstein, A., Rothenstein, A., Robinson, M., Tsotsos, J.: Robot middleware must support task-directed perception. In: Proc. ICRA 2nd Int. Workshop on Software Development and Integration into Robotics, Rome, Italy (2007)
14. Hähnel, D., Burgard, W., Thrun, S.: Learning compact 3d models of indoor and outdoor environments with a mobile robot. Robotics and Autonomous Systems 44(1), 15–27 (2003)
15. Surmann, H., Nüchter, A., Hertzberg, J.: An autonomous mobile robot with a 3d laser range finder for 3d exploration and digitalization of indoor environments. Robotics and Autonomous Systems 45(3), 181–198 (2003)
16. Rusu, R., Marton, Z., Blodow, N., Dolha, M., Beetz, M.: Towards 3d point cloud based object maps for household environments. Robotics and Autonomous Systems 56(11), 927–941 (2008)
17. Rusu, R., Marton, Z., Blodow, N., Holzbach, A., Beetz, M.: Model-based and learned semantic object labeling in 3d point cloud maps of kitchen environments. In: IEEE/RSJ International Conference on Intelligent Robots and Systems, IROS 2009, pp. 3601–3608. IEEE (2009)
18. Roy, D., Hsiao, K., Mavridis, N.: Mental imagery for a conversational robot. IEEE Transactions on Systems, Man, and Cybernetics, Part B: Cybernetics 34(3), 1374–1383 (2004)
19. Hsiao, K., Mavridis, N., Roy, D.: Coupling perception and simulation: Steps towards conversational robotics. In: International Conference on Intelligent Robots and Systems, vol. 1, pp. 928–933. IEEE (October 2003)
20. Cook, D., Das, S.: How smart are our environments? an updated look at the state of the art. Pervasive and Mobile Computing 3(2), 53–73 (2007)
21. Saffiotti, A., Broxvall, M., Seo, B., Cho, Y.: The peis-ecology project: a progress report. In: Proc. of the ICRA 2007 Workshop on Network Robot Systems, Rome, Italy, pp. 16–22. Citeseer (2007)

22. Smith, R.L.: The open dynamics engine (2007), http://ode.org
23. Meeussen, W., Hsu, J., Diankov, R.L.: URDF - Unified Robot Description Format (April 2012), http://www.ros.org/wiki/urdf
24. Diankov, R.: Automated construction of robotic manipulation programs. Ph.D. dissertation, Carnegie Mellon University, Robotics Institute (October 2010)
25. Dietrich, A., Zug, S., Kaiser, J.: Detecting External Measurement Disturbances Based on Statistical Analysis for Smart Sensors. In: Procedings of the IEEE International Symposium on Industrial Electronics (ISIE), pp. 2067–2072 (July 2010)
26. Dietrich, A., Zug, S., Kaiser, J.: Modelbasierte Fehlerdetektion in verteilten Sensor-Aktor-Systemen. In: 11./12. Forschungskolloquium am Fraunhofer IFF. Fraunhofer Institut für Fabrikbetrieb und Automatisierung, IFF (2011)
27. Dietrich, A., Zug, S., Kaiser, J.: Model based Decoupling of Perception and Processing. In: ERCIM/EWICS/Cyberphysical Systems Workshop, Resilient Systems, Robotics, Systems-of-Systems Challenges in Design, Validation & Verification and Certification, Naples, Italy (September 2011)
28. Zug, S., Schulze, M., Dietrich, A., Kaiser, J.: Reliable Fault-Tolerant Sensors for Distributed Systems. In: Proceedings of the Fourth ACM International Conference on Distributed Event-Based Systems (DEBS 2010), Cambridge, United Kingdom, pp. 105–106. ACM Press, New York (2010)
29. Quigley, M., Conley, K., Gerkey, B., Faust, J., Foote, T., Leibs, J., Wheeler, R., Ng, A.: Ros: an open-source robot operating system. In: ICRA Workshop on Open Source Software, vol. 3(3.2) (2009)
30. Foote, T., Marder-Eppstein, E., Meeussen, W.L.: tf - ros (April 2012), http://www.ros.org/wiki/tf
31. Smith, R.C., Cheeseman, P.: On the Representation and Estimation of Spatial Uncertainty. The International Journal of Robotics Research 5(4), 56–68 (1986)
32. Dietrich, A., Schulze, M., Zug, S., Kaiser, J.: Visualization of Robot's Awareness and Perception. In: First International Workshop on Digital Engineering (IWDE), Magdeburg, Germany. ACM Press, New York (2010)

A Case Study of Radio-Based Monitoring System for Enhanced Safety of Logistics Processes

Michael Soffner[1], Mykhaylo Nykolaychuk[2],
Friederike Adler[1], and Klaus Richter[2]

[1] University of Magdeburg, Germany
{soffner,fadler}@ovgu.de
[2] Fraunhofer Institute for Factory Operation and Automation IFF, Germany
{mykhaylo.nykolaychuk,klaus.richter}@iff.fraunhofer.de

Abstract. In many logistics processes, industrial trucks, e.g., forklifts and reach stackers, are used to move heavy load. Their usage often causes serious accidents, e.g., collisions of two trucks or trucks and persons. To reduce the risk of collisions, tracking systems can be integrated into a monitoring of logistics processes. Dynamically changing environments of logistics processes introduce special challenges including changing weather conditions and limited visibilities. In this paper, we describe our approach of a collision detection system based on an industrial radio-based real-time location system (RTLS) and evaluate its accuracy and usability in an application scenario including an outdoor storage of metallic objects.

1 Introduction

Logistics processes often include transportation of heavy load, e.g., container in container terminals or large cargo units in producing industry. To handle heavy load, companies use industrial trucks, e.g., forklifts and reach stackers. The limited view while transporting heavy load and the industrial truck's maneuveribilty cause many serious accidents. As statistics of Berufsgenossenschaft Handel und Warendistribution (BGHW) show, most of the accidents are collisions between trucks or trucks and persons [1].

We develope a collision detection system that warns drivers in critical situations to reduce the number of accidents. Therefore, we equip an environment and objects with embedded technology to automatically track and trace objects, e.g., forklifts. This way, we are able to detect possible collisions in logistics processes. Many industrial application scenarios, e.g., metal producing industries, include in- and outdoor areas. A seemless monitoring of both areas, exclude the use of GPS-based solutions because these systems do not work indoors [2, 3]. Additionally, they do not provide the needed performance and accuracy to implement a collision detection. Furthermore, outdoor areas are dynamically changing environments because of changing weather conditions that excludes video-based systems. Therefore, we implement our collision detection system on top of a local

F. Ortmeier and P. Daniel (Eds.): SAFECOMP 2012 Workshops, LNCS 7613, pp. 477–485, 2012.

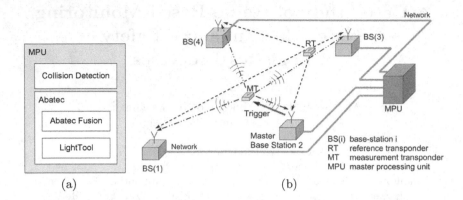

Fig. 1. (a) Software components of the collision detection system and (b) Operating principle of a LPM system [4]

positioning measurement (LPM) system that internally uses radio-based RTLS technology [4–6].

Radio-based location systems include two critical issues that influence the accuracy of measures: (1) line-of-sight and (2) signal multipath [4]. In storage places of logistics processes, objects are continuously placed and removed from stock. Often, these dynamics lead to interruptions of the line-of-sight between system components. Furthermore, these objects reflect electromagnetic waves depending on their material and shape that decreases measure's accuracies and response times of the system.

In this paper, we evaluate accuracies and response times of a radio-based location system for collision detection in non-cooparative environments, a storage area of an industrial metal producing company. In Section 2, we outline the architecture of our collision detection system and describe in Section 3 an application scenario and its characteristics in more detail to make it comparable to others scenarios. In Section 4, we present the method and results of our evaluation.

2   The Collision Detection System's Architecture

Our Collision Detection System (CDS) includes two main components: (1) *software modules* that implement algorithms to detect collisions and (2) *Abatec LPM*[1] to localize objects (see Fig. 1). The Abatec LPM includes two software components, Abatec Fusion and LightTool, and hardware components. It represents a localization abstraction layer, i.e., it determines the position of tagged objects and provides their position data via User Datagram Protocol (UDP) interface at any time. This data is then processed by the collision detection module.

---

[1] Abatec LPM, http://www6.ctm.at/abatec/index_html?sc=791881500

2.1 Collision Detection Component

The goal of our collision detection is to issue warnings to alarm the imperiled persons, e.g., forklift drivers. We distinguish three states: (1) *Normal*, default state, (2) *Warning*, when forklifts work in close proximity to each other (caution area) and (3) *Critical*, when forklifts are on collision course (predicted area). Each tracked forklift owns one state at any time depending on its current position.

The state *Warning* signals a violation of the caution area (see Fig. 2(a)). The caution area is a circular area (threshold) derived by a tracked object's position as its center and a pre-defined radius. If the distance between two forklifts undergoes this threshold the caution area is violated.

To predict collisions (prediction points), we assume a constant linear motion starting from its current position and maintaining its current speed for a pre-defined period of time. These prediction points together with a pre-defined radius set up the prediction area. The state of two forklifts changes to *Critical*, if their prediction areas intersect, i.e., the distance between their prediction points is less then the prediction area's radius (see Fig. 2(b)). If none of both situations occur, the state is set to *Normal*. A formal definition of collision states is given in Definition 1.

Definition 1   *i) Let $S = \{normal, warning, critical\}$ be a set of valid collision states,*

$O = \{o_1, o_2, \ldots, o_n\}$ *with $n \in \mathbb{N}$ a set of tracked objects,*

$T = \{t_1, t_2, \ldots, t_m\}$ *with $m \in \mathbb{N}$ a set of discrete points in time,*

$t_p \in \mathbb{R}$ *the prediction time,*

$r_w \in \mathbb{R}$ *the warning area radius,*

$r_c \in \mathbb{R}$ *the prediction area radius,*

$p_i : T \to \mathbb{R}^2$ *the position of object o_i at a particular time,*

$v_i : T \to \mathbb{R}^2$ *the velocity of object o_i at a particular time,*

$dist : \mathbb{R}^2 \times \mathbb{R}^2 \to \mathbb{R}$ *the euclidean distance between two positions*

ii) The predicted position $p_i^p(t)$ of object o_i at particular time $t \in T$ is
$$p_i^p(t) = p_i(t) + t_p v_i(t)$$

iii) The collision state of object o_i at time $t \in T$ is $cs_i : T \to S$

$$cs_i(t) = \begin{cases} critical, & \text{if } \exists o_j \in O \mid dist(p_i^p(t), p_j^p(t)) \leq r_c \wedge i \neq j \\ warning, & \text{if } \exists o_j \in O \mid dist(p_i(t), p_j(t)) \leq r_w \wedge \\ & \nexists o_k \in O \mid dist(p_i^p(t), p_k^p(t)) \leq r_c \wedge i \neq j \wedge i \neq k \\ normal, & \text{if } \forall o_j \in O \mid dist(p_i(t), p_j(t)) > r_w \wedge \\ & dist(p_i^p(t), p_j^p(t)) > r_c \wedge i \neq j \end{cases}$$

We implemented the collision detection component in C#. The implementation consists of two subcomponents, (a) a listener and (b) collision detector. The listener class represents an interface to Abatec's LPM that looks for incoming UDP packets and generates an event for each received packet. These events

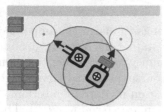 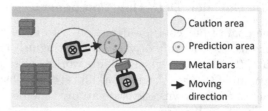

(a) *Warning state* caused by violated caution areas of two forklifts

(b) Prediction areas violations are detected as *Critical state.*

Fig. 2. Differentiation of collision states *Warning* and *Critical*

are then handled by the collision detector. The collision detector contains the detection algorithm.

2.2   Abatec LPM Software and Hardware Components

Abatec's LPM system is an active transponder system (see Fig. 1(b)), i.e., active transponders (MT and RT) are tracked by a set of base stations (BS) [4]. These base stations are connected with a master processing unit (MPU), where the measures are used to derive transponder locations. The system's working principle is to estimate the location of an MT by time-of-flight (TOF) measurements, i.e., the time that electromagnetic waves take to travel from MTs to BSs. Master BS triggers the transponder, which replies with a particular signal. At least three BSs (more for better accuracy) have to receive signals from a MT to compute its position. An accuracy down to a few centimeters is achievable, depending on signal multipaths and line-of-sight (direct visibility). Abatec's LPM provides measures with a frequency of *500Hz*, i.e., 500 values per second for all tracked objects. Since the MTs share this frequency, the measurement frequency for each MT equals the system's frequency divided by number of tracked MTs, e.g., 2 forklifts each with 250 measurements/s. The LPM System operates in the 5.8 GHz Industrial Scientific Medical (ISM) band and has under optimal environmental conditions a measure radius of up to 500 meters.

The LightTool software modul runs on the MPU and collects raw data from BSs to finally compute transponder positions. Then the computed positions are being send by its UDP interface to a specified target. Each UDP packet consists of 17 items, e.g., location, time stamp, speed, and the orientation of the tracked object (which are of special interest for our use case, see Section 3). Additionaly, it is used to make all necessary configurations to set up the system, like creating a list of BSs, specifying the IDs of MT, and setting up the UDP interface.

Multiple antennas can be attached to one transponder (MT) and measured seperately to increase the reliability and accuracy of the LPM. Since you are only interested in the MT's position, the AntennaFusion component merges the multiple positions into one single position and provides all necessary configurations, like specifying arrangements and distances of the antennas.

3 Application Scenario

In the monitored storage place metal bars of $60cm$ in height and approximately $4m$ in length are being handled by forklifts. The in- and outdoor areas of the storage place have a total size of approximately $200x70$ meters. To install base stations and transponders in correct positions three questions have to be answered:

1. What do we want to track?
2. Which environmental influences and characteristics can disturb the tracking?
3. Where do we install the base stations and the transponder?

Tracked objects in this scenario are forklifts. A measurement's accuracy is influenced by the line-of-sight and signal multipaths [4], which determine the positioning of system components. Line-of-sight means that base stations need a direct view to transponders. We installed the transponders (each containing four antennas) on top of a forklift at a height of 3 meters to minimize the possibility that forklifts themselves disturb the line-of-sight between their transponder and a base station.

Non reflective materials in the line-of-sight between transponders and base stations will simply absorb the electromagnetic waves and only a few disturbing signals will be received by a base station. Reflecting materials like metal bars however will reflect the electromagnetic waves and cause many distortions. So high stacks of metal bars, like $3-4$ stacks (with $20cm$ space inbetween), affect the system's reliability because such stacks would be higher $(3-4m)$ than a transponder's height. The same problem occurs when forklifts loaded with metal bars lift their forks higher than their transponder height. In both cases the data has to be filtered or even discarded.

With an increasing height of base stations, the likelihood of limited views would fall and the measurement's accuracy would increase. Still, the distance between base stations and transponders shall not exceed $500m$ to ensure good measurements [4]. In our application scenario, the options where to install the base stations were limited. That is why they were distributed on walls and masts in the area at a height of approximately $5-6m$. We installed 13 base stations to cover the whole storage place area and bypass the limited views caused by walls, other vehicles or stacks of metal bars (see Fig. 3).

4 Evaluation

A collision detection is not reliable if measured values are inaccurate or send delayed. Therefore, we focused in our evaluation on how accurate and efficient

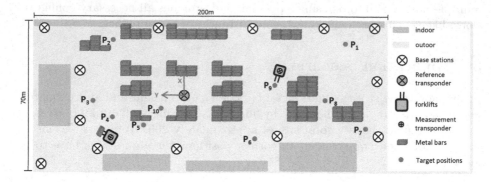

Fig. 3. LPM-system in a 200x70m storage place tracking two forklifts with a measurement transponder on top of their roof. Thirteen base stations including one reference transponder are distributed over the whole outdoor area. The origin of coordinates of measured values lies in the position of the reference transponder.

the collision detection operates within the described application scenario despite multipath and line-of-sight problems.

4.1   Measurement Accuracy of the LPM System

In this application scenario we track forklifts with a size of approximately 5x2x3m. We defined an accuracy requirement of at most 0.5m what might be sufficient for tracking persons as well.

The evaluation procedure included 10 measurements each in a different position (target positions P_i in Fig. 3, with $i \in \{1, ..., 10\}$). We prepared the measurements by choosing the positions accross the storage area, measuring them to know their exact coordinates, and labeling them with markers. Each measurement cycle consisted of two steps. First, forklift drivers approached the labeled

Table 1. Accuracy of the LPM system for a forklift labeled with $Tag = 2000$ at ten pre-defined locations

Num	Tag	target X	target Y	measured X	measured Y	diff	STD X	STD Y	Number of Measurements
P_1	2000	19.39	-68.05	19.22	-68.03	0.17	0.04	0.01	934
P_2	2000	25.23	64.87	25.32	64.76	0.14	0.17	0.16	711
P_3	2000	-1.94	81.28	-1.70	81.45	0.29	0.09	0.06	867
P_4	2000	-16.81	72.15	-16.92	72.10	0.12	0.11	0.06	743
P_5	2000	-28.85	30.18	-28.84	30.18	0.01	0.06	0.02	920
P_6	2000	-28.28	-25.80	-28.33	-25.96	0.17	0.03	0.08	812
P_7	2000	-17.69	-75.91	-17.89	-75.75	0.26	0.04	0.05	943
P_8	2000	-1.21	-77.85	-1.37	-77.85	0.16	0.04	0.06	654
P_9	2000	5.54	-51.28	5.60	-51.22	0.08	0.01	0.01	620
P_{10}	2000	-3.50	8.78	-3.59	8.66	0.15	0.06	0.02	1074

position as close as possible. Second, we measured the forklift's position for $3s$ while it was remaining in this position.

For each target position we measured X and Y coordinates. For each of the generated data sets we determined the coordinate's mean value (*Measured X, Measured Y*), standard deviation (*STD X,STD Y*), and absolute distance between measured and target position *diff* (see Table 1).

For all target positions the highest standard deviation is at P_2 in the X ($0.17m$) and Y ($0.16m$) coordinates for 711 measurments within three seconds. This leads to the conclusion that multipath or visibility problems have occurred more often compared to the other positions. The absolute distance of $0.14m$ shows that the underlying measurements are basically correct. The small difference to the target point can be explained by the fact that the driver can just try to hit the point exactly especially if you think of the forklifts size.

Best results were achieved at P_9, where standard deviation is $0.01m$ in both X and Y coordinates. This means that for all 620 measurements, made within three seconds, the transponder has seen directly a sufficient number of base stations and an accurate position calculation was possible. Finally, we can conclude that the system provides a sufficient accuracy because no measurement exceeded the limit of $0.5m$.

4.2   Efficiency of LPM System and Collision Detection

To ensure a seamless collision detection we need a sufficient rate of collision state calculations. We derive this rate by a worst case assumption. The allowed maximum speed to drive forklifts in the storage place is $15km/h$ ($4.2m/s$) and the forklift's length is 5m. Therefore, we define sufficient as 2 calculated collision states per second, i.e., we know a forklift's collision state every 2.1m when it is moving at maximum speed that is less then half of its length.

The efficiency of the collision detection system was evaluated by tracking 2 forklifts. We basically logged the calculated collision states together with a timestamp. The collision detection system was initialized with following values: prediction area radius with $8m$, warning area radius with $20m$, prediction time $5s$ ($4.2 * 5 = 21m$), an untrusted mode (untrusted - buffers measurements and calculates mean values, trusted - takes Abatec values directly), and 10 values frequency (wait 10 packets before recalculating collision states).

In Fig. 4(a), we show an excerpt of the data over a time frame of $22s$. During this time we measured 6846 valid positions (UDP packets): 3455 for forklift 1 and 3391 for forklift 2. For each forklift we calculated 1370 collision states with an average of 62 states per second. To show how the two forklifter approached each other during these 22s, we show their raw data position trajectories in Fig. 4(b). Dark color marks the time of a critical situation, i.e., the detection of a potential collision state. This means the distance between their predicted locations was less then the threshold defined by the prediction radius (as shown in Fig. 2(b)).

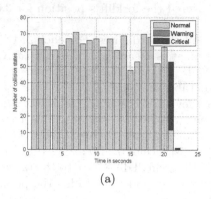 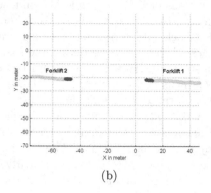

(a)   (b)

Fig. 4. Both subfigures are based on an excerpt of measured values for two tracked forklifts over a time span of 22 seconds. (a) Number of calculated collision states per time interval ($1s$) of the first forklift (b) Motion trajectory of both forklifts.

Finally, we conclude that with a measured average rate of 62 states per second, the collision detection's effeciency was sufficient.

5   Conclusion and Outlook

We showed that the collision detection is reliable in a non-cooperative environment. Despite static and dynamic disturbances in the storage place and inaccuarcies with steering forklifts, a deviation of less than $0.3m$ was achieved.

An open question is the scalability of the collision detection system. In our use case we only compared the positions of two objects with each other. At the moment, a comparision of n objects would result in n^2 collision calculations that could lead to scalability problems. Furthermore, the system's frequency is limited to 500Hz, i.e., 500 values per second for all tracked objects (see Section 2.2), that is another aspect regarding scalability. Here, the question is how a low number of measurements does influence the reliability. We plan to use our installation in the Hanseterminal Magdeburg[2] to run further tests.

Until now, we used only 2 dimensional values of Abatec's LPM system for cardinal directions. In other logistics applications also the 3rd (altitude) dimension can be of interest, e.g., spreader height of a reach stacker or crane trollies. Other extension are interesting as well, like communicating alarms with affected staff or including the tracking of logistics hub staff itself.

Furthermore, we want to integrate the collision detection into our central virtual reality monitoring model that we develope in the context of the project ViERforES[3].

---

[2] http://www.magdeburg-hafen.de/magdeburg-hafen/mdhafen.htm

[3] ViERforES is funded by the German Ministry of Education and Science (BMBF), project 01IM08003C; http://www.vierfores.de/

References

1. Berufsgenossenschaft Handel und Warendistribution (BGHW) (Hrsg.): Zeitdruck ist häufige Unfallursache. BGHW aktuell (1), 14 (January 2010)
2. Hightower, J., Borriello, G.: Location Systems for Ubiquitous Computing. Computer 34(8), 57–66 (2001)
3. Bell, S., Jung, W.R., Krishnakumar, V.: WiFi-based enhanced positioning systems: accuracy through mapping, calibration, and classification. In: Proceedings of the 2nd ACM SIGSPATIAL International Workshop on Indoor Spatial Awareness, ISA 2010, pp. 3–9. ACM, New York (2010)
4. Stelzer, A., Pourvoyeur, K., Fischer, A.: Concept and Application of LPM - A Novel 3-D Local Position Measurement System. IEEE Transactions on Microwave Theory and Techniques 52, 2664–2669 (2004)
5. Uckelmann, D.: A Definition Approach to Smart Logistics. In: Balandin, S., Moltchanov, D., Koucheryavy, Y. (eds.) NEW2AN 2008. LNCS, vol. 5174, pp. 273–284. Springer, Heidelberg (2008)
6. Cyplik, P., Patecki, A.: RTLS vs. RFID - Partnership or Competition? LogForum 7(3), 1–10 (2011)

Visual Approach Facilitating the Importance Analysis of Component Fault Trees

Yi Yang, Patric Keller, and Peter Liggesmeyer

Software Engineering Research Group: Dependability, University of Kaiserslautern,
67663, Kaiserslautern, Germany

Abstract. (Component) fault tree analysis is a safety analysis technique of embedded systems. Importance analysis estimates the respective contributions of potential basic failures to an overall system failure. The analysis results are typically represented in data-aggregated forms. There are only few associations between these forms and component fault tree structures that provide meaningful information. In this paper, we propose a visualization approach that integrates the importance analysis results with structures of component fault trees. This approach facilitates the identification of the critical components and supports the analysis of the influence of the important basic failures.

Keywords: Fault Tree, Component Fault Tree, Importance Analysis, Visualization.

1 Introduction

Fault Tree Analysis (FTA) [1–4] is a commonly used safety-analysis technique for embedded systems. Safety is a state of a system that is *"freedom from unacceptable risk* [1]". The FTA is based upon the usage of a tree-like model called *Fault Tree (FT)* (see Fig. 1 (a)) that consists of a minimum of three types of elements: top event, basic event, and gate. *Top Event (TE)* is the tree root and represents an undesired failure of a system. *Basic Events (BEs)* are leaves and represent the basic failures that may cause a TE to occur. *Gates* logically connect elements of the FT. Each element may have a failure probability. *Component Fault Tree (CFT)* [5] (see Fig. 1 (b)) is an extension of the FT, which allows engineers to encapsulate parts of a FT into CFT components. Each CFT component maps an architectural component of the hierarchical system model. With the help of in- and out-ports, failures may be transferred between CFT components. A CFT component may contain other (sub-)CFT components. This nesting structure corresponds to the hierarchies of the system architecture. In this case, the location of a CFT component in the nesting structure represents the location of the corresponding architectural component in the hierarchical system model. *Importance analysis* [3, 6] is a quantitative measure based on the FT. Vesely et al. [3] concluded that, in general, more than 90% of the failure probability of a TE is due to less than 20% of the BEs. This implies that engineers only need to focus on a small subset of BEs having a

F. Ortmeier and P. Daniel (Eds.): SAFECOMP 2012 Workshops, LNCS 7613, pp. 486–497, 2012.

major contribution. Fussell-Vesely importance measure [7] is a famous method that estimates the respective contributions of BEs to the failure probability of the TE by considering both the logical relations and the failure probabilities of BEs. Each BE is assigned with an importance value between zero and one: the larger the value, the more important the BE. Although a great deal of effort was vested in novel algorithms and methods, very little effort is put toward effective representations. Engineers cannot effectively identify patterns regarding the critical components and analyze influence of the important BEs in the CFT.

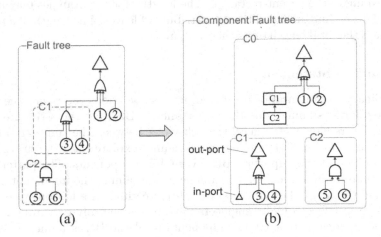

Fig. 1. FT and CFT. There are a main CFT component "C0" and two sub-CFT components: "C1" and "C2". "C2" inputs its failure to "C1" via in-/out-ports.

In this paper, we propose a visualization approach that integrates the importance of BEs with the CFT. Engineers may identify the important BEs and the critical CFT components by taking the hierarchies of system architecture into account. In addition, engineers may dynamically analyze failure propagation.

We organize the rest of this paper as follows: Section 2 describes the previous work as well as their issues. We introduce our visualization approach in Section 3, and show an application example in Section 4. Section 5 shows the experts' review. Finally, we provide a brief conclusion in Section 6.

2   Previous Work

Result of the importance analysis is a set of importance values corresponding to BEs. The result is usually summarized and represented using a data table by most of the FTA tools. BEs are represented in rows, and the importance value as well as the essential data, e.g., the failure probability, are represented in different columns. The graphical data-aggregated forms, e.g., histogram and pie-chart, are also commonly used. *RAMCommander* [8] additionally provides more graphical summary views, e.g., scatter plot, and area chart. *BlockSim* [9] proposes a variant of pie-chart called "square pie-chart" that anticlockwise arranges the BEs in descending order according to the importance values. *ESSaRel* [10] (see Fig. 2 (b)) implements the CFT analysis using the standard graphical symbols defined in [5]. The sub-CFT components are symbolically represented as boxes in the logical structures of their parent CFT components. The logical structures of the (sub-)CFT components are displayed over separate views.

The icicle diagram provides a compact visualization layout that uses stacked rectangles to represent the hierarchies of a tree structure [11]. The child-rectangles are placed under the parent-rectangle. The length of leaf-rectangles may be proportional depending on a quantitative attribute of leaves. The length of a parent-rectangle is the total length of its child-rectangles.

2.1   Problem Statement

The ordinary representations provide few associations between the data-aggregated forms summarizing the importance of BEs and the structure of the CFT. Engineers have to frequently switch views between the summary and the CFT. It wastes much effort and engineers cannot explore the pattern regarding the distribution of the important BEs over CFT components. The pattern supports to analyze the critical CFT components containing the important BEs by considering the hierarchies of the system architecture. In addition, when identifying a given BE in a CFT, engineers have to sequentially go through all the direct and indirect parent CFT components until the BE is found. This issue hampers the analysis of BEs included by the deeper-nested components. Moreover, because the structures of components are displayed over separate views, engineers cannot obtain continuous critical paths describing the failure flow from BEs to the TE.

3   Visualization of the Important Analysis

3.1   Design

To facilitate the identification of the vulnerable system architectural components, we visualize the nesting structure of the CFT. The overall nesting structure in a CFT comprises of the nesting relations between CFT components as well as the case that CFT components contain BEs. To maintain a satisfactory view of a CFT model having a large number of CFT components, we decide to design a compact view for the nesting structure. BEs with the importance values should be represented in this view. The logical structures of CFT components should be dynamically shown for representing failure flow when requested.

The nesting structure is a tree structure that is commonly represented in the form of node-link diagrams and space-filling techniques usually consisting of treemap [12], sunburst layout [13], and icicle diagram [11]. Barlow et al. [14] evaluated readability of these layouts with respect to the interpretation of node relationship, comparison of node size, and user preference. The results showed that the icicle diagram and the node-link diagram were more readable. McGuffin et al. [15] performed a mathematical evaluation for the space efficiency of 2D tree representations. Regarding the metrics of node representation, the authors concluded that the treemap, the icicle diagram, and the sunburst have the similar space efficiency, which was much better than those of different kinds of node-link diagrams. In addition, we consider the layout composition between the compact view and the node-link logical CFT structures (described in the next paragraph). The treemap and the sunburst layout may have aspect ratio issues. In this case, the uniform scale unit cannot be maintained for compact views of different CFT components. In short, the icicle diagram is a suitable layout that cannot only effectively represent the hierarchical relations, but also space-efficiently visualize large-scale data. Thus, we apply the icicle diagram for the compact view representing the nesting structure.

The logical structure of a CFT component is a directed acyclic graph that may be represented by the node-link diagram and the matrix visualization. We finally use the node-link diagram because previous evaluations [16, 17] concluded that the node-link diagram could more effectively represent complex paths. This advantage is beneficial for representing critical paths of logical failure flow.

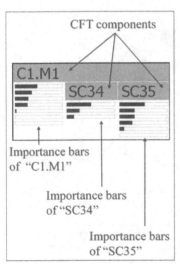

(a) Architectural view.

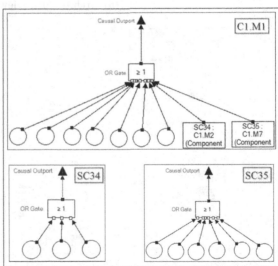

(b) Ordinary representation of a CFT (produced by using ESSaRel [10]). Logical structures of subcomponent "SC34" and "SC35" are represented in respective views. These sub-components are symbolically represented as boxes in the view of the parent component "C1.M1".

Fig. 2. Architectural view. A CFT model is respectively represented using an architectural view (a) and the ordinary concept (b).

3.2 Visualization

Architectural View. We propose an *architectural view* (see Fig. 2) by implementing design concepts of the compact view. We apply the iceray concept of the icicle diagram, where leaf nodes are vertically listed in order to avoid the extreme long view led by a large number of BEs. In the architectural view, a gray rectangle represents a CFT component. The ID of the component is printed on the left side of the rectangle. The sub-components are represented as short rectangles that are horizontally listed under this (parent) rectangle. We developed an *importance bar* to represent a BE, which has a fixed border and a filled part encoding the importance value of the BE: the larger the importance value, the longer the filled part. For a rectangle representing a CFT component, the contained importance bars are vertically listed under the rectangle on the left and sorted according to the importance values in descending order.

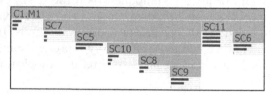

(a) Architectural view.

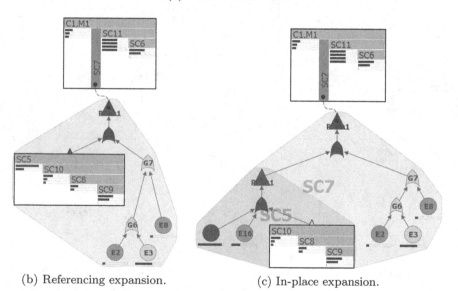

(b) Referencing expansion.   (c) In-place expansion.

Fig. 3. Expansion concepts. (a) Architectural view. (b) Show structure of the sub-component "SC7" using referencing expansion. (c) Show structure of the sub-sub-component "SC5" using in-place expansion.

Representation of Logical Structures. The node-link logical structure of a CFT component is displayed by clicking the corresponding rectangle in the architectural view for analyzing the failure flow. The visible structure may be treated as an expansion of the architectural view. The architectural views of the sub-components and importance bars may be embedded in the logical structure. For example, in Fig. 3 (b) the architectural view of component "SC5" is embedded in the logical structure of the expanded component "SC7". Importance bars are respectively placed under the corresponding BE nodes.

We provide two expansion concepts: referencing expansion (see Fig. 3 (b)) and in-place expansion (see Fig. 3 (c)). By referencing expansion, the structure of a sub-component is linked to the parent architectural view by a dashed curve. In the parent architectural view, a vertical rectangular indicator is drawn to replace the initial part representing the expanded sub-component. This way, engineers may view the structures of the deeper-nested sub-components without needing to care about the higher level parent components. By in-place expansion, the architectural view of the requested CFT component is simply replaced with its logical structure. This way, engineers may obtain the continuous critical paths.

The symbols defined for the CFT are retained in our visualization. In logical structures, the sub-components may be optionally represented as the ordinary symbols (i.e., the boxes) instead of the embedded architectural views for reducing space requirement. To support the analysis of the quantitative failure propagation, we use colors to encode the criticality of the failure probability of CFT elements: red as critical, yellow as moderate, and green as acceptable. We use translucent gray blobs to identify the scopes of structures of CFT components and the nesting of CFT components (see Fig. 3 (c)). Labels of CFT elements (i.e., short descriptions) are allowed to be dynamically displayed.

Analyzing Influence of BEs. A CFT component may be influenced by the nested critical sub-components and the failure flow caused by the important BEs. For a specific BE, in architectural view, the influenced components are highlighted using gradient cyan areas on the left side of the rectangles (see Fig. 4 (a)). In logical structure, critical path of the logical failure flow of the BE is highlighted by a thick border and cyan color (see Fig. 4 (b)).

3.3 Interaction

Besides the interaction of "direct selection", for adapting to different display requirements, we apply zooming interaction for the visualization, which allows engineers to smoothly enlarge and shrink the view of the visualization for clearly showing the interesting parts. In order to show the particular part of the visualization that is currently out of the screen, we provide panning interaction that allows engineers to move the whole visualization for making the part visible. In addition, engineers are allowed to adjust the horizontal and vertical distance between nodes of the logical structure for reducing the space requirement.

3.4 Scalability

The length of the architectural view of a CFT component depends on the number of its sub-components. On a 24-inch screen with a resolution of 1920x1080 an

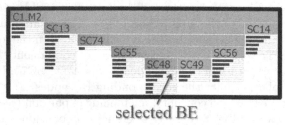

(a) Influence along the nesting structure. Cyan areas on the left side of rectangles highlight the influenced components: "SC48", "SC55", "SC74", "SC13", and "C1.M2".

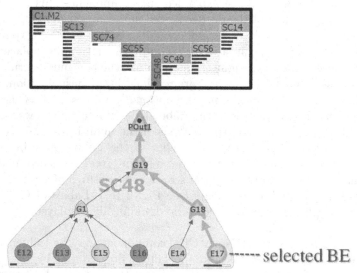

(b) Influence along the logical structure. The highlighted critical path consists of BE "E17", OR-gate "G18", OR-gate "G19", and out-port "POut1".

Fig. 4. Influence of the specific BE

architectural view can display at most 60 CFT components with readable IDs and a maximum of about 10,000 legible importance bars. When showing logical structures, the scalability issue may be serious because the node-link diagrams are sparse and take up much more space.

4   Application Scenario

In order to demonstrate the use of our visualization approach, we present an application example regarding the importance analysis of a CFT model with respect to a mobile robot [18]. The CFT model contains 24 components and 322 BEs. The tasks in this example are to identify the critical CFT components and to analyze the influence of the most important BE.

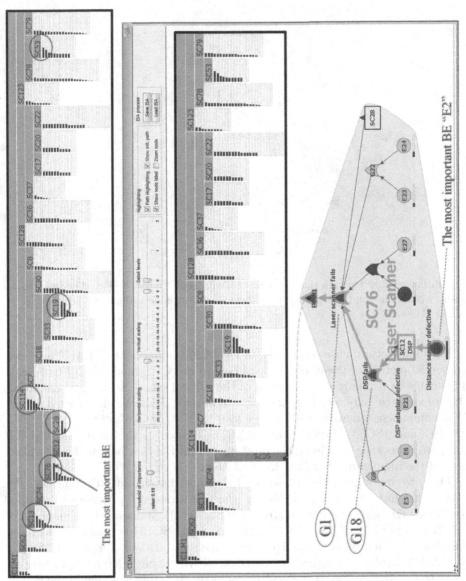

(a) Overview of the (b) Influence of the most important BE. The critical path (with-
importance of BEs.   out out-port) from top to bottom is described as "G1 → G18 →
                      SC12 → E2".

Fig. 5. Application example

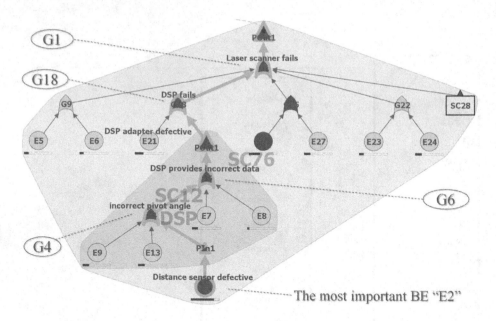

Fig. 6. Failure flow through the structure of component "SC12 (DSP)". The full critical path (without in- and out-ports) from top to bottom is described as "G1 → G18 → G6 → G4 → E2".

The architectural view of the system-level CFT component "C1.M1" provides an overall picture of the importance of BEs of the CFT model (see Fig. 5 (a)). This helps us to analyze the pattern of the critical components. By comparing the importance bars, we find that the important BEs are distributed in six CFT components (marked with red circles): "SC13", "SC76", "SC28", "SC114", "SC19", and "SC53". Component "SC76" is treated as the most critical CFT component because it includes the most important BE that has the longest filled part of the importance bar (i.e., the first bar).

Then, we investigate the influence of the most important BE identified. By clicking the importance bar of this BE, the rectangles of the influenced components are highlighted with cyan areas (see Fig. 5 (a)). It shows that components "C1.M1", "SC62", "SC13", "SC74", "SC76", and "SC12" are influenced by the BE. We then analyze how this BE causes the most critical component "SC76" to fail. We display the logical structure of "SC76" using referencing expansion (see Fig. 5 (b)). To support understanding of the semantic meaning of the failure flow, we optionally show labels of CFT elements. The label of the expanded component "SC76" is printed on the blob and shows that "SC76" corresponds to a laser scanner. We find that the most important BE ("E2") represents the failure of a distance sensor. We perform a top-down analysis starting from gate "G1" to analyze how the failure of the laser scanner is caused by the distance sensor. The highlighted path shows that the laser scanner fails most likely because of DSP problem ("G18") and this problem is most likely caused by wrong data from a

DSP chip ("SC12") rather than a defective DSP adapter ("E21"). In order to analyze why the DSP chip outputs incorrect data, we show the logical structure of "SC12" using in-place expansion that presents continuous failure flow (see Fig. 6). We notice that the cause of incorrect data ("G6") is most probable the wrongly calculated pivot angle ("G4"). The DSP chip makes this mistake because it receives the wrong data from the distance sensor ("E2"). This way, we understand how the defective distance sensor causes the laser scanner to fail.

5 Evaluation

We performed an expert review to evaluate our visualization approach. There were 6 participants with degrees in computer science who worked on CFT analysis at the local university. We introduced our visualization approach and then they were allowed to go ahead and experience using it. The given data was a CFT model having 44 CFT components and 834 BEs. Tasks were provided for the experience including the identification of the important BEs, the critical components, and the influenced CFT components, as well as the investigation of critical paths of those BEs. Finally, for a qualitative evaluation, the participants were asked to fill out a Likert scale questionnaire that has the following questions for estimating whether our approach can facilitate the importance analysis:

- Can the critical components and the influenced components be easily identified in the nesting structure of the CFT?
- Can the important BEs be effectively identified?
- Can logical failure flow be effectively represented?
- Can the critical paths be quickly identified?
- Can the quantitative failure propagation be effectively investigated?
- Can the CFT components along the critical paths be intuitively identified?

Results of the questionnaire (see Fig. 7) showed that in general, our approach was favorably reviewed for the aspects of safety domain, while there were small issues regarding the details of the visualization. The participants commented that the critical CFT components were easy to identify in the architectural view. A participant suggested that sector diagrams could be used instead of the iceray diagram for reducing the space requirement. The importance bars received positive comments, due to their intuitive nature and the universal comparability. The comments regarding the critical path consisted of two aspects: showing paths (i.e., expansion concepts) and highlighting paths. The expansion concepts received positive feedback because the analysis of continuous failure flow was possible and the nested sub-components could be conveniently analyzed. Some participants pointed out that the node-link CFT structure could be sparse and wasted much space. The participants were of the opinion that the highlighting of critical paths was useful. Additionally, the participants commented that the quantitative failure flow along the CFT structures can be intuitively analyzed by the colored CFT nodes. The aggregation blobs were regarded as being effective for identification of the ranges of components while analyzing failure propagation

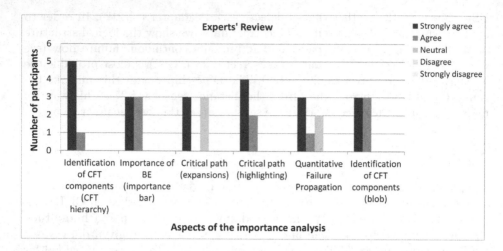

Fig. 7. Experts' review

between CFT components along critical paths. The participants also stated that the blobs for the deeper-nested components could be very dark when representing a multiple-level nesting structure. This could hamper the analysis of the nodes inside the dark blobs. The participants commented that the dashed curves were not suitable because it could confuse the referencing lines with the input lines.

6   Conclusion and Future Work

In this paper, we propose a visualization approach that represents insights for the importance analysis of a CFT by dynamically composing the iceray diagrams and the node-link graphs. Architectural views provide the overview of the importance of BEs by taking the system architecture into account, while the node-link diagrams are aimed at representing the logical structures of CFT components. The expansion concepts support the analysis of failure flow. The referencing expansion allows engineers to quickly investigate the deeper-nested components and the in-place expansion provides continuous critical paths. The translucent blobs are used to enclose the nodes of each expanded CFT component for indicating its scope. Safety experts reviewed the proposed visualization approach and gave positive comments. In short, using our approach, engineers may identify the important BEs and the interesting CFT components, while flexibly investigating the failure propagation. When showing logical structures, the node-link diagrams may take up much space and cause serious scalability issues. Thus, the future work will focus on increasing scalability of the visualization.

Acknowledgment. This work was supported by the International Research Training Group (IRTG 1131) of the German Research Foundation (DFG) and the German Ministry of Education and Research (BMBF) in the context of the ViERforES (Virtuelle und Erweiterte Realität für höchste Sicherheit und Zuverlässigkeit von Eingebetteten Systemen) project. We thank the colleagues at the University of Kaiserslautern and at the University of Utah for their support.

References

1. IEC. Functional safety of electrical/electronic/programmable electronic safety-related systems. International Standard IEC 61508 (2000)
2. IEC. Fault Tree Analysis. International Standard IEC 61025, Geneva (1990)
3. Vesely, W.E., Dugan, J., Fragola, J., Minarick III, J., Railsback, J., Stamatelatos, M.: Fault Tree Handbook with Aerospace Applications. NASA (2002)
4. Vesely, W.E., Goldberg, F.F., Roberts, N.H., Haasl, D.F.: Fault Tree Handbook. U.S.Nuclear Regulatory Commission (1981)
5. Kaiser, B., Liggesmeyer, P., Maeckel, O.: A new component concept for fault trees. In: Proceedings of the 8th Australian Workshop on Safety Critical Systems and Software (SCS 2003), Adelaide, Australia, pp. 37–46 (2003)
6. Stamatelatos, M., Apostolakis, G., Dezfuli, H., Everline, C., Guarro, S., Moieni, P., Mosleh, A., Paulos, T., Youngblood, R.: Probabilistic Risk Assessment Procedures Guide for NASA Managers and Practitioners. NASA (2002)
7. Fussell, J.B.: How to hand calculate system reliability characteristics. IEEE Transactions on Reliability R-24(3), 169–174 (1975)
8. Aldservice. RAMCommander, http://www.aldservice.com (accessed June 15, 2012)
9. ReliaSoft. BlockSim, http://www.reliasoft.com/BlockSim (accessed June 15, 2012)
10. University of Kaiserslautern. ESSaREL, http://www.essarel.de (accessed June 15, 2012)
11. Kruskal, J.B., Landwehr, J.M.: Icicle Plots: Better Displays for Hierarchical Clustering. The American Statistician 37(2), 162–168 (1983)
12. Shneiderman, B.: Tree visualization with tree-maps: 2-D space-filling approach. ACM Trans. Graph. 11(1), 92–99 (1992)
13. Stasko, J., Zhang, E.: Focus+Context Display and Navigation Techniques for Enhancing Radial, Space-Filling Hierarchy Visualizations. In: Proceedings of the IEEE Symposium on Information Visualization 2000 (INFOVIS 2000), pp. 57–65. IEEE Computer Society, Washington, DC (2000)
14. Barlow, T., Neville, P.: A Comparison of 2-D Visualizations of Hierarchies. In: Proceedings of the IEEE Symposium on Information Visualization 2001 (INFOVIS 2001), pp. 131–138. IEEE Computer Society (2001)
15. McGuffin, M.J., Robert, J.-M.: Quantifying the space-efficiency of 2D graphical representations of trees. Information Visualization 9(2), 115–140 (2010)
16. Ghoniem, M., Fekete, J.-D., Castagliola, P.: A comparison of the readability of graphs using node-link and matrix-based representations. In: Proceedings of the IEEE Symposium on Information Visualization 2004, pp. 17–24 (2004)
17. Keller, R., Eckert, C.M., Clarkson, P.J.: Matrices or node-link diagrams: which visual representation is better for visualising connectivity models? Information Visualization 5, 62–76 (2006)
18. The Robotics Research Lab at the University of Kaiserslautern. RAVON (Robust Autonomous Vehicle for Off-road Navigation), http://agrosy.informatik.uni-kl.de (accessed June 15, 2012)

Simulation of Structural Effects in Embedded Systems and Visualization of Dependencies According to an Intended Attack or Manipulation

Sven Kuhlmann, Jana Fruth, Tobias Hoppe, and Jana Dittmann

Multimedia and Security Working Group, ITI Institute, Faculty of computer science
Otto von Guericke University of Magdeburg
University Place 2
39106 Magdeburg
{Sven.tuchscheerer,jana.fruth,tobias.hoppe,
jana.dittmann}@iti.cs.uni-magdeburg.de

Abstract. The purpose of this workshop contribution is the interaction between networked embedded systems (such as controllers, sensors and actuators within a motor vehicle) and how these can be simulated. It aims to assess the potential impacts of IT security incidents in advance and plan protective measures without having to build a complete prototype. The feasibility of recognizing and visualising possible dependencies and structural effects in a complex networked system with embedded components (in this example: A motor vehicle with CAN bus become more and more relevant. One exemplary reason is that in contrast to earlier times, now the vehicle manufacturers are acting just as a systems integrator of supply components. This could result in a leakage of the total understanding and a lost track of the networked system elements. This development is intensified by the growing number of control units, sensors and actuators, which make the complete testing of all system components and their dependencies almost impossible. Derived from this the need for a simulation model that represents these possible interactions as extensively as possible is obvious. In a first research step selected control devices on a CAN network, and related automotive sensors and actuators are modelled by simulation in order to simulate freely and selectable event sequences, e.g. to carry out as part of penetration testing to monitor possible weaknesses in the system and resulting interactions. On the latter, particular attention is given, as the security area is in the main application focus of this simulation.

1 Introduction and Concepts Used

The development of information technology components in motor vehicles is progressing steadily. Current upper-class models often contain up to 100 electronic control units. This large number of IT components, which is present not only in cars but often also in production environments or in the robotics field, is becoming increasingly extensive. Especially to keep track of the behaviour of all IT components, as functions

F. Ortmeier and P. Daniel (Eds.): SAFECOMP 2012 Workshops, LNCS 7613, pp. 498–507, 2012.

are often based on dependencies (e.g. complex sensor information) is hard to estimate by manufacturers. In addition, and especially in the automotive domain the development and production of these IT components is now days often outsourced to different companies; but the assembly of the vehicle takes place, however by the manufacturer. The supplying companies in turn typically provide those IT components as black boxes to avoid knowledge transfer [8]. Therefore, it turns out more and more complex to produce an overall view of all the possible interactions between IT components, especially those who may have undesired consequences [11]. An example (documented in [1]) illustrates this, by two common vehicle components: the air conditioning and automatic parking brake. Seen individually, both have features that offer a comfort plus to the driver. The automatic climate control automatically regulates the power the air condition, based on the current in-vehicle temperature and the desired temperature. The automatic parking brake is able to detect a start-up demand of the vehicle driver and thereupon to loosen itself. These two components resulted in the described case [1] in an unexpected interaction. According to the report, the driver of such an equipped vehicle wanted to drive in a parking garage on a hot day. To unlock the garage door, he had to temporarily get out of the car. Because of the opened door, the temperature increased rapidly in the vehicle, whereupon the air conditioning requested more power from the engine, leading to a brief increase of the engine speed (rpm). The automatic parking brake interpreted the engine speed increase mistakenly as the driver's request for the start-up and loosened the brake. As a consequence of this interaction, the car rolled against the still closed door of the garage.

As this example illustrates in practice, even more or less randomly occurring interactions between automotive IT systems could lead in financial or personal consequential damages. In cases of wilful manipulations the dependencies and interactions are even more critical, for example drivers often try to improve performance or activate restricted functions by themselves (see [7]). On a quantity basis, this should therefore be at least as large as the dimensions of the randomly cases. These findings underline the need to determine, how individual IT components of a vehicle are in interaction and what consequences are included in terms of safety and security aspects, before the start of production (SOP).

The security domain includes those events that occur by intentional acts (e.g. the specific injection of manipulated messages or sensor information). The safety domain (in this article) refers primarily to events that occur through the interaction with the attack and the linkage with other functions or faulty sensor signals. The approach presented in this paper addresses both areas and thus allows a detection and investigation of possible interactions between actuators, sensor information and the control units of a vehicle, visually.

Within this purpose, a generalised model of a vehicular CAN Bus system was created, using the simulation tool AnyLogic [2], containing the most important functions of selected control devices, their sensors and actuators, depicted as realistically as possible. The effects were visualized exemplary, to identify easily the consequences of the attacks, in particular the control devices, affected by the manipulated data.

1.1   Addressed Standards and Used Technologies

The currently most widely used vehicle-bus technology is still the Controller Area Network (CAN) standard. It was developed in the second period of the 1980's and has been used since the early 90's at almost all vehicle manufacturers [3]. Depending on the application context, broadcast-based CAN bus systems are often divided into sub-systems, e.g. in vehicles the domain-cantered "Drive-CAN", "Comfort-CAN" or "Infotainment-CAN". To realize the traffic and the necessary procedures (e.g. collision-avoiding CSMA / CA concept) a CAN message contains of different data fields, including a starter bit, the numeric Message Identifier (the same time indicating the transmission priority), seven control bits (including number of payload bytes) and the actual payload. The correct delivery is ensured by the information in the final field, which is in particular a 15-bit CRC checksum and an acknowledge bit [4] [5].

AnyLogic is a simulation tool that was used in this work in version 6.5.1, developed by XJ Technologies Company. It was chosen, because it supports all three popular modelling paradigms:

- Event-oriented simulation (to simulate manipulation, e.g. sensor event related)
- System dynamics (to update dynamically the whole simulation model, e.g. if one of the sensor data is manipulated, for example changed values)
- Agent-based modelling (to simulate the non-linear dependencies between heterogeneous agents, e.g. the depend functions of more than one control unit)

Based on the simulation models, several types of experiments can be carried out. These include optimizations, which identifies the optimal allocation of an objective function and parameter variations by a given set of variables in which multiple simulation runs are performed and one or more variables are changed. Thus, the selection of the simulation tool was based on specific requirements, including a given possibility of manual intervention in the simulation (e.g. for ingesting engineered messages and manipulation) [2].

After the given introduction to the topic, the following chapters describe which components were selected exemplary, how these were implemented in AnyLogic, how the visualization of the structural effects has been realized and how the simulation of Security-related experiments with focus on the structural-functional analysis can be performed.

2   Modelling an Electronic (CAN) System in AnyLogic

Implementing the principles of automotive IT networks with AnyLogic several simplifying assumptions were made. In particular, an abstraction was made regarding the structure of CAN messages. For example, running in the idealized simulation environment, the transmission of messages is basically free from errors, so the collision and transmission error detection, for example can be dispensed. As essential elements of a CAN message, therefore, the message ID and the user data were mapped in the simulation-model and the creation time was also included. This time stamp allows a uniquely identification of a message to keep track of this message and analyse its origin.

CAN messages are transmitted by the broadcast principle. Thus, each communicator's message is sent to all other participants located on the same CAN-bus. As in an electrical system, however, not every control unit uses each message that is received, each control unit decides on the basis of the message Identification (CAN-ID) in the header, if it processes or rejects the message. To implement this broadcast principle in AnyLogic equivalent to common car-network topologies, a queue-based gateway has been modelled, that allows forwarding the received CAN message to other CAN bus systems (see Figure 1). The distribution of messages to be routed through the gateway to the various buses was realised via split objects. These have one input and two outputs, wherein a copy is forwarded from the second output. However, since events that occur simultaneously are processed sequentially, a delay object is used at the first output to achieve a simultaneous distribution of the messages (otherwise the chain of events of the upper output would be processed initially, until the message is stopped in the simulation model or is removed). The prioritisation according to the message ID was not realised, because within the simulation model there are no bandwidths limits and the focus of this work is on the structural effects, not on the limited resources of CAN busses.

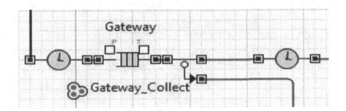

Fig. 1. Modelling of the Gateway

For simplification, the simulated vehicle network forwards all messages from one of the three sub-buses (drive-CAN, comfort-CAN and infotainment-CAN) through the gateway to all bus systems. These buses are implemented as individual classes, which are all built the same way.

They include - as shown in Figure 2 (bottom left) – a message input (Eingang) and output (Ausgang) port, as well as a series of control units, where each of them also includes a split object and a delay. In addition, all messages that pass through the bus system into a collection object are stored for diagnostic and evaluation purposes. This design offers the particular advantage that it is easily extensible, if it is intended to add new control devices, because the basic structure of the individual components is based on a common type.

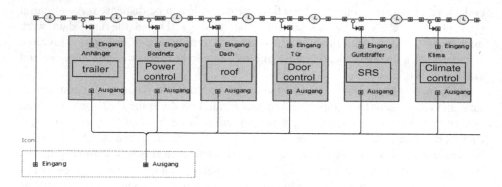

Fig. 2. Modelling the comfort-CAN

2.1   Implementation of the Electronic Control Units (ECU)

Initially, the implementation of the controllers was made as a representative selection for reasons of complexity. This selection is limited to 17 control units, mainly in the area of driver assistance systems. Some control devices were combined into one control device avoiding an implementation of a single function within a separate control unit.

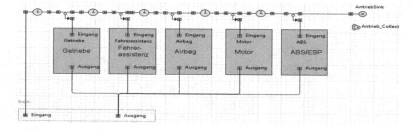

Fig. 3. Modelling of IT components in the drive-CAN

Divided among the three bus systems, the following control units are included:

- Drive-CAN (Fig. 3) contains the controls for the transmission, the driver assistance systems, the airbag, the motor-management and the controller for the ABS / ESP system.
- Comfort-CAN (Fig. 2) contains the controls for the trailer, the vehicle electrical system, electric-roof, doors, air conditioning, windscreen wipers, the steering column and the comfort control unit.
- Infotainment-CAN contains the controls for the radio, instrument cluster and the navigation system.

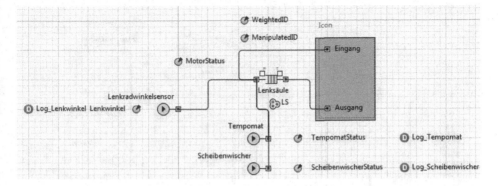

Fig. 4. Modelling of the steering column control unit

Figure 4 shows an example of the structure of the steering column control unit. It includes - as well as the various bus systems - initially an input and an output port that acts as a connection of the different levels in the simulation model. The direct function of a controller is implemented as the functionality of the gateway through a message queue. This approach can be mainly explained by the fact that fair treatment of incoming messages should be ensured. The controllers also include sensors and actuators, each with a data set object in which the value pattern of the sensor or the actuator can be saved.

2.2   Implementation of the Sensors and Actuators

For reasons of complexity a choice of sensors and actuators has been made, as the total number of possible sensors and actuators in a modern motor vehicle would be too extensive for this first implementation. Sensors can either periodically send messages or event-specific, where an event could be for example the occurrence of certain message in the CAN-bus or the operation of a switch. To meet these criteria, source objects were used. Since the definition of the sending message can not be changed directly during the program period, a pre-definition of different payloads must be made for each CAN message, to be sent.

2.3   Implementation of the Overall Model

In addition to the elements, described above, the complete simulation model contains more additional elements. These are implemented either for data or analysis settings. The elements, included for data analysis, contain data set objects that are used to store various data in Excel spreadsheets and a histogram in which the occurrence frequency of message IDs (see Figure 5) are stored. Those elements that are used to carry out changes in settings are divided into two categories. First, those buttons which trigger a plurality of functions: setting the air conditioning or controlling the wipers and much more. The second category of elements is used solely to visualize the set functions, providing a graphical overview of which functions are active, and to what extent.

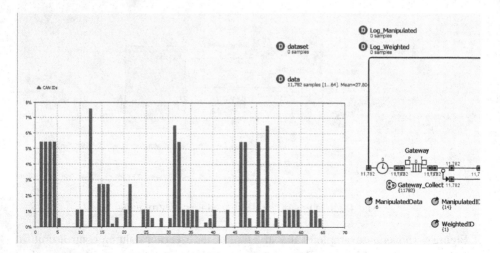

Fig. 5. Overview of the analysis section of the simulation model

One part of these elements is a replica of an instrument cluster that displays data as the current speed, current temperature and turn indicator status. The second part contains simple rectangles that represent a mapping of signal lights.

3   Validation

The methods presented in the previous chapter, which allows security and safety tests were carried out, in the simulation model. So for this simulation model, both, the parameter variation and the use of simulation runs were implemented. The simple simulation runs, in which the user can intervene actively, are based entirely on the overall model introduced in Chapter 2. Within this, the user can manually simulate an arbitrary sequence of operations (e.g. a targeted attack on a sensor or to send a manipulated CAN-message), to identify the effects - related to all control units and functions - in this operation sequence.

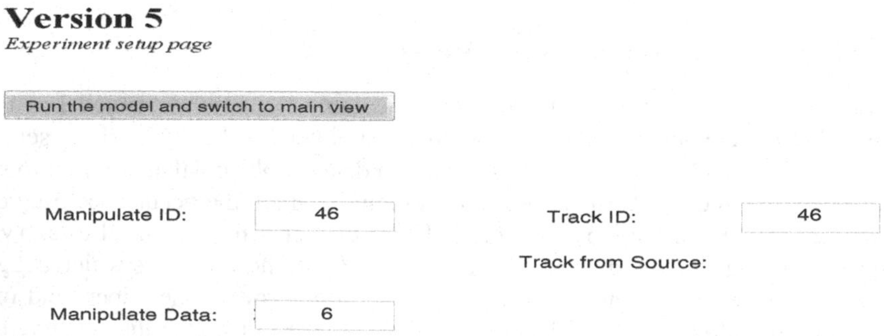

Version 5
Experiment setup page

Run the model and switch to main view

Manipulate ID: 46   Track ID: 46

                                        Track from Source:

Manipulate Data: 6

Fig. 6. Interface for attack simulation

The user interface (Fig. 6) gives the user the ability to set multiple variables. These variables include weighted message-IDs, to check and trace certain paths of this message with the help of highlighting. Furthermore, IDs of messages can be specified and their associated data values can be manipulated. These two functions are used to identify direct and indirect interactions, which are both directly demonstrated in the simulation model as well as in the final analysis. The highlighting of the relevant control devices in the simulation model is implemented either by using a red colour (in the case of manipulated messages) or green (in the case of tracing the weighted-ID, without a manipulation). The parameter variations are based on a slightly modified version of the complete model since users can not directly intervene in the operation sequence (no active AnyLogic allows access to the underlying simulating model). This was solved by using timed events before a fixed sequence of operations has been generated. This sequence of operations can be expanded freely, and thus providing a solid base for the tests. Those parameters that alternate in the parameter variation correspond to the above-mentioned fixed parameters, with the difference that in this case the modified payload is defined as a range in addition to a fixed parameter value. In this range the value of the payload of a message can be defined. Both experimental approaches offer the possibility to perform security-related experiments such as penetration testing or adjustment of known attacks on the system (e.g. for automotive IT forensic analysis) [9]. This is of particular importance because it allows the user to identify and assess hazards and resulting consequences that result from the attacks or manipulation. This makes it possible to identify weaknesses in the system and to identify in early stages of development where security measures or structural changes are necessary. To validate the model, as a practical example, the manipulation of the climate system has been selected (see Chapter 1), with the aim of verifying that the interaction is detected and identified correctly by the simulation as it occurred in reality. The interaction between the electric parking brake and the air conditioning system was identified by the simulation model as indirect interaction with the link engine speed. As a second example the so called "TV in motion" manipulation was tested. This manipulation aims to deactivate the screen-off function when the vehicle speed is above three km/h. This could be done by manipulation of the vehicle-speed sensor data. The manipulation effect the ABS/ESP electronic control unit (ECU) and the navigation system, which includes the TV function as a subsystem since both are depending on a correct vehicle-speed data (Figure 7). The affected ECU and devices (in Figure 7: ABS/ESP and the navigation system) are automatically marked in red colour. This was done to ease the monitoring for the user of such a simulation.

In addition to that a predefined procedure, varying all possible sensor data and vehicle states (these tests are normally performed in expensive real test drive procedures) could be used to identify collisions in dependable functions, that are unknown to developers and would occur in reality – such as the example described in section 1.

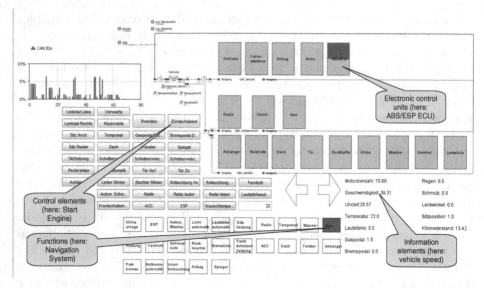

Fig. 7. Result from "TV-in-motion" experiment: Visualisation in the complete model

4   Outlook

Of course, at this stage of development of the simulation model no claim to completeness can be made. This results both from the limited developmental time and the immense amount of potential elements (sensors, actors and control units). Since the extensibility was considered consistently (the simulation model was designed to allow extension of the control devices, sensors and actuators) new elements can be implemented with little programming effort. This is achieved primarily through the use of common concepts for the individual elements. In addition, the CAN standard prioritization for CAN messages can make the simulation model more realistic and consequences caused by prioritization effects can be identified and demonstrated.

For the practical use, those abstract models can be used to derive reactions in cases of automotive-IT manipulation, detected by the automotive intrusion detection systems (IDS, see [6]). If an attack by the IDS (e.g. a bus message inside a vehicle is manipulated), is detected the model can be used to identify which functions and control equipment (through networking and dependencies) could be affected. This information could be used by the Intrusion Management System to choose an appropriate response and for forensic investigations [10]. Those response strategies can also be predefined and therefore much more efficient. Because of the strong causal link between automotive security and safety, particularly in manufacturing, robotics and automotive applications, this approach also improves the road safety [6].

Acknowledgements. Jana Fruth and Sven Kuhlmann are funded by the German Ministry of Education and Science (BMBF), project 01IM10002A. The presented work is part of the ViERforES II Project.

This work was part of the Bachelor thesis of Jens Schiborowski in 2011 at the Otto-von-Guericke University Magdeburg (FIN / ITI / AMSL).

References

[1] Schramm, M.: Organic Computing - "Mr. Self-X "- Wie Computer autonom werden. Bayern 2 (November 2010)

[2] AnyLogic, http://www.xjtek.com/ (last access: September 23, 2011)

[3] Zimmermann, W., Schmidgall, R.: Bussysteme in der Fahrzeugtechnik: Protokolle und Standards, 2nd edn. Vieweg, Wiesbaden (2006)

[4] Bauer, H.: Kraftfahrtechnisches Taschenbuch. Vieweg (2003)

[5] Bauer, H., Dietsche, K.H., Zabler, E., Crepin, J.: Sensoren im Kraftfahrzeug, Bosch. Gelbe Reihe (2007)

[6] Hoppe, T., Dittmann, J., Müter, M.: Decision Model for Automotive intrusion detection systems. In: Automotive - Safety & Security 2010 Sicherheit und Zuverlässigkeit für automobile Informationstechnik, Stuttgart, Juni 22-23. Shaker Verlag, Aachen (2010)

[7] Dittmann, J., Hoppe, T., Kiltz, S., Tuchscheerer, S.: Elektronische Manipulation von Fahrzeug- und Infrastruktursystemen: Gefährdungspotentiale für die Straßenverkehrssicherheit, Paperback, 92 pages. Wirtschaftsverlag N. W. Verlag für neue Wissenschaft (2011) ISBN 978-3869181158

[8] Da: Zulieferer werden für die Automobilindustrie immer wichtiger (July 6, 2001), http://www.welt.de/print-welt/article461473/ (last access: July 15, 2012)

[9] Kiltz, S., Hildebrand, M., Dittmann, J.: Forensische Datenarten und -analysen in automotiven Systemen. In: Horster, P. (ed.) D-A-CH Security 2009, Bochum, Deutschland, May 19-20, pp. 141–152 (2009) ISBN 978-3-00-027488-6

[10] Hoppe, T., Holthusen, S., Tuchscheerer, S., Kiltz, S., Dittmann, J.: Sichere Datenhaltung im Automobil am Beispiel eines Konzepts zur forensisch sicheren Datenhaltung. In: Sicherheit 2010 - Sicherheit, Schutz und Zuverlässigkeit, 5, October 5-7, pp. S.153–S.164. Jahrestagung des Fachbereichs Sicherheit der Gesellschaft für Informatik e.V (GI), Berlin (2010)

[11] Tuchscheerer, S., Hoppe, T., Dittmann, J., Pukall, M., Adamczyk, H.: Herausforderungen an die Absicherung von IT Systemen in der Entwicklung, Betrieb und Wartung von Fahrzeugen. In: Forschung und Innovation - Magdeburg: Univ., insges. 9 S., 2011 Kongress: Magdeburger Maschinenbau-Tage; 10 (Magdeburg), Buchbeitrag, September 27-29 (2011) ISBN 978-3-940961-60-0

From Discrete Event Simulation to Virtual Reality Environments

Sebastian Nielebock[1], Frank Ortmeier[1], Marco Schumann[2], and André Winge[2]

[1] Computer Systems in Engineering,
Otto-von-Guericke University of Magdeburg, Germany
`sebastian.nielebock@st.ovgu.de, frank.ortmeier@ovgu.de`
[2] Fraunhofer Institute for Factory Operation and Automation
IFF, Magdeburg, Germany
`{marco.schumann,andre.winge}@iff.fraunhofer.de`

Abstract. Today's technical systems are often very complex. System dynamics are often hard to predict for humans. However, understanding system behavior is crucial for evaluating design variants and finding errors. One way to cope with this problem is to build logical or virtual simulations. Logical simulations are often very abstract, but can simulate complex behavioral sequences. Virtual reality (VR) simulation is very good for experiencing the system in a view close to reality. However, it is very often static or has only limited dynamics. Until now both approaches exist in relative isolation.

In this paper, we report on our experiences in building a mixed simulation, here a discrete event simulator (DES) is coupled with a virtual reality (VR) environment. We will focus on technical and conceptual challenges, but also present possible use cases for user interaction in this strategy to make more detailed investigations possible. Finally a prototype based on the simulation tool "SLX" and the virtual reality environment "Virtual Development and Training Platform" is used to evaluate the approach.

Keywords: virtual reality, discrete event simulation, synchronization, coupling, model.

1 Introduction

Complex, software-controlled technical systems play a vital role in our modern world. Many processes can't be controlled without them. Nevertheless, this makes it harder for engineers to understand and anticipate the behaviour.

The use of models of the real world system is a well-known strategy to address this problem. There exist a wide variety of models ranging from static, architectural views through formal models including dynamics to precise 3D models. Analysis methods range from best practices through simulation to verification. In this paper, we will focus on 3D models and models expressing abstract behavior. As analysis method, we will only consider (interactive) simulation. Simulation

F. Ortmeier and P. Daniel (Eds.): SAFECOMP 2012 Workshops, LNCS 7613, pp. 508–516, 2012.

has a broad field of applications like in planning of production lines or traffic density[5,9].

Most simulation tools rely on a very abstract representation of physical coordinates and focus on logical places and temporal sequences of events. The common semantic models are discrete event systems (DES). On the other hand, virtual reality simulators typically focus on displaying physical coordinates and orientations very precisely. Temporal evolution is often not possible or implemented in a number of fixed simulation sequences.

As a consequence, each technique itself can give only a limited view on the system: the virtual reality provides understanding of spatial relationships while DES helps understanding temporal understanding. Because of this separation it becomes necessary to model and analyze each of the strategies itself.

The main idea of this paper is to combine the benefits of both in a coupling. So an engineer can use the visualization in parallel to resp. as a front-end of a mathematical DES simulation model. In section 2 it is introduced basic information on "Virtual Reality" and "Discrete Event Simulation" in this paper. The concept of coupling is introduced in section 3 and is evaluated with a prototype presented in section 4. Thereby for illustration, an example system of medium size from logistics scope is considered. Finally the main facts and some future work are summarized in section 5.

2 Related Work

To introduce the topic it is necessary to give an overview about the different techniques and environments and their understanding in this paper. Furthermore some familiar workings are presented.

"Virtual Reality (VR)" is wedded to the definition of a virtual environment. Thereby this environment represents a (mostly) realistic or fictive and visual 3-dimensional presentation generated by a computer. The main element is the user, who controls the actions inside, depending to an underlying control model. The symbioses of visualization and perception of this designed world and its physical properties leads to the term VR [11, p. 3].

In a more technical way the VR-system is a tool to create a set of graphical objects, which are displayed on visualization hardware e.g. a monitor or a CAVE[1]. Using slightly changed images e.g. a different position of an object and play them with a special frame rate[2] leads to the effect of a moving scene, called activities. The state of the objects can be represented as a 6-D-vector: 3 dimensions for the direction and 3 dimensions for the position of the object. There at least 2 special objects: *the path* and *the user*. The path can be used to move an object through the VR, whereby the changing in direction position of the object is automatically done. The user-object is the user interface to interact with the VR like moving through the environment or to grab objects. All graphical information, called *scene* are stored as a *layout*.

---

[1] Cave Automatic Virtual Environment.
[2] Typically given as displayed frames per second.

The Discrete Event Simulation (DES) is a time discrete simulation whereby in every time step one or more events happen. Concerning to the term of simulation, which is defined as the consideration of a system with its corresponding abstract model over time [7, p. 1], an *event* is timeless appearances like an arrival of ship at a harbor. This means that DES does its calculations on specific points in time and jump to the next event-time immediately. Thereby it is possible that in one calculation multiple events are triggered. In opposite to an event an *activity* is a timed element for instance the discharging of a container from a ship. It is necessary to mention that activities are not part of the DES but of continues consideration of a system.

There have been several approaches concerning to the coupling DES with a VR in the last years. So in [13] there is shown different classifications to describe the type of coupling (table 1).

Table 1. Classification of the coupling[13]

Classification	Possible implementations	
Temporal Parallelism	*Concurrent/Online*	*Post-Run/Offline*
Interaction	*Bidirectional*	*Unidirectional*
Hardware Platform	*Monolithic/Homogeneous*	*Distributed*
Visualization Tool Autonomy	*Integrated*	*External*

The categorization "temporal parallelism" distinguishes, whether the DES and the VR are running parallel (concurrent) or sequential (post-run). Another dimension for categorization is how the communication between the both partners is directed. In this case "unidirectional"-case describes that data flows only from the DES to VR. In contrast, the "bidirectional"-case allows both tools to exchange data with each other. Obviously a bidirectional coupling has to be concurrent. Further classifications refer to the used hardware, whether both systems are using a monolithic or distributed platform and the autonomy of the visualization, which characterize whether the DES has an integrated VR or an external one is needed.

Moreover in [13] it is shown that for bidirectional communication messages with timestamps are very useful. Thereby different synchronization methods for those messages are evaluated and a concept of a self-adaptive buffering in the VR system is introduced. Other synchronization methods can be found in distributed simulation, in which conservative and optimistic approaches are used to avoid synchronization faults [4, p. 51ff]. Specific implementations spread from several unidirectional and post-run tools [12,14] to bidirectional solutions[3,10].

3   Concept of the Coupling

The developed coupling may be classified as bidirectional, concurrent, distributed and external. Furthermore the coupling should be created in a way that DES and VR can be run independent (as stand-alone models) from each other. Thereby it consists of 3 parts: The syntactic part (3.1)), which describes time synchronization, the semantic part (3.2)), which describes how semantic information are mapped and the integration of user actions (3.3).

3.1 Temporal Coupling – Synchronization

The main problem to combine the VR and the DES is to synchronize the different views on the time. On the one hand, a DES describes only (discrete) moments in the course of time by events, on the other hand the VR needs a detailed view by representing activities in (fixed) frame rates. In the following, we will assume that time intervals between DES events are much larger - typically several seconds - than those by the VR[3]. Furthermore both, the VR and the DES have a local clock representing their internal simulation time.

During a simulation run the slower clock of the VR runs continuously, while the DES clock has to be delayed between different timestamps. So it becomes possible to visualize activities without interruptions.

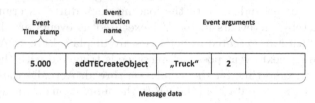

Fig. 1. Structure of a time stamp message

Thereby all events for a specific point in time have to be calculated within the DES and have to be transmitted to the VR. Concerning to a point in time the events can be communicated either parallel, which means one communication message for all triggered events, or sequential, which means one communication message per event. To reduce the size of a message the sequential strategy will be used whereby the delays caused by communication and calculation effort lead different receiving times. To deal with this problems the messages are constructed in way shown for creating a truck object in figure 1 whereby every event has a specific time stamp and specific instruction names and a list of different arguments. The VR is able to interpret and execute these messages by their instruction names. Hereby the messages will be buffered until the VR clock reaches the point in time expressed by the time stamp[4]. The execution of the messages can be either an event e. g. creating a 3D-object or an activity e. g. moving an object on a path. Because the DES doesn't represent activities, further events have to be delayed until the activity is finished, because they can depend on the execution of this activity. For example a truck has to drive to the loading dock before it can be loaded. Nevertheless parallel executions of activities can be done by using multiple simulation threads, which trigger independent events from each other and are displayed in different VR threads.

---

[3] Defined by the frame rate.

[4] It becomes necessary that all events have to be delivered until this point in time is reached.

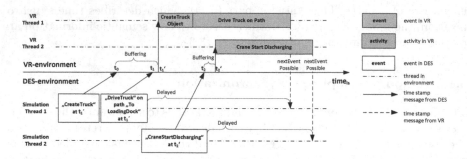

Fig. 2. Communication between DES an VR

A fully communication is shown in figure 2, whereby in this case a truck object is created and drive to the loading dock during a crane is discharging a ship. Hereby the events in the VR executed as events are displayed red and events which are presented as activities are displayed green. At the end of an activity an "a next event possible"-message is triggered with the time stamp to get the next valid time for the simulation thread. Actually these messages can be used to transmit data from the VR to the simulation e.g. measured values by a sensor.

3.2   Spatial Coupling

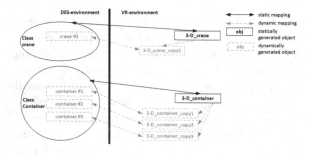

Fig. 3. Class-based semantic coupling

Another challenge is the spatial coupling of the objects in VR and DES. For successful coupling the objects and paths of the virtual reality environment have to be mapped to those in the DES and vice versa. Actually the presentation of the objects is different. A DES sees the objects as logical components, while a VR environment sees them as 3D-polygonal-meshes. To map the objects in a dynamic way a class-mapping is used (see figure 3). Classes of objects from DES (in the example a crane and several containers) are mapped with 3D-objects from the used virtual reality scenario. By doing this it is possible to create or delete meshes in the VR by incarnating or deleting the referred logical objects in the DES. A possible mapping is displayed in 3. However, selecting the mesh is the first step of the mapping. It is also important to set position and orientation. In more general, every state change in the DES must correspond to a (set of) 3D paths in the virtual reality environment. These paths have to be specified manually. However, the current implementation allows easy customization by allocating arbitrary pre-drawn paths to each event. For successful coupling paths and meshes have to couple with each other in the last step.

3.3 User Interaction

The last element in the presented coupling is user interaction. Hereby the knowledge about the system state of the DES resp. the VR has to be considered. The logic controlling the system is within the DES simulation while the VR only provides a visual view on the system. But the user is typically viewing the VR representation. Therefore, it is useful that, users may interact within the virtual reality. For presenting all at a time possible accepted events, the DES must transmit which external events are possible at each time to the VR. User may then select events, which are then passed back to the VR. Of course, in some rare cases update of the list of possible events will conflict with users choices. But this may be solved by informing the user, whenever an invalid events has been passed to the DES.

4 Evaluation

For the test of the approach a real world scenario is used. For evaluating the coupling presented in the previous section a medium sized example of the "Hanse Terminal" in Magdeburg will be used. The "Hanse Terminal" is a harbor for transshipping containers with different loadings from ships to trucks and vice versa. In this logistic process many participants are included e.g. a crane, a reach stacker, trucks and others [8].

The presented example shows a small extract of this logistics process, whereby containers transported by a ship will be stevedored by a crane to be stored on the harbor area. Parallel to this, trucks arrive at the harbor. If containers are stored at the harbor, a reach stacker will load the containers on the trucks. The used DES simulation software tool is SLX [5] by Wolverine Software Corporation [14]. SLX provides an elaborated programming environment to build discrete simulations with parallel threads. As VR-system the VDT-Platform [6] is used. This is a software system that is developed at the Fraunhofer IFF. The VDT-Platform is modular and based on a standardized data model. The architecture of the software system consist three main components [2]

- the Scenario: a certain amount of application specific data that represents the virtual model,
- the Scenario Player: the common set of functionality to handle the Scenario specific data
- the plugin framework: the set of functions for authoring and editing the virtual model and its behavior.

---

[5] Simulation Language eXtended.
[6] Virtual Development and Training - Platform.

In the past, the platform was primarily developed and used for training of maintenance and service personnel. Meanwhile, the increasing availability of 3D data provides more and more fields of application in which this software frame-work can be used. The main idea is to enable interaction with realistic virtual plants, machinery and products on the basis of immersive 3-D virtual environments. That is the basis of the use of the software framework and the virtual environment in the whole product- and production life cycle [1].

Because of the distributed usability an interface also provided by the Fraunhofer IFF, based on the real-time-interface in [6], is used. This interface uses a shared memory, on which reading and writing is synchronized. is used. This interface uses a shared memory, on which reading and writing is synchronized. The implementation of the VDT-Platform is based on plugins. Thereby a plugin for the offline-simulation, which was still build by the IFF, is extended with an interface to communicate concurrently with the SLX simulation. Furthermore this implement also the concepts of the spatial mapping and the user interface. The SLX model is build with 2 modules, whereby one module displays the simulation model to control the current scene and the other provides general functions to communicate with the VR. In this example the controlled model for the example is created as state model, so that incoming user events can change the internal state and so the behavior of the model.

The implementation was successfully done and showed the desired behavior with the "Hanse Terminal" simulation. So it was possible to visualize the activities triggered by the SLX-simulation in the VR under normal conditions [7] just in time. Multiple user events could be triggered and were correctly processed by the SLX-simulation-model. Nonetheless, the distributed functionality wasn't tested, so that no valid conclusions about this can be made yet.

In opposite to integrated visualization tools like used in Plant Simulation [12] this approach sees the VR and simulation as independent to each other by communicating with a centralized interface. So it was possible to simulate the DES separately to the VR. Another benefit is the logging of events created by the DES. This information can be used to replay special situations in the VR using an offline coupling. Because of the independent design this may be done in a different VR-environment.

5   Conclusion

All in all this paper shows that a coupling of a DES and a virtual environment including time, semantic objects and user interaction is possible and useful. The big benefit however lies in analyzing questions, which may not be answered by the DES alone. For example: How close do trucks and reach stackers pass each other? What quality of service could be expected when monitoring the real world system with a camera system?

The basic concept of the coupling – mapping each event of the DES to an arbitrary set of temporal sequences in the VR environment – is very efficient.

---

[7] Normal means with a framerate, which leads to a fluid visualization for the user.

Based on the example of the "Hanse Terminal Magdeburg", these techniques are used to build a prototypical implementation of this coupling. This prototype helped us evaluate the usefulness of the coupling as well as performance and feasibility.

In current work further examples are tested to get a better evaluation about the advantages and disadvantages of this coupling. One aspect is setting up a distributed scenario. Much more interesting, however is moving to full co-simulation: for example having the DES simulation react on (continuous time) sensor values modeled in the VR environment only.

References

1. Blümel, E., Fredrich, H., Winge, A.: Applied Knowledge Transfer to European SMEs by Expertise Networks Using Mixed Reality. In: Niedrite, L., Strazdina, R., Wangler, B. (eds.) BIR 2011 Workshops. LNBIP, vol. 106, pp. 90–101. Springer, Heidelberg (2012)
2. Blümel, E., Hintze, A., Schulz, T., Schumann, M., Stüring, S.: Perspectives on simulation in education and training: virtual environments for the training of maintenance and service tasks. In: Chick, S.E., Sanchez, P.J., Ferrin, D.M., Morrice, D.J. (eds.) WSC. ACM (2003)
3. Franke, R.: Kopplung von diskreter Simulation und interaktiver 3D-Visualisierung. Master Thesis, OVGU Magdeburg - Faculty of Computer Science (2004)
4. Fujimoto, R.M.: Parallel and Distributed Simulation Systems. Wiley Series on Parallel and Distributed Computing. Wiley-Interscience, John Wiley & Sons, Inc., Scientific, Technical, and Medical Devision (January 2000)
5. Goettsch, N.: Planung neuer Produktionsaufgaben: Ohne Simulation kein Angebot beim OEM (March 2007), http://www.it-production.com/index.php?seite=einzel_artikel_ansicht&id=33458 (accessed at March 12, 2012)
6. Kennel, M., Bayrhammer, E.: Eine Schnittstelle zur echtzeitfähigen Kopplung heterogener Simulations-, Steuerungs-, und Visualisierungsapplikationen. In: Forschung vernetzen - Innovationen beschleunigen - 3. und 4. IFF-Forschungskolloquium. Fraunhofer IFF, Magdeburg (April and September 2007)
7. Law, A.M.: Simulation modeling and analysis, 4th edn. McGraw-Hill series in industrial engineering and management science (2007)
8. Magdeburg hafen.de. Hansehafen/GVZ - Hansehafen in Magdeburg-Rothensee (March 2012), http://www.magdeburg-hafen.de/magdeburg-hafen/mdhafen.html (accessed at March 10, 2012)
9. Planung Transport Verkehr AG (2012), http://www.ptv.de/software/verkehrsplanung-verkehrstechnik/software-und-system-solutions/vissim/ (accessed at March 12, 2012)
10. Raab, M.: Mechanismen zur Interaktion zwischen virtuell-interaktiver 3D-Umgebung und echtzeitfähiger Ablaufsimulation. Master Thesis, OVGU Magdeburg - Faculty of Computer Science (March 2007)
11. Schumann, M.: Architektur und Applikation verteilter, VR-basierter Trainingssysteme. PhD thesis, Faculty of Computer Science - OVGU Magdeburg, Fraunhofer IFF, Magdeburg (February 2010)

12. Siemens PLM Software Inc.: Plant Simulation Simulation, Visualisierung, Analyse und Optimierung von Produktions- und Logistikprozessen, http://www.plm.automation.siemens.com/de_de/Images/ plant_simulation_tcm73-62431.pdf (accessed at February 18, 2012)
13. Straßburger, S., Schulze, T., Lemessi, M., Rehn, G.D.: Temporally parallel coupling of discrete simulation systems with virtual reality systems. In: WSC. ACM (2005)
14. Wolverine Software Corporation. Wolverine Web (February 2012), http://www.wolverinesoftware.com/ (accessed at February 8, 2012)

Program Comprehension
in Preprocessor-Based Software

Janet Siegmund*, Norbert Siegmund, Jana Fruth, Sven Kuhlmann**,
Jana Dittmann, and Gunter Saake

University of Magdeburg, Germany
{feigensp,nsiegmun,fruth,gunter.saake}@ovgu.de,
{sven.tuchscheerer,dittmann}@iti.cs.uni-magdeburg.de

Abstract. To adapt to heterogeneous hardware, software of embedded
systems provides customization capacities. Typically, this customization
is achieved using conditional compilation with preprocessors. However,
preprocessor usage can lead to obfuscated source code that can be difficult to comprehend, which in turn cause increased maintenance costs,
bugs, and security vulnerabilities. To profit from the benefit of preprocessors usage, we need to improve their comprehensibility. In this paper,
we describe how program comprehension can be improved and, to that
end, measured. We show that reliably measuring program comprehension requires considerably effort. However, the benefit is that we can
apply concepts that have proven to improve program comprehension,
and thus can e.g. improve maintainability, reliability, and security of
source code.

Keywords: Preprocessor, Program Comprehension, Empirical Software
Engineering, Software Quality.

1 Introduction

Since the development of the first programmable computers, they have become
ubiquitous: We are surrounded by them, especially by embedded systems, which
constitute the major part, about 98 %, of computers [1]. Examples of embedded
systems are PDAs, mobile phones, sensors, or credit cards. The characteristic
of embedded systems, in contrast to desktop systems, are the strict resource
constraints, for example regarding memory capacity or power consumption. Additionally, the heterogeneous hardware of embedded systems leads to challenges
for software, which has to be tailored to specific hardware and application scenarios [2].

To implement software for embedded systems in practice, C and its preprocessor are typically used. The preprocessor supports *conditional compilation*,
which allows developers to write variable software that can be adapted to specific hardware and application scenarios. The C preprocessor uses *ifdef directives*

---

* This author published previous work as Janet Feigenspan.
** This author published previous work as Sven Tuchscheerer.

F. Ortmeier and P. Daniel (Eds.): SAFECOMP 2012 Workshops, LNCS 7613, pp. 517–528, 2012.

```
 1 | static int __rep_queue_filedone(dbenv, rep, rfp)
 2 |   DB_ENV *dbenv;
 3 |   REP *rep;
 4 |   __rep_fileinfo_args *rfp; {
 5 | #ifndef HAVE_QUEUE
 6 |   COMPQUIET(rep, NULL);
 7 |   COMPQUIET(rfp, NULL);
 8 |   return (__db_no_queue_am(dbenv));
 9 | #else
10 |   db_pgno_t first, last;
11 |   u_int32_t flags;
12 |   int empty, ret, t_ret;
13 |   #ifdef DIAGNOSTIC
14 |     DB_MSGBUF mb;
15 |   #endif
16 | // over 100 lines of additional code
17 |   #endif
18 | }
```

Fig. 1. Code excerpt of Berkeley DB, illustrating how conditional compilation is implemented

to enable variability, which we illustrate in Figure 1 with an excerpt of BerkeleyDB[1]. For example, in Line 5, we see such an *ifdef directive*, an **#ifndef**. If the following variable, HAVE_QUEUE, is not set, all according code (Line 10 to 16) is removed, including all *ifdef directives*, by the preprocessor. If HAVE_QUEUE is set, the **#else** branch applies, and source code from Line 6 to 8 is removed. This mechanism allows a developer to adapt BerkeleyDB to for different hardware and application scenarios.

Ifdef directives are used because they offer great variability and flexibility regarding annotations of source code. Furthermore, they are simple to use in many languages or environments (e.g., C, C++, Fortran, and Java Micro Edition) [3,4].

Unfortunately, preprocessors also have drawbacks. In the literature, preprocessors are heavily criticized, because they are considered 'harmful' [5] or even as '#ifdef hell' [6]. The problem is that with *ifdef directives*, we can annotate *everything*, such as a single variable or bracket. This can make it very difficult for a programmer to understand source code that contains *ifdef directives*. We could encourage practitioners to avoid *ifdef directives* and use only contemporary programming mechanisms, such as AHEAD [7], FeatureHouse [8] or AspectJ [9]. In fact, software for mobile phones is developed based on Java or Objective-C. However, in many cases (e.g., sensor networks, cars), *ifdef directives* are still the first choice, and there is lots of legacy code that needs to be maintained. Thus, we need to improve the comprehensibility of preprocessor-based code.

However, understanding source code is what maintenance programmers most of their time do [10,11]. They understand a program top down, meaning that they state a general hypothesis about a program's purpose and refine this hypothesis by looking at details [12]. Top-down comprehension requires knowledge about a program's domain; otherwise, programmers have to use bottom-up

---

[1] http://www.oracle.com/technetwork/database/berkeleydb

comprehension. In this case, developers create hypotheses about a program's purpose by looking at details and grouping them into semantic chunks [13].

Hence, understanding, or *program comprehension*, is an important aspect in software development. We could introduce threats to security or write bugs more often, because we do not understand source code sufficiently. We could waste energy in embedded systems, because we do not efficiently utilize hardware, but concentrate on writing variable code. There are far more problems that come with neglected program comprehension. This can lead to high maintenance costs and introduce threats to security. Hence, we need to deal with program comprehension to allow developers to spend more time improving source code.

In this paper, we describe the importance of program comprehension in the embedded-systems' domain. The primary intent of this paper is to motivate researchers to take more interest in program comprehension. Hence, it should be understood as a position paper.

2   Background

In this section, we take a closer look at the '#ifdef hell' to better understand the risks to program comprehension. Furthermore, we give an introduction to program comprehension models to understand how it can be measured and improved.

2.1   #Ifdef Hell

It can be difficult for a programmer to locate *ifdef directives*, because they can be (i) scattered, (ii) 'hidden', (iii) nested, or (iv) used to annotate long code fragments. First, *ifdef directives* are often scattered over the complete software system. For example, if we want to implement a logging mechanism, this means that we have logging source code in many different locations in different files. Hence, according *ifdef directives* are scattered, as well.

Second, *ifdef directives* can be 'hidden' in code fragments. This is caused by the fine-grained level of annotations, such that single variables or brackets can be annotated. This can be especially problematic, if an opening bracket is annotated, but not the corresponding closing one. In this case, the preprocessor would delete the opening bracket (if the according variable is not defined), but not the corresponding closing one. Hence, trying to compile the preprocessed source code would lead to an error. However, a programmer has problems to detect this error, because in the source code, she actually sees both brackets.

Third, *ifdef directives* can be nested, which means that within an *ifdef directive*, another one is defined. For example, in Figure 1, the *ifdef directives* in Lines 13 to 15 are surrounded by the *ifdef directives* of Lines 5 to 17. In this example, we have a nesting level of 2. However, in typical industrial projects, nesting levels of 9 are typical, and even levels of up to 24 occur [14].

Last, long code fragments can be annotated with *ifdef directives*. For example, in Figure 1, Line 16 states that over 100 additional lines of code are defined, before the `#ifndef` in Line 5 is closed with the corresponding `#endif`. Hence, beginning and end of an *ifdef directive* may not even appear on the same screen, which makes it difficult for a developer to keep track of it.

To sum up, using preprocessors bears considerable risks to program comprehension. Of course, we could encourage practitioners to disciplined annotations or use other approaches for the required flexibility (e.g., subjects [15], aspects [16], mixin layers [17], or combinations thereof [18]). However, introducing novel concepts in industry is a long-term process, such that processors will be used in industry at least in the medium-term future. Hence, we argue that improving their comprehensibility is necessary and can improve maintainability, reliability, and security of source code.

2.2   Program Comprehension

It is important to have an understanding of program comprehension so that we can understand how to measure it. In the literature, we can find three different categories of program-comprehension models: Top-down models, bottom-up models, and integrated models.

Top-down comprehension is the process of deriving and refining hypotheses about the purpose of a program. First, a developer derives a general hypothesis about a program's purpose while neglecting details. During this step, *beacons* (i.e., parts of source code that indicate occurrences of certain structures or operations [12]) help to determine the purpose of a program. Once a hypothesis is formulated, the developer evaluates it by looking at details and refining her hypothesis stepwise by developing and refining subsidiary hypotheses. To be able to determine the purpose of a program top down, the programmer has to be familiar with the domain of a program. Several examples of top-down models can be found in the literature [12,19,20].

Bottom-up comprehension describes how a program is understood when a programmer has no knowledge of a program's domain. In this case, a programmer examines statements of a program and groups them into semantic chunks. These chunks can be combined further until the developer has an understanding of the general purpose of a program. Examples of bottom-up models are described in the literature [13,21].

Integrated models combine top-down and bottom-up program comprehension. For example, if a programmer has some knowledge about a domain, she starts with top-down comprehension. When she encounters code fragments she cannot explain using her domain knowledge, she switches to bottom-up comprehension. Typically, a developer uses top-down comprehension where possible, because it is more efficient. An example of an integrated model is described by Mayrhauser and Vans [22].

What should be clear from the explanations is that program comprehension is an internal cognitive process that we cannot observe directly [23]. Additionally, a programmer usually uses different comprehension models, depending on her familiarity with source code and domain. Hence, reliably measuring program comprehension is rather difficult. In the next section, we explain how we can measure program comprehension.

3 Measurement of Program Comprehension

Since we cannot observe program comprehension directly, we have to find measures to assess it. To the best of our knowledge, there is no standard to measure program comprehension. Instead, several different techniques are used. In this section, we introduce some common techniques to measure program comprehension. We present the methods ordered by how reliable they assess program comprehension, starting with the least reliable. This order also represents the effort of applying the techniques, starting with the least effortless.

3.1 Software Measures

Software measures are popular indicators for several software quality facets, including program comprehension. For example, there is a line of work that compares the quality of aspect-oriented programs to object-oriented programs with preprocessors based on software measures [24]. Software measures are solely based on properties of source code and do not require recruiting any humans to measure the comprehensibility of source code. Instead, tools, such as cppstats[2] or SourceMonitor[3] can automatically analyze source code and compute software measures. Thus, they are convenient indicators for program comprehension.

For better overview, we divide software measures into three different categories: (i) size measures, (ii) complexity measures, and (iii) concern measures. First, size measures analyze the size of source code, for example in terms of lines of code [25]. The assumption is that the more source-code lines a program consists of, the more difficult it is to understand. Hence, a large lines-of-code measure indicates threats to program comprehension.

Second, complexity measures assess how complex source code is. For example, the *complexity* of a method can be defined as the number of branching statements, such as *if*, *for*, or *switch*, of a method [26]. The more branching statements a method has, the more difficult it is to understand. This seems plausible, because a developer has to keep more different execution paths of a method in mind.

Last, concern measures assess properties of the concerns of source code. A *concern* is "anything a stakeholder may want to consider as conceptual unit [...]" [27]. For example, the measure *concern operations* represents the number of operations defined in one concern [28]. The more operations a concern has, the more a developer has to keep in mind, and, thus, the more difficult it is to understand.

---

[2] http://fosd.net/cppstats
[3] http://www.campwoodsw.com/sourcemonitor.html

The problem with software measure is that their relationship to program comprehension is based on plausibility arguments. There is little empirical work regarding how software measures are suitable indicators for program comprehension. Empirical work even suggests that software measures cannot assess program comprehension sufficiently [29,30]. Hence, their reliability is very limited, so software measures should not be used as sole indicators for program comprehension.

3.2   Self Estimation

This and the remaining techniques require recruiting humans and a controlled setting to assess program comprehension. In this context, humans are referred to as participants or *subjects*. Using self estimation, subjects estimate how much they understood from source code. For example, we can present source code to subjects and afterwards ask to estimate how much they understood of source code on a five-point Likert scale [31], 1 meaning *not at all*, 2 *a little*, 3 *about half*, 4 *most*, and 5 *everything*. We can compute a median of the answers of all subjects, and then would have an indicator of how comprehensible the source code used in the experiment is.

However, self estimation is a subjective measure that can easily be biased [32,33]. For example, subjects might over- or underestimate their program comprehension, even subconsciously. Hence, the reliability is questionable, as well. Nevertheless, self estimation is closer to program comprehension, because it actually considers humans and their comprehension process.

3.3   Tasks

Tasks are most frequently used to assess program comprehension [32]. There are different kinds of tasks with different reliability. *Static tasks* require subjects to analyze the structure of source code and are the least reliable. For example, subjects should locate the call of a certain method or the positions of a certain *ifdef directive*. In *dynamic tasks*, subjects should analyze the control flow of programs, for example the possible execution paths of a method. Last, in *maintenance tasks*, subjects should locate and/or fix the cause of a bug or implement additional source code. For example, we can give subjects a typical bug description as a user of a software product might provide it and then ask subjects to fix a bug. This is a typical behavior of a maintenance programmer and requires that subjects closely examine and understand source code.

Hence, tasks are more reliable than self estimation and software measures, because solving the tasks correctly requires that subjects understand source code to a certain degree. Thus, tasks can be a good indicator to assess program comprehension. However, tasks only allow us to observe the result of the comprehension process.

3.4 Think-Aloud Protocols

If we use self estimation or tasks, we cannot observe the comprehension process, but only evaluate whether and to what degree it occurred. To measure internal cognitive processes such as program comprehension, think-aloud protocols were developed [34]. In think-aloud protocols, subjects are instructed to verbalize their thoughts when understanding a piece of source code. This enables us to observe the process itself. Hence, we have a very reliable indicator for program comprehension.

However, applying think-aloud protocols requires considerable effort. First, subjects have to be trained to verbalize their thoughts, because they usually do not talk aloud when comprehending source code. Furthermore, during a session, an experimenter often has to remind subjects to keep talking, even when they are stuck on a piece of source code. Second, think-aloud experiments require much effort to conduct, because they cannot take place in a large group (imagine 10 subjects in one room talking the whole time), and they usually are recorded on tape for the analysis. Third, the taped sessions need to be analyzed to understand how subjects understood a piece of source code [35]. Thus, think-aloud protocols are often too costly to apply.

Reliably measuring program comprehension requires considerable effort. This is one reason why researchers often use software measures, instead of conducting controlled experiments [36]. Nevertheless, the effort in measuring program comprehension and improving it can pay off.

4 Improving Program Comprehension

How can we improve program comprehension of preprocessor-based software? First, we present how background colors can help. Then, we present tools that were developed to improve program comprehension. Finally, we discuss the possibilities of using augmented-reality techniques to support a developer in understanding source code.

4.1 Background Colors

Background colors support a developer in keeping track of source code that is annotated with *ifdef directives*. In Figure 2, we present an example of how background colors can be used to highlight code fragments.

The benefit of colors lies in the fact that humans process colors *preattentively* [37]. Preattentive perception describes the fast recognition of few visual properties, such as colors. Hence, a developer can see at first sight that source code is annotated with an *ifdef directive* and the according variable. For example, in Figure 2, we can immediately see that code in Lines 12 to 14 specify a different variable for the *ifdef directive* than code in Lines 5 to 16.

First empirical results confirm the positive effect of background colors on program comprehension, even for large software systems [38,39]. Furthermore, both

```
 1  static int __rep_queue_filedone(dbenv, rep, rfp)
 2    DB_ENV *dbenv;
 3    REP *rep;
 4    __rep_fileinfo_args *rfp; {
 5  #ifndef HAVE_QUEUE
 6    COMPQUIET(rep, NULL);
 7    return (__db_no_queue_am(dbenv));
 8  #else
 9    db_pgno_t first, last;
10    u_int32_t flags;
11    int empty, ret, t_ret;
12    #ifdef DIAGNOSTIC
13      DB_MSGBUF mb;
14    #endif
15    // over 100 lines of additional code
16  #endif
17  }
```

Fig. 2. Excerpt of Berkeley DB, with background colors to highlight source code annotated with *ifdef directives*. Lines 5 to 16 are yellow, Lines 12 to 14 orange.

experiments revealed that subjects like the color idea, which they in turn reflected back on their performance. Hence, background colors are a good starting point to improve the comprehensibility of preprocessor-based software.

4.2   Tool support

In our line of work, we developed two tools to improve program comprehension. The first is FeatureCommander, a prototype of an IDE that uses background colors consistently throughout the complete user interface [39]. In Figure 3, we present a screen shot to give an impression of the realization of background colors. It uses background colors to highlight source code (1). The left side bar (2) shows highlighted source code of the currently visible source code, whereas the right side bar (3) shows highlighted source code scaled to the complete file. For better navigation, the side bars are interactive, such that clicking them shows the according part of the file. With a slider (4), users can adjust the transparency of the colors. The color palette (5) enables users to assign a color to source code in the editor, in the list of concerns (6), or to files shown in the file explorer (7). With a view ordered by concerns (8), a user can quickly get an overview of which concerns are implemented in which file(s).

The second tool we developed is View Infinity, an IDE prototype that provides semantic zooming from the level of concerns over level of the files to the source code. In Figure 4, we present an overview of this zooming concept. On the bottom, we show the level of concerns. With different levels of detail, users can zoom into the level of files. When users zoom in a certain file, that file is opened in a file editor. Since the zooming concepts is dynamic and difficult to explain with static figures, we encourage the reader to check out the demo video we provide at the project's website (http://fosd.net/vi).

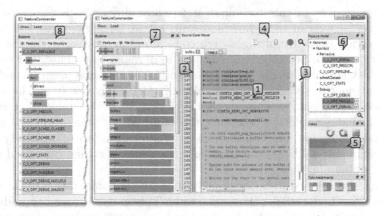

Fig. 3. Screenshot of FeatureCommander. The numbers refer to visualizations we explain in the text.

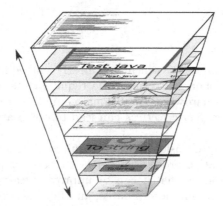

Fig. 4. Screenshot of View Infinity to illustrate the semantic zooming concept.

4.3 Augmented Reality

Augmented reality (AR) is a modern technique to enhance the environment with additional information often displayed in a head-up display. Today, there are already different application scenarios in which AR is used (e.g., Wikitude[4]). However, to the best of our knowledge, the use of AR techniques for software development was not considered until now. We envision using AR techniques to enhance the source code view with additional information to improve program comprehension. Using a head-up display, we can visualize which *ifdef directives* are shown on the screen with information about their purpose, classes in which code annotated with the same *ifdef directive* appear, nesting of *ifdef directives*, etc. This information can be displayed on demand, so we do not change existing source code nor degrade its readability by introducing annotations.

---

[4] http://www.wikitude.org

Another benefit of this technique is to show different views of the source code. That is, we can show how a certain set of *ifdef directives* would affect the generation of the resulting source code after preprocessing. Hence, nested *ifdef directives* can be traced already at the development phase. For example, we see which code fragments are *automatically* included in a program and which not, based on the definition of variables of *ifdef directives* (e.g., the variable HAVE_QUEUE in Figure 2). This allows developers to detect missing constraints (e.g., to include encryption functions, the required key generation and storage, key initialization, and key usage when communication is used) already during the development and helps to understand the cause of errors, bugs, and general potential vulnerabilities.

AR can also be used to automatically show the documentation of classes and methods when investigating the source code. This makes it easier to understand the source code, because a developer is not interrupted in the analyzing process anymore when she would need information of the documentation. Hence, using AR techniques can increase the comprehensibility of source code.

5   Conclusion

We are surrounded by computers, which are mostly embedded, for example in cars, PDAs, or mobile phones. To meet the requirements of resource constraints and heterogeneous hardware, conditional compilation is often used as mechanism. However, using *ifdef directives* can lead to obfuscated and hard-to-comprehend source code.

Measuring program comprehension reliably requires considerable effort, because it is an internal cognitive process. Nevertheless, it is important to measure program comprehension, so that it can be improved. Easy-to-comprehend programs are better to maintain, more reliable, and more secure. Furthermore, we can reduce the cost for software development by ensuring comprehensive programs.

To improve program comprehension of preprocessor-based software, we presented how background colors can be used to highlight annotated code fragments. Additionally, we introduced ideas how augmented reality can help to improve program comprehension.

Acknowledgements. This work is funded by the German Ministry of Education and Science (BMBF), project 01IM10002B.

References

1. Tennenhouse, D.: Proactive computing. Communications of the ACM 43(5), 43–50 (2000)
2. Siegmund, N., Feigenspan, J., Soffner, M., Fruth, J., Köppen, V.: Challenges of Secure and Reliable Data Management in Heterogeneous Environments. In: Proc. Int'l Workshop on Digital Engineering, pp. 17–24. ACM Press (2010)

3. Favre, J.: Understanding-In-The-Large. In: Proc. Int'l Workshop on Program Comprehension, p. 29. IEEE CS (1997)
4. Muthig, D., Patzke, T.: Generic Implementation of Product Line Components. In: Aksit, M., Awasthi, P., Unland, R. (eds.) NODe 2002. LNCS, vol. 2591, pp. 313–329. Springer, Heidelberg (2003)
5. Spencer, H., Collyer, G.: #ifdef Considered Harmful or Portability Experience With C News. In: Proc. USENIX Conf., pp. 185–198. USENIX Association (1992)
6. Lohmann, D., Scheler, F., Tartler, R., Spinczyk, O., Schröder-Preikschat, W.: A Quantitative Analysis of Aspects in the eCos Kernel. In: Proc. Europ. Conf. Computer Systems (EuroSys), pp. 191–204. ACM Press (2006)
7. Batory, D., Sarvela, J.N., Rauschmayer, A.: Scaling Step-Wise Refinement. IEEE Trans. Softw. Eng. 30(6), 355–371 (2004)
8. Apel, S., Kästner, C., Lengauer, C.: FeatureHouse: Language-Independent, Automatic Software Composition. In: Proc. Int'l Conf. Software Engineering (ICSE), pp. 221–231. IEEE CS (2009)
9. Kiczales, G., Hilsdale, E., Hugunin, J., Kersten, M., Palm, J., Griswold, W.G.: An Overview of AspectJ. In: Lee, S.H. (ed.) ECOOP 2001. LNCS, vol. 2072, pp. 327–353. Springer, Heidelberg (2001)
10. Standish, T.: An Essay on Software Reuse. IEEE Trans. Softw. Eng. SE-10(5), 494–497 (1984)
11. Tiarks, R.: What Programmers Really Do: An Observational Study, pp. 36–37 (2011)
12. Brooks, R.: Using a Behavioral Theory of Program Comprehension in Software Engineering. In: Proc. Int'l Conf. Software Engineering (ICSE), pp. 196–201. IEEE CS (1978)
13. Pennington, N.: Stimulus Structures and Mental Representations in Expert Comprehension of Computer Programs. Cognitive Psychology 19(3), 295–341 (1987)
14. Liebig, J., Apel, S., Lengauer, C., Kästner, C., Schulze, M.: An Analysis of the Variability in Forty Preprocessor-Based Software Product Lines. In: Proc. Int'l Conf. Software Engineering (ICSE), pp. 105–114. ACM Press (2010)
15. Harrison, W., Ossher, H.: Subject-oriented Programming: A Critique of Pure Objects. In: Proc. Int'l Conf. Object-Oriented Programming, Systems, Languages and Applications (OOPSLA), pp. 411–428. IEEE CS (1993)
16. Kiczales, G., Lamping, J., Mendhekar, A., Maeda, C., Lopez, C., Loingtier, J.M., Irwin, J.: Aspect-Oriented Programming. In: Aksit, M., Auletta, V. (eds.) ECOOP 1997. LNCS, vol. 1241, pp. 220–242. Springer, Heidelberg (1997)
17. Smaragdakis, Y., Batory, D.: Implementing Layered Designs with Mixin Layers. In: Jul, E. (ed.) ECOOP 1998. LNCS, vol. 1445, pp. 550–570. Springer, Heidelberg (1998)
18. Apel, S., Leich, T., Saake, G.: Aspectual Feature Modules. IEEE Trans. Softw. Eng. 34(2), 162–180 (2008)
19. Shaft, T., Vessey, I.: The Relevance of Application Domain Knowledge: The Case of Computer Program Comprehension. Information Systems Research 6(3), 286–299 (1995)
20. Soloway, E., Ehrlich, K.: Empirical Studies of Programming Knowledge. IEEE Trans. Softw. Eng. 10(5), 595–609 (1984)
21. Shneiderman, B., Mayer, R.: Syntactic/Semantic Interactions in Programmer Behavior: A Model and Experimental Results. International Journal of Parallel Programming 8(3), 219–238 (1979)
22. von Mayrhauser, A., Vans, A.: From Program Comprehension to Tool Requirements for an Industrial Environment. In: Proc. Int'l Workshop Program Comprehension (IWPC), pp. 78–86. IEEE CS (1993)

23. Koenemann, J., Robertson, S.: Expert Problem Solving Strategies for Program Comprehension. In: Proc. Conf. Human Factors in Computing Systems (CHI), pp. 125–130. ACM Press (1991)
24. Figueiredo, E., Cacho, N., Monteiro, M., Kulesza, U., Garcia, R., Soares, S., Ferrari, F., Khan, S., Filho, F., Dantas, F.: Evolving Software Product Lines with Aspects: An Empirical Study on Design Stability. In: Proc. Int'l Conf. Software Engineering (ICSE), pp. 261–270. ACM Press (2008)
25. Henderson-Sellers, B.: Object-Oriented Metrics: Measures of Complexity. Prentice Hall (1995)
26. McConnell, S.: Code Complete, 2nd edn. Microsoft Press (2004)
27. Robillard, M., Murphy, G.: Representing Concerns in Source Code. ACM Trans. Softw. Eng. & Methodology 16(1), 1–38 (2007)
28. Figueiredo, E., Whittle, J., Garcia, A.: ConcernMorph: Metrics-based Detection of Crosscutting Patterns. In: Proc. Europ. Software Engineering Conf./Foundations of Software Engineering (ESEC/FSE), pp. 299–300. ACM Press (2009)
29. Boysen, J.: Factors Affecting Computer Program Comprehension. PhD thesis, Iowa State University (1977)
30. Feigenspan, J., et al.: Exploring Software Measures to Assess Program Comprehension. In: Proc. Int'l Symposium Empirical Software Engineering and Measurement (ESEM), pp. 1–10, paper 3. IEEE CS (2011)
31. Likert, R.: A Technique for the Measurement of Attitudes. Archives of Psychology 22(140), 1–55 (1932)
32. Dunsmore, A., Roper, M.: A Comparative Evaluation of Program Comprehension Measures. Technical Report EFoCS 35-2000, Department of Computer Science, University of Strathclyde (2000)
33. Shneiderman, B.: Measuring Computer Program Quality and Comprehension. International Journal of Man-Machine Studies 9(4), 465–478 (1977)
34. Someren, M., Barnard, Y., Sandberg, J.: The Think Aloud Method: A Practical Guide to Modelling Cognitive Processes. Academic Press (1994)
35. Shaft, T., Vessey, I.: The Relevance of Application Domain Knowledge: The Case of Computer Program Comprehension. Information Systems Research 6(3), 286–299 (1995)
36. Tichy, W.F.: Should Computer Scientists Experiment More? Computer 31(5), 32–40 (1998)
37. Goldstein, B.: Sensation and Perception, 5th edn. Cengage Learning Services (2002)
38. Feigenspan, J., Kästner, C., Apel, S., Leich, T.: How to Compare Program Comprehension in FOSD Empirically - An Experience Report. In: Proc. Int'l Workshop on Feature-Oriented Software Development, pp. 55–62. ACM Press (2009)
39. Feigenspan, J., Schulze, M., Papendieck, M., Kästner, C., Dachselt, R., Köppen, V., Frisch, M.: Using Background Colors to Support Program Comprehension in Software Product Lines. In: Proc. Int'l Conf. Evaluation and Assessment in Software Engineering (EASE), pp. 66–75. Institution of Engineering and Technology (2011)

Author Index